Contents

CHAPTER 3
Thinking Critically About People's Opinions 45

CHAPTER 4
Attitudes and Opinions 67

People and Their Opinions

Thinking Critically About Public Opinion

Eric Shiraev
George Mason University

Richard Sobel

Routledge
Taylor & Francis Group

LONDON AND NEW YORK

To our mentors in public opinion,
Michael Kagay and Vladimir Shlapentokh.

First published 2006 by Pearson Education, Inc.

Published 2016 by Routledge
2 Park Square, Milton Park, Abingdon, Oxon OX14 4RN
711 Third Avenue, New York, NY, 10017, USA

Routledge is an imprint of the Taylor & Francis Group, an informa business

ISBN: 9780321078988 (pbk)

Cover Designer: Nancy Danahy

Library of Congress Cataloging-in-Publication Data

People and their opinions: thinking critically about public opinion/Eric Shiraev, Richard Sobel.
       p. cm.
   Includes bibliographical references and index.
   ISBN 0-321-07898-5
   1. Public opinion. 2. Public opinion--United States. 3. Political socialization.
I. Shiraev, Eric II. Sobel, Richard III. Title.
   HM1236.S52 2005
   303.3'8--dc22

                                                        2004024781

CHAPTER 6
The Media and Opinions 116

CHAPTER 7
Gender and Opinions 143

CHAPTER 8
Social Class and Opinions 166

CHAPTER 9
Race, Ethnicity, Religion, and Opinions 191

CHAPTER 10
Opinions and Voting 222

CHAPTER 11

Opinions About Domestic Issues 249

CHAPTER 12
Opinions About Foreign Policy 284

Conclusion 314

Preface

Though colleges and universities across the country offer courses in public opinion, few current books on this compelling topic capture the imaginations of undergraduate students or their instructors. To engage students and teachers alike as active participants in exploring the world of opinion, *People and Their Opinions* incorporates three distinctive features for learning about public opinion in politics. First, it introduces a **critical thinking approach** that helps develop the skills and knowledge needed to understand and interpret public opinion, particularly as represented in polls. It offers a wide range of assignments, teaching tools, and analytical features to encourage the pursuit of this goal.

Second, the book captures American public opinion in a **comparative perspective**. This takes into consideration major social and political developments in over forty countries of a continuously changing world. Third, the text introduces a wide range of **practical illustrations** from actual studies of how people think and feel about current political and social issues.

People and Their Opinions should be especially beneficial for introductory or middle-level undergraduate courses in public opinion, political science, political communications, and international relations. We have tried to make it understandable by tailoring its style and arguments to college and university students. This book covers important topics, from public opinion formation to the impact of public opinion on policy, and chooses the educational approaches to foster learning about these issues.

The text should also be beneficial to upper-level undergraduate and graduate courses in political science, political communication, sociology, and journalism, and foreign policy service. It will hopefully appeal to educators, professionals, and practitioners from universities, research centers, and service academies. Reflecting the research and teaching interests and experiences of the authors, the approach of this book is cross-national, engaging, and provocative. Because of its comparative focus, international colleges and universities, especially in Canada, Britain, and other English-speaking countries, will find this book relevant and, we hope, engaging.

CRITICAL THINKING

People and Their Opinions describes and uses the major principles of critical thinking in understanding, interpreting, and explaining public attitudes on a wide variety of social and political problems. Applying these tools to public opinion research in the United States and other countries, the text provides an overview of approaches to opinion analysis and alerts readers to common cognitive errors in survey interpretation. The book shows how critical thinking can help comprehend opinion research findings, discover common trends, identify differences in opinion research statistics, and explain the accumulated evidence.

The text incorporates a variety of **pedagogical devices** designed for class preparations and classroom use. For instance, each chapter opens with a vignette and a "Looking Forward" explanation of the concepts and ideas to come. Each chapter also concludes with a summary of the issues, a "Looking Ahead" to the topics to be presented in the next chapters, and a glossary of key terms and definitions. Interspersed throughout are discussion questions, tables, and visual aids. The text provides a wealth of original assignments and interactive exercises for class use. Each chapter also contains boxed Cases in Point and practical examples designed to expand students' thinking on the particular topics of interest. Using engaging examples from opinion research, the authors explain how to interpret and display research data. An original **website**, which will be updated regularly, also accompanies the text. The website contains more cases, exercises, and links to relevant sites about public opinion and politics.

COMPARATIVE PERSPECTIVE

People and Their Opinions provides a comprehensive analysis of **American public opinion in a comparative perspective**. This approach is important for several reasons. First, public opinion trends, including the views of the general public and national leaders, are becoming increasingly significant in policymaking and national security analysis. Second, by comparing trends in American and international public opinion, students become better able to understand the ideological, political, and psychological foundations of opinion formation and expression. Third, the rapid increases in international interactions, cooperation and conflicts, as well as the extension of multilateral military and peacekeeping missions, require a better understanding of national public opinions and their effects on policies across the globe.

AN OVERVIEW OF THE CHAPTERS

The text contains an introduction, 12 chapters, and an **analytical conclusion** that precedes an **appendix of public opinion organizations**.

Chapter 1, "The Nature of Public Opinion," introduces public opinion and discusses three types: consensus, majority opinion, and plurality opinion. The chapter also addresses the social and practical value of opinion polls. Importantly, the chapter explores the relationship of the political system and elections, among other types of political participation, to the impact of opinions on government. It introduces national polling organizations.

Chapter 2, "Measurement of Opinion," explores the difficult task of measuring human psychology and attitudes, particularly through survey research and polling.

Chapter 3, "Thinking Critically About People's Opinions," provides a critical examination of polls and opinions. It also suggests how to examine the circumstances surrounding survey research and how to analyze the survey questions. The chapter examines errors of human perception, including the prejudgments by both pollsters and respondents. It addresses the issue of question wording, and it emphasizes the importance of critically analyzing secondary sources.

Chapter 4, "Attitudes and Opinions," deals with the nature of attitudes, beliefs, and values. The chapter examines scientific approaches to understanding attitudes, particularly the cognitive approach, the regulatory-adaptation approach, and the rational actor approach.

Chapter 5, "Political Socialization," describes political socialization, or learning about politics, and introduces and explores its stages in depth: childhood, adolescence, and adulthood.

Chapter 6, "The Media and Opinions," encourages students to think critically about the media. It discusses the problem of access to information and three types of censorship: political, ideological, and moral. It explores the contents of reported information about opinions and emphasizes the direct impact of the media, including the issues of name recognition and sensationalism. The chapter addresses the process of information dissemination by emphasizing agenda setting, media frames, and political bias.

Chapter 7, "Gender and Opinions," begins the exploration of how additional important factors in political socialization, such as the social differences and similarities between men and women, influence their political attitudes. It examines how gender affects people's opportunities, political attitudes like party identification, and their political involvement. The chapter critically examines the gender gap on important issues like the economy, social welfare, war and peace, and political participation from sociological, cultural, sociobiological and socioeconomic perspectives.

Chapter 8, "Social Class and Opinions," examines the impact of class on attitudes. It analyzes social class as a concept, discusses social class gaps in opinions, and addresses ideological identity and party identification. The chapter also addresses class–related interests, perceptions of economic change, merit, and fairness. It analyzes class–related antagonism, self-identity, access to information, and other social and social-psychological factors in opinion formation.

Chapter 9, "Race, Ethnicity, Religion, and Opinions," addresses cultural issues associated with opinion expression and voting. It presents initial hypotheses of culture studies around ethnicity, race, and religion. It examines diversity of opinions and attitudes of people who are black, Hispanic, and Asian. The chapter also discusses the impact of religion on attitudes and behavior, such as the voting patterns of Catholics, Protestants, Jews, and Muslims in the United States.

Chapter 10, " Opinions and Voting," explores the relationship of opinion to voting as a process and examines several types of voting. It establishes reasons why people vote, including socioeconomic factors, knowledge, legal and institutional features, electoral format, and cognitive, moral, and personality factors. It pays special attention to the low voter turnout typical of some democratic countries and introduces online voting.

Chapter 11, "Opinions About Domestic Issues," looks at the diversity of opinions on a variety of national topics, from abortion, affirmative action, crime and law enforcement, and the death penalty to education, gun control, immigration, the environment, and healthcare. It addresses other ethical issues such as euthanasia, sexual orientation, security, and privacy and explains people's views about the role of government. The book's website contains updates on these issues.

Chapter 12, "Opinions About Foreign Policy," explains the nature and dynamics of attitudes about foreign policy. It covers several distinct types of foreign policy attitudes and how they are influenced by factors including security concerns, ideological perspectives, and partisan beliefs. The website presents a special section on international public opinion and the war in Bosnia (1991–1996) and provides updates on key issues.

ACKNOWLEDGMENTS

Our journey in writing this book was enriched by the thoughtful and in-depth feedback provided by reviewers at every stage of the manuscript's development. We would therefore like to thank the following people for their insights:

Richard Chesteen (University of Texas at Martin)
Amy Gangl (Union College)
Phillip L. Gianos (California State University, Fullerton)
Layne Hoppe (Texas Lutheran University)
Lisa Langenbach (Middle Tennessee State University)
David M. Littig (University of Wisconsin, Green Bay)
Nancy Martorano (University of Dayton)
Scott D. McClurg (Southern Illinois University)
Stephen M. Nichols (California State University, San Marcos)
Clarissa Peterson (DePauw University)
Andree E. Reeves (University of Alabama in Huntsville)
Douglas D. Roscoe (Central Michigan University)
Frank Louis Rusciano (Rider University)
Roger Saathoff (Texas Tech University)
Todd M. Schaefer (Central Washington University)
Robert Y. Shapiro (Columbia University)
Fred Slocum (Minnesota State University, Mankato)
Elaine Willey Tomlinson (Georgetown University)
Rita Whillock (Southern Methodist University)
John K. White (Catholic University)

We would also like to acknowledge with thanks the assistance of other people who contributed to the success of the project. At Longman we would like to thank editor Eric Stano, publisher Priscilla McGeehon, production editors Lisa Kinne and James Hill at Electronic Publishing Services Inc., and Coughlin Indexing Services, Inc. We appreciate the help of copy editor Madeline Perri, editorial assistants Christine Maisano, Kara Wylie, and production manager Ellen MacElree. We thank research assistants Jamal Brathwaite and Ben Kociubinski, as well as colleagues and friends who read drafts of the manuscript and chapters, including Melissa Gallagher, William-Arthur Haynes,

Evan Hinckle, Jens Laurson, Margaret Ormes, Christopher Porter, Jessica Tannebaum, and Paul Turner. We would also like to thank colleagues who advised and encouraged us on this project, including Robert Dudley, David Gergen, Betty Glad, Ole Holsti, Scott Keeter, David King, Cheryl Koopman, Lee Sigelman, Howard Taylor, Sergei Tsytsarev, Sidney Verba, and Vlad Zubok. Finally, we would also like to recognize colleagues and mentors who helped us along the way, particularly James Beniger, Michael Kasay, Everett Ladd, Michael Neustadt, David Sears, Roberta Sigel, Donald Stoke, Howard Taylor, and Richard Ullman.

Eric Shiraev
Richard Sobel

About the Authors

Eric Shiraev is the author, co-author, and co-editor of several books including *America: A Sovereign Defender or Cowboy Nation?*, *International Public Opinion and the Bosnia Crisis*, *Cross-Cultural Psychology*, *Fears in Post-Communist Societies*, *Anti-Americanism in Russia: From Stalin to Putin*, *Accent of Success*, and *The Russian Transformation*. He received a Ph.D. from St. Petersburg University (Russia) and completed a post-doctoral program at UCLA, and he now teaches political psychology and international relations at George Mason University and serves as a research associate at George Washington University. His prime area of interest is the interplay among politics, culture, and psychology.

Richard Sobel is author of *The Impact of Public Opinion on U.S. Foreign Policy Since Vietnam*, editor of *Public Opinion in U.S. Foreign Policy*, and co-editor of *International Public Opinion and the Bosnia Crisis*. He has taught about public opinion and policy at Princeton University, Smith College, University of Connecticut, and Harvard University and has spoken at universities and in the media on the public and policy in the United States and abroad. A Chicago native and graduate of Princeton and the University of Massachusetts, he is a Research Fellow at Harvard Medical School and has been a Senior Research Associate of the Roper Center for Public Opinion Research. His central interests include how public opinion and politics influence foreign policy in the U.S. and internationally.

CHAPTER 1

Introduction: The Nature of Public Opinion

Herein lies the tragedy of the age: not that men are poor—all men know something of poverty; not that men are wicked—who is good? Not that men are ignorant—what is truth? Nay, but that men know so little of men.

W.E.B. Du Bois

D o you want to be known as an average person? Most people don't. We tend to believe we are unique: our bodies, characters, thoughts, and feelings—all features we are born with or acquire over time—become part of our own unique existence and knowledge. And yet, day after day, people often refer to other people as average. We frequently say "people believe" or "people don't understand," having in mind the "average other." Politicians and pundits speak for the average individual and repeat standard phrases that begin "The American people want. . . . " Economists lecture about average workers, typical buyers, and ordinary investors. Political scientists refer to the average voter. Sociologists describe the behavior of the average man, woman, teenager, suburbanite, and adult. Social scientists seldom deal with single individuals; experts have to find and interpret averages—the trends, the tendencies, and the majorities. The scientific understanding of people's views on society and politics—this textbook's subject—is impossible without the use of averages and percentages. Although every individual human being is distinctive, when we describe social processes and tendencies we must make generalizations.

Welcome to the world of statistical averages! In this opening vignette, we make judgments about the opinions, values, and views of the average American: one who lives in the beginning of the 21st century and who represents public opinion, the values and views of the American majority. What are the attitudes of the average American? What do majorities think these days about social and political issues, problems, and dilemmas? Let's generalize at this moment about what hundreds of opinion polls reveal.

The average American today is generally satisfied with the way things are going in the United States; favors the death penalty for people convicted of murder; opposes laws prohibiting possession of handguns; believes the courts do not deal harshly enough with criminals; opposes same-sex marriages; supports the right of women to obtain an abortion; approves a greater government role in environmental protection; supports limited military engagements of the United States abroad; does not have distinct views on affirmative action and school vouchers. . . . But wait! Where did these conclusions come from? The answer: surveys conducted by respected polling firms. Hold on! Isn't it true that analyzing the same surveys suggests that the average American supports a life sentence without parole for murderers rather than the death penalty? Isn't it correct that when there are casualties, the average American is less likely to support military engagements overseas? Don't these polls reveal that the typical American has serious reservations about when and why a woman has a right to an abortion? Don't these surveys show that if there is a choice between preventing crime and punishing criminals, the average American prefers prevention? If so, which analysis gives us more accurate and objective information about the average American or the average citizen of another country?

The answer is both, depending on the point of view. This textbook presents different angles of, or approaches to, the analysis of public opinion. Therefore, we direct your attention to the principles of critical thinking in the process of interpreting surveys. Studying people's opinions is not about taking one snapshot of their thoughts about an issue. It is about examining averages, tracking tendencies, and establishing similarities among and differences between people's collective opinions. This book is an attempt to canvass the diversity of human attitudes and to sketch a few underlying reasons for the differences. Yet, keep in mind that behind numbers and averages are survey respondents—human beings—who answer specific questions under specific circumstances.

Looking Forward. This first chapter, "Introduction: The Nature of Public Opinion," describes the nature and types of public opinion, its social role, value, and impact on contemporary society. The chapter describes kinds of public opinion and illustrates how public opinion translates into political involvement. It also introduces the influence of opinion on government and public policy, and it briefly sketches a history of polling.

WHAT IS PUBLIC OPINION?

Public opinion is the predominant idea, sentiment, or attitude held by members of a social grouping on specific social and political issues. It typically describes sentiments held by members of large populations—of states, territories, or, more commonly, entire nations. Occasionally, the term is used to describe opinions in smaller social groups—a political party's membership, a school's student body, or a corporation's workforce. In exploring how people express their ideas, this book pays particular attention to opinions and attitudes about issues, dilemmas, and problems of social and political significance. Although public opinion is more than the results shown in polls, public opinion and popular attitudes are typically identified through polling, the scientific method of measuring opinion.

Any attempt to examine public opinion involves making generalizations. Take, for instance, surveys that ask Americans to evaluate their satisfaction or dissatisfaction with the way things are going in the country. How is it possible to make generalizations about people's diverse opinions of this issue? Our mood can change daily, and it affects our perception of reality. Each of us can feel good about our own life today but feel less optimistic when something goes wrong. Events can go well in society, yet—because of personal unfavorable circumstances—an individual may see the world painted in gray. On the other hand, events may not be going well in society, but for some individuals, life is beautiful. In answering questions on public opinion surveys, people express their own unique outlooks.

Polls do not, however, reflect our individuality and uniqueness. What they show is how opinions are distributed within a social group or across an entire society. Let's return to the issue of people's satisfaction with the events around them. For example, in May 2004, 37 percent of Americans were satisfied with the way things were going in the United States at that time (Gallup/CNN/*USA Today,* May 7, 1,003). On the other hand, in 1992, a similar survey registered the lowest satisfaction of the early 1990s: just 21 percent felt satisfied (Gallup News Service, 2002). These findings do not give us any information about *why* respondents expressed opinions in that particular way. What the findings show is that more people in 2002 than in 1992 expressed satisfaction with the events around them.

Types of Public Opinion

People convey at least six levels or kinds of popular opinion. Public opinion can be divided into three major categories. The first is **consensus,** typically defined as midway between a majority and unanimity in a population, or at least 75 percent agreement on an issue (McClosky, 1964). Consensus represents a very widely held view that dominates an issue; for instance, in 2002, consensus was that the federal government programs for healthcare needed to be expanded (77 percent) (Bouton & Page, 2002, p. 24).

The second is **majority opinion,** which is registered when more than 50 percent of a population expresses a similar opinion on an issue. In a 2003 survey, 60 percent of Americans said the United States spends "too much" on foreign aid to developing countries; 21 percent said the amount is "about right," and 9 percent said "too little" (Princeton/Kaiser/Harvard, October 2002, 1,201). According to this survey, the majority of Americans believed the government spends too much on foreign aid. In democratic countries, the sentiment of a majority about important social issues carries a special political meaning for both citizens and leaders. A 50 percent threshold generally allows candidates to win elections, legislators to pass laws, and committees to establish a policy. Majority rule is one of the most common features of democracy.

A third category of opinion is **plurality opinion,** which occurs when the largest proportion of people that has a similar opinion on an issue that is smaller than a majority. For example, poll respondents expressed four types of opinions about one of the major foreign policy problems of the past decade—the anti-U.S. stance of Saddam Hussein and his government in Iraq. In a survey conducted in 1998 (Princeton Survey Research, February 1998, 751), long before the 2003 war with Iraq, 18 percent supported "limited air strikes" against Iraq; 36 percent supported "all-out air and ground military action"; and 39 percent supported "continued diplomatic efforts." The idea of "diplomatic efforts" was the plurality opinion here.

It is important to emphasize that public opinion, typically, represents a range or distribution of opinions. In a democratic society, people are not expected to have unanimous views on social and political issues. In most cases, opinions are distributed among dissimilar points of view. Surveys rarely show that 90 percent of the population supports or opposes an issue, idea, or person. For example, during the first months after the September 11, 2001, terrorist attacks on the United States, polls showed that between 85 and 92 percent of Americans supported the president's performance. This was one of the highest approval ratings in history. In periods less fraught with perceived dangers, presidents typically receive far lower support from the public.

A fourth kind of public opinion is called **intense minority opinion.** Some issues, such as whether or not the government should allow abortions, permit gay marriages, or establish a system for rating Hollywood movies, intensely concern some individuals but not others. Some people have a personal interest in specific policies; some care a great deal about particular issues or values, and some are simply better informed about certain aspects of life. Intense minorities often express their opinions in political behavior, such as protests, demonstrations, and single-issue voting.

A fifth and related category is the **attentive public,** or the group of people who pay attention to a particular policy area or social issue. The attentive public may express intense minority opinions or represent a group with special interests or knowledge of a topic, such as foreign policy or civil rights programs. The attentive public may include opinion leaders with special knowledge of a particular issue area.

Over the past 50 years, with the exceptions of the Vietnam War and the period in 2001–2002 when homeland security became the most important problem, few foreign policy issues have become areas of intense concern for the majority in the United States. When people are asked to answer an open-ended question by naming the most important issue in deciding their vote for president, they typically mention the economy, education, and healthcare. In 2003, as an example, one in every three Americans (33 percent) mentioned the "economy in general" as the most important issue; 15 percent mentioned employment. Terrorism was suggested by 8 percent and education by 7 percent (Gallup, May 2003, 1,005).

One of the paradoxes of public opinion is that even without detailed knowledge of national and international affairs, most people still have views on a great variety of issues, including the death penalty, abortion, affirmative action, the military budget,

A CASE IN POINT 1.1 Elitist Commentators or Next-Door Neighbors?

Do the American media elite represent the opinions of the American public? Do they speak on behalf of working people, students, small entrepreneurs, farmers, teachers, police officers, technicians, and nurses? Or do they represent the views of engineers, physicians, CEOs, college professors, lawyers, and software designers? The media elite and the public may be as widely separated in their views as the south and north poles. Reporters and commentators, on the other hand, are closer to the government in their views and activities; the media and government often blend by means of professional affiliations and family ties. Examples? The principal ABC analyst and anchor George Stephanopoulos was a close adviser to Bill Clinton. A star analyst of MSNBC, Chris Matthews, was a speechwriter for Jimmy Carter. CNN star correspondent Christiane Amanpour married former State Department spokesman James Rubin. Tony Snow, a popular columnist and television and radio commentator, was a speechwriter in the Reagan and Bush administrations (1989–1992). ABC's Diane Sawyer was a Richard Nixon press aide. NBC's leading policy expert, Tim Russert, was special counsel to Senator Daniel Patrick Moynihan, a powerful Democrat in Congress. *New York Times* political columnist William Safire was a speechwriter for President Nixon. While Andrea Mitchell reported for prime-time NBC news programs, her husband, Alan Greenspan, served as the chairman of the Federal Reserve. A journal editor and television expert, William Kristol, was Vice President Dan Quayle's chief of staff. Can you continue this list?

Some critics argue, "So what?" They imply that political correspondents and anchors have to have a good knowledge of American politics and international relations, and what better place to obtain this knowledge than in the government? Besides, Larry King, Tom Brokaw, Bill O'Reilly, Dan Rather, and many other television analysts and anchors did not work for presidents, vice presidents, or other high government officials. Journalism, some argue, is a profession like any other, drawing people of different backgrounds and political platforms.

Questions:

Do you think media commentators usually represent your opinions on social and political issues? Which commentators or reporters have a greater impact on your views than others?

and U.S. response to developments in other countries (Delli Carpini and Keeter, 1996). Opinion polls typically do not distinguish between people who are seriously concerned about an issue and those who answer the question just because they are asked do to so. However, the attentive public, in contrast to uninterested and unconcerned individuals, attempts to engage in various forms of political participation with a goal in mind: to make their views heard and to translate them into social or political action. Among forms of participation are volunteer community activities, voting, campaigning, direct communications with representatives, and protest (Sobel, 1993a).

The sixth kind of public opinion is **elite opinion.** This is the prevailing sentiment among policymakers and those individuals capable of influencing the direction of domestic and foreign policy through their roles as security and defense executives, analysts, problem definers, gatekeepers, watchdogs, experts, and commentators (Page & Shapiro, 1988). Although elite opinion may be less familiar to the general public, it typically becomes known through public debates, briefings and statements, televised interviews, printed publications, and talk shows in which these individuals voice their opinions about domestic and foreign issues. These individuals may not only speak on behalf of "the people," but they may also become a source of others' opinions.

PUBLIC OPINION AND SOCIETY

It is necessary to consider people's opinions within the social context in which they are expressed. Nations and regions differ, and no society is homogeneous. No single factor influences all individuals' opinions. However, each person lives in a society that has a set of norms, values, and expectations of its members. In democratic societies since ancient Athens, government policy has been meant to reflect the will of the people. In short, governments are supposed to express public attitudes in legal forms.

Customs and laws determine the boundaries of acceptable actions and illegal behavior. Societal norms and values determine appropriate and inappropriate attitudes. In some countries, the law even establishes what opinions are considered illegal, so a person who expresses forbidden ideas may be punished. What factors should be considered in analyzing survey results? We present these as guidelines.

- The overall political environment in which a poll is taken—primarily the nature of government and its institutions—affects the content of both survey questions and respondents' answers.

Knowledgeable observers, for instance, are cautious about accepting opinion polls conducted in totalitarian or authoritarian states (such as former communist countries and contemporary North Korea, China, Iran, and Cuba) for at least three reasons. First, many people living under totalitarian regimes are reluctant to give their true opinions, especially about social and political issues, because they fear retribution from the authorities for their politically incorrect answers. Second, the ruling regime or party would oppose sponsoring or at least publicizing the results of any poll whose outcome was unfavorable to the government. Third, poll results can be "corrected," or tampered with, to produce an outcome more desirable to the authorities. In many developing democracies in Eastern Europe—including Russia, for instance—governments control some or most national polling and media organizations. When an authoritarian state is in charge of opinion polls, there is little hope the government would be willing to publicize unfavorable opinions revealed in surveys.

- People's pragmatic evaluations of what is useful to them and what is not, as well as cultural, ideological, and religious values, determine popular views and orientations about events and issues—in short, what is public opinion.

Let's give several examples. During the past decade, in most developed democratic nations, the majority of adults were against the death penalty for murder. A remarkable exception to this opinion pattern appears in two countries: Japan and the United States. Rooted in a variety of cultural and ideological beliefs, this tough approach to criminals has been reflected in a predominant opinion in both countries for more than 30 years (see Chapter 11 on domestic issues).

Here is another example. Traditionally, Canadians are more attentive to foreign affairs than Americans and show more willingness to intervene for humanitarian reasons in ethnic conflicts abroad than do Americans (Carriere et al., 2003). This support, according to many observers, stems largely from a belief shared by a majority of Canadians about their country's humanitarian mission in the world and the government's involvement in international affairs.

When the United States and its North Atlantic Treaty Organization (NATO) allies began air strikes against Yugoslavia to stop Serbian aggression against Muslim minorities in Kosovo, most people in Europe expressed support of the military action, initiated in 1999. However, the majority of people in Greece, though a NATO country, criticized the United States and condemned the bombing of Serbian cities. Why? One reason was that most Greeks are Orthodox Christians, as are most Serbs. The Greeks and Serbs share not only a common border and religion but also a long history of trade, cooperation, and endless struggle against foreign invasions. Similarly, in 2003, most people in predominantly Muslim Turkey and Pakistan opposed the invasion of Iraq, another Muslim nation, though ultimately their governments lent some support to the United States and its close allies.

- Social norms and practices affect what types of survey questions are asked and how people answer. If social norms and values change, opinion polls reflect these changes.

Consider the evolution of societal values related to sex and sexual behavior and their influence on the evolution of opinion polls. Until the 1930s, the United States had an unwritten prohibition of public discussion of venereal diseases. In the 1940s, the situation changed; the media picked up the discussion about these diseases' causes, prevention, and treatment. Gallup and later Roper (major polling organizations) started to use survey questions about venereal diseases to measure people's views on the government's actions targeted to curb this growing problem. Although human sexual behavior was discussed in survey questions as early as the 1930s (the Kinsey Report was released in 1948 and revealed a wider variety of sexual behaviors than was previously recognized), surveys with questions about homosexuality did not appear regularly until the early 1970s. In that period, which featured what is often called the sexual revolution, opinions of many Americans—including opinion leaders—on sex and sexual orientation became more

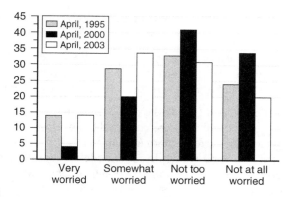

FIGURE 1.1

Distribution of answers to the question: "How worried are you that you or someone in your family will become a victim of a terrorist attack—very worried, somewhat worried, not too worried or not worried at all?"
Sources: Princeton/Pew, April 2003, 674; Gallup/CNN USA Today, April 2000, 1,006; Gallup/CNN and USA Today, April 1995, 1,008.

tolerant than they had been in previous decades. Social acceptance of particular topics changes, and these changes affect the contents of the questions asked in polls and the willingness of survey subjects to respond sincerely.

- People tend to become attentive to events and issues when something dramatic or outstanding happens around them.

Think about opinions and fears about possible terrorist attacks. After the attacks on New York City and Washington, DC, on September 11, 2001, when thousands of lives were destroyed, 43 percent of survey respondents expressed "a great deal of concern" that there would be more major terrorists attacks on the United States (*Washington Post,* September 28, 2001, 1,215). A year before, in 2000, when asked if they were worried about becoming attack victims, 24 percent expressed such a worry about terrorists. In April 2003, during the war with Iraq, 42 percent were concerned about terrorism. We all tend to worry more about things that appear to represent immediate dangers or can affect our lives in a destructive way. (See Figure 1.1.)

SOCIAL VALUE OF OPINION POLLS

Opinion polls have become part of daily life in contemporary democracies; the results of surveys are published in newspapers, posted on the Web, and broadcast on television. While some people do not pay attention to them, many others do. Why do they pay attention to opinion polls?

Practical Value

Surveys convey important information about issues, products, or services, and some people base their decisions about these on survey results. Consumer surveys help businesses learn about the popularity of their products and services. A measure of overall success of multibillion-dollar television and radio industries, for example, is based on the ratings or assessments of popularity of shows like *ER* and *60 Minutes* (we discuss TV in Chapter 6 on the media and opinion). Based on what they learn from surveys, broadcasting companies charge more money for advertising on popular programs like the annual Super Bowl and less for ads shown during less popular shows like the *Nightly Business Report*.

Some individuals use survey information to determine how a particular product—an item for sale, political candidate, public official, or social policy—is perceived by the public. What do potential voters think about a possible change in the death penalty laws? Do people want to see their taxes spent on new defense initiatives? Does a candidate for president have a chance to win the White House? If people do not like the product, it can be changed; policies can be modified; product quality can be improved; an issue can be withdrawn from a campaign platform; and goods can be pulled off the shelves. Candidates may drop out of campaigns in response to polls. In certain situations, people's knowledge of the results of recent surveys may motivate them to decide whether or not to vote. For example, some people respond to the results of a preelection poll by thinking, "If 80 percent of voters in my district are going to vote for this candidate, why should I bother showing up at the polls on Tuesday? My vote won't make a difference." On the other hand, if surveys show a race is too close to call, many people may decide to cast their ballots to help to prevent a particular candidate's victory. This happened, for example, in Louisiana in 1992, when a record turnout on Election Day was determined primarily by most voters' desire to prevent a reactionary candidate, David Duke, from being elected U.S. Senator.

Comparative Value

Some people want to keep their eyes on what other people think or do. By comparing our own opinions to those held by other people, we learn not only about them but also about ourselves. "How do I vote as compared to others? What do other people think about this issue? Are my views off track or in line with the majority?" These thoughts sometimes cross our minds when we read material about other people's

---

A CASE IN POINT 1.2   Specific Opinions on Particular Policies

Surveys can help policymakers determine specific details about public support of particular policies. Consider an example related to environmental issues. When answering the question "Would you be willing to pay another 10 cents in taxes per gallon of gas, which would fund more research and development of alternative energy sources and encourage people to use less gas?" 58 percent of surveyed Americans said yes and 39 percent said no. When the question was reformulated as "Would you be willing to pay another 50 cents in taxes per gallon of gas, which would fund more research and development of alternative energy sources and encourage people to use less gas?" support waned significantly; just 24 percent supported the idea, while 73 percent refused to endorse it (Princeton/*Newsweek*, November 2001, 1,001). People approve of certain policies but, apparently, attach price tags to them.

views and behavior. Research shows that many individuals seek other people's opinions before they formulate their own. In these cases, public opinion itself becomes news (Lenart, 1994; Bardes, 1999). One poll showed that 57 percent of Americans are very interested and 31 percent are somewhat interested in other Americans' attitudes about enduring social issues, such as gun control, abortion, and affirmative action (Gallup, July 1999, 1,021).

As discussed in Chapter 4, many people express an opinion in order to be in line or consistent with the majority of other people. For instance, 71 percent of Americans supported the death penalty for a person convicted of murder (Gallup, May 2004, 1,000). Some reason that "If most individuals support the death penalty in America,

---

A CASE IN POINT 1.3 When Pollsters and Their Sponsors "Go Wrong"

Push Polls

Surveys may not only inform us about other people's opinions; they can influence our own opinions. Sometimes deliberately, occasionally inadvertently, pollsters use surveys to influence views. Push polls are an example. A weekly poll on the website of the Democratic National Committee (DNC) in 2000 asked visitors: "As the nation approaches a new millennium, what are the most important priorities facing our next president? Saving Social Security, strengthening Medicare and paying down the debt, or implementing George W. Bush's $1.7 trillion risky tax scheme that overwhelmingly benefits the wealthy?" (Suellentrop, 2000). This wording of this survey was meant to bias the reader in a particular direction. A similar poll would have resulted if Republicans called people by phone to ask how potential voters felt about Democratic attempts to raise taxes "unfairly" on hardworking Americans.

These are examples of a push poll or advocacy poll in which telephone calls or online surveys give people biased and negative information about a candidate or a policy. The poll organizers want to push people away from a candidate or toward support of an issue. In these cases mentioned here, the pollsters did not care much about polling or any other kind of research. Both parties use polls to advance their positions. The Democrats deliberately called the Bush's plan "risky" and accused it of benefitting the rich. The Republicans organized a counterattack by asking supporters to send pro-Republican political messages to the DNC site.

Representatives of both major parties as well as other political parties and organizations occasionally conduct these types of pseudo surveys. However, push polls violate the American Association for Public Opinion Research (AAPOR) Code of Ethics because they tend to mislead respondents, whereas well-conducted and well-designed polls accurately ask about and represent the opinions of a population or group. Because push polls can easily be confused with real polls, they damage the reputation of legitimate polling, thereby discouraging the public from participating in legitimate survey research (AAPOR, 1996). As discussed in Chapter 3, it is important to think critically about the quality of any poll.

this means that this policy is generally okay; there cannot be so many people totally wrong about this issue!" A 1999 poll taken in Japan revealed that almost 80 percent of the nation supported the death penalty, a record level of approval compared to six similar polls conducted in Japan since 1956 (*The Daily Yomiuri,* 1999). Knowing that 60 or 80 percent of the population shares an opinion may cause some individuals to express the same view, especially if the issue under consideration is relatively remote from the individual's immediate concerns. We should not forget, however, that certain people like to express an opinion that contradicts the majority's views. They may reason, "If most people think this way, I'll think the opposite." Studies show that some adolescents develop their opinions in this way (Rice & Dolgin, 2002).

Political and Ideological Value

Opinion polls can show which issues draw greater support of potential voters and which problems leave voters indifferent. Individuals running for public office want to know how strong their support is among potential voters. Knowledge about the level of support has tremendous implications, and it influences campaign strategies (as we discuss in Chapter 10 on voting). Specific information about voters' choices in districts and states, issue preferences of women and men, support of different age and income groups, and many other facts about voters' preferences and participation are extremely valuable to political parties and candidates (Wayne, 2000).

Polls, viewed in perspective, reflect predominant tendencies of public opinion. Supported by the majority of the population, these views often become principles on which domestic and foreign policies are built (Sobel & Shiraev, 2003). Recognizing such patterns helps in the formation of a national consensus by demonstrating the knowledge and understanding among informed citizens about long-term policies and societal institutions. For example, most Democratic candidates in recent campaigns have not promised to initiate measures to stop the death penalty or ban possession of firearms because they were aware of a trend of American public opinion in support of capital punishment and against outlawing guns. Most Republican candidates, similarly, do not promise to initiate laws to prohibit all abortions because most Americans are not likely to support these measures (see Chapter 11 on domestic issues).

Overall Resistance to Polling

Have you heard and read about the poor reputations of opinion polls? Some people say polls are *useless* because public opinion is so volatile that it is impossible to take an accurate snapshot of it. Others suggest surveys are *biased* because they are sponsored by politicians and large corporations that want to get information from people and then use it in pursuit of their own goals. Here is one of many critical proclamations against polling found on the Web. It suggests that people who are unhappy with surveys take steps to resist further polling. <personal.riverusers.com/~thegrendel/polls.html>

> So, what to do about this polling scam? *Refuse to participate.* If called upon by a pollster, answer "No thanks." Remember that the polling industry makes big bucks from the opinions of the people who take part in a poll or opinion survey, but the suckers themselves get nothing. Moreover, you can have a greater effect on the poll by opting out than by joining in. If a small but significant proportion of the population outright refuses to participate in a poll, then the pollster's "representative sample" becomes a joke. Oddly enough, your opinion weighs more heavily if kept secret.

There are several reasons why some people dislike polls and pollsters. One reason is *social-psychological:* Certain individuals or groups whose views are not dominant in society tend to downgrade the importance of opinion polls that show differences between them and other people. It is common for such individuals to be critical of the knowledge level of respondents, the design of the survey, the quality of the questions posed, and the timing of the polling. There are also *ideological* reasons. Believers in a conservative ideology, for example, call for less control over individual activities. An opinion poll, from this ideological standpoint, can be viewed as an invasion of an individual's privacy. Can you think about other reasons some individuals hold skeptical or negative opinions about polls?

GOVERNMENT: DOES PUBLIC OPINION MATTER?

Comedian Dennis Miller once joked about his attitude toward U.S. presidents: "Do what you are supposed to do, and leave us alone!" Millions of people are not concerned about what a local or national government does. Some individuals express little interest in public affairs and do not care much about a wide range of social and political issues. Many people do not pay attention to domestic or foreign policy and hardly recognize the name of their state senators or gubernatorial candidates. They neither petition the government nor vote in elections.

Some people care strongly about and take notice of what the government does. Therefore, they vote. Others not only vote but also give financial support to political candidates, sign petitions, and participate in rallies. Millions of people want their opinions to be heard in federal, state, and local offices. Letters and phone calls flood state and national capitals. In the mid-1990s, people started to use email to express their opinions. For instance, the number of email messages flowing into the U.S. House of Representatives doubled between 1998 and 2000 and by 2005 should approach 100 million a year. These are all forms of expression of public sentiment that is potentially different from those reflected in polls.

Two Views on Government and Polls

Walter Lippmann, the classic analyst of public opinion, once wrote that people desire democratic government not for its own sake but rather for its results (Lippmann, 1922). Therefore, many people expect their government to do what they, the citizens, believe it should do. Does the government respond to the people's voice? To what extent does public opinion influence the policies enacted by the government? There are two views on how public opinion should affect policy.

- According to the first outlook, in a democracy, people's representatives should be relatively independent decision makers, or trustees. Acting on behalf of their constituencies, officials nevertheless should not rush to address every grievance of the citizens or to satisfy every wish of their voters. The government is obliged to represent only the public's true and stable concerns and global interests, and not the public's emotional reactions to changing events (Nisbet, 2000). The uninformed or poorly informed public can be a source of instability in politics. To summarize this view, government should pay selective attention to certain public opinion.

- According to the opposing view, the people's elected representatives in the government, or delegates, should conduct policy in response to their constituents'

A TOPIC FOR CLASS DISCUSSION Factors Mediating Public Opinion's Influence on Policy (see Figure 1.2)

Government institutions and communications.

The structures of political institutions and political communications include the type of republic, that is, parliamentary or presidential; formal distribution of roles among policy institutions; frequency of national and local elections; design and ownership of the media; basic socioeconomic conditions; and level of institutionalization of opinion polls by the government.

Political arenas and elections.

Policy debate takes place in specific political arenas that reflect political interests pursued by the government and its opposition. Special areas of attention include existing government coalitions with other parties; debates and struggles within the government; political struggles between the ruling party and other political forces; domestic and international political issues relevant to election campaigns; and decision makers' anticipation of public reaction to policy-related issues in their attempts to either maintain or boost their popularity.

Political participation.

Less knowledgeable and unmotivated individuals have little impact on policy. An ill-informed public is subject to manipulation by elites who are able to solicit public support for their policy initiatives. Voters and nonvoters often have very different opinions, especially about economic issues.

requests and wishes. Prominent pollsters of the 20th century hoped polling would increase the impact of public opinion on policy. A pioneer in modern polling and an advocate of democracy, George Gallup (1985), for example, contended that almost any opinion held by ordinary people should be taken into account by governing elites. Louis Harris, another prominent pollster, in *The Anguish of Change* (1973) also promoted the need for officials to closely follow public opinion and stop underestimating the public's knowledge and intelligence.

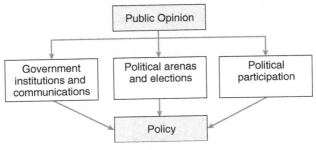

FIGURE 1.2

Factors mediating public opinion's influence on policy. (Shiraev & Sobel, 2003)

What do the Americans think about public opinion polls and their influence on government? On the one hand, a substantial proportion of people want public opinion to matter in government affairs. A Washington, DC, pollster, Steven Kull, and his colleagues (2000) found that, in general, most people feel politicians should pay more attention to public opinion. On the other hand, they also expect public officials to develop rational and independent policy on behalf of their electorate. In a 2003 poll, 33 percent of respondents said opinion polls have too much power and influence in Washington, whereas 48 percent disagreed and said the polls have too little influence (Harris, February, 1,010).

A 2000 poll asked registered voters a multiple-choice question: "In general, when elected officials decide how to vote on important issues, do you think they should pay the most attention to: their own knowledge and conscience, experts involved with that issue, their constituents who contact them about the issue, their campaign contributors, or public opinion polls?" No predominant opinion was expressed in response to this question. Twenty percent of respondents mentioned *experts;* 18 percent suggested *opinion polls*; 22 percent pointed out *constituencies,* and 19 percent mentioned officials' *own knowledge and conscience*. The only minimal category was campaign contributors: only 1 percent wanted elected officials to pay attention to this group (Fox, May 2000, registered voters, 900).

Politicians pay attention to public opinion and polls to govern better and to get reelected. Sometimes they try to ignore or manipulate public opinion to support the politician's own policy preferences.

What about governmental responses to public opinion? Overall, public opinion constrains and stimulates policy (Sobel, 2001). In fact, studies that compared public opinion with actual policy outcomes show relative consistency between opinion and policy; in more than 500 issues examined during a 30-year period beginning in the 1960s, the consistency between the predominant views and corresponding policy was found in approximately 60 percent of cases (Monroe, 1998; Weissberg, 1978). High congruence between public opinion and policies (66 percent) was found in a study of 300 policy-related issues and problems between 1935 and 1979 (Shapiro & Page, 1999). Although these studies did not show whether public opinion influenced sentiments expressed through polls or whether government decisions shaped people's views on domestic and foreign affairs, by and large, a correspondence between policy and public opinion exists.

However, just because the public maintains strong and stable opinions about a specific issue does not necessarily mean that people's hopes and expectations should automatically translate into new laws and policies. Circumstances mediate, or act as means to translate, the impact of public opinion on policymaking. (Figure 1.2.) The impact of public opinion on government derives from several mediating factors or conditions, including political institutions and communications, political competition, election, and other forms of political participation.

Political Structure: Institutions and Communications

National political systems are organized in particular ways so that public opinion may or may not act as a catalyst to domestic or foreign-policy actions. A country's political structure, including parties, bureaucracies, political competitors, and pressure groups, may or may not transmit opinions to the policy process. National governments have different traditions of soliciting and considering public opinion as a factor in policymaking. This process is called the **institutionalization of polling.** Look at some trends in the ways polls are institutionalized.

- Historically, the leaders of nondemocratic regimes care less about public opinion than do democratic governments. A dictator or military ruler may discount public opinion because his policies are not implemented through democratic means.

- Public opinion is expected to influence policy more directly in two-party parliamentary settings (such as the United States) than in coalition-based multiparty assemblages (such as Germany and Italy). Stronger parties should be better conduits of public opinion than weaker ones (Risse-Kappen, 1991).

- National systems with concentrated and sophisticated channels of communications, involving parties, interest groups, bureaucracies, and the media, generally provide better conditions for public opinion expression than systems with underdeveloped or fragmented communications.

Political Landscape and Elections

Public opinion sets limits on the actions of elected representatives largely because most public officials want to be reelected. Thus, policymakers tend not to act against overwhelming public support of or opposition to certain issues (Serafino & Storrs, 1993). Mistakes cost the decision maker politically. In the United States, within a presidential administration, major elected officials, cabinet secretaries, and other high-level executives confirmed by the Senate are typically more responsive to public opinion than nonpolitically appointed career officials (Sobel, 2001).

The desire to be elected or reelected creates pressing incentives for politicians to respond to public opinion in order to avoid falling too far out of line with most voters. Assumptions about a positive public reaction to a proposed action or policy contribute to a permissive policy climate, whereas anticipation of criticism may contribute to a nonpermissive climate. Political opposition is less likely to challenge policy decisions if the public support of such actions is overwhelming. On the other hand, the opposition is more likely to challenge the government if public reactions are negative, split, or expected to be negative or divided.

Political Participation

Political elites and activists tend to be more influential than people who do not have particular interests in social issues. People who pay attention to politics and social events are more knowledgeable about how government works and how to influence it (Delli Carpini & Keeter, 1996). An ill-informed public typically becomes subject to manipulation by elites who have both power and resources to create or boost temporary public support for their policy initiatives. On the other hand, many politicians actively seek or pay attention to opinion polls that support their views on issues. Public officials often cite supportive polls as a justification for a decision or policy.

WEB

Go to
ablongman.com/shiraev
for more information
on this topic.

The history of polling in the United States goes back to the 19th century, when interest groups and newspapers attempted to investigate voting preferences of local audiences. By the middle of the 20th century, opinion polls were a customary feature in newspapers and magazines. Some early polling, such as the *Literary Digest* prediction that President Franklin Roosevelt would lose in 1936 and the *Chicago Tribune*'s declaration that New York governor Thomas Dewey beat President Harry Truman in 1948, turned out to be disastrously wrong. Many elements of survey procedure—research design, compilation of a sample, design of questions, and training of pollsters—came from psychological research and, in particular, from advertising studies conducted by behavioral scientists. Despite setbacks, polling accuracy increased. Advances in methods of statistical analysis, such as random selection, brought greater understanding of the role of sampling in describing large segments of population. George Gallup founded the American Institute of Public Opinion in 1935. In the same year, *Fortune* magazine introduced its new survey, administered under the direction of two market research experts, Elmo Roper and Paul Cherrington. In 1956 the polling firm of Louis Harris and Associates was founded and quickly gained reputation and popularity. In the 1970s, most polling companies switched from face-to-face interviews to telephone surveys. In that decade and the next, media polls became popular in newspapers like the *New York Times* and the *Washington Post* and for television networks like CBS and ABC. Many of these polls are now archived for research use at the Roper Center for Public Opinion Research at the University of Connecticut or the Survey Research Center at the University of Michigan.

Links to Important National Polling Organizations

American Association for Public Opinion Research: www.aapor.org

The Center on Policy Attitudes: www.policyattitudes.org

The Gallup Organization: www.gallup.com

Harris Polls: www.harrisinteractive.com

Inter-university Consortium for Political and Social Research: www.icpsr.org

National Election Studies: www.umich.edu/~nes

The National Opinion Research Center: www.norc.uchicago.edu

The Pew Research Center for the People and the Media: www.people-press.org

The Roper Center for Public Opinion Research: www.ropercenter.uconn.edu

The Survey Research Center: www.isr.umich.edu/src

ASSIGNMENT 1.1   PROLIFERATING INFORMATION SOURCES

Americans today are exposed to an increasing variety of information sources. Facing increasing amounts of written, digital, visual, and audio information on radio, television, and the Internet, the average citizen reaches a media threshold—a type of information overload under which the individual is exposed to more information than she or he can handle. The inability of individuals to handle the intensifying informational avalanche leads to a reduction in the number of media sources (channels, programs, etc.) to which the individual listens. As a result, viewers tend to minimize the number of sources they use for personal education, information, and entertainment. The individual tries to find a stable package of channels and programs to which he or she feels attached. These channels, programs, print sources, and websites begin to play special, sometimes exceptional and exclusive roles in the person's life. In short, people tend to narrow the sources of information for their views.

"When it comes to your most important views and beliefs about life, which influences have had a greater impact on your life or had the biggest influence on your thinking?" Over the years, a question about information sources was asked by different polling organizations. In 2001, answering a similar multiple-choice question about information sources, responses were split among several answers.

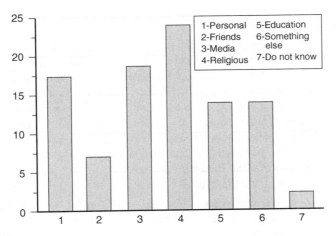

1-Personal   5-Education
2-Friends   6-Something
3-Media   else
4-Religious   7-Do not know

FIGURE 1.3

Distribution of answers to the question: "Which of the following has had the biggest influence on your thinking on. . . ?"
Source: Princeton/Pew, March 2001, 2,041. (Average scores on the following issues: euthanasia, human cloning, government's help to the poor, use of the military against genocide, same-sex marriages, help people in need, and death penalty for murder.)

Figure 1.3 lists the distribution of answers to the question "Which one of the following has had the biggest influence on your thinking on . . . ?"

What are the main information sources of your opinions on social and political issues, such as human cloning and government help to the poor? For each issue, identify the most influential source. Is it personal experience, family, friends, media impact, religious beliefs, education, or something else? (If the last, please identify it.) Find a partner in class and exchange your answers. After you finish, conduct a poll of the class. Tally the individual results. Use the following table for answers. Compare the class data with the results of the national survey (see Figure 1.3).

	Personal experience	Friends/ Family	Media influence	Religious beliefs	Education	Something else	Don't know
Euthanasia							
Human cloning							
Death penalty							
Same-sex marriages							
Military aid to countries							
Helping people in need							
Taxes							

CHAPTER SUMMARY

- Public opinion is the predominant sentiment held by members of a social group on social and political issues. There are at least six kinds of public opinion. First, *consensus* (75 percent) is halfway between unanimity and majority. *Majority opinion* is identified in cases when more than 50 percent of a population expresses a similar opinion on an issue, and *plurality opinion* is the largest proportion of people sharing an opinion on an issue. A segment of a population may express concerns and beliefs called *intense minority opinions*. The *attentive public* are those who pay particular attention to specific policy areas. Finally, *elite opinion* is the prevailing sentiment among policymakers and other individuals capable of influencing the direction of domestic and foreign policy.

- Opinions must be understood within their social context. Several factors should be taken in consideration. The overall political environment in which a poll is taken affects the content of both survey questions and respondents' answers. Cultural, ideological, and religious values often affect respondents' views about and orientations to events and issues. Social norms and practices affect what questions are asked in surveys. If social norms and values change, questions in opinion polls reflect these changes. People tend to become attentive to events and issues when something dramatic happens around them in their community, in their country, or around the world.

- The practical, comparative, political, and ideological values of surveys are also determined by a variety of circumstances. Published surveys convey important information about issues, products, or services, and some people base their decisions about these on the survey results. Many people tend to keep their eyes on what other people think or do. By comparing our own opinions to those held by others we learn not only about those others but also about ourselves. In the world of politics, opinion polls can show which issues draw the support of potential voters and which problems do not. Politicians and public officials running for office turn to polls to estimate the strength of their support among potential voters.

- In the ongoing discussion about the impact of public opinion on policies enacted by government, there are two basic views on how public opinion should affect policy. According to the trustee outlook, in a democracy, people's representatives should be relatively independent decision makers. Acting on behalf of their constituencies, they should not address every grievance of the citizens or satisfy every wish of their voters. According to the delegate view, people's elected representatives should conduct policy in response to their constituents' requests and wishes.

- Specific circumstances mediate the impact of public opinion on policy. Among them are the structure of government institutions and communications, political competition and elections, and the level of people's engagement in politics. Overall, political elites and interested groups tend to be more influential than people who are not interested in social and political issues. Likewise, individuals who take active roles in the political process, join forces in effective groups, and command greater resources are typically more influential than the unorganized public.

Looking Ahead. After learning about the nature and types of public opinion in this introductory chapter, Chapter 2 on "Measuring Public Opinion" explains methods of survey research—in short, how to poll. Polls prepared according to professional standards produce results that are likely to be accurate and representative. The next chapter explores surveys, sampling, measures of relationship, problems with question wording, and ways to identify public attitudes other than polls. It offers critical suggestions about the process of gathering information and interpreting data in research studies.

DEFINITIONS OF KEY TERMS

Attentive public—Those who pay particular attention to a specific policy area or social issue.

Consensus—Agreement of at least three-quarters of a population on an issue.

Elite opinion—The prevailing sentiment among policy makers and other individuals capable of influencing the direction of domestic and foreign policy.

Institutionalization of polling—The process of soliciting and considering public opinion as a factor in government's policymaking.

Intense minority opinion—Views supported by a group of people who are attentive to a particular policy area or social issue.

Majority opinion—The view of more than 50 percent of a population in a distribution of opinions.

Mediate—To act as a means to translate one factor into another.

Plurality opinion—The opinion supported by the largest proportion of respondents when no group forms a majority.

Public opinion—The predominant sentiment held by members of a social grouping on a particular issue.

Push poll—A technique in which telephone calls or Web-based surveys are used to give people critical and often biased information about a candidate or a policy.

CHAPTER 2

Measurement of Opinion

One of the more intriguing
approaches to public opinion
is to study its accuracy.
Allen Wilcox and Leonard Weinberg, 1974

Movie characters create memorable phrases. Playing the ostentatious teacher Mr. Keating in the classic movie *Dead Poets Society*, Robin Williams declared, "No one can measure poetry!" His remark referred to a textbook author who dared to introduce a quantitative method of poetry measurement. Perhaps unintentionally, Mr. Keating touched on a centuries-old debate about whether it is possible to measure phenomena of the human mind.

Science should be based on reliable assessment of reality. The quality of research on people's opinions depends on the quality of its measurement (Kuhn, 1970). Today, the question is not only whether or not we can quantify opinions but also whether or not we can measure them accurately. To understand the diversity of human opinions, intentions, and values, to predict electoral outcomes with the smallest error, and to gauge consumers' product preferences, the specialist—a pollster, social or political scientist, or marketing expert—must gather reliable evidence. The information needs to be verifiable, and the data must be interpreted impartially.

Whether or not we can measure poetry is debatable. People's opinions, of course, are not poems; they are expressed as oral or written responses to one or a set of questions. Moreover, people read poetry and examine opinion polls for entirely different reasons.

Looking Forward. This chapter on "Measurement of Opinion" explains research methodology in studies of public opinion by providing an overview of the methods pollsters use today. The chapter explores surveys, samplings, correlations, and question wording, as well as ways to gauge public attitudes other than polls. It also offers

TABLE 2.1

A comparative analysis of average differences between national presidential polls and actual outcomes of presidential elections. In 1996, 1992, 1980, 1976, and 1968 a third candidate was included in the assessments. (In percentages.)

	1996	1992	1988	1984	1980	1976	1972	1968	1964	1960	1956
M1	1.7	2.2	1.5	2.4	3.0	1.5	2.0	1.3	2.7	1.0	1.8
M2	1.8	1.3	1.4	2.2	3.0	1.0	1.3	1.3	2.7	1.0	1.8

Source: Panagakis (1999).

critical suggestions about how to gather and interpret data in quantitative and qualitative studies.

MEASUREMENT AND HUMAN EXPRESSION

What kind of useful information can an observer find looking at the results of the following study? Nick Panagakis (1999) examined how close predictions were to the actual voting results in 11 U.S. elections from 1956 to 1996. He used two methods to calculate errors in national presidential polls. The first method (M1) calculates the average of the differences between national poll estimates and the election result. The second method (M2) establishes the average differences between the actual winning election margin of the Republican and Democratic candidates and national poll's predicted winning margin. The results of these two analyses are presented in Table 2.1.

What does this study suggest? First, it reveals the trend in relative accuracy in surveys about presidential preferences. A skeptical person may look at the table and see that the largest error (3 percent) was registered in the 1980 elections. The smallest percentage was in 1960 (1 percent). In fact, in 12 out of the 22 examples, the error was less than 2 percent. The study results also suggest that a considerable proportion of people are relatively certain about their voting preferences before Election Day. Finally, polls may help draw a conclusion: People are somewhat consistent in their presidential preferences, and it is useful to continue studying opinion because polls can provide a reasonably accurate preview of electoral outcomes.

By and large, **survey research** in public opinion is organized as a set of steps or stages, each of which requires special preparation. A brief description of these steps precedes a more detailed account of each.

STEPS IN SURVEY RESEARCH

Researchers need to follow certain rules as they conduct a study of people's opinions. Although research strategies differ, they share common rules, stages or steps.

1. Choose and describe a problem or issue to investigate. A survey sponsor may suggest this issue. Review the available literature related to this problem (including journals, magazines, online databases, and newspapers) to identify similar studies and their results.

2. Identify the research goal or an outcome you want—for example, new data reflecting people's opinions about a social or political issue, suggestions about why people expressed certain opinions, or a forecast of future elections. You can use at least two strategies. You can collect information and then make a conclusion, a generalization based on the available facts. Or, if you begin with a theoretical concept, you can collect information to test its validity.

3. Identify and describe the sample to be selected for your study. For example, depending on your goals, you can use a national sample, a local sample, a number of experts on social policy, fellow students, or other groups. Determining the composition of the sample is one of the most important steps in any survey research. Learn more about sample selection in opinion research later in this chapter.

4. Choose a methodology, a research method or methods you have to use to achieve your research goals. Using more than one method usually increases the validity of the conclusions.

5. Put together a schedule (timetable) for your project. Remember, most tasks take longer to accomplish than expected.

6. If possible, conduct a preliminary study (often called a pilot study) to see how well your methodology works, how people react to your questions, and whether or not you encounter probable or real obstacles to data collection.

7. Collect your research data from the field survey. Record the answers and prepare them for analysis.

8. Analyze your data and interpret them using basic methods of critical thinking (Chapter 3 is devoted to this topic).

9. Present the results in a report and display your data. Survey data are usually displayed as tables, charts, or graphs. Though space for a report is often limited, detailed explanations and comments are often needed. A data presentation describes the goals and results of your search and breaks down your description into easily followed subtopics. Finally, describe any problems in the survey. Suggest where and how your data could be or should be used to understand a social or political issue.

SAMPLE SELECTION
Types of Sampling

If a pollster wants to examine the opinions of residents of a particular state or country, he or she will find it is impossible to obtain responses from every individual. High cost and time limitations imposed on most surveys preclude a complete enumeration. Therefore, public opinion studies examine attitudes within samples, or specially selected groups of relatively small numbers of individuals, that represent a whole population (Hennessy, 1965; Vijver & Leung, 1997).

Sample selection in opinion research may be achieved through several strategies. One strategy is called **convenience sampling;** here, the researcher chooses a sample based on a particular reason, such as location of his or her professional or personal contacts in the area. For example, Hofstede (1980) examined opinions of several thousand IBM employees in various countries. He did not study employees of other international corporations. It is not unusual in survey research conducted by professors to ask college students to fill out questionnaires. It is also common for international graduate students to conduct comparative opinion research by selecting two samples, one in the United States and the other in their home country (Levin et al., 1998).

A better sampling strategy, called **random sampling,** chooses a group of respondents in a way that every member of the sample has an equal chance of being selected. Simple random sampling chooses respondents from an entire eligible group called a population. Systematic random sampling begins at a randomly chosen respondent, and then samples in consistent intervals, such as every 20th respondent. Random sampling is used in most public opinion polls. One of the main goals the researcher pursues is the creation of a sample that closely reflects the category of the population under investigation. Such a sample is called a **representative sample.** Random sampling, if it is planned and conducted correctly, is one of the most reliable methods of designing a representative sample of a large population.

A random sample represents a group (a city, a state, a nation) that may be thousands of times larger than itself. The average proportion of responses from a representative sample is likely to be a good estimation of the entire population. That is why a poll taken from a random sample of people mirrors the opinions of a country with a multimillion population. However, this is a general expectation about random sampling. Even random sampling may occasionally produce an unrepresentative sample, which differs significantly from the larger group it represents.

Sampling Error

The **sampling error** (or margin of error) indicates the extent to which a percentage estimated from a sample differs by chance from the figure calculated based upon the entire population it represents. In fact, sampling error exists in every sample except an entire population. It has been established, based on probability statistics, that in a country the size of the United States, in a national random sample consisting of roughly 600 individuals the odds are 95 out of 100 that the poll results are within less than 4 percent of the population value. For example, if a Gallup poll conducted in May and June 1984 found that 54 percent of Americans believed there were "too many" immigrants from Latin America, the true percent was likely to be between 58 and 50 percent (because the studied sample was 615 people). Major polling companies often use larger national samples: 1,000 or sometimes larger. In these cases, the probability is very high (95 percent) that the sampling or margin of error is not more than 3 percent. So if you find out that according to a *Newsweek* poll (October 2001), 71 percent of 1,004 Americans stated that the government should permit antiwar protests, this is likely to indicate that the actual percentage for the entire population was not higher than 74 percent, but it was probably no lower than 68 percent.

Determining the size of a representative sample is a problem in practically all opinion studies. Several statistical methods allow the researcher to choose the size and type of the sample (Heiman, 1996). Because sampling error declines as sample size grows, larger samples are generally more representative than smaller ones. However, non-sampling errors like poor study design or ambiguous question wording may also affect the validity of the findings of a survey.

Even though data collected from very small samples may yield trustworthy predictors of a population's opinions, humans tend to commit the error of overgeneralizing from too small a sample. Let's illustrate this concept in a simple hypothetical example. You conduct a preelection poll that measures students' support of one candidate for the Student Senate. You ask 110 students on campus and find out that out of 10 women you approached, 7 support one candidate. Out of 100 men who also gave their opinion, 59 said they would vote for the candidate. It looks like the candidate is getting more support from female students! Why? Because, based on an immediate assessment, "7 out of 10" is more convincing than "59 out of 100." However, which of these statistics is a more reliable indicator of how the entire college will vote? The more reliable indicator is the "59 out of 100" because it is drawn from a larger sample. The main error committed in this survey interpretation is that women's answers were gauged from a small sample of 10 respondents, which would be less representative than the larger sample. We should mention, however, that a sample of 110 people may not be representative of a campus population unless it is chosen randomly.

In review. The smaller the sample, the greater the sampling error. The larger the sample, the lower the sampling error. Estimates derived from larger random samples are typically more reliable than estimates derived from smaller samples.

Sampling and Accuracy of Polls

Some surveys are less accurate than others. Take, for example, so-called **straw polls,** which are informal snapshots of public opinion designed to establish some understanding of how opinions and preferences are distributed. Television networks, other news organizations, and websites carry out many of these polls. For example, MSNBC.COM, CNN.COM, and FOXNEWS.COM conduct online polls on topics ranging from politics to sports and photography. Although tens of thousands of emails may be sent to the site by Web visitors, these surveys hardly reflect the distribution of opinions of the entire nation. They are likely to reflect the opinions of the population of individuals who are young, have Internet access, and have a particular interest in answering questions on these polls.

How do pollsters put together an accurate sample? For instance, a researcher wants to find out how foreign-born residents and citizens of the U.S. identify themselves politically—as Democrats, Republicans, Independents, or with some other party. A national random sample of 2,000 foreign-born citizens should be representative of the whole population of foreign-born U.S. voters. The 2000 Census found roughly 4.6 million naturalized Americans born in Europe, 5 million born in Asia, 800,000 born in Canada, 400,000 born in Africa, 9 million born in Latin America, and 110,000 born in Oceania. Applying these groups' proportions to a proposed sample of 2,000, the researcher creates targets for each category of the foreign-born population. An ideal sample would thus have 460 Europeans, 500 Asians, 900 Latin Americas, 80 Canadians, 40 Africans, and 11 Oceanians. Will this sample accurately represent the studied population? Yes, if the sample also reflects the foreign-born population in terms of gender, education, income,

A CASE IN POINT **2.1** The 1948 Polling Disaster

Although major polling mistakes are relatively rare in today's professional opinion research, the history of polling does feature a few embarrassing moments. One of the most remarkable misjudgments took place in the presidential election of 1948. The major polling organizations predicted the defeat of incumbent president Harry Truman (D) by New York governor Thomas Dewey (R). The *Chicago Tribune* ran the headline "Dewey Beats Truman." *Life* magazine featured Dewey's picture on the cover with a caption reading "The Next President of the United States." In fact, Truman won. Two top polls, Gallup and Crossley, favored Dewey to win with 50 percent of the votes against Truman's 45 percent. The Roper poll was even more certain, predicting Dewey would win with 52 percent of the votes to Truman's 37 percent. When the actual voting results showed the polls were wrong, a study by the Social Science Research Council cited three major reasons, largely related to sampling, for the failure. First, a disproportionate number of college-educated voters was polled; second, polls were not conducted through the final days of the electoral campaign, when a substantial proportion of voters make their decision; and third, a large proportion of undecided voters was erroneously eliminated from the poll analyses. These mistakes were corrected in subsequent preelection surveys.

These questions were asked in November 1948 after the election about the presidential candidates. Gallup asked, "Did you vote for Dewey, Truman, Wallace, or Thurmond (for President 1948)?" Fifty-one percent stated they voted for Truman and 45 percent said they voted for Dewey (Gallup, November-December 1948, in person, 1,500.) The gap between the candidates was 6 points. When the question was asked with the names in a different order: "Did you vote for Truman, Dewey, Wallace, or Thurmond (for President 1948)?" Truman got 57 percent, Dewey received 39 percent; the gap between the candidates was 12 points, twice the other version of the poll. A month later, Gallup asked, "Did you happen to vote in the presidential election on November 2?" and "Did you vote for Truman, Dewey, Wallace, or Thurmond?" In response, 43 percent said they voted for Truman and 31 percent said they voted for Dewey (Gallup, December 1948, in person 1,500). The Roper poll asked an open-ended question: "For whom did you vote for President (in 1948)?" Dewey was mentioned in 47 percent; Truman received 44 percent; the rest didn't recall (*Roper/Fortune Poll*, November 1948, in person, 3,481). Actual results differed from the predicted: Truman won 49.6 percent of the popular vote, whereas Dewey received 45 percent.

and area of residence. To assure the appropriate proportions of subgroups in a study, pollsters often use stratified random sampling with the known percentage of respondents, for instance, in smaller groups or strata. To poll more economically, clustered or multistage sampling, while not strictly random, also produces representative samples. More detailed discussions of sampling and polling can be found in statitstics or research methods textbooks (Erikson & Tedin, 2005).

In this example, the number of respondents selected from Africa and Oceania are, respectively, 40 and 11. The chief concern of the researcher in this and similar cases may be that such limited samples are too small to represent the entire population of these ethnic groups. In such cases, pollsters use *oversampling*—that is, they select a disproportionately large number of respondents in these subgroups in order to draw more reliable conclusions about these populations. Oversampling is normally used in national surveys that study opinions of smaller groups identified by ethnicity, profession, and other variables when small groups are oversampled. The results then need to be statistically corrected ("weighted") to reflect the appropriate known proportion that the subgroup represents in the population.

A sample needs to be representative of a larger social, ethnic, professional, national, or other group. A researcher may not claim that a sample is representative of the U.S. population if it comprises, for example, only suburban middle-class professionals from Boston and college students from Eugene, Oregon. In this case, any difference in opinions between students and suburban residents is not representative of the nation as a whole. Even the results of the famous Hofstede study on values, mentioned earlier, which was based on a large sample of 88,000 IBM employees in more than 60 countries, should be accepted with caution. Why? Because all of the individuals were employees of a large international corporation, the sample did not represent a diverse population. When selecting or analyzing samples, especially for comparative purposes, beware of potential differences in the samples' demographic and social characteristics from the overall population.

The specialist should also be aware of *nonresponse rates*—the percentage of potential respondents that do not reply to questionnaires. The U.S. Bureau of the Census published interesting data on nonresponse rates for mailed census questionnaires among various groups in the United States (Table 2.2).

What do these numbers suggest? According to the Bureau's estimates, the most responsive individuals—that is, those likeliest to complete and return questionnaires—are those who own property and live with a spouse. This means the researcher is likely to get responses not from a random sample of households but rather from a sample in which married individuals with relatively high income (because they can afford to buy property) and, predictably, high educational levels are overrepresented. Nonresponse

TABLE 2.2

The nonresponse rates for individual households for mailed census questionnaires.

Population	Nonresponse Rate
White Non-Hispanic	22.0%
Black	43.4%
Hispanic	36.6%
Asian or Pacific Islander	33.9%
American Indian, Eskimo, or Aleut	36.9%
House/Apartment owner	17.7%
Renter	38.7%
Spousal household	19.4%
Nonspousal household	38.1%

Source: The U.S. Bureau of the Census, Population Division Working Paper No. 19, July 1997.

A CASE IN POINT **2.2** The Use of Nonrepresentative Samples

A reporter for a newspaper in Ohio obtained the results of a survey according to which cell phone users tend to be polite and respectful to others. Most people understand that there are times and places in which they must turn off their phones or not make calls. The reporter disagreed with the survey results. What did he do? Instead of looking critically at the questions and the method by which the survey was conducted, or searching for other surveys on the subject, he conducted his own "informal survey" by asking a few people whether other people's cell phones affect their work performance. For example, he interviewed a wedding administrator and a funeral director about cell phones ringing during ceremonies. Using this graphic and impressive but anecdotal evidence, the reporter raised doubts about the original survey's results. Although many people would support his claim that cell phone users do not exhibit much courtesy in public, the argument is weakened by poor reasoning and by surveying a nonrepresentative sample.

rates can introduce errors to survey results because the people who do not respond may have different views from the people who do.

Many comparative surveys examine the opinions and beliefs of two groups of college students—one American and one from another country. Even if the student samples used in the studies are representative of all students and the surveys are accurately translated, a possible methodological problem related to fundamental differences between national educational systems could occur. These differences may be indirectly responsible for incompatible samples. Why? In many countries, including Germany, Russia, Korea, and Japan, college admission is highly competitive. In these countries, to become a college student one must take and pass difficult qualifying exams in several subjects. Many young men and women fail and, as a result, do not become college students that year. In the United States, most colleges accept a higher proportion of applicants than in countries with more competitive college systems. Therefore, critical evaluation of the subject pool of these comparative studies often reveals that the surveys do not measure differences between compatible representative samples of students. Instead, they uncover differences between (a) highly educated, motivated, and relatively successful Japanese, Russian, and German men and women, and (b) a randomly selected average group of American college students who did not go through as difficult a process of pre-college selection as did their counterparts overseas (Shiraev & Levy, 2001). In sum, national educational practices affect the representativeness of the samples and the results of the polling based on these samples.

LOOKING FOR LINKAGES

Anyone who conducts opinion research must identify a relationship, or **correlation,** between two or more variables, or measures of social characteristics. Correlations may be positive, negative, or zero. Correlations are positive if, in one set of data, scores on variables, like income and education, are similarly high; correlations are also positive when scores on a variable, like popularity of political candidates, are low and the number of votes they receive is also low. Correlations are negative, however, if scores on a variable, like age, are high but scores on a variable, like number of rap concerts attended, are low (or the other way around).

Here are additional examples of positive and negative correlations. In the United States, the relationship between people's support of the Republican Party and their support of conservative ideas illustrates a positive correlation: Republicans are likely to be politically conservative, not liberal. An example of a negative correlation is a cross-national correspondence between per capita income in a city and the amount of money a city needs to spend on fixing streets; the higher the income per capita, the lower the rate of street repair. In Italy, a survey shows that an individual's friendliness and openness is positively correlated with political affiliation with the center-left political parties. What does this finding mean? It is likely that people who score high on such individual traits as friendliness and openness also affiliate with political parties closer to the political left. In contrast, those who score low on these individual traits are likely to associate with the Italian political right (Caprara et al., 1999).

The strength of correlations can vary from strong to weak. This is determined by a measure of correlation called the **correlation coefficient,** which has two components. The first is the sign indicating either positive or negative linear relationship (correlation). The second is a number representing the size of the correlation; this number can range from +1 (the highest positive correlation) to −1 (the highest negative correlation). In other words, the larger the numerical value (positive or negative) of the correlation coefficient, the stronger the relationship between the two variables under investigation. A correlation of 0 means there is no linear relationship between the variables.

Today, every college textbook that deals with methodology reminds students that correlation does not establish a cause-and-effect relationship between two variables. Indeed, correlational studies often leave the question of cause and effect unanswered. Let's demonstrate. In the United States, individual beliefs that social inequality is normal are negatively correlated with support for helping the needy, and the score is relatively high: −.55 (Pratto et al., 1999). It is difficult to make a definite conclusion about which, if either, factor is the cause and which is the effect. Do people's beliefs in inequality cause them to oppose helping the needy, or does their opposition to helping the needy cause their attitudes about inequality? Correlations in opinion studies do not prove causation.

In review.   A link between events does not prove a one-directional causal relationship. If a researcher presents two sets of events and shows that these events happen at the same time, do not accept a conclusion that one causes the other. Although knowing about a link enables us to predict one variable, given the other, it does not permit us to draw unequivocal conclusions about the source or direction of causes and effects.

SURVEYS

Surveys are the most common technique for data collection in opinion studies. In a typical survey, a trained interviewer asks the respondent to express an opinion about a particular topic or issue. This can be done in direct or indirect surveys. In **direct surveys**, the interviewer is in actual communication with the respondent (a phone call, for instance) and can provide feedback, repeat a question, or ask for additional information. In **indirect surveys**, the interviewer has no direct communication with the respondent. The questions are typically mailed or sent electronically to the respondents in their homes, classrooms, or workplaces.

Direct surveys are conducted in several ways, the most common being face-to-face or by telephone. In face-to-face surveys, the interviewer sees the respondents, who are usually at their residence or workplace. Telephone surveys, although they typically do not allow visual contact between the respondent and the pollster, are also based on direct interaction. This type of survey is usually the least expensive of most survey types and can be successfully used where the population has unlimited access to telephones. Nevertheless, even in the 21st century there are many regions around the world in which telephones are either unavailable or prohibitively expensive. In these areas, people who have telephones are likely to have a higher socioeconomic status than those who do not. Therefore, face-to-face interviews (or a combination of telephone and face-to-face surveys) are necessary to assure the representativeness of the sample. As an example from the 1990s, uneven access to telephones was the reason many opinion polls in Ukraine, a former republic of the Soviet Union, were conducted face to face (Paniotto & Kharchenko, 2000).

Internet-based surveys are a relatively new form of interviewing. The advantages of so-called web surveys are that they are cheaper and faster to administer than most traditional polls (Schaeffer & Dilman, 1998). One of their major drawbacks, however, is that they cannot generate a representative national sample because only a proportion—although a growing one—of the population has access to computers either at home or at work. In many foreign countries, even if a person has a computer, his or her access to the Internet and email may be limited; because of the high price of service, many people use the Internet for short periods only.

Not much is known yet about the advantages and disadvantages of computer-assisted surveys, in which respondents generate their answers on a computer rather than a piece of paper. There is evidence that computer-assisted surveys increase respondents' willingness to make potentially embarrassing admissions, such as number of sexual partners and use of marijuana and other substances (Tourangeau & Smith, 1996). Researches from Temple University (Wright et al., 1998) found that adolescents reported by computer significantly higher levels of alcohol use, illicit drug use, and psychological distress in the computer mode than on paper questionnaires. Statistics for 12- to 18-year-olds appear here, with the computer-assisted survey result first and the paper survey result second: "Ever smoked a cigarette" (49/43); "smoked in past 30 days" (28/17); "ever used marijuana" (30/25); "used marijuana in past 30 days" (15/7); "ever used an illicit drug other than marijuana" (7/2); "ever used an illicit drug other than marijuana in past 30 days" (7/2); "ever drank alcohol (56/52); "drank alcohol in the past 30 days" (27/23). The computer results show higher drug use.

We return to Internet-based surveys in Chapter 10, when we discuss voting behavior.

SURVEY QUESTIONS

The most typical forms of survey questions are dichotomous, open-ended, and multiple choice. **Dichotomous questions** give the subject two choices only: to respond "yes" or "no," or to "approve" or "disapprove" certain policies, decisions, or activities of politicians and public officials. As an illustration, presidential approval ratings in the United States are frequently based on dichotomous survey questions, the most common of which is "Do you approve or disapprove of the way [name] is handling his job as president?" In 2003 alone, at least 75 national surveys contained this question about President Bush. Researchers and politicians frequently use these and similar surveys related to the U.S. Congress to find out the public's attitudes about specific decisions and policies (Kagay, 1999). We should note too that in most polls, the respondent is given a third alternative: "don't know" or "no opinion."

Open-ended questions, which typically begin with "What do you think . . ." or "What is your opinion about . . . ," give respondents an opportunity to express themselves, explain their thoughts and feelings, and produce answers and suggestions the pollster might have overlooked in multiple-choice questions. However, several cognitive and methodological obstacles make open-ended questions less valuable and attractive for polling than multiple-choice ones. Open-ended questions require a certain mental effort to recall information and to reason, which some respondents do not want to exert during the interview. Of course, not all people dislike thinking when they answer survey questions. As many professionals in the polling field agree, the point is that many survey participants expect to give short answers based on clear choices. Therefore, open-ended questions may appear as unexpected challenges to which some respondents may answer "I don't know." Also, some respondents have never encountered or thought about the problem posed by the question and therefore are reluctant or unable to give a meaningful answer. They might choose an answer, however, if the question were formulated dichotomously.

Multiple-choice (or close-ended) **questions** are easier to analyze than open-ended and, like dichotomous questions, limit the respondent's choices in that they offer clear answer options. Common forms of multiple choice questions are the selections of answers from a list of options on an ordered scale of, for instance, agreeing or disagreeing, strongly or somewhat (i.e., agree strongly, agree somewhat, disagree somewhat, disagree strongly). Even respondents who have little idea about their position can easily choose the option that appears most attractive at that moment (Zaller, 1992). Common forms of multiple choice questions are the selections of answers from a list of options on an ordered

TABLE 2.3

Americans respond to an open-ended question: "What do you think is the most important problem facing this country today?" (In percentages.)

Education	16	Welfare	3
Ethics/family/moral decline	15	School shootings/violence	2
Crime/violence	11	Youth/Teen pregnancy	2
Dissatisfaction w/government	11	Environment	2
Taxes	11	Abortion	2
Medicare/Social Security	9	Foreign aid/focus overseas	1
Healthcare	8	Immigration/illegal aliens	1
Guns/Gun control	7	Judicial system/courts/laws	1
Economy in general	6	Care for the elderly	1
Poverty/Homelessness	5	Kosovo/Serbia/Milosevic	*
Federal budget deficit	4	Iraq/Saddam Hussein	*
Drugs	5	AIDS	*
International/Foreign affairs	4	Other noneconomic	6
Racism/Race relations	4	No opinion	6
Military/Defense issues	3		

*Indicates less than 0.5 percent of responses.
Source: CNN/*USA Today*/Gallup, March 12, 2000, national adult, 1,006, telephone.

TABLE 2.4

Americans respond to a multiple-choice question (A).

Let me read you a list of issues and ask which one or two are the most important to you personally. . . . Banning partial-birth abortions, offering tax-funded vouchers to help parents afford the cost of sending their children to private or religious schools, allowing the Ten Commandments to be displayed in public schools and government buildings, including a mandatory period of silence for prayer or meditation during the school day, putting strict limits on the growth of gambling. (In percentages.)

Banning partial-birth abortions	29
Offering tax-funded vouchers to help parents	25
Afford the cost of sending their children to private or religious schools	24
Allowing the Ten Commandments to be displayed in public schools and government buildings	24
Including a mandatory period of silence for prayer or meditation during the school day	24
Putting strict limits on the growth of gambling	13
All equally important (volunteered response)	5
None/Other (volunteered response)	10
Not sure	2

Source: Hart and Teeter Research Companies/NBC News/*Wall Street Journal,* March 5, 2000, national adult, 1,213, telephone.

scale of, for instance, agreeing or disagreeing, strongly or somewhat (i.e., agree strongly, agree somewhat, disagree somewhat, disagree strongly).

Look at the results of three national polls taken in March 2000 about problems facing the United States at that moment. Table 2.3 displays the answers to the open-ended question. Tables 2.4 and 2.5 display the answers to multiple-choice questions. What do you notice of particular interest in the distribution of answers in these polls?

When an open-ended question is asked and the choice of answers is unlimited, respondents typically produce a variety of answers, and the pollster must invest significant time in categorizing and coding them. This process alone may bias the poll interpretations. For instance, if the largest response category is education, answers ranging from "quality of education" to "low teacher salaries" to "school lunches" to "prayer at school" may be included in the same category.

In general, open-ended questions are not expected to produce an undisputed account of the problems viewed as most important. According to the results of the multiple-choice poll (Table 2.4.), abortion (and the issue of partial-birth abortions in particular) occupied the first place (29 percent) on the list of personal concerns; this is higher than educational problems, which were at the top of the list (Table 2.3). In the previous case (Table 2.3), abortion was named only by 2 percent of the respondents, and in the third poll (Table 2.5), it constituted 13 percent of answers. The issue of immigration, which, according to other polls (see Chapter 11), is a cause of serious concern for the majority of Americans, was a top priority for only 1 percent of respondents to this survey (Table 2.3). Often, when a respondent must choose from or rank several options, the answer is "All of them are equally important" (5 and 10 percent, respectively, in the polls under analysis), which may merely reflect the respondent's unwillingness or inability to compare the alternatives.

TABLE 2.5

Americans respond to a multiple-choice question (B).

I'd like to read you a list of legislative priorities that Congress is working on this year (2000). Please tell me which one you feel is the most important priority for Congress to pass. . . . Passing tougher gun-control restrictions, adding prescription drug benefits to Medicare coverage, ending the "marriage penalty" in the income tax system, which sometimes requires married couples to pay higher taxes, banning late-term abortions, increasing the minimum wage, protecting the privacy of consumers' health and financial records, passing a patients' bill of rights. (In percentages.)

Passing tougher gun-control restrictions	21
Adding prescription drug benefits to Medicare coverage	16
Ending the "marriage penalty" in the income tax system, which sometimes requires married couples to pay higher taxes	14
Banning late-term abortions	13
Increasing the minimum wage	10
Protecting the privacy of consumers' health and financial records	8
Passing a patients' bill of rights	6
All equally important (volunteered response)	10
None/Other (volunteered response)	1
Not sure	2

Source: Hart and Teeter Research Companies/NBC News/*Wall Street Journal,* March 5, 2000, national adult, 1,213, telephone.

When an issue or event is exciting, or dangerous, or vital to people's existence, open-ended polls typically produce clearer results. For instance, in answering the open-ended question "What do you think is the most important problem facing this country today?" on November 11, 2001 (two months after the September 11 attacks), 37 percent of respondents mentioned "terrorism," which was named far more often than "economy" (16 percent), the second-ranked issue (Gallup, November 2001, 1,005).

In review.   Question format may significantly affect both the distribution of answers and the process of interpreting opinion polls. Open-ended questions give respondents the widest choice of answers but may seriously limit the ways in which the survey can be interpreted. Multiple-choice questions give respondents fewer options but have a significant methodological advantage: The answers to these questions are easily coded.

In general, people whose understanding of English is limited have difficulty articulating responses to open-ended survey questions. Lack of familiarity with response scales may also affect individual reactions and answers. Keep in mind that "standard" paper-and-pencil surveys or one-on-one interviews are not common in all countries. In some communities, the use of written questionnaire techniques is limited by low literacy rates and people's reluctance to deal with the unfamiliar.

STRUCTURE AND ORDER OF QUESTIONS

Imagine you are answering the following survey question: "Which baseball team do you like better: the Cubs or the Red Sox?" Will your answer be affected by the order in which the two teams are mentioned? In other words, how great is the chance you would answer differently if the question was "Which baseball team do you like better: the Red Sox or the Cubs?" Perhaps a reasonable person would say "none." Why? "If I like one team better than the other," this person may argue, "or if I prefer iced tea to water, why should the order of the items in the question affect my response?" This reasoning seems plausible. However, what if you see little difference between the objects of evaluation? To explain this point, let us turn to elections.

Imagine you are running against three other candidates for public office in your city. You can choose to list your name on the ballot in the first, second, third, or fourth position. Which should you choose? Most people would choose to be listed first! And for good reasons. Since the 1950s, several lawsuits have been filed in the United States in which the plaintiff claimed he lost a local election because his name was not listed first on the ballot. Does this claim have any scientific substance? Is the order of names on the ballot important in determining the outcome of an election?

Several studies show that there is an order-of-appearance bias in decision making. For instance, analyses of 1992 election returns in Ohio (for U.S. president, U.S. Senator, county commissioner, prosecuting attorney, and common pleas judge, among others) revealed name-order effects in 48 percent of 118 races. This translates into an advantage of approximately 2.5 percent for candidates listed first. The effect was even stronger when no incumbent was on the ballot, when the candidates' party affiliation was not listed, and when the campaign had been minimally advertised (Miller & Krosnik, 1998). No one filed protests or claimed mistreatment in the Ohio elections because the order of candidates' names was varied randomly on the different ballots.

To explain this effect, some researchers turned to cognitive theories of decision making, which focus on how people process information. A voter may come to the polls undecided about whom to vote for and knowing very little about the candidates. When this voter looks at the ballot, he or she sees a list of unfamiliar names. When facing this little problem ("I have to vote but I don't know yet who my choice is") some individuals may use the principle of *low information rationality*—that is, they selectively pay attention to a small and salient chunk of available information (called a *heuristic*). Thus, some may reason that the first name listed must be that of the front-runner or most important candidate and that front-runners deserve a vote. Likewise, the sort of person who is inclined to vote for the underdog may choose the candidate listed last (Popkin, 1991).

To summarize, the order in which items appear in a survey may affect responses. This is true in the United States and in other countries. For instance, on a survey conducted in Hong Kong during its unification with China in 1997, the order of questions affected the way people evaluated the likely impact of the political transition on their future (Raghubr & Johar, 1997).

 How can this problem be avoided? The most reliable way is to rotate the questions, items for evaluation, or names presented in each survey so no particular item is kept in one place on the list.

Some people say "yes" to a survey question without contemplating its meaning. Instead of retrieving all relevant information from memory and giving a balanced response, the respondent just jumps ahead and replies, "agree." This can happen for many reasons. Some people are tired, distracted, or uninterested in participating. This resistance may be caused by the perceived ambiguity of the question. Individual psychology also plays a role. Many years ago, Couch & Keniston (1960) showed that some people

A CASE IN POINT **2.3** **The Way Questions Are Asked**

Individuals are susceptible to bias not only by the order in which questions are asked but also in the manner in which they are asked. For example, several studies show that questions or statements of the agree-disagree type can cause response bias. Only one view is explicitly presented to respondents, and alternative options appear under the "disagree" option. As an illustration, a 1997 study of 1,986 adults in Kazakhstan, a former republic of the Soviet Union (47 percent of respondents were ethnic Kazakhs and 34 percent were ethnic Russians), contained questions about people's attitudes toward ongoing reforms. Respondents were supposed to either agree or disagree with statements, such as "Free prices are necessary for Kazakhstan's economic recovery" and "It is necessary for the state to control prices in order [for Kazakhstan] to recover economically." The study revealed a strong agreement bias—the propensity of respondents to agree with an assertion regardless of its contents (Javeline, 1999). The bias was stronger for ethnic Kazakhs than it was for ethnic Russians. Why did this acquiescence bias occur? How does this bias work? As authors of this study proposed, Kazakhs have a long history of following rules of respect to others and learn from childhood not to offend a guest. Therefore, many Kazakh respondents did not want to express disagreement with the pollster's statements. In addition, people in the Russian sample were slightly more educated than the Kazakhs, which could have contributed to the bias.

are prone to give "yes" or "I agree" answers no matter what question is asked by the interviewer.

HAZY, KNOTTY, CORNY, AND OTHER BAD QUESTIONS

Pollsters do not want difficult and ambiguous questions in surveys because they waste time, money, and effort; they measure very little, if anything. That is why the wording of each question is a long and meticulous process. Usually this is collaborative work: Staff members of polling firms or research teams typically read and verify the meaning of all words and phrases in a survey questionnaire. Some questions are rewritten multiple times. Keep in mind that a respondent may not answer the intended question but rather what he or she thinks the pollster meant by asking it. Researchers often pretest their questions repeatedly with a diverse range of respondents to establish with confidence that the vast majority understand the survey questions correctly.

Consider an example. In answering questions about housing, people often do not accurately indicate the number of people who live with them. Additional probing is often needed in surveys that ask for an exact number of household residents. Some people do not want to answer for a reason (such as a live-in nanny being undocumented). Others have confused living situations involving family members who stay, leave, and come back again (Martin, 1999). Of course, if someone does not want to say exactly how many people are in a household, no questionnaire can elicit this information. Plenty of people, however, are sincere in their answers but still misinterpret the question or do not have accurate information. Therefore, they may unintentionally give ambiguous or wrong information.

A question is considered bad when it is phrased in such a way that it generates ambiguous reactions or the same answer. In fact, many questions can be considered bad because there is no guarantee that words will not be ambiguous or misunderstood, or will cause the respondent to give an answer that does not reflect the situation under study. Consider, for example, this simple question: "How old are you?" The respondent may not want to answer it. What is the problem? The potential snag is that some people are sensitive to the word *old* because they are concerned with own aging and *old* to them does not measure age but rather is an indicator of their aging. As a result of this mental association, these individuals may skip the question or report a younger age. The wording "What is your age?" may satisfy most people.

There are at least three other categories of error in survey questions: linguistic, swaying, and cognitive.

Linguistic errors typically include blunders and typographical slips (for example, *on* instead of *one, four* instead of *for, pour* instead of *poor*); imprecise usage of *this, it, their* (for example, "If the government decides to deploy the troops, what would be their biggest obstacle to overcome?" It is not clear who should overcome the obstacles, the government or the troops); and double-negative questions (for example, "Does it seem impossible that you will not vote for this candidate?"). Using words such as *former* and *latter* to describe the order of nouns in the question may also be confusing. Of course, linguistic errors include many other mistakes.

Swaying errors relate, in general, to the power of persuasion. In these cases, the question is designed to sway the respondent to give a particular answer. Such questions may preclude the respondent from giving a different answer simply because it can be perceived as inappropriate, unsuitable, or even morally wrong. Some respondents may think less about the question and more about the impression their answer should produce. For example, the question "True Americans are known as generous people who give money to charity. Do you also intend to make a donation?" is persuasive because it deliberately puts respondents in a moral predicament: If they do not donate, they are not a "true American" or generous.

Swaying questions appear relatively rarely in surveys prepared by professional polling firms. However, mistakes of this kind do occur. As an illustration, look at the following question asked in a Russian opinion poll in which respondents had to assess a statement and express their agreement or otherwise: "It is better to have an orderly society than to allow 'freedom' to disrupt order?" You may sense the biasing aspect of the question in its separation of "freedom" from "order" so that "freedom" appears as incompatible with order, undesirable, or evil.

Cognitive errors are represented by so-called hazy, knotty, and corny types of questions.

- Hazy questions either preclude unambiguous interpretation or, if they are multiple-choice, do not offer all available options as answers. For example, when a respondent reads the following question: "How often do you discuss problems such as school violence and drugs with your family members?" he or she faces two sets of alternatives to choose from. The individual may discuss violence quite often but not pay attention to drug problems. However, the answer "often" will be interpreted as if both of these problems are discussed, which is not true. In this case, the question should be separated into two. (See Assignment 2.1 in the end of this chapter.) To avoid this type of ambiguity, polling companies provide multiple-choice answers. For instance, for the question "Does your household currently subscribe to cable TV (television) or a satellite dish service?" the pollster offered these answers: "cable only," "satellite only," "both," and "neither" (ICR and AAOHN, October 2003, national employed adults, 504).

Here is another example. The following question is addressed to naturalized citizens: "What is your birthplace—South or Central America, Europe, Africa, Australia, Asia, Oceania?" But the list of possible answers does not include Canada, Mexico, or the United States itself (some people are born in the United States but are not citizens). This question is not complete because it excludes an entire continent (North America) from the possible answers.

A question such as "Can you recall who was president(s) when you were a child?" is also hazy or ambiguous because people tend to interpret the chronological boundaries of childhood differently. For some of us, it is from birth to age 18. For a child psychologist, it could be from 2 years of age, right after infancy, to puberty. All in all, hundreds of frequently used words and expressions that are heard and read in the media, require exact interpretations because, otherwise, their ambiguity will distort people's reactions. Expressions such as *gun control, late-term abortion, school vouchers, affirmative action, illegal immigration, tax cuts,* and *gays in the military* evoke a variety of interpretations and associated meanings. We discuss this issue again in Chapter 11 on domestic issues.

■ Knotty questions are those that are difficult to understand and correctly interpret. There are plenty of reasons why a question may be misunderstood, but one of the most obvious is the presence of one or more technical terms, or even several of them. The educational level of respondents, their proficiency in the language, their familiarity with the survey's subject, and their fatigue affect the process of understanding. As a result, a respondent may say "Don't know" or choose an answer by chance, even though the answer might be different if the person knew the real meaning of words in the questions.

Try to read the following survey question, the length of which could be a serious obstacle to many respondents: "Now, which one part of the Republican statement on corporate scandals made you most likely to agree with the Republican candidate for Congress—would it be . . . prosecution of Arthur Andersen and investigation of Enron, penalties that include jail time, requiring corporate executives to repay any money made on falsified financial reports, retirement security reforms that give workers more control over their 401(k) and pension funds, or guaranteeing that seniors' Social Security benefits can never be cut?" (Greenberg/POS and NPR, July 2002, 721). This is a knotty question!

■ Corny questions, even though they are not persuasive, typically produce only one answer. For instance, a respondent can choose to agree or disagree with this statement: "People immigrate to the United States because they look for better lives." The overwhelming majority of students who answered this question agreed. Indeed, if someone disagrees, does she mean people move to the United States because they look for something worse than they had before? Corny questions do not necessarily distort public opinion. The main problem with them is that they do not add anything new to the understanding of what people think about particular issues.

QUESTION TRANSLATION

Professionals who work on international surveys face an additional set of problems. The majority of comparative projects require translation from one language into another language or languages. A difficult task faces the investigator: to make sure the translated version of the questionnaire is as close to the original version as possible. However, even a well-translated survey is different from the original. Languages have different grammar rules and sentence structures. Sometimes one sentence in English requires two sentences in other languages to convey its meaning. The word *privacy* has no counterpart in Russian. Metaphors (like *pie in the sky*) and imprecise words (like *probably* and *frequently*) should also be avoided in comparative studies because they are difficult to translate (Brislin, 1970). Some words and phrases common in the vocabulary of the average American may have no equivalent in other languages. For example, the phrase *sexual harassment* requires detailed explanation when translated into some other languages. If you have trouble believing this, ask a Spanish-, Arabic-, Urdu-, Vietnamese-, or Hebrew-speaking person to translate *sexual harassment* into her language. They may come up with a phrase in their native tongue—but then ask another person from the same country to translate this phrase back to English. The translation is likely to be something other than "sexual harassment."

Following these three rules improves the likelihood of successful translation of survey questions.

1. First, arrange that the translation be conducted by bilinguals, that is, by people proficient in both languages, who test their work via back-translation. This involves translating the original version of the survey, retranslating the translation back into the original language, and comparing the result with the original.

2. Second, obtain translations from several people. Compare their versions and convert them into a consistent one.

3. Third, administer both versions of a questionnaire to bilingual individuals. Both versions yielding similar results is a good indicator of a successful translation (Sechrest et al., 1972).

NON-SURVEY METHODS

Although non-survey methods are not used often as polls, they provide researchers with important data, especially when polling is unavailable or inappropriate. Let's describe some of these methods.

Experiment

In **experiments,** the researcher randomly assigns subjects to particular testing conditions. By varying the conditions, the researcher tries to detect specific changes in the subjects' opinions. In an experiment, the condition(s) created by the experimenter are called the **independent variable(s).** The aspect of human activity, such as an opinion, that is studied and expected to change under influence of the independent variable is called the **dependent variable.** The experimenter controls the independent variable—that is, changes the conditions of the experiment to see the effect on the dependent variables.

A simple illustration of an experiment can be drawn from a study of flag preference in two groups of very young schoolchildren: Arabs and Jews (Lawson, 1975). The researcher measured how often children of the two groups, both living in Israel, would choose symbols representing their national and political identity, either Israeli or Palestinian flags. The dependent variable in this study was the decision to choose a picture with a particular flag on it. The independent variable was pictures of various flags, and that variable was manipulated or alternated by the experimenter. This experiment revealed that the youngest Arab and Jewish schoolchildren in Israel were significantly different in their flag preference depending on their ethnic origin (Lawson, 1975). This study also showed that children in the areas of conflict learn about politics and political symbols much earlier than their counterparts in conflict-free countries.

Content Analysis

Content analysis is a research method that systematically organizes and summarizes both the manifest content of communication (what was actually said or written) and the latent content (the meaning of what was said or written). Usually, a researcher examines the information in transcripts of speeches, interviews, television or radio programs, letters, newspaper articles, and other forms of reports. The main investigative procedure of content analysis consists of two steps. Initially, the researcher identifies coding categories. These can be nouns, concepts, names, or topics. First-level coding is predominantly concrete and involves identifying aspects of information that are clearly evident in the text. Second-level coding is more abstract and involves interpreting the first-level categories.

Content analysis of responses is especially valuable when researchers cannot use standard questionnaires. For example, during a study of undocumented aliens in the United States (Shiraev & Danilov, 2004), the vast majority of the subjects selected for this research did not want to give written answers. Although all of them were employed at the time of the survey, lived in the United States for many years, and paid income taxes, most expressed fear of detention by the Department of Homeland Security. The subjects preferred oral communication with the interviewer, and most did not want to be tape-recorded. For this reason, a coded version of the interview

 containing numerical scales could not be used. Instead, a qualitative version of the interview was prepared to fit the new requirements of an oral interview. The answers were recorded in a notebook by the researchers and then analyzed for content later.

Focus Groups

Focus groups are used intensively both in academic and marketing research. The most common approach is to gather a small group of people to respond to specific social, political, or marketing messages. The typical focus group has 7 to 10 participants who are experts or represent potential buyers, viewers, or voters. Based on the goal of the research, the group may be homogeneous or heterogeneous in terms of age, gender, ethnicity, educational background, and occupation.

Focus groups present a number of problems for comparative pollsters because they do not represent randomly selected samples (Kern & Just, 1995). The principal advantage of the method is the opportunity to analyze specific issues, such as whether or not a particular campaign slogan would succeed among potential voters (for instance, among senior citizens or people under 25) and whether or not a certain political initiative would find support among members of a particular constituency or social group.

Meta-Analysis: Research on Research

Suppose you are studying the effectiveness of so-called negative campaigning on voters' choices. The research question is whether voters change their mind under the influence of negative and antagonistic statements made in campaign ads or remain unaffected under the influence of negative campaigning, thereby making it ineffective? After collecting all available books, articles, and reports on the topic by different authors across time, can you make a scientific generalization from all these studies? Is it possible to analyze these data and draw a conclusion about the linkages, if any, between the extent or nastiness level of negative campaigning and changes in the voter's mind? These studies are difficult to compare because they are extremely diverse. Some are based on interviews with a few dozen potential voters, others included hundreds of participants from availability samples of different countries; finally, some others were based on national samples.

A statistical method called **meta-analysis** allows pollsters to analyze quantitatively a large collection of survey results and integrate the findings. In brief, meta-analysis means the analysis of analyses, usually called *combined tests*, of a large group of individual results in an effort to make sense of diverse and often differing findings (Wolf, 1986). Attractive features of this method include its reliance on statistical formulas for summarizing different results. It is imperative to analyze a large selection of studies, not just those that appear to be fair and interesting.

For example, Richard Lau and Lee Sigelman and their colleagues (1997) did a meta-analysis of dozens of studies that dealt with the effects of negative campaigning on electoral results. While many experts believe negative campaigning can help win elections, according to the meta-analysis, negative political ads were no more likely than positive ads to produce the results their sponsors wanted.

Meta-analysis has some disadvantages, though. The method attempts to compare opinion studies whose variables are defined differently. For example, if two studies identify "affirmative action" differently, comparisons of the two would produce unreliable results. Moreover, many studies use different measuring techniques and are often based on results obtained from dissimilar groups of subjects. Finally, meta-analysis is usually applied to published studies that represent statistically significant findings. Nonsignificant findings may be unpublished, overlooked, or ignored, which may bias the process of sample selection for meta-analysis.

Qualitative Approaches

Qualitative methods are typically employed when variables are difficult or impossible to measure, or when the researcher wants to examine people's opinions in detail. In one such study, Jennifer Hochschild (1981) conducted in-depth face-to-face interviews with Americans of different educational and income levels to determine what they consider fair and unfair distributions of justice in their country. Some researchers try to detect and describe implicit or unspoken aspects of communication, hidden rules, and innuendo—the contexts so difficult to measure by standard quantitative procedures (Marcella, 1998). Items studied in this way include street graffiti, popular jokes, and song lyrics. Swedish researcher Tom Bryder (2003), for example, conducted a comparative study of anti-communist attitudes in visual propaganda, such as posters, caricatures, and visual aids. In some cases, nontraditional survey methods are used to take into consideration particular cultural traditions of the population (see A Case in Point 2.4).

Standardized measures are not suited for certain circumstances. Many respondents are illiterate, unable to use multiple choices, or afraid to write down their answers or speak on the phone for various reasons (Paniotto & Shiraev, 2002). Measuring opinions about topics and variables that are not adequately conceptualized or operationally defined is fraught with difficulty as well. For example, as we examine Chapter 11 on domestic issues, Americans tend to assign conflicting

---

A CASE IN POINT 2.4 Culture-Bound Surveys

What kind of obstacles should researchers anticipate when conducting a survey in a country located thousands miles away? Can they use a telephone survey? Not if there are few phones around. Can they ask people at random and in person? This might create a problem. Imagine a foreign researcher in a small town asking people questions and writing their answers on a piece of paper. Can we expect people to be open with the researcher? Perhaps alternative survey methods should be used in such situations. For example, Ho (1998) describes a procedure used in opinion research in the Philippines. This is a special unobtrusive survey procedure called *pagtatanung-tanong* that can be used in relatively small, stable, and homogeneous communities. The researcher asks survey questions in natural, calm contexts and appears to be conversing with people, or asking around. He may ask the questions in sequence. The answers may lead to the formulation of new questions and clarifications if needed. Inconsistency in the answers indicates a diversity of opinions among interviewees. Consistency might indicate an opinion pattern. This type of research does not disturb people and allows the researcher to address sensitive issues that would not have been answered in a standard opinion poll.

meanings to expressions like *affirmative action, school vouchers, national debt,* and *stem sell research.*

Psychobiographical research, or analysis across time of particular individuals—usually outstanding personalities, celebrities, and leaders—is a form of qualitative research. Specialists examine diaries, speeches, comments, letters, memoirs, interviews, and witness accounts in an effort to compose a profile of particular individuals, usually prominent political personalities. The goal of psychobiographical research is an in-depth description of how the person's opinions and subsequent behavior are formed and transformed. Examples appear in books on Harry Truman by David McCullough (1992); on Richard Nixon, edited by Lawrence Friedman and William Levantrosser (1987); on Jimmy Carter by Betty Glad (1980); on Mikhail Gorbachev by Archie Brown (1996); and on other world leaders by Ofer Feldman and Linda Valenty (2001). A psychobiographical study shows that Ronald Reagan started his political life as a moderate liberal and was a founding member of the Americans for Democratic Action. Once elected president of the Screen Actors Guild, he became heavily involved in the fight against the union's takeover by alleged communist sympathizers. This struggle and the experience gained from this ordeal influenced his views about communism. Reagan's second wife, Nancy, also influenced his attitude change during his union years (Renshon, 1989). Raisa Gorbachev played the same role of mentor and close advisor to her husband, the last Soviet leader, Mikhail Gorbachev, when he was a student at Moscow State University in the 1950s (Glad & Shiraev, 1999).

ASSIGNMENT 2.1   PROBLEMS WITH QUESTIONS

Can you detect what is wrong with the questions below? Find hazy, knotty, and corny questions, and then correct and rewrite them.

1. Do you think that people change jobs because they look for better conditions and higher pay?

   _____

2. How often do you discuss local or national news with your parents?

   _____

3. What is your favorite TV or radio talk show?

   _____

4. How often do you feel depressed, frustrated, or angry watching the evening news?

   _____

5. If prejudice is caused by unconscious factors, to what extent do these variables overlap with previously established contextual conditions?

   _____

6. What is your parents' ethnic background?

   _____

7. Are you single or married?

_____

8. Do you think the creation of the Internet is an important informational achievement?

_____

ASSIGNMENT 2.2   ERRORS IN SAMPLING

Identify potential errors in the following cases:

Case 1. A research group studies police officers' ethnic stereotyping and asks them to answer 15 survey questions. There are 155 officers in a squadron. On Monday evening, 85 officers show up for the survey. The researchers ask them to fill out questionnaires, assuming that a group this size is a representative sample of the squadron.

Case 2. A student union conducts a poll among English as a Second Language (ESL) students by collecting 300 responses from 150 men and 150 women. The interviews took place in the college library, where patrons are approached seemingly randomly and asked to answer a few questions. The assumption is that a sample of 300 is big enough to represent the student population of this campus.

Case 3. A radio talk show host decides to study opinions about affirmative action and asks listeners to email their responses to the station. Listeners from all states and of all ages and both sexes send 1,500 messages to the station. The host assumes that 1,500 is a large enough sample to be representative.

CHAPTER SUMMARY

- Quantitative research methods examine social characteristics and opinions as variables primarily through observation and measurement. Because opinion measurement deals with a large number of respondents—individuals who express their opinions—the most common indicator is the average.

- Public opinion studies examine opinions within samples, or specially selected groups, relatively small numbers of individuals, chosen to represent a whole population or universe. The sampling error indicates the extent to which the sample differs by chance from the population it represents.

- One of the main goals the researcher pursues is the creation of a sample that closely resembles the whole category of people under investigation. Such a sample is called a _representative sample,_ whose characteristics should accurately reflect those of the population. Random sampling, if planned and conducted correctly, is one of the most reliable methods of designing a representative sample. A random sample is expected to be representative of a group (a state, a nation) thousands of times larger than itself.

- A specialist or student conducting opinion research often needs to establish relationships, or correlations, between two or more variables. The strength of a correlation is expressed by a correlation coefficient. Correlation does not prove causation between variables.

- The survey or poll is the most common technique for collecting data in opinion studies. In a typical survey, a trained interviewer asks respondents to express their opinion about a particular topic or issue. Survey questions typically are dichotomous, open-ended, or multiple-choice.

- The type of questions asked and the order in which they are presented may significantly affect the distribution of answers as well as their interpretation.

- A survey question is considered bad when it is worded in a way that generates ambiguous reactions or causes all respondents to produce similar answers. The three categories of survey question errors are linguistic, swaying, and cognitive.

- A variety of psychological and other context-related factors affect each respondent's answers.

- Several non-survey methods are used in opinion studies. Although used less often than polls, they may provide important data, especially when polling is unavailable or inappropriate. Among these non-survey approaches are experiments, content analysis, focus groups, meta-analysis, and qualitative methods.

Looking Ahead. After exploring appropriate ways to measure and avoid errors in public opinion surveys here, Chapter 3 develops an approach to critical thinking that helps to evaluate the strengths and accuracy of public opinion research and the conclusions drawn from studies of public attitudes. It alerts readers to looking critically at how questions are asked and becoming aware of prejudgments participants and users of polls may make. It suggests looking critically at descriptions and labels, and advises knowing how to interpret correlations and understanding multiple causes of opinions.

DEFINITIONS OF KEY TERMS

Cognitive error—Mistake in interpretation due to people's cognitive abilities or caused by difficult or ambiguous types of questions.

Content analysis—A research method that systematically organizes and summarizes both the manifest content of communication (what was actually said or written) and the latent content (the meaning of what was said and written).

Convenience sampling—A sampling procedure in which the researcher chooses a sample based on availability.

Correlation—An indication of the strength and direction of the relationship between two or more variables.

Correlation coefficient—A number between -1 and $+1$ that summarizes and describes the type of relationship present and the strength of the linear relationship between two variables.

Dependent variable—The aspect of human activity (or effect) that is studied and expected to change under the influence of an independent variable(s).

Dichotomous question—A survey question formulated to give the respondent only two response choices such as "yes" or "no."

Direct survey—A survey procedure in which the interviewer maintains or can maintain direct communication with the respondent and thus is able to provide feedback, repeat a question, or ask for additional information.

Experiment—The investigative method in which the researcher alters some condition in order to detect specific changes in the subjects' behavior, attitudes, or emotions.

Focus group—A small group used to gather responses to specific social, political, or marketing messages.

Independent variable—The condition controlled by the researcher.

Indirect survey—A survey procedure in which there is no direct communication between the respondent and the interviewer.

Linguistic error—A type of survey question error, typically a grammatical blunder or typographical slip.

Meta-analysis—The analysis of analyses, usually called *combined tests*, of a large collection of results. The goal is to make sense of a diverse collection of studies.

Multiple-choice question—A type of survey question offering a limited list of response options.

Non-sampling error—Non-random error in the results of a study because of problem in the way the study was designed or conducted such as using poor question wording.

Open-ended question—A type of survey question that gives respondents the opportunity to express themselves and to explain the nuances of their thoughts and feelings.

Psychobiographical research—An analysis over time of a particular individual, usually an outstanding person, celebrity, or leader.

Random sampling—A sampling procedure whereby each and every member of the sample had an equal chance of being selected.

Representative sample—A sample whose characteristics accurately reflect those of the population being studied.

Sampling error—Also called *margin of error*. A measurement indicating the extent to which an estimate drawn from a sample differs by chance from the population it represents.

Straw poll—Informal snapshot of public opinion designed to generate evidence of how people's views and preferences are distributed.

Survey research—The investigative method in which groups of people answer questions about their opinions or their behavior.

Swaying error—A type of survey question error that results from trying to persuade respondents to give a particular answer.

CHAPTER 3

Thinking Critically About People's Opinions

In order to generalize about fruit, it is perfectly appropriate to combine apples and oranges.

Robyn M. Dawes

Y ou go to the *New York Times* online archives, look through the headlines, and see one that catches your eye: "One in five nurses tell survey they helped patients die." You anxiously scan the content and find out that according to a national survey, many intensive care nurses reported speeding a patient's death, acting alone or with at least the unspoken consent of doctors or families (Kolata, 1996). This news shocks you. Millions of Americans have been in intensive care units. Does it mean that many of them died or may have died because of their nurse's decision? Could this story be true? Can this national survey be wrong? Searching for answers, you come up with three explanations. The first: Twenty percent of ICU nurses performed euthanasia, deliberately putting a patient to death to end his or her suffering. The second: One hundred seventy of 850 nurses participating in the survey, from across the country, deliberately lied to the researchers by saying they were killing patients. The third: Many nurses either misinterpreted the survey questions or misperceived their own behavior, that is, interpreted medical procedures they performed plus circumstances surrounding them as hastening patients' deaths. It is also possible they misinterpreted both the questions and their own behavior. Which of these options is most likely to be correct?

By presenting this case, we do not intend to imply that we really know what the nurses meant. We cannot look inside their minds to determine what motivated them to give these answers. We can make a few suggestions, however. Perhaps the questions on this medical survey were ambiguous and therefore misinterpreted by some respondents. The nurses' responses revealed their concerns, anxieties, and confusion about where palliative care ends and euthanasia begins. Most nurses participating in this study evaluated their own behavior as in a gray zone of intensive care where the distinction between hastening death and providing care is unclear. For example, the most frequent procedure the nurses described was administering pain-relieving medications to patients, understanding that these drugs might hasten death. Doubt, regret, and even guilt may have contributed to some nurses' self-incriminating responses; if so, we have a good illustration of *post-hoc error,* a type of reasoning mistake. A post-hoc error is the mistaken logic that because event *B* (death of a patient) *follows* event *A* (medical procedure or drug administration performed by a nurse), then *B* must have been *caused* by *A*. In short, people erroneously jump from "This *could have happened* because of my actions" to "This *must have happened* because of my actions." In fact, event *B* may have been caused by a number of factors.

It is up to you to interpret this survey. Perhaps some nurses indeed performed euthanasia, as they reported. Others may have misinterpreted several questions of the survey. It is also likely that some misjudged their own actions. ICU nurses are more likely to experience life-and-death situations than other nurses (Kolata, 1996a). Surveys are difficult to interpret and easy to misinterpret. But no matter what results you analyze—those of a small college survey or a national poll—your rational, critical, and balanced assessment of the expressed views will help you make more accurate judgments about other people's opinions.

Looking Forward. This third chapter, "Thinking Critically About People's Opinions," presents basic "tools" of critical thinking necessary to understand, analyze, and interpret surveys. It provides guidelines for critical thinking that help to evaluate the strength and accuracy of polls and other public opinion studies and the conclusions from studies of public attitudes. It alerts readers to looking at how questions are asked, become aware of their and respondents' biases and prejudgments, and how to look critically at descriptions and labels about people and events. It advises how to interpret correlations and understand multiple causes of opinions.

CRITICAL THINKING ABOUT POLLS

How to interpret survey results is one of the most important questions in public opinion studies. What is concealed behind the numbers, graphs, percentage points, and columns? Do surveys accurately reflect people's opinions? People express a wide range of views about opinion polls and their accuracy and usefulness. In the early days of scientific polling after World War II, more than 50 percent of Americans believed opinion polls are "right most of the time" in predicting results of elections, and only slightly more than 20 percent suggested that the "record is not good" (NORC, November 1948, personal, 1,288; NORC, October 1952, personal, 1,291). In the 1970s, Gallup asked a national sample, "How do you feel about public opinion polls?" Thirty-seven percent replied that they are an accurate/good idea; 31 percent believed they are a good method to find what people think; and only 10 percent replied they did not believe polls are accurate (October 1975, personal, 1,558).

In the 1980s, 75 percent of survey respondents believed opinion polls work for "the best interests of the general public"; 8 percent disagreed (Roper, March 1985, personal, 2,000). In the 1990s, approximately two-thirds of Americans believed polls worked in the "best interest" of public, and one-fifth said they "work against the best interests of the general public" (Princeton, June 1997, 1,000; Gallup, April 1996, 1,001). Americans these days tend to be more skeptical about survey accuracy. When Fox News asked registered voters whether opinion polls represent what people think about important issues, two-thirds of respondents were skeptical. Almost one-third, nevertheless, believed the surveys are accurate (Figure 3.1).

Although curious people may be interested in other people's opinions about polls, these opinions about opinions (or **meta-opinions**) provide little information about how a particular poll reflects particular opinions. To establish how closely a poll reflects reality, the inquiring mind needs a way to analyze numbers, percentage points, and proportions developed through polls. **Critical thinking** is such an approach—an active and systematic intellectual strategy to examine, evaluate, and understand opinion polls on the basis of reasoning and valid evidence (Levy, 1997). Learning how to think critically in analyzing and interpreting survey data is a vital and indispensable component of learning about public opinion. Critical thinking is not simply about criticizing, disapproving, and passing judgment on opinion polls and the professionals who conduct the surveys. It is a process of inquiry that is sometimes skeptical, sometimes cautious, sometimes supportive and enthusiastic. Critical thinking about surveys also generates new questions and encourages us to look at an issue from a different perspective by producing new ideas and inviting rival explanations (McBurney, 2001).

Anyone who reads can read opinion polls. A person with elementary education should be able to compare two or three figures in a table. However, to *interpret* these numbers calls for more than a simple comparison. Critical thinking requires the observer to display three important virtues: curiosity, doubt, and patience. Critical thinking is not

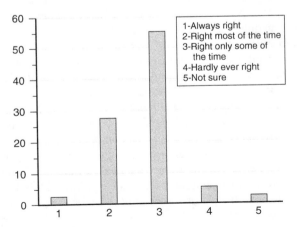

FIGURE 3.1
Opinions about opinion polls. Fox News. May 2000, 900. (In percentages.)

a magical or mysterious gift. It is not an exclusive gift miraculously bestowed on the intellectual elite. It is a skill set that can be taught, learned, and mastered.

This chapter discusses a set of principles and procedures called *the guidelines for critical thinking*. These guidelines will help you interpret and explain people's opinions as expressed in surveys and help you analyze polls by reducing bias and inflexibility in your judgment. They are grouped in four categories or sets.

1. *Thinking About Context:* The first set of guidelines deals with the *circumstances* under which the poll was conducted—that is, the context in which the survey was taken, plus its design.

2. *Thinking About Bias:* The second set of guidelines for critical thinking takes into consideration individual *prejudgments* in the process of understanding and interpretation of surveys.

3. *Thinking About Wording:* The third set deals with the way we use language in *descriptions* of survey results.

4. *Thinking About Explanations:* The fourth set describes how to form a better understanding of the *reasons and causes* that influence people's opinions.

THINKING ABOUT A SURVEY'S CONTEXT
Circumstances Surrounding a Survey

Current issues may divert the respondent's attention and affect his or her responses to survey questions. Among these factors are local economic and social developments, national events, media attention to the survey's subject, and general knowledge about the topic. Americans' attention to the legal aspects of abortion, affirmative action, and the death penalty grows significantly when the Supreme Court considers related cases. During most military campaigns abroad—especially if they are short and successful—the approval ratings of U.S. presidents go up. Conversely, casualties among U.S. troops typically reduce people's support for military actions on foreign soil. In the past 20 years, Israelis' support for a peace agreement with the Palestinian Authority declined greatly after terrorist attacks against Israel. Let's demonstrate the impact of contextual factors on opinions with more examples.

A large comparative study of attitudes among residents of formerly communist Eastern European countries, conducted in the late 1990s, revealed a surprising finding: People in Belarus, whose government officials were criticized by foreign observers for systematic violations of basic human rights, reported substantially higher levels of satisfaction with their lives and current state of affairs than did people in neighboring countries with fewer violations. For example, the opinion gap between Belarusians and Ukrainians was 24 percentage points (in Ukraine, only 2 percent of people expressed satisfaction with their life). Could the surveys be wrong? If we look at these surveys' contextual factors, we see that wages were one factor contributing to the somewhat favorable perception of economic conditions in Belarus (Titarenko, 2002). A crucial element of Belarus's economic policy was governmental responsibility for most people's salaries—and the salaries were paid. Only 10 percent of Belarusians reported being owed back wages, while in Russia and Ukraine delays in payment were widespread and persistent during the entire decade in the 1990s. Many Belarusians were aware of the difficult wage situation in neighboring countries, and this could have affected their relatively favorable evaluations of their own circumstances. If this assumption is correct, it may partially explain why, unlike Russian and especially Ukrainian workers, the majority of Belarusian workers tolerated low wages and generally refrained from strikes, rallies, and other political actions: Economically, they felt relatively secure (Golovaha & Panina, 1999).

The next example suggests how cultural circumstances affect the way survey questions are answered. The Center for Health and Gender Equity evaluated dozens of national surveys comprising 140,000 women in about 50 countries. One of the most commonly reported forms of domestic abuse against women was wife-beating. It occurred in all countries and in all socioeconomic, religious, and cultural groups (Smit, 2000). In some countries, 10 percent of women reported violence against them, while in others the percentage was six times greater. However, these survey data do not necessarily suggest that men in some countries are six times more abusive than men in others. A careful look at the circumstances surrounding the surveys shows that in traditional cultures and, in particular, among the poor and in rural communities, it is considered inappropriate to complain about one's husband because the complaint can hurt the reputation of the family. Moreover, many women are afraid to tell the truth because they fear retaliation from their husbands. Therefore, what these surveys more likely reveal is also the level of restraint some women show when asked to report violence against them. To reduce bias in cross-national studies and to increase the survey's validity, as Chapter 2 on measurement suggests, quantitative polling methods need to be supplemented with qualitative techniques, such as in-depth interviews.

Circumstances and events may change the distribution of answers in unexpected ways. For example, when do you think people were more concerned about a possible nuclear attack against the United States—in 2000 or in 2001? Any reasonable person would guess that after the events of September 11, 2001, Americans expressed more anxiety about being vulnerable and unprotected. The polls do not show this. In 2000 (Gallup, May 2000, 1,011), 32 percent of Americans believed a nuclear war was either "fairly likely" (23 percent) or "very likely" (9 percent). In the fall of 2001, levels of concern were lower: 17 percent and 9 percent, respectively (Hearst/NBC/*Wall Street Journal,* November 2001, 809).

Surveys conducted on behalf of a client are supposed to be ideologically and politically neutral; they are not supposed to sway people's opinions in a particular direction (Owen, 2000). Nevertheless, many survey sponsors are *not* neutral observers; they have a vested interest (which they often try to conceal) in particular poll results. Public opinion expressed in support of a cause may attract more supporters and media attention. Favorable survey numbers may translate into more publicity. Publicity may be linked to changes in policy. Therefore, when interpreting a survey, it is vital to recognize who the sponsor is, especially if it is a political or social organization and detect possible biases. In Chapter 6 about media, we discuss political bias in the interpretation of preelection surveys and other polls.

You have already learned that choosing a representative sample is one of the most important tasks in survey design. Making sure the survey examines a valid sample is vital for poll developers and critics. You can review sampling issues by looking back at Chapter 2. In Chapter 6, we also explain how the media's attention to particular issues affects people's perception of certain social and political events.

The Way the Question Is Asked

How would you interpret a 1998 survey showing that 76 percent of Americans believed it is "more important to be tough on criminals" and only 17 percent said it is more important to "protect the rights" of the accused (WP/Kaiser/Harvard, August 1998)? You would, perhaps, say that by a 5:1 ratio Americans prefer a tougher approach to the treatment of criminals and reject a softer one. However, a more careful analysis of the questions asked in this poll would bring you to a more cautious evaluation of the results. Why? Because of the way the question was asked. The respondents were offered only two options: They were asked to choose between "to be tough" or "protect the rights." But is it possible to pursue both goals—that is, to be tough on criminals *and* to protect their rights? Or some may prefer to leave things as they are in how criminals are treated? We can only guess, of course, about how many people would have chosen these two possible answers had the question been asked with different options. However, it makes sense to anticipate that the 5:1 ratio in this survey would have been different.

If you think the previous example was based on hypothetical assumptions and is not convincing enough, consider a real-life scenario. When public officials responsible for bus service in a county near Washington, DC, looked at the results of a survey designed to gauge public sentiment about metro transit, they realized their problem was more than the unsatisfactory bus service. The problem was the survey's questions, which were designed so respondents had only one possible way to answer them: by choosing either to (1) continue poor bus service or (2) increase taxes to pay for better roads (Ginsberg, 2000). As a result, the officials faced a lose-lose situation: Because of the poorly designed poll, residents did not have a chance to consider options that included improved bus service. The only alternative to poor bus service, according to the poll questions, was to support financing of new road construction projects.

The history of public opinion research offers many examples of how biased questions affect respondents' answers. In a national survey conducted by the Roper Organization in June 1980 (personal, 2,006), 80 percent of respondents agreed the government should reduce the number of immigrants who can enter the United States legally each year, and only 16 percent disagreed. The answers appeared very anti-immigrant, an unusual tendency for the time; most people in other polls conducted in the 1980s expressed tolerance for immigration. Was that year special? Did something terrible happen on the U.S.-Mexican border? The first step in addressing these issues is to look carefully at the question respondents were asked to answer:

> "At its present rate of growth the population of the United States will double in about 40 years—to over *400 million people.* Some people are concerned about this and others are not. Here are some different points of view as to what, if anything, should be done with respect to population growth. Would you go down the list and for each item on the list tell me whether you agree with it or disagree with it?"

How did the organizers of this survey come up with the number 400 million? Why didn't they suggest a smaller number, such as 300 million or even less? Let us assume the 400 million prediction was made by an authoritative source. Who determined that the anticipated population growth would be based on immigration alone? An impressively large figure could have swayed many respondents to express negative, restrictive opinions about immigration and immigrants.

The impatient observer tends to form an opinion about a poll by looking only at the distribution of answers to the opening question. Why? Sometimes the percentages seem impressive enough to discourage further analysis. Nevertheless, the answers to follow-up questions may provide the patient observer with a clearer and more detailed picture of the opinion distribution. In Chapter 4, which examines attitudes, you will learn more about how the order of survey questions may change the distribution of answers. To review the subject of question design, refer to the sections entitled "Structure and Order of Questions" and "Hazy, Knotty, Corny, and Other Bad Questions" in Chapter 2.

In review. How to apply context rules or guidelines.

1. When you try to understand and interpret an opinion poll, learn more about social and political context or conditions under which the poll was taken. See if any specific events could sway people's opinions in a particular way. Find, if possible, a similar poll taken earlier.

2. Make sure that the survey is based on a representative sample.

3. If possible, find out who was the survey's sponsor and whether this organization has a vested interest in the survey's results.

4. Look at the survey's question or questions and try to determine whether the respondents' answers could have been affected by the question's design.

THINKING ABOUT BIAS IN SURVEY INTERPRETATION

In the classic TV series *Star Trek,* Mr. Spock, a half-human, half-Vulcan, had no emotions. He did not experience empathy, sadness, or passion. His behavior was directed by pure logic. In reality, emotional commitments are inevitable elements of human life. However, people's likes and dislikes sometimes say more about the individuals themselves than about the objects they consider. Our personal attachments, interests, preferences, and values can bias our thinking; often we equate our description of what *is* happening in the world with our perception of what *should be*. The nature of human cognitive process is that most people experience an automatic launch of so-called **social attribution,** a complex cognitive mechanism by which people interpret events and behaviors of others and themselves.

Be Aware of Your Own Prejudgments

What happens when people come across information that is different from their preconceptions? Put another way, what do people do when they perceive a clash between the empirical evidence and their opinions? There are several possibilities.

People may modify their opinions to fit the data. Example: "I thought people in this country were always against military actions abroad. But polls show that most people support an interventionist military policy. Perhaps I was wrong in my judgment."

People can interpret the data to fit their existing opinions. Example: "I thought people in this country were always against military actions abroad. But polls show that most people support an interventionist military policy. I think the polls were wrong. Respondents either did not understand the questions properly or were brainwashed by the media."

Which one of these approaches is chosen more often? Psychological research shows that individuals are inclined to make data fit their existing opinions (Aronson, 1997). Moreover, people may pay attention to polls that confirm their views and completely miss others that challenge them. Suppose, however, that a survey contradicts current expectations—that is, the new data do not fit the old theory. Now what? In the pursuit of knowledge, fair observers put aside their stubbornness and alter their theory to accommodate accurate facts. Some people, however, will not do that. They would rather defend their opinions and claim that the facts are wrong. It is easier and less frustrating to maintain a point of view than to reassess it. Some people may say, "Don't confuse me with the facts!" Others suggest, "*I* know what most people think about this issue. Your poll is wrong!" Some sound upset: "People are stupid; they should not have answered the question in this way." Research provides significant evidence that most people tend to be inaccurate in assessing the attitudes of others. Moreover, people often hold beliefs simply because these beliefs have useful implications, not necessarily because they are supported by clear evidence (Lenart, 1994; McBurney, 2001).

Look at a series of polls, taken over almost 50 years, in which Americans were asked to assess the meaning of two important values, religion and freedom of speech, in a difficult yet realistic predicament. People were asked to explain how they might choose between freedom of speech and religious values (Table 3.1). Now try to interpret these results from two personal positions: (1) a civil libertarian who believes individual freedom is greater than all other human values, and (2) a religious advocate

TABLE 3.1

"There are always some people whose ideas are considered bad or dangerous by other people. For instance, somebody who is against churches and religion. If such a person wanted to make a speech in your city/town/community against churches and religion, should he be allowed to speak or not?" (In percentages.)

	1954	1974	1984	1994	2002
Yes, allowed	37	62	68	73	77
Not allowed	60	37	32	26	22
Don't know	3	1	0	1	1
Respondents	n/a	1,484	1,473	2,992	2,765

Source: NORC-GSS, national samples.

who believes religious values are in decline and only religion is capable of guiding the lives of human beings. Compare these two interpretations.

What does Table 3.1 say? The results of these surveys suggest that the proportion of people who support the first choice (allowing the individual to speak) was growing over the years. Likewise, the proportion of people who choose the second option (not allowing the individual to speak) was declining. Can we say that religious values are in decline among Americans? Can we further infer that freedom of speech is becoming a priority for the average American? Neither those who believe religious values are declining nor those who think freedom of speech is becoming Americans' priority can claim with certainty that the results of these polls confirm their views. Little in these polls suggests the absolute worth of these values (freedom of speech and religious values) to those surveyed.

It is possible that feelings about these values strengthened, declined, or remained unchanged since 1954. One of a few meaningful conclusions the critical observer can draw from these data is that people comparing two sets of values in a particular hypothetical situation were changing their priorities over the years toward endorsing individual rights over religious values. However, if one suggests this change is due to some *recent* social developments in the country—an influx of "uncultured immigrants," "destruction of the family," or "hip-hop and rock music"—one is likely to be wrong. Why? The most significant changes took place, according to these surveys, between 1954 and 1974 rather than more recently.

Be Aware of Respondents' Assumptions

When people answer survey questions, many of them assume they understand the subject matter correctly. When participants in a 1997 national survey were asked, "Do you think that a random sample of 1,500 or 2,000 people can accurately reflect the views of the nation's population, or not?" almost two-thirds of the respondents (65 percent) said "cannot"; far fewer, only 30 percent, suggested otherwise (PSRA/Pew,

---

A TOPIC FOR CLASS DISCUSSION "Right" and "Wrong" Issues

One important way in which personal views can bias thinking is when people equate a description of what *is* with a prescription of what *ought to be*. This occurs, for instance, when people define what is good in terms of what is typical. The observer should learn to differentiate objective descriptions from subjective prescriptions (Levy 1997).

Question:

Do you think that statistical frequency of people's support of a social issue should make the issue right or appropriate for society? If most people do not support an issue, does it make the issue they reject wrong and inappropriate?

June-August 1997, 1,201). Did people know about the nature and statistical meaning of random sampling, or did they just guess?

To **assume,** as dictionaries explain, is to expect something with certain confidence. Many individuals answer survey questions by expressing their assumptions rather than actual knowledge of facts. Let's illustrate. People in the United States earn different incomes. We can group them according to their yearly earnings. For this case, we assign people who make from $20,000 to $30,000 a year to one group and those who make from $50,000 to $75,000 to another. They all (or so the government hopes) pay income taxes. Can you guess, without access to government statistics, what share of the total individual income tax paid by all U.S. taxpayers is paid by these two groups? Do these income groups each contribute 3, 5, or 10 percent, or does one group pay more in taxes than the other?

We collected responses to this question from 100 college students. In 90 of these guessed responses, the main assumptions were that the share was either equal or that people in the higher earning bracket contributed about twice as much as those who make less. Do you agree with this estimation? How would you answer this question? Setting the book aside, spend a few moments considering the cognitive processes you used to reach your conclusions. How, specifically, did you go about arriving at your estimates?

Now here is the answer. According to official data, people in the higher income group pay 16 percent of the total, while people in the lower income group pay 1 percent, so the ratio is 16:1 (CTJ, 2000). Why is this case important to the discussion of critical thinking in survey analysis? Because people may base their opinions on very little information. And very often, this information is the person's own perception of reality rather than actual evidence.

What are the implications of people's relative lack of knowledge about taxes? Think, for example, about the never-ending debate about tax cuts. Who deserves them more: people who make less money or people who pay more taxes? People may develop strong opinions for or against tax cuts on the basis of individual perceptions, either accurate or inaccurate, of what some income groups pay relative to others.

How do assumptions work? Individuals tend to use information that is easily available or more accessible from memory. As a result, many people tend to overestimate or underestimate actual occurrences of events. This cognitive strategy is termed the **availability heuristic** (Tversky & Kahneman, 1973). A *heuristic* is a mental shortcut for problem solving that allows the individual to reduce complex information to simple judgments. The availability heuristic is the process of drawing on instances that are easily available from memory. This heuristic helps people answer questions concerning the frequency ("How many of them are there?"), incidence ("How often does this happen?"), or likelihood ("What are the odds that something like this will occur?") of particular events. And what types of instances are likely to stand out in memory? In general, people are prone to think more quickly of instances that are easy to imagine, and they tend to assume that easily imagined events occur rather frequently. For instance, if you have no trouble bringing to mind a survey in which a majority of American women opposed a U.S.-led foreign military intervention, you are more likely to judge that this opinion is common among women. By contrast, if it takes you a while to think of illustrations of Jewish or Hispanic voters overwhelmingly supporting a Republican candidate, you are prone to conclude that members of these groups rarely support Republicans.

In review. How to apply the bias guidelines.

1. Keep an open mind when you interpret polls and evaluate evidence by knowing that your opinions can be biased.

2. To reduce the impact of bias on your evaluations, ask yourself in what ways your explanations might be wrong. One specific method of doing so is to imagine an opposite explanation.

3. When faced with a discrepancy between your expectations about the result of an opinion poll and the actual result, resist the tendency to assume that your expectations are correct, and the facts must somehow be wrong.

4. Be aware that expectations and assumptions influence answers to survey questions. Incorrect assumptions can lead to inaccurate opinions. When assumptions change, corresponding opinions can change too.

WORDING: LOOK CRITICALLY AT DESCRIPTIONS

Because we use language to communicate, we name things and people by attaching verbal labels to them. Labels are easily converted into beliefs that can appear as facts (Ward, 1999). "Women in this country vote for Democrats." "Republicans are against abortion." "Hispanics would never support this candidate." "Retirees will definitely approve this initiative." These are examples of how labeling simplifies and distorts individual perceptions of reality. Why? Because millions of American female voters do not cast their votes for Democratic candidates, plenty of Republicans maintain pro-choice beliefs, and individual members of demographic or cultural groups express a wide variety of opinions. This means we should be aware of the extent to which labels affect both understanding and interpretation of opinion polls.

Pay Attention to Labels

People's best attempts to remain neutral or objective are constrained by the limits of language. It is nearly impossible to find words that are devoid of evaluative connotations, so evaluations tend to be biased. Few neutral adjectives are available to describe people's opinions. Even if such words did exist, many people would still be likely to utilize the ones that reflect their personal preferences. Individuals routinely apply social- and personality-related terminology. Consider the names applied to various groups: *pro-choice* and *pro-life, hawks* and *doves, hardliners, religious right, environmentalists,* and many others. How accurately do these tags describe people's complex views and perceptions? The cases described below and throughout the textbook illustrate how social reality can be shaped by language.

A headline posted on a popular website reads: "A new survey shows a public hungry to buy tickets for suborbital jaunts above Earth." The idea of space cruises looked impressive indeed, according to the headline. Do you imagine hundreds of thousands of people eagerly waiting in long lines to pay for their suborbital space flight experience? Don't rush to get your place in line. The survey's actual results are different from what the headline said. Although 51 percent of those surveyed in the United States and Canada said they *would* purchase a space trip, there was little indication of their "eagerness" to do so. According to the polls' predictions, at a price of $100,000, only 10,000 people would actually become space travelers (David, 2001). Now, can you calculate what proportion of the U.S. and Canadian populations combined a sample of 10,000 people would represent?

Remember that people may, deliberately or not, misread or even overlook certain numbers revealed by surveys. For example, this statement distributed by CNN in 1998 may not contain actual misinformation: "Poll shows Bill Gates' popularity growing" (http://www.cnn.com, January 23, 1998). It does contain bias, nevertheless, that is subtle. Look at the actual numbers of the CNN/*Time* magazine poll. According to the survey, 42 percent of those polled had a favorable opinion of Gates in 1998, compared to 31 percent in 1995. His popularity grew. However, a slightly higher percentage of people expressed an unfavorable view of Gates than in 1995: 15 percent versus 11 percent. This means the number of people who think unfavorably of the Microsoft founder also grew! To present a more accurate assessment of the poll, how would you rewrite the headline?

Pay attention to verbal interpretations of what are insignificant statistical differences. If you find, for example, that according to the National Restaurant Association's 2000 poll 27 percent of senior Americans (age 65 and older) said they prefer to dine out on Easter, it was only 2 percent higher than in 1996. These results do not indicate with certainty that "More families are dining out on Easter" (CRA, 2001). As noted in Chapter 2 on measurement, in samples of 1,000, the margin of error is such that any figures (such as the intent to vote for one candidate or another) less than 6 percentage points apart are likely to be within the margin of error and cannot be said to be statistically different. Therefore, it can be misleading to talk about one candidate being "in the lead" or "ahead" of the other candidate, if the difference between the opponents is 3 percent (Cunningham, 1992).

Also, beware of so-called obvious statements in descriptions of opinions of a particular group. These obvious descriptions and evaluations are true for practically all people. Nevertheless, such statements are frequently used in everyday descriptions of people and their opinions (Levy, 1997). Over the years, we have come across numerous obvious statements our students used to describe the results of opinion polls (Table 3.2).

How can one avoid obvious statements? One can add qualifiers, modifiers, or adverbs. One can describe and interpret not in general terms but rather in terms of magnitude or degree. Rather than writing, "Women pay attention," use a more specific phrase such as "Compared to men, more women. . . ." Instead of suggesting, "Republicans worry," write, "A higher percentage of Republicans, compared to Democrats, worry. . . ."

Question Secondary Sources

In the beginning of this chapter, we introduced a case about nurses that demonstrates how easy it is to misinterpret a survey and make an inaccurate assumption about the respondents' views based on information from a secondary source, such as a report in a newspaper. An important tool of critical thinking is your investigation of the original source of the polling data. If you can look at the numbers and see the results firsthand, you might find that an interpretation of this poll is inaccurate or biased. Consider an example. In a recent conference presentation, a colleague said that Americans,

TABLE 3.2

Examples of obvious statements.

Obvious statements	Critical-thinking comment
"Survey suggests that immigrants who came to these shores looked for a better life."	This statement is correct. However, it does not provide useful information about the immigrants. Do other people also look for a better life? Differences in responses between immigrants and nonimmigrants, or among different groups of immigrants, should be noted in the description.
"Republican supporters in this poll worry about excessive government."	This statement is accurate. Nevertheless, it does not provide useful information about the Republican supporters. The word "excessive" means that something is unnecessary, unwarranted, or too much. It is only reasonable for most people, not only Republican supporters, to worry about excessive government.
"Women pay attention to issues related to education."	This statement does not provide useful information about women's opinions about education. Both men and women pay attention to education-related issues. If a poll reveals specific gender differences, describe them.
"There is a feeling of insecurity in the people of Czech Republic."	This statement does not provide adequate useful information about the Czech respondents. Feeling insecurity is a universal human emotional state that varies from person to person and among social groups.

according to polls, so irrationally hated the former Soviet Union in the 1980s that most of them, due to their biases, preferred to die rather than live under socialism. It took a while before we found the opinion poll to which our colleague referred. Indeed, according to this poll, 53 percent of Americans surveyed in 1985 by CBS and the *New York Times* said they would rather risk the "destruction of the United States" than be "dominated by the Russians" (CBS/*New York Times,* September 19, 1985). How should we interpret this result? According to our colleague, the poll respondents were mostly uninformed Russophobes and zealots. On the other hand, we can also assume that Americans who answered this question were rational and informed individuals. They preferred self-destruction to a Soviet invasion. However, and most importantly, it was a highly hypothetical case that did not indicate most Americans were actually ready to die.

Vivid examples, spectacular events, personal testimonies, accidents—in contrast to statistical data—are likely to exert a disproportionate impact on people's judgments. In this way, emotional descriptions can be more persuasive than evidence. Consider, for instance, the abortion issue. Politicians, radio and television commentators, and newspaper and magazine reporters frequently mention the debate between "pro-life" and "pro-choice" groups regarding this problem. Does abortion appear to be a key political issue in this country that seriously affects election results? In fact, opinion polls show that only a small percentage of Americans in the 1990s—about 10 percent—considered abortion a crucial issue that affected their voting behavior (Andersen, 1997).

Sometimes, despite our expectations, outstanding events do not change attitudes much; in October 2001, 81 percent of Americans said preventing the spread of weapons of mass destruction should be a top governmental priority. Yet, the same proportion had expressed the same opinion earlier that year, before the terrorist attacks on September 11 (Pew, October 2001, 1,281).

The easier it is to bring an explanation to mind, the more valid the explanation appears to a person. For example, conversations about contemporary Americans' intimate relationships are common these days. People often talk about couples who live together without being married. These conversations are heard on campus, at home, and in the media. Many people have unmarried friends who live together. Exactly what proportion of heterosexual couples do you think live together without being married to each other? One-half? One-third? One-quarter? In fact, the number is much lower. Surveys show that only 5 percent of heterosexual couples in the United States living together in the late 1990s were unmarried (Strong et al., 1998).

In review. How to apply the wording guidelines, Part 1.

1. Remember that descriptions, especially general statements about people's opinions, are often biased.

2. Try to be specific in descriptions. Instead of stating "According to a poll, people want change," say or write, "*This* percentage of people supported the proposed change, and *that* percentage was opposed."

3. Avoid making obvious statements in survey descriptions and interpretations. Cast such statements not in general terms but rather in terms of their specific magnitude or degree.

4. Accept anecdotal evidence with caution. Although personal testimonies and vivid cases may be persuasive, they are not inherently trustworthy indicators of fact.

5. Use the data, whenever possible, from representative surveys rather than a researcher's interpretation of them (or headlines above them).

Be Aware of Dichotomous and Continuous Variables

Critical thinking is about making comparisons. People often say, "These two groups are different in their opinions," or "These two groups are similar in their views." How-

---

A CASE IN POINT **3.1** Headlines About Survey Results

This headline appeared on the National Education Association website on March 5, 2001: "Bipartisan Poll Shows Public Undivided on Key Education Reforms." However, the poll itself does not present evidence of unity among people who replied to the survey question. Majorities of 55 to 60 percent supported government's more active role in education and an increase of federal spending in the area. However, large proportions of people did not support these measures. The public is not "undivided."

ever, nothing can be absolutely identical to or entirely different from anything else. Similarities and differences are based on the perspectives from which you choose to view them. Thus, most people and events can be seen as both distinct from and similar to others. In general, we tend to formulate easy conclusions about similarities and differences. It is so convenient! People frequently assign observable phenomena to one of two discrete categories rather than perceive them as lying along a continuum—that is, people tend to dichotomize variables.

When you read interpretations of opinion polls, you will find that dichotomous descriptions are common. Such interpretations include approval and disapproval, support or opposition, acceptance and rejection, voting for a candidate or against her. For instance, if 51 percent of respondents supported national independence and 49 percent did not, an observer can suggest, "The supporters of independence prevailed." This is the way democracy works and majority rules. Nevertheless, even when two groups of individuals express two different opinions, this does not mean the groups are totally in opposition. Further, the strength of the attitudes is unclear, and it is quite likely that respondents in opposite categories share a number of similar opinions in other areas. As a result, the **dichotomous variable** "supporters/opponents" appear as more continuous, for example, "strong supporters/weak supporters/weak opponents/strong opponents."

Take, for instance, a study conducted by the Feldman Group (Price, 1999). The researchers administered a survey of American attitudes about gay rights to a sample of 1,000 likely voters. Studying the reported survey results, readers may develop the impression that only two sets of opinions among Americans exist: supporting and opposing gay rights. However, a critical inquiry would reveal a more complex picture that attitudes toward gay people are not blatantly dichotomous; people are not necessarily either for or against.

Let's illustrate. In some circumstances most Americans support gay rights; they say they think it ought to be illegal to fire someone for being gay and believe anti-gay attacks are hate crimes. However, at the same time most Americans believe gay marriages should not be legalized (see Chapter 11 on domestic issues for more details). Does this mean that if you disapprove of firing someone based on his or her sexual orientation you support gay rights and, at the same time, if you oppose the legalization of gay marriages you are against gay rights? You see how dichotomous conclusions may distort reality and misrepresent people's opinions; a respondent can be on

TABLE 3.3

Continuous versus dichotomous distributions of attitudes toward gay rights.

Accepting	Supports gay rights, including marriage; supports measures to enhance equality for women and racial minorities.
Tolerant	Supports most gay rights, except marriage and adoption; supports measures to enhance equality for women and racial minorities.
Traditionalist	Against hate crime and anti-gay job bias; supports measures to enhance equality for women and racial minorities but not gay people.
Socially conservative	Against many measures to enhance equality for women, racial minorities, and gay people.

one side on one issue and disagree with others. This illustration clearly shows a continuum of people's attitudes about gay rights. At least four categories of opinions emerge (Table 3.3). We suggest further analysis would likely reveal that these four types of opinions ("accepting," "tolerant," "traditionalist," and "socially conservative") themselves contain a range of views.

Similarities and differences between two phenomena are relative. Similar things are different to some degree, and things that appear different can share features. For example, are people who belong to the extreme political left different from those who belong to the extreme right? Apparently so. However, when we examine carefully their opinions on a variety of issues, we may find these two groups sharing certain features. In particular, classic studies of political behavior show that members of these two groups share a set of authoritarian beliefs and practices, including inflexible and uncritical adherence to particular beliefs, an exaggerated need to identify with strong authority, and intolerance of opponents (Adorno et al., 1950; Eysenk, 1954).

In review. How to apply the wording guidelines, Part 2.

1. Learn to differentiate between variables that are dichotomous and those that are continuous.

2. Most opinion-related phenomena are not dichotomous; they lie along a continuum.

3. When making judgments and comparisons, try to be specific and use percentages and proportions (such as majority or minority) to describe the distribution of opinions.

4. When comparing and contrasting social groups and their opinions look for both similarities and differences between these groups.

EXPLANATIONS: UNDERSTANDING SOURCES OF OPINIONS

Why did black voters in the United States primarily support the Republican Party before the 1960s? Why did most of them subsequently choose Democratic candidates? Why do most American women today vote for the Democratic Party? Why are the United States and Japan the only two developed free-market democratic nations in which the majority of people support the death penalty for convicted murderers? Explaining *why* people express particular views is always difficult because human behavior is not fully understood. Often, we can detect only visible causes and tend to believe they are the sole contributors to expressed opinions. In fact, many causes determine people's attitudes, social preferences, political choices, moral judgments, and voting behavior.

Know How to Interpret Correlations and Co-appearances

In Chapter 2, which discusses measurement, you learned that a correlation is a measure of the relationship or association between two (or more) variables. Correlations enable observers to base predictions about one variable or event on another, that is, if two events are correlated, then the presence of one event provides information about the other. Take, for instance, a typical U.S. voting pattern: People's yearly income and their identification with a political party are correlated. In particular, among Americans who make less than $15,000 a year there are fewer Republican supporters than among those who make $30,000. Furthermore, there are more Republican backers among those who make $50,000 a year than among those who make $30,000 (see Chapter 11 on domestic issues). What kind of a prediction can one make based on these data? It is reasonable to suggest that Republican candidates, in general, receive greater support from people who make more money, as compared to people who make less. If so, why does this pattern exist? Here is one explanation: When a person makes more money, he becomes supportive of Republican ideas about tax cuts, for example, that protect the interests of people who make more money. This is, however, only a generalization. Of course, some people base their party preference on their income. It is quite possible, nevertheless, that many people who express support for the Republican Party have always supported it, and that their income has little to do with their voting preference. For example, 10 years ago, these people could have been making very little money and still could have been supporting the Republican Party. Today they have more money than those who do not support Republicans. But we do not know exactly whether their status derives from their affluent parents and grandparents, their own efforts, or both.

It is important to bear in mind that a correlation does not establish a causal relationship between the variables. In other words, we cannot say exactly, based on the correlation, why A (income) and B (party identification) are linked. Let's move on to another example. Consider the correlation between educational level and interest in politics. According to surveys, the more educated people are, the more interest in politics they express (Delli Carpini & Keeter, 1996). Based on research evidence, what may we conclude? Can we state that educational advancement causes greater interest in politics? Perhaps, but maybe greater interest in politics causes people to study. Then again, isn't it possible that educational advancement and interest in politics affect one another? To complicate matters further, what about the possibility that some other variable, such as socioeconomic status, causes both educational advancement and greater interest in politics? Put another way, given a correlation between A (educational advancement) and B (interest in politics): Does A cause B? Does B cause A? Do A and B cause each other? Does C (level of income, for instance) cause A and B? A correlation caused by a third variable is called **spurious**. Unfortunately, a correlation alone, in fact, *cannot* provide us with definitive answers to these questions.

One mistake in judgment relates to the appearance together of two events. This mistaken logic concludes that simply because Event B follows Event A, then B must have been caused by A. This error, also known as **post-hoc error** or **parataxic reasoning** (Sullivan, 1954), occurs when despite a lack of evidence, people conclude that two temporally close co-appearing events are causally linked. For example, polls show that Asian Americans express less interest in politics than do members of other cultural groups in the United States. At the same time, this group expresses the strongest opposition to same-sex marriages (see Chapter 9 on cultural issues). Following parataxic or post-hoc reasoning, one may conclude that opposition to same-sex marriages among Asian Americans stems from their relative lack of knowledge about political rights and civil liberties. In fact, this interpretation is inaccurate because we do not know the degree to which interest in politics affects views on marriage or homosexuality.

Although some people tend to think of causal relationships as being one-directional (Event *A* causes Event *B*), frequently they are two-directional (Event *A* causes Event *B, and* Event *B* causes Event *A*). In other words, variables can, and frequently do, affect one another. This relationship is called a causal loop or, depending on our subjective evaluation of a particular situation, either a "healthy spiral" (if we happen to like it) or a "vicious cycle" (if we do not). As an illustration of this principle, find your own answer to this widely debated question: "Do conservative beliefs cause people to join the Republican Party, or does association with the Republican Party cause people to develop conservative beliefs?" If the relationship between ideological views (i.e., conservative or liberal) and political affiliation (i.e., Republican or Democratic) is viewed as a demonstration of a two-directional relationship, the argument may be moot; clearly, each view can affect the other.

Although correlations may provide accurate and frequently useful information about an existing relationship, they cannot be counted on to answer the questions *why?* and *how?* Even when a correlation strongly *implies* causation, it does not *prove* causation.

Look for Many Causes

A strong majority of Americans said they support the United States providing assistance to people in poor countries, whose governments sponsor family planning (PIPA, 2001). Is there a particular reason why most Americans hold this attitude? Actually, the question should be asked not about one particular reason but rather several reasons. Virtually any significant behavior has many determinants, and any single explanation is inevitably an oversimplification. Thus, we must consider a wide range of possible factors, all of which could to varying degrees be involved. For example, some respondents may believe overpopulation is the most significant economic and social problem in the world and, therefore, something should be done to overcome it. Others do not believe

---

A CASE IN POINT 3.2 What the "Average" American Thinks About Correlation and Causation

The reasoning rule that "correlation does not prove causation" is discussed in many college textbooks. Perhaps you already studied this rule in psychology, sociology, or research methods classes. But what does the average American think about the relationship between causation and correlation? According to a Gallup poll, about 64 percent of Americans answered "yes" to the question "Do you believe correlation implies causation?" whereas 38 percent replied "no" and another 8 percent were undecided (Gallup, October 1998, 1,009). Does this mean that almost two-thirds of Americans cannot reason properly? Think critically. Look carefully at the survey question. The question did not ask, "Do you believe correlation *always* implies causation?" Because correlation *may* suggest causation between two variables, some respondents may have used this reasoning to answer this question. In addition, do you think some respondents simply did not understand how to interpret the words *causation* and *correlation*?

in the threat of overpopulation; however, they support the United States helping other countries. Others believe people in poor countries should have better access to contraceptives and the United States can help in this matter.

Numerous surveys consider the multiple determinants of prejudice, or the negative evaluation of an ethnic, racial, religious, or social group formed without knowledge or examination of the facts. Why do people hold prejudiced views of groups, such as immigrants? It is important to understand that a single person may be prejudiced for several reasons. Likewise, a large group may express prejudiced views based on a wide variety of factors. For example, some people have unpleasant experiences with a few immigrants and tend to generalize this negativity to all members of this large and diverse group. What other factors can contribute to prejudice? List as many as you can think of. Compare your answers to the list of reasons posted on the book's website. See also the section on immigration in Chapter 11.

What causes many people in former communist countries, such as Russia, Poland, Belarus, and Ukraine, to support communists in local and national elections? Are they concerned with their social benefits, which may be threatened by free-market policies but guaranteed by the communists? Or are they disappointed with the results of democratic developments? Are they simply longing for the past? Or maybe they have been enticed by skillful electoral campaigning conducted by well-funded communists? Now, try replacing each *or* with *and*. In fact, communists' support may be viewed as a result of all these factors (Shlapentokh & Shiraev, 2002).

In review. How to apply the explanation guidelines.

1. Correlation between two variables or co-appearance of two events is not, in itself, proof of causation.

2. Keep in mind that correlations enable us to make predictions from one event to another; they do not, however, provide explanations as to why the events are related.

3. When a correlation is observed, consider all possible pathways and directions of causation. For example, if Event *A* and Event *B* are correlated, does *A* cause *B*? Does *B* cause *A*? Do *A* and *B* cause each other? Does *C* cause *A* and *B*?

4. In attempting to explain why an event occurred, do not limit your search to one cause. Instead, explore multiple plausible causes, all of which may be responsible for producing the effect.

In short, when you evaluate opinion surveys, keep your mind open to different points of view. If you look to confirm your expectations, do not cling to them in the face of disconfirming evidence. Be empathetic, that is, try to understand ideas you do not like and to see things from the position of people with whom you disagree. Although emotional occasions and vivid events may be persuasive, they do not necessarily tell us about general tendencies. Try to find additional information about the event you are examining. When faced with a discrepancy between your beliefs and the evidence, resist the tendency to assume your beliefs are right and the facts are wrong.

Are we, the authors, free of cognitive errors in our analyses of polls? Do we follow our own advice? We hope so, but we may be wrong at times. We may make mistakes or errors of judgment, and we say without reservation that if you find the mistakes, *you are thinking critically*. This is one of the goals we want to achieve.

ASSIGNMENT 3.1   SIMILARITIES AND DIFFERENCES

When comparing and contrasting, try to explain the ways in which things are similar and different. Choose several standpoints from which to evaluate your subject. Despite what appears to be overwhelming similarity between two phenomena, search for and take into account their differences. Conversely, regardless of what may seem to be the absence of commonalities between two events, search for and take into account their similarities. Choose three pairs from this list and find and describe at least three similarities between each pair.

Republican public officials and Democratic public officials (besides that they are all U.S. citizens and public officials)

Pro-life and pro-choice supporters in the United States (besides that they are concerned about abortion)

Chicago Cubs and Chicago White Sox baseball fans (besides that they live in Chicago and vicinity)

Voters who support the death penalty and voters who oppose it (besides that they are adults)

North Koreans and South Koreans (besides that they are Korean)

After you finish this assignment, think about whether or not your feelings about these pairs have changed.

CHAPTER SUMMARY

- Critical thinking is an active and systematic intellectual strategy for examining, evaluating, and understanding opinion polls on the basis of sound reasoning and valid evidence. Learning to think critically in analyzing and interpreting survey data is a vital and indispensable component of the process of learning about people's opinions.

- There are verifiable facts, and there are assumptions. Many individuals answer survey questions by using and expressing their assumptions rather than actual knowledge.

- Some people tend to maintain preconceptions and expectations about certain issues without verifying the accuracy of their opinions. In some situations, preconceptions are helpful in anticipating events. People also make logical mistakes.

- The rules or guidelines of critical thinking fit into four categories or sets. The first set of rules deals with the *circumstances* under which the poll was conducted. This includes the examination of the context in which the survey was taken and the survey's design. The second set of guidelines helps you take into consideration *prejudgments* in the process of understanding and interpreting of surveys. The third set deals with the way we use language in *descriptions* of survey results. The fourth set provides suggestions about forming a better understanding of the *reasons and causes* that determine people's opinions.

- Many events capture a respondent's attention and affect his or her responses to questions. Among these are local economic and social developments, national events, media attention to the survey's subject, and knowledge about the subject. If interpretations of an event are easily retrieved from memory, that event seems more prevalent than an equally frequent event that does not evoke easily retrieved interpretations. Vivid examples, spectacular events, personal testimonies, and accidents are likely to exert a disproportionate impact on people's judgment.

- The way survey questions are asked can influence the responders' answers. The observer must determine whether the design and order of the survey's questions might have affected the respondents' opinions.

- Generalizations about opinion patterns and social groups that carry them are likely to be incomplete or inaccurate. The observer may see respondents as belonging to a homogeneous category; however, the diversity within that group may be wide.

- Many people tend to make data fit their opinion rather than fit their opinion to the data. Moreover, people may pay attention to polls that confirm their views and miss others that challenge their views.

- When interpreting a survey, it is vital to recognize who the sponsor is, especially if the sponsor is a political or social organization.

- A fundamental and pervasive human psychological activity is the propensity to name things and people, to attach labels to them. Labels are then easily converted into opinions, and opinions into facts.

- An important element of critical thinking is its reliance on the original source of the polling data. If you can see the results firsthand, you might find that an observer's interpretation of this poll is inaccurate or biased.

- People naturally tend to dichotomize variables that are more accurately conceptualized as continuous. Many observable phenomena that lie along a continuum, somewhere between point A and point B, are frequently presumed to fit into *either* category A *or* category B.

- One type of post hoc judgment error is related to the co-appearance of two events. People may mistakenly conclude that, simply because Event B follows Event A, then B must have been caused by A. They misconstrue temporal linkage as causal linkage despite lack of supporting evidence.

- Virtually every significant behavior, or its results (including expressed opinions), has many determinants, and any single-factor explanation is inevitably an oversimplification.

Looking Ahead. Now armed with tools of critical thinking from Chapter 3, we turn to Chapter 4 on "Attitudes and Opinions" to explore in more detail how people form and express their views. The chapter describes major theories that shed light on how people form beliefs, attitudes and values, and express opinions relatively consistently in various circumstances, in particular, in surveys. It discusses balance, adaptation, and rational actor theories, and ways to look critically at attitudes.

DEFINITIONS OF KEY TERMS

Assume—To expect something with confidence.

Availability heuristic—The process of drawing on instances that are easily accessible from memory.

Critical thinking—An active and systematic cognitive strategy for examining, evaluating, and understanding opinion polls on the basis of sound reasoning and valid evidence.

Dichotomous variable—Any variable divided into two opposites. This division often takes place in the observer's mind.

Meta-opinion—A judgment expressed about an opinion or opinions.

Post-hoc error—Also called **parataxic reasoning.** The assumption, despite lack of evidence, that temporally related events or co-appearances are also causally linked.

Social attribution—A cognitive mechanism by which people interpret events and behaviors by applying easily available explanations.

Spurious correlation—A correlation between two variables produced by a third variable.

CHAPTER 4

Attitudes and Opinions

I share no man's opinions; I have
my own.

Ivan Turgenev

Dilemmas, comparisons, evaluations. . . . People have to make choices every day; they make judgments and endorse policies, decisions, and political candidates. Based on personal preferences, people elect presidents, reach verdicts in courts, and answer survey questions. Can you guess what answers Americans provided when asked to choose between different alternatives?

For example, which is more important: to develop a belief in God or to acquire the scientific viewpoint? Critics complain that the United States is a materialistic society in which everything is calculated and based on the pragmatism of science. However, according to a poll, Americans prefer "encouraging a belief in God" (78 percent) to "a modern scientific outlook" (15 percent).

Some observers say Americans are preoccupied with freedom and individual rights. However, "defending standards of right and wrong" is considered more valuable (55 percent) than "protecting rights of individuals" (39 percent). "Being tough on criminals" was chosen by 76 percent, whereas only 17 percent preferred "protecting rights of accused." Moreover, "guaranteeing law and order" was chosen by 56 percent of Americans over "guaranteeing individual freedom" (34 percent).

Some say Americans are more concerned about the economy than about any other social issue. True, the goal of "increasing economic growth" was selected by 55 percent over "narrowing the gap between the rich and the poor," chosen by 37 percent. However, "protecting the environment" (52 percent) won more support than "increasing jobs and economic growth" (37 percent). What comes first in terms of its importance, "family values" or "rights of women?" "Preserving family values" received support from 60 percent, whereas "working for the rights of women" received the backing of 31 percent (*Washington Post*/Henry J. Kaiser Family Foundation/Harvard University, August 10–27, 1998, national adult, 1,200).

How do people come to such decisions? How stable and consistent are their opinions? In discussing the nature of attitudes, we describe prominent theories that shed light on how people form their views and express opinions in various circumstances—in particular, in surveys.

Looking Forward. The fourth chapter, "Attitudes and Opinions," explains how people form and express their views, in short, the nature of opinion. It describes prominent theories that shed light on how people form attitudes and express opinions under various circumstances, in particular, in surveys. It discusses balance, adaptation, and rational-actor theories, and ways to look critically at attitudes. It examines how people come to decisions about what is important to them and the relative consistency and stability of their opinions.

THE NATURE OF ATTITUDES

Critical appraisal of public opinion requires an analysis of **attitudes,** the psychological representations and evaluations of features of the social world. Attitudes are, in fact, the psychological links or associations between cognitive images and their evaluations (Fazio et al., 2000). Attitudes are based on personal experience. An individual's memory retains an image along with its appraisal. However—as we discuss later in the chapter—people may also express attitudes about issues and problems they have never seen, thought about, or dealt with.

Attitudes are not easy to depict because they are not directly observable. Any description of attitude is, in fact, an act of imagination. Although no one can see gravity as a form of energy, people can observe and measure its effects: Apples fall from the tree; they do not fly up. Let's use this analogy to describe attitudes. Although we do not see attitudes, we can deduce them from people's oral or written responses to questions, and sometimes we can infer them from behavior: If a woman puts a bumper sticker on her SUV that reads "Jones for Governor," she probably supports Jones's quest for the governorship.

One common view of attitudes is based on a two-dimensional model, according to which an attitude has at least two major components or dimensions: cognitive and affective.

- *The cognitive component.* This is the individual's knowledge and thoughts about a certain object (such as a nuclear plant), person (such as a presidential candidate), or issue (such as speed limits and the legal age for voting), including memorized facts, experiences, and assumptions. Here are some representative statements that reflect an individual's knowledge or beliefs: "My older brother is going to vote for the Libertarian party." "In our country, the rich get richer and the poor get poorer." "Clinton said he would not run for public office again."

- *The affective component.* Often known as the emotional component, this is an evaluation of an object or issue linked to one or several basic human emotions, such as joy, fear, disgust, sadness, anger, and surprise. Consider the following statements: "My older brother is going to vote for the Libertarian party, *and I do not like his choice.*" "The rich get richer and the poor get poorer, *and I am pleased to say this is how things should be.*" "Clinton said he would not run for an office; *this is dis-*

appointing to me." The affective component need not be dichotomous, that is, a positive or negative evaluation. Ambivalence, or the presence of both positive and negative evaluations, may exist in many attitudes (Lavine et al., 2000).

Both emotional and cognitive components are likely to affect the individual's behavioral readiness to act in a certain way regarding an object or issue he or she evaluates (Allport, 1954). By suggesting, for example, that you do not like your brother's decision to vote for the Libertarian party, you may also express your willingness to (a) criticize your sibling, or (b) talk him out of doing so, depending on the circumstances. An impact of an attitude on behavior is mediated by a mixture of factors, including the strength of cognitive-affective links within the attitude itself (Yadov, 1977). What does this mean? An attitude is expected to be "strong"—that is, resistant to change—when the emotional-cognitive links are based on substantial knowledge and reinforced by a sound emotional commitment to the object or issue (Kalgren & Wood, 1986). Such strong attitudes, in fact, are likely to influence individuals' behavior. For example, it was shown that so-called early voters, U.S. citizens who are allowed, for different reasons, to cast their absentee ballots before Election Day, demonstrate a greater interest in politics and have stronger ideological ties with political parties than other voters (Stein, 1998).

In review.   An attitude is expected to be resistant to change when the emotional-cognitive connection is based on substantial knowledge and reinforced by a sound emotional commitment to the object or issue.

A CASE IN POINT **4.1** Culture and Attitudes

Cultural influences may contribute to the development of attitude components. Such cultural factors are occasionally discussed in the media and have become subjects of theoretical speculations. Here, for example, is what Gavriil Popov, a renowned Russian economist, reformer, and ex-mayor of Moscow, said in an interview with a major Russian weekly newspaper: "Polls are created by psychologists and sociologists of Anglo-Saxon, mainly west-European mentality. . . . Here in Russia, a poll reflects not a [rational] decision of a person but his mood" (*Argumenty I Facty* 8, 1996, p. 3). The emotional nature of Russians' attitudes was also emphasized by Andrei Kokoshin, a former deputy defense minister and prominent social scientist: "[The] Russian man is somewhat fatalist. He does not program his life rationally as German, Anglo-Saxon, or French men do. . . . " (*Argumenty I Facty* 25, 1996, p. 3). Some Russian experts explained a dramatic shift of public opinion during the presidential elections of 1996, when support for President Boris Yeltsin climbed from the single digits to almost 50 percent in a three-month period, by emphasizing the role of the *emotional* and *irrational* (something that lacks a conscious cognitive effort) in the Russian voter's attitude. Likewise, in 1999, Vladimir Putin, a security official virtually unknown to the general public, quickly earned mass support (POF, November 27–28, 1999) and a few months later was elected president. Some experts explained this election result reflected people's volatile mood and their support of any authority figure who appears tough and powerful. Do you agree?

Attitudes can be described in a variety of ways and forms. Let's examine two attitudinal types: beliefs and values. Is there any significant distinction between them? If there is a difference, what is it?

BELIEFS

J.J. has two beliefs: that people in Latin America speak Latin and that all politicians in Washington, DC, are corrupt. A **belief** is a perceived relation between an object and its attribute, that is, its quantity, quality, or other characteristics. Individuals initially form beliefs on the basis of their life experiences, and these beliefs, in turn, influence the formation of new ones (Davidson & Thomson, 1980). In their beliefs, individuals typically establish cognitive relationships between two or among several objects or issues. As a demonstration of beliefs, let us turn to the results of a survey conducted in 1995. According to this national poll, 49 percent of respondents believed the CIA was involved in the assassination of President John Kennedy; 50 percent believed that flying saucers are real, and 9 percent believed the 1969 Apollo moon landing was a massive hoax designed to scare the Soviet Union and boost the American people's confidence in their own government (*Washington Post,* July 23, 1995). In a 2002 poll, 57 percent of Americans believed in extrasensory perception or "other experiences that cannot be explained by normal means" (CBS, February, 861). In another 2002 poll, 11 percent of registered voters said they believed President Bush knew about the September 11 attacks ahead of time (Fox, April 16, 900). Beliefs are not facts; they represent perceptions of reality.

Beliefs typically do not contain evaluations. For example, an answer to the question "Have you used illegal drugs?" (*Time,* November 24, 1997) should reflect the respondent's belief, because her answer is likely to indicate the way she understands the words "to use" and "illegal drugs," and the relationship between them. A hypothetical follow-up question, "Do you approve or disapprove of some people using illegal drugs?" requires a more complex evaluative statement from the respondent. In this case, most likely, disapproval or approval of illegal drugs would reflect the respondent's attitude toward drug use.

The way people express and interpret beliefs may play an unexpected role in political battles. In 1999, George Lundberg, a 17-year veteran editor of the *Journal of the American Medical Association (JAMA)* was fired by Association officials for "inappropriately and inexcusably interjecting *JAMA* into a major political debate" (Smith, 1999). Why was he fired? The problem was that the editor decided to publish a . . . research article. What was inappropriate about this decision? The issue containing the article was published during the Congressional debate about President Clinton's affair with Monica Lewinsky. The authors of the article, entitled "Would You Say You 'Had Sex' If . . . ?" conducted a survey in 1991 that asked students at a Midwestern university whether or not they defined oral sex as having "had sex." According to the survey, 60 percent did not think oral sex was having sex (Sanders & Reinisch, 1999). The editor was fired because it appeared to critics that the only reason to publish this research finding in a prominent journal was political, that is, to aid President Clinton (Smith, 1999; *Washington Times,* 1999).

Beliefs about intimate issues can quickly become a focus of the media's attention. Americans' beliefs about the meaning of the expressions *sexual relations* and

TABLE 4.1

What Americans thought in 1998 about sexual behavior. (In percentages.)

Does "sexual relations" cover more than "sexual intercourse"?	Yes	No	Don't know	Number of respondents
Princeton Survey Research, 1/1998	76	12	12	757
ABC News, 8/1998	73	22	5	1,023
ABC News, 9/1998	81	13	6	525
Gallup, 9/1998	73	20	7	631

sexual intercourse—Clinton cited the variety of meanings of such expressions in his videotaped self-defense testimony—were also examined by major polling organizations in 1998. According to these surveys, from 19 to 27 percent of Americans may not believe the expression *sexual relations* covers more than *sexual intercourse,* thus somewhat supporting Clinton's deposition (Table 4.1).

VALUES

In older English, the word *value* was used mostly as a verb meaning "to esteem." Today the term *values* is used predominantly as a plural noun meaning "beliefs or attitudes" (Will, 2000). A **value** is a complex attitude that reflects a principle, standard, or quality the individual uses to distinguish the most desirable or appropriate objects and issues. Values are stable and enduring preferences for a specific behavior (often called *instrumental value*) or goal (called *terminal value*) over others (Rokeach, 1973). For example, two New Yorkers, Jay and Fay, may dream about a happy, interesting, healthy, and trouble-free life. This is their terminal value. However, they may differ in their choice of instrumental values. Jay would like to move to a small town in Idaho. His goal is to live far away from the excruciating noise and debilitating stress of the big city. Fay, on the other hand, would like to choose an ambitious business career, since her goals are money, power, and interpersonal connections, which, in her view, will bring happiness into her life.

Values hold a more central, stable position than attitudes and can influence the expression of attitudes and behavior toward a variety of objects and situations (Rokeach, 1968). Consider a few examples. We anticipate that a person who is against abortion because of his deeply seated religious *values* is likely to join the Republican Party and support its political program and candidates during elections. It is likely that a Hindu woman will not eat a roast beef sandwich at a friend's party because abstinence from beef (a Hindu religious *value*) is stronger than the attitude of being polite to her host. Likewise, an Italian autoworker strongly attached to the *value* of equality is likely to support government actions aimed at helping people from neighboring Yugoslavia (Belucci & Isernia, 2003). A deep commitment to the *value* of nonviolent resolution of social conflicts prevented Mikhail Gorbachev from using drastic and violent measures to thwart the collapse of the Soviet Union in the 1991 (Glad & Shiraev, 1999).

In review. Beliefs establish cognitive relationships between two or among several objects or issues. Values are stable and enduring preferences for a specific behavior or goal over others.

Individual values are connected to the way people cope with basic social problems, and these coping strategies are influenced by culture. Smith and Schwartz (1997) investigated three basic issues that differentiate cultures: (a) the extent to which people are independent of or dependent on groups; (b) people's views on prosperity and profit; and (c) people's views on whether it is appropriate to exploit, fit in with, or submit to the outside world. An analysis of people's responses revealed their basic views as distributed between two ends of a spectrum of human values.

> **Type 1. Social Order versus Autonomy.** People who value social order believe in the status quo, advocate moderation and self-discipline, and care about orderliness and tradition. People who value autonomy emphasize the rights of individuals to pursue their own ideals and to enjoy life for the sake of pleasure and excitement.

> **Type 2. Hierarchy versus Egalitarianism.** People with hierarchic values justify the legitimacy of an unequal distribution of power, resources, and social roles in society. People who who stress egalitarian values see individuals as equals who share basic interests and should receive equal access to society's resources.

> **Type 3. Mastery versus Harmony.** People with stronger mastery values encourage individuals to exercise control over society and exploit its natural resources. Ambition and high self-esteem are important individual traits that accompany mastery values. People with higher harmony values believe the world should be kept as it is—preserved and cherished rather than exploited.

In a 1996 study, Hofstede showed important national and cultural differences in the way people expressed their value preferences. A sample of 40 countries was divided into several groups: West European (France, Germany, etc.), Anglo (Great Britain and the United States), East European, Islamic, East Asian, Japan (as a single country), and Latin American. People in East Asian nations gave especially high marks to hierarchy and social order values and low marks to egalitarianism and autonomy. West European participants, as a group, gave somewhat more autonomous answers compared to the East Asian sample. The Anglo profile fell between the West European and East Asian samples. One interesting finding established a correlation between the size of the household and the values of social order and hierarchy. Values such as stability, discipline, and compliance were supported more often in large families living under one roof than in smaller family units.

ATTITUDES: APPROACHES TO UNDERSTANDING

When you pick up your phone and respond to a pollster's questions, how do you generate your answers? Do you have attitudes about issues and simply share them with the polling organization? Do you make some decisions on the spot? Do you feel uncertain about some questions and sure about others? To explain how humans form and express attitudes, let's examine several empirical theories.

Some theories focus on how attitudes are organized and function in the individual's mind. According to the **cognitive approach,** the focal point is how the individual represents and organizes his experience cognitively. Cognitive processes, such as perception, memory, recognition, and decision making, play a critical role in attitude formation and expression. Particular attitudes depend on the presence of other attitudes and cognitive mechanisms by which individuals receive, understand, and interpret incoming facts they encounter.

According to the **regulatory-adaptation approach,** attitudes represent reactions or habits. People learn particular attitudes as they learn certain behaviors. Therefore, attitudes are merely labels people attach to certain oral reactions or written responses. Attitudes that prove useful are retained. Other attitudes are not retained because they prove useless or unrewarding.

THE COGNITIVE APPROACH
Attitude Accessibility Theories

When ABC News asked Americans in 2003 whether they "favor or oppose the death penalty for persons convicted of murder," 64 percent were in favor. Only 31 percent were opposed, and 5 percent did not give a definite answer (ABC, January 16, 1,006). However, when the same survey asked another question, "Which punishment do you prefer for people convicted of murder, the death penalty or life in prison with no chance of parole?" the answers were distributed in a decidedly different way. Now 49 percent chose the death penalty, and 45 percent said they prefer "life without parole." The difference in the answers is remarkable. Why did it happen? Which of the answers more accurately represents respondents' true attitudes? In Chapter 2 on measurement, we already saw the impact of survey question design on respondents' answers. However, we did not pay much attention to the cognitive-psychological mechanisms that determine these effects. One such mechanism is **attitude accessibility,** a measure of availability and easiness of expression of an individual's specific attitude.

Overall, an attitude's accessibility is determined by the strength of the cognitive connections between an image and its evaluation (Fazio et al., 2000; Millar & Tesser, 1986). Certain information and evaluations are easily retrievable from memory, others less so. Several factors determine attitude accessibility. The first is the frequency of the attitude's expression (Fazio, 1989). Researchers show that if someone expressed an attitude several times, it should be easily accessible from memory (Doll & Ajen, 1992; Fazio & Zanna, 1981). Overall, anyone interested in an issue or problem—the death penalty, for instance—is expected to have more accessible attitudes related to capital punishment than people who do not have any interest. Pragmatic appeal of a social issue (for instance, lower taxes), group attachments (political, ethnic, religious, and other affiliations), fundamental values (for example, nonviolence), or several other factors determine the accessibility of particular attitudes (Boninger et al., 1995).

On the other hand, a wide variety of factors can block the accessibility of the person's memories and attitudes. For example, victims or witnesses of assault may not recall important details of the violent act because of the tremendous associated emotional pain. If, however, the process of retrieval involves facing few cognitive and emotional obstacles, this knowledge becomes highly accessible.

Quite often, the content of the question sways the respondent to give a particular reply. Earlier in this book, in Chapter 2 on measurement, we learned that the order of options available to the respondent affects their answers; many people tend to choose items that appear earliest on the list. Early studies of how individuals make decisions show that many people tend to agree with or settle for the first available solution (Simon, 1957).

Let's go back to the death penalty example. When respondents are given just two possible answers to the question, those who have previously expressed their general support or opposition to the death penalty find it easy to remember their position. When several options are offered, respondents are likely to consider these new choices and may produce new answers based on a wider variety of accessible attitudes.

The accessibility of an attitude is also defined in terms of the speed with which the attitude is retrieved from memory. Specialists use reaction time as a way to distinguish responses that stem from strong versus weak attitudes. Individuals with stronger associations tend to respond faster than those with weaker associations. Fletcher (2000) showed, for example, that differences in survey question response times among groups of respondents is attributable to the different degrees of importance the groups attach to the questions. The most controversial questions are typically associated with a delay in responding.

How does the issue of accessibility affect the answers themselves? Attitudes that are more accessible are more likely to be expressed and more likely to affect behavior than attitudes that are less accessible (Snyder & Swann, 1976). Easily accessible attitudes are considered more important to the individual and tend to have a stronger influence on other attitudes and actions than attitudes that are not easily accessible (Roese & Olson, 1994). In addition, people are less likely to hold accessible attitudes if these conflict with other attitudes.

A CASE IN POINT 4.2 The Art of Asking Questions

The popular Swedish children's author Astrid Lindgren created a famous character named Karlsson—a funny little rascal with a propeller on his back who does inappropriate things like asking puzzling questions. Consider one question he addressed to a mean, discipline-obsessed housemaid: "Have you stopped drinking cognac in the evenings or not?" How should she, who never tasted alcohol, answer? There are two easily accessible answers: "yes" and "no." If she says "yes," this implies she used to drink cognac in the evening. If she says "no," this implies she continues to drink cognac in the evening. A simple answer to this question is not readily accessible. To answer this question, the housemaid needs a more sophisticated answer, like "Look, I have never tried alcohol."

Such inquiries are called *provocative questions*. What they do is raise the odds of the respondent giving the most available answer—that is, the simplest and most probable. This answer, however, could get the respondent in trouble.

Here is an illustration involving two groups. The first group is composed of both individuals who share liberal values but oppose abortion rights and individuals who share conservative values but support abortion rights. The second group consists of liberals who support abortion rights and conservatives who oppose abortion.

Historically, conservative values and support of abortion rights do not match. Neither do liberal values and anti-abortion attitudes. As a result, people in the conservative group are less likely to express abortion-related attitudes than those in the liberal group (Huckfeldt & Sprague, 2000). In practical terms, conservatives who support abortion rights will tend to be less outspoken on the subject than liberals who support these rights.

An attitude becomes more accessible if it contains a strong emotional evaluation of an issue—either positive or negative—but not both. Attitudes with a uniform composition of the affective component are called **single-evaluation attitudes.** Attitudes that contain a mixed emotional component are called **dual-evaluation attitudes.** If an individual develops a dual-evaluation attitude, the process of responding to a related question requires the integration of positive and negative evaluations. The process of retrieving ambivalent elements is thus more time-consuming and requires a greater cognitive effort than retrieving a single-evaluation attitude. Ambivalent attitudes, therefore, are expected to be less accessible for the individual than single evaluation attitudes (Lavine et al., 2000). For example, a woman who is against abortion rights and does not want to consider abortion for herself under any circumstance is likely to have more accessible abortion-related attitudes than a woman who is against abortion but might consider one for herself under certain circumstances.

In review. The accessibility of an attitude from memory is determined by the strength of the cognitive connections the individual makes between images and their evaluations.

Cognitive Balance Theories

Cognitive balance theories hold that people seek consistency among their attitudes and try to avoid any mismatch among them or between their attitudes and behavior. One classic balance theory (Heider, 1959) examines consistency pressures within a simple three-element cognitive evaluation process.

The first element (A) is a person who develops evaluations. The other two elements (B, C) are objects, issues, or people being evaluated. If (A) (a husband, for example) loves his wife (B), and she wants to donate $100 to a political candidate (C), the husband is likely to support this decision ("My sweetheart always does the right thing"). If, however, he dislikes the proposed donation, his attitude toward his wife may change from positive to less positive or even negative ("Why does she waste the money I earned?"). In general, a balanced cognitive system is one in which individuals agree with people they like and disagree with people they do not like. This theory proposes that we attach a greater value to things we like and a lesser value to things we dislike (Pratkanis, 1988; Davidson & Thomson, 1980). Experimental research also shows that the principles of cognitive balance are common in various countries (Triandis, 1994).

A state of balance between two attitudes may significantly influence behavior. As a demonstration, research shows that in the Canadian federal election of 1993, the intentions of voters with balanced partisan views were expressed faster than the intentions of those who had unbalanced views (Bassili, 1995). Individuals with balanced partisan attitudes were also most likely to vote in the election, and when they voted, they tended to do so consistently with their preelection voting intentions. People with unbalanced attitudes, on the other hand, after they decided to vote, were unlikely to vote consistently with their voting intentions.

According to Festinger (1957), whenever an individual must decide between two or more alternatives, the final pick is almost always inconsistent with some of his attitudes. Imagine Mark voted for Arnold Schwarzenegger for governor of California in 2003 because Schwarzenegger promised to cut taxes and keep social programs. Right after the inauguration, the new governor made a series of policy statements about cutting social programs that Mark does not want eliminated. This perceived inconsistency between intention and actual result generates in Mark an unpleasant state of emotions often called **cognitive dissonance.** Social psychologists have long established that most people seek to avoid cognitive dissonance and reduce its negative emotional impact on behavior. In general, people feel compelled to either seek actions or form new attitudes to reduce the dissonance. They can do this in at least three ways:

1. By assigning a greater value to the chosen alternative. Mark could reason, "If I wanted Arnold Schwarzenegger in the office, I should trust him and support him no matter what."

2. By downgrading and devaluating the alternative that was not chosen. Mark could think, "Overall, it is much better to have this governor than any other. Electing anyone else would have been a complete disaster. Meanwhile, I can cope with what Mr. Schwarzenegger does."

3. By avoiding thinking or talking about the decision they have made. Mark can bring the issue to a conclusion: "I have voted. The topic is closed."

According to cognitive balance theories, if an individual has an attitude about a particular issue, she is motivated to seek selectively information that affirms the correctness of her initial attitude (Lavine et al., 2000). For example, two groups of participants agreed to participate in a study. One group was strongly against capital punishment, and the other was strongly in favor of it. The groups were given two reports to consider. Report #1 provided evidence in support of capital punishment and contained arguments suggesting it prevents murder. Report #2 provided evidence against capital punishment and suggested it does not deter murder. Respondents with positive attitudes toward capital punishment found Report #1 (the one supporting capital punishment) more convincing than Report #2. Exactly the opposite was true for the group against death penalty; most found the second report more convincing than the first one (Lord et al., 1979).

Why do most people strive to balance their attitudes and avoid dissonance? The main motive is to avoid unpleasant emotions caused by cognitive tension. A simple, harmonious, consistent, and meaningful view on issues is normally free of tension. To achieve a harmonious view, people tend to use the **least-effort principle:** They minimize the number of cognitive operations needed to reach a goal. Therefore, people who are liberal or conservative on one issue tend to be relatively liberal or conservative on a wide range of issues (Converse, 1964). To avoid a potentially frustrating dissonance, the individual acquires specific types of explanations, assessments, and behaviors. An optimist is likely to explain the economic slowdown of the early 2000s as an expected market correction, while a pessimist may see in it compelling signs of a global economic failure. A person who likes a certain television network may stop watching other networks ("Why should I watch something I do not like?"). Likewise, a person who thinks the media distort information may stop watching television and reading newspapers, turning instead to alternative websites for the latest updates and analyses, or avoid media overall.

Balance theories also suggest that an individual's active voluntary participation in an organization or political campaign should increase his positive feelings toward that organization or project. For example, Cann (1995) found that American activists who worked for candidates in the 1988 elections became more committed to the candidates and their ideologies as a consequence of their participation. Direct and successful involvement in an ideologically charged campaign typically reinforces the activist's commitment to his party or candidate.

Attitudes Expressed via Balanced Responses

Imagine a pollster asks whether you support a $1,000-a-year per-person tax increase in your state. Suppose you do not like this idea at all! Without hesitation, you express your negative opinion to the pollster. The **response theory** assumes that people react to incoming information by immediately generating positive or negative thoughts. If the information stimulates a strong counterargument, a negative attitude is activated and then expressed in the form of an opinion. If the message stimulates mostly favorable comments, a positive attitude emerges and is expressed (Greenwald, 1968). If, for example, Peter Jennings, the ABC news anchor, expresses a cautious and skeptical view of Israeli settlements on the West Bank, a person who knows very little about the situation in the Middle East, but admires Jennings, may form an attitude and produce an opinion about the settlements based on the anchor's comments. If Jennings sounded reasonable, the person is likely to agree. On the other hand, if Jennings evokes critical evaluations in the person's mind, the response reflecting these critical evaluations is likely to be different, and the person will disagree.

In the context of the response theory, compare, for example, rational and rationalized voting. The rational vote occurs when a voter first decides on her own position and then decides to vote for a candidate who represents this position. The rationalized vote is a reversal of this causal order: The voter first chooses a candidate and then takes a position on issues as influenced by that candidate (Brody and Page, 1972). The rationalization may occur in two forms. The first is projection: The voter favors a candidate by assuming the candidate agrees with her on many important issues. The other form is persuasion: In this case, the voter forms her issue positions according to those of the selected candidate.

Dogmatism

Dogmatism is close-mindedness, rigidity, and inflexibility with respect to attitudes and subsequent behavior. It is a well-protected cognitive organization of attitudes and beliefs, usually organized around one central idea or issue that has absolute authority over the individual's other beliefs and provides a framework for patterns of opinions and intolerance toward other people or issues (Rokeach, 1954). The dogmatic individual has a limited way of thinking about ideas regardless of their content; he will reject ideas that differ from his own. Dogmatism also makes the individual uncritical of people who share his views and hostile to those who do not.

Political psychologist Ofer Feldman (1996) used a questionnaire to compare dogmatism in politicians of the United States, Italy, and Japan. He found the Japanese members of parliament were neither as high in dogmatism as the Italian parliament deputies nor as low as the American state legislators. In other words, he found Japanese politicians less dogmatic than Italian legislators but more dogmatic than their American counterparts. We can understand these findings better if we recognize the differences in political party systems in these three countries. Italy, at the time the survey was conducted, had eight major ideologically diverse national political parties, each advancing a different political doctrine and philosophy of life. In-group ideological pressure on the members of each party was high. In the United States, in contrast, the two major political parties were weakly organized and highly decentralized, and in-group ideological pressure was not expected to be high. Feldman argued that the Japanese political system contains characteristics of both Italian and American political systems: high ideological solidarity and relative independence from the central party structures. One methodological fact should be noticed, however. The data for the American sample were gathered from state legislators, whereas the Italian and Japanese samples were of national legislators.

In review.   People tend to maintain a simple, consistent, and personally meaningful view on issues. Overall, they seek consistency among their attitudes and try to avoid any mismatch among attitudes or between attitudes and behavior.

THE REGULATORY-ADAPTATION APPROACH
Attitudes as Learned Reactions

According to the **learning approach**, people acquire information about events and objects, and in doing so they also learn how to feel and think about them. In line with the behavioral tradition in social sciences, this approach pays little attention to the cognitive aspect of attitudes and mostly deals with opinions and behaviors, habits, and norms that derive from these opinions (Eysenk, 1954/1999; Hovland et al., 1953).

People learn about the rules of law as well as about lawlessness. For example, in Northern Ireland, a country devastated by ethnic and religious tensions between the Catholic and Protestant populations, children from the areas with the highest levels of tension and violence scored lower on a measure of non-aggressive attitudes (Ferguson and Cairns, 1996). Likewise, opinions may be affected by the absence of learning. Thus, Kinder and Mendelberg (1995), analyzing survey data, found that opposition to marriage between black people and white people is stronger among white people who do not interact with black people.

A central assumption of the learning approach is that the expressed content of attitudes is strongly mediated by specific experience. In a comparative study of the

United States and Great Britain, college-educated respondents were asked whether elected politicians should follow their party's line or whether they should make up their own mind regardless of how their party wants them to act. In the United States, respondents were more likely to say politicians should act independently. In Great Britain, respondents were more likely to say politicians should follow their party's line. How can one interpret the difference in responses? Members of major political parties in the United States are not typically bound by strict rules and strong party discipline. In Great Britain, political activities are based on a high degree of party discipline. The British respondents knew about the existing party discipline and the rules and gave responses based on their learning experience (Cain et al., 1987).

Here is another case. During the Great Depression of the 1930s, most American workers vented their frustration with economic and social policies by turning to the politically moderate Democratic Party. In Europe, however, much more radical and even extremist movements developed: German Nazism, Italian Fascism, and Spanish authoritarianism are the exemplars. Why did this happen? Perhaps the differences in stability between social and political institutions of the United States and Europe (for example, a relative weakness of political parties in the United States and their strength in Europe) as well as historical circumstances (such as the prevalence of nationalistic and xenophobic attitudes in Europe after World War I) channeled the learned political attitudes in different directions (Delli Carpini, 1989).

The Rational Actor Approach

The **rational actor approach** was formulated by the classic thinkers, mostly economists and philosophers, of the 18th and 19th centuries (see Smith, 1776/1937). According to this approach, human nature is self-interested. Individuals (referred to as *actors*) satisfy their needs by pursuing goals. Each actor's behavior results from a process that involves conscious choice. Actors pursue goals and have preferences (attitudes) that are consistent and stable. Among many options, actors choose the alternative that appears most attractive to them. People usually gauge other people's actions using rational calculations (Simon, 1983).

According to Edwards (1954), when facing choices, people compare options and then adopt the alternative they think will provide the best result for them. Moreover, people not only act directly according to their attitudes and self-interest, they also take into consideration the context of their actions. For example, a person may appreciate, at least in theory, radical socialist ideas about taxation but consider such views naïve and inappropriate in the "real" world when governments rely on taxes.

The rational actor perspective focuses primarily on responses to current, immediate balances of alternatives. It pays less attention to psychological constructs, such as promise or duty, which may determine what the person likes or dislikes regardless of her rational calculations. Certain kinds of attitudes emerge primarily from one's childhood or adolescent experiences. For example, many ethical judgments arise from deep-seated predispositions that are acquired early in life and relate to the psychological identity of the individual (Monroe, 1995). Critics say attitudes and behaviors based on such attitudes are not typically influenced by immediate rational calculations.

For example, read the following real-life stories.

A TOPIC FOR CLASS DISCUSSION Difficult Choices

Daniel Crocker was a 38-year-old professional who lived in suburban Virginia with his wife and two children. One day he quit his job, consulted his minister and family, and boarded a plane to Kansas, where he willingly confessed to a murder he committed nineteen years before. During World War II, Soviet dictator Joseph Stalin refused to exchange his son, a Red Army officer and prisoner of war, for a German general captured earlier by the Soviet troops. Stalin allegedly said one shouldn't exchange a captured soldier for a general. Stalin's son was later killed by the Germans.

What kind of irrational calculations forced these people to make such tough choices? Obviously, some people argue that if rational and pragmatic calculations prevailed, different decisions might have been made: Daniel Crocker would have stayed home with his family and Stalin would have exchanged the general for his son. However, it seems that in these stories, another type of rational calculation took place. The decisions perhaps were made according to moral values of responsibility, duty, or honor.

As these cases suggest, both people's expressed opinions and the decisions they make are often based on values and not only on pragmatic calculations. Most people do not carry a behavioral calculator and consciously assess, survey, and choose what set of attitudes or values to express in various social situations. Rather, adherence to certain moral values becomes a major motivational force in some people's decisions and actions (see Leinder & Kiewiet, 1981, on sociotropic approaches).

Despite its appeal, the rational actor approach has cultural limitations. Consider an example of how people perceive the values of other cultural groups. For some Western observers, Islamic fundamentalists appear as rational actors who use cost-benefit models of attitude formation. However, Islamic fundamentalism constitutes a complete way of looking at the world, a view that differs from the traditional view dominant in much of the West as reflected in rational actor theories (Monroe and Kreidie, 1997). The fundamentalist perspective is best understood in reference to a worldview that (1) makes little distinction between public and private; (2) assumes that truth can be discovered by revelation; and (3) suggests that reason is subservient to religious doctrine. Religious values dictate and dominate all basic issues, and only within the confines of the fundamentalist identity are choices made by cost-benefit calculations. Islamic fundamentalism taps into a quite different political consciousness, one in which religious identity determines the range of options, including behavior and attitudes.

Attitudes as Temporary Constructions

The temporary constructions approach focuses on how attitudes are expressed. According to this view, people often construct evaluations on the spot, even though they have never before considered the subject (Converse, 1964/1970). Most individuals lack attitudes on a wide variety of issues. However, when asked to express their attitudes, they tend to engage in a response-construction process by politely choosing between the response options offered them by a pollster (Zaller, 1996; Tourengeau & Rasinski, 1988). When asked a survey question, many people call to mind ideas that are immediately accessible from memory and use them to make choices among the options offered to them. However, people are likely to make these choices off the top of their head and without careful examination and evaluation of available facts. Therefore, attitudes formed and expressed during surveys, according to this view, often represent a single aspect of respondents' feelings toward an attitude object. Within this approach, as a challenge to cognitive dissonance theory, the opinions people express may be seen as manifestations of strong and enduring predispositions or as casual verbal statements (Bem, 1972).

Imagine a fellow student knocks on your door and asks for a donation to a local environmental group. You do not have much time to talk to the student; besides, you are in a good mood, so you quickly donate the requested five dollars. When your roommates ask why you donated the money (in their opinion, you should have refused because you do not share the views of environmentalists), you explain you "simply did not want to look cheap; besides, this particular environmental group seems different from the others."

The process of communication between a pollster and a respondent is explained in similar terms. In most situations, people try to cooperate with pollsters, researchers, or reporters by giving or constructing plausible answers. Often, individuals are not really sure what their position is; nevertheless, they may infer their answers from the situation itself. Davis (1997) reports, for example, that in face-to-face surveys, the investigator's race may affect answers of respondents of another race; some people "act nice" and give answers they assume will please the interviewer. In a survey, black interviewees expressed less willingness to vote for Jesse Jackson, the renowned civil rights advocate, when approached by a white pollster compared to another sample interviewed by a black pollster. In a classic experiment, Chester and Newcomb (1952) showed that Catholic respondents were more likely to give answers consistent with church doctrine if, just before questioning, a priest made a brief appearance in the room where the survey was conducted.

Empirical research backs up assumptions that the ad hoc opinion-construction process is more likely to occur when the individual's knowledge about an issue is vague and ambiguous (Taylor et al., 1997). That is why it is possible for most people to express an opinion that did not exist seconds earlier (when it was a "non-attitude") about a new and unfamiliar issue. Imagine you are asked about a new bill being considered by the Congress. You know nothing about this legislation, including whether or not you support it. Nevertheless, instead of saying "I don't know," you give either a "yes" or "no" answer after you quickly assess the information about the bill available in the question.

An individual may more easily construct and communicate an opinion if he believes other people hold the same opinion. Support from others and the knowledge that some individuals, or even just one person, can reinforce an individual's positions on issues (Lenart, 1994). There is a small but statistically significant relationship between the degree to which a person believes others hold similar opinions and his willingness to express those opinions. Moreover, many people tend to not express opinions that, as they believe, contradict the majority's view. These findings were based on an analysis of 17 studies of 9,500 participants from six countries (Glynn et al., 1997).

Why do people care about other people's opinions? According to Noelle-Neuman (1986), many of us dislike the social isolation associated with private opinions. To understand this, consider a hypothetical case. Maria gets a new job. To avoid being isolated and to become acquainted with coworkers, she tries to determine what opinions they hold. If she subscribes to the perceived dominant opinions, she will feel free to express and discuss them. The absence of resistance or criticism from others is likely to strengthen Maria's attitudes, that is, others think in the same way. On the other hand, if she realizes not many people share her views, Maria will try to avoid social isolation and will not express her true attitudes at work. This situation results in a "spiral of silence." In fact, minority opinions, being less publicly shared, appear less discussed compared to situations in which opinions are shared by a majority.

That somebody else shares his attitude helps an individual improve his self-image. Many people constantly look for validation to signal that they are accepted and approved by others (Renshon, 1994). Some forms of political participation may be influenced by a desire to communicate with people who share one's view and interests. For instance, a study of political participation in both pro-life and pro-choice volunteer organizations found that among the most important reasons given for participation was so-called group solidarity, expressed in statements such as "to be among like-minded people," "to make new friends," "because many of my friends are members," and "to attend lectures and other organizational events" (Gross, 1995).

The Regulatory Model of Attitude Expression

In a 1902 lecture, famed sociologist Emile Durkheim used the following example. Three or four lines of different length were drawn on a board and shown to children who were asked to look at them carefully. Once they became familiar with the lines, the children were asked to find their equivalent on another blackboard on which were drawn lines of the same length mixed with lines of greater or shorter length. When a child said he had found and designated the line corresponding to the one shown on the first blackboard, the observer expressed disbelief by asking, "Are you sure this is the only right one?" This question alone was sufficient to persuade 89 percent of the elementary-school children to change their answer. Overall, 56 percent of children of all ages, including those who had given the right answer, abandoned their first opinion (Durkheim, 1925). Why did the children change their opinions so readily?

In the classroom, individuals, and children in particular, may face quesions based on relatively limited information. A word of doubt from the teacher may be interpreted by the child as a suggestion to change his opinion. The consequences of a mistake in judgment are not vitally important for the child. In reality, people face consequences for their actions and therefore tend to choose opinions and judgments that help reach particular goals or match particular situations. For instance, a person may laugh at a joke when surrounded by adults but be very angry if the same joke is told when small children are present. Another person may support a small property tax increase after attending a meeting of the county school board; a few hours later, this individual may oppose the tax hike after realizing how much credit card debt he has accumulated. Opinions, in fact, are adaptive mechanisms that help the individual adjust to the changing environment.

The situations in which people express attitudes can be described as organized on three levels (Yadov, 1977). The *first level* comprises relatively brief cognitive-emotional representations of changeable social realities. Such short-lived attitudes regulate the individual's behavior in limited situations within a short period. A staunch supporter of the president may get angry with the president's remarks during a press conference and then calm down later. Another person, a strong supporter of nonviolent measures in international relations, may temporarily express a wish to punish a foreign government after seeing evidence on television suggesting this government supports terrorism. These attitudes are not long-lasting, are not likely to be interconnected, and can easily change when the situation changes or the individual obtains new information.

The *second level* comprises attitudes that regulate the individual's behavior in her principal social activities: the family, education, job, hobbies, and personal relationships. Attitudes on this level are typically linked to one another and attached to self-image because they reflect personal goals and interests in major areas of life. These attitudes are relatively stable. Nevertheless, they can evolve with time or when the principal activities change, for example, the person starts a new job, gets married or divorced, experiences other major relationship changes, starts school, or graduates.

Here is an example. The birth of a child may affect the parents' social attitudes for several reasons. First, new parents often reassess their financial situation and plans for the future. In general, at the top of the list are long-term economic concerns that change parents' views about their savings plans and spending policies (for example, how to pay for day care, orthodontia, and college education). This forecast may shift the parents' attitudes about the taxes they pay. Parents may become concerned about the quality of public schools, the allocation of money in their state and district, and a wide variety of policies that may affect the well-being of their children. Parents change their television viewing patterns. Many abandon their favorite shows because of the lack of time. Other young parents spend less time watching the news. Some stop watching educational programs. Parents may spend less time with their friends and acquaintances, thus cutting off channels of interpersonal communication used before for exchanging comments and views (Merida, 1996).

Attitudes of the *third level* are the most general mental representations of the social and political world, or *values*. These are the most stable sentiments because through them the individual understands and communicates the most important principles of her behavior (see the section on values earlier in this chapter).

How are attitudes expressed according to the regulatory model? People evaluate the direct significance of situations or issues to their behavior, finances, security, well-being, social identity, or values (Lavine et al., 2000). They then choose or construct a temporary attitude for dealing with a current situation and perhaps another attitude for dealing with a situation of greater social significance. Finally, they may base their response on a certain value. For example, an individual who maintains a fundamental value of economic freedom may see an environmental protection policy, despite its advantages, as a threat to the value of freedom and therefore express a negative opinion about a specific environmental measure.

The popular expression "not in my backyard" (NIMBY) demonstrates the regulatory model in action. People can be sympathetic in principle toward particular issues without wanting to make these issues part of their daily existence. For example, several studies show that people can be strong supporters of equality and have strong negative attitudes against ethnic discrimination; however, the same people can be against the affirmative action or for tougher anti-immigration policies (Glaser & Gilens, 1997; Sears, 1996).

Contrary to an understanding of attitudes as simple and changeable responses to a pollster's questions, the regulatory approach suggests that only some attitudes are unstable and changeable. For example, an analysis of the 1996 U.S. presidential campaign showed that during the peak of the media coverage, people's attitudes about their presidential choice remained mainly unchanged. Most people decide to vote for a particular candidate before the general election campaign begins (Erikson & Wlezien, 1999).

Different individuals may mean something different by and anticipate different consequences of the same position on an issue. Even two individuals sharing the same view of a particular issue may arrive at that view for different reasons. For example, an attitude about abortion may be based on an individual's knowledge of and beliefs about women's rights, privacy rights, and/or religious values and beliefs (Huckfeldt & Sprague, 2000).

Broad cultural norms and traditions influence the ways people view the world. Although general moral principles of behavior appear similar across social groups, the interpretation of these principles is strongly influenced by politics, ideology, and culture. In Japan, for instance, moral relativism is often based on a distinction between "formal" and "informal" interpretations of behavior and morality. The same moral act may be viewed formally as a social obligation and informally as a natural feeling and caring for others (Benedict, 1946). It appears that these two attitudes toward an issue may coexist in the individual (Gilbert & Shiraev, 1992). Contradictions between the two views need not reflect inconsistency. However, the individual may feel a psychological conflict between the inward (true inner feelings) and outward (public moral standards) ways of expressing the opinion. Those who accept this conflict maintain their confidence. Those who reject the conflict may experience social alienation and insecurity (Naito & Gielen, 1992). Japanese subjects, for example, may accept discrepancy between their public and private selves; they act according to the group norm. Most American respondents, in contrast, try to eliminate inconsistencies between public and private self (Iwato & Triandis, 1993). Research shows that the principles of cognitive balance can be applied to all cultural groups and that most people tend to eliminate the mismatch between public and private attitudes. Nevertheless, there is evidence that the balance principle operates more strongly in the West than elsewhere (Triandis, 1994).

In review.   Attitudes serve the individual in her quest for a particular goal, and they help filter incoming information and mediate behavior. They also help the person adjust to changing social situations.

THINKING CRITICALLY ABOUT ATTITUDES
The Context

As we learned in Chapter 3 about critical thinking, a question's format may have substantial impact on respondents' attitudes. Let's illustrate this with two examples. In 1997, CBS News and the *New York Times* conducted a poll about affirmative action. Approximately 47 percent of respondents said affirmative action programs in hiring, promoting, and college admissions should be abolished (CBS/NYT, December 1997, 1,258). However, when the same respondents were asked another question, "What if abolishing affirmative action programs (in hiring, promoting, and college admissions) meant there would be far fewer minority doctors, lawyers, and other minority professionals? Then, would you say affirmative action programs should be continued or abolished?" the majority that opposed affirmative action (57 percent of those who initially opposed) remained undaunted: The program should be abolished anyway. However, 31 percent, almost one-third, said that the program should continue. The remaining 12 percent of respondents did not have an opinion.

A skeptical analyst would raise doubts about the validity of this survey. How can people support a position and a few seconds later change their opinion? A more careful and critical look at this poll, however, reveals that the respondents were somewhat consistent. Why? Because they were answering specific questions about specific issues. It is quite likely that many of those who opposed affirmative action believed that abolishing the policy would not result in a negative outcome—that is, the proportion of minority lawyers and doctors would be unchanged. On the other hand, if they perceived obvious negative consequences of abolishing affirmative action, some respondents might change their opinion. A detailed analysis of this poll also reveals the volatility of opinions on affirmative action in the context of social and ethnic status. The highest percentages of respondents who changed their opinion in the second condition were black people (62 percent) and people with an income of less than $15,000 (44 percent). The highest percentage of those who did not support affirmative action were people making between $50,000 and $75,000 (66 percent), closely followed by those making more than $75,000 (65 percent), Republicans (64 percent), college graduates (63 percent), and people of Jewish descent (63 percent).

Here is another example. A poll conducted in the 1970s asked whether people should allow a communist journalist to get accreditation in the United States. Only 37 percent said "yes." A second group of respondents was asked the same question *after* being asked about allowing an American journalist to work in the communist Soviet Union, which the vast majority supported. In this second group, the proportion of respondents who agreed to allow Russian reporters in the United States was 73 percent. Why did the answers of the two groups differ so dramatically? Perhaps when the respondents were only asked about the communist reporters, the answers were influenced by anti-communist attitudes. When the question was preceded by one about American reporters working overseas, the answer was influenced by the previous reply: If we send our journalists to the Soviet Union, we might expect the Soviets to send their reporters in the United States, and we expect reciprocal treatment from both countries (Schuman & Presser, 1981).

Whenever possible, look at the survey's questions and try to determine whether the respondents' answers could have been affected by the questions' design and meaning. Sometimes percentages in an opinion poll are so impressive that further analyses appear unnecessary. Nevertheless, the answers to follow-up questions may provide the patient observer with a clearer, more detailed, and more accurate picture about what people think about important social and political issues.

Bias

As you remember, balance theories propose that people tend to avoid contradictions among their attitudes. However, in reality, a person's attitudes may well be contradictory and "unbalanced." Throughout the book, we show how people often express biased and contradictory opinions. Table 4.2 represents a compilation of several opinion polls about the last four American presidents in the 20th century. The question was "Which comes closest to your opinion of the president?"

Examine the data critically. As you can see, it was quite common to like a president personally but disapprove of his policy. It was less common to dislike a president and approve his policy. About 30–40 percent of responses distinguished between and separated from each other the evaluation of the president's (1) political profile and (2) psychological profile.

When people answer survey questions, they often assume they understand the issues. The next example suggests the extent to which this is so. In the 1990s, as a reaction to increasingly fierce competition in media markets, a wave of corporate mergers started in broadcasting. Did Americans recognize a difference in media coverage? A 1998 telephone survey asked Americans their opinion of media mergers: "Do you think these media mergers have improved the quality and accuracy of news reporting, made it worse, or haven't had much effect either way?" About 14 percent believed both quality and accuracy improved. A little less than a half, 46 percent, said they had not noticed any difference. More than one-third, 35 percent, said the developments made quality and accuracy worse (Princeton/*Newsweek*, July 1998, 752). Although people made these evaluations not only about the quality of news but also about the source of the changes they noticed, they did not necessarily know that the differences occurred because of the mergers. (See the section on cause-and-effect relationships in Chapter 3 on critical thinking.)

Wording and Labeling

The language we speak, as noted in Chapter 3, allows us to name things and people by giving them verbal labels. Labels can then be easily converted into beliefs that may, in turn, appear as facts. Perhaps you have read and heard comments that good values

TABLE 4.2

People's like, dislike, and approval of three U.S. Presidents. Compiled by K. Bowman from polling by the *Washington Post*/ABC News and the *Wall Street Journal*/NBC News.

	Reagan 9/86	Bush 10/91	Clinton 4/98	Bush 11/03
Like personally, approve of policies	53%	43%	33%	40%
Like personally, disapprove of policies	21%	35%	45%	28%
Don't like personally, approve of policies	9%	7%	2%	6%
Don't like personally, disapprove of policies	14%	12%	19%	20%

Source: Washington Post, August 16, 1998, p. A25; *Los Angeles Times*, November 20, 2003, www.latimes.com.

are disappearing or evaporating. Can we really say people have lost their values? When people name things, they tend to treat abstract issues as if they were concrete objects (Levy, 1997). Values do not necessarily disappear. They can rise or fall in our estimation of their relative importance. For example, consider the decline in support of affirmative action in the United States in the 1990s. People do not destroy their views on affirmative action and throw them out. Instead, some individuals no longer attach as much importance to affirmative action as they or others once did (Mayton et al., 1994).

Here is another illustration. A 1998 poll examined the opinions of Americans about a range of social issues. Among the respondents, a 55 percent majority believed there should be clear community's standards for right and wrong (WP/Kaiser/Harvard, August 1998, 1,200). Some people may interpret the results of this survey as suggesting Americans are too conservative. However, the poll result should not cause us to believe that 55 percent of Americans follow moral standards. It only suggests that so many people wish such principles existed. The poll does not identify the specific moral standards people hold; indeed, as many as 35 percent of respondents said in this poll that every individual should live by his own moral standards. Again, this does not mean that more than one-third of Americans are against moral standards. The numbers suggest that 35 out of 100 people do not want to see any collective or standard rules for moral behavior.

Try to avoid making general assumptions about gender, ethnic, national, religious, and other social groups. Remember, these variables (such as "women," "Asians," and "college graduates") may not represent discrete types. They stand in continuums. An observer, for example, should not describe a large ethnic group as either "collectivist" or "individualist." Rather, the description should reflect a continuum that shows different degrees of collectivist and individualist traits. For instance, in many publications, China is identified as a collectivist nation. Therefore, some people anticipate that Chinese respondents always give collectivist replies to survey questions. That was not the case in one study reported by Lien (1994). In 1993, 77 percent of Chinese respondents (5,455 respondents in six provinces) disagreed with the statement "In a lawsuit involving an individual and a collective entity, the judgment should favor the latter." When asked, "Should police officers detain a person for the sake of public safety even though they were unable to determine his guilt?" 47 percent opposed detention, and only 28 percent supported it. As you can see, the answers were at least somewhat individualist.

Explanations: Causes and Reasons

We encourage you to think critically about national and cultural differences in values and the extent to which they differ among nations. Being a member of a particular national or ethnic group does not necessarily mean one's values are different from those of a person with a different national or ethnic identity. Of course, symbols, names, and traditions bear special meanings for each national or ethnic group. If you ask them to associate the word *freedom* with a particular name in history, many Americans will mention George Washington or Abraham Lincoln; many South Africans will mention Nelson Mandela; many Egyptians will mention Gamal Nasser. But whether these names and other symbols stand for different values is questionable. Although two groups may have different values, this need not cause different behaviors. Besides, millions of individuals in every nation and every cultural, religious, and ethnic group express a wide range of attitudes and values. The variety of values within a group is typically greater than the value gap between two groups. As you read in Chapter 3 on critical thinking, people tend to dichotomize or divide their perceptions into categories that, more accurately, should be conceptualized as continuous. Instead of seeing values as a continuum, we often and easily cluster them into overly simple divisions, such as Western and non-Western.

ASSIGNMENT 4.1   PATTERNS IN OPINION FORMATION

Ask five people to read these two statements and identify which statement they consider true (in fact, both statements were made up).

> **Statement 1.** (From *USA Today*) A well-known London-based international organization, Truth in Broadcasting, has given its yearly Honor and Truth Award to Howard Stern, an American radio talk show host. "By doing this we support truth and enlightenment all over the world," said Rachel Bell, the organization's spokeswoman.

> **Statement 2.** (From *USA Today*) A well-known London-based international organization, Truth in Broadcasting, has given its yearly Lies and Shame title to Howard Stern, an American radio talk show host. "By doing this, we condemn lies and indecency all over the world," said Rachel Bell, the organization's spokeswoman.

Then ask each person to identify his or her opinion about Howard Stern using the scale below:

> *I love Howard Stern (5)*   *I like Howard Stern (4)*   *Hard to tell (3)*
> *I don't like Howard Stern (2)*   *I hate Howard Stern (1)*   *I don't know this person (0)*

Describe the results of your mini-survey in a brief summary or critique. Were respondents consistent in their evaluation of the stories and their attitude toward Howard Stern? Bring the results to class for discussion.

ASSIGNMENT 4.2   COGNITIVE DISSONANCE

Consider the following statement: "The mythology, the shared beliefs, the heroes of American history are part of the cement that binds together this diverse society. They are part of the common heritage of all Americans, which every citizen should know."

Ask five people (not in this class) to assess their agreement or disagreement with this statement on the scale:

Definitely agree   *Somewhat agree*   *Somewhat disagree*   *Definitely disagree*

After asking them the question, tell them Patrick Buchanan wrote this on June 4, 1975, for the *Chicago Tribune*. (Buchanan is a well-known conservative journalist, political strategist, and former presidential candidate.) Then listen and write down the respondents' immediate comments about this assertion or the writer. Does the mechanism of cognitive dissonance work? Do those who both *agree* with the statement and *like* Buchanan begin to explain their position to you even though you did not ask them to comment? Did you notice that those of your interviewees who *agree* with the statement and at the same time *dislike* Buchanan and his views comment either on the "true meaning" of his words, his "real" intentions, or the context of his statement?

CHAPTER SUMMARY

- Attitudes are not easy to depict because they are not directly observable. Therefore, any description of attitude is an act of imagination. Attitudes are commonly viewed according to a model whose two dimensions are the cognitive and the affective.

- In their beliefs, individuals typically establish cognitive relationships between two or among several issues. Beliefs typically do not contain evaluations. Values are stable and enduring dispositions that indicate a preference for a specific behavior or goal over others.

- Values can be categorized according to several approaches. One approach investigates three basic issues: (a) the extent to which people are independent of or dependent on groups; (b) people's views on prosperity and profit; and, (c) people's views on whether they should exploit, fit in with, or submit to the outside world.

- According to the cognitive approach to attitudes, the expert should focus on how the individual represents and organizes her experience cognitively. Cognitive processes, such as perception, memory, recognition, and decision making, are critical to attitude formation and expression.

- According to the regulatory-adaptation approach, attitudes should be treated as reactions or habits; people learn attitudes that prove useful in particular cultural and social circumstances.

- Some attitudes are easily accessible; others are not. Overall, an attitude's accessibility is determined by the strength of the cognitive connections between an image and its evaluation. Several factors determine attitude accessibility.

- Cognitive balance theories state that people seek consistency among their attitudes by trying to avoid any mismatch among them or between attitudes and behavior.

- The response theory assumes that people react to incoming information by generating positive or negative thoughts. If the information stimulates a strong counterargument, it activates a negative attitude.

- According to the learning approach, people acquire information about events and objects and, in the process, learn their feelings about and behavioral responses to these objects.

- Rational actor theories suggest that people pursue goals and have preferences (attitudes) that are consistent and stable for them. Among many options, people (actors) choose the alternative that appears most attractive to them.

- According to the temporary construction theory, most individuals lack strong feelings on a wide variety of issues. However, when asked to express their opinion, they tend to engage in a response-construction process by politely choosing among the response options the pollster offers.

- The regulatory model suggests that in each moment, people make evaluations to see whether a particular situation or issue has direct significance to their well-being or social identity, or whether it is relevant to one of their values. Based on these evaluations, certain attitudes are activated.

- Broad cultural norms and traditions influence the way people view the world. Even though general moral principles of behavior and attitude formation appear universal across large social groups, interpretation of these principles may be strongly influenced by politics, ideology, and culture.

Looking Ahead. After examining attitudes and opinions here, we turn to Chapter 5, on political socialization, to explore how attitudes develop. It presents stages of political learning from childhood to early and later adulthood. It identifies types of values and theories of stages of moral judgment, and encourages thinking critically about the roles of education and work as areas of political learning.

DEFINITIONS OF KEY TERMS

Attitude—The psychological representation and evaluation of various features of the social world.

Attitude accessibility—A measure of the availability and ease of expression of an attitude.

Belief—The perceived relation between an object and its attributes (the object's quantity, quality, or other characteristics).

Cognitive approach—The tradition in social science that focuses on reasoning and the mental processing of information, that is, the perception, recognition, conception, and judgment of facts.

Cognitive dissonance—The perceived inconsistency between two or among several attitudes or between behavior and attitudes.

Dogmatism—Closed-mindedness, rigidity, and inflexibility in opinions and subsequent behavior.

Dual-evaluation attitudes—Attitudes containing an ambivalent emotional component.

Learning approach—A view of attitude formation according to which people acquire information about events and then learn to think and feel about them.

Least-effort principle—A mechanism that allows a person to minimize the number of cognitive operations needed to reach a goal.

Rational actor approach—Theories proposing that human beings, given options, will choose the alternative with the highest expected utility for them.

Regulatory-adaptation approach—The tradition focusing on attitudes as reactions or habits. People may learn particular attitudes because they prove useful in political, cultural, and other social circumstances.

Response theory—The assumption that people react to incoming information by generating positive or negative thoughts.

Single-evaluation attitudes—Attitudes whose affective component has a uniform composition.

Value—A complex attitude that reflects a principle, standard, or quality the individual uses to distinguish the most desirable or appropriate things and issues.

CHAPTER 5

Political Socialization

By nature, men are nearly alike; by practice, they get to be wide apart.

Confucius

We live in an age of fateful challenges. As a nation and a people, we are [being tested]. Each of us can look forward to many years of uncertainty and peril—but also of work and hope. The revolutionary forces shaking the earth have converged, presenting us with hard choices, with a need for action, for ideas, for concerted and sustained commitment as a nation and as individual citizens. We are challenged by the revolution of hope in continents long captive by stagnation and despair. We are challenged by the revolution in science and technology bringing new boons and new dangers to humanity. We are challenged by their revolution in international relationships. Nation has begun to work with nation to solve mankind's problems. New international bodies are exploring uncharted paths of world cooperation and interests of worldwide peace, justice, and freedom (Advertising Council, 1963).

President John F. Kennedy addressed these words to the American people in 1963. Do people today face the same challenges about which he spoke so passionately many years ago? Or was the world of the 1960s dramatically different from today? It is a convenient assumption that past social and political realities differed dramatically from today's issues. However, in thinking critically, can we say this with certainty? Kennedy talked about new hopes for starving peoples. Have starvation and despair ceased? Have Americans stopped their pursuit of equality, wider opportunities, and greater dignity for our nation? Have we charted all paths of world cooperation? Can modern technologies threaten democracy and international peace? Have people stopped being concerned about international security? Do we need action, ideas, and sustained commitment in politics? Perhaps individuals have faced similar challenges throughout history, and young people in the 21st century should have little difficulty understanding the concerns of John Kennedy and the youth of the 1960s. What remains different are the specific content of those challenges. Influenced by historic, political, and cultural circumstances, such as Kennedy described, individuals develop unique values, attitudes, and political affiliations.

The 2004 elections in the United States showed that, while many voters considered specific issues, including the economy and the war in Iraq, in their decisions, a significant group turned to their deeper values, fundamental beliefs, and long-term political concerns to determine their choices.

This chapter explores political socialization, the process of acquiring attitudes and behaviors related to politics. The development of individuals' political opinions takes shape under the circumstances common and unique across the lifespan. Theories discussed in this chapter explain the effects of life circumstances and other factors on political attitudes, opinions, and activities.

Looking Forward. Chapter 5, on "Political Socialization," explores the process of acquiring attitudes and behaviors related to politics. It explains how the development of individuals' common and unique experiences takes shape under various life circumstances across the lifespan from childhood to later adulthood. It discusses theories of values and moral development and the effects of life circumstances and other factors on people's political opinions and actions.

WHAT IS POLITICAL SOCIALIZATION?

Most of us have opinions about society and politics. Individuals express views about the distribution of income and resources, crime, taxes, terrorism, national security, and scores of other issues. Some know little about how state governments allocate funds for construction projects, but most people have an opinion about whether or not it is necessary to build a new highway through their hometown. Without knowing much about issues, many people have opinions about political candidates, international conflicts, and whether or not people should be allowed to carry concealed weapons.

Where do these opinions come from? Individuals' fundamental views on social and political issues are formed within **political socialization,** a lifelong process during which the individual acquires attitudes and behaviors related to politics (Langton, 1969). Political socialization is part of the broader socialization process by which an individual becomes a member of a society and takes on its values and behaviors (Bronfenbrenner, 1979). People are not born with social and political ideas; they develop them as they acquire political orientations, including knowledge, values, and attitudes. Transmitted from one generation to another, social and political ideas become powerful forces that, in the form of public opinion, may influence government's decisions and determine not only the direction of policies but also a nation's way of life. Thoughts produce actions that transform society. Social transformations, in turn, influence people's attitudes and values.

Political socialization is a complex process of lasting conversions, changes in direction, and sudden transitions. In big cities in Texas and small villages in China, people constantly change their attitudes and acquire new beliefs. They may lose interest in one area of life while developing expertise in another. An actor or writer may become president; Ronald Reagan of the United States and Vaclav Havel of the Czech Republic are two examples. Ex-presidents become writers; you can buy the memoirs of Richard Nixon and Bill Clinton in bookstores. Some people change political parties and embrace new religions. Others remain committed to attitudes developed in their early years.

Socialization agents, including family, schools, peers, religious institutions, media, and the workplace, mediate the development of political ideas. In addition, the **political community,** a collection of individuals, groups, and institutions that support the government and its underlying political system, has a special role in political socialization (Deutsch, 1954; Juviler & Stroschein, 1999). People and socialization agents transmit political ideas either vertically or horizontally, that is, from one generation to the next or among members of the same generation.

Not only socialization agents but also the general conditions of society affect political socialization. In communist societies, such as China, North Korea, Cuba, and the former Soviet Union, most people developed their political views under the influence of an official ideology. Today, many authoritarian governments around the world control education and the media, which allows the ruling elite to regulate the flow of information. In contrast, young people in industrialized democracies face a wider range of opportunities and options. Social roles under such governments are more variable because they are not likely to be strictly regulated. Studies show that in democratic countries, individuals become members of a wide variety of subgroups and express a greater assortment of opinions than people who grow up in authoritarian or totalitarian societies (Camilleri & Malewska-Peyre, 1997).

In countries with egalitarian (pro-equality) social traditions, the value of equal opportunity dominates in the process of socialization. Historically, for example, Scandinavian countries promote active government participation in education, healthcare, and social security programs. Because these programs require sizable subsidies, income tax rates in Scandinavian countries are considerably higher than those in the United States. Although people in Sweden or Denmark differ in their opinions on how much they should pay in taxes, the overall principle of governmental involvement in social welfare remains unchallenged. In countries with strong non-egalitarian traditions, such as the United States, the concept of merit, according to which people are entitled to benefits in proportion to their contribution to society, is a dominant view. Remember, the division between egalitarian and non-egalitarian societies is not always distinct, and every society has elements of both of these traditions.

Social ideals that represent the wishes of an entire nation, particularly if endorsed by popular political leaders, have a significant impact on the process of political socialization. Beliefs in the exceptionality and special mission of Israel (Merom, 1999), Russia's special calling as a Eurasian nation (Shiraev & Zubok, 2001), and the destinies of Taiwan (Bullard, 1997) and Palestine (Abu Sada, 1997) to resist an enemy create powerful psychological predispositions in young individuals of these nations.

STAGES OF POLITICAL SOCIALIZATION: CHILDHOOD

Although a child's early thinking is largely apolitical, childhood nevertheless has a significant impact on the development of political attitudes. There are two basic approaches to this issue. According to the **primacy approach,** childhood is the most important period of political socialization, that is, each person's basic values reflect experiences of his pre-adult years, and each person learns his political attitudes by the time he is an adolescent (Hyman, 1959). The **recency approach** is based on the assumption that the closer a particular learning experience is to relevant adult opinions or decisions, the greater is its impact. In other words, childhood might not be as important as some experts think. During childhood, individuals do not fully form political attitudes; rather they form **political predispositions** to certain attitudes (Zaller, 1996). Nonetheless, political predispositions, formed during the early stages of socialization, regulate the acceptance or nonacceptance of the political information the developing person receives.

Which approach, primacy or recency, is more consistent in explaining and predicting attitudes? Research suggests that both views are legitimate and are empirically supported.

More so than the young of most other species, human children come into the world weak and helpless, and the period of complete physical and social dependency on care-givers is relatively long. Nevertheless, young children are capable of making judgments about the world around them. One study showed that between second and fourth grade, over half of the U.S. children asked were able to identify their political party attachment, which was, primarily, a reflection of their parent's party preference. Studies show that by elementary school, most children were able to clearly identify themselves as a member of their ethnic group, nationality, and social class (Dawson et al., 1977). Similar results were obtained in other studies. In the Middle East, for instance, both Arab and Jewish elementary schoolchildren showed significant differences in their flag preference, clearly divided by Arab or Jewish origins (Lawson, 1975). In regions of political instability or ethnic conflict, such identities are formed even earlier.

Critics argue, however, that political learning is different from general learning. For most children living in a stable society, the world of politics is far removed from their daily experience, and there are important differences between learning about politics and learning about other aspects of the world. Children's political ideas differ from their thoughts about such well-examined features of the physical world as number, weight, and volume. Political objects are not immediately accessible to the child. As a result, adults, and parents in particular, frequently intrude on children's thinking process by supplying their own adult concepts and reasoning, thus helping form children's attitudes about the social and political world (Connell, 1971).

Learning About Politics

How do children learn about politics? Political psychologist Stanley Renshon (1975), in his pioneering research on the topic, maintained that basic beliefs about the nature of the world are acquired in an attempt to eliminate confusion and clarify uncertainties about life. By seeking answers to questions such as "Why do people die?" "Who will help the homeless?" and "Why is it wrong to lie?" the child acquires basic knowledge about social and political events. Easton and Dennis (1969) developed comprehensive views on political socialization. They studied how American grade-school children learn about political authorities, identifying four basic stages in the process. The first stage is *politicization*. Here the child begins to understand the presence of the authority outside the family and develops knowledge about supervisors, bosses, and managers. The second is *personalization*, when the child acquires an awareness of certain highly recognizable political authorities. Among the most salient authority figures for the American child are usually the police officer and the president; in other countries they may be a king, a religious leader, a party official, or a military officer. During the *idealization* stage, the child views some authorities as good and benevolent. They offer help, punish bad people, and get things done. During *institutionalization,* as the child grows up, she begins to transfer feelings about known authorities to other institutions of government. Thus, the child builds diffuse support for or rejection of the political system.

This theory, of course, should be applied through the prism of circumstances. For instance, children living in the same neighborhood may, depending on their ethnic origin, view police officers as protectors or oppressors. These perceptions are likely based on the children's direct experience. Moreover, presidents are not always idealized and admired by the majority. As an illustration, children interviewed in the midst of the Watergate scandal, after President Nixon was accused of unlawful conduct, showed a sharp decline in idealization of the president (Dawson et al., 1977).

Cognitive scientists assert that the same basic thinking processes support the development of political attitudes and conceptual thinking. In an early study of political socialization, researchers examined the development of children's understanding of the noun *country.* The study showed a gradual development of reasoning. The child begins without any concept at all; then she gradually includes more elements in the concept as she moves through cognitive stages. In the second stage, the child understands spatial relations, so she is aware that, for example, a city may be located in another state or province. However, the child may have trouble comprehending that one may be both a resident of a particular state or province *and* a citizen of the country. Only later, in the third stage, does the logical connection or synthesis occur (Piaget & Weil, 1951).

Direct experiences with events also significantly affect children's political socialization. Tangible or observable events are more easily comprehended and memorized than abstract models. As an example, several studies in England, Japan, and Norway suggested that children tend to develop elaborate conceptions of war earlier than they do of peace. The conceptions of war focus on features of conflict, such as killing, fighting, and weapons. Children's conceptions of peace are largely defined in abstract terms, typically, as an inner state of tranquility or the absence of war. Why are these concepts so differently constituted? Conflicts are pervasive and have concrete aspects that can be observed and experienced directly. Peace, on the other hand, is a much less concrete and more abstract phenomenon of experience (Rosenau, 1975).

In review. According to the primacy approach to political socialization, initial learning is the most resistant to change. According to the recency approach, the closer in time a particular learning experience occurs to the individual's need to develop relevant opinions or decisions, the greater its impact.

FAMILY AND POLITICAL SOCIALIZATION

Earlier studies introduced the family as one the most powerful agents of political socialization (Hyman, 1959). According to the primacy approach, as you know, early experiences and initial learning are the most resistant to change. Therefore, family-related experiences ought to be, in theory, the most important in the individual's life (Easton & Dennis, 1967). Family environment thus should be viewed as the context within which the development of the individual's political attitudes and values takes place. As a result, the family should be the child's fundamental source of social and political ideas. These assumptions are generally supported by research.

Political party identification is also typically transmitted from parents to their offspring. For example, several studies showed that a high parent-child correlation in party identification was consistent across countries and in fact usually higher than the correlation of other political attitudes (Dawson et al., 1977; Campbell et al., 1960). The transmission of attitudes from the parent to the child was often based on interfamilial communication. Political scientist Paul Beck (1977) argued that the extent to which political and social events are discussed by family members, for instance, at meals, significantly affects the child's political attitudes. Nevertheless, simple frequency of discussion is not the only factor affecting attitudinal developments. The more accurate the child's perception of his parents' views, the more they will affect the child's attitudes. Likewise, the greater the importance of a particular issue to the parents, the more their view will influence the child's attitudes (Tedin, 1974; Connell, 1972).

The extent to which parents agree on political positions affects the transmission of their attitudes. When both parents agree on an issue, they both may discuss it with their child and provide her with similar arguments (Jennings & Niemi, 1974). Sometimes, however, reverse political socialization occurs, and children influence their parents' attitudes. For instance, children may affect their parents' choice of presidential candidate.

Social-psychological conditions, including mutual trust, ability to communicate, hostility, and perception of generational differences, also influence the socialization process that takes place within the family (Bengston & Black, 1973; Maccoby et al., 1954). Psychologists maintain that parents who have greater control over their children's lives also have greater odds of influencing their ideas and beliefs. On the other hand, parents who prefer not to influence the child's choices in life are unlikely to influence many of his social attitudes (Rice & Dolgin, 2002). Does this mean that families in authoritarian societies have greater control of children's socialization than families in democratic countries? As one comparative study reveals, Turkish parents from a sample tended to restrict their young children's influence on the parents' own affairs and tended not to let children discuss family matters, whereas German parents were generally indulgent and accepted

A CASE IN POINT 5.1   Political Efficacy

The individual's belief that one can effectively participate in politics and therefore has some control over the action of political decision makers is likely to be formed during his early years (Langton, 1969). Almond and Verba (1965) established that **political efficacy** is related to a general feeling of self-worth, which is also typically developed in the family. Political efficacy is usually linked to one's perception of personal competence, control, and power (Renshon, 1975a).

their children as participating members with influence in the family (Schonpflug et al., 1990). It is an oversimplification, however, to consider the relationships among family members as a simple dichotomy of controlling and authoritarian parenting (for example, in countries with few democratic traditions) and independent and nonauthoritarian (for example, in democratic countries). There are restrictive and nonrestrictive parents in every society. Moreover, interdependence within the family is a continuous variable based on many factors (Kagitcibasi, 1996), one of which is socioeconomic. Studies show that in many working-class communities in the United States as well as in pre-industrial communities in Africa and the Pacific, parents have only a limited willingness to instruct their children about social and political issues and tend to assume that children can and should learn things at school and on their own (Rogoff, 1990). Middle-class parents tend to answer children's questions with more elaborate explanations than do less educated parents of lower social classes (Berger, 1991).

ADOLESCENCE

The teenage years of **adolescence** are a period of rapid transition from childhood to adulthood. While biological changes in adolescents are universal, the social-psychological attributes of the transition reflect social and cultural circumstances. For instance, extended schooling in many developed countries spreads adolescence over longer periods than in many non-industrialized cultures whose members take on adult roles very early.

Adolescents commonly develop their understanding of freedom, equality, democracy, duty, and social responsibility as teenagers. Their views of the good citizen, a person who takes an interest in public affairs as well as obeys the law, is also formed during this period (Jennings & Niemi, 1974). Individuals whose status, income, and position in community are relatively secure are likely to display *inclusive* attitudes, which are generally tolerant to other groups and individuals. Conversely, young individuals whose status and security are questionable or tenuous may exhibit mainly *exclusive*, intolerant attitudes to other people. In addition, those who perceive themselves and their parents as members of a relatively high-ranking and stable social elite are more likely to display inclusive attitudes than those who rank themselves among lower-status groups (Pollock, 1975).

Surveys reveal differences in political knowledge between adolescents and their parents. Kent Jennings compared such knowledge of parents and their adolescent children over several years. He examined how well both groups knew facts pertaining to the United States government, current political developments, and historical events. In general, young people were better informed than their parents (see Table 5.1). Small exceptions were related to historic facts such as President Franklin D. Roosevelt's political affiliation (Jennings, 1996; Jennings & Stoker, 1999). Better educated children were thus more familiar and better able to analyze contemporary events.

A hallmark of adolescence is rebelliousness. Long ago, Stanley Hall (1904), a renowned expert in human development, wrote that this inevitable upheaval is caused by biological factors and therefore should be common to all adolescents in every country. Contrary to this suggestion, empirical studies show that adolescence is not nec-

TABLE 5.1
Correct Identifications of Political and Historical Details. (In percentages.)

	1965 Parents	1965 Children	1973 Parents	1973 Children	1982 Parents	1982 Children
U.S. Senate term (length)	33	50	32	43	33	43
Number of members of U.S. Supreme Court	25	40	26	34	26	32
Location of WWII concentration camps	85	86	85	90	85	93
Marshall Tito's home country	46	28	46	39	39	41
Franklin Roosevelt's party affiliation	94	67	94	71	92	69

Source: Jennings (1996).

essarily turbulent for a majority of teenage boys and girls (Kon, 1977; Petersen, 1988; Dolan, 1995). Furthermore, the adolescent years may be associated with the development of withdrawal, skepticism, and **political cynicism,** the belief that politicians and public officials repeatedly violate prescriptive moral standards for their behavior and, therefore, the average honest person has no incentive to participate in politics (Glad & Shiraev, 1999; Schwartz, 1975). In countries where the media are free of ideological censorship, political cynicism is likely to be common because adolescents are exposed daily to discouraging information about certain politicians and their actions. However, cynical views also developed in adolescents living in countries without a free press (Sigel, 1989; Gozman & Edkind, 1992).

ADULTHOOD

Political socialization continues in the adult years. As a socialization period, adulthood is typically divided into three stages: early, middle, and late (Levinson, 1978). Early adulthood is usually a period of learning and change, while the middle and late stages are associated with relative stability of political attitudes. The borders separating these periods are imprecise, of course. Many people accomplish great things early in adulthood. For example, George Washington won his first battle as a colonel at age 22. Martin Luther was 29 when he started the Reformation of Christianity. Einstein published his famous theory of relativity at 26. Fidel Castro became Cuban leader at 32.

Two hypotheses, **persistence** and **openness,** attempt to explain the process of adult political socialization (Renshon, 1989). According to the persistence hypothesis, people acquire attitudes early in life and are not likely to change them later. For example, children reared in a religious, conservative family are likely to retain religious, conservative values as adults. Common generational experiences are important influences on political attitudes. Significant events, especially of early adulthood, may have a long-term impact on party identification, issue positions, and cultural attitudes. In the United States, the World War II generation, born in the 1920s and earlier, developed positive and respectful attitudes toward the military. The baby boomers, born in the 1940s and 1950s, became sharply divided about the military primarily because of the Vietnam War.

The persistence hypothesis is intriguing. Nevertheless, empirical studies repeatedly show that political socialization continues in adulthood and that transitions in attitudes and political behavior therefore continue throughout life, as the openness hypothesis states (Sigel, 1989). Many people adjust their attitudes and behavior later in life in response to changing social and political situations. These attitudinal transformations can be substantial. In other words, an individual's experiences in early childhood and adolescence do not necessarily determine what she thinks about taxes, speed limits, and

political candidates today. During adulthood, the formation of a *political self* takes place; this includes national, ethnic, or religious loyalty, identifications with political, social, and ideological groups, and political orientation (Dawson et al., 1977).

A person's political attitudes may be influenced by his perception of time (Cutler, 1977). The dominant perception in early childhood is that time is never-ending. Early adulthood brings the realization that time is a scarce resource. Middle age and later stages lead to the perception that time is seriously limited. Gergen and Black (1965) pointed out that among public policy attitudes, orientation toward constructive solutions to problems of international politics are substantially related to perception of time; the less time the leader has, the harder he works to solve a problem. Renshon (1989) referred to the world of creative arts, in which the phenomenon of late-age creativity is well researched. The final works of Michelangelo, Shakespeare, Rembrandt, Verdi, Beethoven, and Tolstoy suggest that the last stages of life often bring release from conventional concerns and free artists to make major creative statements that represent a culmination of their vision. The great German poet Goethe completed his seminal work, *Faust*, when he was 80. Lamark completed *The Natural History of Invertebrates* when he was 78. Ronald Reagan became president when he was 70. Mohandas Gandhi reached the peak of his popularity at 75. Therefore, an individual's aging does not necessarily indicate social or political disengagement.

In review. Political socialization continues during adulthood. Social and political events affect the attitudes of adults. Life conditions and transitions, such as change in family, social, and occupational status, including a new job or retirement, may also influence political views.

What factors affect political socialization during all these stages? Let's discuss several theories of socialization, beginning with those that focus on quality-of-life issues.

QUALITY OF LIFE

Consider a few examples. In 1933, during the Weimar Republic, almost one-third of Germans voted for Adolf Hitler. In the 1990s, after the fall of the communist government, almost one-third of Russians still voted for Communist Party candidates. In 1980 and 1992, respectively, presidents Jimmy Carter and George Bush lost their second elections as incumbents. What common features tie these events together? As the

A CASE IN POINT 5.2 The Generation Gap

In 2002, the *Washington Post*, the Henry J. Kaiser Family Foundation, and Harvard University surveyed the political beliefs of Americans of different ages and created a forecast of their future political opinion and behaviors based on population patterns and recent voting habits (August 2002, 2,886). These were the major findings of the study:

In 1974, voters younger than 30 slightly outnumbered those 65 years and older. By 1998, this pattern changed: Older voters outnumbered the young by more than a 2:1 ratio. If the trend continues, by 2020 more than 30 percent of all voters will be 65 or older, while only 8 percent will be younger than 30.

In the beginning of the new millennium, fewer people strongly identify with either political party than voters did 20 years before. Four of every 10 people younger than 30 described themselves as neither a Democrat nor a Republican; 2 in 10 people over 65 said the same.

All groups, the young (under 30), middle-aged (30–65) and older people (over 65), were similar in their mistrust of the government, with more or less equal percentages of each group saying most politicians were crooks and that average people had little say in government. But young people who held such skeptical views were 30 to 40 percentage points less likely than older pessimists to plan to register or to vote.

In 2002, approximately 45 million young adults under age 30 were eligible to vote. Younger people were markedly more enthusiastic than older age groups about privatizing what have been public responsibilities. Nearly 6 in 10 young adults in the survey said they favored tax vouchers that would help families pay tuition at private and religious schools. This idea, supported largely by the Republican Party, was approved by only one-third of elderly voters. About 60 percent of younger people said Social Security should be redesigned so workers could invest some of their payroll taxes in the stock market; this proposal was favored by less than half of those between 30 and 65, and only by approximately 25 percent of people 65 and older.

Young adults held attitudes usually regarded as liberal. They expressed more tolerance of diversity than previous generations and were more resistant to government interference with personal choices. For instance, people younger than 30 were the most likely to believe gay people should be allowed to marry. They were more sympathetic to affirmative action programs that aid minorities. When asked whether it is more important for the country to work for family values or for the rights of women, young adults were more than twice as likely as the elderly to put the emphasis on women.

saying goes, people vote their pocketbooks. College textbooks have long suggested that economic security or insecurity is the most important concern motivating people to vote for particular political candidates (Macionis, 2003). Politicians promise better economic times and opportunities, and people tend to believe such promises. Amidst economic chaos, Hitler promised prosperity to German people. The Russian communists promised protection and security, which most people lost after the collapse of the Soviet Union. Carter and Bush were both voted out of office during economic recessions. Some experts predicted an easy victory for Vice President Al Gore in 2000 because the U.S. economy in the late 1990s was strong, credited by many to Bill Clinton's presidency (*Washington Post*, May 2000). However, despite economic difficulties in the early 2000s, George Bush was reelected as president in 2004.

Life circumstances largely determine the way individuals make important decisions, such as voting for a political candidate. A fundamental feature of human existence is **quality of life,** the overall availability of and access to resources essential for well-being. Although cultures differ on what constitutes well-being, typically it includes material security, good health, and a sense of happiness or the absence of unnecessary suffering. Availability of food and water, type of environment, living conditions, quality of education and healthcare, rate of violence, and a wide variety of other factors contribute to the overall quality of life. Geographical location, climate, natural disasters, type of government, and governmental policies determine the amounts of resources available to individuals in each country or region.

Quality of life may directly or indirectly affect what individuals do, want, and think about. When an economic crisis hit Japan in 1997 and destroyed many families' hopes for a secure future, the rate of violent crime rose 40 percent over the rate for 1996, especially among Japanese teenagers, according to the Ministry of Health and Welfare of Japan (1998). Access to resources is another important factor that both unifies and separates people and nations from one another and affects individual behavior and attitudes. Many Egyptians, Indians, Ukrainians, and Romanians do not mind looking for jobs in Kuwait or Germany, but not the other way around; economic conditions are much better in Germany and Kuwait than in many other countries in the world. Similarly, millions of undocumented workers want to start new lives in the United States. However, it is unlikely that many American citizens try to live and work without proper documentation in a foreign country. The presence of resources in a region does not mean they are equally available to all. Geographical isolation, economic and political inequality within a country or territory, and the extent of such inequality may influence people's activities, well-being, and socialization. Most empirical studies of ethnic and cultural minorities point at inequality and oppression as major causes of perceived psychological differences between minorities and mainstream groups (Jenkins, 1995). Oppression itself is often defined on the individual level as the unequal or unfair distribution of resources (Fowers & Richardson, 1996).

Materialist and Post-materialist Values

Life is not static. People and groups may change their social status and, therefore, their access to resources and power. If an individual grew up in poverty but later prospered, this transition may influence her attitudes and values. People modify their attitudes along with changes in their lives. The extent of such changes, however, is not clear. According to the **scarcity hypothesis** (Inglehart, 1990), the maturing individual attaches greatest subjective value to those objects that were in relatively short supply during childhood, and this attachment carries through to adulthood. As an illustration, if a young girl grew up poor in a single-parent home without appropriate healthcare, as an adult she is likely to care about, more than anything else, her economic security and financial stability. Issues, such as humanitarian aid to foreign countries and civil liberties, although she may consider them important, are not likely to be high on her list of major concerns.

People who pursue economic goals such as the accumulation of money and wealth tend to develop materialist values and to support government policies that promise security and safety. People who never lived in poverty and whose economic and physical security were assured during their pre-adult years tend to develop a higher regard for less tangible goals, such as quality and diversity of life, human dignity, peace, harmony, and aesthetics. The values based on these concerns are called *post-materialist*. For example, someone whose parents were highly educated and had secure jobs and a stable income is likely to develop post-materialist values. She will tend to express concerns about humanitarian problems, equality, and freedom, and be less concerned with economic issues.

The scarcity hypothesis is supported by empirical studies. For instance, an examination of attitudes of 3,000 women who grew up receiving public assistance in the state of Washington showed that, overall, women raised by adults who experienced economic hardships that put their families on public assistance later gave greater priority to materialist values. Conversely, women who were raised in economic security placed somewhat greater emphasis on post-materialist values (Sangster & Reynolds, 1996).

Research in formerly communist countries also supports the scarcity hypothesis. According to numerous surveys, most people in these countries care more about national security and personal safety than about individual liberties, democratic values, and universal peace. Most generally prefer "security" and "order" to "democracy" and "civil rights" (Shlapentokh & Shiraev, 2002). Bardi and Schwartz (1996) studied the values of 2,770 people from eight East European countries that were experiencing the political and social transition from socialism to democracy. They found

A CASE IN POINT **5.3** Mario's Revolution

An in-depth study of a Venezuelan revolutionary named Mario showed how both psychological and social factors influenced the development of his political beliefs (Slote, 1996). A series of critical conflicts coupled with poverty and lack of education contributed to his radical, revolutionary choice. His parents' divorce and peer pressure contributed to Mario's seeking resolution for many difficult personal problems. In addition, he was looking to rationalize his anger and frustration. Marxism, a theory that advocates equality and clearly identifies enemies of working people, became a convenient source of his rationalization attempts. As a result, Mario vented his negative feelings at a convenient target: institutional authorities and government officials, whom he perceived as oppressors. Some of Mario's acquaintances took advantage of his commitment to the values of integrity and idealism. A trusting and sincere man, he was easily manipulated by his radical leaders, some of whom used revolutionary slogans to pursue their own selfish interests.

that preferences for the values of equality, social justice, and peace ("universality" values) were highly correlated with hopes for social order and individual safety ("security" values). Remarkably, for individuals in Western democratic societies, universality and security values were negatively correlated.

How can we interpret these findings? The social transition from totalitarianism to democracy is long and stressful. Despite the numerous limitations socialism imposed on individual freedom and economic opportunities, that social system generally provided relative social order and a sense of protection and security. Democratic changes, inevitably and unfortunately, coincided with the destruction of the major social institutions that had provided that sense of security. The development of a market economy forced many individuals to be concerned about daily bread, a worry they did not have under socialism. These changes inevitably produced anxiety and frustration in millions of individuals, causing many of them to long for order and guaranteed material security (Klicperova, 2002), to feel safe and secure again. In Slovakia, for instance, most senior citizens, the age cohort that experienced the most difficulty in the transition to a free market, did not consider "prosperity" and "market economy" characteristics of democracy. The vast majority of younger respondents, in contrast, who lived only briefly under socialism, associated democracy with prosperity and market economy (Moodie et al., 1995).

THE IMPACT OF ENVIRONMENT

Political socialization is part of a broader socialization process. Understanding the developing individual cannot be separated from understanding his social and political environment. People constantly exchange messages with others in their environment as they transform each other (Goodnow, 1990). The individual is not a passive and static entity influenced by his surroundings but rather a dynamic and open system (Harkness, 1992). As mentioned earlier in the chapter, social problems influence people to form particular beliefs about social change; the beliefs cause particular actions; the changing environment, again, influences people's belief systems.

John Berry (1992; 1971) identified the major environmental factors influencing individual socialization as ecological and sociopolitical settings, the natural contexts in which humans and their environment interact. The **ecological context,** including the economic activity of the population, factors such as the presence or absence of food, the quality of nutrition, heat or cold, and population density, has a tremendous impact on the individual's needs and beliefs. The **sociopolitical context** is the extent to which people participate in both global and local decisions. It includes ideological values, the organization of the government, and the presence or absence of political freedoms. The maturing individual adjusts to existing realities and acquires roles as a member of a particular group.

Daily surroundings are part of a larger social and political system. Individual growth takes place within a developmental niche that can be viewed as a combination of situations or settings (Harkness & Super, 1992). First, individuals live in physical and social settings comprising people, available products, and services. Second, they encounter collections of customary practices whereby they convey and receive messages. Finally, their caretakers express beliefs and expectations that become part of the social environment. These three types of settings mediate individuals' development within society.

Bronfenbrenner (1979) divided the environment in which individuals develop skills and attitudes into four interdependent entities: Microsystem, Mesosystem, Macrosystem, and Exosystem. The Microsystem involves immediate family members, schoolteachers, friends, and others who interact directly with the individual. The Mesosystem comprises the linkages between two or more environmental settings; for example, a child may attend a religious school once a week, and a teacher from this school and the child's parents may work together on improving his understanding of moral imperatives. The Macrosystem consists of customs and beliefs most valued in a particular society. Finally, the Exosystem includes the media, extended family, legal and social organizations, political institutions, and other influencing agents that may indirectly affect the individual. Among such agents are charismatic personalities, celebrities, and leaders whose life (and death) can have significant meaning for the individual. By providing information and images that shape perceptions, the media, television, radio, newspapers, magazines, and the Internet affect individual attitudes and behaviors. The media are the major sources of information and images for most people, especially the young. (Chapter 6 addresses media impact on people's opinions.)

Tragic deaths of popular personalities—political figures, journalists, and celebrities—cause shock, denial, anger, desperation, and similar strong emotional reactions in many people. Almost any American adult born in the 1950s and earlier can tell you where he was and what he felt upon getting the news about the assassinations of President John F. Kennedy and Dr. Martin Luther King, Jr. Most people in the United States can say where they were and what they experienced on the morning of September 11, 2001. Similarly, people in Sweden have shocking memories of the deaths of Prime Minister Olof Palme and foreign minister Anna Lindh; many Chileans remember the death of President Salvador Allende; Italians recall the violent death of politician Aldo Moro; Russians point to the death of popular journalist and television star Listiev; Indians remember the murder of their prime ministers Indira Gandhi and Rajiv Gandhi. Britons especially recall the death of Princess Diana. The deaths of John Lennon and Kurt Cobain speak especially to many Americans and Britons.

But what is the impact of the death of a popular personality on people's attitudes and behavior? In a 1998 study, Elliott suggested that due to the increasing importance of celebrities' impact on socialization, their deaths may cause traumatic recollections for some individuals and change their views on life, because popular figures tend to be nostalgically idealized. Such idealization may become the psychological foundation for future attitudinal changes. For instance, Raviv and colleagues (1998) studied the reaction of Israeli youth to the assassination of Prime Minister Yitzhak Rabin in 1995. For most left-oriented young people, the leader's death catalyzed an identity search and boosted their sense of ideological partisanship.

PSYCHOLOGICAL THEORIES

To understand better the mechanisms of political socialization, specialists often turn to psychological theories of individual development. The approach developed by Erik Erikson, one of the most respected and controversial psychologists of the 20th century, exemplifies such a theory. Erikson (1950) believed all humans pass through eight developmental stages that stretch from birth to death. Each stage is characterized by a developmental conflict or crisis. If the crisis is resolved, the developing person successfully adjusts to her social environment. If the crisis is not settled, the person continues to have related problems. For instance, if a teenage girl's conflict between a desire to make independent decisions and the fear of retribution from parents for demanding independence has a positive resolution, she will emerge with a strong self-identity. A negative outcome, however, will result in her sense of frustration and confusion (see Table 5.2).

Erikson defined the healthy or mature personality as one that possesses the eight virtues of hope, will, purpose, competence, fidelity, love, care, and wisdom that emerge from the positive resolution of each developmental stage. Despite the suggestion that this theory is applicable to a wide variety of national and cultural settings (Gardiner et al., 1998), Erikson's stages indicate a general sequence not always paralleled in countries other than the West. For most adults in economically developed societies, healthy and financially independent retirement is a prime area of concerns. Savings and investments, taxes and tax exemptions become a source of either elation or frustration for millions of individuals in the United States, Canada, Germany, Japan, and other developed countries. At the same time, billions of human beings in other parts of the world have no money to save. Hunger, civil and ethnic wars, violence and oppression imposed by authorities, chronic ecological problems, and other cataclysms are in the focus of daily concern. Unpredictable disturbances lead to unpredictable problems, and the sequence of these problems is not as straightforward as Erikson's classification would have it. Therefore, in many cases, more immediate strategies of survival may dominate people's lives.

Consider another point. In wealthy industrialized democracies, people exercise relative freedom of choice. They have available to them food, places to live, schools to attend, job opportunities, ideologies, lifestyles, and even religions. The problem is that the process of individual development may be stressful when people are confronted with a wide variety of choices and possibilities. Conversely, in less affluent

TABLE 5.2

Developmental Stages According to Erikson.

Stage	Ego Crisis	Age	Positive Outcome
1	Basic Trust versus Mistrust	0–1	Hope
2	Autonomy versus Shame and Doubt	2–3	Will
3	Initiative versus Guilt	3–5	Purpose
4	Industry versus Inferiority	5–12	Competence
5	Ego Identity versus Role Confusion	Adolescence	Fidelity
6	Intimacy versus Isolation	Young Adult	Love
7	Generativity versus Stagnation	Adulthood	Care
8	Ego Integrity versus Despair	Maturity	Wisdom

Source: E. H. Erikson, *Childhood and Society,* 1950.

A TOPIC FOR CLASS DISCUSSION Insecurity and Values

In Western Europe and the United States, the 1970s was a period of inflation, growing unemployment, and relative economic scarcity and insecurity. These developments influenced the value orientation toward materialistic life goals of people who were adolescents at the time. Could this materialism be a reason why the Republicans were in the White House for 12 years, until 1993? The 1990s brought relative stability and the sense of abundance to the West, particularly to the United States. Therefore, the attitude pattern should be changing, especially among those who grew up in the 1990s and became adults in the early 21st century. If this hypothesis is correct, should we anticipate that between 2005 and 2010 public interest in the United States will shift toward humanitarian issues? Or should we anticipate that the threat of terrorism, recession, and economic insecurity of the early 2000s will affect the development of materialist values?

countries, individual identities and lifestyles may be prescribed at birth. People accept, generally without questioning, where to live, a religion, a political ideology, a government, an occupation, and many values. When people have fewer choices, their transitions from one stage to another may go more smoothly than those of Western people who have more options to choose from. In other words, Erikson's theory may be more applicable to societies with **broad socialization practices** that emphasize independence and free self-expression than those with **narrow socialization practices** prescribing an ideology that strictly identifies both right and wrong behaviors. In addition, that in many countries, social maturation is not associated with increased independence, as Erikson believed, but rather with increased interdependence.

STAGES OF MORAL JUDGMENT

When people answer a question asked by a pollster or discuss breaking news with their friends, they are often asked to weigh moral dilemmas based on their perceptions of right and wrong. People routinely express opinions about giving or not giving financial aid to the needy, keeping or cutting support for social projects, helping or not helping the oppressed, bombing or sparing foreign cities, and executing or imprisoning convicted criminals. How do they make these moral judgments? Are the judgments immediate reactions to questions, or are they the products of other processes? A developmental theory of moral judgment created by Laurence Kohlberg (1981) suggested an explanation. Kohlberg described and empirically tested six types of moral judgment associated with six stages of individual moral development. In brief, according to this theory, people develop moral reasoning by moving from stages in which they justify moral actions from the standpoint of reward and punishment to higher stages in which they choose social norms and values as guidelines for moral actions (see Table 5.3).

TABLE 5.3

Kohlberg's Stages of Moral Development.

Stage 1. Preconventional level. Judgments about what is right and what is wrong are based on fear of punishment. *Example of judgment: "It is absolutely appropriate to freeze the assets of this country in our banks so long as no one can retaliate against us for what we are doing."*

Stage 2. Preconventional level. Moral conduct produces satisfaction, whereas immoral conduct results in unwanted consequences. *Example of judgment: "We have to help undocumented aliens to get affordable health services; otherwise they will be responsible for spreading diseases and we will all suffer because of our inaction."*

Stage 3. Conventional level. Any behavior is good if it is approved by significant figures. *Example of judgment: "I will support airstrikes against this country because the decision was made by the president of the United States, our commander-in-chief."*

Stage 4. Conventional level. The existing laws determine what is moral and immoral. *Example of judgment: "It is OK to execute this convicted felon because the laws of this state permit the death penalty."*

Stage 5. Post-conventional level. Moral behavior is based on interpretations of individual rights and underlying social circumstances. *Example of judgment: "We should recognize same-sex marriages because it is not up to any government to tell people whom they should and shouldn't marry."*

Stage 6. Post-conventional level. Moral conduct is regulated by universal ethical principles that may rise above government and laws. *Example of judgment: "There is no such category as illegal aliens. We are all children of earth."*

Source: Kohlberg (1981)

Snarey (1985) examined 45 empirical studies of moral judgment conducted in 27 countries and showed that the first four developmental stages appear to be universal in this population. However, other studies revealed serious shortcomings in cross-national validation of Kohlberg's theory (Shweder et al., 1990). Why? The methodology used in comparative cross-national studies on moral development was based on hypothetical stories of moral choices faced by American respondents. For example, in one such story a woman suffering from a serious illness is prescribed an expensive drug that should save her life. However, the pharmacist charges an excessive amount of money for the lifesaving prescription. The woman's husband does not have enough money to pay the bill. The moral predicament is whether or not it is morally acceptable for the husband to steal the drug. It appears that this hypothetical story should be easily understood and interpreted all over the world. However, in many countries, healthcare is under government control, and pharmacists cannot charge market prices. Moreover, in some countries, physicians distribute medication directly to their patients.

Another serious criticism of Kohlberg's theory is that the six developmental stages are closely linked to values of Western liberalism and individualism based on moral choice. In many countries, moral judgment is based on existing traditions rather than on free will and choice. The Bible, the Koran, the Torah, and other religious scriptures describe moral behavior. Moreover, some studies point out that individuals' moral judgments in some non-Western countries are produced by circumstance and are not necessarily based on their level of moral development (Matsumoto, 1994; Vassiliou & Vassiliou, 1973).

An interesting examination of Kohlberg's theory was conducted in a study that compared the moral judgment of more than 1,000 Hong Kong, Chinese, English, and American college and high school students (Ma & Cheung, 1996). The test consisted of four stories that described a moral problem. The authors argue that the moral judgments of the Chinese are reinforced by traditional norms and regulated by conformity to primary groups. Chinese tend to see issues, such as the concern for social order, consensus, and abiding by the law from a collectivist perspective. Chinese socialization is also influenced by the Confucian concept of the Five Cardinal Relationships, which emphasizes the harmonious connection between sovereign and subject, father and son, husband and wife, siblings, and friends. The authors argue that respect for social order, consensus, and law-abiding behavior are attached to a Chinese collective mentality. In contrast, people in Western societies tend to be concerned primarily with individual rights and want their interests protected by the law, which often mediates interpersonal relationships. The Chinese, on the contrary, tend to not resolve their conflicts in legal institutions. Most prefer instead to resolve their conflicts via interpersonal contacts. This practice, however, is a double-edged sword. It may appear that interpersonal orientation is more humane and appealing than the law-based system of relationships, that is, it seems healthier to settle a conflict than to litigate it. However, an emphasis on the interpersonal system of communications may stimulate nepotism and corruption, two serious problems that Hong Kong and Chinese officials often recognize.

In review. Major developmental theories of socialization gauge this process as the individual's transition from one developmental stage to another. Each stage has distinct behavioral and cognitive characteristics. People are expected to form particular reactions and ideas during particular stages. However, the process of individual socialization is not linear. Many factors, such as social environment and individual experiences, influence an individual's development.

EDUCATION AND POLITICAL SOCIALIZATION

A political system survives by developing supportive expectations and behaviors among its members (Weaver, 1998). Formal education often serves as a conductor of such support to the younger generation. However, education may be conducted in different ways. In totalitarian and most authoritarian countries, political socialization resembles political **indoctrination,** wherein the learning of a specific political ideology requires its uncritical acceptance. Indoctrination intends to provide knowledge about why the ruling political regime is good. Totalitarian regimes, such as communism and Nazism, considered that schools' essential task was to indoctrinate students to the ruling ideology.

In most democratic countries, a major learning mechanism of political socialization is also education. Political ideas can circulate in society, and the individual is relatively free to choose or to not choose any view. Moreover, some dedicated supporters of liberal education have long asserted that the goal of good teaching about politics in a democratic society is to help students come to an independent position. Sociologist Max Weber suggested that the teacher's job is to help students develop their own critical perspectives and to confront students with the difficult political choices they must make (Weber, 1946). The teacher must present the facts about political institutions and behaviors rather than act as a moralist who prescribes values to guide political action. According to this view, political advocacy has no place in the classroom.

A number of studies stressed the importance of education in determining individual's political opinions (Bennett, 1998a). Classic research suggests that educational institutions change people's attitudes. In a study of students at Bennington College, Newcomb (1943) showed that the relocation from affluent and conservative homes to a predominantly liberal college campus was followed by a leftward direction in political preferences in many students that persisted into later life (Alwin, Cohen & Newcomb, 1988). Earlier studies of political socialization revealed that better educated people are more interested in politics, have a stronger sense of duty, are more apt to feel they can influence the political process, and vote at a higher rate than less educated people. Better educated individuals tend to pay more attention to political campaigns, get involved more often in political discussions, and have a wider range of political attitudes than less educated individuals. Better educated people are more likely to join a political organization (Dawson et al., 1977).

There are more recent illustrations of this tendency. A set of surveys in three states that use caucus conventions to choose presidential delegates (Iowa, Michigan, and Virginia) suggested that delegates who attended either a Democratic or Republican nominating caucus were better educated than citizens in the general electorate. Reportedly, 42 percent of the Democratic sample and 51 percent of the Republicans had a college degree (Cann, 1995). Less than 30 percent of Americans have college degrees. The National Survey of American High School Seniors conducted by the University of Michigan showed that the more civics courses a student had, the more likely he was to (a) be knowledgeable, (b) participate in political discourse, (c) feel efficacy, and (d) show civic tolerance (Langton, 1969). This finding does not explain, however, whether civics courses influence political attitudes or whether students with particular political attitudes prefer to take political science courses.

Special training programs may help individuals from former authoritarian regimes learn more about democracy, its main principles, and functioning (Frost & Makarov, 1998). Similarly, the atmosphere and authority relations in the classroom also affect political attitudes and later behaviors (Bowles & Gintis, 1976). Emphasis on critical thinking, moving away from stress on memorization toward emphasis on argumentation, shape students' current and future approaches to political involvement. People who learn independent approaches in school tend to pursue independent political positions later in life (Sobel, 1993).

Other studies demonstrate links between education and training, on one hand, and political behavior, on the other. For instance, occupational involvement such as decision making on the job is positively correlated with political participation (Sobel, 1989). According to Ehrlich (1999), education in political science is more effective when it is based on at least three principles: (1) problem-based learning (students focus on problems and conflicts); (2) collaborative learning (special interaction between students and teachers); and (3) community service learning. Glanville (1999) examined the role of extracurricular activities in predicting adult political behavior and found that participation in student government positively predicts political involvement, political interest, and political awareness in early adulthood.

THINKING CRITICALLY ABOUT POLITICAL SOCIALIZATION

Research methodology is a first critical point to consider about studies of political socialization. How do researchers gather evidence of how people acquire political ideas and values? Surveys are the most common method; people recall personal experiences and report their responses to political and social events of their childhood or adolescence. Yet, survey research faces a potential problem. In studies of party identification of parents and children, for instance, the party preference of the respondents' parents is usually reported by the respondent himself. Is his recollection inaccurate? Can he misinterpret his parents' voting record? After children spend 10 or 20 years away from home, they may easily overestimate or underestimate the strength of their parents' partisan affiliations.

It is always important, in comparative surveys, to pay attention to the similarity or otherwise of social conditions to which research subjects were exposed. Let's look again at the English-Indian-Japanese survey mentioned earlier in this chapter. The authors of that study stated that the samples were compatible because all of the subjects were randomly selected from suburban areas of the selected countries, and their income was approximately the same in terms of its purchasing power. However, direct comparisons can be misleading. Although a family in one country can purchase, in theory, the same amount of food as a family in another country, the quality of purchased food may be dramatically different. The quality of medical care in a first country may be significantly lower than the quality in a second country, despite comparable access to care. Educational systems and therefore children's knowledge about political and social events are likely to differ. In addition, the scope and depth of the problems some countries face—overpopulation, infectious disease, corruption, and environmental problems, to name a few—can only remotely resemble the daily problems of average American, Canadian, or Japanese children.

In another study, 1,500 high school students from Finland and Estonia participated in a survey that measured attitudes on a variety of social issues (Keltikangas-Jarvinen & Terav, 1996). Estonian adolescents, as a group, were found to be more aggressive and less socially responsible than their Finnish counterparts. Moreover, avoidance was found to be the most typical way of dealing with problems for Estonian students. How can we critically interpret these findings? Estonia and Finland are geographically close and share many elements of culture and history. The authors explain the results of the study by appealing to social and political factors. For more than 40 years, Estonia was part of the Soviet Union, whereas Finland remained an independent country. Western values of individual freedom and democracy were persistently promoted among Finnish children. In contrast, in Soviet Estonia, public education and socialization promoted collectivism, obedience to authority, and a sense of social responsibility. Why did the young Estonians in this study show attitudes of avoidance, aggression, and lack of responsibility? Despite the communist government's efforts, according to the authors, most young people in Estonia rejected the main values promoted by the authorities. Other factors may also have contributed to the socialization of Estonian youth of the 1990s. The unprecedented political and ideological struggle in the country, after it gained independence, a rapid growth in crime and corruption, increasing social inequality, and a loss of guaranteed social security may have triggered a sense of disappointment and frustration in the population. Perhaps these and other negative developments of more recent times, not only the experiences of the early 1980s, affected the attitudes of Estonian adolescents.

Here is another example from the field of socialization that demonstrates how the social conditions of respondents influence survey answers. Women from India, Japan, and England were asked to tell the age at which they expect their child to achieve confidence and maturity in his judgments, important goals of socialization. Differences between Japanese expectations and English expectations were insignificant (Joshi & MacLean, 1997). However, the expectations of Indian mothers were considerably different from those of the other two national groups. Indian mothers expected competence at a later age than mothers in England and Japan. Why? The Japanese and English respondents were from urban areas. Children in those regions live primarily in small families, and the mother, who is likely to have a job, needs to encourage her child's early independence. Indian children from the studied sample lived mainly in large extended families with many relatives representing two or three generations in one household. The Indian mothers may have been under less pressure to encourage their child's independence early.

Many findings about political socialization reported here were based on studies conducted in the 1960s and 1970s. Some of these findings reflected common, cross-national patterns related to the individual's socialization and the acquisition of political knowledge. Other data reflected developments that may or may not be applicable to contemporary society of the 21st century. In the 40-year period since the classic works in political socialization were published, the American family has undergone a fundamental transformation. There are significantly more working mothers than there were in the 1970s. The average American family is getting smaller. Parents today tend to be more educated than their parents were 30 and 40 years ago. Contemporary research in political socialization does not yet adequately interpret the effects of these changes.

ASSIGNMENT 5.1   BIRTH ORDER

According to Sulloway (1996), firstborn children tend to be more supportive of the status quo and the existing social and political establishment than their younger siblings (later-borns). The author mentions many exceptions to this rule, and many are known to historians. For example, during the French Revolution, royalists (supporters of the king) were largely firstborns, but so were the most irreconcilable opponents of monarchy. Moderates tended to be middle children. In the National Convention that voted on whether or not to execute King Louis XVI, firstborns were the most sharply divided group. Those firstborns from the upper classes were more likely to vote for mercy; those from the lower classes, to vote against it. Consider two notorious political personalities of the 20th century: Adolf Hitler of Germany and Vladimir Lenin of Russia. Hitler was a firstborn; Lenin had older siblings.

Identify from their biographies the birth order of a half-dozen U.S. presidents of the 20th century. Were there older or younger brothers or sisters in their families? What were their party affiliations? Now try this. U.S. presidents have been the target of assassination attempts. Investigate whether the assassins had older or younger siblings.

ASSIGNMENT 5.2   ATTITUDES OF TEENAGERS AND THEIR PARENTS

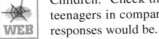

Log onto the textbook's website. Click on Chapter 5. Find a link called "Parents and Children." Check the results of a survey that measured attitudes of U.S. teenagers in comparison with what their parents thought their children's responses would be.

Assess the similarities and differences between the opinions of children and parents about money, social issues, and social trends. What do you think is the source of the differences? Describe several factors that may contribute to the differences.

CHAPTER SUMMARY

- Political socialization is a lifelong process by which individuals learn political attitudes and behaviors. It is part of the broader socialization process whereby an individual becomes a member of a particular society and takes on its values and behaviors. Social and cultural conditions mediate political socialization.

- Across nations, human development and socialization take place in stages. Specialists refer to social and cultural norms, on one hand, and attitudinal and behavioral changes, on the other, associated with each life stage.

- The recency approach suggests that the closer in time a learning experience is to relevant adult opinions or decisions, the greater is its impact. The primacy approach views childhood as the most important period of political socialization; accordingly, individuals' basic values reflect the experiences of their pre-adult years; they most likely learn political attitudes by the time they are adolescents.

- Family environment is the major context within which the individual's development of political attitudes and values takes place. The family develops a child's most fundamental ethnic, religious, party, and social-class identifications.

- Fundamental components of a person's social and political identity, such as conceptions of freedom, equality, and religious and ethnic affiliations, commonly develop during adolescence. The view of the good citizen, that is, a person who takes an interest in public affairs as well as obeys the law, also forms during this period.

- Political socialization continues during adulthood, particularly in the community and the workplace. According to the persistence hypothesis, adults acquire attitudes early in life and tend to not change them later. In contrast, according to the openness hypothesis, people adjust their attitudes and behavior when situations change; these transformations can be substantial. Political socialization continues during late adulthood.

- The availability of and access to resources determine the individual's quality of life. Quality of life may directly or indirectly affect the process of political socialization.

- An environmental approach considers political socialization as part of a broader socialization process. The developing individual cannot be separated from his or her environmental context. People constantly exchange messages within the environment, thereby transforming each other.

- Many prominent theories of socialization, such as that of Erikson and Kohlberg, interpret this process as the individual's transition from one level to another. The person going through these stages tends to develop distinct behavioral and cognitive characteristics.

- Formal education plays a critical role in the process of political socialization. Each political system must develop supportive expectations of and behaviors among its members. Formal education serves as a conductor of such support to the younger generation.

- While interpreting data from studies on political socialization, it is crucial to look at the context in which the studies were conducted. In comparative studies, multiple factors, such as significant political events, specific circumstances, the type of political regime, the type of educational system, family values, and other cultural traditions, should be taken in consideration.

Looking Ahead. The next chapter on media and opinions discusses an important and fascinating cultural source of political socialization: the press and electronic media. It critically explores access to and restrictions on information, and it examines the direct impact of the media and extraordinary events, the spread of news, agenda setting, media frames, and political bias. It identifies media impact on attitudes, behavior, and policies, and the extent to which this influence is exaggerated.

DEFINITIONS OF KEY TERMS

Adolescence—Period of transition from childhood to adulthood.

Broad socialization practices—Socialization practices that emphasize the development of independence and free self-expression in the individual.

Ecological context—The natural setting in which humans and the social environment interact.

Indoctrination—The teaching of a specific political ideology intended to provide beliefs about why the ruling political regime is "good."

Narrow socialization practices—Practices prescribing an ideology that identifies "right" and "wrong" behaviors.

Openness hypothesis—The suggestion that people change their attitudes and behavior, sometimes substantially, in response to changing situations.

Persistence hypothesis—The suggestion that adults acquire attitudes early in life and tend to not change them later.

Political community—A collection of individuals, groups, and institutions that promote the government and its underlying political system.

Political cynicism—The belief that politicians and public officials repeatedly violate prescriptive moral standards in their behavior.

Political efficacy—The individual's belief that he can effectively participate in politics and therefore has some control over the action of political decision makers.

Political predispositions—Stable traits of individuals that regulate the acceptance or nonacceptance of political communication.

Political socialization—A lifelong process whereby individuals acquire political attitudes and behaviors.

Primacy approach—A set of assumptions that the individual's basic values reflect the experiences of his pre-adult years and that political attitudes are learned, most likely, by the period of adolescence.

Quality of life—The availability of and access to resources essential for the individual's well-being.

Recency approach—A set of assumptions that the closer a particular learning experience is to relevant adult opinions or decisions, the greater its impact.

Scarcity hypothesis—The suggestion that the developing individual attaches greatest subjective value to those objects that were in relatively short supply during childhood and carries this attachment throughout adulthood.

Socialization agents—The family, schools, peers, religion, workplace, and the media as creators of social learning.

Sociopolitical context—The extent to which people participate in global and local decisions.

CHAPTER 6

The Media
and Opinions

The way in which the world
is imagined determines at any
particular moment what men will do.
Walter Lippmann

The new electronic interdependence
recreates the world in the image of a
global village.
Marshall McLuhan

Multimedia activist Joey Skaggs is an artist, satirist, hoaxer, and dedicated proponent of independent thinking and media literacy. He is a journalist who not only reflects reality in the usual way journalists do but also "creates" reality by the media and for the media. Over the course of more than 30 years, Skaggs has hoaxed TV networks, wire services, newspapers, magazines, and radio stations around the world. His tactics are amazingly simple. First, he creates an idea about something that is not happening or does not exist. Then, with the help of resourceful friends, he begins to act on this story as if it were real, and then the story is conveyed to anyone who wants to pay attention to it. The result? The story is picked up by the media, begins to live on its own, and, in fact, becomes reality itself. In 1976, he organized a fake auction of rock star sperm. The event drew the attention of newspapers and radio stations and was broadcast on national television. Then he fabricated a story about a bordello . . . for dogs. The phone rang off the hook as hundreds of people called to talk to New York's first and only pimp for canines. In 1987, Skaggs organized "Save the Geoduck Campaign," a fake protest action to solve a nonexistent problem. This campaign received great media coverage and drew huge support. In 2000, he created a stir by announcing the foundation of a memorial theme park, "The Final Curtain," with a traveling time-share program, roller coasters, and other attractions, all designed for the dead. What does Joey Skaggs want? He is not looking for money or a prestigious job. His goal, as he explains, is to have fun and send people a warning signal: Be careful, because the media easily buy into disinformation and hype and then feed it to the public. The media are becoming increasingly powerful in the business of influencing people's thinking. Skaggs asks us, indeed all independent thinkers, to follow simple bits of advice: Question authority in all forms; do not forsake critical analysis for wishful thinking; look to more than one source for information; challenge preconceived notions and prejudices.

Is this sound advice?

Looking Forward. Chapter 6, on "The Media and Opinions," discusses the press and electronic media as important and impressive cultural sources of political socialization. In thinking critically about the media, the chapter explores access to and restrictions on information, including censorship. It examines the direct impact of the media, extraordinary events, the spread of news, agenda setting, media frames, and political bias. It explores as well media influence on attitudes, behavior, and policy, and the extent to which this influence is exaggerated.

THE MEDIA FACTOR

Do the media represent reality objectively? This story about Joey Skaggs, who deliberately misrepresents real events by faking and staging nonexistent ones, raises that question. Skaggs does not claim a place of honor on the media Olympus. He simply claims that his distortions of reality are almost the same as some of those manufactured by the mainstream press, networks, and news services. A classic sociological study in the 1980s revealed that television snapshots of contemporary reality were widely inaccurate: They showed significantly more men than women on television; the women were much younger than the men; children, the elderly, and ethnic groups were grossly underrepresented (Gerbner et al., 1986). In another acclaimed book, *Out of Order*, Thomas Patterson showed that the media routinely distorted issues by focusing mainly on controversy, conflict, and failure (Patterson, 1993).

People who work for the media have their own opinions and tastes. They may paper over one event, cover another overzealously, or become concerned with or indifferent to others. Let's look at examples. When the FBI investigated an explosion during the 1996 Atlanta Olympic Games, Richard Jewell, a security guard at the Olympic Park, was unceremoniously scrutinized by the media and presented as a mastermind behind the bombing. Sixty-nine percent of Americans in 1996 said the media treated Jewell, who was innocent, "unfairly" (ABC, August 1996, 511). David Westin, news president of ABC in 1998, killed a story planned for the newsmagazine *20/20* about pedophilia at Disney World because it could have hurt ABC's parent company, Disney. Defective Firestone tires, the subject of one of the biggest consumer-safety scandals in the late 1990s, were first reported by local TV stations in 1996, yet it took nearly four years for the national media to catch on and tell the story. We know that the media overexpose certain crimes while leaving dozens of similar crimes unreported. Most Americans know about ethnic conflicts in the world's hot spots, such as the Middle East. However, only few are aware of what is happening to the Roma in Europe and ethnic groups in China and Rwanda, or what is wrong in Nagorny

Karabakh, or Jammu and Kashmir. The reason is that without media coverage, the public has little awareness of the shadowed parts of reality.

These points, however, may be taken out of context, as critics argue. Nobody says the media can always cover the world with perfect accuracy. Some events are actually more newsworthy than others. The First Amendment gives U.S. media many resources by which to express their opinions and report stories. They can not be blamed if some of their opinions turn out to be mistaken. Moreover, as the argument goes, they should be free to report or not report a story if they so choose. People should think critically and distinguish for themselves information they believe is inappropriate and useless from what is appropriate and useful. No matter how objective a reporter tries to be, it is almost impossible to satisfy insiders, people who automatically reject information that differs from what they already believe (Efron, 2001).

Which side in this discussion do you support? Do you hold the media at fault for misinforming us, or do you praise them for doing a good job?

THE MEDIA AND ACCESS TO INFORMATION: THE RIGHT TO CENSOR?

Not all people have the same quality of life. We live in dissimilar environments; while some have plenty of resources, others have limited access to them. In theory, all people can be educated and have free access to information. This does not happen in the real world; knowledge is unequally distributed. Numerous factors, including technological backwardness, laws, political pressures, social class differences, and cultural norms, prevent millions of individuals from obtaining at all what other people obtain easily. The media may be used by governments or particular social groups to filter information into two large categories: information that is "appropriate" versus "inappropriate" for people's consumption. This restrictive practice of reviewing and determining what is appropriate for publication or broadcast according to moral, ideological, or political considerations is called **censorship.** Camouflaged under labels, such as *regulations* and *restrictions,* censorship is a powerful tool used by governments, social and religious institutions, and the media themselves to filter out certain information that then becomes nearly unavailable to the public. Several rationales are used to justify the practice of censorship.

Political Censorship

Defenders of the political form of censorship argue that restrictions on information are necessary to protect social order and stability. For the sake of this goal, people should not be allowed to disseminate information that undermines the political authority of the government. Freedom of speech may be granted formally to the media, but it is limited; people may receive information from the media on all subjects except those concerning criticism of the government, its representatives, and political leaders. Many totalitarian as well as authoritarian regimes, especially those established by the forceful seizure of power, endorsed **political censorship:** Communist Russia until the 1990s, Nazi Germany and Fascist Italy in the 1930s, Greece in the late 1960s, Chile in the 1970s, Nicaragua in the 1980s, Iran and Sierra Leone in the 1990s, to name a few. Some governments argue that political censorship is a temporary means to providing social stability and therefore will be abolished as soon as the desired stability is achieved.

Ideological Censorship

In Germany today, it is against the law to publish or air any material that endorses Nazism. However, such material may be published or produced in the United States or Russia. Under **ideological censorship,** the government or the media themselves establish a set of ideas or principles about a society's past, present, and future. Information challenging these principles and measures is prohibited from publication. In former communist countries, ideological censorship was compulsory. Articles, reports, and essays about the advantages of the free market, ideological freedom in Western countries, and details of the personal lives of the founding fathers of communism have been generally prohibited from publication. Government censors working for major newspapers and magazines in the former Soviet Union received higher pay than the chief editors of these publications (Korotich, 2000).

Religious censorship is one facet of ideological censorship. In many countries, criticism of the dominant or official religion is strictly prohibited by law. In the most fundamentalist governments of the beginning of the 21st century, such as Iran and Saudi Arabia, a journalist who dares publish critical materials about Islam, the official religion in these countries, may be prosecuted. In various forms, ideological censorship is enforced today in many countries.

Moral Censorship

Societies develop standards of decency and public morality and may also enact laws prescribing the standards to be followed in communications among businesses, institutions, and the media as **moral censorship.** For example, in the United States, sexually explicit materials are excluded from major prime-time television network programming. Radio and television commentators may not say certain words on the air. Violating these rules typically results in sanctions. For example, the vast majority of daily newspapers in the United States will not print photographs of nude bodies or images that may be considered sexually graphic. In Russia, on the other hand, this type of material was relatively common in many mainstream newspapers and magazines of the 2000s.

Totalitarian and some authoritarian governments exercise strict control over the media by regulating what may be printed and broadcast and what must not be. In fact, the media played and still plays an important role in the political socialization of the citizens of these countries (Schneider, 2000). In a free democratic society, the government does not determine what is broadcast on radio and television or what is published in newspapers. Nevertheless, democracy does not provide individuals with total freedom to disseminate all materials regardless of content. Although the First Amendment of the American Constitution guarantees freedom of speech, the mass media are subject to a variety of government rules and regulations. Broadcasting on radio and television, for instance, is regulated by a government agency, the Federal Communications Commission (FCC). All media are subject to *libel* laws, which hold broadcasters responsible for false information that defames or harms others. In addition, media are subject to local laws on *obscenity*. Therefore, nudity, extreme violence, and

A CASE IN POINT 6.1   Censorship in the Egyptian Media

Often, political, ideological, and cultural reasons for censorship are inseparable. Here is a list of issues and themes likely to be censored and not be published in the *Middle East Times* published in Cairo.

> Reports on human rights abuses in Egypt
>
> Criticism of the Egyptian president or his family
>
> Criticism of the Egyptian military
>
> Reports about the poor treatment of Egyptians in friendly Arab countries, especially in Saudi Arabia
>
> Discussions of modern, unorthodox interpretations of Islam
>
> Reports on discrimination against Coptic Christians in Egypt.

Source: Middle East Times, http://www.metimes.com.

verbal profanity are banned from most shows aired by radio stations and television networks. People in a democratic society have different opinions about the extent of media censorship. In 2003, 38 percent believed there was "too much media freedom" in the United States, but the same percentage said there was too much "government censorship" (CSRA/FFMS, June 2003, 1,000).

WHAT IS REPORTED?

The media disseminate at least four categories of news. **Available news** contains information that is easily obtainable, such as basketball and baseball scores, weather forecasts, reports about public events, and decisions made by politicians and public officials. If one radio or television station does not report on these events, other stations may. **Discovered news** is typically the result of journalistic investigation. This information is not easily obtainable, so it remains unknown to the average reader or viewer until a newspaper or radio station decides to print or air it. Available and discovered news can be practical, entertaining, or both. **Practical news** serves an individual's pragmatic goals, whereas **entertaining news** has primarily enjoyment value. Mixing these types of news has become a common practice. Actor Leonardo DiCaprio interviewed President Clinton in 2000, and Arnold Schwarzenegger announced his 2003 bid for California's governorship on Jay Leno's *Tonight Show*. Were these events sources of practical or entertaining information? Similarly, in 2004, celebrities like Bruce Springsteen and the Dixie Chicks campaigned for John Kerry, while Schwarzenegger and Red Sox World Series star Curt Schilling worked for George Bush.

Obviously, not every event that happens in your town, county, province, state, and country becomes news. Many factors determine what is covered, why it is covered, and how much of it is covered (Norris, 2000). What makes an event newsworthy?

Direct Impact

Events become newsworthy when they have direct impact on individuals. At the start of 2001, millions of Americans were reading, listening to, and watching business reports about the falling numbers of the stock market. In 2003, stocks were climbing back. Reports about ups and downs of the market are important because these numbers tell many Americans about their personal earnings and losses, about their college savings and pension funds. When information about a national event or regional news becomes less important to many individuals, this news will be reported less frequently. As an example, from the end of the Cold War in 1991 to 2001, media coverage of foreign affairs, especially the number of reports from Russia and East European countries, dropped significantly, along with declining public interest to that region (Rielly, 1999). In the fall of 2002, among all television broadcasts, the highest rating was given to newscasts about the deadly shooting incidents in Washington, DC, called the Washington sniper case.

Name Recognition and Sensationalism

Newsworthiness occurs when important and recognizable people are involved in inappropriate activities. An event becomes media-worthy when it involves the famous or well known (Patterson, 1993). Over the past 50 years, major political and social events, scandals, and state funerals attracted extremely large audiences. The coverage of events, including the funerals of presidents John F. Kennedy and Ronald Reagan, the live broadcast of Neil Armstrong walking on the moon, the wedding of the Prince and Princess of Wales (Charles and Diana), and the O. J. Simpson murder trial, kept tens of millions of Americans in front of their television sets and radios. In every country, heads of state, speakers of parliament, or prime ministers are typically the center of national political and social life; therefore, events in which they figure are newsworthy. These people get media exposure by virtue of doing or not doing something required by their status. Even the absence of leaders may become news. During the 1980 Winter Olympics in Lake Placid, New York, U.S. President Jimmy Carter did not participate in the opening ceremony, which is traditionally hosted by the head of state of the country holding the games. The president kept a low profile and stayed away because of the ongoing hostage crisis in Iran. Twenty years later, in the summer of 2000, Russian President Vladimir Putin did not interrupt his vacation at a sea resort after receiving reports about a tragic accident to the Russian nuclear submarine *Kursk,* in which more than 100 sailors drowned. He knew about the tragedy but was absent from his office. In both cases, because the media vigorously discussed the whereabouts of the presidents, their absence was newsworthy.

Until the 1980s, the media observed an unwritten rule that the private lives of political figures and public officials should remain private. Americans knew little about public officials' personal problems, illnesses, love affairs, divorces, and details of their personal relationships, faults, and hobbies. Because of the lack of media coverage, many Americans were not aware, for example, that President Franklin Roosevelt was paralyzed and used a wheelchair. No special law was passed to limit privacy in the media, but newspapers and networks realized that private behavior may have public ramifications. The so-called "privacy statute" was effectively abandoned by the 1980s. Scandals involving public officials and celebrities sell newspapers and boost television and radio ratings.

Moreover, by publishing controversial reports and revealing scandalous facts about politicians, the media established themselves as a powerful political force that could elevate or bring down almost any political career. One of the most prominent examples is the case of former U.S. Senator Gary Hart, a major contender for the 1988 Democratic presidential nomination. While rebuffing journalists' questions about a suspected extramarital affair, he challenged the press to "catch" him. The challenge was accepted. As a result, the senator's affair was exposed on the front pages of leading newspapers and on prime-time television news, and Hart was forced to drop out of the presidential race. Accusations of sexual harassment created enormous media hype about Clarence Thomas's 1991 Supreme Court nomination. In 2001, the media widely debated California representative Gary Condit's relationship with a missing congressional intern, thus derailing his political career.

During an interview with the former White House intern Monica Lewinsky, Barbara Walters asked her about the thrills of phone sex with the president of the United States. Even though many people felt this discussion was inappropriate, 40 percent of the households watching television that night tuned in to the Lewinsky interview. With an average audience of 48,530,000 viewers over the two-hour telecast, this interview became the most-watched television news program ever broadcast by a single network (http://www.abcnews.go.com). Stories about President Clinton's personal life, and especially his relationships with women, began circulating in the media in 1992, when he was campaigning for the presidency. The stories continued after he left office eight years later. At times, such tales overshadowed reports about his reelection campaign. For example, between Labor Day and Election Day in 1998, the number of stories about the election appearing on network evening news was 72. During the same period, the number of stories about Monica Lewinsky on network evening news was 426. Table 6.1 displays the media coverage of President Clinton in the years before he left office in 2001.

As you can see from this table, *taxes* was the most frequently used keyword in publications over an eight-year period. Only during the impeachment debate in December 1998, was the Lewinsky scandal given more attention than other issues. However, references to scandals were more frequent than references to terrorism or

TABLE 6.1

Number of publications in Lexis/Nexis database dedicated to Bill Clinton and containing these keywords: *scandal, Lewinsky, infidelity, taxes, terrorism,* and *immigration.*

December	Scandal	Lewinsky	Infidelity	Taxes	Terrorism	Immigration
1992	24	0	2	527	11	49
1993	68	0	40	427	37	35
1994	45	0	0	938	18	41
1995	57	0	1	385	27	37
1996	78	0	0	164	19	20
1997	113	0	1	226	35	28
1998	568	1,613	48	182	59	16
1999	87	156	2	130	75	30
2000	50	69	1	184	50	28

Source: Lexis/Nexis.

immigration, two important American policy issues. Even though 44 percent of Americans strongly believed in 1997 that journalists spent too much time reporting on the personal lives of public officials (Roper/Freedom Forum Media Studies Center, January 1997, telephone, 1,500), these reports continued to draw high popularity ratings.

Interpretation of Events

Events also become newsworthy if the media have the opportunity to provide ratings-boosting interpretations. In many countries with strong political parties, candidates are able to communicate their messages through party organizations in voting districts. In the United States, however, political parties are relatively weak. Therefore, to mobilize as many voters as possible, political candidates rely mostly on the media. Examples? Billionaire presidential candidate H. Ross Perot paid millions of his own dollars to tape and broadcast television addresses to the American people in 1992. However, for the vast majority of political campaigns, this expense would be too high. Therefore, most candidates use the media to communicate with voters in two ways: free coverage on news programs and brief paid ads, called spots.

Paid advertisement is important if little or no free coverage is given to the campaign. Free news coverage is most important when the candidate or developments around him become newsworthy (Ansolabehere et al., 1993). But how do candidates achieve newsworthiness? The media are a powerful political force in their position to determine which events are more newsworthy than others. In fact, coverage of an event and related discussions may become more important than the occasion itself. Critics call this phenomenon "media hype" (Safire, 1978), referring to events that are less significant than the media portrays them. In 2000, answering a question about whether the media made the Florida election recount seem more of a crisis than it really was, 67 percent said yes, referring to television networks, and only 26 percent disagreed. The majority also believed cable television was responsible for the Florida hype (54 versus 28 percent). In addition, a plurality of 49 percent attributed hype to national newspapers and magazines (Princeton/*Newsweek,* November 16, 2000, 1,000).

"Media hype," on the other hand, does not necessarily affect the people's opinions as expressed in the polls. In 2004, Senator John Kerry apparently "won" the debates against President George Bush, yet that victory did not boost opinion in the polls significantly in favor the the challenger.

Extraordinary Events

Events become newsworthy when they are extraordinary. Did you know that in the old Soviet Union, government-owned radio stations provided live coverage of Moscow *fireworks* on major state holidays? All the listener could hear was symphonic music accompanied by a rumbling thunder. Radio stations in communist countries did not care about profit; all their bills were paid by the government. But market-driven media must woo their listeners, readers, and viewers, who want to be not only informed but also entertained. People tend to pay more attention to news reports that cause emotional reactions, such as joy, fear, sadness, surprise, or anger. The desire to be entertained is one of the main reasons people turn to the media, which must touch human sentiments in order to receive attention. As the old joke goes, "If a dog bites a man, it's not news. If a man bites a dog, that's news!" Not surprisingly, you may expect that a mayor's speech at the dedication of a public park would attract few viewers, while a serious car accident would attract more. If a doctor treats her patients well, she will rarely make the news. However, if she makes a mistake, especially one with grave consequences, a story about it is "good enough" for newspapers, the Internet, or television news. A television station is not likely to run a story about a building being built well but rather one about a building being destroyed by fire, flood, or other disaster. If things are going well in El Salvador or Cameroon, these countries have little chance to be mentioned by the U.S. media. However, if events turn bad, Americans are more likely to hear about these countries. The worse the events, the likely more news reports will follow.

From the political candidate's viewpoint, one of the most important goals of campaigning is to avoid noticeable mistakes that could damage his image (Ansolabehere et al., 1993). Newspaper photographs of Michael Dukakis in a tank in 1988 and Bob Dole falling off a wooden stage in 1996 did not garner those presidential candidates additional rating points or votes. However, many candidates, especially when trailing in opinion polls, may take a risky approach to campaigning: They would welcome even a blunder that got them additional media coverage. Some candidates run simply to increase their name recognition for future campaigns; they may feel they can afford mistakes just because the media will mention them more often.

Emotional expressions by presidential contender Howard Dean in 2004 may have cost him the lead in the Democratic Primaries: media stories began to portray him as an "unstable" candidate.

HOW NEWS SPREADS

Agenda Setting

Of the innumerable events of a given day, only a few are chosen for coverage in the regular news or in special reports. Among the thousands of topics people discuss every day, only a few are debated on television. Among the many subjects that deserve attention, only some are addressed in newspaper articles and editorials. As we mentioned earlier, editors and journalists often exercise their control over determining what becomes news and what does not. This process is called **agenda setting,** and because of it, the media can choose the topics about which their audience is likely to think and talk later.

As we learned in Chapter 4 on attitudes, opinions that are easily accessible from memory tend to be expressed more often than less accessible attitudes. Because of agenda setting, some attitudes become more accessible than others. This means that many individuals distinguish between *more important* issues and *less important* ones based solely on how the media cover them. As experimental research shows, people exposed to television reports dedicated to particular topics later tend to regard these topics as more important than others (Iyengar & Kinder, 1987).

The media can affect the accessibility of the individual's attitudes through agenda setting. The relationship between agenda setting and attitudes can be reversed; the media may simply follow public opinion. That is, producers, editors, and journalists choose what stories to cover based on whatever the audience considers significant and interesting. If a situation occurs that the public follows with great interest, for example, a military conflict, the media are likely to jump on the story.

Media Frames

Besides agenda setting, the media provide viewers with **media frames,** a form and context for interpreting the news. Consider illustrations. One day in the spring of 2001, websites of two leading news organizations posted their evening headlines. MSNBC's headline for a story about an air accident involving an American and a Chinese military plane read: "Diplomatic dogfight: U.S., China trade blame for spy-plane collision." CNN's headline was: "U.S. says China is intercepting U.S. military planes in unsafe manner." Above a posted article about the situation in Yugoslavia after its former president was arrested, CNN's headline read: "War crimes tribunal wants Milosevic." MSNBC offered the less dramatic "Milosevic fate is far from sealed." Notice the difference in the way details were presented and emphasized in these four headlines.

Media frames serve several functions. *First,* they serve an agenda-setting role by directing attention to or from particular social or political issues, emphasizing or deemphasizing their importance. *Second,* they may offer a way to interpret issues or events, thus suggesting the meaning of issues at hand. *Third,* they may present favorable or unfavorable interpretations of issues and events, thus promoting particular attitudes in the audience toward these issues and events. *Fourth,* they may propose particular actions or responses with respect to the issues or problems covered. Let's discuss common kinds of framing.

Quantitative framing is the type of framing in which events, circumstances, and human actions involve numerical values. Take, for example, the most common type of quantitative framing, called *horse-race framing,* which presents politics as a contest, competitive game, or race. A special role in this framing is allotted to the results of opinion polls and their interpretation: Someone is ahead and someone is behind and by how much. The 2000 U.S. presidential election may have been the most quantitatively framed because it was the most strongly poll-driven election in history. The media organizations conducted more than five times the number of horse-race polls during the first seven months of 2000 than in an equivalent period 20 years ago when Carter ran against Reagan. Twenty-six surveys were conducted in 1980 versus 136 in 2000, more than four polls per week. In the final weeks of that presidential campaign, the vast majority of the media reports discussed tracking polls and the candidates' reactions to them (Steinhorn, 2000). The 2004 campaign was similar.

Quantitative frames tend to be relatively simple: X is ahead (bigger, stronger) and Y is behind (smaller, weaker). For example, in the late 1990s, ABC launched the tag line calling itself the network "watched by more people than any other network." At the same time, CBS's famous claim was almost identical: "the most watched network." Which network was telling the truth? The answer is that both networks were correct. They based their claims on different computations, that is, on different quantitative framing. CBS counted the number of people watching television and divided the total by the number of minutes each network was viewed. ABC based its claim on the number of people who watched at least six minutes of one ABC show per week (60.3 percent of the total audience compared to 58.3 percent for CBS).

Priming is another form of framing; it is the capacity and ability of the media to highlight particular issues and events as criteria for evaluating politicians (Ansolabehere et al., 1993). Every public figure has a great variety of characteristics and can make both great and objectionable decisions. Nevertheless, the media often dedicate a great deal of coverage to a single issue, with the result that the name of a particular politician is chiefly associated with this highlighted issue in the mind of the public. Priming not only allows the media to create the politician's personal and political image with the help of solid arguments based on meaningful facts, it also provides conditions for uncritical acceptance of the primed material (Petty & Cacioppo, 1979). For example, from January 1 to

March 1 of 1992, the print media published 301 reports in which the first President Bush was mentioned in conjunction with the 1991 Gulf War. In the same period, the number of reports in which the president was mentioned in conjunction with the economic recession was three times as high: 986. The international military campaign to liberate Kuwait, for which President Bush is given credit, drew significantly less attention than the state of American economy. Media priming is listed among the reasons the incumbent Republican president was defeated by Governor Bill Clinton, the Democratic candidate. Bush's name was often associated with the recession and, therefore, with difficulties and problems (Schlesinger et al., 1994).

Episodic framing allows journalists and commentators to describe individuals in the context of particular circumstances: Interviews, live pictures, personal stories, and footage of developing events. **Thematic framing,** on the other hand, is based on presenting generalized knowledge and more systematic and abstract analysis of a topic. Mixed framing, or hybrid coverage, is common as well; it features both information about a case or problem and an analysis or discussion with generalizations and conclusions. For example, MSNBC.COM (March 19, 2001) posted an article about a research project that found most email messages sent to the House of Representatives in Washington, DC, are unanswered by the lawmakers' staff. It cited two reasons. The first was the spam emails many lobbying groups send; these messages were generally ignored because they were not sent by individuals from personal computers. The second was the lawmakers' lack of funding, which results in too few personnel to handle the volume of email correspondence. Then the article framed the situation. It did not suggest that money is needed to train and fund congressional staffers to improve the handling of incoming email. The article's main topic (thematic

---

A CASE IN POINT 6.2   *Quantitative Framing or "Misframing"*

Watch for irregularities journalists or commentators commit in reporting on opinion polls.

- No information is given about the sample, such as who was surveyed and when—for example, "a poll was conducted" or "in a survey. . . ." Misrepresenting the sample may lead people to assume the poll is national when in fact it is not.

- No information is given about the question or questions asked in the survey, but the results are interpreted anyway. A hypothetical example: "Twice as many Americans like tall politicians than short ones," with no reference to the exact wording of the question.

- Labeling even a single percentage-point difference between two samples as ups or downs, gains or losses, when, in fact, the difference is statistically insignificant. In other words, the evidence is that there is no difference between the samples.

- The survey sponsor is not mentioned (we addressed this problem in Chapter 2 on measurement).

framing) was the lack of contact between ordinary people and their congressional representatives. Email is not the cause of the problem; the article emphasized that the lack of response by Congress has deep cultural roots. Conclusion? There has long been a divide between the citizen and the elected official.

Viewers exposed to thematically framed news tend to explain the problems covered in those reports as caused by social factors, such as socioeconomic conditions, the inaction of government officials, and cultural norms. Viewers exposed to episodic coverage tend to explain the issues presented in the reports by referring to the individual traits of the people involved in the stories. In other words, if a report on school violence is framed to focus on national statistics and research in the field, people will tend to conclude that social problems cause the problem. If a journalist reports on a particular incident of school violence, people are likely to blame the perpetrator himself for what happened (Ansolabehere et al., 1993; Nisbett & Ross, 1980).

Episodic framing is a series of snapshots of reality. For example, the American public tends to overestimate the proportion of African Americans among the poor. At the same time, television networks and national printed sources tend to portray the poor as composed of a higher proportion of blacks than is really the case. For example, between 1988 and 1992, *Time, Newsweek,* and *U.S. News and World Report* published 182 stories and 206 pictures about poverty. Sixty-two percent of people in those reports were black (Gilens, 1996). In fact, black people comprise less than one-third of the American poor (U.S. Bureau of the Census, 2000). This example, however, does not necessarily suggest the media were responsible for people's mistakes in their evaluation of social reality. Many other factors, including lack of knowledge or prejudice, could have contributed to the misperception of the racial composition of the poor. Journalists are also members of the public and, as such, have views and stereotypes that are reflected in their broadcast work.

Political Bias

Most people are sensitive to the preferences, choices, and agendas pursued by journalists in interviews and reports. More than half of Americans, 57 percent, believed in 2000 that members of the news media "often" let their political preferences influence the way they report the news; 32 percent said "sometimes" (Princeton/Pew, October 2000, 1,331). **Political bias** in media-based event coverage may derive from the journalist's identification with certain political principles and the interests of a particular party. Through the 20th century and today, the mainstream media in the United States are largely nonpartisan. Unlike many other democratic countries, major political parties in the United States today do not own mainstream newspapers and magazines. And yet, for many years, American media were charged with so-called liberal bias, that is, hidden and overt support of the Democratic Party and liberal values (Rothman & Lichter, 1987; Lichter et al., 1986; Margolis & Mauser, 1989). You can find similar arguments about whether or not the media have a liberal bias in recent arguments of journalists themselves on television news and commentary programs such as *Meet the Press* (NBC), *Crossfire* (CNN), or *Hannity and Colmes* (Fox News). The following arguments represent both supporters and opponents of the liberal bias theory (Croteau, 1998; Holhut, 1996).

- Most newspaper and television reporters do not represent the "real" America. Because of high salaries and educational degrees, most reporters, editors, and producers tend to reinforce values of the white liberal wing of the highly educated upper and upper middle class.

- On the other hand, most people from the upper classes tend to vote Republican, and there are linkages between the individual's social status and his or her ideological beliefs (see Chapter 8 on social class).

- Because contemporary liberal ideology focuses on active social involvement in issues, such as welfare, unemployment, healthcare, and the environment, reporters with liberal views have a better chance of having a report published or aired.

- On the other hand, these complaints about how easy it is to promote compassion are groundless and represent little more than camouflage for the lack of captivating ideas among conservatives.

- The liberal bias can be easily detected by looking at the content of major television networks and mainstream newspapers. It is true, for instance, that many large newspapers, such as the *New York Times* and the *Washington Post,* regularly endorse Democratic presidential candidates.

- On the other hand, empirical research on the content of the media, journalists' opinions, and arguments they use in the reports suggests a balance between opposing political views. Some argue that the conservative Fox News television network counterbalances the liberal CNN. Even though reporters and editors tend to be Democrats, publishers tend to be Republicans. The *Wall Street Journal* regularly endorses Republican candidates for president.

One argument frequently made about the political bias of major newspapers is that public opinion polls sponsored or conducted by news organizations, such as television networks and newspapers, are also biased. In this view, news organizations may conduct so-called push polls (see Chapter 1) so that respondents give answers the pollsters want them to. As a result, major newspapers and networks help their candidates with positive public-opinion images. Table 6.2 displays a comparison of opinion polls

TABLE 6.2

Measurement of voters' intentions in forthcoming 2000 presidential election: A comparative analysis. (In percentages.)

Fox News Polls			*Washington Post*/ABC Polls		
Dates	Gore	Bush	Dates	Gore	Bush
November 1 (likely voters, 1,000)	43	43	November 1 (likely voters, 1,495)	45	49
October 18 (likely voters, 900)	42	45	October 18 (likely voters, 1,920)	45	48
October 5 (likely voters, 900)	43	42	October 6 (likely voters, 925)	46	44
September 20 (likely voters, 900)	46	43	September 28 (national, 1,801)	47	44
September 6 (likely voters, 900)	46	43	September 6 (reg. voters, 925)	46	49

Source: September-November 2000, Fox News Polls and *Washington Post*/ABC Polls.

A CASE IN POINT **6.3** Partisan Media?

The debate about partisanship in American media continues. Look, for instance, at arguments used by both Republican and Democratic commentators about the 2000 presidential campaign and the media's handling of Al Gore and George Bush (Kurtz, 2000).

The Republican View	*The Democratic View*
Most journalists philosophically are liberal Democrats, and they cannot set aside their biases and report objectively. Take, for example, Clinton's presidency. Partly because of favorable media coverage, Clinton was able to maintain public support despite his numerous political and personal setbacks.	There was no favorable coverage of Clinton's presidency. Major newspapers led the way in unearthing scandals involving Clinton: The *New York Times* broke the Whitewater story, the *Los Angeles Times* was out front on the 1996 fundraising abuses, and the *Washington Post* broke the Monica Lewinsky story.
In September 2000, according to the Center for Media and Public Affairs, comments about Gore on the ABC, CBS, and NBC evening newscasts were 55 percent positive, compared with 35 percent positive for Bush.	Preferences change during the campaign, and so does the coverage. By contrast, Bush got 62 percent positive evaluations in July of 2000, according to the same report. There were negative evaluations of Democratic candidates, in general.
Democrats received primarily balanced coverage, whereas most Republicans received biased coverage; the reports about them shifted toward more negative evaluations. Bush was painted a soon-to-be loser in September 2000.	Bush enjoyed largely favorable press coverage, while Gore was depicted as a bumbling, wardrobe-changing stiff. When Gore was behind in the spring of 2000, his campaign was portrayed as constantly making mistakes. When Bush started losing in the polls, the coverage of Gore changed favorably.
Bush portrayed himself as a "compassionate conservative," yet he was stereotypically evaluated as a heartless person who cared only about the oil, the rich, and the execution of convicted criminals in Texas.	Journalists have been overly critical of Bush's combination of "compassionate" and "conservative" positions. The press has a hard time with candidates who try to invent new labels for themselves.

conducted by two news organizations, Fox News, which is frequently mentioned as a supporter of the Republican Party, and *Washington Post*/ABC, which is frequently mentioned as a supporter of the Democratic Party. As you can see, the results are nearly identical; the differences between two sets of opinion polls are statistically insignificant (with two exceptions, in which the *Washington Post*/ABC gave George W. Bush a slight lead).

TABLE 6.3
Types of Media Framing: A Summary.

Type of Framing	Description
Quantitative	A type of framing in which the events, circumstances, and human actions in a story or report are assigned numerical values or described with the help of numbers.
Priming	The capacity of the media to highlight issues and events as criteria for evaluating politicians.
Episodic	A type of framing that allows journalists to explain a certain issue or problem using descriptions of specific people in specific circumstances.
Thematic	A type of framing based on generalized knowledge and systematic analysis of a topic.
Political/Ideological	A type of framing based on identification and explanation of issues and individuals in terms of ideological or political principles.

THE MEDIA IMPACT

To what extent do media organizations affect people's opinions about important social and political issues? Do television reports and newspaper articles matter in determining individual votes? Surely, weather forecasts and traffic reports change our intentions and subsequent behavior. But in most situations, the influence of the media on the individual's opinions and behavior is less obvious. Moreover, in many situations it is difficult or even impossible to measure media effects. Overall, two opposing views about the impact of the media are widely debated (Table 6.3).

Media: A Significant Impact

Many Americans remember the events of 1982, when seven unsuspecting people in Chicago died after taking Tylenol laced with cyanide. It appears now that just one person in only one area of the country committed this criminal act. However, complaints about suspected poisoning multiplied across the country to epidemic proportions; apparently, thousands of people across the country reported experiencing alarming symptoms caused by something they had bought recently. *ABC News* and the *Washington Post* conducted a survey in October 1982 that showed that 100 percent of Americans knew about the Tylenol poisoning story (October, 505). Although 40 percent of surveyed people said the story was sensationalized (ABC, October 11, 505), 57 percent of Americans said that because of that tragic incident, they would be reluctant to buy nonprescription medications (NBC and Associated Press, October 18, 1,595). Elliot Aronson (1995) reported about a film, *Cry Rape,* that told the story of a rape victim who mistakenly identified an innocent man as her assailant. In 1973, in the weeks after the film was aired by CBS, the number of reported rapes decreased dramatically. Do you think people feared police would not believe them, as happened in the movie? Sociologists demonstrate that copycat crimes, such as robberies, assaults, and suicides, take place in bunches after the media publicize certain cases of criminal or deviant behavior.

Supporters of this view argue that people tend to respond to messages to which they are exposed (Geiss, 1987). In politics, as in commerce, people are inclined to buy things about which they know. Advertising often works.

Ideas about media impact are supported by authoritative sociological and psychological research. Bandura (1969) showed in experiments how people absorb the content of television programs by "observational learning" or "modeling." In Bandura's model, observational learning is more likely to occur when behavior is rewarded (or punished), when rewards or reinforcemens are administered by someone of high status, or when the observer can identify with the speaker. The observed behavior later is generalized and used by the individual (McBride, 1998). Furthermore, experimental evidence indicates that even a single viewing of value-laden programming can influence thoughts and behaviors as much as six weeks later (Ball-Rokeach et al., 1981). Media effects also result from exposure to public affairs programming, and they are cognitive, affective, and behavioral in their consequences (Ansolabehere & Iyengar, 1996).

Short-Term Effects

Arguments about media impact often refer to short-term effects, illustrated in the following examples: the presidential races between Jimmy Carter and Ronald Reagan (1980), George H. W. Bush and Michael Dukakis (1988), and Al Gore and George W. Bush (2000). Though the circumstances of these campaigns and their outcomes were different, they give rise to the same assumption: The media influenced some people's opinions at the last minute so their votes affected the outcome of elections. In 1980, the last Carter-Reagan debate was held one week before the elections. After the debate, several polls registered last-minute swings of preference; Reagan was gaining more support than Carter was. This rapid switch of preference by some voters may have cost Carter the electoral victory.

In 1988, then–Vice President George Bush ran a series of campaign ads designed to persuade the public that his opponent, Democratic candidate Michael Dukakis, was "soft on crime" during his tenure as governor of Massachusetts. To press the argument, the Bush campaign used the case of Willie Horton, a convicted felon briefly released from prison in a furlough program. During his furlough, Horton committed another crime by raping a woman. Absolutely unknown to Americans a few days earlier, Willie Horton was correctly identified by 24 percent of survey respondents in October of that year (*Times-Mirror,* October 1988, 2,006). Moreover, during this ad campaign, Bush gained many supporters. Did this advertising tactic help Bush attract votes? Many experts believe that was the case (Anderson, 1995).

In the fall of 2000, it was generally expected that Vice President Gore, because of his fine public speaking skills, would do a better job in the television debates than Texas governor Bush. Gore's supporters expected this outcome to lead undecided voters to choose the vice president. Unfortunately for the Gore campaign, post-debate polls showed that most Americans did not believe he scored a clear victory in the debates. As a probable result of this perceived tie, Gore gave the impression of underachievement and apparently did not get enough undecided votes in several highly contested states, and, eventually, he lost the election there.

Does the reporting of exit polls, which show how an election is going and which candidates are currently ahead or behind, on Election Day affect other voters' decisions? Some studies say no, it does not affect behavior (Graber, 2002); others say yes, it does (Morin, 2000). Researchers argue that the three major television networks and online journalists, in violation of a 1985 promise, released exit poll results long before the polls closed. Republican pundits complained that the early projection of Gore as the winner in the crucial state of Florida might have affected voting on the West Coast, where the polls were still open. In congressional hearings in 2001, news executives from ABC, CBS, CNN, NBC, and the Associated Press outlined several voluntary reforms for future election coverage. For example, the networks pledged not to declare the winner of any state's election until after all the polls closed there. CNN said it would not project a winner when the margin of victory was less than 1 percent. ABC said it would insulate its own election analysts from competing networks (WWW.MSNBC.COM; Feb 14, 2001). A similar problem occurred in 2004 when exit poll results were leaked to the media in the early afternoon, showing an initial lead for John Kerry (Morin, 2004).

Nevertheless, the assertions about the impact of early reporting are based on assumptions. A critically thinking individual can make at least two suggestions about possible effects of early reporting on turnout (see Table 6.4):

Some researchers conclude that the impact of the media on voter behavior is largely negative. The essential form of citizens' participation in politics, community affairs, and election campaigns changes from direct personal involvement to spectatorship. Political television shows concentrate on apparent problems rather than on their causes. They create a false impression of personal involvement in the viewer. Mesmerized by colorful pictures and emotional analyses, the viewer fails to participate and tends to delegate responsibility for representing his interests to analysts who appear on the shows or who write editorials and reports (Swanson & Mancini, 1996). Thomas Patterson (1993), in his popular book *Out of Order,* wrote that the U.S. news media grew more negative and more cynical in political coverage over the past 40 years, that this had matched a growing popular distrust of politicians and government and a general disengagement from civic life, and, as the result, that cynicism in the news contributed to cynicism in the electorate.

Other researchers are less critical of the media. For Norris (2000), the existence of "media malaise" (suggestions that media and political communication reduces civic activism, diminishes trust in government, and retards knowledge of and interest in public affairs) has little empirical support. In fact, people who follow the news know more about politics than those who do not. They are as trusting of political institu-

TABLE 6.4

Effects of Early Reporting: Alternative Explanations.

Early reporting may decrease turnout	*Early reporting may increase turnout*
Some voters who had planned to vote may choose not to vote late on Election Day when their candidate is trailing the opponent and their vote would not change the outcome.	Some voters who had not planned to vote may choose to vote because they feel their vote may help their candidate who is trailing or because they feel satisfied casting a vote for the sure winner.

tions as those less attentive to news. Media-driven malaise, according to Norris, does not exist. The best evidence, in fact, goes in the other direction: Active, politically engaged people attend to the news more than others, and that attention reinforces their political involvement. In industrial countries, people who attend to the news are significantly more likely to participate in political campaigns by voting, contributing money, or discussing politics. Watching hour after hour of entertainment television may be a factor in disengaging Americans from political and civic life (Putnam, 2000), but watching TV news is not. Norris does not find any relationship between increasing negativism in the news since the 1980s and popular trust in governing institutions, which has risen, fallen, and risen again in the same period.

Media: The Impact Is Exaggerated

Quite a few experts believe the impact of the media on people's opinions and decisions is generally overestimated. When Americans were asked about which influences have had a great impact on their life, only 5 percent mentioned media (Barna, January 1993, 1,205). Using content analysis, Patterson (1993) showed a substantial and growing gap between what reporters and the public consider important and meaningful issues.

A history of research of media effects on people's attitudes and subsequent behavior shows a remarkable picture of both surging enthusiasm and skepticism. Before the 1930s, empirical research on persuasion showed that radio and newspapers became major sources of daily information in economically developed countries. Once a luxury item, the radio became a necessary possession for every family and an important means of communication in nondemocratic societies as well. Stalin in the Soviet Union, Hitler in Germany, Franco in Spain, and Mussolini in Italy used the radio for propaganda. It was generally believed by researchers in the 1920s and 1930s that despite psychological resistance, people were vulnerable to persuasion, and therefore radio and newspapers can change people's opinions. John Watson, a founding father of American behaviorism, earnestly supported this view. The enthusiasm for it, however, began to wane in the 1940s. Numerous studies conducted at that time measured the effects of media exposure on the individual's attitudes and behavior. The conclusion was muted: Most studies found that only some messages, under particular circumstances, in some individuals, produce only small changes.

For example, sociologists examined the effects of exposure to information on voters' intentions (Lazarsfeld et al., 1948). A main finding of this study was disappointing and surprising: Little evidence was found to support the view that the greater one's exposure to news and information, the higher the likelihood that initial attitude would change. For some people, however, exposure to newspapers reinforced their initial attitudes. Other studies showed that voters tend to be attentive to articles or radio messages that confirm their initial beliefs or intentions (Klapper, 1960). Messages conflicting with their personal beliefs were routinely ignored or forgotten (Nimmo, 1970).

Skeptics imply that presidential debates seem to influence a limited number of people. For example, answering a survey question about whether anything they learned from or about the 2000 presidential debates made them change their minds about whom to vote for, 86 percent of respondents said "no" and only 14 percent said "yes" (CBS, October 2000, 617). A bit more detailed are results of a poll asking whether voters changed their opinion about the presidential candidates after watching them debate (Table 6.5).

TABLE 6.5

After tonight's (Oct. 3, 2000, presidential) debate, how has **your** opinion of Al Gore and George W. Bush changed? (In percentages.)

	Al Gore	*George W. Bush*
Changed for the better	32	35
Changed for the worse	22	21
No change	46	44

Source: CBS, October 3, 2000, registered voters, 812.

As you see from the table, almost half of the surveyed voters did not think they changed their opinion about the candidates, yet more than half believed their opinion did change. Nevertheless, these results are likely to indicate that many people who like a particular candidate tend to change their opinion about him for the better. Likewise, many individuals who dislike a candidate changed their opinion for the worse. As the percentage points in this table show, Al Gore and George Bush had approximately equal numbers of supporters whose opinions switched.

We must think critically, however, to avoid overemphasizing the impact of a single debate or a single political ad on people's choices. Likewise, one negative issue, one problem associated with the candidate, even when it is primed by the media, does not necessarily cause a decrease in voters' support. Many other factors and circumstances affect voters' opinions and subsequent voting decisions.

People tend not to change their initial attitudes after watching television, reading newspapers, or listening to the radio. In 1998, after the allegations that President Clinton had had an affair with a White House intern spread over the media, 63 percent of Americans said this information did not change their opinion about the president's credibility. Only 13 percent of survey respondents suggested that their opinion of Clinton became much less favorable. The largest proportion of those who said Clinton became much less credible, in their opinion, were Republicans, 17 percent of whom said their perception changed (*Los Angeles Times,* January 1998, 1,191). Only 14 percent of surveyed voters in the United States believed media coverage of electoral campaigns has the most impact on deciding the presidential election (VNS/ABC News, CBS News, NBC News, Fox News, CNN, Associated Press, November 1996, exiting voters 16,637). Seventy percent of respondents said the candidates themselves have the most impact.

THE MEDIA IMPACT: CRITICAL THINKING EVALUATIONS

Which argument is a more realistic assessment of the media's impact on people's opinions? The extent of the impact depends on several intervening and contextual factors. Among these factors are the individual's prior knowledge, exposure to information, and the trustworthiness of the information source. For more detailed analyses of factors affecting public opinion, look back at Chapter 4 on attitudes, and Chapter 5 on political socialization.

Direct Exposure to Issues

For people who lack direct exposure to an event, such as the outbreak of a deadly virus in a foreign country, media images can be crucial to their understanding of and reactions to the information received (McBride, 1998). To illustrate, let us return to the 1992 presidential campaign in the United States. The third-party candidate, H. Ross Perot, decided to launch a series of self-sponsored television lectures in which he tried to educate Americans about his economic and social views. Did people change their opinions about him? We would anticipate that most of them did not. Do you remember the survey results that indicate little change in people's opinions of candidates after televised presidential debates? Yet, in the case of Perot, 41 percent of the surveyed registered voters who saw the lecture/commercial said their opinion did change (CBS/*New York Times*, 1,854), maybe because he appeared alone.

Previous Commitments

Frustrated, fearful, excited, or motivated individuals are more susceptible to information relevant to their state of mind than are less motivated or uninterested individuals (Hovland et al., 1957). Furthermore, people tend to expose themselves to information and images they already like, approve of, or support. This phenomenon is called **selective exposure.** Therefore, the messages disseminated by the media are more likely to reinforce predispositions than to convert people from one view to another. Political ads rarely convert partisan voters to a different party. However, the media impact can still be significant; it was shown that ads can solidify support among those already committed to a particular candidate or among undecided individuals (Ansolabahere & Iyengar, 1995). Supporters of a politician are likely to continue supporting him or her, no matter what kind of negative information is presented. Partisan views affect the way information is filtered. Thus, after President Clinton's speech on February 17, 1993, on his economic policy, only 9 percent of Democrats said their opinion about the president changed to less favorable, whereas 40 percent of Republicans said the same (Gallup/*Newsweek*, February 1993, 753).

Extraordinary events receive significant media exposure and influence people's opinions about what they see. John F. Kennedy was considered an above-average president during his presidency, and his approval ratings were high. However, his assassination produced an upward shift in people's perception of his life and presidency. In 1983, 20 years after his assassination, 26 percent of Americans referred to Kennedy as one of the greatest presidents of all times (Harris, November 1983, 1,252). Although Americans have diverse opinions about who is the "greatest president," Kennedy is ranked very high. In 2003, for instance, he and Abraham Lincoln were named the "greatest" by 17 percent of Americans (Gallup, November 2003, 1,004).

Knowledge and Education

Responses to messages vary substantially with the level of political knowledge and sophistication of the individual (Zaller, 1992; Kimball, 1995). Thus, argument-based messages tend to be more effective to an audience that is knowledgeable about the issue presented in the message. Image-based information is more effective when the audience has little or no knowledge of the issue. More educated people have greater access to media sources; therefore, they are potentially exposed to a greater variety of information than are less educated people (Hibbing & Theiss-Morse, 1998). At the same time, the more educated tend to not be persuaded by a single report or article because they can recall or tune into other informational sources that cover the same issue. Knowledgeable people tend to be less gullible than those who know less. People who are less educated and have limited access to information sources tend to be more persuadable because they do not have enough opportunities to recall conflicting reports or to seek additional information on the issue at hand (McGuire, 1968).

The Communicator's Features

One important factor contributing to media's influence on attitudes is the credibility of the source in the eyes of the audience. Early studies in cognitive psychology indicated that the more credible the source, the better the information is received by the audience (Heider, 1949). In particular, Hovland and Weiss (1951) showed that in situations of uncertainty, when asked to evaluate a printed text, an individual tends to express more sympathetic views if the source is attributed to trustworthy authors.

The second important factor contributing to the effectiveness of communication is people's trust in information sources. To illustrate, 52 percent of Americans said they trust either "all" or "most" of what local television anchors state in their reports; 42 percent said the same about major network anchors (FFMC, March 1998, 1,001). In 2003, the expression of trust remained practically unchanged; 41 percent said they trusted television news anchors (CSRA, September 2003, 1,005).

The Overall Impact of the Media

The critical analysis of the impact of the media on attitudes and behavior continues as an exchange of arguments and counterarguments about the role and functioning of media in today's society.

Argument.   The media today are a powerful force that influences the lives of millions of individuals. From direct propaganda and brainwashing to the most sophisticated concealed spins, the media help sell policies, promote political ideas, and endorse politicians. Mass media can put anyone on a pedestal or destroy him. Many politicians modify their behavior because they know they will be in the news (Semetko et al., 1991). Because people spend more time reading news and watching moving images, they have less time available for other important social activities (McBride, 1998; Putnam, 2000). At the end of the 1990s, the average adult American spent more than 1,000 hours per year watching television, a mean of more than three hours per day. Eighty percent of employed Americans said they had either cable television or satellite dish service in their homes (ICR, October 2003, 504). In 2002, 52 percent of Americans said they regularly watch an evening news program, such as *ABC World News Tonight, CBS Evening News,* or *NBC Nightly News* (Princeton/Pew, April 2002, 3,002). Computers and the Internet also keep Americans glued to their chairs. In a 2000 survey, people were asked how much time they spent online the day before. Fifteen percent said they spent more than three hours, 20 percent spent between one and three hours, and another 36 percent spent from 30 minutes to one hour online (Princeton/Pew, March 2000, 3,533). One study estimated that if this pattern persists, the average person will spend the equivalent of nine years in front of the television or computer by the time she reaches the age of 65 (Woodward, 1997). Overall, the media have become almost an omnipotent social power with an agenda of their own.

Counterargument. The media are very important in contemporary life and able to influence public opinion. However, the influence goes in both directions: People's needs, interests, and demands influence the media to follow public opinion. The mass media in the United States, as in most democratic countries, are mostly privately owned. Money is needed to run newspaper, TV, and radio businesses, and the funds come almost exclusively from advertising. Commercial time and ad space are sold in America like any other product. Therefore, media professionals try to create and select those programs that will attract large audiences so advertisers will pay more money to run commercials. It is simple: If only a few people watch a show, sponsors will not buy advertising on it, and if there is no money, there will be no show. People use mass media for entertainment and education. From weather and traffic reports to stock market updates, the practical value of the media is enormous. For instance, why do local television stations broadcast weather reports so often? Because these reports receive the highest rating among viewers; people want to know what it's like outside! Since the 1990s, the Internet has provided access to all kinds of information that was previously unavailable. Almost 8 out of 10 Americans in the late 1990s believed the growing informational power of the Internet is a positive development (NFOR/ Ogilvy, July 1998, mail 500). Overall, people can choose what they watch, read, and browse. If they do not want to, they can do something else.

Argument. Consumers today have significantly more sources of information, radio stations, television networks, websites, cable companies, or newspapers, than they did 5 or 10 years ago. Technological opportunities available to journalists are growing at an unprecedented speed. Innovations, such as digital recorders, cell phones, and laptop computers, were introduced to reporters relatively recently. Not long before, satellite connections, cellular networks, the Internet, and email were science fiction props. Today, instant access to new technologies allows news organizations to receive, analyze, and disseminate information 24 hours a day. Breaking news is no longer distributed by morning and evening newspapers. In the era of electronic journalism, reporters are expected to grind out stories around the clock and bring the viewer "live" to almost any place on earth.

Counterargument. It is a paradox, but the vast technological advances and increased competition among media news sources create additional pressures on those responsible for printing, posting, and broadcasting. Competition was limited when newspapers were the only medium in the United States. Then came radio. After that, three major television networks were established that dominated the American market before the rapid development of cable and satellite television and the Internet. As a result, broadcast news has struggled for profits since the 1990s. Christiane Amanpour (2001) of CNN mentioned in an interview that "it actually costs a little bit of money to produce good journalism, to travel, to investigate, to produce compelling viewing on-screen and to give people a reason to watch us." The cost of gathering and reporting information rose in the face of a steadily declining audience. News broadcasts from major television networks lost millions of dollars every year since the mid-1990s. Live coverage of important developments is typically commercial-free and, therefore, financially unattractive for radio and television networks. In the 1990s, major networks lost market share, which led to less money, which led to downsizing and restructuring. On the corporate level, the concentration of media sources accelerated. Because of corporate mergers, television networks, newspapers, and magazines have become part of large media companies. The results? Sameness is replacing diversity in contemporary mass media. One quick look at the headlines of major newspapers and the websites of major networks reveals similar pictures. Day after day, virtually the same topics and issues are the focus of attention of journalists and editors.

How does the Internet affect television viewers' habits? Do people spend less time watching television and reading newspapers because of the new online sources of information? Most studies show that the impact of the Internet on the distribution of viewing patterns is not significant. According to one study of Internet users, fewer than 2 percent said they were trading time spent watching television solely for Internet usage. Only 1.5 percent of the more than 17,000 randomly selected Internet users surveyed in the study of nine television network sites said they watched less television because they were spending time online (Burke, 1999). In 2000, Americans were asked to name their favorite activities; 23 percent mentioned "watching television" and only 6 percent suggested computers (Harris, June 2000, 1,015). Things change, however. The integration of television and the Internet should transform some viewing and net-browsing habits.

Argument.   Freedom of choice is a prized value of democratic society. Everyone has access to the power button or remote control. These devices help filter meaningful news from that which is less important and make it easier to turn to information sources that do the best job. All information in a variety of forms and genres becomes available to the people, who decide what they want to read or watch, and in what quantities. Viewers are not duped by just one website or television channel. People exercise their choices. Some choose appointment television and watch their favorite news daily at a certain time. Others prefer a 24-hour news coverage format (for example, CNN Headline News or Fox News) so they can check recent developments when they want to. It is increasingly common for viewers to check a network's website, get information about an event or program, and then watch this network's programming. Surveys show that, after watching a program, people go to its network's website for more information (Burke, 1999).

Counterargument.   Because of the way the news is produced today, the line between significant and unimportant news is blurry. Years ago, experts began to express concern about the impact of sensationalism; being preoccupied with flashy images, the media were replacing heroes with celebrities (Safire, 1978). This negative tendency has developed further since the 1970s. As John Sommerville (1999) points out in *How the News Makes Us Dumb,* people used to get the news only when something newsworthy happened. Today, because of competition, newsworthiness is often artificially created and inflated by journalists, editors, and producers. Intimate details of people's lives become news. Professional rewards seem to flow toward reporters who expose or accentuate inter-

 personal conflict and scandals. Kerbel (2000) compares the techniques used by networks' news divisions to those of talk show hosts. Local television news anchors also adopt a format similar to that of the talk shows: brevity, simplicity, and shocking entertainment.

ASSIGNMENT 6.1 BEER COMMERCIALS

Note: This assignment is based on a dramatization.

Situation and role:
You are an independent media consultant hired by the attorney general's office of your home state to create a report.

Political plot:
Both the governor and the attorney general seek reelection in three years on their pledge to balance the state budget. It is obvious this goal cannot be achieved without a substantial revenue increase. However, public opinion in the state is against new taxes. Efforts to tax certain products and services failed as well. For example, previous attempts by the governor to raise taxes on beer sales through legislation have failed. Beer companies use their economic power in the political system of the state. (It is the rare state legislator who can afford to turn down campaign contributions from the beer industry.) Litigation is the best chance for the state to challenge beer companies. A lawsuit against beer companies has been filed.

Issue explained to you:
Why the lawsuit? The beer industry has a long history of denying that its products have harmful effects. This strategy, so far successful, was developed to refute reports of health risks, public safety risks associated with beer drinking, the addictive nature of beer, and the targeting of adolescents and young adults by beer commercials on television. This policy of beer giants has limited discussion of how society should address beer drinking. Meanwhile, the state pays millions of dollars for a wide range of problems resulting from or related to beer consumption, such as drinking-related crimes, teenage drinking, car accidents and injuries, alcohol rehabilitation programs, and medical care for beer-related health problems. By advertising beer on television, beer companies promote drinking. In fact, the taxpayer is a victim and should be compensated by the beer industry. All in all, how are beer companies able to continue making large profits in the face of significant evidence that use of their product can be dangerous and sometimes fatal, especially for the young? Attorneys for the beer industry suggest that neither children nor adolescents pay attention to beer ads. Beer advertising's purpose is to get drinkers of competitive products to switch. This is virtually the only way a beer brand can immediately increase its business.

Goals to achieve:
Analyze beer commercials on television. Look for evidence, or lack thereof, that:

1. Beer commercials promote social acceptance of beer drinking.
2. The beer industry's claims that beer drinkers are overwhelmingly a mature market are wrong.
3. Beer imagery appeals to adolescents and, often, to children.
4. Beer commercials appeal to the adolescent need for autonomy.
5. Beer commercials give the product friendly familiarity for the young.
6. Beer commercials *deliberately* target the young.

Background:

Evidence: According to several studies, including the Alcohol Advertising on Television project (camy.org/research/tv1004/), (a) adolescence is a time of identity formation and advertising attentiveness, and youth are persuasion-susceptible novices; (b) no isolation protects youth from beer ads; (c) for beer companies, youths are strategically more attractive than adults; and (d) teens are more responsive than adults to beer ads. (See also Schooler et al., 1996.)

Procedures:

Select and videotape 10 beer commercials. Specify the network, date, and time of broadcast. Analyze the commercials using the strategies above. Pay attention to the following: Who appears on the commercials—that is, what is their age, sex, occupation, social role? What do they say; what do they do? Compare the "childishness" and the maturity of the commercials. Examine music and sound effects. Note the program during which each commercial appears (a sports show, a soap opera, a sitcom, etc.).

Reports:

Submit both qualitative and quantitative reports to your sponsor's office (700 words minimum). Support your arguments with empirical evidence. Use charts and/or tables. Give numbers and percentages. Do not use phrases such as "In many commercials I found . . ." or "In some ads there are some men who. . . ." Be precise. Do not forget, you are participating in an important political campaign, and your report will be used in court hearings.

CHAPTER SUMMARY

- The role and function of the news media are widely debated. On the one hand, they are viewed as powerful and intrusive forces that influence the lives of millions of individuals. On the other, people's needs, interests, and demands influence the media to follow public opinion.

- On the one hand, the consumer today can choose from many more sources of information (radio, network television, cable television, websites, newspapers) than were available 5 or 10 years ago. On the other, sameness is replacing diversity as the contemporary mass media merge; the contents of major newspapers and networks are becoming more similar.

- On one side, the viewer can clearly judge what is important and what is not. On the other, because of the way the news is produced today, the line between significant and unimportant news is blurring.

- Camouflaged under labels, such as *regulations* and *restrictions*, censorship is a powerful tool used by governments, large corporations, and the media to make certain information unavailable to the public. Political, ideological, and moral reasons are used to justify the practice of censorship.

- At least four categories of news are disseminated by the media: available, discovered, practical, and entertaining.

- Circumstances and conditions make some events newsworthy. Events are newsworthy when they have direct impact on the individual; when they become important and recognizable people are involved in them; when they give the media an opportunity to provide ratings-boosting interpretations of these events; and when they are extraordinary.

- At least two mechanisms exist whereby the news can make an impact: agenda setting and framing. Types of framing include quantitative, qualitative, priming, episodic, thematic, ideological, and political.

- Political bias in media-based event coverage may derive from the journalist's identification with political principles and the interests of a particular party. Due to 20th-century historical and economic developments, the mainstream media in the United States are largely nonpartisan.

- Two opposing views about the media's impact on attitudes are widely debated. According to the first view, the media have a tremendous impact on people's opinions and behavior. According to the second view, the impact of the media on people's opinions and decisions is grossly overestimated.

- Several factors mediate and determine the effectiveness of the media impact on the individual. Among them are direct exposure to issues, previous commitments, knowledge and education, and the communicators' features.

Looking Ahead. Chapter 7, on "Gender and Opinions," begins the exploration of important factors other than the media that affect public opinion. As a formative element of individuals and their social environment, gender affects people's social opportunities and opinions. The chapter critically examines the gender gap from sociological, sociobiological, and socialization approaches.

DEFINITIONS OF KEY TERMS

Agenda setting—The process that determines what becomes news and what does not.

Available news—Information that is easily obtainable, such as sports scores, weather forecasts, reports about public events, or decisions made by politicians and public officials.

Censorship—The practice of government or other sources to restrict for moral, ideological, or political reasons the information made available for publication or broadcast.

Discovered news—Information that is typically uncovered by means of journalistic investigation.

Entertaining news—Information that has primarily an enjoyment value.

Episodic framing—The type of framing that allows journalists and commentators to describe specific people in specific circumstances.

Ideological censorship—The practice of endorsing a set of ideas or principles about society's past, present, and future and of restricting access to information that challenges these ideas and principles.

Media frames—The form and context used by journalists for interpreting news.

Moral censorship—The practice of endorsing a set of standards of decency and public morality.

Political bias—In media-based coverage of events, the journalist's identification with the principles and interests of a particular party or group.

Political censorship—The practice of a government to ban information that undermines the authority of the state or that of a ruling party.

Practical news—Information that serves an individual's pragmatic goals.

Priming—A type of framing that refers to the capacity of the media to highlight issues and events as criteria for evaluating politicians and officials; a type of framing.

Selective exposure—The tendency of people to expose themselves to information and images they already like, approve of, or support.

Thematic framing—The type of framing that is based on a systematic analysis of a topic.

Quantitative framing—The type of framing in which events, circumstances, and human actions are assigned numerical values.

CHAPTER 7

Gender
and Opinions

We hold these truths to be self-
evident, that all men and women are
created equal.

Elizabeth Cady Stanton (1815–1902)

As part of a project that included in-depth interviews of people who recently acquired U.S. citizenship and were planning to vote in upcoming elections, an interviewer sat down with Kasa, a 27-year-old single mother and immigrant from Cameroon. She was a college junior pursuing a nursing career. The interview was not supposed to be long, and Kasa worked quickly on her answers. At the end, she was asked to identify her political party affiliation. Kasa seemed puzzled and, after hesitating for a few seconds, asked for examples to help her assess her party preference. "Sure," the interviewer said. "Here are a few examples. What do you think about . . . the extent of the federal government's involvement in running the country?" "As little as possible," she replied swiftly. "Well, this is a Republican view. What is your position on abortion?" "It is up to the woman." "Quite Democratic. Now what is your position on the affirmative action?" "Good idea." "Death penalty?" "Keep it." "U.S. military actions abroad?" "Bring every soldier back." "Non-military help to foreign countries?" "It has to be increased." "State-sponsored healthcare?" "Good idea." "School prayer?" "Kids should pray." The interviewer stopped asking questions. "You know, you are answering both ways; it is difficult to say whether you are a Democrat or Republican. Maybe you should study the issues a bit and make your decision later." "Sure," Kasa replied with a big smile. "Perhaps I will make my choice from the perspective of a woman."

Contrary to what some popular books say, men and women are not from different planets. Every man and woman was born and bred on Earth; all breathe the same air, eat the same food, walk down the same streets. They hope for, worry about, and believe in similar things. Or do they?

Looking Forward. Chapter 7, "Gender and Opinions," begins the exploration of how important factors in political socialization other than the media, such as the differences (and similarities) between men and women as social groups, affect public attitudes. As a formative element of individuals and their social environment, gender affects social opportunities, attitudes, party identification, and the likelihood of political involvement. The chapter critically examines the gender gap in attitudes on important issues, such as the economy, social welfare, war and peace, and political participation from sociological, cultural, sociobiological, and socialization perspectives.

GENDER GAP

How different are the opinions of men and women as groups? Studies of the so-called **gender gap** in voting choices and opinions began in the 1960s. The first research articles on a gender gap in attitudes reported it was small and had little significance. Later, however, researchers paid more attention to the gap as a serious issue of political consequence (Trevor, 1999). They uncovered not only opinion differences between men and women but also differences in the ways women of different backgrounds, age, and social groups expressed their attitudes and values. Studies conducted in the 1960s and the early 1970s showed that women as a group tended to be more oriented than men toward local political issues, especially those pertaining to schools and education. Men, in contrast, displayed greater interest in national and international affairs (Jennings & Niemi, 1981).

Studies in the 1970s showed that women were more supportive than men of a guaranteed annual income, wage and price controls, wealth equalization, guaranteed jobs, state-provided healthcare, and government-assisted student loans (Shapiro & Mahajan, 1986). In the late 1970s, politically active working-class women, when they expressed their concerns for family values, were in fact exposing conservative views of gender roles. These women emphasized that their main goals were realized at home, with their families, and not necessarily in the workplace (McCourt, 1977). Overall, studies showed that political conservatism was negatively correlated with women's educational level; in other words, women who earned higher educational degrees tended to be more liberal than their less educated peers (Welch & Sigelman, 1982) and voted accordingly. Early research on women's opinions also addressed violence, safety, and overall well-being. Look, for example, at the results of the 1971 American Women's Opinion Poll (VS, October, personal 4,000), in which women and men were asked to identify their top five concerns from a list. Figure 7.1 shows the distribution of answers.

As you can see, even though the differences between the assigned ranks and expressed views were not overwhelming (although statistically significant, except attitudes toward crime), women were more concerned than men with two deadly issues: the Vietnam War and curbing drug abuse.

Contemporary Polls and the Gender Gap

What do more recent polls reveal about the gender gap? Look at a relatively contemporary selection of issues for which a statistically significant gender gap was established (Table 7.1). Compare this to survey results in which the differences between opinions were not statistically significant (Table 7.2).

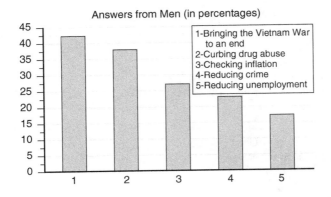

Answers from Men (in percentages)

1-Bringing the Vietnam War to an end
2-Curbing drug abuse
3-Checking inflation
4-Reducing crime
5-Reducing unemployment

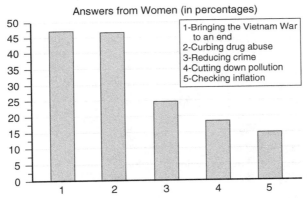

Answers from Women (in percentages)

1-Bringing the Vietnam War to an end
2-Curbing drug abuse
3-Reducing crime
4-Cutting down pollution
5-Checking inflation

FIGURE 7.1

Five top choices of men and women answering the question: "If you had to choose, which two or three problems on the list do you feel should be attacked first?"
Source: VS, October 1971, personal, 4,002.

In most surveys, the differences between men's and women's responses are not particularly large; in many cases, they are in single digits (as you can see from other tables and charts in this chapter). Differences within a 5-point range are typically not statistically significant. Other polls, however, demonstrate a larger gender gap. Among the issues about which men and women, as social groups, tend to express different opinions are violence and safety. For instance, in 2003, nearly 44 percent of American women voters said their religious beliefs would be an important factor in the 2004 elections, compared to 33 percent of men who said the same (Pew, December 2003, registered voters, 867). Pew Research Center for the People and the Press revealed in another study that when asked which was more important, gun owners' rights or gun control, 49 percent of the men polled chose rights and 46 percent control. In contrast, 28 percent of the women chose gun rights and 67 percent gun control (Pew, May 2000, 1,303).

Here is another example. Overall, 56 percent of Americans, as reflected in a 1997 study, believed that "A person who has been convicted of drunk driving should be

TABLE 7.1

Gender Gap in Attitudes About Various Issues (1993–2003).

Issue (Date, organization, sample)	Overall	Women	Men	Gap
Faith would be extremely or very important to help shape my vote for president in 2004 (Pew, December 2003, registered voters, 867)	39	44	33	11
Support of death penalty (ABC/WP, January 2003, 1,133)	64	55	74	− 19
Strongly approve of the way George W. Bush is handling his job as president (WP, November 2001, 759)	69	66	71	− 5
Military retaliation against terrorism even if innocent people are killed (CBS, September 11, 2001, 402)	66	57	75	− 18
Freedom of speech should not extend to groups like the Communist Party or the Ku Klux Klan (Pew, November 1997, 1,165)	38	45	31	14
The government should ban all cigarette advertising (ABC, June 1997, 1,001)	53	59	46	13
The ground war in Iraq would be worth the cost of several thousand American troops (CBS/NY Times, February 1998, 1,153)	30	23	39	− 16
Nude magazines and X-rated movies provide harmless entertainment for those who enjoy it (Pew, November 1997, 1,165)	41	36	46	− 10
There should be a law barring illegal immigrants from public schools, public hospitals and other state-run social services (ABC/WP, August 1996, 1,514)	49	45	54	9
Very interested in politics (Princeton/CRP/Pew, April 1997, 1,404)	29	24	33	− 9
Profanities in movies are not offensive to me (Gallup/CNN/USA Today, July 1999, 1,031)	24	28	20	8
Federal spending on foreign aid should be decreased (NY Times, April 1998, 1,395)	49	44	53	− 9
Sexual materials lead people to commit rape (GSS, February–April 1993, personal, 1,606)	57	62	50	12
Everyone convicted of drunk driving should have a special sign on their license plate so that everyone would know (Princeton/Newsweek, January 1995, 753)	51	54	49	5

prohibited from purchasing a gun," while 41 percent disagreed. A closer look at the gender factor reveals a significant disagreement between men and women: 52 percent of men rejected the idea of linking drunken driving and gun purchase restrictions (45 percent supporting), but 66 percent of women supported it (30 percent opposing) (ICR/Hearst, August

TABLE 7.2

Gender Similarities in Attitudes About Various Issues (1993–2001).

Issue (Date, organization, sample)	Overall	Women	Men	Gap
Support for military retaliation against countries supporting terrorism (Gallup, September 14–22, 2001, 2,042)	89	88	90	– 2
Oppose the legality of same-sex marriages (May 1993, *U.S. News,* registered voters, 1,000)	74	73	74	– 1
Consider an extramarital affair always harmful to a marriage (*Newsweek,* September 1996, 751)	70	68	72	– 4
Abortion should be illegal (CBS, January 2003, 814)	22	24	20	4
When a woman becomes pregnant through rape, abortion should be legal (AP/ICR, January 1998, 1,012)	74	75	73	2
The death penalty for someone convicted of rape (*Time*/CNN/Yankelovich, June 1997, 1,024)	47	49	46	3

1997, 2,016). In an October 1999 poll of public attitudes and social values, Pew Research Center found that 60 percent of women agreed with the statement "Books that contain dangerous ideas should be banned from school libraries," while only 48 percent of men supported this view. Forty-four percent of women said freedom of speech should not extend to groups such as the Communist Party or Ku Klux Klan; about 33 percent of men agreed. (Note, however, that despite the opinion gap, a majority of both men and women disagree with the idea of free speech restrictions.) About 50 percent of women thought the police should be allowed to search the houses of known drug dealers without a court order. In contrast, 40 percent of men thought it would be acceptable (Loth, 2000).

Women, as compared to men, tend to express greater concern about economic issues. As an example, in Great Britain there was a significant gender gap in attitudes about adopting a single European currency (the euro), which was officially established in 2002 in other European countries. During the debates about the proposed new currency, more women than men feared adopting the euro would mean higher interest and mortgage rates (47 percent of women to 35 percent of men) and would be bad overall for the British economy (41 percent to 31 percent) (Perkins, 1999). Nevertheless, in the bigger picture, a majority of both men and women in Great Britain did not think the euro would harm the economy.

Many polls on economic and social security issues yield small to nonexistent differences between the opinions of men and women. In a 2000 poll, American respondents were asked about Social Security. Sixteen percent of men and women wanted to keep Social Security unchanged. Overall, 33 percent of men and 37 percent of women opted for minor reforms to protect current beneficiaries; and 44 percent of men and 39 percent of women agreed to allow individuals to take responsibility for their future earnings by investing a portion of their payroll taxes in personal retirement accounts (DiVall, 2000). As you can see, the gap here is slight.

Fewer women than men support the death penalty (Delli Carpini & Keeter, 1996; Ellsworth & Gross, 1994). In the 1980s and 1990s, many polls revealed consistent 10-point differences between the sexes with respect to capital punishment. When answering the question "What do you think should be the penalty for murder committed by a woman—the death penalty or life imprisonment with absolutely no possibility of parole?" 50 percent of Americans supported the death penalty and 38 suggested life imprisonment (CNN/*USA Today,* January 1998, 1,004). In this survey, men overwhelmingly supported the death penalty compared to life in prison (a 62–28 percent ratio), whereas more women supported life sentences (47–38 in favor of life terms). In the 2000s, men continued to be significantly more supportive of capital punishment than were women. Nearly three-quarters of men (74 percent) supported the death penalty in 2003, compared to 55 percent of women (ABC/WP, January 2003, 1,133).

American women, in general, were less enthusiastic than men about defense spending. Expressing their views on U.S. military actions abroad, consistently more men than women agreed with interventionist options, such as air strikes and troop deployment. Since 1975, men generally have been more willing than women to increase government defense spending (Holsti, 1992; Smith, 1984). Of virtually all military campaigns abroad, beginning with World War II and the Korean War in the 1940s and 1950s and continuing through the Vietnam campaign in the 1960s and 1970s and later involvements in the Caribbean, Central America, the Persian Gulf, and Afghanistan, women were less supportive than men. However, the gender gap on foreign involvement issues was small, mostly in single digits (Fukuyama, 2000; Holsti, 1996).

Women show greater support than men for school prayer, social welfare measures, jail terms for drunk drivers, and bans on cigarette advertisement. They are also more likely than men to oppose legalized gambling, legalized drug use, and prostitution. Women are more likely than men to see candidates' stand on abortion as an important component of their voting decisions. They also tend to maintain more tolerant (pro-choice) attitudes toward abortion than men do (Andersen, 1997; see Chapter 11 on domestic issues). Research also indicates that women are generally more inclusive and tolerant and less prejudiced than men on a variety of ethnic and racial issues (Sidanius & Pratto, 1993; 1999).

Are there gender differences in voting turnout and other political activities? For many years, fewer women than men participated in national and presidential elections. In the 1968 presidential elections, for example, 5 percent more men than women voted. Eight years later, when Jimmy Carter was elected president, for the first time women outnumbered men at the polls. In the 1990s and the early 2000s, women con-

---

A CASE IN POINT 7.1   The Gender Gap in Surveys of Other Countries

The gender gap in Great Britain concerning people's interest in politics is noticeable. Although the gap between men and women who reported reading major newspapers is small (10 percent), expressed interest in politics is bigger. For example, 63 percent of women in Great Britain proclaim themselves "not interested" in politics, compared with 31 percent of men (Toynbee, 2000).

stituted from 52 to 54 percent of the presidential electorate (Page, 2000). Higher voter turnout provides the basis for women's wider political influence.

Table 7.3 shows a gender gap in party identification. Analyses of American National Election Studies conducted from 1952 to 1996 show that women usually identified slightly more than men did with the Democratic Party. During the last 30 years of the 20th century, women were less likely than men to support Republican candidates. There were exceptions, however, and the gap was primarily in single digits. Since the 1980s, a higher proportion of men lean toward the Republican Party. In addition, men are more likely than women to consider themselves political independents, and women are more likely than men to claim a partisan identity (Norrander, 1999, 1997). In 2004 more women voted for Kerry than for Bush.

As you can see from the table, changes in party affiliation began to appear in the 1970s. There was a slow but steady decline in men's identification with the Democratic Party, a slight increase in women's identification with the Democratic Party, and a decrease in the identification of both sexes as political independents.

In recent years, however, a change occurred among younger voters: The partisan gender gap has been diminishing. As a 2002 *Washington Post* poll shows, one of the most prominent trends is that young women are rejecting the Democratic Party more often than did their mothers or grandmothers (WP/Kaiser/Princeton, September 2002, 2,886), but most of these do not choose the Republican Party instead. They have become more likely to describe themselves as independents or supporters of a minor political party. Approximately 34 percent of women between the ages of 18 and 37 identified with the Republican Party, compared with 32 percent of similarly younger men. Meanwhile, 30 percent of the younger women and 23 percent of the men said they were Democrats. This poll also showed a 9-point Democrat-Republican gap between younger women and men. The gap between senior Americans (75 and older) is 20 points.

Combined with higher female voter turnout, the partisan gender gap creates the potential for women to support and implement social and political policies more

TABLE 7.3

American National Election Studies.
Party identification (D—Democratic, R—Republican, I—Independent). (In percentages).

	1992	1982	1972	1962	1952
Men D	32	39	37	50	48
Women D	40	50	44	47	49
	1992	1982	1972	1962	1952
Men R	28	26	23	27	26
Women R	23	23	24	32	30
	1992	1982	1972	1962	1952
Men I	38	35	39	24	26
Women I	32	27	32	20	21

Source: American National Election Services, 1952–92.

A CASE IN POINT **7.2** Women and the Use of Military Force

Richard Eichenberg analyzed gender differences on the use of military force by the United States in 455 public opinion surveys from 1990 to 2002. Several important conclusions emerge from the analysis. First, on average, women are less supportive of the use of military force for any purpose. Second, variations in the magnitude of gender differences largely confirm the reasoning of past theory and research: Women are relatively more sensitive to humanitarian concerns and to the loss of human life than are men. Third, it is nonetheless also true that women are hardly pacifists, and men are not uniformly bellicose. Any difference occurs at the margins in response to specific circumstances and the specific military actions contemplated. Fourth, given their magnitude on some issues involving military force, gender differences have the potential to be a significant factor in political decisions to use military force and in the political response to that use of force (Eichenberg, 2002).

favorable to their common concerns. If, for instance, more women are concerned with educational policies and vote regularly in elections, over time we can expect more resources to be devoted to school and other educational programs. To evaluate this prospect, look at national spending on education since the 1980s, when the gender gap began to take on political significance, to see if school spending has risen more than spending for other types of programs, and try to explain why or why not.

UNDERSTANDING THE GAP: A SOCIOLOGICAL APPROACH

If a gap between men's and women's opinions exists, are there plausible approaches or theories to explain it? Although the differences are typically small, they are consistent. Will the gap persist? Will it grow? Could it eventually disappear? There are several approaches to explaining the gender opinion gap.

Those who explain gender gap using a **sociological approach** share a general view that primarily social factors create differences between men and women. Several prominent sociological theories hold that society exists objectively, apart from individual experience, and that aspects of society can be explained by other society-related factors. For example, poverty is caused by unequal distribution of resources, which is caused by the way society is organized. Social institutions, norms, and values, therefore, become significant regulators of all human activities (Weber, 1922; Durkheim, 1924; Parsons, 1951).

According to fundamental sociological traditions, women and men differ in their opinions because of social differences. The gender gap is a product or result of social developments. If society changes, the gap should change as well. For example, norms of violence and beliefs associated with violence are passed from one generation to the next. If a particular generation in society, through its institutions, customs, and values, displays less violence and less aggression than previous age cohorts, it is likely that the new generation will produce fewer incidents of aggression than its predecessors (Kelly, 1997).

Men and women play different roles, established by society, and regulate the activities of the two groups by means of different ideas, prescriptions, and symbols. In traditional societies, behavioral and attitudinal differences between men and women are expected to be large because of the social pressure on both sexes to perform their prescribed roles. In contemporary democratic societies, on the other hand, the differences should be insignificant due to social equality and a convergence of the social expectations of men and women. However, **gender role** differences persist in contemporary society, thus determining the gap between men and women in many areas (Elshtain, 1991; McDonagh, 1999). For example, even though American women had been able to exercise political choice through voting, education of children, and community work, their participation in politics was still comparatively limited at the end of the 20th century (Carroll, 1989). In short, according to the sociological tradition, women and men tend to differ in their opinions because of different social influences on their behavior.

For both men and women, not only individual social experiences but also personal interpretation and evaluation of those experiences may influence attitudes. In the middle of the 1990s, a new cliché, "angry white man," began to circulate in the media. As commonly explained, angry white men were those expressing frustration about the government, which persistently and deliberately, they felt, deprived them of their fundamental rights. According to this view, discrimination against women and other disadvantaged groups was basically over in the 1980s. However, a new form of gender discrimination was advancing in the United States: discrimination against men. The angry white man argues that women (and, in fact, any other social group that claims discrimination against itself) not only enjoy equality with men but also, and this is particularly unfair, demand special privileges and advantages. Affirmative action, for instance, with its demands for equal representation in the workforce, may be, as they claim, discriminatory against men in employment and promotion practices. Gender inequality exists, but it should not be replaced by new **reverse gender discrimination.** Overall, contemporary men should not be punished for the discriminatory practices and traditions of the past they did not create. Finally, as some men imply, the media are extremely sympathetic toward women's issues and readily cover cases of sex discrimination against women, but do not give men positive media coverage. Frustration over what is seen as anti-male policies causes many men to contribute to the gender gap by expressing critical views on social issues and especially on social programs, including affirmative action, job promotion, college admission, and welfare.

The angry white man case suggests that the gender gap in attitudes may be explained, if we understand better how individual perception works. Many men and women experience and perceive reality in similar ways. Many others perceive society and their experiences from different angles not because they are naturally different but rather because they have different experiences and attempt to protect their individual and group interests. As a result, it is quite likely that plenty of men did not pay attention to gender inequality because it did not affect them. Assuming contemporary gender policies affect them directly, some men began to express serious concerns about reverse discrimination.

Overall, despite significant progress achieved on civic and economic rights, the claim that gender discrimination is over is premature. The law may protect people from discriminatory practices, but people still see discrimination in their daily activities. For instance, a survey of nearly 2,000 doctors working at 24 of the nation's leading medical schools found a sense of discrimination against female clinicians, researchers, and teachers. In fact, 77 percent of women polled, and women now make up about 25 percent of all medical school faculty, said they felt they had been discriminated against because of their sex (Lasalandra, 2000). A critic may point out that the data in this survey are based on people's opinions. Neither opinions nor beliefs are evidence that actual discrimination took place. Nevertheless, plenty of evidence shows, directly and indirectly, that discrimination and inequality between men and women persist.

SOCIOBIOLOGY: A DESTINED FUTURE?

Few approaches stir as much debate and criticism in social sciences as **sociobiology** despite the support of new arguments. Sociobiology is a multidisciplinary theoretical model that explores the ways in which biological factors affect human social activities—including socialization and opinion formation. This paradigm explains society and human activity by means of biological laws of behavior. Two prime goals of humans as living creatures are survival and procreation. To endure, humans need food and other resources. People look for mates, conceive, give birth, and then protect the offspring until they are mature enough to take care of themselves. Like animals, humans of all cultures strive to avoid unnecessary pain and to eliminate threats to their well-being.

Sociobiologists generally hold that the behavior of men and women, despite tremendous social changes, is regulated by biological processes and therefore that gender gaps will not diminish. Biological differences between men and women, such as size, strength, hormones, and reproductive behavior, lay the foundation for behavioral norms, cultural customs, and written laws that reinforce differences between the sexes. Proponents of this approach offer natural and evolutionary explanations for the development of attitudes, cooperation and competition strategies, aggression, prejudice, sexual preference, and a wide range of human actions ranging from competitiveness in sports to voting (Davies, 1963; Fukuyama, 2000). Moreover, some anthropologists claim that through evolution, men developed behavioral patterns that suited the basic need for group cooperation in hunting and warfare. For women, such patterns were less essential for survival (Schubert, 1991). Sociobiologists often directly compare humans and other animals, especially primates, to argue about differences between men and women (Tiger, 1969; Fox, 1971). They believe that humans are, like other animals and despite a seemingly endless variety of possibilities, programmed to act in certain ways to fit changing social and environmental conditions and to respond by instinct and hormones to threats and challenges.

A favorite sociobiological theme is male aggressive behavior. Males have to be tougher than females because, with few exceptions, they are destined by thousands of years of evolution to protect their offspring. Men and the males of other animal species are different, of course, but they are similar in that they all compete for scarce resources and females. Some scientists suggest rather pessimistically that the nature of violence has not changed over the years and that human males continue to dominate other species through intimidation and cruelty (Wrangham & Peterson, 1997).

Women are less prone to violent acts than are men, though some women are capable of aggression and violence. The history of modern world leadership contains many examples of tough female politicians. Israeli prime minister Golda Meir and British prime minister Margaret Thatcher could hardly be called soft on issues. Anthropologists and historians accumulated evidence suggesting that women in various times and in dissimilar social situations also supported retaliatory violence, military campaigns, and violent insurgences. Nevertheless, according to sociobiologists, more women than men have antiviolence and antimilitaristic attitudes because of their biologically predetermined roles of mother and nurturer. Most men, on the other hand, primarily due to genetic, hormonal, and other biological factors, are prone to aggressive acts.

According to the sociobiological tradition, for these natural reasons women are relatively apolitical because politics is about dominance and violence, which are not good for female nature (Hess & Torney, 1967). In 1999, 9 percent of American men reported membership in the National Rifle Association, but only 2 percent of women (Gallup, February 1999, 1,054). From the sociobiological view, the answer is that there *should* be more men than women who are prone to violent means of self-defense and aggression.

In comparing men and women, sociobiologists typically use the concept of **sex,** a term that refers to the biological differences between men and women. Most opponents of this approach come from a **gender** perspective, which refers to socially constructed differences between men and women based on social norms and values. Newborn boys and girls acquire these roles and by means of gender socialization become men and women.

In review.   Sociobiologists emphasize, and are often criticized for emphasizing, the biological, physiological, and genetic factors that contribute to differences between men and women.

GENDER SOCIALIZATION

In attempting to understand the gender gap and in generally accepting the crucial impact of social conditions on human lives, many researchers turned to studying the links between society and the individual. These specialists focus on psychological, cognitive, and behavioral mechanisms through which society influences men and women. Theories of socialization and **gender socialization,** the process whereby individuals acquire a gender role, became the foundation for an approach to the attitudinal gender gap. In Chapters 5 and 6, we examined major institutions and mechanism of political socialization and their role in attitude formation. Here we discuss gender-related aspects of political socialization.

Studies in gender socialization produced a large variety of empirical data that challenge the main postulates of sociobiology. Take, for example, the assumption that women are naturally predisposed to hold conservative attitudes and seek peaceful solution of conflicts. According to this view, women tend to maintain the status quo and therefore prefer responsibility to recklessness, order to rebelliousness, and incumbency to challenge. Research in socialization seriously questions this assumption. Let's give just a few examples.

Early studies in the 1960s suggested that conservatism or liberalism in women tended to be a function of educational factors (Sigel & Reinolds, 1979–1980) and social-psychological factors, such as interaction with peers (Feldman & Newcomb, 1971). The Feldman and Newcomb study also showed that a desire for social recognition and acceptance could drive women to acquire increasingly liberal attitudes. Contrary to what sociobiology suggests, it found that if a married couple has different political views, the direction of change does not necessarily go from husband to wife; husbands also frequently change their political views and come to agree with their wives on political issues (Steckenrider & Cutler, 1989).

Early research in political socialization also described and analyzed specific gender differences in the socialization process. For example, cross-culturally, most boys were typically and more often than girls encouraged to be fighters in their daily activities, including play, whereas most girls were led to grow up as peacekeepers, to respect authority, and to seek consensus (Hess & Torney, 1967; Langton, 1969). Also, aggression is generally inculcated in boys more than in girls (Gilligan, 1982).

Ideas about the conditions under which the development of the individual takes place became central in many socialization theories. According to a champion of socialization research, Urie Bronfenbrenner (1979), the human environment is part of a larger cultural world. Both the environment and the individual are open and interchangeable systems, and each child's development takes place within a particular developmental niche that can be viewed as a combination of life circumstances or settings (Harkness & Super, 1992). Among these settings are adults' beliefs and expectations about boys and girls, their social roles, the goals of education, and the means to achieve these goals. Altogether, these circumstances, along with the child's experiences, represent **anticipatory socialization.** What adult men and women express as opinions and voting behavior is the product of their learning as children, adolescents, and younger adults through interactions with parents, peers, school, the media, coworkers, and other factors (Renshon, 1975).

A study conducted by the American Association of University Women (AAUW) showed that in the last decade the gender gap was widening in technology education and technical careers. The study found that, compared to boys, fewer girls were entering computer fields. Among high school students taking advanced placement tests in computer science, only about 17 percent were female. Women receive less than 28 percent of all computer science bachelor degrees. The proportion of women in information and technology fields dropped from 40 percent in 1996 to 29 percent in 1999. Some experts suggested that differences between men and women were based primarily on the latter's relative lack of interest in computers (Schorow, 2000). However, this explanation does not explain why women, as a group, are less interested in computer technologies than are men. The reasons, for the gender gap, perhaps, can be found in socialization experiences, such as parents' views about their children's career choices, teachers' expectations, and peer pressure.

Of course, the law, social norms, and religious values influence individual practices that form the building blocks of socialization. Gender roles are defined according to larger cultural norms. Which country, do you think, shows a greater gap between gender roles: the United States or Turkey? One study of attitudes found it was Turkey (Sunar, 1992). Specifically, men and women interpreted their gender roles in line with cultural traditions of their countries. Unlike most Americans' views on gender, most

Turkish respondents defined gender roles distinctly, without much gray area in between.

As you remember, sociobiology pays special attention to male violence. Indeed, studies link the higher testosterone level in males' bodies and their incidence of aggressive behavior. However, critics of the natural factor in aggression also identify socialization conditions, such as poverty, domestic abuse, street violence, lack of male role models, the glorification of war and lawlessness, and drug use, as the major contributors to deviant and destructive behavior in young men (Eagly, 1995).

As Plutzer and Zipp (1996) show, the identity-related experiences of early socialization play an extremely important role in determining the gender gaps in attitudes and voting behavior. For instance, several studies found that women, as compared to men, are more likely to pay attention to the candidate's sex in determining their vote choice (Dolan, 1998; Burrell, 1994; Hershey, 1977): that is, women are more likely than men to vote for a female candidate because she is a woman. Such attitude and voting patterns may occur as the result of **gender identification,** the process of accepting the social view of oneself in terms of gender. Many women may decide to vote for female political candidates based not only on issues but also because their shared gender identity: "We are women, and women should support each other." The finding that women in the United States are more likely than men to express strong party identification may also be explained by social-psychological factors, such as some women's active pursuit of group affiliations and the attractiveness of sisterhood (Sigel, 1996; Norrander, 1997).

However, women's gender solidarity was less obvious in the past. Many American voters expressed prejudice against female candidates because of their gender. For example, for many years both men and women maintained less than enthusiastic opinions about women as politicians. Support for women's involvement in American government remained low among both men and women up to the 1960s. In 1936, for instance, only 36 percent of Americans believed there should be more women in politics. Fewer than a third of Americans in the 1930s and 1940s favored the hypothetical appointment of a woman to the presidential cabinet. In 1952, only 31 percent of men agreed the country would be better governed if more women were in Congress or held important government positions. Although 47 percent of women supported this idea, less than a majority, a 16-point opinion gap between men and women, was significant (Erskine, 1971; Andersen, 1997).

How can we interpret these findings? The view that cultural factors rooted in socialization experiences are major causes of gender bias has significant support in research. From this point of view, society through its socialization practices maintains a general belief that politics is a manly pursuit that requires masculine traits, such as autonomy, lack of remorse, and high levels of achievement motivation. Women, assumed by many to lack these traits, are thus considered unskilled for public service. Of course, not all people who enter politics must have these characteristics. Moreover, if a woman has developed these so-called masculine traits, does this automatically qualify her to become a political leader or public official? The problem with perceptual bias of any kind is that it does not allow the observer to escape from an unfairly imposed view of people and issues. If a woman displays masculine traits, she runs the risk of being viewed as pushy or preoccupied with career and therefore unqualified for office (McDonagh, 1999). This negative, stereotypical perception of

A CASE IN POINT **7.3** Interpreting Results from the Past

When Gallup Polls asked Americans in 1962 (June–July, personal 2,313), "In Russia nearly nine out of every ten medical doctors are women. Why, in your opinion, are there so few female doctors in the United States?" the vast majority of respondents pointed out that American women have too many household duties and prefer caring for their families (45 percent). Only 19 percent offered a more critical opinion, suggesting that American women have harder time being recognized for their skills and talents and are discriminated against by men. The results of this survey, though, are not easy to interpret; it is simplistic to suggest that American women in the 1960s valued their home-related activities as more important than careers. If almost one-half of Americans suggested that women in this country had many household duties and had to take care of their families, was this a proud statement or a regretful apology for the fact that many women couldn't pursue professional careers because of a lack of choice?

women in politics may be one of the factors contributing to the existing attitude gap; some people may vote against a candidate simply because she is a woman.

In the decades following the 1960s, however, the gender gap in attitudes about women in power became smaller, and support for women in politics grew (Simon & Landis, 1989). While only one-half of Americans supported a hypothetical woman candidate for high political office in the late 1960s, 15 years later a 1984 poll found that nearly 9 out of 10 Americans would vote for a woman candidate for mayor, governor, senator, or congressional representative (Gallup, 1985). This supportive attitude has remained relatively steady, including 87% for a woman as president (Gallup, May 30, 2003).

In review.   Instead of referring to universal laws of human development, whether biological or social, many specialists in socialization rely on measurable and replicable empirical evidence. Contemporary studies focus on socialization patterns, especially on differences between boys and girls in their early learning experiences. All in all, social roles, stereotypes, anticipatory socialization, and personal gender-related experiences influence the process of political socialization of both men and women.

ONCE AGAIN, INEQUALITY

In the social sciences, the idea of inequality and its effects on human behavior is long-standing. There is no shortage of concepts that underline unequal social position of men and women as a fundamental factor determining gender gaps in many areas. For example, **feminist** critics have long insisted that liberal democracy generally fails to produce equality between men and women. Indeed, the proclamation of individualism and human rights as basic principles of human relations did not in itself result in a great political inclusion of women in social and political life (McDonagh, 1999). As political scientist Rogers Smith pointed out in his acclaimed book *Civic Ideals* (1997), the inequality of men and women was expressed in the American political tradition itself,

TABLE 7.4

Earnings of Full-time, Year-round Workers.
Median Income of Men and Women in the United States.

	Number	Median earnings
Women	41,639,000	$29,680
Men	58,712,000	$38,884

Source: U.S. Census Bureau, Washington, DC, Income in the United States, September 2003.

which originally combined ideas of freedom, equality, and civic virtue with postulates about inherently unequal groups: slaves, servants, immigrants, minorities, and women.

In addition to political inequality, for many years in the United States and other democracies, men and women experienced income inequality. Although this gap began to diminish after the 1950s, the earning gap between men and women was large and remains significant; men as a group continue to make more money than women. According to the U.S. Bureau of the Census, by 2000 women in the United States earned about 73 cents for every dollar men made, a one-cent *drop* since 1996. In 2000, the median income for married-couple households was $59,300. The median for a family maintained by a man only was $38,884, while the median for a family maintained by a woman was only $29,680 (see Table 7.4).

Earning disparities are evident in other countries (Shiraev & Levy, 2003). For example, experts estimate that highly skilled women in Great Britain earn over their careers an average of $200,000 less than male colleagues of the same qualification (Benett, 2000). Although several explanations of the earning gap can be offered (Headlee & Elfin, 1996), nobody disputes its existence (see Table 7.5).

A gender gap also exists in academic degrees earned. Although women surpassed men in the number of college degrees, as shown in Table 7.6, significantly more men than women in the United States earn doctoral degrees. This degree is increasingly important today for the highest-paid positions in many branches of private business and government. As a rule, low-paying jobs do not require advanced educational degrees from employees.

TABLE 7.5

Earning Gap Between Men and Women in Some Countries (women's earnings as a proportion of men's).

Country	Wage	Country	Wage
New Zealand	.81	The Netherlands	.78
France	.80	Canada	.72
Britain	.79	Portugal	.66
Germany	.79	Switzerland	.65
United States	.78	Japan	.63

Sources: Organization for Economic Cooperation and Development, International Labor Organization, Statistics Canada, Bureau of Labor. Statistics prepared by Smith (2000).

TABLE 7.6

Educational Attainment of Adults by Sex.

	Bachelor's degree	*Master's degree*	*Doctoral degree*
Women	16,056,000	5,322,000	599,000
Men	15,656,000	5,205,000	1,433,000

Source: U.S. Census Bureau, Washington, DC, 2000.

In a capitalist society, the more money one makes, the more chances and opportunities one gets to complete one's education, pay medical bills, purchase property, buy products, enjoy free time, and choose entertainment. As discussed in Chapter 8, on social class, economic inequality is a contributing factor to the way in which our attitudes are formed, retained, and changed (Fowers & Richardson, 1996). In Chapter 5, on socialization, we referred to the concept of quality of life. If two groups of individuals, men and women, have different qualities of life, the group with fewer resources and less power may wish to change this unequal situation. *How* to change it depends on a number of factors. This perception of inequality and accompanying desire for change could contribute to a gap in attitudes between the sexes. In the early 1990s, according to an assessment (Frankenhauser et al., 1991, p. 257), women owned less than 1/100th of the world's property and received only 10 percent of the world's income. Men owned and earned most. No recent radical changes have been made to the world's distribution of property, so this tremendous economic disproportion continues in the 21st century.

It is unrealistic to expect that male opinion leaders and politicians in the United States and around the world would alone suggest, lobby for, and implement policies directed at the elimination of the existing gender gap. The problem is not just the gap itself; the problem is that women are in a disadvantageous position and that this situation affects their attitudes and voting behavior.

Recent political efforts have been directed at equalizing the conditions of political campaigns and elections to give women greater access to politics, traditionally a men's arena. One such equalizing idea is the establishment of electoral quotas (for example, exact numbers of how many men and women can be elected to city council) and party lists. For example, party lists, and not just individual candidates appearing on ballots, give female voters a chance to achieve two goals simultaneously: (1) to choose a person with a particular political orientation or supporting particular policies, and (2) to choose a woman. The idea of establishing quotas as a remedy for past discrimination does not appeal to the majority of Americans (in Chapter 11, on domestic issues, we will get back to this problem). However, in Europe, such policies are increasingly common. Some political parties, such as the Greens, established a 50-50 policy for male and female candidates on the party voting list. In Sweden, one of the most advanced countries in terms of women-friendly policies, political parties have established gender quotas allocating a certain percentage of parliamentary seats to women (McDonagh, 1999).

Consider these examples. According to the United Nations Development Fund for Women's report, by 2000 only eight countries (Denmark, Finland, Germany, Iceland,

A TOPIC FOR CLASS DISCUSSION Economic Influences on Preferences

Economics may determine the political attitudes and voting preferences of men and women. Consider, for example, a substantial shift of many American women's attitudes in favor of the Democratic Party between the late 1980s and the early 2000s. Demographic and financial factors, among many others, of course, influenced this shift. For instance, there has been a steady increase of divorce in the United States, as approximately one-half of all marriages break up. Four out of five divorcees remarry; however, the remaining 20 percent do not. Half of divorced fathers do not pay mandatory child support. This means that there are millions of families who have just one earner whose prime concern is likely to be economic security of her family (Luker, 1996; Galbraith, 1998). How would this economic situation, in your view, contribute to the voting preferences of single or divorced women with children? Which party's candidates are they likely to support? Were they more likely to vote for Bush, Kerry, or Nader in 2004?

the Netherlands, Norway, South Africa, and Sweden) enrolled both girls and boys in secondary schools in equal numbers and maintained at least 30 percent female membership in national parliaments. Sweden, at 43 percent, has the highest representation of women as elected parliamentarians (Mathi, 2000). Internationally, in the second half of the 20th century, women were elected head of state or government in 40 countries, including Canada, Great Britain, Finland, India, Pakistan, Turkey, and Nicaragua (McDonagh, 1999). In the 1992 U.S. elections, 53 women, a record number, were elected to Congress. Although the proportion of women in state legislatures and the U.S. Congress did not increase significantly in the 1990s, recruitment of women to executive-branch posts did (Davis, 1997; Norris, 1997; Norris & Lovenduski, 1995).

GENDER GAP: THINKING CRITICALLY

Explanations

Earlier we examined several approaches to explaining the differences in attitudes of men and women. Of course, biological factors may determine an individual's temperament, skin color, metabolism, predisposition to illness, and even operatic vocal quality. On the other hand, biology is not destiny: People's lives are not programmed in advance. Human predispositions and potentials remain latent unless they interact with the environment. A qualified expert can predict social developments and trends; however, having knowledge of society is not sufficient to correctly predict the attitudes of men and women and how widely they differ. We have to look deeper into the particular situation and scrutinize both macro- and micro-factors, global social trends, and local, cultural, community developments that together influence the opinions of women and men as groups.

The case of the 1990 electoral victory of Violeta Barrios de Chamorro in Nicaragua is a fine illustration of how closely commingled all these factors are. Chamorro was elected president as the candidate of a multiparty coalition (Sobel, 1993). In her campaign she repeatedly portrayed herself as the widow of a national hero and as a self-sacrificing and committed mother who promised to bring peace to Nicaraguan families torn by the devastating civil war. She appeared to be a traditional, conservative, and patient wife, the educator and role model for her children. In her speeches, she often mentioned the name of her late husband and showed her dedication to his ideas. Her opponents rarely challenged her political traditionalism because the electorate apparently liked what they saw in her as a political candidate (Kampwirth, 1998). Chamorro employed neither feminist slogans nor demands for equality and equal opportunity during the campaign, but women still supported her in great numbers. Trying to understand Chamorro's victory and the reasons for her enthusiastic support, we should not forget the impact of culture and context on people's voting behavior. Nicaragua is a country with a strong Catholic tradition and pervasive emphasis on custom, family values, and personal sacrifice. Moreover, the campaign was also meant to symbolize the ending of the civil war, and Chamorro's pleas to the people to get back to their families, fields, workshops, and kitchens, to take care of their children, were appealing and timely.

Cultural and social conditions are changing everywhere in the world, at varying speeds and to different degrees. In the United States, for instance, an increasing number of women work outside the home. The average age at which women marry and have children has risen. The fertility rate has declined dramatically since the 1950s. Single parenthood rates are on the rise. The educational level of American women is increasing faster than that of men. These and many other factors influence the size of the attitudinal gender gap.

Family relationships are among the micro-factors that influence attitudes. Thorton and Freedman (1979) found that divorce tends to be associated with an individual's shift toward egalitarian (pro-equality) attitudes. The birth of additional children, on the other hand, is associated with the retention or development of traditional gender role attitudes. The cause-and-effect relationship in this case is not clear. It is possible that some unhappily married women's lack of traditional attitudes could give them more options in choosing whether or not to get divorced. Likewise, it is possible that a woman who accepts traditional gender-role attitudes, that is, the role of a dedicated mother and wife, is willing to have more children than women who do not have such traditional attitudes.

Bias

Several theories explain attitudinal differences between men and women as the reflection of social conditions; the more similar the conditions, the more compatible attitudes and the narrower the gender gap. Nevertheless, equality may exist on paper but not in reality. Certain conditions can be changing for one gender; they may remain largely unchanged for the other. Here is an example. Women in the United States are making progress in male-dominated professions. According to the U.S. Bureau of Labor Statistics, in 1983 only 7 percent of dentists were female. By 2000, this proportion had more than doubled to 17 percent. In 1983, only 15 percent of lawyers were women. By 2000, the proportion had doubled to 29 percent. The number of women police officers and security guards is rising, to 21 percent from 13 percent in 1983. However, men's pursuit of traditionally female professions, such as nursing, elementary and high school teaching, and airline service has not risen. While the proportion of male nurses increased from 3 percent in 1983 to 7 percent in 2000, there were fewer men, compared to 1983, teaching in elementary and high schools; the percentage of male teachers had dropped from 29 to 25 percent. The number of male flight attendants also dropped, from 26 to 16 percent. The professional gap has narrowed in male-dominated fields, but it did not narrow and in fact somewhat widened in female-dominated professions (McClain, 2000).

Would you expect differences between men and women in their attitudes about the family? Do you assume that women are more family-oriented than men? Not every survey provides evidence that women care more about family issues than men do. A national survey by the Radcliffe Public Policy Center at Harvard University showed that, contrary to what some observers anticipated, 70 percent of men in their 20s are willing to give up pay for more time with their families compared with 63 percent of women of the same age (Brooks, 2000). Although 85 percent of women ages 21 to 39 put a work schedule that allows for family time at the top of their list of important job components, nearly the same percentage of men chose similarly. It should be considered, however, that some respondents may have given socially desirable answers just because it seemed nice or correct to express that opinion.

Wording

We know that oral and written interpretations of statistical differences found in opinion polls are often constrained by choices in language. If more American men than women express support for the death penalty, this does not mean that most women oppose it. In fact, more than 50 percent of women are in favor of capital punishment for people convicted of murder. A more appropriate interpretation of the gender gap regarding the death penalty is simply that more men than women support it. Likewise, it is tempting to call women liberal, pro-Democratic, or egalitarian, based on their survey responses. However, assumptions about women's tendency to support liberal, social-democratic ideas are stereotypical and largely inaccurate. For instance, both in Western Europe and the United States, women tended to express more conservative attitudes than men did, especially prior to the 1960s (Campbell et al., 1960; Lipset, 1960). Throughout the 1990s, conservative attitudes and values were supported by majorities of women from the transitional post-communist societies of Eastern Europe (Kharchev, 1994; Shlapentokh & Shiraev, 2002). Among these opinions were traditional moral and religious attitudes, a tough stance on crime, an emphasis on self-reliance, and intolerance of homosexuality.

According to most surveys, the attitudinal gender gap, as this chapter suggests, is not large. The preeminent specialist on gender socialization, Roberta Sigel, showed in the 1980s and 1990s that most American women adopted attitudes of self-reliance. In the 1990s, many women claimed they had not personally experienced discrimination and that it was up to them as individuals to rise above whatever bias they encountered (Sigel, 1996). Although most women admit that political and socioeconomic inequality persists between men and women, their emphasis on self-reliance may keep their attitudes politically more conservative even as they defend liberal values.

Context

What is the future of the attitudinal gender gap? How big will its impact be on public opinion and electoral politics? The significance of the gender gap should be analyzed in the context of social and cultural changes taking place today.

The the gender gap in attitudes may increase in the near future due to demographic changes in most economically advanced democratic societies. For the most of the 20th century, the median age of Americans was below 30. With steadily increasing life expectancy and decreasing fertility rates, the median age is climbing and is expected to pass 40 and, in some countries, 50 years. Women have an advantage of five to seven years over men in life expectancy; as a result, the proportion of active and healthy women is increasing relative to men. Moreover, as scores of sociologists now assume, older women are becoming one of the most important demographic groups affecting survey results and voting outcomes in many democratic countries. For instance, women constituted 52 percent of the electorate in the 1996 U.S. presidential election, men 48 percent (Page, 2000).

Let's hypothesize, perhaps optimistically, about the future of the gender gap, relying on the information already discussed and spicing it with optimism and hope. Wider abundance and availability of resources should create a society in which political struggle for economic equality between men and women, as well as among social, religious, national, and ethnic groups, may eventually subside. Social and political systems that were foundations of traditionalism and gender-based discrimination should gradually ease their grip. Women in these societies should be able to expand their rights and the limits determined by their country's social and cultural customs.

In the United States, women's attitudinal emphasis on care and caregiving is expected to continue in the forthcoming decades because of a significant demographic trend of the 2000s: the massive retirement of baby boomers who will live longer than previous generations and will demand high-quality healthcare (West, 2000). However, centuries-old cultural practices of socialization are likely to continue to reinforce a difference between the genders' behavioral patterns and attitudes. On the other hand, some experts predict that more women will be elected to public office. Although it is impossible to predict exactly what policy changes will take place as a result, society is likely to benefit because of fewer wars, greater security, and more care provided for citizens.

Life expectancy may also contribute to opinion differences when comparing male and female samples. Why? For several reasons, women tend to live longer than men. For instance, in Canada, life expectancy is 77 years for men and 83.6 for women. In the United States, it is 79 for women and 74 for men. In Switzerland, it is less than 76 years for men and 82 for women (Lem, 2000). Compared to women, men tend to occupy more dangerous and risky jobs. More men serve in the police and the armed forces; more fatal car accidents involve men than women. Men are more likely to engage in aggressive, reckless, and risk-taking behavior (DSM-IV; Schubert, 1991). As a result, each adult age cohort has more women than men, and the disproportion increases with age. For comparison, in 2000 in the United States there were approximately 18 million men between 20 and 30 years of age and 18.5 women in the same age category. In the 40–50 age group, the gap grew to 21.4 million women and 20.7 million men. Among people 65 and older, the gap is substantial: 14 million men and 18.7 million of women (U.S. Census Bureau, 2000).

What do these numbers suggest? Statistically, more men die younger than do women, and the male population gets thinner faster. This demographic development should affect polling samples, which should represent more women than men, particularly older women. People who are older tend to have attitudes indicative of their primary concerns, wishes, and worries. Therefore, the pattern in opinions should indicate a steady change toward a family-oriented, nonmilitary outlook and such issues as moderation, peace, social security, and responsibility.

ASSIGNMENT 7.1   SOCIAL DOMINANCE AND GENDER

SDO (Social Dominance Orientation) expresses the individual's general support of anti-egalitarianism and hierarchically structured relationships among social groups. In other words, SDO indicates that the individual believes in inequality among social groups. SDO correlates with political conservatism, ethnocentrism, authoritarianism, opposition to increased taxation of the wealthy, belief in the Protestant work ethic, opposition to interracial marriage, support for interventionist wars, opposition to wars in support of humanitarian values, opposition to social welfare, and negative attitudes toward foreign immigrants. SDO, nevertheless, is not reducible to these constructs. Social psychologists suggest that members of high-status groups are more anti-egalitarian (that is, against equality) than members of lower-status groups. Therefore, as access to resources becomes more open to all social groups and the groups become more equal in social status, the differences in SDO between the groups should become smaller. Likewise, the further apart the groups are in status, the more substantial will be differences in their egalitarian attitudes. For example, if we compare Sweden (a predominantly egalitarian culture) and Saudi Arabia (a non-egalitarian culture), we should expect that men and women in Sweden hold significantly closer views on equality than do men and women in Saudi Arabia.

However, survey research does not support this hypothesis. Data collected in the United States, Sweden, Israel (including the West Bank), the Soviet Union, Poland, England, and Australia showed that men in all countries, regardless of their social composition, have significantly higher levels of social dominance than women. Men turned out to be less egalitarian (less supportive of equality) than women across cultures and social groups.

Question:
Why do you think men tend to be less egalitarian than women? Do you believe socialization is the main determinant of how men and women think about equality among social groups? Or is anti-egalitarianism in some men a weapon they use to protect their dominant position in society?

Source: J. Sidanius and F. Pratto, *Social dominance: An Intergroup Theory of Social Hierarchy and Oppression* (Cambridge: Cambridge University Press, 1999).

CHAPTER SUMMARY

- Studies of the gender gap in voting choices and attitudes began in the 1960s and 1970s. The first research on gender gap in attitudes identified it as having little significance. Later, however, attention to the growing political impact of the gap gradually increased.

- Overall, according to polls, women as a group, compared to men, tend to be more egalitarian and more concerned with domestic issues, social security, safety, and violence. Women are more reluctant than men to send U.S. troops abroad and prefer stricter gun control. In general, women are less supportive of the death penalty and more tolerant toward abortion. More women than men vote during national elections. More women in the United States vote for the Democratic Party than for the Republican Party.

- Several scientific approaches explain the nature of the gender gap in attitudes. Sociological approaches share a general view that social factors cause differences between men and women. According to the sociological tradition, women and men differ in their opinions because of the different social influences on their behavior. The gender gap, therefore, is not a natural, biological construct; it is rather a product of society.

- Sociobiology, as a theoretical model, explores the ways in which biological factors affect human social activities, including socialization and opinion formation. Genetic, hormonal, and physiological factors are believed to contribute to behavior of both sexes.

- According to the socialization perspective, boys and girls are socialized to their roles as men and women. Social norms influence individual practices that become the building blocks of anticipatory socialization. Development and socialization can be viewed as a dual process. On one hand, a child's physical growth and certain psychological skills are biologically determined. On the other hand, the developing child is closely attached to his or her social environment.

- Theories of economic inequality suggest that access to resources determines the roles of women and men play in society. These roles are unequal, and the inequality affects the attitudes, values, and behavioral patterns of men and women as social groups.

- The political significance of the gender gap in attitudes may increase in the near future with demographic changes in women's numbers in most economically advanced democratic societies.

Looking Ahead. To complement this exploration of gender's influence on opinions, the next chapter, "Social Class and Opinions," examines the impact of socioeconomic or social class factors, including income, education, and occupation, on people's values and opinions. Social class affects party identification and attitudes on social and political issues from affirmative action to the death penalty to taxes and foreign policy. Class also affects involvement in work, which affects wider political participation.

DEFINITIONS OF KEY TERMS

Anticipatory socialization (gender related)—Experience in the predominant beliefs and expectations about gender roles, the goals of childrearing and education, and the means to achieve these goals.

Feminist—Supporter of feminism, a political movement and social philosophy that advocates women's economic, political, and cultural equality with men.

Gender—The socially constructed role distinction between men and women.

Gender gap (in public opinion studies and voting)—The difference between men and women in their expressed opinions and electoral behavior.

Gender identification—The process of viewing oneself in terms of gender.

Gender role—A social expectation about what boys, girls, men, and women should and should not do as males and females.

Gender socialization—The process through which individuals acquire their basic roles as men and women.

Reverse gender discrimination—The alleged practice of discrimination against majority men as a by-product of overcoming consequences of discrimination against women and other minorities.

SDO (Social Dominance Orientation)—Expression of individual support for anti-egalitarian and hierarchical relationships among social groups.

Sex—The biological and genetic distinction between males and females.

Sociobiology—A multidisciplinary theoretical model that explores the ways in which biological factors affect human activities, including socialization and opinion formation.

Sociological approach (in public opinion studies)—A general view that differences between men and women are caused primarily by social factors.

CHAPTER 8

Social Class
and Opinions

The ruling ideas of each age have
ever been the ideas of its ruling
class.

Karl Marx and Friedrich Engels,
The Communist Manifesto

The enthralling H. G. Wells novel *The Time Machine* is not only about the possibility of time travel, it is also a vivid and pessimistic vision of the future of humankind. In Wells's imagination, in a million years human civilization will consist of two antagonistic classes: the delicate and weak *Eloi* and the primitive and cruel *Morlocks*. The Eloi live on the surface. Descendents of the contemporary upper class, they spend their lives effortlessly walking, talking, and playing in the sun. Descendants of the working class, the repugnant and physically powerful Morlocks live underground and operate machinery. Thousands of years before, they were forced to work and settle beneath the surface. These nocturnal creatures are uneducated and cruel. They prey on the defenseless Eloi, who virtually surrendered to their sorry fate. The harmony of humankind in the author's mind ends up with a distressing discordance; class divisions seeded in the 19th century produce the future decay, regression, and violence of one class against the other.

Social prophecies of this kind are usually improvised as semiscientific speculations embellished by the author's creative imagination. We are free to accept or reject Wells's ideas. The question he poses, however, has been and continues to be the subject of relentless debates about money and power. What is the role of resources in determining who we are and what we think? Look at the events around you. Some people make more money than you, and some make less. The partition of the human world into the rich and the poor continues. Are the major divisions among people today largely determined by their money and resources? To what extent do money and resources affect the ways people think and act?

Looking Forward. This chapter examines how social class, or socioeconomic status, as measured by income, education, and occupation, influences people's opinions.

Social class affects party identification and attitudes on a variety of values and social issues, from affirmative action to the death penalty to taxes to foreign policy. Class also influences involvement in work that affects wider political participation.

CLASS AND SOCIAL BACKGROUND

A great variety of social, political, psychological, and developmental factors shape individuals' opinions and determine their behavior. Being born a woman or man, in the United States or Mexico, with certain ancestral roots affects a person's attitudes and actions. Social background affects what people think about the death penalty, abortion, nuclear weapons, and life in general and for whom he votes. Altogether, educational background, ancestral origin, and gender, among many other features that distinguish individuals, may alter the type and amount of resources one has, the money one makes, the medical care one receives, the type of job one does, the home in which one lives, and the ways one sees the world and acts politically. The factors that contribute to people's quality of life also determine their position in society, or **social status.** Let's state the obvious: Even with equal rights in theory, people are not equal, nor are social groups. Some people make more money, receive better benefits, attend better schools, and live in better houses than other individuals do. Society, including the one in which you live, is stratified. Large social categories are ranked in hierarchies. A rank or level within this hierarchy is typically called a social status, or social class. Class affects attitudes and behaviors.

SOCIAL CLASS AS A CONCEPT

Discussions about the impact of social class on opinions start with the nature of class. A **social class** is a large social grouping of people who occupy similar levels in the social hierarchy by sharing common relations to productive resources (Sobel, 1989). Income, wealth, living conditions, opportunities, and access to resources link people to different social classes. Membership in a social class is associated with social position and determines quality of life. The placement of people into higher and lower categories or classes is at the core of all social stratification systems. In practically all known human societies, people of higher classes have greater access to resources and possess more power than do members of lower classes.

But what determines the individual's social class? According to our definition, it is her relationship to productive resources. Some people own billions of dollars in factories, oil refineries, television networks, publishing companies, and sports teams. In the United States, there are more than 300 billionaires. Some 23 million other Americans own small businesses: print shops, bakeries, dry cleaners, farms, and taxicabs. Other people own investments in businesses and banks that bring them income and profits. Over 100 million people in the largest social group in the United States (and many other countries) work for the most part for salaries or wages.

Occupation, income, and level of educational attainment are other features that determine people's social class. Some occupations require lengthy training, access to which is highly competitive. It is extremely difficult, for example, to become a physician, head coach of a professional football team, or career diplomat. Professors, attorneys, doctors, and architects spend from 7 to 10 years in college and university before they start working as professionals. If we include all the years of formal schooling in elementary, middle, and high school, plus the years of undergraduate college and graduate training, we find that a typical university professor or physician spends almost a quarter of a century preparing for his or her job. At the end, the individuals who occupy these positions typically receive higher compensation and better benefits than most people. In comparison, some jobs require only basic education, little training, and limited skills. Traditionally, pay and benefits for people who work these jobs are average or below.

A number of features that determine social class membership are conferred at birth or during childhood. For example, Ted Turner, the billionaire founder of CNN, acquired his initial capital from his father. Bill Gates, cofounder of Microsoft, also grew up in a wealthy family. Certainly, these men multiplied their initial capital many times because of their own effort and favorable circumstances. But their adult membership in the upper class was prepared for them by their parents. In some countries, certain people inherit membership in the social elite, including the nobility or royalty. In contrast, other people earn or achieve higher class status by their deeds; their property, money, degrees, and titles are earned, not inherited.

Class Stratification

Throughout history and across schools of thought, there have been differing views of social class. For example, Marxists recognize at least two major and antagonistic social classes, distinguished by their relations to productive means: landlords and tenants, capitalists and proletariat. In contrast, according to Max Weber, the ownership of productive resources is important but not the only factor in determining class. A person's class position is also based on his or her income, occupational prestige, education, and social power, the ability to change things in society. Therefore, each society has more than two social classes.

Contemporary definitions of social class are based on an assumption of more than two classes; upper and lower divisions and subdivisions exist in each social class. A main criterion for classification is personal income. One of the most common systems of stratification includes four major categories: upper class, middle class, working class, and lower class (Macionis, 2003). This distinction, of course, is imprecise. In the United States, if we distribute all people according to their annual income and pick 5 percent from the top of the distribution, we find that these individuals make more than $150,000 a year. We also find out that the people in this category tend to be well educated, hold prestigious jobs, and develop a system of group relationships that tie them together through marriage, friendship, and partnership.

The next group, the middle class, represents from 40 to 50 percent of the United States population. Members make between $35,000 and $100,000 dollars per year per household. Almost half of these individuals have college degrees. Middle-class Americans are typically employed in white-collar jobs in many sectors of the economy, and their work generally requires advanced education and training to reach the upper middle class. Some people who work in average-paying occupations, such as sales representatives, teachers, or middle managers, are middle class. Others who work in average-paying occupations, but at jobs requiring less skill, such as repair technicians, building contractors, and medical assistants, are lower middle class.

About one-third of Americans belong to the working class; these people often are called blue-collar workers. Their jobs usually involve manual labor and typically do not require a college degree. The remaining 10 or 15 percent of Americans constitute the lower class, whose income is around or below the national poverty level. When employed, they hold low-prestige jobs that pay only minimum wage. People belong to a lower class mostly because they have lower education or job skills. Some working-class are members of the so-called working poor, who are employed in low-paying jobs. Some cannot work or hold very low-paying jobs, for instance, due to illness, physical condition, or family situation.

Classification has many exceptions. It is relatively easy to determine the social class of a wealthy individual who lives in a million-dollar house near New York or San Francisco, has completed an advanced educational degree, and works as a chief surgeon in a hospital. Similarly, we would have little problem identifying the lower social class of a person who is unemployed, has six dependents, did not complete high school, and lacks a spouse or close relatives to help. In other cases, however, determining class is more complicated. Another way of identifying social class is to ask people about their class identification: which class they think they are in. This method does not provide a precise picture, however. The vast majority say they are in the middle class.

SOCIAL CLASS ATTITUDE GAPS

Folklore, fairy tales, anecdotes, and literary masterpieces around the world reflect the fundamental differences between the haves and the have-nots. It is commonly perceived that in socially polarized societies, the attitudes of people from upper classes differ from those of lower classes. The well-off do not fully understand the views and opinions of the poor and underprivileged; similarly, the poor do not readily accept the views of the rich. Individuals of dissimilar social backgrounds and opposite social categories and classes tend to have different political orientations and ideological beliefs and support different candidates in elections. More conservative assessments hold that class-related factors play an increasingly minor role in predicting attitudes, party identification, and political ideology, especially in contemporary Western democracies, with constantly growing middle classes (Lafferty, 1989). If economic growth is sustained and social opportunities are preserved, the divisions among people may become less significant.

How different are attitudes of people in different social groups? Two self-identified criteria were chosen for analysis: yearly income and education (Table 8.1). What do these numbers suggest about the relationship of social class and attitudes?

Interest in politics.   A person's educational level and income, on one hand, and interest in politics, on the other, are positively correlated. In surveys, the higher an individual's income and educational level, the more interested he or she is in politics. Interest in politics does decline slightly among the highest-paid group of respondents relative to the groups that earn between $15,000 and $75,000.

Ideological identity.   Overall, ideological orientations, such as moderate, conservative, or liberal, are only loosely correlated with income. There is no gap between individuals of higher and lower income groups in terms of their self-identification as

TABLE 8.1

Distribution of Opinions, Party Identity, and Ideological Issues by Income. (In percentages.)

Issues	<15K	15-30K	30-50k	50-75k	>75k
Very interested in politics (Princeton/CRP/Pew, April 1997, telephone, 1,404)	23 ($10–20K)	24 ($20–30K)	29	40	30
Consider themselves Republican (Pew, September 1999, national adult parents, telephone, 597)	15 ($10–20K)	20 ($20–30K)	36	37	40
Consider themselves Independent (Pew, September 1999, national adult parents, telephone, 597)	36 ($10–20K)	26 ($20–30K)	27	36	32
Consider themselves Democrat (Pew, September 1999, national adult parents, telephone, 597)	43 ($10–20K)	43 ($20–30K)	30	26	25
Consider themselves conservative (Gallup/CNN/ USA Today, July 1999, national, 1,031)	39	38	45	39	37
Consider themselves moderate (Gallup/CNN/ USA Today, July 1999, national, 1,031)	36	39	37	44	43
Consider themselves liberal (Gallup/CNN/ USA Today, July 1999, national, 1,031)	24	19	16	17	19

Distribution of Opinions on Social and Political Issues by Income.

Issues	<15K	15-30K	30-50k	50-75k	>75k
Say the amount of federal income tax they have to pay is too high (Gallup/CNN, USA Today, July 1999, telephone, 1,031)	52	53	63	62	70
Federal spending on foreign aid should be decreased (NY Times, 1998, telephone, 1395)	54	50	53	49	42
Supported U.S. military strikes against Yugoslavia (Gallup/CNN/USA Today, April 1999, telephone, 1,055)	50	56	62	66	58
Support a law barring illegal immigrants from public schools, public hospitals, and other state-run social services (ABC/WP, August 1996, telephone, 1,514)	35	43	52	56	58
Abolish affirmative action programs (CBS/NY Times, 1997, national, telephone, 1,258)	36	48	59	66	65
Death penalty for a person convicted of murder (Gallup, February 1999, telephone, 1,054)	81	70	72	85	66
Freedom of speech should not extend to groups like the Communist Party or the Ku Klux Klan (Pew, November 1997, telephone, 1,165)	27 ($10–20K)	21 ($20–30K)	20	14	13
When a woman becomes pregnant through rape, abortion should be legal (AP, 1998, telephone, 1,012)	59	65	84	78	80
A person who has been convicted of drunk driving should be prohibited from purchasing a gun (ICR/ Hearst, August 1997, national, telephone, 2,016)	62	59	55	49	53
Unfavorable opinion about Microsoft (Gallup/CNN/ USA Today, April 1999, telephone 1,055; Gallup, March 1999, telephone, 1,078)	19	14	17	9	14

TABLE 8.2

Distribution of Opinions on Party Identity and Ideological Issues According to Respondents' Education. (In percentages.)

Issue	Less than high school	High school graduate	Some college	College graduate	Post-graduate
Consider themselves Republican (Pew, September 1999, national adult parents, telephone, 597)	25	32	31	36	38
Consider themselves Independent (Pew, September 1999, national adult parents, telephone, 597)	24	33	31	33	31
Consider themselves Democrat (Pew, September 1999, national adult parents, telephone, 597)	41	29	30	25	29
Consider themselves conservative (Gallup/CNN/*USA Today*, July 1999, national, telephone, 1,031)	41	40	42	42	35
Consider themselves moderate (Gallup/CNN/*USA Today*, July 1999, national, telephone, 1,031)	32	42	38	47	39
Consider themselves liberal (Gallup/CNN/*USA Today*, July 1999, national, telephone, 1,031)	23	15	19	12	26
Say the amount of federal income tax they have to pay is too high (Gallup/CNN/*USA Today*, July 1999, telephone, 1,031)	53	62	61	62	56

Distribution of Opinions on Social and Political Issues According to Respondents' Education.

Issue	Less than high school	High school graduate	Some college	College graduate	Post-graduate
Supported U.S. military strikes against Yugoslavia (Gallup/CNN/*USA Today*, April 1999, telephone, 1,055)	50	56	61	63	67
Unfavorable opinion about Microsoft (Gallup/CNN/*USA Today*, April 1999, telephone, 1,055; Gallup, March 1999, telephone, 1,078)	19	17	10	16	17
Abolish affirmative action programs (CBS/*NY Times*, 1997, national, telephone, 1,258)	57	52	58	63	59
Death penalty for a person convicted of murder (Gallup, February 1999, telephone, 1,054)	73	79	76	74	62

Continued on next page

Table 8.2 *(continued)*

Distribution of Opinions on Social and Political Issues According to Respondents' Education.

Issue	Less than high school	High school graduate	Some college	College graduate	Post-graduate
A person who has been convicted of drunk driving should be prohibited from purchasing a gun (ICR/Hearst, August 1997, national, telephone, 2,016).	60	58	57	50	50
Recognizing the legality of same-sex marriages *(U.S. News & World Report,* 1993, registered voters, telephone, 1,000)	18	16	24	24	48
Freedom of speech should not extend to groups like the Communist Party or the Ku Klux Klan (Pew, November, 1997, telephone, 1,165)	28	25	19	13	3
A person having an extramarital affair can also be a good spouse *(Newsweek,* September 1996, telephone, 751)	42	46	47	48	55
Support a law barring illegal immigrants from public schools, public hospitals, and other state-run social services (ABC/WP, August 1996, telephone, 1,514)	48	47	48	57	47
When a woman becomes pregnant through rape, abortion should be legal (AP, 1998, telephone, 1,012)	50	72	80	90	79
Federal spending on foreign aid should be decreased *(NY Times,* 1998, telephone, 1,395)	50	52	53	42	39
Very interested in politics (Princeton/CRP/Pew, April 1997, telephone, 1,404)	14	24	33	35	45

conservatives. Only those who make between $30,000 and $50,000 are more likely than other income groups to consider themselves conservative than other income groups; this group difference, however, is not substantial. Liberal identification is also relatively stable across all income groups, with a minor increase of self-identified liberals among people in the lowest income category. There are slightly more moderates among higher-paid groups than other groups. Slightly more than 40 percent of Americans of all educational levels, except the postgraduates, consider themselves conservative. The least conservative group, according to self-identification, consists of people with advanced college degrees. The gap between the groups, however, is only in the single digits. College graduates have the highest proportion of ideological moderates; the lowest proportion of moderates is found among the least educated Americans.

Party identification. The party identification gap between groups of higher and lower income is significant. The more money people earn, the less likely they are to identify themselves with the Democratic Party and the more likely they are to identify themselves with the Republican Party. There are three times as many Democrats as Republicans among those who make less than $15,000 per year; there are almost twice as many Republicans as Democrats among those who earn more than $75,000. People of the lowest income category are as likely to identify as independents as individuals of higher income categories. Education and party identification are also related; more education indicates a higher possibility that the person will identify with the Republican Party. In contrast, identification with the Democratic Party generally decreases with educational advancement. The lowest proportion of self-identified independents is found among the least educated Americans. The proportion of those who identify as independents changes little across other educational groups. The Institute for America's Future showed that whites without college degrees had significantly more positive feelings toward the Republican Party than toward the Democratic Party. Nevertheless, Al Gore, the Democratic presidential candidate in 2000, won in the districts with the highest percentage of people with academic degrees (Edsall, 2001). Chapter 5 discussed the impact of education on political socialization.

Taxation. Small class differences appear in people's opinions about taxation. Surveys show that, overall, most people believe they pay too much in taxes, both federal and local. Opinions about high taxes are correlated with the individual's income; as a rule, the more money people make, the more likely they are to believe their taxes are too high. Correlation between people's opinions about taxes and their educational level is slight, though fewer people among the least-educated Americans than among other groups believe they pay too much to the federal government.

Foreign aid. The relationship between social class and support for giving foreign aid is positive. As a rule, individuals of higher income groups tend to support foreign economic aid to a greater extent than members of lower income groups. Likewise, the most educated express the highest level of support to foreign aid, while the least educated show the least support.

U.S. military action abroad. Income and education also correlate positively with opinions about U.S. military action abroad. When joint forces of the North Atlantic Treaty Organization (NATO) conducted air strikes against Yugoslavia in 1999, during the two-month conflict a sizable majority of Americans supported the action. Those who made the least money and were least educated expressed the least support. The middle class and the most educated individuals expressed the strongest support. Those with income above $75,000 were a little less enthusiastic about the strikes than the middle class was.

Undocumented immigrants. Among the most fundamental questions human societies face are whether or not to help people who are least fortunate, who will provide this help, and how much assistance will be provided. American public opinion shows generational patterns on this issue. In certain periods of history, people tend to express more willingness to help than in other times. In the United States, despite the tremendous economic success of the 1990s, people tended to be less willing to share with others, compared to previous decades. For example, consider opinions about undocumented (or "illegal") immigrants, technically called "illegal aliens." Upper and lower socio-economic groups differ in their opinions about whether undocumented immigrants should have access to state services and facilities. The more money people make, the less willing they are to use taxes to help the undocumented. On the other hand, with the exception of college graduates, all educational groups express similar opinions about government help to illegals: Across four out of five educational groups, less than 50 percent of Americans would support a law banning undocumented immigrants from using educational and healthcare benefits. College graduates, as a group, expressed a slightly different opinion: 57 percent said they would support the ban.

Affirmative action.   Support of affirmative action programs decreases with increased income. Differences among income groups are remarkable. Just over a third of people in the lowest income category support the abolition of affirmative action, whereas almost two-thirds of people of the two highest income groups support its abolition. College graduates, more than every 6 out of 10, express the most negative opinion of affirmative action across all educational groups. High school graduates express the most supportive attitude about the affirmative action, although 52 percent said they would support its abolition. There are also racial differences in attitudes about affirmative action.

The death penalty.   Opinions about the death penalty vary greatly and depend on the types of the questions asked, as we will see in Chapter 11 on domestic issues. Yet, most opinion polls reveal that income is not a substantial factor in determining people's opinions about capital punishment. Most Americans currently support the death penalty, and the differences between income groups are not significant. The only

---

A TOPIC FOR CLASS DISCUSSION   Income and Attitudes About Foreign Policy

Is it possible to predict foreign policy attitudes of social groups based on their income? One theory suggests that low-income individuals should oppose overseas military engagements because they regard them as a diversion of taxpayers' money from solving pressing domestic problems. As Chapter 5 on political socialization mentioned, the availability of resources throughout an individual's life may stimulate the development of post-materialist values. The core of these values is the support of world peace, harmony, and protection of the weak and oppressed, so an individual with post-materialist values is expected to support humanitarian military engagements overseas. Results of opinion polls (Table 8.2) show that both support of and opposition to U.S. military actions abroad show modest differences as income rises across income groups. That means that either (a) both hypotheses work or (b) neither does. What do you think?

group that shows relatively lower support for the death penalty is that with the highest income. Education does not seem to substantially affect opinions about capital punishment. Only individuals with postgraduate degrees are more reluctant than other groups to support the death penalty. Still, sizable majorities across all educational groups support the death penalty for a person convicted of murder.

Abortion. People in the upper classes express more tolerance for abortion than do other groups. Like survey questions on the death penalty, the wording of questions about abortion significantly influences people's opinions. Although a more detailed analysis of abortion views is presented in Chapter 11, regardless of the wording of the question on abortion, the gap between groups placed high and low according to income and education is substantial, often reaching 20 or more percentage points. Income and time spent in school are positively correlated with support for women's right to have an abortion, and more educated people as well as individuals with greater earnings are more tolerant about abortion (Princeton/*Times Mirror,* July 11, 1991, national adult, 1,212). In general, the support for women's right to abortion increases with educational level and reaches its maximum, 90 percent, among college graduates. The support drops slightly among the most highly educated Americans.

Free speech and individual rights. Low-income and low-education groups, compared to other groups, take a more restrictive stance on deviant behavior and controversial opinions. Consider, for example, possible sanctions against individuals who have been convicted of drunk driving. A gap of approximately 10 percentage points divides individuals of the two highest and two lowest income groups regarding a measure such as prohibiting drunk drivers from purchasing guns. A single-digit gap exists between high school and college graduates. A more distinct trend characterizes opinions of low-income citizens about the extension of freedom of speech to unpopular groups such as the Communist Party and the Ku Klux Klan. In fact, people of higher income are more likely to tolerate radical and reactionary groups than individuals of lower income categories. A substantial difference in opinions about the rights of unpopular groups exists between the highly educated and the least educated.

Overall, it is clear that with the increase of years of schooling, there is a growing understanding of human rights. About one-fourth of high school graduates believe certain groups may be deprived of their political rights. The same opinion is shared only by 3 percent of individuals with graduate degrees. Americans with the highest educational degrees tend to expand their tolerance with respect to social issues such as same-sex marriage. While support for this nontraditional type of marriage is relatively small among most Americans (only about one out of three), almost half of postgraduates would recognize the legality of same-sex marriage.

SOCIAL CLASS, ECONOMIC INEQUALITY, AND ATTITUDES

An individual's position in a particular social class does not automatically predict how someone thinks and acts. Nevertheless, membership in a social class may affect the

> ### A CASE IN POINT **8.1** The Information Rich and the Information Poor
>
> Economically successful people are far more knowledgeable about politics than are disadvantaged people. Studying surveys that examined how well Americans were informed about political and historical topics, names, and subjects, Delli Carpini and Keeter (1996) found that the average gap in political knowledge between the highest-paid group and the lowest was 40 percent. Many would argue that the opinion gap is easy to explain: Poor people are not interested in topics outside their sphere of immediate interest. Nevertheless, the gaps in knowledge about facts of more immediate relevance to the economically disadvantaged were about as large. Low-income citizens fell far behind the affluent in knowledge of people and parties committed to the problems of the disadvantaged as in knowledge of presumably less relevant facts. As these authors observed in their well-known book *What Americans Know About Politics and Why It Matters*, knowledge that can be useful in the expression of political interest is still "the province of those fortunate enough to advance educationally and financially" (p. 216). In other words, the distinction between upper and lower classes is also the distinction between the information rich and the information poor.

person's everyday experiences. Thus, economically troubled individuals are likely to draw their opinions from experiences that are quite different from the experiences of individuals who are economically successful. Likewise, members of the middle class are likely to develop opinions in the context of experiences that do not resemble those of either wealthy or poor people.

How do economic conditions and related experiences affect personal attitudes? Here are several possible explanations:

- Economic conditions have a direct impact on people's concerns and interests.
- These concerns are related not only to current social position but also to the changes that occur or might occur to that social position.
- Perceived economic inequalities affect people's views on whether or not these inequalities are justified.
- The perceived inequality between upper and lower social classes may spark the development of negative attitudes toward social classes or groups other than one's own.
- Economic inequalities affect the psychological process of self-identification, which may influence individuals to seek protection from certain political ideas and the forces that promote them.
- Economic disparity creates informational inequality that contributes to the attitudinal gap between upper and lower classes.

Class-Related Interests

Social class affects the major interests of individuals. One hundred and fifty years ago, Karl Marx was one of the staunchest supporters of this approach. The Marxist postulate **class interest** based on the assumption that each social class pursues an objective interest that exists independently of individual will. The realization of this goal is the fulfillment of their class interest. Thus, the oppressed should express a fundamental goal of redistributing resources and obtaining an equal share of the wealth. The oppressors, on the other hand, should have the opposite fundamental interest: to defend their resources from attempts to redistribute them.

Although most political and social scientists reject Marx's class struggle perspective, many scholars supported the assumption that people's economic condition and attitudes are linked (Edwards, 1954; Simon, 1983). Each person's economic situation largely determines the spheres of his or her *awareness and concerns*. People are anxious to gain more than they currently possess or to retain what they have, including their social status (Krugman 1997). People of lower classes typically support high taxes imposed on the upper classes. They are likely to endorse social programs that promote equality. They are also likely to support legislative measures that help them, as members of their social class, obtain more resources and benefits. On the other hand, people of the upper classes endorse lower taxes for themselves and oppose many social programs because they drain social resources and reward people who, they feel, do not deserve assistance. A person with no savings or investments is likely to be only slightly concerned with the swings of the stock market. Real estate owners are more aware of property taxation than nonowners. High-income earners pay more attention to income tax than to sales taxes (Bowler & Donovan, 1995). Individuals whose financial opportunities are relatively limited by the small size of their income are more concerned with wages and the availability of inexpensive products and services. For people with more secure positions, major concerns are investment opportunities and individual liberties.

In review. Ideas about class-related interest help explain the process of political socialization of individuals occupying lower or higher social status. Nevertheless, social classes contain a diverse collection of individuals who may pursue different goals.

Perception of Economic Changes

The opportunity for social mobility contributes to the way people identify with a social class. Social destination, and the process of moving from one status to another, not necessarily the status of origin, contributes strongly to attitudes, political orientations, and priorities (Turner, 1992). A person's social class or place in the social hierarchy does not necessarily determine what she likes or dislikes about government, religious freedoms, school vouchers, and foreign policy. People often base their attitudes on comparisons of themselves and others of their economic situation in the past. The perception of changes and anticipation of future positive or negative outcomes can significantly shape the opinions of people of any social class.

As an illustration, for 30 years after World War II, virtually every social group in the United States experienced rapid and sustained economic advancement. Every year, most people brought home more money than they did the year before. The economy was strong and expanding. As a result, when affirmative action programs were first introduced in the 1960s, they were met with a significant degree of social support (Trump, 1991). At a time of confidence in the present and hopefulness for the future, these programs, designed to promote equality and remedy past discrimination, were perceived with optimism by many people (see Chapter 5 on political socialization).

This optimistic attitudinal pattern began to change in the 1970s, through the 1990s. Average earnings continued to grow; however, when adjusted for inflation, the vast majority of Americans' incomes showed no real growth, and some families even experienced financial decline. The slowing economic growth coupled with increasing inflation resulted in changed perceptions of economic security. Yesterday began to look better than today, and many people anticipated the future with a great deal of anxiety. As a result, support for social equality programs declined (see Chapter 11, on domestic issues, for a more detailed analysis of opinions on affirmative action). What can explain this? Many individuals base their attitudes on a comparison of their past and present economic situation. If the comparison produces satisfying results, people tend to become more egalitarian (express pro-equality opinions). If the comparison is not satisfactory, their opinions are likely to become less egalitarian (Wilson, 2000).

Comparative studies show that the loss of social and economic security, which millions of people in former communist countries have faced since the 1990s, had a profound impact on their attitudes toward a free market and democracy (Shiraev, 1999). Links are direct between the loss of social class status and negative evaluation of free-market society. In the minds of millions of people in these countries, democracy was responsible for economic insecurity and other social problems (Fischer, 1999; Gryzunov, 1995; Moodie et al., 1995). Economics not only affects the direction and focus of social awareness but also influences people's general view of how resources should be *managed* and *distributed*.

How does the loss of social status affect an individual's attitudes and behavior? Belonging to the unemployed intensifies attitudes in some people and deepens the indifference in others. The loss of social status is frequently and distinctly associated with the growing indifference of workers toward work and social activities. Hans de Witte's study of German youth (1992) who lost their jobs found that a substantially larger proportion, compared to working youth, held either radically left, ultra-right, or completely apathetic attitudes. It is possible, too, that not only does unemployment influence attitudes but also that initially held attitudes (such as being undisciplined or apathetic) have something to do with losing a job.

Perceptions of Merit and Fairness

People want to protect what they have and secure access to resources they do not have. At least two broad views of the just distribution of resources and power in society stand out (Sears, 1996). According to the first view, the distribution should be based on **merit.** Because individuals cannot receive identical shares of everything, people normally compete for resources. As a result, people who, due to their adaptive individual traits or merits, are able to obtain access to more than others do deserve what they attain.

According to the other view, society should distribute its resources according to the principle of **fairness.** People may have different traits and skills and face dissimilar life circumstances. The outcomes of these circumstances, however, should not divide men and women into superior and inferior classes. Human society should provide all humans with equal chances and opportunities. Equal conditions should be provided for all people, not only the select few.

Which view is more acceptable to which category of people? Individuals who attempt to preserve their social class status, occupational prestige, or other privileges are more likely to develop merit-based attitudes. People from social groups that are relatively deprived of resources and privileges and who have limited access to high-paid jobs are more likely to adopt fairness-based attitudes.

Consider an example. Individual incomes in the United States grew rapidly from the end of World War II through the early 1970s. Later, however, the annual income of working people, adjusted for inflation, declined. The median wage for Americans dropped 10 percent and economic inequality began to grow. Incomes of the highest-paid 5 percent of Americans exceeded the entire income of the lowest-paid 20 percent. Workers without a college degree, almost three-quarters of the U.S. labor force, lost more than other groups in real wages (Wilson, 2000; Faux, 1997).

As a result, the more successful upper and upper-middle classes accumulated more wealth and guaranteed themselves greater economic security than the working class and the poor (Freeman, 1999). This social disparity yields two opposite ideologies. The upper class tend to support the merit-based principles and endorse conservative, pro-Republican views. The poor and the working class, on the other hand, endorse fairness-based ideas and vote for Democratic candidates.

Despite the simplicity and clarity of these assumptions, they do not necessarily predict political attitudes or voting behavior. Consider, for example, the 2000 presidential campaign. Contrary to what the merit and fairness hypotheses predict, most working-class districts supported the Republican candidate, George W. Bush. Most people in affluent districts supported the Democratic candidate, Al Gore (Edsall, 2001). A similar distribution of votes occurred during the 2004 presidential election.

Class-Related Antagonism

History provides vivid examples of the impact of economic factors on attitudes. Many people make conclusions and form new ideas based on their interpretations of their own socioeconomic situation. During periods of economic instability, when a feeling of financial insecurity expands across social groups, many people grow impatient and become susceptible to simplistic ideological messages about easily identifiable causes of economic troubles. As a rule, particular individuals or social groups are identified as causes of economic hardship. Different social, ethnic, and religious groups have been accused of causing such hardship. In the socialist revolutions of the 20th century, the prime targets of ideological and political attack were ruling classes. Religious and ethnic minorities were frequent targets as well. In Russia, the Bolsheviks blamed the royalty and the capitalists for the country's problems. In Germany, the Nazis blamed Jews for Germany's financial and economic turmoil of the post–World War I decades. All over the contemporary world, in Bosnia, Mexico, Rwanda, Northern Ireland, Russia, and other countries, ethnic groups are routinely accused of causing economic troubles. In the United States, many people commonly associate their problems, real or imaginary, with the impact of racial, ethnic, and religious minorities, including immigrants (Wilson, 1978; Parillo, 1997). Because of such beliefs, unfortunately, many groups turn against each other—race against race, ethnic group against ethnic group, and citizens against immigrants.

Self-Identity and Other Psychological Factors

Self-identification helps explain the relationship between social class and attitudes. People perceive themselves as members of large social groups, such as social classes. This perception affects their attitudes on a wide variety of issues; people express opinions and vote as members of a certain social class. Working-class individuals who strongly identify with that class are likely to develop similar attitudes. Working-class individuals who identify with the middle class are more likely to express different attitudes than those of the majority of working-class individuals (Sobel, 1993).

Marxist theories maintain that people of the same social class tend to express **class solidarity** and display similar opinions because they share common objective interests. Although class solidarity appears to be rational, antagonistic attitudes may be held by members of the same social class. According to one study, white working-class taxpayers tended to reveal their resentment toward black working-class welfare recipients because, according to the white respondents, their hard-earned tax dollars go to feed people who are not willing to work (Greenberg, 1995). In another study, most of the white unemployed individuals on welfare saw themselves as deserving such benefits but tended to see people from minority groups as undeserving (Fine & Weis, 1998).

Many people express their social position by distancing themselves from people of other social classes (Jennings, 1992). This produces a psychological acceptance barrier between the less successful and fortunate, on one hand, and the rest of society, on the other (Figure 8.1).

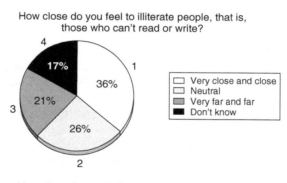

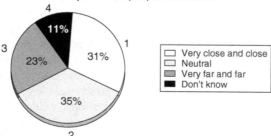

FIGURE 8.1

Opinions About the Less Fortunate.
Source: PSRA/NCCJ, January 2000, 2,584.

Sizable proportions across nations maintain a predominantly negative opinion about the poor. A telephone survey conducted in Hong Kong showed that most respondents evaluated poor people negatively: 68 percent said a lack of confidence and self-esteem were characteristics of the poor. Most respondents connected poverty with lack of individual responsibility. Almost 70 percent said laziness and a failure to strive for excellence cause poverty in most cases (Wong, 2000).

Members of upper classes tend to interpret the attitudes of people of lower classes, especially attitudes different than their own, as challenging the status quo. Conversely, opinions expressed by people from upper classes are often seen as attempts to further deprive the less fortunate of the opportunity to establish a fairer world. For example, the opposition of the upper class to higher taxation is frequently interpreted by lower classes as a lack of good will or sheer greed. Conversely, the support of the lower classes for higher taxation is often interpreted by the upper class as class envy.

Many individuals simply do not want to identify with a lower class. Consider another example. Many Americans from the lower class have high expectations for their future standard of living. Because of these expectations and the reluctance to identify themselves with lower social classes, many poor people avoid low-paying jobs perceived by them as demeaning (Jaynes, 2000). Hoping not to be identified as members of the lower class, some people remain stagnant in their social status because they are not eager to undertake actions they see as inappropriate even in order to improve their socioeconomic situation.

Access to Information

Social class affects individuals' educational advancement, which, in turn, influences their attitudes. Socioeconomic conditions affect individuals' access to information resources. Throughout history, lower social classes have faced limitations in their attempts to gain knowledge. Lack of knowledge prevents individuals from understanding their problems and needs as members of larger social groups. For many years and in various countries, most people from lower classes have faced serious restrictions and limitations on their access to schooling and knowledge. Today, social class membership depends, significantly, on individuals' educational advancement and how much they know. Across countries, the less people know about their position and about how resources are distributed in society, the less likely they understand their social situation and, therefore, the less able they are to protect their rights and defend their interests (Delli Carpini & Keeter, 1996).

In general, poor families have fewer opportunities than upper-class ones to encourage their children's educational skills (Rice & Dolgin, 2002; Douglass & Bloomfield, 1968). This disparity between upper and lower socioeconomic classes have grown larger in the computer age after the 1980s. More than 9 out of 10 Americans who made more than $75,000 per year had a computer by the end of the 1990s; only 28 percent of those who made less than $15,000 had computers (Gallup/*USA Today*, December 1999, 1,011). By the late 1990s, 87 percent of Americans with postgraduate degrees had computers in their homes. Most people who graduated from college or had several years of college education also had computers at home: more than 7 out of 10, according to the same survey. Only half of Americans with a high school degree and 32 percent of those who did not finish high school had a computer at home.

In review.   Social position influences quality of life. People may justify their social status to preserve their access to resources or challenge the status quo, aiming for personal achievement and fairer distribution of resources in society.

OCCUPATION AND OPINIONS

In *The Time Bind* (1998), Arlie Hochschild describes an undisclosed Fortune 500 company whose workers willingly shifted their interests and creative energies from families to work. They put in long hours not because the company's management demanded it but because many found their jobs more rewarding than their home lives. The company created work groups that began to provide greater psychological satisfaction and fulfillment than their families did.

Though this situation is not typical of most working Americans, Hochschild has a point. Professional groups are capable of bringing meaning into people's lives. Think about this: No matter what we do, groups to which we belong have a notable impact on how we think, what we want, and what we try to avoid. Sociologists call them "small groups," but their impact on attitudes is not minor. Many views, including important social and political outlooks, are formed, sustained, and altered by the groups with which people identify. Professional groups continue to be an important institution of socialization (Latane, 1981).

Studies of totalitarian societies provide a plethora of examples of how work groups influence attitudes and behavior of their members. For example, work units in urban China are assigned by the ruling communist government to carry out political, economic, and social functions. These functions range from serving as political censors for the government to distributing social benefits such as retirement plans, vacations, and apartments. Work units help provide education, assist in solving marital problems, and play a substantial role in maintaining order within the community. Because of work unit pressure, the vast majority of Chinese urbanites must be engaged in pro-government political activities, that is, they attend meetings, vote in local elections, and criticize dissidents (Shi, 1997).

Democratic societies avoid most oppressive forms of government and do not assign work units to control and brainwash individuals. Nevertheless, views on practically everything, from street violence to the budget deficit, from overseas military engagements to movie ratings, are routinely communicated and tested at work and among friends and coworkers. Social scientists have repeatedly shown that both general and specific working conditions can shape and transform people's political attitudes (Savage, 1985; Habermas, 1984; Kohn, 1969). It has also been long established that close friends and work associates tend to look at the social and political world in similar ways (Dawson et al., 1977).

As the socialization process continues well beyond the pre-adult years people with similar views attract each other. Friends may create and develop mutually acceptable views on many issues. Similar professional experiences may create similar interests and attitudes toward professional issues that can be extrapolated to broader social problems. Doctors, lawyers, and military officers share many beliefs and attitudes as groups (Steckenrider & Cutler, 1989). It is tempting to believe that many attitudes of professionals develop in the course of their working careers.

A CASE IN POINT 8.2   Selected Attitudes According to Region of Residence

There is little regional difference in people's opinions about whether the taxes they pay are too high: 57 percent of Southerners agreed, and 61–63 percent of people in other regions expressed the same attitude. In the South, 42 percent considered themselves conservative, as did 43 percent in the West. In the East, the proportion was lower—34 percent—and 33 percent of Midwesterners considered themselves conservative. Only 54 percent of people in the Western states supported air strikes against Yugoslavia; in other parts of the country, support was somewhat stronger: between 58 and 61 percent (Gallup/CNN, *USA Today*, April 1999, telephone, 1,055). Regional differences exist in tolerance of illegal drug use. Most Americans do not tolerate illegal drug use (NBC/*WSJ*/Hart, March 1998, 2,004). The greatest opposition, 77 percent, was expressed in the South. The East and West have 65 and 64 percent, respectively, of those who opposed, and Midwest showed 70 percent opposition. There was no regional difference in support of the death penalty for a person convicted of murder; in all four regions, support was between 73 and 76 percent (Gallup, February 1999, telephone, 1,054). Support for a law barring illegal immigrants from public schools, public hospitals, and other state-run social services (ABC/WP, August 1996, 1,514) was highest on the Midwest (51 percent) and lowest in the East (46 percent). Same-sex marriages were supported by 27 percent in the East and Midwest and 25 percent in the Western states. The lowest support, 17 percent, was expressed in the South *(U.S. News & World Report*, 1993, registered voters, telephone, 1,000).

However, following the rules of critical thinking, you should consider that these professionals may have developed their attitudes and values before they started their careers.

Higher education is akin to an occupation in providing a group experience. Typically, college students form and join campus groups for a variety of personal and educational reasons. Similarities in their experiences create similarities in expectations and interests. College education and training give many individuals broad knowledge and a sense of control. In a well-known comprehensive study of political socialization, Jennings and Markus (1986) showed how college experience changed the attitudes of young people. In the 1960s, before entering college, many of the participants of this study were conservative on a wide spectrum of issues. However, after going to college during the Vietnam era, many became more liberal on a number of social issues.

Work Engagement, Attitudes, and Participation

If economic situation shapes the direction of interests and affects the development of specific attitudes, why are the poorest social groups also the least interested in politics?

Why do more than one-third of low-income individuals identify as ideological moderates when they are, according to class-related assumptions described earlier, supposed to resist the status quo and attempt to change it? Another approach that links social class to attitudes examines this relationship from a different perspective. It pays attention to the issue of work participation and its impact on attitudes, social participation, and citizenship behavior. The individual's social class matters; however, exactly what that individual does at work matters too in determining views on social and political issues.

Specifically, opportunities to participate in workplace decisions are seen as crucial in determining social and political attitudes and the type of political participation. Individuals in subordinate work situations are likely to expect to be in similar relationships in their social life and politics. In contrast, people who participate in a wide range of social decisions at work are likely to extend these activities into social and political fields (Almond & Verba, 1965). For instance, enterprise ownership is related to a higher level of activity in local affairs than nonowning workers (Greenberg, 1981).

The workplace, according to this approach, is a micropolitical system in which participation in decision making, or occupational involvement, constitutes a significant form of social and political involvement (Oppenheimer, 1972; Sobel, 1993). There are four types of **occupational involvement.** The first is *authority,* which involves the rightful ability to tell others what to do. The second is *supervisory responsibility,* which involves the ability to direct the work of subordinates. The third is *work participation,* which includes involvement in workplace decisions that are permitted or required according to job description. The fourth is *job participation,* which includes involvement in running one's own job. Relations involving authority are, in fact, political relations on a micro level. The closer in structure or organization work relations are to those that occur in the outside political world, the stronger should be the transference of attitudes between work and politics (Sobel, 1993).

In practical terms, owners and managers are expected to be more active voters in local and national elections than other employees because managing and voting are both formally organized activities. In the United States, those who exercise formal authority at work tend to participate in formal political acts such as voting more frequently than those who do not exercise authority (Sobel, 1993).

People who are active participants at work also tend to play more active roles in the community and sometimes in protests. The sense of being successful in work often transmits to a feeling of obligation for community involvement. An early comparative study (Almond & Verba, 1963) found that workers who reported that they were consulted on the job had considerably higher scores on feelings of overall political efficacy or competence than did workers who were not consulted. Conversely, a lack of occupational success or fulfillment can lead to low levels of community involvement (Steckenrider & Cutler, 1989). Low self-esteem, rigidity of judgment, and political conservatism may be the consequence of monotonous, nondemanding work routines (Kohn, 1980). Because political participation and work involvement are positively correlated, it is difficult to make categorical statements about cause and effect in this relationship. However, studies today suggest that attitudes and values related to work participation more often stimulate attitudes and values related to political participation than vice versa. Moreover, occupational involvement should generate political participation because those empowered by activities within the workplace pursue similar political involvement outside since they learn to be political on the job. Those who do not participate in work-related decisions, or participate only in decisions affecting their own jobs, typically do not learn skills that carry over to the political sphere.

Some people may be active in both social participation at work and political activity because they are predisposed to seek authority, engagement, and opportunities for decision making. These individuals express their social and political attitudes in activities including work, community, and family. They transfer their political attitudes from work to politics and from politics back to work. As an example, a person may be actively involved in pressuring the local board of education to spend more money on children's activities; at the same time, this person may be actively promoting among his coworkers the idea of workplace childcare. On the other hand, some individuals, due to personality traits such as shyness, avoid engagement in both politics and work-related social activities.

As you remember from Chapter 5 on political socialization, there is a strong positive relationship between socioeconomic status and political efficacy. Individuals who have resources and a secure economic future tend to believe their voting and other forms of political participation matter for society and can make a difference in people's lives (Renshon, 1975; Almond & Verba, 1965). This does not mean, of course, that social class is the only factor determining political efficacy. The direction of this relationship can be the reverse. It is quite possible that an individual's beliefs can determine what she does and, subsequently, what social position she achieves.

Economic success influences an individual's place in a social class system and affects his views on politics. Individuals in higher-status positions tend to express greater interest in and to participate more actively in politics than people of lower social status. The data displayed earlier in this chapter (Table 8.2) and other studies show that people who are financially successful tend to express more interest in politics than those who make less money. Satisfactory or improving personal financial conditions, along with rising expectations of future success, are likely to stimulate interest in social life and public politics. Economic success is inseparable from economic independence. Women who are economically independent of their husbands were more likely to make political decisions that reflect their own political interests rather than their husbands' views (Carroll, 1989).

"Equal wealth and equal opportunities of culture have simply made us all members of one class," wrote the renowned American writer and utopian socialist Edward Bellamy (1850–1898) in a description he made in 1888 of human society in the year 2000. His forecast, however, did not come true. People possess neither equal wealth nor equal opportunities. But even if they achieved equality in these areas, it is doubtful they would share the same attitudes on who is "right" and "wrong" for public offices, moral and immoral actions, religion, environment, abortion, and many other features of human affairs and social life. Position in social class affects but does not determine opinions, attitudes, and values.

A CASE IN POINT 8.3 **A Study of Military Professionals**

In a study conducted in the late 1980s, American military professionals were found to be more nationalistic, and valued order and discipline in political life more highly than their civilian contemporaries (Lovell & Stiehm, 1989). Ten years later, a massive study based on 4,900 interviews examined a growing gap in attitudes between prominent U.S. civilians and the nation's military elite (Graham, 1999). The military officers polled were those considered on a fast track to top jobs; the prominent civilians were selected randomly from special biographical works. The study concluded that over the past quarter-century, elite military officers have largely abandoned political neutrality and become partisan Republicans. Overall, 64 percent of the officers identified themselves as Republicans. An ideological divide matches this partisan gap too. Military officers, for instance, are far more likely to identify themselves as conservative (66 percent) than are civilians (42 percent). Military officers tend to see civilian society in a moral crisis and think civilians should adopt more of the military's values and behaviors. Civilians tend to agree that a moral crisis exists but strongly oppose the notion that military values are the answer.

THINKING CRITICALLY ABOUT SOCIAL CLASS AND OPINIONS

Wording and Labeling

No matter how objective and impartial we want to be, when we assign people to groups, such as the upper class, the poor, or the middle class, we tend to introduce a bias. As soon as we label a group of people in terms of social class, we attribute to many members social characteristics that are likely to be inaccurate. How can we determine, for example, the social class position of white-collar employees, such as computer engineers? We may say that white-collar employees are middle class because of their income and the type of work they do. We may also say that white-collar workers are part of a managerial class. Alternatively, we may hold that some white-collar employees constitute a new type of working class when they engage primarily in manual work. Or, we may consider that white-collar labor is a special class between the middle and working classes. When we assign a social class label to a large group of individuals, we also tend to assign them a set of characteristics we think are typical for members of that class. In reality, being white collar, working class, and management each has separate effects on an individual's opinions and subsequent behavior (Sobel, 1989).

Social situation varies on a spectrum. As you remember from Chapter 3 on critical thinking, people tend to dichotomize variables that, more accurately, should be conceptualized as continuous. Many observable phenomena occur along a continuum but are frequently presumed to fit into one of two discrete types: either owners or workers. Social classes, for example, should be more accurately described not as distinct categories but rather along a continuum. To illustrate, how do we determine the social class of a woman born to working-class parents when she is about to receive her college degree? How do we assign social class to someone who was born to upper-class parents, received a good education, and later chose to live and work on a farm? There are approximately 5 million millionaires in the United States. Do they belong to the same social class as Americans who make more than $150,000 per year?

Another difficulty in determining a person's social class is that social status may change over one's lifetime. This transformation in social position is called **social mobility.** In some societies, social mobility is extremely difficult due to cultural constraints and political infrastructure. A classic Indian caste society, for example, is based on individuals' inherited status, which determines the occupation, income, and lifestyle of most people. In 20th-century totalitarian societies such as the Soviet Union, China, Cuba, and Cambodia, some social groups were encouraged or forced to migrate, become educated, and learn new professions, while other groups were held back and given little chance to change their social status. In addition, some relatively open systems allow considerable social mobility without serious regulation. Social scientists have long noticed that the lines between classes in these open systems are somewhat less delineated (Bell, 1960). Capitalist democracy is one such system. From 70 to 80 percent of people in the United States in the past 20 years experienced some sort of social mobility (Hout, 1998). This provides additional support for the view that social categories should be assigned with caution.

Context

The realization that survey questions are not serving their intended purpose may cause a pollster to change the study design. This happened with an unemployment rate survey administered by the Bureau of Labor Statistics and the Census Bureau in the early 1990s (*Washington Post,* 1993). To be counted as unemployed, an individual must meet two criteria: (1) being out of a job but available for one, and (2) having taken some action to find work in the four weeks before the interview. However, people routinely misinterpreted a key question: "Did you do any work at all last week, not counting work around the house?" Some unemployed people answered "yes" because they volunteered to help a friend or neighbor. A new survey contained a modified question: "Last week, did you do any work for pay?"

Accurate unemployment numbers not only satisfy the curiosity of researchers; they also form a significant measure of the overall economic situation in the country. In addition, the rate of unemployment is also a factor in people's evaluation of presidential performance and hence has political meaning.

Explanations

In survey analyses, it is important to use a comprehensive approach to examining factors that may influence attitudes. For instance, are the attitudes of middle-class black people distinctive from those of working-class black people? Do black-white attitudinal differences come largely from differences in income, education, and occupation? Tuch and Sigelman (1997) showed that race and class factors shape attitudes together. In particular, on the question of whether it is government's responsibility to provide jobs for those who need them, lower-class whites and higher-class blacks occupied an intermediate position between the strong opposition expressed by higher-class whites and the strong support expressed by lower-class blacks. Race and class reinforced one another among higher-class whites and lower-class blacks and cut across one another among lower-class whites and higher-class blacks.

Bias

Preconceived judgments are often caused by the way people interpret others' actions and attitudes. Social psychologists have established that when an individual judges other people's opinions, she tends to explain them as a product of their internal traits. At the same time, the importance of situational impact on opinions is frequently minimized. For example, imagine a person who does not say hello to you in passing. The person is rude—or isn't he? Maybe he did not see you or was preoccupied with an urgent problem. Maybe you did not say hello loud enough for him to hear you. What other interpretations are possible?

An interesting illustration of the influence of information on judgment is available from journalism studies. Television viewers see many reports about poor, unemployed, or homeless people in the United States. These reports either cover real-life stories about certain individuals or provide general information about unemployment, homelessness, or poverty in a state or in the country. The viewers tend to interpret reports about real homeless, jobless, or poor individuals in a specific way: Most consider that their problems are caused primarily by themselves (that is, they are lazy or unmotivated) and not by the way society is organized (that is, lack of opportunity, no healthcare). The viewers' opinions about such reports typically change when the reporter pays more attention to facts and figures representing issues on the state or national level. In these cases, viewers tend to attribute poverty and homelessness to social maladies rather than to personal causes (Iyengar, 1991; Mills, 1959).

ASSIGNMENT 8.1   CLASS INTERESTS
IN POLITICAL RHETORIC

During the first round of presidential debates in 2000, the Republican candidate, George W. Bush, met face-to-face with the Democratic nominee, Al Gore. An analysis of the debates' transcript showed that one candidate used the words and phrases "working people," "workers," and "the poor" 15 times. His opponent used these words only three times. Which was Gore? Let's consider this. In the United States, over the decades, supporters of the Democratic Party have tended to identify it with the working class and economically underprivileged groups. Their opponents, the Republican Party, are portrayed as supporters of big business, Wall Street, and the wealthy (Carmines & Berkman, 1994). So the candidate who avoided mentioning the working people was Bush? Wrong; it was Gore. Because the Democratic Party had already established its reputation among the working class, the pressure was on Bush to discuss issues from a perspective that would get the attention of members of this social class.

Now think about this. How often did other candidates appeal to "working people," "workers," and "the poor"? Using the key phrase "presidential debates," find online transcripts of the debates between Bush and Kerry (2004), Bush and Gore (2000), Clinton and Dole (1996), Clinton and Bush (1992), Bush and Dukakis (1988), and Carter and Ford (1976). Locate the words "working people," "workers," and "the poor." Which candidate used these words most often? Did Republican candidates

(Bush, Dole, Bush, and Ford) use these words more often than their Democratic counterparts (Kerry, Gore, Clinton, Dukakis, Carter)? Explain the findings.

CHAPTER SUMMARY

- Social class is a concept that refers to members of a large social group who occupy the same level in the social hierarchy by sharing common relations to productive resources. Income, education, living conditions, opportunities, occupation, and access to resources link people to different social classes. Membership in a social class is associated with people's positions in society and subsequently affects the quality of their lives and their attitudes.

- Contemporary definitions of social class or status are based on the supposition that society is stratified beyond two different classes, the middle versus the working class. Each class has several upper and lower divisions and subdivisions. The main criterion for class membership is personal income, though education and occupation also affect class situation.

- A person's educational level, income, and interest in politics are positively correlated. Ideological orientation is not necessarily correlated with income. A significant party-identification gap exists between groups of higher and lower income; generally, the more money people make, the greater their belief that their taxes are too high. Higher-income groups tend to support foreign economic aid to a greater extent than lower income groups. The most educated express the highest level of support for foreign aid, while the least educated support it least.

- Support of affirmative action programs decreases with higher income. Income is not a substantial factor in determining people's opinions about the capital punishment. Education does not impinge on people's stance on capital punishment. People in the upper classes express more tolerance toward abortion than do members of other groups. The support for women's right to abortion increases with level of education. Lower-income and low-education groups tend to take a more restrictive and authoritarian stance on deviant behavior.

- Economic conditions have a direct impact on people's concerns and interests. These concerns are related not only to their current social position but also to changes that might occur. Perceived economic inequalities also cause people to develop particular views on whether or not these inequalities are justified. The perceived inequality between upper and lower social classes may spark members' development of negative attitudes toward social classes or groups other than their own. Economic inequalities affect the psychological process of self-identification, which may cause individuals to seek protection from certain political ideas. Economic disparity creates informational inequality that contributes to the attitudinal gap between upper and lower classes.

- Similar work experiences may create similar interests and attitudes toward workplace issues that can be extrapolated to broader social and political problems. Opportunities to participate in workplace decisions are seen as crucial in determining social and political attitudes and types of political participation.

Individuals in subservient work situations are likely to expect to be in similar relationships in their social life and politics. On the other hand, people who participate in a wide range of social decisions at work are likely to extend these activities into social and political fields.

Looking Ahead.   Related to social class are ethnicity, race, and religion, in short, culture, that affect people's beliefs and attitudes. Chapter 9 explores the diversity of opinions expressed by and about different racial, ethnic, and religious groups on issues and in voting. Theories of social power and prejudice explain some of these differences in political opinions and behaviors.

DEFINITIONS OF KEY TERMS

Class interest—Objective interests of a class that exist independently of the wills of the individual members.

Class solidarity—Agreement of opinions and interests among members of a group belonging to the same social class and sharing common objective interests.

Fairness principle—The belief that society should provide its members with equal chances and opportunities.

Merit principle—The belief that people should earn access to resources and opportunities.

Occupational involvement—Four types of participation in decision making in the workplace.

Social class—A large social group whose members occupy the same level in the social hierarchy by virtue of common relations to productive resources.

Social mobility—The process of movement from one social position to another.

Social status (or socioeconomic status)—The individual's position in society, as measured by income, occupation, and education.

CHAPTER 9

Race, Ethnicity, Religion, and Opinions

Culture is simply how one lives and
is connected to history by habit.

LeRoi Jones

In the spring of 2000, the tens of thousands of demonstrators who took the streets of the United States capital in the cold rain to protest the meeting of the World Trade Organization had a common attribute: They were overwhelmingly white and young. In July 1998, when France won the World Soccer Cup, the Canadian city of Montreal erupted in elation. Hundreds of thousands of people rushed out of their homes to cheer and celebrate. The dancing and singing crowd was overwhelmingly French-speaking Canadian, or Quebecois. English-speaking Toronto was quiet that night. In the summer of 2000, 92 percent of blacks and 76 percent of non-Hispanic whites in Miami, Florida, said that the Cuban boy named Elian Gonzales, brought to the United States by his mother, who died en route, should be returned to Cuba. Only one group overwhelmingly objected this plan: Cuban Americans, 83 percent of whom said the boy should remain in the United States (Witt, 2000). In upstate New York in 1999, a man refused to join 11 other jurors in convicting several defendants of cocaine charges, saying he was sympathetic to the defendants' struggles as blacks to make ends meet. In deliberations, this juror proclaimed that the government's case wasn't worth "a bag of beans." This man was African American (Biskupic, 1999).

Look around. Check opinion polls. Read newspapers. You do not have to be a professional to notice the obvious tendency of people to express opinions along the lines of their national, ethnic, racial, and religious groups. Why do these culture gaps in opinions occur? How substantial are such divisions?

Looking Forward. Ethnicity, race, and religion, or culture, separately and together, affect people's beliefs and attitudes. This chapter explores the diversity of opinions expressed by and about different racial, ethnic, and religious groups on issues and in voting. The theories of social power and prejudice help explain differences in political opinions and behaviors among groups.

CULTURE: ETHNICITY, RACE, AND RELIGION

Before we start our analysis, we should define culture. What is culture and what role do ethnicity, race, and religion play in an individual's cultural identity? For the purposes of this textbook, we define **culture** as a set of attitudes, behaviors, and symbols generally shared by a large group of people and communicated from one generation to the next (Shiraev & Levy, 2004). No society is culturally homogeneous. No two cultures are entirely similar, and no two are entirely different. One cultural cluster can comprise significant variations and dissimilarities.

Take, for example, the term commonly used for European countries, the United States, Canada, and English-speaking Australia and New Zealand: Western culture. This group of countries may represent one cultural cluster; however, each of these countries is diverse and stratified. Furthermore, some Western countries are more diverse than others, while others achieve relative equality. Use the term *culture* cautiously, recognizing that whenever you do, you describe general patterns. People who belong to the same culture do not necessarily have identical traits and opinions.

Cultures are created by people, and people tend to identify with particular cultures. Race, ethnicity, and nationality, among other characteristics, are recognizable variables or components of cultural identification. What meaning do people attach to the words *race, ethnicity,* and *nationality?* There is no single understanding of these terms. For this reason, and because the definition debate is far from over, we introduce widespread, common, and prevalent views on these concepts.

A **race** usually indicates a large group of people distinguished by certain similar and apparently biologically transmitted physical characteristics. It is essential to mention the high or low frequency of occurrence of such physical characteristics because practically *all* physical traits appear in *all* populations. Race is also a social category. Why? It indicates, first and foremost, experiences shared by most people who happen to belong to a racial category (Brace, 1995; Dole, 1995; Gould, 1994, 1997; Langaney, 1988). In some countries, race is used as an official demographic category. For instance, in contemporary United States, the government recognizes the following racial categories (Table 9.1).

TABLE 9.1

Racial Categories in the United States.

White (includes people of European, Arab, and Central Asian origin)
Black (includes people of African origin)
Native American (includes people of American Indian, Eskimo, and Aleut origin)
Asian (includes people of East Asian and Pacific Islander origin)
Hispanic (includes people of South and Central American origin)

Source: U.S. Bureau of the Census.

Pakistani-Americans, Palestinian-Americans, and Finnish-Americans, according to this categorization, are considered white. A person who was born and raised in South Africa and then immigrated to the United States would not be considered black if his ancestors were from the Netherlands (even though they settled in Africa a hundred years ago). The Hispanic category incorporates people of every racial group. For example, a person of African ancestry who was born and raised in the Dominican Republic and later immigrated to the United States would be considered Hispanic.

How many people of each race or group of origin live in the United States? Below in Table 9.2 are estimates by the U.S. Bureau of the Census, the government organization that provides statistical analysis of American population, of the distribution of races in the United States in 2005.

In the United States, the term **ethnicity** usually indicates an individual's cultural heritage, the experience shared by this person and others with a common ancestral origin, language, traditions, often, religion, and geographic territory. Ethnicity is often confused with **nationality,** which is commonly defined as a person's identification with a geographical territory unified as a political entity as an independent state recognized by other countries.

The Diversity of Opinions

Representatives of ethnic and religious groups express a miscellany of opinions. Among them are, however, some common patterns. As a general pattern, for instance, black and Hispanic U.S. citizens, compared to white and, in some cases, Asian citizens, are more supportive of the government's active involvement in policy issues such as employment, job security, and education. Assessing their own **political tolerance,** the willingness to support the extension of citizenship rights to all members of society and to permit the expression of political ideas or interests one opposes, many Americans do not want to give their least-liked groups (such as communists or Ku Klux Klan members) free speech rights or the right to hold rallies, teach in public school, and run for public office. However, black people tend to be less tolerant of their least-liked groups than are whites and Hispanics (Davis, 1995). Look at the data presented in Table 9.3 and compare the expression of political tolerance toward communists. In these examples, white people show a lower level of intolerance than other groups. However, blacks

TABLE 9.2

U.S. Population by 2005. (In estimates.)

Race/Origin	People by 2005	%
Total	285,981,000	
White (including Hispanic)	232,463,000	81.3
Hispanic origin (of any race)	(36,057,000)	(12.6)
Black	37,734,000	13.2
American Indian, Eskimo, and Aleut	2,572,000	0.9
Asian and Pacific Islander	13,212,000	4.6

Source: The U.S. Bureau of the Census, Current Population Reports, Series P25-1130, "Population Projections of the United States by Age, Sex, Race, and Hispanic Origin: 1995 to 2005."

TABLE 9.3

Distribution of Agreement in Answers to Opinion Polls According to the Respondent's Ethnic/Racial Affiliation. (In percentages.)

	Overall	White	Black	Hispanic	Asian
Very interested in politics (Princeton/CRP/Pew, April 1997, telephone, 1,404)	29	29	28	20	6
Approval of President Clinton's job performance (CBS, January 1998, 855)	73	69	90	85	84
There should be a law barring illegal immigrants from public schools, public hospitals, and other state-run social services (ABC/WP, August 1996, telephone, 1,514)	49	53	28	23	n/a
When a woman becomes pregnant through rape, abortion should be legal (AP/ICR, January 1998, telephone, 1,012)	74	74	73	72	n/a
Favor the Supreme Court ruling that women have the right to have an abortion during the first three months of their pregnancy (Yankelovich/*Time*/CNN, May 1998, telephone, 1,234)	55	55	62	50	60
Nude magazines and X-rated movies provide harmless entertainment for those who enjoy them (Pew, November 1997, telephone, 1,165)	41	39	57	39	31
Profanities in movies are not offensive to me (Gallup/CNN/*USA Today,* July 1999, telephone, 1,031)	24	24	18	28	n/a
Federal spending on foreign aid should be decreased (*NY Times,* April 1998, telephone, 1,395)	49	52	35	39	40
Sexual materials lead people to commit rape (GSS, February–April 1993, personal, 1,606)	57	57	58	n/a	n/a
Everyone convicted of drunk driving should have a special sign on his/her license plate so that everyone would know (Princeton/*Newsweek,* January 1995, telephone, 753)	51	50	61	n/a	84
The government should ban all cigarette advertising (ABC, June 1997, telephone, 1,001)	53	53	54	49	n/a
The ground war in Iraq would be worth the cost of several thousand American troops (CBS/*NY Times,* February 1998, telephone, 1,153)	30	30	28	35	42
Oppose the legality of same-sex marriages (*U.S. News,* May 1993, registered voters, 1,000)	74	74	72	100	100
Consider an extramarital affair always harmful to a marriage (*Newsweek,* September 1996, telephone, 751)	70	71	66	n/a	66

TABLE 9.3 *(continued)*
Distribution of Agreement in Answers to Opinion Polls According to the Respondent's
Ethnic/Racial Affiliation. (In percentages.)

	Overall	*White*	*Black*	*Hispanic*	*Asian*
The death penalty for someone convicted of rape (*Time*/CNN/Yankelovich, June 1997, telephone, 1,024)	47	46	50	59	25
Freedom of speech should not extend to groups like the Communist Party or the Ku Klux Klan (Pew, November 1997, telephone, 1,165)	38	26	49	40	44
Paparazzi have gone beyond their constitutional guarantees of free speech (*LA Times,* September 1997, telephone, 1,258)	75	76	69	70	83
No type or level of illegal drug use should be tolerated in the United States (NBC/*WSJ*/Hart, March 1998, telephone, 2,004)	70	67	82	79	60

and Hispanics are more tolerant of the undocumented immigrants (commonly called *illegal aliens*), compared to whites, and the opinion gap between these groups is significant. Asians express more intolerant attitudes toward paparazzi photographers—hunters for sensational photos of celebrities.

The table shows that the groups hold somewhat similar attitudes about cigarette advertising, extramarital affairs, and abortion in the case of rape. The groups do not differ substantially in the ways they connect rape with "sexual materials" (that is, videos and magazines); most Americans across ethnic groups see the materials causing the assaults. Blacks and whites typically express the same level of interest in politics, which is slightly higher than Hispanics. Relatively small but statistically significant differences appear in how groups perceive women's right to abortion during the first three months of pregnancy. Blacks express the most support to this law and Hispanics the least, with a 12-point gap between them. The table shows clearly the substantial opinion gap between Asian Americans and other groups with respect to interest in politics.

Black respondents appear more sensitive to ethics issues, such as profanities in movies, and less judgmental of erotic publications than other groups; the attitudinal gap, though, is small. Asian Americans distinctively approve punishment for drunk driving; most support public humiliation of offenders by requiring special license plates. Overall, 51 percent of Americans support this measure, 30 percentage points less than the Asian American group alone. The groups differed in their willingness to risk American lives in the military operation against Iraq. Whites, compared to other groups, are more in favor of decreasing federally funded foreign aid.

The difference in attitudes about same-sex marriage, an issue in the 2004 presidential campaign, of Hispanics and Asians, on one hand, and the rest of the country, on the other, is remarkable. Whereas sizable majorities of Americans, slightly less than three-quarters of the population, oppose the legalization of same-sex marriage, Asians and Hispanics show little diversity in opinion on the subject; practically all of them oppose such a measure. Most Asians express strong opposition to death penalty, demonstrated in their opinions about the death penalty for rape. While the opinion gap between blacks and whites is not statistically significant, there is a considerable gap between (a) black and whites and (b) Hispanics. Overall, almost 6 of every 10 Hispanics supported the death penalty for rape and only 1 in 4 Asians supported this measure. Blacks express the most intolerant attitudes about the use of illegal drugs, compared with Asians and whites.

Before we examine theories that attempt to explain the similarities and differences in attitudes among ethnic and religious groups, let us describe some attitudinal trends in several major groups in the United States.

Blacks

The U.S. Bureau of the Census projects a population of approximately 37 million black people in the United States by 2005, the overwhelming majority born and raised in this country. In 2000, fewer than 500,000 people in America were born in Africa (U.S. Bureau of the Census, 2000). The legacies of slavery and segregation, hidden behind the hypocritical legal principle of separate but equal in education, work, marriage, political participation, recreation, and even school tests, have left scars on the lives of African Americans almost a century and a half after slavery was abolished.

Polls suggest that black people, in general, are more dissatisfied with the American political system than are whites and other groups. People's attitudes on this matter are substantially affected by their perception of the process of desegregation, on which there are three major views (Morris et al., 1989; Bobo, 1997). According to the first position, the United States continues to be a racist country. Segregation has, in fact, never ended; it only changed its forms and continues to exist in many institutionalized but subtle structures (Willie, 1979). Supporters of the second view criticize the first and state that racism as an institutional obstacle has disappeared and that it is up to blacks themselves to advance and achieve in American society (D'Souza, 1995). In the third view, racism had a devastating impact on black people; however, a combination of social efforts to remedy the misfortunes of racism and of the sustained effort of African American themselves has stimulated progress.

About 6 in 10 blacks identify as Democrats, less than 10 percent are Republicans, and the rest are Independent or lean to other parties (WP/Kaiser/Harvard, June–August 1999, 2,197). In the 2000 presidential and the 2002 midterm elections, about 90 percent of black voted for Democratic candidates. In 2004, about 11 percent of blacks voted for George Bush (*NYT*, 11/7/04) (see Chapter 10 on voting). Blacks, in general, are supportive of vigorous governmental efforts to address employment, job training, and other work-related issues. According to data published by Tuch and Sigelman (1997), there is a black-white consensus in favor of providing help for the elderly and assistance to college students from low-income families. Almost 80 percent of blacks support government's involvement in employment and unemployment issues. However, the support of whites of this issue was relatively modest: between 40 and 50 percent. Moreover, most whites refuse to endorse measures such as quotas in college admissions, government involvement in housing, and choosing members

A CASE IN POINT 9.1   Perception of Discrimination

There is a notable attitudinal gap between blacks and whites in their perception of discrimination, according to most national and local surveys. For example, consider a study of 1,000 students conducted at the University of Washington (Rivera, 2000). Students were asked to rate racial conflict on campus on a scale of 1 to 6, with 6 being the most serious. Black students had the mean score of 3.53, whereas white students' mean score was 2.57. Other groups scored closer to each other (Filipinos, 3.02; Asian-Americans, 2.97; Hispanics, 2.94; and Native Americans, 2.86). For an item about being exposed to a racist atmosphere in the classroom, black students had a mean score of 2.91, which was significantly higher than the 1.73 score of white students.

of a particular group over others on the basis of racial or ethnic identity (see also Chapter 11 on domestic issues).

Blacks and whites also differed in their perceptions of how affirmative action is covered by the media. Among those who said the media are biased in covering affirmative action, 50 percent of whites and 17 percent of blacks said the media deliberately support affirmative action; 73 percent of blacks said the media are negatively biased (PSRA/*Times Mirror,* July 1997, 1,212). Black people's opinions are about evenly split between supporters and opponents of the death penalty, while whites are predominantly in favor of capital punishment (Gallup, February 1999, 1,054).

As a group, despite their overwhelming support of the Democratic Party, blacks express opinions almost as conservative as opinions of whites. Overall, consistent with the study by Tuch and Sigelman, less than 40 percent of blacks consider themselves liberal, and 25 percent call themselves conservative. By comparison, about 25 percent of whites are self-proclaimed liberals, and slightly over 33 percent are conservatives. In general, comparative studies show that the attitudinal gap between blacks and whites began narrowing in the 1960s (Jennings & Niemi, 1981). This trend continued in the 1990s and early 2000s due to several factors, including the rapid growth of the black middle class.

African American representation in the U.S. House of Representatives leaped dramatically in 1992 after the creation of numerous districts with black majority populations. But blacks no longer experience the same post-redistricting gains. With the 1993 *Shaw v. Reno* ruling, the Supreme Court sharply curtailed the deliberate drawing of majority-black districts. One argument against such districts is that making race the dominant factor in redistricting violates the Constitution's equal protection clause. In addition, Democratic strategists understand creating majority-black districts drains blacks from other districts, which are then more likely to vote Republican (Lublin, 2002; Guinier, 2000).

Hispanics

Nearly one in four registered Hispanic voters is less than 30 years old, and 13 percent of Hispanic voters were naturalized as citizens since 1996. Since 2000, the Hispanic population of eligible voters has been one of the fastest-growing groups in the country, increasing by 700,000 in just two years (*Washington Post,* October 4, 2002). As the statistical data presented earlier show, Hispanics, an extremely diverse group with respect to national roots, income, education, occupation, and social position, represent almost 13 percent of the American population. The number of U.S. citizens born in Latin America is approximately 10 million. Hispanic voters, as a group, began to draw the attention of experts and politicians in the early 1990s. Today, campaign experts understand that neither Republicans nor Democrats can win California, New York, or Texas without securing at least a third of the Hispanic votes at the polls. Any presidential candidate today clearly needs Hispanic votes to win the White House (Booth, 2000).

The political and social views of many people of Latin origin (also called *Latinos*) are closely related to the way they see themselves: (1) as a minority group and, therefore, disadvantaged persons, or (2) as U.S. citizens enjoying all the rights and opportunities of citizenship (Garcia, 1997). The influence of Catholicism is inescapably a critical factor in any assessment of Hispanic attitudes since both South and Central America are predominantly Catholic.

As we noted earlier, Hispanics are slightly less interested in politics than the general population but significantly more interested, as a group, than are Asians. Surveys demonstrate that 26 percent of Hispanics describe themselves as liberal, 34 percent as moderate, and 34 percent as conservative. In 2000, by a ratio 2 to 1, Hispanic citizens favored the Democratic Party over the Republican Party (Booth, 2000). In 2002, 49 percent of Hispanic voters surveyed identified themselves as Democrats, 20 percent as Republicans, and another 20 percent as Independents. However, specific survey questions show less support for Democrats; when participants were asked whether they had more confidence in congressional Democrats or in President Bush, 43 percent favored Democrats and 42 percent chose the president (Pew/Kaiser, September 2002, Hispanic voters, 1,329). Big differences also exist within the Hispanic voting bloc. As an example, in the 2000 election, Cuban-Americans in Florida voted overwhelmingly for George W. Bush, while Hispanics as a whole (including non-Cuban Hispanic voters in Florida) voted 60 to 40 for Al Gore. Hispanic voters in 2000 backed Al Gore over Bush, 62 to 35 percent (Eilperin, 2002). In mid 2004, John Kerry had a 2 to 1 lead over Bush among Hispanic registered voters (Morin & Balz, 2004), though 43 percent of Hispanics voted for Bush (*NYT*, November 7, 2004).

Hispanic men and women show less support for abortion than the national population; more than half the respondents of the Pew/Kaiser 2002 poll believed abortion should be illegal in most (30 percent) or all (24 percent) cases. At the same time, Hispanics are similar to a national sample of Americans in their attitudes toward the death penalty. Almost 72 percent of Hispanics supported the death penalty for a person convicted of murder, and 24 percent were against it, compared to the overall national support rate of 71 percent and opposition of 22 percent (Gallup, February 1999, 1,054).

More than half (55 percent) of Hispanic voters in 2002 preferred to pay higher taxes to support a bigger government that provides more social services. Almost half (48 percent) thought there were too many immigrants in the United States; nevertheless, 76 percent believed the United States should allow more Latin Americans to work in this country legally.

Hispanics tend to express conservative attitudes about same-sex marriages, overwhelmingly rejecting the idea of legalizing them. On the other hand, their more tolerant opinions regarding extramarital affairs are not much different from the majority's views. U.S.-born Hispanics are more likely to vote than are naturalized citizens. However, among Hispanics with yearly incomes of less than $15,000, the reverse tendency is true. Almost 53 percent of naturalized low-income Hispanic citizens, compared with 42 percent of U.S.-born Hispanic citizens with low income, voted in 1996. Among those in the lowest income bracket (less than $10,000 per year), 47 percent of naturalized citizens voted, compared with 41 percent of the U.S.-born (Bass & Casper, 1999).

Asians

Less than 5 percent of Americans claim Asian ancestry and are a majority only in one state, Hawaii. The second-largest group of Asians is in California, where they represent more than 12 percent of the population. The Asian population of Washington, New York, and New Jersey is above 5 percent. Like Hispanics, Asian Americans tend to live in families that are larger than the average and typically have several working adults. They also tend to concentrate in metropolitan areas with high costs of living and are internally stratified according to social class, national origin, and ethnic lines (Taylor, 2002).

Many ethnic groups in U.S. history, especially during the initial periods of immigration and settlement, have experienced the painful pressure of expulsions, national origin quota systems, repatriation campaigns, selection tests, and other immigration hurdles. Historically, the relationship between the U.S. government and Asian population was complicated by a variety of anti-immigration laws and regulations (Ancheta, 1997). Asian Americans faced discriminatory laws including the Chinese Exclusion Act of 1882, anti-miscegenation acts prohibiting Asians (and blacks) to marry whites, the World War II detention of Japanese Americans, and postwar restrictive immigration bills. Despite these and other difficulties, Asian Americans have largely succeeded in the United States and now are one of the most economically prosperous and educated groups in the country.

As Chapter 8 on social class explained, two reliable criteria typically predict high levels of political participation in the United States: high educational level and high median family income. Asians, as a group, are a clear exception to this rule (Lien, 1997). More educated and economically advantaged Asian citizens, in general, are no more active voters than other educational and income groups. As a group, Asian Americans show a participation deficit; that is, they underparticipate in electoral politics. Among the 10 million Asian Americans, no more than 2 million are believed to be registered voters. Moreover, as you saw in Table 9.3, Asian Americans are also, as a group, less interested in politics than are whites, blacks, and Hispanics.

Low interest and modest participation, obviously, do not preclude Asian Americans from expressing diverse attitudes on a number of political issues. For instance, Japanese and Filipinos tend to be more Democratic, whereas the majority of Koreans and Southeast Asians tend to vote Republican (Tilove, 2000). On the other hand, attitudinal consistency makes this group stand out. For example, Asian Americans show overwhelming support for the punishment of people convicted for drunk driving, almost unanimously oppose same-sex marriage, support the death penalty, and are not particularly strong opponents of illegal drugs.

TABLE 9.4

Some Major U.S. Religious Populations.

Religious Body	Number of Members
Protestant (Christian)	85–86 million
Roman Catholic Church (Christian)	62 million
Orthodox Christian (Russian, Greek, Ethiopian, and others)	5.6 million
Jewish	5.2–5.6 million
Church of Jesus Christ of Latter-day Saints (Mormon)	4.2 million
Muslim	1.6–4 million
Buddhist	1.8 million
Hindu	795,000

Sources: Yearbook of American and Canadian Churches (1999); U.S. Bureau of the Census (2002); National Jewish Population Survey (2002); Religious Congregations and Membership (2000). When the direct count is unavailable, assessments are made by other groups based on different criteria.

RELIGION AND ATTITUDES

How many people in the United States claim affiliation with a major religion? Table 9.4 displays the top eight religious affiliations of Americans. The most prevalent religious group in the United States is Christians, with over 158 million of followers. For every 25 Americans who consider themselves Christian there is one Muslim or Jewish person.

Now let us look at religious affiliation and attitudes. Table 9.5 displays a sample of attitudes expressed in the late 1990s by people who identified themselves as Catholic, Protestant, or Jewish, and for comparison, a group that did not identify with any religion. This selection of attitudes on issues ranges from the death penalty to foreign aid. Despite a tremendous diversity of opinion within these religious groups, there are some noteworthy patterns. Across religions in the United States, orthodoxy increases the chances that an individual votes Republican.

Individuals who claimed no religious identification were more eager than the other three groups to risk American lives in the confrontation with Iraq. Nonreligious individuals demonstrated more liberal views (except on the death penalty and federal spending issues, on which the differences in opinions were not statistically significant), compared to Christians. Overall, as a comparative analysis shows, the Jewish group, compared to Christians, expressed more liberal opinions. The differences on many issues are remarkable, and the attitudinal gap is over 20 to 30 points on issues such as the death penalty and federal spending on foreign aid. The gap is in double digits on other issues.

Catholics and Protestants

Mormons and white evangelical Protestants are predominantly Republican, and the large majority of them voted for Bush in 2000 and 2004. Those of these groups who attended church less frequently split 55–45 between Bush and Gore in 2000 (Barone et al., 2002). Liberal reforms, gay rights activism, feminism, and pro-choice policies, which are likely to be associated with the Democratic Party, tend to alienate religious voters. For example, in the 1950s and 1960s, most Catholic voters were Democrats. The

Democratic Party's movement in a liberal direction may have contributed to a majority of Catholics voters switching party affiliation; most Catholics voted Republican in the presidential elections of 1972, 1980, 1984, and 1988. This tendency reversed again; in 1992 and 1996, a majority of Catholics voted Democratic (Prendergast, 1999; Layman, 1997). Although in 2000, practicing Catholics favored Bush by 14 percentage points, less religious Catholics backed Gore by 18 points (Barone et al., 2002). In 2004, the majority of Catholics (52 percent) voted for George Bush though John Kerry is a Catholic (*NYT*, November 7, 2004). A solid majority of Catholics today are economic liberals; they tend to support taxation related to social issues and support labor unions, foreign aid, pro-environmental protection, and strict government regulation of industry and consumer products—all traditional Democratic themes. On the other hand, the majority of Catholics are social conservatives that support the death penalty and oppose abortion and drugs. These are all traditional Republican themes (Prendergast, 1999).

According to surveys (Table 9.5), Catholics and Protestants tended to express similar opinions on many issues, with the exception of a small 6-point gap in their views on whether or not sexual materials lead people to commit crime. In other instances, the differences were insignificant because they did not exceed 3 percentage points.

TABLE 9.5

Distribution of Agreement in Opinion Questions According to the Respondent's Religious Affiliation. (In percentages.)

	Protestant	Catholic	Jewish	None
Consider self a Republican (Pew/Princeton, September 1999, 597)	37	25	18	6
Consider self a Democrat (Pew/Princeton, September 1999, 597)	28	34	57	24
The ground war in Iraq would be worth the cost of several thousand American troops (CBS/*NY Times*, February 1998, telephone, 1,153)	30	29	14	42
Federal spending on foreign aid should be decreased (*NY Times*, April 1998, telephone, 1,395)	50	47	24	49
Sexual materials lead people to commit rape (GSS, February–April 1993, personal, 1,606)	62	56	40	36
Nude magazines and X-rated movies provide harmless entertainment for those who enjoy it (Pew, November 1997, telephone, 1,165)	38	41	62	56
Freedom of speech should not extend to groups like the Communist Party or the Ku Klux Klan (Pew, November 1997, telephone, 1,165)	40	40	24	22
Abortion should be illegal in all circumstances (Gallup/CNN/*USA Today*, January 1998, telephone, 1,004)	17	19	0	7
The death penalty should be the penalty for murder (CBS, February 1998, telephone, 620)	45	44	15	41

Protestants and Catholics do, however, tend to vote differently. In 1992, 44 percent of Catholics voted for Clinton, while only 34 percent of Protestants did so. In 1996, 53 percent of Catholics voted for Clinton and only 35 percent of Protestants did so (Weber, 2000).

Catholics make up 24 percent of the electorate, some 62 million citizens, and in 2000 actually voted at a rate 4 percent higher than Protestants (the difference would be even more significant if Hispanic turnout were not relatively low). The impact of the Catholic vote is greater than numbers alone because the Catholic population is heavily concentrated in key states with high Electoral College votes, including Massachusetts (54 percent of the electorate), New Jersey (46 percent), and New York (44 percent) (Weber, 2000).

Jews

Almost half of more than 5 million American Jews live in two states: New York and California. The 2002 National Jewish Population Survey found that 24 percent of American Jews hold graduate degrees, compared with 5 percent of the general population, and the median income of Jewish households is $50,000, compared with a national figure of $42,000. A fifth of Jewish households are low-income, defined as earning $25,000 or less, which reflects recent Russian immigration and the aging of the Jewish population (Cooperman, 2002). Historically, Jewish voters support Democratic presidential candidates with 65–80 percent of their votes. The campaign of 1980 was a rare exception: When Ronald Reagan, the Republican, and Independent candidate John Anderson divided the Jewish vote and reduced support of the Democratic party by 19 percent, 39 percent of Jews voted for Reagan against Jimmy Carter. In 2000 and 2004, 19 and 25 percent, respectively, of Jews voted for George Bush (*NYT,* November 7, 2004).

In state elections, however, Jews have frequently supported Republican candidates. For example, as Zogby (1998) points out, three prominent New York politicians of the 1990s, Senator Alfonse D'Amato, Governor George Pataki, New York City mayor Rudolph Giuliani (and his successor, Michael Bloomberg, elected in 2001), all received strong and consistent support from Jewish voters. American Jews account for more than half of the large individual contributors to the Democratic Party and, in recent years, between 20 and 30 percent of the contributors to the Republican Party (Zogby, 1998).

The Republican agenda is supported by Jewish voters in at least three categories. The first category of Republican backers is Orthodox Jews, whose attitudes toward a wide range of social issues tend to be conservative. The second category comprises middle- and upper-middle-class Jews who live in suburban areas and tend to support the Republican agenda on taxation and economic policy. The third category comprises recent Jewish immigrants from Eastern Europe and countries such as Iran. They modify their anticommunist and anti-authoritarian views into a set of pro-Republican attitudes like lukewarm support of affirmative action, new taxation, and immigration.

Polls continue to show that the vast majority of Jews support abortion rights and oppose the death penalty and school prayer. Jews are more tolerant of the content of the media, more permissive regarding social behavior, and show greater support than do Americans in general for U.S. aid to foreign countries. Traditionally, most Jews also support government aid to poor and needy people. Since the 1990s, most American Jews have supported the Middle East peace plan and an independent Palestinian state (Cohen & Liebman, 1997).

Muslims

Islam has more than 1 billion adherents across the world. Although Muslim immigration to the United States was relatively small, the Immigration and Nationality Act of 1965 signaled a substantial increase of immigrants from Arab countries, the Middle East, and other Islamic states. From 2 to 6 million Muslims live in the United States (Table 9.4), not all of whom have Muslim ancestors. According to some estimates, about 30 to 40 percent of American Muslims are blacks who embraced Islam in the United States (Parillo, 1997) and black converts make up the fastest-growing segment of the American Muslim population. Up to 90 percent of all U.S. converts to Islam are black (Sperry, 2002).

Research conducted by the American Muslim Council in New York City (Culver, 1999) provides one of the first in-depth views of the attitudinal patterns of this large religious and cultural group. According to a 2001 Zogby poll, 40 percent of American Muslims considered themselves Democrat, 23 percent said they were Republicans, and about 35 percent Independents. In 2004, 50 percent of American Muslims considered themselves Democrats, 12 percent were Republican, and 31 percent were Independents, with 1 percent undecided (www.projectmaps.com). The vast majority of Muslims in the United States favor the rights of Palestinians and oppose military actions against Iraq. American Muslims are overwhelmingly against abortion. Remarkably, most Americans tend to see this religious group as significantly disadvantaged; the results of a 2000 poll suggest that almost 42 percent of Americans, the largest proportion that expressed this opinion about any religious or ethnic group, believe Muslims in the United States suffer at least some discrimination (PSRA/NCCJ, January–March 2000, 2,584). In the same poll, 31 percent said Muslims have too little influence in American society (36 percent said the influence is about right).

American Muslims have formed several organizations to promote their interests and start voter registration drives. In 2000, for the first time, Muslim advocacy groups endorsed a U.S. presidential candidate: George W. Bush. The Council on American-Islamic Relations sent a post-election questionnaire to mosques. Of 1,774 respondents, 72 percent reported voting for Bush, who actually got about a third of Muslim votes (Gore about half, Nader an eighth). Of those, 85 percent said their decision was influenced by the endorsement of Muslim groups (Murphy, 2000). In 2004, over two-thirds voted for John Kerry (Bakhari et al, 2004).

In review. Most U.S. minority groups tend to support the Democratic Party; however, this support depends on several situational factors. Hispanics divide their votes, but the majority tend to vote Democratic. Among the exceptions are Asian Americans and Muslims, who are about evenly split between Democratic and Republican preferences. Religious orthodoxy, as noted earlier, increases the chances an individual express conservative attitudes and will vote Republican.

THEORIES OF DIFFERENCES

So far, we have discussed cultural factors such as ethnicity, race, and religion that affect attitudes of large cultural groups. Why do culture gaps exist? Perhaps the explanations sound alike: "Well, the differences in attitudes are based on cultural differences among people." In fact, such an explanation, called *tautological reasoning* (Levy,

1997), does not explain much. We know that cultures are different as well as similar in many ways and forms. So the question is what specific factors associated with culture have an impact on individuals' attitudes?

Several approaches help us understand why factors such as religion and ethnicity influence people's views. Remember that these approaches are not cohesive theories but rather standpoints from which to make assessments and judgments.

From the **social power** standpoint, availability of and access to resources are the most significant factors influencing the values and opinions of ethnic and religious groups. Taking the **cultural identity** approach, the strength and content of cultural identity are the most significant factors affecting people's behavior and attitudes. In the **cultural prejudice** view, people form stable negative perceptions of and attribute negative traits to other cultural groups and, based on these negative assessments, form their own beliefs and values. Finally, from the **cultural variables** standpoint, each culture has distinct and measurable characteristics; these can be viewed as mechanisms that influence, shape, and reshape people's attitudes.

The Social Power Perspective

According to the social power perspective, economic factors drive society. If a social group gains access to resources, it obtains social power and can thus dominate other social groups. Groups dominated by others are deprived of resources and, subsequently, kept out of power.

Perhaps the simplest way to contrast one group to another in terms of socioeconomic advancement is to compare the income people in each group earn. Figure 9.1 displays the median income per household among major groups of origin (racial groups). Median scores in this table indicate that 50 percent of the families in each category make more than the median and 50 percent of the families make less than the median.

The top income group in the United States is Asians, followed by whites. Blacks and Hispanics, as groups, make significantly less money. Overall, according to the

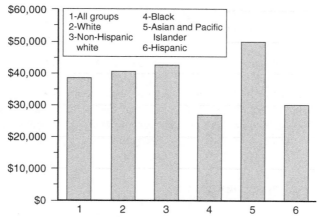

FIGURE 9.1

Median Income per Household, 2002.
Source: U.S. Bureaus of the Census, Current Population Survey.

social power approach, this economic inequality determines differences among the groups with respect to their access to political power and a wide range of resources, including health and preventive care, high-quality food, good living conditions, and job, educational, and recreational opportunities. These factors determine the overall quality of life. In short, racial and ethnic attitudes reflect the perceived competition among groups for limited resources (Bobo, 1988; Sigel, 1970).

Domination and hierarchy influence the way groups see society and each other. In other words, not race or ethnicity, the indicators of individuals' ancestral roots, but rather association with a certain social class creates major behavioral and attitudinal differences among groups (Blauner, 1972; Wilson, 1978; Sowell, 1981). For instance, people from a certain ethnic or religious group who belong to the economic middle class are expected to associate with the middle-class representatives of other ethnic groups. As an illustration of an assumption based on this approach, lower-class whites should experience similar problems and concerns as lower-income blacks and Hispanics; therefore, there should not be a substantial gap in their attitudes. From this perspective, minorities' rise to prosperity and their assimilation into the mainstream of American middle-class society should decrease racial or ethnic group differences in attitudes and voting.

Supporters of this approach believe that education and occupational advancement can bring groups closer together and make their attitudinal differences less pronounced (Juviler & Stroschein, 1999). This may apply not only to white/non-white relationships. For example, misunderstanding, mutual disappointment, and even tensions between blacks and Cuban Americans in Miami may be caused by the way these two ethnic groups share, or rather are not able to share, political power in the region (Witt, 2000).

However, oppression and discrimination may also contribute to passivity and avoidant behavior in subordinate individuals. Such people become uninterested in social issues and politics because, in their view, little can be done to change their circumstances. The ruling class may also discourage the oppressed from participation in democratic institutions. As Morris and colleagues (1989) argued, among the reasons why only 20 percent of eligible black voters were registered to vote in 1952 were obstacles beyond legal impediments in voting rules, such as hostile and violent actions against black voters, especially in the South, as well as discriminatory literacy tests, and poll taxes. As an alternative to political apathy and lack of participation, the protest tradition developed that taught young blacks to question the system of white political domination. This tradition not only promoted disaffection with the majority society but also encouraged black pride and group solidarity (Scheepers et al., 1992; Wirt, 1997).

The social power perspective offers clear and simple ideas that explain why people prefer particular ideological and political affiliations, including liberal and conservative values. Although the differences between conservatism and liberalism are complex, in general, the conservative tradition emphasizes the importance of property rights and basing the distribution of resources in society primarily on merit (Sniderman et al., 1984). The liberal tradition, in contrast, emphasizes individual liberties and proposes that the distribution of resources in society be based primarily on need. Following these rules of reasoning, one might expect that those social groups that have access to power and resources would lean toward conservative ideology, while

> ## A CASE IN POINT **9.2**   Black Support of Political Parties
>
> When Americans of all backgrounds were asked about why they think black Americans have overwhelmingly voted against Republicans and for Democrats over the years (HT/NBC/*WSJ*, March 2000, 1,213) the top choices were predominantly social and economic explanations. Compare the answers in the table. (*Note:* Respondents could pick more than one choice.)
>
> | Responses About Why Blacks Did Not Support Republicans. (In percentages.) | |
> | --- | --- |
> | Republicans' position on social issues such as education and welfare | 24 |
> | Republicans' lack of support for affirmative action programs | 19 |
> | Republicans' lack of support for civil rights policies | 19 |
> | Republicans' position on economic issues | 17 |
> | Republicans have very few black-elected officials and party leaders | 15 |
> | All/none/not sure | 27 |
>
> | Responses About Why Blacks Supported Democrats. | |
> | --- | --- |
> | Democrats' position on social issues such as education and welfare | 30 |
> | Democrats' support of civil rights policies | 24 |
> | Democrats' support of affirmative action programs | 19 |
> | Democrats' position on economic issues | 15 |
> | Democrats have more black-elected officials and party leaders | 11 |
> | All/none/not sure | 34 |

oppressed groups such as ethnic and religious minorities should embrace liberal values. Likewise, political affiliation should be connected to people's acceptance of either liberal or conservative values. For many decades in the United States, Democrats traditionally attracted the votes of less affluent groups, including ethnic minorities. Not surprisingly, the suggestion that the Republican Party should "improve its stance towards minorities" appeared in a 1999 survey as the most important condition that would encourage people to vote for the party (Tarrance/BAPAC, May 1999, national adult blacks, 800).

Beware of simple generalizations and stereotypical pigeonholing since the statements "You are poor, so you are a Democrat" and "You are wealthy, so you are a Republican" are far from accurate. For example, a sizable proportion of working-class Americans vote Republican. Consider another example. American Jews are among the wealthiest religious groups in the United States. Do they vote Republican? Only a few of them. Consistently, over many years, most Jews identify as liberals and vote Democratic. As Cohen and Liebman imply (1997), such "passion" for liberalism is rooted in the Jewish socialization process that promotes in children values of universal compassion and collective responsibility for the less fortunate. One of the most consistently oppressed groups in world history, Jews, in general, associate themselves with minorities, as a minority themselves, and understand the needs of people who are deprived of society's resources.

Access to resources determines access to power. Access to power determines many attitudes of the powerful. After the Civil War, although the majority of white Americans accepted the abolition of slavery, they did not accept the achievement of equality. The idea that black people and other minorities would live in the same neighborhoods, go to the same schools, and share the same resources as whites was unacceptable to many of them. As a result, segregation laws called "Jim Crow" lasted decades and left a deep impact on American society (Sears et al., 1997). Similarly, in the 1960s, most Americans accepted the idea that racism should be eliminated once and for all. In the last 35 years, Americans have changed many of their beliefs about race and equality. In general, they have become increasingly supportive of racial integration. However, their support of specific policies to bring about integration has been inconsistent and ambiguous (Ball-Rokeach & Loges, 1994). Since the late 1980s, while supporting racial and ethnic equality in principle, many white Americans expressed their opposition to further implementation of egalitarian policies such as affirmative action and redistribution of resources according to principles of fairness (Sears, 1988, 1996).

Overall, major differences in opinion formation and its expression by groups reflect realistic assessments of their social, economic, and political position in America. Despite the apparent logic and simplicity of the social power perspective, there are many objections to its way of explaining differences in attitudes. Without diminishing the importance of socioeconomic factors, many critics turn instead to emotional and cognitive factors. One of them is prejudice.

Theories of Cultural Prejudice

Imagine you agree to participate in a national survey and answer this question: "For each of the following groups, please tell me whether you feel that they are receiving too many special advantages, receiving fair treatment, or are being discriminated against." The list of groups follows. How would you answer this question? What criteria would you apply in your opinion? Table 9.6 displays the results of a 2000 national poll that asked this question about treatment of a variety of minority groups.

TABLE 9.6

Perceptions of Fair Treatment, Special Advantages, and Discrimination Against Selected Groups. (In percentages.)

	Asian Americans	Evangelical Christians	Catholics	Hispanics	Blacks
Too many special advantages	11	14	9	15	19
Fair treatment	60	52	75	46	42
Discriminated against	18	12	6	30	34
Not sure	11	22	10	9	5

Source: NBC/*WSJ*/Hart, March 2000, telephone, 1,213.

Of course, some people believe they use objective criteria to evaluate people. Others, however, judge solely on the basis of their feelings and perceptions. Everyone simply likes and dislikes some things and people. Many of us do not even try to explain why we do not like something or someone. To be prejudiced is to hold a negative opinion about particular people or a group just because you do not like them. **Prejudice** is an adverse, preconceived, and unsubstantiated judgment. The stronger an individual's prejudice is, the less likely she will hold a positive opinion about a negatively evaluated person or a group (Levine et al., 1999). How does prejudice affect other attitudes? As many theories of attitude suggest (see Chapter 4 on attitudes), a negative or positive opinion can cause a chain reaction of corresponding opinions.

Prejudice can develop and be expressed against age, racial, or ethnic groups (for example, the elderly, blacks, or Germans), social groups (for example, working-class people, lawyers, or professional athletes), or religious groups (for instance, Christians, Hindus, or Sikhs), men and women, political groups (such as pro-life and pro-choice activists, liberals, or conservatives), and many other group targets. Prejudice is measured in several ways such as emotional closeness. Look at the distribution of answers to a

TABLE 9.7

Americans' Feelings Toward Certain Ethnic and Religious Groups.

Question: "Here are some groups that have been in the news. Please tell me how close you feel to each of them: very close, close, neutral, far, very far, or don't you know enough about the group to say. How close do you feel to...?" "Have contact" stands for the percentage of those who said they have contact with a particular group. (In percentages.)

	Whites	Blacks	Hispanics	Asians	Native Americans
Very close	36	15	10	6	11
Close	39	44	34	26	25
Neutral	21	31	35	36	31
Far	2	4	6	10	10
Very far	—	2	2	5	4
Don't know/refuse	1	3	13	21	18
Have contact	87	83	66	52	41

	Immigrants	Muslims	Jews	Fundamentalist Christians	Atheists
Very close	8	4	7	12	3
Close	24	9	29	21	9
Neutral	34	27	36	26	25
Far	13	14	8	9	14
Very far	4	11	4	11	24
Don't know/refuse	17	36	17	22	25
Have contact	49	24	51	48	28

Source: PSRA/NCCJ, January–March 2000, 2,584.

national poll that asked people to estimate their emotional closeness to various ethnic and religious groups (Table 9.7).

Prejudice is also interpreted in a variety of ways. Some prominent scientists view it as an internal form of aggression (Dollard et al., 1939). Others interpret it as a reflection of an unconscious need to have enemies (Volkan, 1988), while many treat prejudice as a result of learning experiences (Gielen et al., 1992). Prejudice is also often interpreted as a cognitive phenomenon, an attitude produced and enhanced by other attitudes and values. For instance, some experts trace the roots of American's prejudices back to early Americans' belief in the rightness of control of the country by white, male, Protestant northern Europeans (Smith, 1997). Sidanius and Pratto (1993, 1999) showed, for example, that positive attitudes toward market capitalism influences beliefs in social inequality. In contrast to the views of supporters of the social power approach, Gilens (1995) suggested that negative racial attitudes are, in fact, the most important source of opposition to welfare policies among whites. Stereotypes of blacks as lazy and irresponsible individuals are still widespread among whites and may continue to have a profound impact on whites' social and political thinking. In particular, some whites view blacks as violating traditional values of American individualism and not possessing positive trait characteristics such as competence, industry, moderation, and self-control (Bobo, 1997). Researchers also argue that many anti-black attitudes of the 1950s have been largely replaced by a more subtle form of modern prejudice called *symbolic racism* that is based on assumptions that racism is officially over and blacks together with other minorities demand too much from society (Sears, 1988; Raden, 1994).

Prejudice is commonly understood as an irrational feeling that may be reduced by a variety of means, including education. As a rule, people who are more educated tend to be less prejudiced than those who are less educated. This rule has exceptions, however. An analysis of attitudes collected in an American National Election Study shows that highly educated individuals still maintain strong negative opinions about religious fundamentalists (Bolce & De Maio, 1999). Specifically, the respondents in this study were asked to locate their feelings about certain groups on a 100-point scale from 100 (most positive), 50 (no feeling at all) and 0 (most negative). Religious fundamentalists received 47 points. The lowest levels of sympathy were expressed toward liberals (46 points) and illegal aliens (average 35 points); the highest points were given to the poor (68 points).

Age-related experience can also affect prejudice. In the 1990s, age groups born soon after 1945 were less prejudiced against minorities than older groups born prior to the 1940s. This trend did not continue, though. The younger adults born in the 1970s, for example, are somewhat more prejudiced than their parents (Wilson, 1996).

Prejudice is not only a state of mind; it often translates into behavior (Kirschenman & Neckerman, 1991; Farley et al., 1994; Bobo & Zubrinsky, 1996). Prejudice-based behavior evokes new perceptions and new prejudice (Du Bois, 1940). Prejudice, for example, affects evaluations of political candidates and actual voting. Black candidates for office typically encounter a degree of difficulty securing white votes that is based partly in racial prejudice (Citrin et al., 1990; Kinder & Sanders, 1996). In a study of the influence of the race factor, Moskowitz and Stroh (1994) found that black political candidates need to overcome at least two big psychological obstacles. The first is a prejudiced reaction of voters to the candidate's

TABLE 9.8

Meta-stereotypes: Mutual Assessments Between Whites and Blacks. (In percentages.)

Stereotype	Percentage of Whites Who Endorse This Sterotype (Davis & Smith, 1990)	Percentage of Blacks Who Perceive Most Whites as Endorsing This Stereotype (Time/CNN, April 1991, 504)
Prefer to live off welfare	59	75
Violent	54	82
Lazy	47	69
Unintelligent	31	76
Unpatriotic	18	44

Source: Sigelman and Tuch, 1997.

race. The second is a set of distortions of the candidate's issue positions, common in cross-cultural perception and communication. For example, Sigelman and Tuch (1997) showed that blacks and whites not only perceive each other inaccurately but also misrepresent what other groups think and feel (Table 9.8). Overall, as this study suggests, blacks and whites have stereotypes of other groups and often act according to these stereotypes.

In review.   Prejudiced individuals tend to reason about other groups in stereotypical ways: "They are different from us; there is nothing in common between us and them. They are evil. They are all the same, monolithic and unified. They are threatening and take advantage of us. They do not change." Prejudice may be used as a convenient explanation for the differences in attitudes among ethnic, national, and religious groups. However, this point of view, in most cases, does not explain why the negative evaluations occur in the first place.

CULTURAL IDENTITY

When John F. Kennedy was nominated for the U.S. presidency in 1960, his opponents openly argued that he, as a Catholic, would report to the Pope in the Vatican to receive policy directions and other orders. When Connecticut senator Joseph Lieberman, an Orthodox Jew, was the 2000 vice presidential nominee of the Democratic Party, a few prominent figures raised concerns about whether the senator would put the interests of his religion and Israel before the interests of American people (Watanabe, 2000). During the election year of 2004, issues such as abortion, stem cell research, and gay marriage were frequently debated from religious points of view. This is an old question: When do we express our individual views and act on our own, and when do our thoughts and actions represent the groups to which we belong?

Theories of social identity suggest that people tend to think, feel, and act in line with their personal identifications. Their emotional and cognitive attachments to particular **reference groups** serve as standards for behavior and attitudes. Two psychological principles, liking and similarity, explain why reference groups can be effective determinants of attitudes (Holtz & Miller, 1985). Knowing that you are similar to the members of an ethnic or religious group can bring a variety of psychological rewards. According to the social categorization theory (Tajfel, 1982), individuals identify with "in-groups" in order to promote their self-esteem, basing this on a belief that their group is greater, better, or more advanced than out-groups. Thus, voting for a candidate of one's own race or ethnic group may enhance a person's self-esteem by creating a sense of empowerment. This psychological process of self-empowerment may compensate for feelings of inadequacy created by a perception of personal economic and social deprivation (Bovasso, 1993).

Members of religious, ethnic, national, and other groups tend to develop a sense of collective identity on the basis of two kinds of perceptions: perceptions of shared features within the group, and perceptions of the differences between these features and those of other social clusters. This creates in members of the group a sense of uniqueness. Thus, Chinese mainland identity is different from Taiwanese identity because the latter was initially formed under years of exceptionally difficult conditions of blockade, isolation, resistance to threats, and continuous reliance on military power (Bullard, 1997). In seventeenth-century England, many educated individuals considered themselves exceptionally rational and scientific, not like their peers in other European countries. In today's Israel, the sense of uniqueness is based on the concept of continuous struggle, endurance, and success (Merom, 1999). Many Americans share beliefs in their own distinctive identity as an exceptional nation that represents the most just society in the world. Boykin (1994) suggested that the uniqueness of people of African ancestry is that many of them share nonmaterialistic and community-oriented beliefs to a greater extent than other group do. Many Russians share a belief in their own Eurasian exceptionality rooted in cultural legacy and superior intellectual and military strength (Shiraev & Zubok, 2001).

A CASE IN POINT 9.3   Culture and Democracy

Can most people in a country be unready for democracy? If a political system has free elections and the rule of law, how can a country not be ready? For many years, Western politicians and opinion leaders have pressured African countries to adopt multiparty systems for an apparently indisputable reason: Free democratic elections should produce governments accountable to the citizens. For Schaffer (1998), such a "mechanical" approach to political transformation is not always effective. He showed that the culture of Senegal, a country in Western Africa, is one of the reasons democracy does not seem to work there, at least from the standpoint of a Western observer. Most Senegalese base their political decisions not on free choice but rather religious and tribal solidarity and perceptions of social hierarchy. Under such conditions, candidates' agendas, policy preferences, and character mean little, especially compared to patron loyalty and the expectation of immediate material rewards when their candidate is elected. How does this differ from the U.S. and Europe?

However, belonging to a particular group of ethnic Americans does not necessarily make an individual share every aspect of that identity. A poll by the *Washington Post,* the Henry J. Kaiser Family Foundation, and Harvard University (June–August 1999, Hispanic adults, 2,417) showed an interesting pattern. About 50 percent of Hispanics think they, as a cultural group, share only a few political interests and goals with each other. Many Puerto Ricans said they did not have much in common with Mexican Americans, and Cubans suggested they had little shared interest with immigrants from Central America (Booth, 2000).

A crucial element in understanding how cultural identity influences attitudes is identity strength. The stronger an individual feels about his or her own identity, the more influence the identification will impose on the person. In surveys of religiosity, more than 95 percent of Americans, consistently over the years, say they believe in God (Table 9.9). However, people interpret God in a variety of ways (Bishop, 1999).

It is not easy to gauge the strength of an individual's attachment to a particular religion because there are different kinds of religiosity. In terms of rituals, some people frequently observe them, and some do not. Degree of belief in religious doctrine varies tremendously. The extent to which religious beliefs figure in an individual's daily behavior and how well he is informed about the history and doctrines of his religion differ (Glock, 1962). According to the Barna Research Group (January 1994, 1,206), 67 percent of Americans agree that God is "the all-powerful, all-knowing, and perfect creator of the universe who rules the world today." However, others have different ideas. About 10 percent of Americans think of God as "a state of higher consciousness." Approximately 8 percent consider God "a realization of personal human potential," 3 percent of people mentioned many gods, and another 3 percent imply that "everyone is God." As you can see, even if there is an overwhelming consensus about belief in God, people differ in the ways they understand the deity (see Table 9.9).

A special category of religious attitudes and behavior is **religious fundamentalism.** Typically, fundamentalists insist on literal interpretations of sacred books or teachings and call for a restoration of the original interpretation of religious concepts. They frequently reject scientific explanations and guidance about how to live. Fundamentalists often display psychological intolerance of other people's opinions and behavior; they tend to not accept religious pluralism and a multiplicity of choices. In their eyes, only their own religious views have validity, and those of others do not.

TABLE 9.9

Americans Answering the Question "Do you believe in God?"
After 1976, the question was, "Do you believe in God or a universal spirit?" (Gallup).
The question in 2003 was "Do you believe in God, or not?" (QUPI). (In percentages.)

	November 1944	*August 1967*	*December 1988*	*December 1994*	*June 2003*
Yes	96	98	95	96	92
No	1	2	5	3	6
Don't know	3	1	1	1	3
N (sample size)	1,500	1,525	750	1,016	1,015

Source: Gallup and QUPI.

Fundamentalists generally preach social and political conservatism. With few exceptions, they are pro-life, in favor of religious education at school, against divorce and gay rights, and for tougher control over the content of media and the arts. Generally, religious fundamentalists stand for clear and definite moral principles.

Less than 10 percent of Americans in 1996 considered themselves religious fundamentalists (CBS/*NYT,* June, 1,200), a drop from 1994, when 17 percent reported such membership or association (CBS/*NYT,* September, 1,161). Since the late 1980s, voters have begun to orient their political attitudes and behavior according to their feelings about Christian fundamentalists, who began to play, at least to some minds, the role of a negative reference group (Bolce & De Maio, 1999). As you can see from Table 9.10, approximately a third of Americans in the past had either an antagonistic or moderately antagonistic attitude about Christian fundamentalists. In a 2000 poll, "mostly unfavorable" and "very unfavorable" opinions about this group were held by 36 percent of Americans, and a favorable opinion was expressed by 48 percent (Gallup, March 2000, 1,024).

The strength of religious identity is associated with beliefs in whether the government should protect American religious heritage from secular activists. The separationists who want to see no government involvement in advancing religion were losing ground in the 1990s (Servin-Gonzalez & Torres-Reyna, 1999). Increasingly larger numbers of Americans supported the idea that the government should protect the country's religious heritage. In 1987, 32 percent supported this idea (CCD, 1,889); in 1998, the number reached 48 percent (WP, August, 2,025). However, the question was asked with one small but potentially substantial difference. In the 1987 poll, the question was asked about the "Judeo-Christian heritage," whereas the 1998 poll referred to the more neutral "religious heritage." The proportion of Americans who support the idea that clergymen may discuss political candidates or issues from the pulpit has risen over time. In 1965, this approach was supported by 22 percent of respondents (Gallup, October, 2,783); in 1998, the proportion was 34 percent (WP, October, 1,018).

Overall, individuals can maintain their cultural identity and at the same time be active citizens who contribute to the community. A democratic nation can be culturally diverse but at the same time unified if its members accept the political order, share a common identity with other citizens, and exercise full equality of rights and obligations.

TABLE 9.10

Attitudes Toward Christian Fundamentalists. (In percentages.)

	1988	1992	1996
Antagonistic	22	17	20
Moderately antagonistic	14	13	15
Indifferent	54	56	55
Moderately positive	6	8	6
Positive	4	6	5
N (sample size)	780	1,179	821

Source: American National Election Studies.

THINKING CRITICALLY ABOUT CULTURE AND OPINIONS

Context

Pollsters examining the views of racial, ethnic, or religious groups need to learn about the racial and ethnic composition of the regions in which the survey was conducted. For example, more than one-quarter of American Muslims (approximately 1.5 million) are black. Approximately half of American Jews live in just two states, New York and California. Chicago has the largest Jewish population of any U.S. city after New York and Los Angeles. In Chicago, the number of Muslims now exceeds 300,000, making them the area's third-largest religious group, after Catholics and Protestants. By the beginning of the 2000s, Minnesota was home to the largest settlement of Somalis outside Africa. In Massachusetts, 54 percent of registered voters are Catholic, while among registered voters in Texas only 23 percent are Catholic. Florida's largest Hispanic group comprises Cuban immigrants and their descendants. New York City's largest percentage of Hispanics are Puerto Ricans. Washington, DC, and nearby northern Virginia have large proportions of immigrants from El Salvador. Southern and southwestern states have large populations of Mexican Americans. Overall, Mexican immigrants constitute 60 percent of the nation's Hispanics. To understand immigrant groups, it is crucial to remember that many immigrants come to the United States from economically underdeveloped countries and that many do not have, or did not have when they first arrived, the educational and professional skills that they may later attain that would allow them to find high-paying jobs.

When pollsters ask a respondent to identify his race or ethnicity, the answers are often based on the person's decision about his ancestral origins. Does having a Hungarian grandmother make her grandson John, born in Philadelphia in 1983, a Hungarian? If Dina's grandparents were Jews raised in Latvia, why does Dina consider herself Jewish but not Latvian? If Rahim's great-grandfather lived in an area of Africa now called Togo, does this indicate that Rahim is black? And what if Mike's mother is Irish, his father is from Samoa, and their parents have mixed backgrounds? More than 2 million people born in the United States before 1990 were children of mixed marriages. This category is especially imprecise because no criteria define the term *mixed*.

The racial and ethnic composition of society is typically considered a solid sociological fact. Nevertheless, people's opinions about their own identity may affect not only how surveys are interpreted but also many policy-related issues. Remember, in the contemporary United States, many people's identification with their ancestral cultures has become a matter of choice (Clausen, 2000). The 2000 Census forms allowed Americans to choose from 63 possible racial combinations, and each of these could be combined with Hispanic for a total of 126 choices (Cohn, 2000). It is up to respondents to choose one race or to indicate multiple backgrounds. However, some critics vigorously opposed this array of choices on the grounds that if many Americans identify as mixed ancestry, the number of people in previously existing racial categories would be significantly reduced. The result, these critics argue, would be multiple revisions in the distribution of federal funding for minorities, would affect educational and social programs, and would even change the racial composition of juries.

Overall, when you analyze surveys that involve respondents' identifiable cultural backgrounds, try to identify factors and events that could have influenced people's answers. Examine the poll's design and the context in which the survey was taken.

Bias

In attempting to understand the world in which we live and to navigate our way through life, we adopt a wide variety of beliefs and expectations. The content of these ranges from the mundane (the best brand of detergent, the most flattering hairstyle) to the profound (the meaning of life, the existence of God). Of course, our expectations vary in the degree to which we become personally invested in them. What happens, then, when our expectations are challenged by new facts in survey data? What happens to those assumptions we particularly like or have come to accept as truths? If we responded to such challenges in a purely rational manner, we would simply detach our personal feelings from the dispute, evaluate the substance of the challenge objectively and dispassionately, and then, if appropriate, modify our conclusions accordingly.

But people are not always rational. Specifically, when our assumptions are challenged by new facts, we are prone to feel we are personally being challenged as members of a social, ethnic, or religious group. Our first impulse, typically, is to protect our beliefs, as if to protect ourselves. Thus, some people cling to their assumptions and expectations, even in the face of contrary evidence. This bias in thinking is called the **belief perseverance effect** (Lord et al., 1979). When people engage in belief perseverance, they usually respond to challenges by discounting, denying, or simply ignoring information that runs counter to their beliefs. Belief perseverance can lead to stereotyping, and these assumptions can lead to erroneous expectations. Consider the following examples.

As shown in this chapter, the vast majority of Hispanic voters in the United States support Democratic candidates over Republicans. Should we anticipate that this voting pattern is unchangeable? Not necessarily. For instance, in Texas, according to several polls, from 39 to 49 percent of Hispanics voted for the Republican governor-to-be George W. Bush when he ran for office in 1998. In the 2000 presidential election, Cuban Americans voted overwhelmingly for George W. Bush, while Hispanics as a whole (including non-Cuban Hispanics in Florida) voted 60 to 40 percent for Al Gore. Seventy-five percent of Cuban Americans said they would vote for Bush in 2004 (WP/Univision/TRPI, Hispanic registered voters, July 6–16, 1,605). The majority of Russian immigrants in Israel are staunch supporters of that nation's conservative and right-wing parties. Should we anticipate the same tendency in the political preferences of Russian immigrants in New York? That expectation has been proved incorrect. According to surveys, more than 70 percent of Russian immigrants support a liberal ideology and voted for Democrats in 2000 (Krieger, 2001).

Ethnic or religious identity does not automatically indicate how a person expresses her views or votes. For example, many commentators in the British press who claimed the majority of the South Asian population in Britain did not support the anti-terrorist military campaign in Afghanistan in the fall of 2001 (Hodgson, 2001). Polls, though, showed a different picture; nearly 90 percent of British Asians were broadly supportive of the international intervention in Afghanistan.

Wording and Labeling

An opening statement from an online article reads: "Asians prefer to surf the Internet at home rather than from work." The article describes the results of an international comparative survey of Internet users. What does this statement reveal? Does it suggest non-Asians do not like to surf the Net from their homes? Does it mean all Asians prefer to go online from home? If not, how many of them do? The actual results of the poll are not disclosed. No country-by-country breakdown of the sample is provided. No description of the types of professionals interviewed is offered. What appears in the article is a set of verbal categorizations.

As we already learned, verbal categorizations tend to reduce large numbers of diverse people to an "average" person. Individuals may belong to a certain ethnic group, but diversity within that group may be considerable. Comparing large groups such as American whites, blacks, Hispanics, Asians, or any other of the world's national, ethnic, or religious groups, we should bear in mind that these groups are far from homogeneous. People of the same ethnic group may have quite different lifestyles, attitudes about social issues, and treasured values. Immigrants include esteemed scientists and skillful engineers who emigrated for economic reasons as well as political refugees. People in China and Taiwan may be part of a single culture in the view of some; however, these nations, despite many common features, remain different ideologically, politically, and philosophically. In every large group, we find individuals who are educated and illiterate, wealthy and poor, live in cities or small towns. People of different racial or ethnic backgrounds often have similar beliefs and share the same values.

How can we avoid the impact of generalizations and labeling in survey descriptions? As we learned in earlier chapters, we should accept with caution phrases such as "Hispanics support" and "Asian Americans do not approve." Look for exact percentages and try to find out more about the distribution of answers in these polls. Newspaper headlines and the headings on popular websites are designed to draw attention. They often appear interesting and exciting. "Most Mexican Americans prefer conventional medical care for their diabetes rather than alternative and traditional treatments," reads a headline on a popular website. How was this conclusion drawn? In fact, the headline describes a scholarly article published in a professional journal (Hunt, 2000). In their original article, the authors did not make sweeping generalizations about the results of a survey they had conducted, as they had interviewed only 43 low-income Mexican Americans. The label implying the reference was to all Mexican Americans was made for visitors to the website. The authors of the professional article should not be criticized for the misleading statements of the online article's author.

In analyses of survey responses or voting results, beware of dichotomization of the findings. Here is an example: More American Catholics tend to vote for Democratic than Republican candidates. There is also a positive correlation between liberal attitudes and support of the Democratic Party. If Catholics tend to vote Democratic, does this mean their attitudes are predominantly liberal? In fact, this question has no conclusive answer. Why? On one hand, as surveys show, a solid majority of Catholics hold liberal views on a range of social and economic issues such as progressive taxation, labor unions, foreign aid, environmental protection, and government regulation of industries. On the other hand, the majority of Catholics are also social conserva-tives: They support the death penalty, maintain anti-abortion views, and possess strong anti-drug attitudes (Weber, 2000). That majority voted for Bush in 2004.

Explanations: Influences and Reasons

Previous chapters note that in attempting to explain why people express certain opin-ions, patient observers should not limit their search to just one influence. Most likely there are multiple plausible causes, each of which may be partly responsible for pro-ducing the effect. If we understand this important rule of critical thinking, we will be cautious in our efforts to determine the role of ethnicity, race, and religious affiliation in the expression of people's attitudes.

Does the race, ethnicity, or religious affiliation of a political candidate play a role in voters' evaluations? If a Hispanic candidate named *Gomez* runs for state office, would he get more votes if he were white or Asian? If people did not elect candidate *Levandowski,* who is Polish American and Catholic, was the rejection based on neg-ative attitudes about her ethnicity, religion, or both? Was the candidate's ancestral background irrelevant? Was the most important factor influencing voters' choice the candidate's accomplishments? Were both the candidate's past performance and cul-tural background the factors? Without careful examination of the contributing factors, simple explanations of the causes of voting preferences will be erroneous. Most likely, as we emphasize throughout this textbook, multiple factors and multiple causes affect voters' choices. Of course, some factors have a greater impact on attitudes and elec-toral choices than others. Thus, Hispanic voters in the United States are predominantly Catholic and tend to oppose abortion. At the same time, this general opposition to abortion does not seem to motivate the majority of Hispanic voters to vote for Repub-lican candidates in local and national elections (see Chapter 11 on domestic issues).

Surveys typically yield little information about how people utilize race or eth-nicity in determining their support of a candidate. For instance, Colleau and colleagues (1990) asked people to evaluate a hypothetical written profile of a candidate running for U.S. Senate. One group of participants received a profile stating that the candidate was black. The other group was handed a profile that did not mention about the can-didate's race. The black candidate was evaluated higher that his white competitor. If we assume that all experimental conditions were equal and the people in both groups were chosen randomly, can we infer with confidence that race was the factor deter-mining people's positive perception of the black candidate? It is difficult to give a def-inite answer. The hypothetical candidate's race was perhaps one of the contributing factors, but other contributing influences could exist as well. What was the initial atti-tude of the participants to candidates of various races before the experiment? Can we assume that some participants wanted to appear nice and express a politically correct evaluation of the minority candidate because they did not want to appear prejudiced against black people? Anyone can argue that many people might not have taken the questions seriously because they knew they were participants in an experiment, which is different from real polling or actual voting.

Direct questions about a candidate's ethnic background or religious affiliation may help determine people's attitudes about her. In 2001, a *Washington Post*/ABC poll (August 12, A1) asked Americans, "Does the fact that Lieberman is an orthodox

A TOPIC FOR CLASS DISCUSSION Why Do Blacks Support the Democratic Party?

Before the 1960s, most blacks in the United States voted for Republican candidates. After the 1960s, blacks voted overwhelmingly Democratic. This voting trend continued in the 1996, 2000, and 2004 presidential elections and in the intervening midterm elections. For more than a hundred years, black-elected officials were generally Republican. In 1869, the first black congressional representatives were members of the Republican Party, establishing a trend that continued until 1935, when the first black Democrat was elected to Congress. In recent years, most blacks elected to public offices nationwide were Democrats. What factors have contributed to this change in voting pattern? Which, in your view, contributed most? Can you think of factors not on this list?

Democratic leaders' pro–civil rights actions in the 1960s

The Democratic Party's growing attention to urban and minority problems

Increased voting turnout among blacks

Growing educational level of black voters

Growth of the black middle class

Jew make you feel more favorable or less favorable toward him?" Half (51 percent) reported a "more favorable" opinion about the candidate, 16 percent said "less favorable," and 33 percent said it made no difference. Apparently, according to this survey, Senator Lieberman's religious affiliation was a factor in people's opinion about him. Nevertheless, other motivating factors (for example, overall support of the Democratic Party, concerns about political correctness, and respect for religiosity) were involved. In addition, a person may have a favorable opinion about a political candidate but still be reluctant to vote for her on Election Day.

Easily identified features such as race, ethnicity, and religion are simple to imagine as explanatory causes of people's attitudes. Some people may say that a candidate was not elected because he is Korean American. Others may say that voters in a certain state are against abortion because of their conservative religion. These assessments are partially correct; some people hold negative opinions about specific groups, and many individuals express certain opinions because they follow a religious doctrine. These statements about the causes of people's attitudes, nevertheless, are too simplistic. To avoid unsophisticated, one-dimensional conclusions about the sources of people's opinions, pay attention to socioeconomic factors. Try to weigh the impact of current social events on what people say in opinion polls. Do not forget about the individual socialization experiences of the respondents. In short, think about the multiple factors that shape human experience, attitudes, and behaviors.

ASSIGNMENT 9.1   BIRTH RATES AND SUPPORT FOR WAR

Edward Luttwak, in his book on the logic of war and peace (1990), expressed the controversial idea that there is a correlation between the availability of human resources and people's willingness to support war and military actions. To exemplify, the continuous decline in family size (from two-parent families with many children to single-parent, single-child families) makes people in the countries with low birth rates more opposed to military casualties than are people in less technologically advanced agricultural societies. Why? Agricultural societies often have a "surplus" of young males because of high fertility rates.

Question:
What do you think about this hypothesis? You can examine its validity by looking at polls. If Luttwak's suggestion is correct, it predicts that the lower the fertility rate in a particular ethnic, racial, or religious group, the less supportive its members will be toward U.S. military engagements abroad. Check this hypothesis using opinion polls about foreign military engagements by ethnic groups. Refer to Chapter 12, on foreign policy attitudes, for examples of military interventions.

CHAPTER SUMMARY

- Culture is a set of attitudes, behaviors, and symbols generally shared by a large group of people and communicated from one generation to the next. No society is culturally homogeneous. No two cultures are entirely similar, and none are entirely dissimilar. Each cultural cluster can show significant variation.

- Race is usually defined as a large group of people distinguished by biologically transmitted physical characteristics. Ethnicity usually indicates an individual's cultural heritage, the experience shared by this person and others with a common ancestral origin, language, traditions, and, often, religion and geographic territory. Nationality is commonly defined as a person's identification with a geographical territory unified as an independent state recognized by other countries.

- The ethnic, religious, and racial groups in the United States express both similarity and difference in attitudes. Most U.S. minority groups tend to support the Democratic Party. Hispanics may differ somewhat, but the majority still tend to vote Democratic. The exceptions are Asian Americans and Muslim Americans, who are evenly split between Democratic and Republican preferences.

- Several approaches allow researchers to examine and explain why factors such as religion and ethnicity affect people's views. From the social power standpoint, availability of and access to resources are the most significant factors influencing opinions. Domination and hierarchy determine the way groups see society and each other. In other words, not race or ethnicity but association with a certain social class determines major behavioral and attitudinal differences among groups.

- From the cultural identity standpoint, not resources but rather the strength and content of cultural identity are the most significant factors affecting behavior and attitudes. Members of religious, ethnic, national, and other kinds of groups tend to develop their sense of collective identity on the basis of two kinds of perceptions: shared features within the group and differences between these features and those of other social clusters. This collective identity gives members of the group a sense of uniqueness.

- From the cultural prejudice standpoint, people form stable negative perceptions of and attribute negative characteristics to other cultural groups. Prejudice is commonly understood as an irrational feeling that can be reduced by a variety of means, including education. As a rule, people who are more educated are less prejudiced than those who are less educated.

- When examining the views of racial, ethnic, or religious groups, it is important to learn about the racial and ethnic composition of the region in which the survey was conducted. Another area of concern is the impact of generalizations and labeling on survey results. Easily identifiable features, such as race, ethnicity, and religion, are simple explanatory causes of people's attitudes. A person's ethnic or religious identity does not automatically indicate how she will express her views or vote.

Looking Ahead.   The next chapter explores voting as a process and reasons, from socioeconomic status to knowledge and institutional factors, that affect voting. It explores why people do not vote and the complexity of voting decisions. It explores the influence of ideology and partisanship on voting.

DEFINITIONS OF KEY TERMS

Belief perseverence effect—The tendency to cling stubbornly to one's beliefs and expectations in the face of contradictory or disconfirming evidence.

Cultural identity perspective—The approach to attitudes that suggests the strength and content of cultural identity are the most significant factors affecting behavior and attitudes.

Cultural prejudice perspective—The approach to attitudes based on the assumption that people form stable negative perceptions of and attribute negative characteristics to other cultural groups and use these negative assessments when forming their beliefs and values.

Cultural variables perspective—The approach to attitudes according to which each culture has distinct measurable characteristics that can be viewed as the mechanisms that form people's attitudes.

Culture—A set of attitudes, behaviors, and symbols shared by a large group of people and usually communicated from one generation to the next.

Ethnicity—An individual's cultural heritage; the experience he shares with others who have a common ancestral origin, language, traditions, and, often, religion and geographical territory.

Nationality—One's identification with a geographical territory unified as a political entity or independent state recognized by other countries.

Political tolerance—The willingness to support the extension of rights to all members of society and to permit the expression of political ideas or interests one opposes.

Prejudice—An adverse, preconceived, and unsubstantiated judgment.

Race—A large group of people typically distinguished by apparently biologically transmitted physical characteristics.

Reference groups—Social groups that serve as standards for individuals' behavior and attitudes.

Religious fundamentalism—The belief in strict interpretations of religious doctrine often associated with social and political conservatives.

Social power perspective—The approach to attitudes that suggests the availability of and access to resources are the most significant factors influencing ethnic and religious groups' values and opinions.

CHAPTER 10

Opinions and Voting

A President needs political
understanding to run the government,
but he may be elected without it.

Harry Truman

Imagine that a day before an election you see a poll that reports a difference of one percentage point between two candidates for office. Does this indicate the one-point leader will win? Can it accurately predict the outcome of the election? An educated person would argue that in opinion polls, differences of one, two, three, or four percentage points are likely to be insignificant. Election results, however, are based on ballots cast. No matter how small the difference between the number of votes for each of two candidates, a one-vote difference is sufficient to declare a winner. A difference of one vote or one percentage point is political reality; some people and political parties win offices; others lose them. In 2000, George W. Bush was elected with 271 electoral votes, only one above the minimum requirement to decide who would live in the White House for the next four years. When the 2000 electoral dispute over the way votes in Florida should be counted reached its height, the United States Supreme Court voted 5–4 for Bush. These close votes decided the U.S. presidency (Broder, 2000). After the election was over, the media covered arguments that such a narrow margin did not give Bush a legitimate mandate to lead the country because his opponent, Democratic candidate Al Gore, actually won the national popular count by more than five hundred thousand votes! However, the presidency went to Bush because the United States Constitution set the procedures for presidential elections: Each candidate gains electoral votes until one gains more than half.

Opinion polls project possibilities within a measure of certainty; polls are not elections themselves. Elections produce and institutionalize results according to law. Thus, an election is a game with a set of rules, and in this game, every vote counts.

Looking Forward. This chapter explores the process of voting and factors from socioeconomic status to knowledge and institutional setting that affect voting. It explores why people don't vote and the complexity of voting decisions. It pays particular attention to the influence of ideology and partisanship on the voting decision.

THE "SIMPLE" ACT OF VOTING

Democracy is inseparable from **voting**, the formal expression of preference for a candidate for office or for a proposed solution on an issue. Throughout the centuries, philosophers, sociologists, and political scientists have debated the nature of people's opinions expressed through voting and the impact of those opinions and voting on government and society. The vote has long been understood as a fundamental right, a basic freedom, and an expression of civic responsibility.

From a behavioral perspective, voting is a simple, rather ordinary sequence of human actions. A person goes to a polling place during specified hours on a certain day (or submits an absentee ballot before). The polling place may be miles from home or just around the corner. It may be in a local elementary school, city hall, or library. The person arrives at the facility, waits in line a few minutes, has his name checked off a registration list, and enters a voting booth. Inside the booth, the voter makes a decision about whom he wants to be mayor, governor, president, or representative in local, state, or national government. The voter may push a button, touch a screen, mark a box, or punch a hole through a paper ballot. He may write in a name or cross one out. Although actual voting takes just a few minutes, opinions people express in the process of voting move democratic society in a new direction or maintain it at the status quo.

How do people express their views in elections? What makes them vote for candidate Smith and not for candidate Bartlett? Quick generalizations about voting behavior such as "It's all about pocketbooks" or "Incumbents always win" are not necessarily correct. In 1945, Great Britain and its allies won the bloodiest war of the 20th century. British prime minister Winston Churchill, who had led his country to victory, was logically expected to win again easily in the national elections. Against expectations, he lost. In 1996, ignoring five painful years of economic turmoil, skyrocketing inflation, and rampant crime, two-thirds of Russian voters elected Boris Yeltsin to a second term as president. In 2000, after almost eight years of unprecedented economic growth during the presidency of Bill Clinton, his vice president, Al Gore, was not elected to succeed him. In 2004, in an era of terrorism, and despite problems in the Iraq war, incumbent George Bush was reelected.

Voting takes place in a variety of places and circumstances. As we observed in previous chapters, scores of variables must be considered in an analysis of public opinion and political behaviors like voting. No single theory can embrace the whole of democratic voting and explain why and how people make their decisions on Election Day.

Voting As a Process

Although voting may be viewed as a single event, it is far from simple. Pushing a lever, punching a hole in a ballot, checking off a name, touching a computer screen, or dropping a sheet into a ballot box is the culmination of the electoral process, which begins weeks, months, or sometimes years before the scheduled voting. For example, in the United States, presidential, congressional, and gubernatorial campaigns last for many months. In presidential elections, the process formally begins with a series of battles during the winter and spring in state-by-state primaries and caucuses. This period ends in the summer with national conventions of the Democratic and Republican parties. Then, after the traditional Labor Day kickoff in September, two major candidates compete against each other (and sometimes against third-party candidates) until Election Day in early November. In many parliamentary democracies, such as Germany and Canada, the executive branch of government is determined by a coalition of parties in the national legislature. Therefore, competing candidates think in advance about possible political coalitions so they can attract votes and win legislative seats. In many democratic countries, national elections may be called before the end of the legislature's tenure, a process unknown, except in the case of recalls, in the United States. Early national elections, for example, have been called during the past 10 years in many countries, including Israel, Japan, Italy, Peru, and Russia. The duration and dynamics of electoral campaigning vary, often significantly from nation to nation, and each country's legal regulations as well as political and cultural traditions determine the campaign process.

TYPES OF VOTING

Voting as a complex behavior can be divided into several categories. An **election** is a process of selecting candidates by vote for a public office, typically a position in an administration, legislature, or court. Another major type of voting is the **referendum** (plural *referenda*) or initiative, an electoral event in which eligible voters express their opinion about a specific problem or policy issue. A referendum is different from an opinion poll. Surveys are designed to measure people's *attitudes*. Referenda represent an official process regulated by the government and designed to determine a political *decision*.

There are several types of referenda. A *compulsory referendum* is popular voting organized by the government. This referendum's results direct the government to a specific action (Gish, 2000). Such actions may include, for example, decisions about the independence of a territory. In recent history, referenda on independence took place in countries of the former Soviet Union, Czechoslovakia, Ukraine, Quebec, Puerto Rico, and Bosnia. Compulsory referenda affect local issues, such as building a nuclear power plant or financing a new baseball park with taxpayers' money. As an example, in 1999, residents of Missouri cast their ballots in support of or opposition to a proposition that would allow people 21 years of age and older to apply for permits to carry concealed handguns.

In some U.S. states and several countries, people, not the government, can start a *ballot initiative*, which can lead to the creation of a new law in that state, province, or nation. For instance, Proposition 5, the 1998 ballot initiative passed by almost two-thirds of California voters, would have allowed Indian tribes to offer video slot machines and card games. Successful ballot initiatives, however, do not automatically become law. Courts may determine if, when, and how they do. As an example, the state Supreme Court reversed the Proposition 5 decision about gambling on Indian reservations (Reuters, August 23, 1999). In Oregon, since 1902, the people have passed more than one hundred initiatives through referenda.

A *petition referendum* may veto certain laws or executive decisions. These decisions can be big political issues or smaller problems, such as business contracts signed by local governments (*Los Angeles Times*, January 11, 2000). Another form of referenda is the *recall*, whereby an elected official can be voted out of office before the end of his term. Democratic Governor Gray Davis of California was recalled in 2003 and replaced by actor Republican Arnold Schwarzenegger.

TABLE 10.1

Main Goals of a Political Campaign.

- **Energize the loyal.** Ensure that the individuals who are supposed to vote for a candidate will indeed vote for that candidate.

- **Motivate the unmotivated.** Make sure people who are unenthusiastic about voting but who support a candidate vote this time.

- **Persuade the undecided.** Be certain everything is done to convince undecided voters, especially those who do not know whether they will vote and who will be their choice, to cast their ballots for a candidate.

- **Disenchant the opponents.** Convince some of a candidate's opponents not to vote.

- **Woo the opponents.** Persuade some of candidate's opponents to change their mind and vote for another candidate.

Finally, an *advisory referendum* is organized as a measure of people's opinion on an issue or policy. The government may or may not take these results in consideration. In one such case, the people of Stoddard, a small community in western Wisconsin, voted in 2000 to disband the town police department by a narrow vote of 251–247 (Lagosi, 2000). The state disagreed, and the department was spared.

Voting, as mentioned earlier, is preceded by a preparation period. This may be long or short, depending on circumstances. The multistage preparation process is called **campaigning,** or the deliberate and systematic effort to win an election. To campaign is to strive for a political nomination, office, or, in cases of referenda, a certain decision. Campaigning can also be viewed as a deliberate attempt to achieve a set of electoral goals (see Table 10.1). Forms of electoral participation besides voting and campaigning include volunteering, making financial contributions, and attending political rallies. Demonstrating in non-electoral rallies is considered a form of protest.

To campaign is to persuade potential voters to cast a ballot in a certain way. But what do we know about voters' intentions? Why are some people eager to vote while others are unenthusiastic and indifferent? Research on voting behavior has established several major motivational factors for voting. Let's start with this question: Why do people vote?

WHY PEOPLE VOTE

Ask three or four people why they voted during the last election and you will receive answers like these: "Voting is my right"; "It's my responsibility and duty"; "I liked the candidate." Some may refer to their family traditions. Others may say they did not have any particular reasons; they just voted. Still others may recall very specific reasons. Overall, several factors motivate people to vote.

Socioeconomic Factors

Individuals' social status and economic conditions, such as income, education and occupation, and demographic variables, including age and race, predict their political participation and voting (Verba & Nie, 1972). What does this mean? People who are more likely to vote are those with higher educational degrees and higher occupational statuses than nonvoters. Older individuals are more likely to vote than those who are younger. People of higher income vote more frequently than those who make less money (Hughes & Conway, 1997; Wolfinger & Rosenstone, 1980). Cross-national data suggest that class affects voting behavior even in democratic societies (Moreno, 1999; Klicperova, 2002).

Knowledge and Voting

Citizens with greater or lesser degrees of knowledge tend to differ in their voting behavior. Overall, knowledge and electoral participation are positively correlated; people who know more about social and political events are more likely to vote than those who know less. More knowledgeable people know more specific details about how, where, and when to vote. Poorly informed citizens hold fewer, less stable, and less consistent opinions about candidates than those who are better informed. Knowledge is typically correlated with political interest and political efficacy, that is, the individual's belief that she and her vote can make a difference, which may increase her motivation to vote. The overwhelming majority of the most knowledgeable 10 percent Americans vote; in contrast, only a small portion of the least informed Americans cast their ballots (Delli Carpini & Keeter, 1996; Neuman, 1986).

Political knowledge is not equally distributed. Some people know more about politics than others. How does this knowledge disparity affect society through its social or political consequences? If the most informed people tend to vote more often than those who are least informed, the more knowledgeable have a greater opportunity to influence politics through voting than those who are less knowledgeable. The knowledgeable have more political power than other people.

Legal and Institutional Factors

During "elections" in former communist countries (although one could hardly call them true democratic elections), governments typically announced voter turnout of 99 percent. Although government operatives blatantly exaggerated these numbers for bureaucratic and ideological purposes, actual voter turnout was quite high. One reason for such active participation was mandatory electoral laws. Even when no sanctions were imposed on nonvoters, many people turned out to vote, just in case there might be (Shlapentokh & Shiraev, 2002).

Compulsory voting is not just an antidemocratic attribute of totalitarian governments. Many liberal democracies, such as Australia, require voting (Jackman & Miller, 1995). Even though, in most cases, governments lack power and resources to enforce such laws, voter turnouts in countries with compulsory voting are higher than in other nations (Hall, 1997). Table 10.2 displays comparative data on legislative elections.

Electoral Format

Electoral format and other procedural rules established by national or local governments increase or decrease turnout. One of the most common electoral formats is the single-member district, in which a candidate needs either a plurality or majority of the votes to

TABLE 10.2

Average Turnout Rates, 1960s–1990s.

Country	Mandatory Election Law	Average Turnout Rates (%)
Australia	Yes	95
Italy	Yes	91
Venezuela	Yes	83
Costa Rica	Yes	80
Germany	No	86
Canada	No	74
Ireland	No	74
Japan	No	71
Switzerland	No	52
Columbia	No	44
United States	No	44

Source: Moreno, 1999.

win. For example, U.S. congressional representatives and members of the Commons, the Lower House of British Parliament, are elected from single-member districts.

How does an electoral system based on single-member districts affect voting behavior and campaigning? On the national level, the system based on single-member plurality districts does not provide parties with sufficient incentives to mobilize *all* voters in *all* electoral districts. As a result, turnout is low because some districts or regions are practically excluded from campaign mobilization efforts if victory or defeat there seems predetermined (Blais & Carty, 1990). Why? If a party or candidate is projected to win clearly or lose soundly in a certain district, there is little reason to spend much time and money there in an attempt to mobilize voters. U.S. presidential candidates in 2004 spent less or no time in states in which they are expected to lose or win big. In such situations, many voters, especially those who intend to support these presidential candidates, may feel discouraged about participating. People are more likely to vote if they feel their vote may affect the electoral results. Potential voters' perception that their vote will not affect the outcome of an election dispirits them and decreases turnout (Downs, 1957). Voters who live in a so-called **banner district**, one in which a party or candidate makes a better showing than anywhere else in a current election, are also less motivated to vote because the outcome of the election is predicable. On the other hand, if a district's election is too close to call, campaigners try to do a lot there to encourage the highest possible turnout of potential supporters.

Multiseat electoral districts, such as in Japan, or proportional-representation districts in countries like Israel and Russia, allow voters to choose more than one representative to the legislature. Voter turnout in places with these electoral systems is typically higher than in single-seat districts (Moreno, 1999).

Election timing may also significantly affect turnout in two ways. First, the frequency of elections is negatively correlated with the rate of turnout in national legislative elections, that is, turnout goes down when elections occur frequently. In other words, if the frequency of elections increases, fewer voters show up (Hoskin 1997; Powell, 1986). Second, when congressional elections are held at the same time as presidential elections, turnout tends to increase because many voters are drawn to the polls by the high-profile presidential race. In contrast, when local elections are not held concurrently with salient national elections, turnout is typically lower. A number of empirical studies have confirmed these observations, known as the surge and decline thesis (Campbell, 1960; Cox, 1997).

Personality Factors

Many individual psychological factors, such as personality traits, influence individuals' decisions to vote or not to vote (Barner-Barry & Rosenwein, 1991). Recent social-psychological studies indicate that personality is organized around five basic behavioral tendencies or traits (Costa & McCrae, 1997).

1. Openness to experience (the extent of original, intellectual interests, curiosity, and imagination)

2. Conscientiousness (the extent of organized and productive behavior, planning abilities, dependability)

3. Extraversion (the extent of assertive, goal-directed, expressive behavior)

4. Agreeableness (the extent of appreciative, forgiving, kind, and trusting behavior)

5. Neuroticism (the extent of anxious, tense, emotionally unstable behavior)

How might these traits affect voting? For example, neuroticism is related to anxiety. Some people experience greater anxiety than others. Some individuals with persistent anxiety may strive for perfection in practically everything they do by following the rules of "appropriate" or "good" behavior. Therefore, voting, for these individuals, is an important act of good citizenship that they *must* undertake. Due to individual circumstances and socialization experiences, some people are more conscientious than others. Conscientiousness as a personality trait can affect responsible, socially appropriate behavior and political efficacy (see Chapter 5 on political socialization), which, in turn, contribute to conscientiousness. Some individuals tend to be more extroverted than others: certain people actively express their attitudes verbally or through behavior, whereas others do so less often. Activists, therefore, are more likely to vote than nonactivists.

Individual psychological traits, however, are likely to be randomly distributed, so it seems implausible that in one voting district we would find more extraverted or conscientious individuals than in another. Nevertheless, personality traits develop and transform under the influence of external circumstances. Social factors, such as education and access to resources, may activate particular traits of large numbers of individuals and make them more or less likely to vote.

Cognitive Factors

People tend to undertake actions they expect to be beneficial. According to this logic, voting behavior can be based on purely rational calculations; anyone would want to vote, if the benefits of voting exceed the costs (Tullock, 1967). Many people vote because they have had positive experiences with other forms of electoral participation, such as campaigning or fundraising (Almond & Verba, 1965).

One cognitive factor that can affect voting is a sense of personal control. Social psychologists link voting behavior to the way individuals perceive their control over their world. Julian Rotter (1996) suggested two categories of people. *Internals* prefer to explain events as influenced by controllable internal factors, such as their own will, determination, or wishes. *Externals* prefer to explain events as influenced by uncontrollable external factors, such as luck or fate. What is important here is that internals, those who believe in personal control over things, are more likely to vote than are externals (Gore & Rotter, 1963). The individual's belief in his ability to influence the outcome of an election is based on several attitudes. Among them is the belief that a person can influence the political system and that one political party or candidate is better than the other or others (Timpone, 1998).

Some people vote because they want to avoid possible regrets and frustration over not voting if their candidate or party loses by a close margin (Blais et al., 1995; Riker & Ordeshook, 1968). For instance, half of U.S. adults who did not make it to the polls in 2000, the closest presidential election in recent history, said they regretted not having voted (*Newsweek*/Princeton, November 9–10, 2000, 1,000). In a 1996 poll, a third of people expressed less motivation to vote if the electoral result seems predetermined (see Figure 10.1).

Moral Factors

As we learned in Chapters 4 on attitudes, and 5 on political socialization, the desire to gain is not the only source of motivation. Laurence Kohlberg (1981) proposed that people, in their judgments of right and wrong behavior, often choose to use social norms and values as guidelines for action. Voting can be viewed as a moral act, a civic duty (Downs, 1957). Many people, if not most, vote without expectation of immediate benefit. Voting, for many people, is a low-cost, low-benefit action (Aldrich, 1993). Some people have a strong sense of civic responsibility; others do not. Campaigns may thus play an important role not only in educating individuals about candidates' views, but also in activating voters' civic conscience: "Vote because this is your duty!"

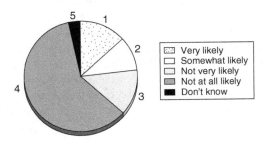

FIGURE 10.1

Likelihood of Voting. "If the final opinion polls show Bill Clinton as a virtually certain winner with a big lead over Bob Dole, how likely do you think it is that you may feel that there is no real point in your voting—very likely, somewhat likely, not very likely, not at all likely, or don't know?"
Source: Harris, October 1996, registered voters, telephone, 943.

In review.   People who know more about social and political events are more likely to vote than those who know less. Turnout is usually higher in countries with mandatory voting. Overall, people vote for several reasons, including obvious, salient, and recognizable factors as well as subtle, contextual influences. These include electorate rules, participatory factors, and cognitive and moral factors.

LOW TURNOUT OR ALIENATION?

Citizens in democratic societies have the right to vote. Thousands of people fought and died for this right on the barricades and in trenches, in revolutionary wars, and in battles for independence. Voting is one of the ultimate prizes in the struggle for freedom from tyranny, oppression, and autocracy.

How many people today exercise this right? In democratic countries, the freedom to vote routinely comes together with freedom not to vote (Naumetz & O'Neil, 2000; Shen, 2000). For example, the 1999 national elections in Ukraine drew 74 percent of potential voters. More than a quarter of eligible voters in this young democratic country did not bother to vote. In Zimbabwe, another country struggling to build a political sys-

tem, 40 percent of eligible voters did not cast their ballots in 2000. In Romania's parliamentary elections in 2000, turnout was 54 percent. It is not difficult to find an election that took place in a relatively new democratic country in which more than a third of eligible voters did not vote.

How about older, established democracies? Turnout in American elections was high in the 19th century, often 80 percent, when the eligible electorate was much smaller. Then the turnout declined slowly and steadily (Schudson, 1999). When Americans elected John F. Kennedy president in 1960, national turnout was 63 percent. A generation later, in 1996, voter turnout in the presidential election was below 50 percent. Nonpresidential elections typically draw even lower numbers; voter turnout in the 1994 congressional elections was 39 percent and dropped to 36 percent in 1998 (Shen, 2000; Neal & Morin, 1998). In some local elections, voter participation is consistently under 20 percent of registered voters and sometimes under 10 percent of eligible voters (Chapman, 2000). Overall, turnout in presidential elections is lower than in most other democracies; the U.S. ranks close to the bottom among democratic nations (Mair, 2000). But in 2004, turnout was 60 percent, the highest since 1968 (WWW.CNN.COM, November 3, 2004).

While turnout in national elections in most European democratic countries is higher than in the United States, it also has declined. In the 1960s, an average of more than 85 percent of eligible voters in Western Europe, and nearly 90 percent in both Germany and the Netherlands, cast their votes in national elections. But the rates decreased consistently so that by the late 1990s, a sizable group of European countries, including Austria, Finland, Iceland, the Netherlands, Sweden, and Great Britain, recorded their lowest national election turnouts in 50 years. Switzerland had the lowest turnout; less than 4 out of 10 eligible voters participated in national elections in the 1990s. Especially low numbers of voter participation were recorded in European parliamentary elections; in 1999, turnout in most participating countries was between 24 and 45 percent. In one ward in northern England, only 17 out of 1,000 eligible voters showed up. Of course, some countries produce more favorable voting records. For example, in Belgium, where voting is compulsory, the turnout is high. Malta now consistently records one of the highest turnouts of any democracy (Mair, 2000).

A TOPIC FOR CLASS DISCUSSION What to Do About Low Turnouts?

Most media reports portray low voter turnout as a negative social tendency. What kinds of remedies are offered to reverse this? What specific measures are proposed that could push turnout higher? To suggest that "We must increase voter's awareness" or "People should be more responsible" is to state the obvious. The question is *how* to enhance awareness and responsibility. How can more people be persuaded to vote? In this critical thinking exercise, consider the advantages and disadvantages of each of the following measures. What other measures can you suggest? Write down your opinions and discuss them. One possible turnout-increasing measure, online voting, is described on the website.

Make Voting the Law

Pro: Mandatory voting strengthens democracy. In countries such as Costa Rica and Australia, regulations require citizens to vote. In Australia, the law requires voting if the participation rate in previous elections falls below 60 percent.

Con: Mandatory voting is undemocratic and authoritarian. If today the government makes people vote, tomorrow it could make them vote for a particular party. Mandatory voting laws, therefore, should not be implemented in contemporary democratic society.

Change the Election Date

Pro: Establish a national Election Day holiday. Move Election Day to a weekend. Reasons? Citizens would feel that voting is a special event. It would give many people a chance to feel responsible for their civic activities.

Con: All proposed changes regarding dates or special holidays will face serious legal challenge. Further, formal changes in scheduling are not enough to reverse a trend in people's voting behavior; those who typically do not vote would not vote even on a special election day.

Repeal the Registration Requirement

Pro: Make registration automatic for everyone at the age of 18. The less bureaucracy we have in our country, the better.

Con: Without voter registration, fraud could become a serious problem; the experience of other countries and our own problems in Florida in 2000 provide enough evidence of voting irregularities.

Computerize Voting

Pro: Online voting is a great new way to reach people who cannot get to polling places because of long commutes, lack of time, busy work schedules, or disabilities.

Con: Online voting is discriminatory because people who do not have computers or cannot pay for Internet services are left out; the advantage is given mainly to voters who are more educated, younger, and make more money.

Why are the voting rates in many countries so low? At least two theories or explanations can be offered. Some observers describe the low-turnout phenomenon as a sign of **alienation,** or the individual's disengagement and withdrawal from contemporary society. Further, these observers argue, this process is inevitable in any capitalist democracy. It indicates growing indifference and hostile attitudes toward the political or economic system in general (Marcuse, 1964). In the more prosperous world, most people are caught up in the race for material possessions. Many grow selfish and increasingly uncaring about social and political events around them. The voting situation deteriorates because big businesses and interest groups rather than voters influence politicians. People figure that once politicians are elected, they do more to help their wealthy contributors than assist average citizens. Therefore, ordinary citizens see little use in voting (Shen, 2000).

Critics of this view argue that low turnout is a normal phenomenon that does not mean that voter inaction smothers democracy. The historic emphasis on individualism and suspicion of government is part of both American and, more broadly, Western tradition, especially when society is not in crisis (Samuelson, 1998). If things are going well in most people's daily routines, these people may not care who is in public office; the government plays a small role in their lives. Some people vote only when they worry about their well-being; they turn out in large numbers when there are important and urgent problems to decide (Neal & Morin, 1998). For example, low turnouts in the European parliamentary elections mentioned earlier might be caused by the nature of people being asked to choose representatives to a transnational legislature with limited power to influence local events. Therefore, most citizens skip the process altogether.

Finally, in most democracies, new ways to alter social policy have proliferated in the last 30 years. The role of the watchdog of democracy is increasingly assigned to interest groups and the media. If things go in the wrong direction, people can appeal to the courts, government organizations, and the media (Schudson, 1999). All these opportunities have, in a way, reduced the importance of elections; in contemporary democracies, outcomes of regular elections are not expected to cause radical political transformations. Nevertheless, if some groups care more about social and political issues than others, they could have greater influence on electoral outcomes. As an example, in the 2002 midterm

elections in the United States, the higher turnout of Republican voters (51 percent) than Democratic voters (45 percent) was a crucial factor that allowed the Republicans to retain majority control of the Senate and the House of Representatives (More & Jones, 2002).

THE COMPLEXITY OF VOTING DECISIONS

What motivates a person to vote for candidate *Bush* but not for candidate *Kerry*? Most individuals are able to identify the reasons for their voting decisions. For some people, voting for a certain candidate is the expression of their views on issues; for others, it is an act of support for a favorite candidate; for still others, it is their expression of resentment of an opposing candidate. Some voters form blocs to promote an initiative or candidate and therefore express the opinions of their groups; others never join groups and even avoid discussing politics publicly (Barner-Barry & Rosenwein, 1991). Conformity may play a powerful role in the decision-making process; some individuals make decisions because of indirect pressure from friends, significant others, or colleagues.

Many voters are partisan, or *party-oriented*, and support one political party and its candidates in elections. Identifying with this party is the main reason these people vote for certain candidates. In 2000, for example, registered U.S. voters were asked about "the most important one or two reasons" they would be more likely to vote for one candidate than another. Twenty-four percent of Vice President Gore's supporters and 19 percent of Governor Bush's supporters reported voting the party line as their chief reason (Gallup, April 2000, national registered voters, 998).

In 2004, exit polls showed "moral values" as an important factor in Bush voters' choice (WWW.CNN.COM/ELECTION/2004). The expression of personal dislike as well as the manifestation of personal approval and support is common in *candidate-oriented* voters. These voters tend to support or reject a candidate as an individual because of her character and skills; they tend to pay less attention to the person's political views. *Issue-oriented* voters have a particular opinion about a social issue or problem and select a candidate or party that represents their view.

Seven months before the 2000 presidential election, Gallup polls asked: "As you may know, people take many different kinds of things into account in deciding on whom to vote for President. What about you? What is the most important factor for you as you decide on your vote for President this year?" (Gallup, March 2000, 1,205). Almost 42 percent of respondents mentioned personality traits or the individual style of their candidate, including honesty, integrity, trustworthiness, competence, experience, character, leadership ability, and personality. The importance of specific issues was mentioned by 58 percent of the national sample. Another poll taken in 2000 (Princeton/*Newsweek*, February 2000, registered voters, 750) revealed that 71 percent of Democratic supporters and 74 percent of Republican backers said none of the issues specified in the poll (abortion, the economy, education, gun control, healthcare, protecting Social Security, and poverty) was the most important factor determining their choice.

In the 2002 midterm elections (when the entire House of Representatives, one-third of U.S. senators, and a number of state governors were elected), Democrats were generally supported by voters who rated the economy as poor. Republicans were supported by voters who gave the economy high ratings. Those who thought the performance of the economy was only fair split their vote about evenly, although they leaned toward the Republicans (More & Jones, 2002). Overall, decision making is a complex process, and many people may not have enough opportunity, especially when answering a brief survey, to contemplate all the reasons why they support one candidate or another.

In their evaluation of candidates, voters can use at least two strategies. In **prospective evaluations,** people assess the ability of the candidate to fulfill her promises if elected to the office. In **retrospective evaluations,** the public considers how the candidate performed in the past (Levine, 1992). Voters also distinguish between salient and complicated issues. Voters tend to respond to salient issues rather than to conceptually difficult ones (Zaller, 1992). Any salient issue may become crucial for retrospective evaluations. For example, retrospective evaluations associated

Hubert Humphrey and the Democrats in 1968 with the war in Vietnam, protests, and major social reforms. Richard Nixon's troubles in the Watergate scandal were among the major issues his successor, Gerald Ford, confronted in the 1976 elections. Jimmy Carter's crucial problems were rampant inflation and the American hostages in Iran in 1980. A sluggish economy became a critical theme working against George H. W. Bush in 1992.

Not every voter clearly intends to back a particular candidate. Some individuals use their voting not to support but to defeat someone running for office. **Protest voting** is based on the desire to express disagreement or disappointment with a particular candidate or with proposed policies. When people exercise this type of voting, they wish to express their disagreement with a candidate by voting against or sending him a message.

Many voting decisions are not based on reason and rational calculations. **Prejudiced voting** occurs when candidates or issues are rejected because of voters' negative prejudgment. Polls have long asked whether Americans would vote for a well-qualified Catholic or Jewish presidential candidate (Table 10.3). Although the U.S. Constitution set no qualification regarding the religion, gender, or ancestry of the president, only one president in the twentieth century has been Roman Catholic, and none has been Jewish. As shown in the table, up to the late 1950s, as many as one in every four Americans was reluctant to vote for a qualified candidate because of his religion. However, this had changed significantly by the 1970s and remains similar in later polls.

Overall, men tend to show weaker support for women candidates and greater support for men in senatorial and gubernatorial races. Women show a significantly greater tendency to vote for women candidates for the House of Representatives than do men (Dolan, 1998; Burrell, 1994; Cook, 1994). Is this an example of gender-biased and prejudiced voting of some men and women? Many women voters are drawn to women candidates because they address problems uniquely important to women such as gender discrimination, sexual harassment, and abortion, and they are deemed by women voters to be more competent at handling them than men (Plutzer & Zipp, 1996; Paolino, 1995). Party affiliation also matters. Because women voters are more likely than men to vote for Democratic candidates, and most women running for Washington offices are Democrats, the gender gap in support of women candidates may be a reflection of the partisan gender gap (Cook, 1994).

TABLE 10.3

"If your party nominated a generally well-qualified man (person) for president this year, and he (or she) happened to be a Catholic/Jew (Jewish) would you vote for him (or her)?" The questions were asked in slightly different ways. (In percentages.)

	August 1958	March 1969	July 1978	June 1983	February 1999	June 2003
Yes	69/62	87/86	91/82	92/88	94/92	90/85
No	24/28	7/8	4/12	5/7	4/6	8/10
No opinion	7/10	5/6	5/6	3/5	2/2	2/5
Number polled	1,621	1,634	1,555	1,517	1,014	2,002

Source: Gallup, 1958–1999; Pew, 2003.

A CASE IN POINT 10.1   *"None of the Above" as a Form of Protest Voting*

During a referendum, a voter can support or oppose a law or legislative initiative. What happens when the voter does not like any of the options that appear on the ballot? Answering "none of the above" is a form of protest voting whereby voters express their dissatisfaction with the available options. They may hope that their indecision will postpone the implementation of any change. Consider an example in 1998, when Puerto Ricans voted in a referendum to determine the future status of their island. The following options were offered to voters: (1) U.S. statehood, (2) independence, (3) current commonwealth status, and (4) sovereignty under a treaty with the United States. Almost 71 percent of Puerto Rico's 2.2 million registered voters added their voices to a century-old debate over the territory's relationship with the United States. The votes were narrowly split, with more than 46 percent supporting statehood and more than 50 percent choosing "none of the above." This protest vote rejected statehood while showing people's dissatisfaction with the island's version of commonwealth status (Gonzalez, 1998).

IDEOLOGY AND OPINIONS

Ideology as a comprehensive set of ideas about society and its past, present, and future affects opinions and politics. Although an ideology may contain rules for individual behavior intended to accomplish the goals set out by that philosophy, its main feature is a particular view of society and people as a large group. In theories of political behavior, it is common to refer to **political ideology**, a comprehensive set of ideas about the nature and goals of politics and government. Modern ideologies often serve as tools that help governments or political groups mobilize people and call on citizens to join in collective efforts. In the world of information and the exchange of ideas, ideology may give individuals an opportunity to make sense of reality and put forward ideas about how to bring about a better future.

Ideologies are categorized along several dimensions. Among these are views on the scope, sources, and direction of social change, attitudes about property rights, and opinions about the rights of the individual. Most commonly, ideologies are divided into liberal, moderate, and conservative (with the frequent addition of radical and reactionary). Radical and liberal views are typically labeled as leftist or left-wing ideas, which advocate government activism and change, while conservative and reactionary are typically called rightist or right-wing; these advocate maintaining or returning to the status quo. Throughout history and across countries, the meanings of these labels have varied.

Radical ideologies reflect a fundamental critique of society, its government, institutions, or current policies, and contain a plan offering a rapid and massive restructuring of society or its elements. Reactionary ideologies are based on principles that proclaim the necessity of a rapid return to the past and its social institutions and policies. According to reactionary thought, traditional social institutions, policies, practices, and laws should be reinstated.

Liberal ideologies accept many elements of the status quo while advocating the reorganization and substantial improvement of society and its institutions and policies, not necessarily by radical means. Liberals believe in government action to meet individual needs. Liberal ideologies affirm the inevitable transformation of social institutions, including the family, education, religion, social norms, customs, and values. They are based on the belief that human nature is good and that individuals, if they act reasonably and responsibly, are able to achieve social progress. Liberals place the greatest emphasis on human rights and relatively lower emphasis on property rights. Liberals also tend to believe that human beings are essentially equal in terms of their entitlement to social benefits and that inequalities ought to be corrected.

Conservative ideology is generally a shield of status-quo defenders. Conservative ideology holds the assumption that social change does not necessarily lead to social improvement, especially if government or other institutions direct the attempted change. However, when change is necessary, transition should come slowly and in moderation. According to conservative ideologies, society is based on tradition and not on the good intentions of a few reformers. Conservative ideologies imply that people are not able to apply reason and goodwill when they intend to make social changes. Conservatives assign greater value to property rights than to political rights. Human beings are not equal to each other in terms of their access to social benefits; they should have equal rights but may achieve unequal results in free competition.

Moderate ideologies endorse a general satisfaction with society and acceptance of the wide range of liberal and conservative views. Moderates tend to see matters from several perspectives and to consider the relative benefits of both liberal and conservative alternatives to social problems. In the 1998 congressional elections, approximately 54 percent of those who identified themselves as moderates voted for Democrats, compared with 43 percent for Republicans (Neal & Morin, 1998).

There are many cross-national similarities in the way people understand and interpret conservative and liberal beliefs and values. For instance, a woman's right to choose or not to choose an abortion is commonly recognized by liberals around the world. People with conservative views generally support the importance of religious education. Social programs and financial help to the poor and needy frequently top liberal agendas. Conservatives are less inclined to spend money on such programs, often considering them wasteful. Traditionally, in attempts to solve international conflicts, liberal ideologies are bases for negotiations for mutual concessions. On the other hand, conservatives tend to rely on leadership strength, especially on military strength. Conservatives are likely to spend less money on government services for immigrants and try to restrict immigration. Liberals, in contrast, are likely to support measures that help immigrants and their families.

Attitudes of individuals who consider themselves either liberal or conservative vary from country to country. The interpretation of these attitudes is often based on specific circumstances and local political developments. For instance, conservatives in the United States are likely to support less federal involvement in economy and finances, while in China and Russia, conservatives are those who support more central planning and governmental involvement in economy, business, and banking.

How can you evaluate your own ideological views? Ideally, you should review a comprehensive list of issues and values that represent contemporary liberal and conservative ideologies and then assess your attitudes about the items on the list. Accurate ideological self-evaluation is difficult to achieve. First, developing an indisputable account of conservative and liberal views is hard. Second, ideologues themselves may not agree on many issues. Moreover, as the interview with the young woman called Kasa in Chapter 8 on gender shows, many find themselves in agreement with several conservative and liberal values at the same time.

Overall, conservatism-liberalism is not a dichotomous but rather a continuous variable. The vast majority of people have a conservative view of some issues and a liberal view of others. Some people in this situation call themselves moderate, whereas others may still identify as conservative or liberal. Over the years, people showed relatively consistent tendencies in the way they identified their ideological position as liberal, conservative, or moderate. As shown in Table 10.4, which presents opinion polls taken as early as 1964, moderates are usually the largest ideological group. Note also that fewer Americans considered themselves liberal than conservative.

TABLE 10.4

Distribution of Ideological Self-assessments, 1964–2003. (In percentages.)

	1964	1970	1975	1980	1985	1990	1995	2000	2003
Liberal	26	22	15	17	19	22	17	21	19
Conservative	28	41	43	32	30	33	33	34	36
Moderate	37	37	40	51	42	37	46	41	40

Surveys: 1964 – Which one of the phrases listed on this card do you think best describes you, yourself, when it comes to political matters? Gallup/Potomac Associates, personal, 1,564, dk answers 9 percent; 1970 – How would you describe yourself—as very conservative, fairly conservative, middle-of-the road, fairly liberal, or very liberal? Gallup, personal, 1,507; 1975 – Do you think of yourself as conservative, moderate, liberal or radical? *Time*/Yankelovich, Skelly and White, telephone, 1,014, radical 2 percent; 1980 – On most political matters, do you consider yourself conservative, moderate, or liberal? CBS News/*New York Times*, voters as they left voting booths, self-administered questionnaire 15,202; 1985 – How would you describe your views on most political matters? Generally, do you think of yourself as liberal, moderate, or conservative? CBS News/*New York Times*, telephone, 1,509; dk answers 8 percent; 1990 – How would you describe your views on most political matters? Generally, do you think of yourself as liberal, moderate, or conservative? CBS News/*New York Times*, telephone, 1,370, dk answers 8 percent; 1995 – How would you describe your views on most political matters? Generally, do you think of yourself as liberal, moderate, or conservative? CBS News/*New York Times*, telephone, 1,111, dk answers 4 percent; 2000 – How would you describe your views on most political matters? Generally do you think of yourself as liberal, moderate, or conservative? CBS News/*New York Times*, telephone, 947, dk answers 5 percent; 2003 – Thinking about your general approach to issues, do you consider yourself to be liberal, moderate, or conservative? HT/CNN/*Time*; telephone, 1,507, other answers 14 percent.

Source: National adult samples.

In review. Historically, political parties and movements in the United States and most democratic countries tend to identify their platform as leaning in either a liberal or a conservative direction. Political struggles in developed democracies today also reflect the competition between liberal and conservative ideologies. Since in the United States the Republican Party accepts many elements of conservative ideology and the Democratic Party embraces many liberal ideas and principles, in theory, conservatives are likely to vote for Republican candidates and liberal voters for Democratic candidates. In reality, this does not always happen. More conservatives would mean that more American presidents after 1964 should have been Republican. In fact, among the eight presidents between 1964 to 2004, three were Democrat and five were Republican.

Between one in six and one in four Americans identified as liberal in the end of the 20th century. From the 1980s onward, almost one in three American identified as conservative. Ideology plays an important role in the formation and expression of attitudes. However, it may play a relatively lesser role in determining for whom people vote. One of the most important factors contributing to voters' electoral choices is party identification.

PARTISANSHIP AND OPINIONS

To have partisan sentiment is to support the views, values, and policies of a **political party,** an organized group structured around certain social ideas and competing for political power. Each political party develops a set of ideas and policies, and support or otherwise of these ideas and policies determines a person's partisanship. In the United States, people who support government programs designed to boost employment and help the poor are likely to vote Democrat. In Great Britain, they are likely to vote for the Labor Party. In Ukraine, they are likely be Communist Party supporters.

Political parties around the world are extremely diverse in terms of organization, membership policies, and party discipline. So-called strong parties demand discipline and unity of their members, who are supposed to support particular ideas and participate in party activities. Weak parties do not demand obedience from their members and are often based on the so-called big tent theory, which regards a political party as a spacious home for debate. Unlike strong political parties, which typically maintain accurate account of membership, weak parties cannot exactly determine the number of their members since they often have official membership mechanism, people can switch alliances relatively easily. The United States has a weak party system. One of the most difficult tasks in predicting American elections is determining which voters remain *standpatters*, or continue to support the same party during all elections, and how many become *switchers*, or move to another party in subsequent elections (Key, 1966; Kirkpatrick & Jones, 1974).

Because of the relative weakness of party affiliation here, surveys are often the only reliable method of determining how many people support which party. Polls, of course, give only an approximate evaluation of party affiliation. People tend to understand and report their association with or membership in political parties differently. Some people do not reveal their party identity; others do. Therefore, answers vary from poll to poll. Let's demonstrate.

Polls show a relatively clear picture of partisanship in the United States over recent years (Figure 10.2). A study of self-reported political affiliation from 1952 to the early 1990s (Green & Palmquist, 1994) revealed that over the period of 50 years, a slight preference was generally given to the Democratic Party. A turn to the left in respondents' opinions took place in 1964, when Lyndon Johnson, a Democrat from Texas, was elected President. A slight swing toward the Republican Party occurred in the 1980s, when two Republicans occupied the White House (first Ronald Reagan and then George H. W. Bush). Independents have also grown. Remember, people's identification with a political party often depends on the question asked, and different polls may bring different results.

Do these fluctuations in party identification indicate real changes in people's attitudes toward political parties? Because cross-sectional surveys typically do not examine the same pool of respondents over time, every survey includes new individuals in the sample. Most likely, party identification remains relatively stable for most people. The most significant changes in survey results are likely to be caused by the inclusion of the new voters in the samples, those who were too young to vote in the two or four years before the survey was taken. Why? According to the classic work of Glenn and Hefner (1972), the generational groups (people of the same relative age) tend to maintain relatively stable partisan attachments despite broad political fluctuations in the country. The overall shift in party identification is probably caused by the younger age cohorts, who bring new balance to party affiliations. During the years of Republican presidency, more young people developed alliances with the Republican Party than in any other age cohort. Similarly, during the Democratic years, more young people than any other age group formed their identification with the Democratic Party.

In some states, citizens do not declare party affiliation; therefore, it is difficult to say exactly how many registered voters belong to the two major political parties. Over the last 15 years, less than 30 percent of voters registered as Republican and more than 30 percent registered as Democrat, so registered Democrats traditionally outnumber registered Republicans. Growth in independent voter registration is significant; it increased from 20 percent in the 1960s to 30 percent in the 1970s and 1980s and to even higher proportions in the 1990s and the 2000s.

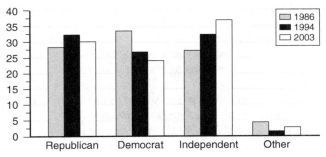

FIGURE 10.2

Party identification. *Question:* "In politics, as of today, do you consider yourself a Republican, a Democrat, or an Independent?" (In percentages.)
Source: Gallup/*Newsweek*, 1986, 756; Gallup/CNN/*USA Today*, 1994, 1,010; Gallup/CNN, 2003, 1,006.

EXPLANATIONS FOR PARTISAN VOTING

At the dawn of voting behavior studies, Belknap and Campbell (1952) showed that voters' party identification generally predicted electoral choice. Campbell, Converse, Miller, and Stokes (1960), in a groundbreaking work for American political science, *The American Voter*, suggested that although the great majority of people identify with a political party, this affiliation is based primarily on psychological factors and to a much lesser extent on pragmatic calculations. Citizens are generally not interested in and are unfamiliar with most political issues. Although this conclusion of *The American Voter* is now questioned about the nature, origins, and strength of party identification, it sparked a long debate (Keith et al., 1992; Miller & Shanks, 1996). Why do people develop and maintain attachments to political parties? Let's gauge at least three points of view.

Identity

According to one outlook, partisanship is a form of self-identity that may contain gender, professional, ethnic, religious, and other psychological components. A relatively strong psychological bond links the individual to his political party. Just as one may consider himself Irish, Nigerian, Buddhist, or Texan, he may also identify as a Democrat, Libertarian, Republican, Social Democrat, Tory, or as a member of any other political party. Partisans may also see themselves as members of social groups. Such membership may be established in the process of socialization and become a stable feature of the individual's self-image, which can further affect behavior. Party identification is not likely to be formed by rational calculation. It is rather caused by attitudes formed at some point in the individual's early years. Many people are unfamiliar with, misinformed about, or uninterested in political issues. Nevertheless, they can express strong partisan support and clearly identify partisan preference in elections (Converse & Pierce, 1985). Party identification in stable democracies is not particularly susceptible to shifts in political currents. Therefore, despite the swings in political or economic fortunes, partisanship in democratic countries generally changes slowly (Green & Palmquist 1990, 1994; Schickler & Green, 1994).

Rational Assessment

Some people develop partisan attachments early in life and do not change them. Others, as Downs (1957) and Fiorina (1981) argue, act as rational individuals who constantly evaluate their options and try to make rational voting decisions. If a party's voting platform does not suit an individual and its representatives did a poor job as politicians or officials in the government, this party will not likely get support from this person in the future.

According to the rational voter view, people vote because they are capable of assessing which party should provide them with greater benefits. Partisanship is likely to be based not on long-term attachment but rather on approval or disapproval of specific policies. Parties' programs on issues such as taxation, education, and immigration policies may have a more significant impact on people's party identification than their socialization experiences (RePass, 1971; Pomper, 1975). Party attachments, for example, have been found to shift when a political party changes its previous political course (Schickler, 1996; Brody & Rothenberg, 1988). In sum, continually updated in light of current information, partisanship may undergo considerable change. The public adjusts its assessment of parties rapidly in the wake of changing national or international conditions (Page & Shapiro, 1992).

Identity Based on Reasoning

According to another view, the previous two approaches to partisanship should be combined. Voters are both partisan *and* rational; they form political beliefs in their early years and then update their attitudes based on new information (Zechman, 1979; Calvert & MacKuen, 1985). People care about issues but, at the same time, they also consider strongly the image of the party they support when making voting decisions (Gerber & Green, 1998; Nie et al., 1976). If a candidate and a voter belong to the same party and the candidate's reputation was shattered by a recent scandal, the voter may reconsider her intention to support both the candidate and the party.

According to this view, voters are susceptible to partisan changes, but to different degrees; some people are more resistant to change than are others. Age, for instance, is an important factor. Younger voters tend to be more susceptible to partisanship changes, whereas older voters have more stable partisan affiliations (Achen, 1992; Alwin & Krosnick, 1991). Psychological factors also contribute to partisanship, as people tend to defend done deeds such as actual voting. For example, after the 2000 elections, 98 percent of those who reported having voted for a presidential candidate say they would not switch candidates if they had it to do over again (*Newsweek*/Princeton, November 9–10, 2000, 1,000).

THINKING CRITICALLY ABOUT VOTING

Contextual Factors

Predicting elections is often as tricky as predicting the weather; a multitude of contextual variables have to be considered. Sometimes results can be forecasted with little difficulty. For example, the electoral victories of Bill Clinton in 1996 and Ronald Reagan in 1984 were almost certain and forecasted by pollsters weeks before Election Day. On the other hand, some electoral predictions based on polls turn out to be incorrect. For example, Harry Truman in the 1948 U.S. presidential vote and John Major in the 1994 British national elections were both projected to lose. Most pundits and commentators were certain about the outcome of these elections. The results proved them wrong. History shows a number of other examples of electoral miracles or disasters that demonstrated substantial changes in voters' decisions. For instance, George H. W. Bush enjoyed very high approval ratings in 1991 at the end of the first Gulf War, one year before the presidential elections, but he lost to Arkansas governor Bill Clinton the next year. In 1996, Russian president Boris Yeltsin had approval ratings as low as 6 percent only five months before the scheduled elections. He was reelected anyway by a solid majority of votes.

One of the most important contextual factors that affect voting is incumbency. Public officials who are already in office tend to remain there if they run for reelection. For example, the reelection rate for U.S. representatives is close to 90 percent.

The reelection rate for U.S. senators is lower, but consistently above 60 percent over the past 20 years. Since World War II, eight U.S. presidents have run for reelection; seven were successful. Their opponents defeated three sitting presidents, Gerald Ford in 1976, Jimmy Carter in 1980, and George H. W. Bush in 1992.

Voters tend to support incumbents for several reasons. Elected officials, because of their status as executive officers or legislators, establish contacts in their constituencies and may develop a base of donors who support their reelection campaigns. The incumbent typically has better access to the media; her activities are likely to be covered by local stations, newspapers, or national networks. Media exposure helps officials build name recognition among potential voters. If an official maintains a good reputation so that his name is not associated with scandals, shameful events, or other unpleasant developments, name recognition can be very helpful. Overall, little-known challengers have only a slim chance of defeating incumbents, especially when the economy is relatively strong and the incumbent has a good record and his name is not associated with dishonorable actions.

Incumbency, nonetheless, is not always a positive factor contributing to reelection. A phenomenon called *incumbent fatigue* represents voters' general inclination to replace the official in the office—not necessarily and only because of political or ideological views but primarily because of the electorate's psychological weariness with the current official (Balz & Morin, 1999). Term limits are a response to the sense that incumbents stay in office too long.

A CASE IN POINT 10.2   The Third-Party Candidate Factor in Elections

In 1980, a moderate Republican, John Anderson, after losing his bid for the Republican nomination, decided to run as an independent candidate; that year, the incumbent president, Jimmy Carter, was defeated by Ronald Reagan, a Republican. In 1992, Texas billionaire H. Ross Perot announced his candidacy for the presidency; that year, the incumbent Republican president, George H. W. Bush, was defeated by Bill Clinton, a Democrat. In 2000, Ralph Nader, the presidential candidate of the Green Party, drew 3 percent of the national vote. This was lower than he and his supporters hoped for. Nonetheless, in that year, the incumbent vice president and Democratic presidential candidate, Al Gore, lost the election.

Third-party candidates tend to affect the reelection chances of incumbents negatively. Anderson, Perot, and Nader drew enough votes from Carter, Bush, and Gore, respectively, to make them lose their bids for presidency. A *Wall Street Journal*/NBC poll (2000) showed that the Green Party candidate, Nader, took twice as many votes from Gore as Patrick Buchanan, a conservative candidate who finished a distant fourth, took from George W. Bush. Nader's strong showing in the national elections, particularly in close states like Florida, was a major factor in Gore's defeat (Fund, 2000).

In U.S. presidential elections as well some other national races, the presence of third-party candidates may have a significant impact on electoral outcome. The votes cast for these candidates are usually those that would have been given, in the absence of the third-party option, to major-party nominees. If the third-party candidate is popular, the most damage is typically done to the major-party candidate whose views are closer to the views of the third-party challenger. This occurred in 2000 but not 2004.

Chapter 3 on critical thinking, mentioned studies that assessed the impact of the undecided vote. An **undecided voter** is registered and eligible to vote but does not make up his mind about who to vote for until late in the campaign. In the 1993 New Jersey and the 1994 New York governors' races, the incumbents were leading in polls in the closing days of the contests. Governor James Florio was leading in four of five polls and Governor Mario Cuomo was ahead in all five major polls. Despite the forecasts of respected polling organizations, both incumbents lost. Most likely, the analysts did not adequately take into consideration the undecided voter factor.

The undecided voter brings uncertainty to electoral forecasts. These voters are typically tracked through trial-heat polls in which representative samples of potential voters are asked about their decision as if they were voting at that moment. How can pollsters and election campaigns determine the potential distribution of undecided votes during the election? One approach is to split them 50-50 in a two-candidate race. This approach, however, will not necessarily lead to an accurate assessment and prediction. Several electoral studies showed, for example, that challengers are more likely than incumbents to get undecided votes, so incumbents leading a single challenger but securing less than 50 percent of the polls are at high risk of losing the election (Gruca, 1996; Panagakis, 1989). Why does this happen? Constituents usually know the incumbent's record. If a voter is undecided late in the campaign, this is probably bad news for the incumbent because it indicates the voter doubts the incumbent deserves another term. Given the incumbent's advantages of name recognition and a

---

A CASE IN POINT **10.3** Incumbents and Challengers

Consider the following hypothetical situation: A senator from Pennsylvania seeking reelection is facing a challenger. The results of a preelection poll among those who intend to vote are 45 percent for the incumbent and 40 percent for the challenger, with 15 percent undecided. Now imagine you are a journalist covering this election for a local television station. How would you report these numbers? Would you say that, according to surveys, the incumbent has a 5-point lead, or would you rather cite all the numbers: "45 to 40 with 15 undecided"? Even though these two ways of reporting seem equivalent, they are not. If you quote the point-spread situation (5 percent) as an anticipated outcome on Election Day, your reasoning is based on the assumption that the two candidates will split the undecided vote equally. However, this is not likely to happen. In fact, as we learned in this chapter, most of the undecided vote usually goes to the challenger. In our hypothetical senate race, the final result is more likely to be too close to call (50-50) than a 53-47 win for the incumbent.

record in office, undecided votes at this stage are likely to be a predictor of the incumbent's problems with these voters (Kolbert, 1993).

In countries such as India, Italy, and Russia, the multiparty political system also contributes to a large number of undecided voters. This increases the difficulty of predicting how they will vote (Rao, 2002).

As we learned about critical thinking in Chapter 3, many survey sponsors are not neutral observers; rather, they have stake in particular polling results. Public opinion expressed in support of a political party or candidate may help attract or sway more supporters and draw media attention. Favorable survey numbers may translate into publicity, monetary support from individual and interest groups, and favorable voting decisions. Therefore, when an observer interprets an electoral survey, it is vital to recognize who the sponsor is, especially if the sponsor is a political or social organization. For instance, in publications about elections, it is common to read critical opinions about surveys conducted by the Democratic or the Republican party. Polls conducted by independent sources are more reliable partly because they are expected to be nonpartisan.

Wording

If you think critically, you may find confusing the way the labels *conservative* and *liberal* are used. A conservative may be a dedicated opponent of abortion and call herself a pro-life supporter. At the same time, she may be a vigorous supporter of the death penalty, agreeing that the state has the right to put a human being to death. A liberal may back international peace, actively support negotiations, and advocate peaceful deals between conflicting groups. At the same time, looking at other cases, she may endorse military intervention and violent confrontations with particular countries responsible for genocide. Supporters of liberal policies such as affirmative action and social welfare that were established several decades ago may be labeled *conservative* by their critics today because of the supporters' unwillingness to revise them. Remember that ideological identity is a continuous and changeable variable. It is easy to imagine dichotomous divisions and label people according their ideological labels. Therefore, when making judgments about large groups of people and their ideological affiliations, be specific and use percentages and proportions (such as majority or minority) to describe the distribution of opinions.

Overreporting Bias

Some people tend to "overreport" their voting. Some say in polls that they voted in a particular election when, in fact, they did not. Why does this occur? Some people give socially desirable answers because they believe voting is what they are supposed to do as citizens and feel ashamed if they did not. Others may confuse the elections in which they participated. Because many Americans vote every two years or more often, some may confuse having voted in one of the previous elections with having voted in the last election (Belli et al., 1999).

Explanations

To see deeper into the survey numbers, it is important to analyze the group surveyed, its composition, and its diversity. Here is an illustration. A 1997 poll about affirmative action by Princeton Survey Research Associates (PSRA, July, 1,212) asked Americans whether they think news organizations tend to favor one side in the way they report about civil rights, including affirmative action. Those who said yes were then asked: "Do [news organization] tend to favor the side that supports affirmative action, or do they tend to favor the side that is against affirmative action?" The answers, remarkably, divided about equally; 44 percent said the media favor supporters of affirmative action, and 42 percent said the media favor opponents of affirmative action.

Why did this distribution occur? People who answered these questions may have had access to different sources of information; they read different newspaper and watched different television programs. Or they may have formed an opinion about affirmative action and deliberately paid attention to sources that confirmed their opinion. What if people did not have an opinion about affirmative action and gave their answer without serious thought? These explanations are based on the assumptions that the sample was relatively homogenous and the only differences among respondents were based on cognitive factors, that is, the way they accessed and processed available information. This information was available about this sample, making more informative descriptions possible (Table 10.5).

How substantial are the differences between groups on the two civil rights questions after the sample is broken down into categories? In general, respondents belonging to one group have similar views about media bias. Significant differences can be detected between black and whites; the gaps are 33 and 37 points. The gaps between Republicans and Democrats are 23 and 19 points. The differences among other groups are also substantial. The answers were not distributed randomly among the respondents, and there are links between political affiliations and racial or group identity, on the one hand, and the way individuals assess the media with respect to their coverage of affirmative action, on the other.

Knowledge about the distance voters must travel to polling places may help predict voter turnout; people who live relatively close to polling places are more likely to vote than those who live farther away (Schlichting & Tuckel, 1994). Think critically. These results do not necessarily mean that the only reason some people decide not to vote is that they are unwilling to spend time traveling to their polling place. Socioeconomic factors can affect voter turnout significantly in that people who have

TABLE 10.5

Looking at Composition Groups Within the Sample: Media and Affirmative Action.
Distribution of answers among those who said that news organizations tend to favor one side over the other in the way they report about civil rights, including affirmative action. M—male, F—female, B—black, W—white, R—Republican, D—Democrat, LI—low income (less than $15,000), HI—high income ($50,000 and greater), CG—college graduate, HG—high school graduate. (In percentages.)

	M	F	B	W	R	D	LI	HI	CG	HG
Media favor the side that supports affirmative action	53	38	17	50	56	33	36	53	56	39
Media favor the side that opposes affirmative action	36	46	73	37	33	52	46	33	36	46

Source: PSRA, July 1997, 1,212.

their own cars (or families with two or three cars) are more likely to drive and vote than those who do not have cars and therefore have to rely on their feet or public transportation. Overall, the more information you have about voters, the more accurately you can predict an election.

ASSIGNMENT 10.1   PARTISAN HOUSEHOLDS

After studying partisanship patterns in voting, Gelman and Little (1998) described an interesting pattern. They found that people who live in one- and three-person households tend to vote Democratic, whereas people who live in two-person households tend to vote Republican. **Question:** How would you explain this voting pattern?

ASSIGNMENT 10.2   INCUMBENTS AND CHALLENGERS

In parliamentary electoral systems such as in Italy, Great Britain, and Japan, both the executive branch and the legislature are chosen simultaneously; the party or coalition that wins the majority of the votes is responsible for forming a new cabinet. In countries with presidential electoral systems, such as the United States, Mexico, and France, people elect presidents who later appoint members of the executive branch. In theory (if not practice), the multiparty competition of parliamentary electoral systems should lead to higher voter turnout than those of presidential systems (Moreno, 1999).

Your task:
Find and compare data on voter turnout in recent national elections in (a) five countries that have a parliamentary electoral system and (b) five countries that have a presidential electoral system. Compare election turnouts. Which cluster of countries had higher voting rates? What factors could have contributed to the voter turnout in the studied countries?

CHAPTER SUMMARY

- Voting is both a simple and a complex behavioral act influenced by a wide variety of economic, social, and psychological factors. There are at least two major types of voting: elections and referenda. Voting is preceded by campaigning, a deliberate and systematic effort to win an election.

- Several factors motivate individuals to vote: socioeconomic status; knowledge of social and political realities; legal and institutional features such as mandatory electoral laws and voter registration requirements; single- versus multiseat electoral formats; personality characteristics; cognitive and moral factors.

- Low electoral turnout can be viewed in at least two ways. In most democracies, electoral turnout has tended to decrease over the past 50 years. Some observers describe this phenomenon as a sign of alienation, or the individual's disengagement and withdrawal from contemporary society. Critics of this view argue that low turnout is a normal phenomenon that does not indicate that inaction smothers democracy. The historic emphasis on individualism and suspicion of government is part of the Western tradition in general and the American tradition in particular, especially when society is not in crisis. Among the many suggestions for increasing electoral turnout are online voting and dropping registration requirements.

- The voting choice can be a combination of issue-oriented, candidate-oriented, or party-oriented decisions. People tend to evaluate political candidates both prospectively and retrospectively. Protest voting is based on a voter's desire to express disagreement and disappointment with a particular candidate or proposed policies. Prejudiced voting is rooted in negative prejudgment of a candidate or policy.

- Political ideologies are categorized along several dimensions, among them the scope, sources, and direction of social change; attitudes about property rights; and attitudes about individual rights. Most commonly, ideologies are divided into three categories: liberal, moderate, and conservative (plus radical and reactionary). There are many cross-national similarities, but also some differences, in the ways people understand and interpret conservative and liberal beliefs and values.

- Overall, conservatism-liberalism is not a dichotomous but rather a continuous variable. In the United States, since 1964, moderates tend to represent the largest ideological group. In general, fewer Americans considered themselves liberal than conservative. No less than one in six and no more than one in four Americans called themselves liberals in the end of the 20th century. Since the 1980s, almost every third American has identified as conservative.

- Polls give an approximate evaluation of party identification. People's understanding and reporting of their association with or membership in political parties across the country differ. Over the past 15 years, slightly less than 30 percent of registered voters were registered Republicans and slightly more than 30 percent were registered Democrats. The rate at which voters registered as independents grew significantly, from 20 percent in the 1960s to 30 percent in the 1970s and 1980s. The proportions were even higher in the 1990s and the 2000s.

- Partisanship can be a form of self-identity that may contain gender, professional, ethnic, religious, and other psychological components. According to the rational voter view, people vote because they are capable of assessing which party should provide greater benefits to them. According to another view, voters are both partisan and rational; they form political beliefs and then update their attitudes as new information becomes available.

- Polls conducted by independent sources are more reliable than sponsored polls partly because independents are expected to be nonpartisan. Self-identification in political and ideological terms is imprecise. Many individuals inaccurately recall whether or not they voted in a particular election. Some people over-report their voting, saying they voted in a particular election when they did not. In sum, when analyzing studies that explain the reasons for partisan voting, look for multiple causes.

Looking Ahead.   The next chapter explores domestic issues on which people have a diversity of opinions. These include abortion, affirmative action, criminal justice, the death penalty, education, immigration, and health care. The chapter also examines ethical issues about euthanasia, sexual orientation, and privacy.

DEFINITIONS OF KEY TERMS

Alienation—An individual's disengagement and withdrawal from society.

Banner district—The voting district in which a party or candidate makes a better showing than anywhere else in a current election.

Campaigning—A deliberate and systematic effort to win votes in an election.

Election—A process of selecting candidates by vote for a public office, typically a position in an administration, legislature, or court.

Ideology—A comprehensive set of ideas about society, its past, present, and future, and measures to be undertaken to accomplish the goals set by the ideology.

Political ideology—A comprehensive set of ideas about the nature and goals of government, typically characterized in the United States as liberal, moderate, or conservative.

Political party—An organized group of individuals structured around certain social ideas and competing for political power.

Prejudiced voting—The approach to voting in which the voter rejects certain candidates or issues because of negative prejudgment and unwillingness to reconsider it.

Prospective evaluations—Potential voters' assessment of a candidate's ability to fulfill her promises if elected.

Protest voting—A type of voting based on the desire to express disagreement of disappointment with a candidate or with proposed policies.

Referendum—An electoral event in which eleigible voters express their opinion about a specific problem or policy issue.

Retrospective evaluations—Potential voters' assessment of a candidate's past performance.

Undecided voter—An eligible voter who does not make up his mind in advance of Election Day.

Voting—An individual's formal expression of preference for a candidate for office or for a proposed resolution for an issue.

CHAPTER 11

Opinions About
Domestic Issues

Nothing in the world can one
imagine beforehand, not the least
thing. Everything is made up of so
many unique particulars that cannot
be foreseen.

Rainer Maria Rilke

President John F. Kennedy didn't want the public to know he was using polling data to develop a better strategy for civil rights issues; in those days, referring to surveys was seen as an obvious weakness in a president. Most Americans believed then that the highest representatives of the people were elected to public offices as trustees to use their own judgment and not to depend on pollsters—political fortunetellers. Politics has changed since the early 1960s, and more people seem to accept that presidents should respectfully respond to polls reflecting the opinions of their constituencies. President Lyndon B. Johnson, for example, learned from the polls not to raise the Vietnam War as an issue in the 1964 presidential campaign if he wanted to be reelected. President Richard M. Nixon turned to polling as part of the art of presidential politics in bringing many of his domestic decisions in line with the people's opinions during his five-year tenure. President Jimmy Carter got help from survey specialists and was the first president to witness one of his pollsters, Patrick Caddell, achieve celebrity status. Unfortunately, Carter's reelection team made serious mistakes when Caddell underestimated the strengths of presidential candidate Ronald Reagan, who won the 1980 election. Despite some accounts, Reagan persistently used national opinion polls to avoid making obvious mistakes on domestic policies. George H. W. Bush, who succeeded Reagan as president, did not regularly use surveys and suffered a loss of popularity over the economy. However, Bill Clinton, who became president in 1993, gave opinion polls serious consideration throughout his eight years in the White House. Moreover, he gave some of his poll-savvy senior advisers like Dick Morris direct access to the Oval Office. Since 2001, President George W. Bush has considered polling on issues important to the American people part of his domestic strategy. He gets help from a polling center in Texas that conducts national polls four or five times a month (Judson, 2002; Sobel, 1993).

Presidents over the past 40 years accepted, sometimes reluctantly, that following polls means keeping in touch with voters' opinions. This strategy can assist not only with important policies but also can help win elections. Knowing what the American people think about domestic issues is an essential part of presidential politics today.

Looking Forward.   This chapter examines a range of domestic issues on which people have a variety of opinions. Important domestic issues include abortion, affirmative action, criminal justice, the death penalty, education, immigration, and healthcare. The chapter also examines ethical issues about euthanasia, sexual orientation, and privacy.

DOMESTIC ISSUES

If you ask people whether they want to live long and happy lives, it is only reasonable to expect the answer "yes." Nevertheless, when you ask them what is supposed to be done, preserved, or changed in their lives and in society to achieve long and happy lives, the answers will vary. In totalitarian societies, people are likely to give similar responses about society and the ways it should be managed. This similarity is explained by the power of tradition or the power of intimidation; the ruling authorities do not want to allow deviation from the correct, government-approved way of thinking. In democratic societies, a diversity of ideas about issues and problems represents the norm.

Americans express a great variety of opinions. The chapter deals with a range of controversial topics such as abortion, affirmative action, crime and law enforcement, the death penalty, education, gun control, immigration, the environment, healthcare, ethical issues, and government. The sections begin with a brief description of the issue followed by a discussion of competing arguments and critical thinking. Special attention is given to a critical evaluation of contextual factors and other circumstances likely to affect people's opinions. The chapter also compares opinion trends over the years and discusses the relationship between people's ideological and voting preferences and their attitudes about specific issues.

ABORTION

Nearly 50 million abortions are performed worldwide each year. Almost 60 percent take place in developing countries and are mostly illegal because of official restrictions and the opposition of religious institutions. In countries such as China, however, the government encourages abortion as a birth control method. Countries vary in terms of frequency of abortions performed. The number of legal abortions in the United States increased from 1970 to an all-time high in 1984 of 36.4 for every 100 live births. The rate declined to 31.1 in 1995 and continued to decline in the early 2000s (WHO, 1999; Henshaw et al., 1999; Alan Guttmacher Institute, 2000).

General Arguments

In the historic 1973 case of *Roe v. Wade,* the U.S. Supreme Court ruled that states could not restrict abortion in the first three months of pregnancy and only within limits in the second three. However, later rulings of the Court, in particular decisions in 1989 and 1992, gave states the limited right to regulate abortion by establishing waiting periods and requiring parental consent for underage women (Cook, 1997). These developments reflected and renewed vigorous political debates between opponents and supporters of abortion. Since the 1970s, the term **pro-life** has become a convenient label for the stance of people who oppose abortion. The counter-term **pro-choice** emerged in 1978 to describe people who support the right of women to choose or not choose to have an abortion (Richler, 1999).

Arguments on both sides focus on several principal points. One is the question of when life begins. People on the "pro-life" side argue that human life begins at conception, and so all abortion is murder. People on the "pro-choice" side maintain that determining when life begins is a matter of political definition; religious, cultural, and legal arguments about the meaning of conception have varied and been accepted or rejected by different people. Supporters of pro-life arguments say women do not have the right to decide whether their unborn children should live or die because the child's life does not belong to the woman. Backers of the pro-choice position argue that an embryo is a part of the woman's body and that she, not the government, should decide what to do with her body. Table 11.1 compares the basic arguments of pro-choice and pro-life backers.

How are abortion views distributed among Americans? As shown later in the chapter, it is difficult to draw far-reaching conclusions and to compare polls because of differences in questions. However, some generalizations can be made. In 2002,

TABLE 11.1

Abortion: Arguments Pro-choice and Pro-life.

Pro-choice	*Pro-life*
An embryo doesn't have a beating heart; at earlier stages, it is merely a collection of cells made by the joining of the egg and sperm.	Abortion stops a beating heart; it interrupts the life of a human being.
Women have the right to decide whether or not to have an abortion and to be responsible for their body. No one should tell them what to do with it.	Abortion is the murder of an innocent child; women have no right to decide whether the child lives or dies.
Different legal, religious, and cultural standards are used to determine when life begins. People have the right to establish or change these standards.	Human life begins at conception. No one should establish new standards.
It is not against the law to have an abortion as long as it is performed legally. If abortion is outlawed, women will obtain the procedure illegally, making ordinary citizens criminals.	Abortion is both an immoral and a criminal act that should be outlawed through litigation or legislation.

according to CBS and Gallup polls, approximately one-third of Americans believed that abortion should be legal under any circumstances. Around 50 percent of respondents believed abortion should be legal under certain specified circumstances. The remaining one-fifth of respondents wanted abortion illegal under all circumstances (Gallup, May 2002, 1,012; Gallup, April 2000, 998; CBS/*NYT,* February 2000, 1,225). Among those who agree with the woman's right in principle to interrupt her pregnancy, nearly a fifth consider this action morally wrong (Smith, 2001).

Americans' views on abortion are sharply divided on a number of dimensions. The pro-choice position is mostly endorsed by residents of large metropolitan areas, by people who are better educated and moderately religious, and by political liberals. In contrast, pro-life supporters are likely to be found among religious individuals, political conservatives, rural residents, and older age cohorts. The gender gap, if it exists at all, is slight: About 40 percent of men and 37 percent of women believe abortion should be generally available. Approximately 20 percent of men and 24 percent of women think it should not be permitted. Younger and older women hold nearly identical views on abortion (CBS, January 2003, 814). Among people older than 65, approximately 30 percent are pro-choice, 10 percentage points less than those between the ages of 30 and 49. Among people under 30, pro-choice attitudes are shared by 34 percent. Support for abortion rights also increases with education level. Among those who earned less than a high school degree, only 20 percent are pro-choice. However, almost 50 percent with a bachelor's degree or higher favor abortion rights (Smith, 2001; Cook, 1997).

People who believe abortion should remain permitted are almost evenly divided between those who think it should be generally available and those who think it should be more restricted than it currently is. The great majority of Americans also believe that abortion will remain legal in some way. There are regional differences in the United States on the abortion question. Southerners and Midwesterners are more likely to believe abortion should not be permitted, while Westerners and Northeasterners are more likely to think it should be generally available.

Most Americans have little knowledge of actual abortion rates. For example, more than a third of those surveyed in 2000 (35 percent) thought current rates are the highest in over 20 years. Another third (37 percent) thought abortion rates were either at their lowest in over 20 years or remained the same. The rest did not know or want to give an answer (Princeton/Kaiser, February 2000, 1,006). Here is another example of many people being uninformed on the topic. A drug called mifepristone (also known as RU-486 or the abortion pill), which interrupts pregnancy in its early stages, was approved by the U.S. Food and Drug Administration (FDA) in 2000. While activists on both sides exchanged intense arguments about the legal and moral aspects of RU-486, less than half of survey respondents (45 percent) had heard about this drug (Gallup, April 2000, 998).

Specific Circumstances

Respondents' answers are based on their interpretation of the survey questions. Therefore, we must look carefully at how each question is asked. For example, according to a Gallup poll (May 2002, 1,012), to the question "With respect to the abortion issue, would you consider yourself to be pro-choice or pro-life?" 47 percent of respondents answered "pro-choice," while 46 percent answered "pro-life." Do these results contradict the data obtained by CBS and the *New York Times* in 2000 that showed pro-life supporters at 20 percent? Why is there a 26-point difference between the polls?

The discrepancy is due to the way the questions are worded. For example, when people are asked a direct question such as "Do you think abortion should be illegal, or not?" the proportion answering "should be illegal" is greater than in surveys in which people are given the opportunity to consider circumstances such as threats to the mother's life, illness, and rape. Thus, in a 2000 national poll (NBC/*WSJ*, March 2000, 1,213), 35 percent said abortion should be illegal. According to the 2002 CBS poll mentioned earlier, only 20 percent of Americans wanted to have abortion illegal. In that survey, people were given information about circumstances under which some abortions could occur. In a national survey conducted by Virginia Commonwealth University, an even lower proportion of respondents (14 percent) replied that abortion should be illegal in all circumstances (September 2001, 1,122). In this survey, people were asked to consider abortion under circumstances such as endangered health, rape, and incest.

Another possible reason for the inconsistency in survey results is the division of attitudes about abortion into either/or categories. The labels *pro-life* and *pro-choice* are misleading, especially the latter. The vast majority of pro-choice individuals do not believe that women have the right to terminate a pregnancy at any time, but some people mistakenly attribute this belief to pro-choice supporters. The main point of a strong pro-choice view is that a woman should be allowed to obtain an abortion for specific reasons within established time limits (see Table 11.2). Strong backers of pro-life views, on the other hand, tend to oppose abortion under all circumstances and to advocate alternatives such as adoption.

What about people who agree with only one of the items on the list? Most people are neither completely for women's freedom to have an abortion nor totally against it; their views are somewhere between the two extremes. For example, an individual may reject abortion in principle but agree that under extreme circumstances, a woman can choose to terminate her pregnancy. For instance, 74 percent said abortion should be legal in cases of pregnancy through rape (AP, January 1998, 1,012).

TABLE 11.2

Criteria for Establishing Strength of Attitudes about Abortion.

Criteria: If you support the view that a woman should be allowed to have an abortion during the legally established period for these reasons, your views are more or less pro-choice. If you oppose these reasons, your views on abortion are more or less pro-life.

- If the woman's own health is seriously endangered by the pregnancy
- If there is a strong chance of serious defect in the child
- If the woman became pregnant because of rape or incest
- If the woman is not married and does not want to marry the father
- If the family has a very low income and cannot afford more children
- If the woman is married and does not want any more children

Source: Smith, 2001.

> ## A CASE IN POINT **11.1**   Survey Questions on Abortion
>
> Let us consider the results of three surveys taken in 1991 by different polling organizations. Answering the question "Do you think abortions should be legal under any circumstances, legal under only certain circumstances, or illegal in all circumstances?" 33 percent responded they should be legal under any circumstances and 14 percent said they should be illegal in all circumstances (Gallup, September 1991, 1,005). In another survey, 44 percent said a woman should be able to get an abortion if she decided she wants one no matter what the reason. In this case, only 10 percent said abortion should be illegal in all circumstances (Yankelovich/*Time* and CNN, July 1991, 1,000). When the third survey asked whether a woman should be allowed to have an abortion in the early months of pregnancy, if she wants one, 43 percent completely agreed and 20 percent completely disagreed (Princeton/*Times Mirror*, July 1991, 1,212).

When asked directly "Are you for or against abortion?" many individuals prefer to give the pro-life answer because they do not endorse abortion in principle. However, when respondents must decide about specific circumstances, the answers change. See Table 11.3 for the distribution of opinions about abortion under various circumstances.

The vast majority of Americans believe abortion should be legal if the mother's life is in danger. Only a few people out of a hundred believe abortion should be legal in the last three months of pregnancy. Opinions on abortion are generally split when people consider the circumstance of potential physical or mental impairment of the child.

Americans are far less enthusiastic about considering conditions such as low income, absence of the other parent, and the unwillingness of a married woman to have another child as justifications for abortion. In one of the earliest polls on this issue, taken in 1969, 67 percent of respondents disagreed that abortion

TABLE 11.3

Opinions About Circumstances Under Which Abortion Should Be Legal.
Question: For each situation, please say whether or not you think abortion should be legal. (In percentages.)

Condition or circumstance	Legal	Illegal	Other
When the woman's life is endangered	82	15	3
When the pregnancy was caused by rape or incest	50	46	4
When the child would be born with a life-threatening illness	60	35	5
When the child would be born mentally disabled	72	24	4
When the woman does not want the child for any reason	41	56	3

Source: Gallup, May 2003, 1,014.

should be legal if the family does not have enough money to support the child. Only 23 percent agreed. Seventy-eight percent also said that parents not wanting to have more children should not legitimize a termination of pregnancy (Gallup, 1969, personal, 1,560). Throughout the 1980s and 1990s, from 4 to 5 Americans out of every 10 agreed that low income was a significant reason for a woman interrupting her pregnancy. Consistently, after 1972, more than 40 percent considered single motherhood or the unwillingness of the woman to have more babies as unacceptable reasons for an abortion. Opinions were evenly split about whether legalized abortion encourages sexual promiscuity and leads to a decline in morals; the 45 percent of those who disagree with this statement surpass the supporters by an insignificant 3-point margin (Harris, 1970, personal, 1,600).

Attitudes About Abortion and Voting Behavior

When answering open-ended questions about America's problems, only 3 percent of Americans mentioned abortion in 2000 (Fox, January 2000, registered voters, 900). In 2002, before the midterm elections, only 2 percent of respondents said they would most like to hear the electoral candidates talk about abortion (Pew, October 2002, 1,513). In other surveys, when people are asked to address the importance of a candidate's abortion stance to their voting choice, most people say it is indeed important. For example, in a poll by ABC/*Washington Post*, more than three-quarters of Americans said abortion is important to them in forthcoming presidential elections, and significantly fewer people (23 percent) said abortion was not important to them (ABC/WP, March 2000, 1,083). For the vast majority of voters, the candidate's position on abortion is not the most crucial factor in choosing who to vote for (Gallup, April 2000, 998).

Partisan differences on abortion exist. In 2003, 43 percent of Democrats believed abortion should be generally available, and 35 percent thought it should be more strictly limited. Among Republicans, 29 percent said believed abortion should be generally available, while 41 percent supported stricter measures. In addition, 28 percent of Republicans and 21 percent of Democrats said abortion should not be permitted. Independents' views on abortion are close to the opinions of Democrats (CBS, January 2003, 814). Pro-choice policies drew the strongest support from mostly white, highly educated professionals (Edsall, 2001). Not surprisingly, because more individuals express pro-choice views than pro-life views, more people (31 percent) believed in 2000 the Democrats would handle abortion policy better than Republicans (23 percent) (NBC/*WSJ*, March 2000, 1,213). However, in 2004 the gap disappeared; 35 percent preferred Democrats, while 33 percent favored Republicans (HT/NBC/*WSJ*, January, 1,002).

AFFIRMATIVE ACTION

The Civil Rights Act of 1964 was designed to promote equal opportunity and treatment for all individuals regardless of race, color, religion, sex, or national origin. Title VII of the Act, which covered employment, stimulated the creation and implementation of policies collectively called **affirmative action** to end discrimination and create opportunities for minorities and women. The advocates of affirmative action say social justice is not achieved by ending discrimination and by good intentions alone. Equal justice and equal opportunity should be achieved by legal and political means (Hill, 1997). Specifically, affirmative action calls for minorities and women to receive special consideration in employment, education, and business decisions. As an illustration, affirmative action may call for a personnel executive or a college admission officer faced with two similarly qualified applicants to choose the minority person over the white or to recruit and hire a qualified woman for a job instead of an equally qualified man.

General Arguments

Supporters of affirmative action assert that hundreds of years of discrimination in the United States, especially against African Americans, benefited mostly one category of population: white men. They conclude that granting modest advantages to minorities and women is not only fair but also imperative. Affirmative action, in the view of its proponents, provides qualified people with a better opportunity to succeed in education, employment, and business (Bowen et al., 1998). In contrast, a central argument of opponents is that affirmative action is a form of reverse discrimination; in this attempt to remedy past injustice, white men are singled out as the target of new forms of bias. Opponents also argue that affirmative action results in giving jobs and scholarships to less qualified candidates. Supporters of affirmative action, on the other hand, say the policy has been beneficial to millions of people who otherwise would have had fewer chances to advance in society (Plois, 1996; Rivera, 2000).

Attitudes about affirmative action in the 1990s were relatively evenly split between opponents and proponents. Answering a 1997 question about what affirmative action programs generally do, 42 percent said the programs "ensure minorities get access to schools and jobs," and 49 percent said they "give preferential treatment to minorities" (Gallup/CNN and *USA Today*, November 1997, 1,019). Table 11.4 displays the pro and con arguments about affirmative action programs.

Although the U.S. Supreme Court, in 1978 and 2003 decisions, limited affirmative action, it upheld the idea that temporary racial preferences are necessary to achieve diversity, particularly in light of evidence of ongoing discrimination against minorities. The continuing debate about affirmative action revolves around the definition of terms such as *diversity*, *discrimination*, and *preferential treatment*.

Specific Circumstances

When the survey question about affirmative action is phrased "Do you support or oppose affirmative action?" people express support more often than opposition. In a 2000 poll, for example, 58 percent expressed support and 33 percent expressed opposition to affirmative action (Gallup/CNN and *USA Today*, January 2000, 1,027). However, small changes in wording can affect the distribution of answers. When the question asks about eliminating affirmative action programs that give "special consideration to minorities and women in decisions about admissions, hiring, or promotions," more than half favor eliminating affirmative action and only 40 percent want to keep it (Hart & Teeter, NBC/*WSJ*, June 1999, telephone, 2,011). In 2002, a question about affirmative action that would "give preferences to blacks and other minorities" yielded only 38 percent of support; in contrast, 58 percent disagreed

TABLE 11.4

Affirmative Action: Arguments Pro and Con.

Pro	Con
Most supporters of affirmative action oppose quotas and believe that merit and skill are important criteria for qualified candidates. Affirmative action offers help to such candidates.	Affirmative action means preferential selection procedures that favor less qualified candidates over more qualified ones. Quotas become more important than merit and skills. Affirmative action is a form of favoritism.
Despite the progress that has been made, society still does not offer equal opportunity for women and certain minority groups.	Affirmative action may have been necessary 30 or 40 years ago, but social conditions have changed for the better.
Discrimination is grounded in prejudice and exclusion, whereas affirmative action is an effort to overcome prejudicial treatment through inclusion.	Society cannot cure discrimination with another type of discrimination and new forms of exclusion. This practice creates new prejudices without curing the old ones.
The reality is that colorblind policies often put racial minorities at a disadvantage.	The only way to create a just society is to adopt colorblind policies.
Important gains in racial and gender equality are a direct result of affirmative action.	Affirmative action has not succeeded in significantly increasing female and minority representation.
Support exists if the results of opinion polls are properly interpreted.	According to polls, most people in the United States no longer support affirmative action.

(Princeton/WP/Kaiser, August 2002, 2,886). Also, mentioning "quotas" and "special privileges" in survey questions about affirmative action significantly reduces expressed support for these programs.

The vast majority of Americans reject the idea of using numbers and quotas in affirmative action policies. Most people (86 percent) see the goal of affirmative action as ensuring that minorities have equal opportunities to compete in the workplace. Only 11 percent suggest the goal is ensuring that minorities are adequately represented in the workplace (PSB/DCL, January 2000, national registered voters, 1,000). In another survey, 33 percent of respondents said they felt strongly in support of affirmative action programs. These programs, however, should not impose rigid quotas to counteract the effects of discrimination. Almost one-quarter of respondents (26 percent) strongly agreed that affirmative action programs have gone too far in favoring minorities and should be phased out because they unfairly discriminate against whites. The remaining 41 percent either did not have an opinion or felt "not so strongly" about the programs (Hart & Teeter, NBC/*WSJ*, March 2000, 1,213). When the question was asked about the overall impact of affirmative action policies, a majority (58 percent against 33 percent) believed that, on the whole, affirmative action had been good for the country (Gallup, November 2001, 1,523).

Socioeconomic status of respondents is correlated with attitudes toward affirmative action. In the 1990s, 45 percent of those earning less than $15,000 a year supported affirmative action programs in hiring, promoting, and college admissions, whereas the support of the upper middle class (making $75,000 and more) was much thinner, only 30 percent, with 61 percent of this group wanting to end these programs (CBS/*NYT,* December 1997, 1,258). There is also a significant attitudinal gap among white, black, and Hispanic respondents. The majority of blacks and Hispanics (60–70 percent, depending on the poll) support affirmative action, whereas the majority of whites (above 50 percent) tend to express a lack of interest in the continuation of affirmative action (see Chapter 9 on race and ethnicity).

Political Affiliations

Party identification correlates with attitudes about affirmative action. People who identify with the Republican Party are more likely to express negative attitudes and generally support policies that would reduce the impact of affirmative action or repeal it completely. Many blue-collar voters cited the Republican Party's negative view on affirmative action as an important reason for voting for that party in the 2000 elections (Edsall, 2001). Supporters of the Democratic Party lean toward the continuation of affirmative action policies. In a 1997 poll, for instance, 56 percent of Democrats supported the continuation of affirmative action programs, twice the proportion of Republicans (28 percent) (CBS/*NYT,* December 1997, 1,258). The same tendency was observed in the early 1990s; 34 percent of Republicans supported and 42 opposed affirmative action, whereas 71 percent of Democrats supported and 24 percent opposed (Hart & Teeter/NBC and *WSJ,* June 1991, 1,006). Although most blacks support affirmative action, black conservatives argue that continuing federal intervention in the form of affirmative action only perpetuates the dependency of blacks on outside help and deepens their sense of reliance on the government. Black liberals, in contrast, embrace government intervention through affirmative action programs as a remedy to past discrimination (Curry & West, 1996; Edley, 1998).

CRIME AND LAW ENFORCEMENT

A 1999 survey asked Americans an open-ended question about the ways in which life in the United States has gotten worse compared to the 1950s. "More crime" or "more violence" was mentioned in 44 percent of responses, far more than 19 percent of those who cited a decline of morals (Princeton/Pew, April–May 1999, telephone, 1,546). Crime was a central concern in the 1990s and remains an important issue today despite a steady decline of crime rates throughout the 1990s and the beginning of the 2000s.

General Arguments

The debate about the sources of criminal behavior and therefore the means by which it can be restrained has gone on for decades. Two views have emerged. Proponents of the first view believe that crime is inevitable. Whether it is caused by human nature or social ills, it will always remain part of human civilization. Therefore, tough law and its unremitting enforcement are the only effective remedy. Proponents of the other view consider crime, in most forms, a function of social problems. As long as society does not solve these problems, its members will have to deal with crime (see Table 11.5).

TABLE 11.5

Arguments About the Nature of Crime and Its Prevention.

Crime is a byproduct of social ills. If society cures its ills, then crime will substantially diminish.	Crime is an inevitable evil, part of our lives. Both human nature and social problems create conditions for crime.
People and government should pay more attention to the prevention of crime.	Major social effort should be placed on law enforcement and the punishment of criminals.
Isolation and punishment of criminals have limits; they may deter crime, but the overall impact of punishment is insignificant and it's costly.	Punishment and isolation of criminals deters crime; if people know that punishment is inevitable, they commit less crime. It is worth the cost.

Arguments about crime and law enforcement also deal with the principal question of whether prevention or punishment is a more important and efficient way of dealing with crime. On one hand, a get-tough approach continues to draw supporters. In 1992, 83 percent of Americans believed the criminal justice system was not tough enough in its handling of crime. In 2000, fewer people than 10 years earlier but still a clear majority (70 percent) expressed the same opinion. Only 2 percent of Americans believed in 2000 that the criminal system was too tough (Gallup Polls News Service, 2001). Moreover, when people were asked to choose between "being tough on criminals" and "protecting the rights of those accused of crime," 76 percent supported the first option and only 17 percent the second (WP/Kaiser and Harvard, August 1998, 1,200).

At the same time, a majority of Americans see deeper causes of criminal behavior and accept prevention as a valuable means of reducing crime. For example, in a 2000 survey, respondents were asked to choose between two approaches to lowering the crime rate in the United States. The options were rotated in the survey to reduce the impact of position on answers.

A. More money and effort should go to attacking the social and economic problems that lead to crime through better education and job training.

B. More money and effort should go to deterring crime by improving law enforcement with more prisons, police, and judges.

More than two-thirds of the sample (68 percent) selected money and effort, and only 27 percent opted for law enforcement (Gallup, August 2000, 1,012). The vast majority of Americans (94 percent) support special federal programs on crime prevention. More than 70 percent of respondents considered such a policy as either extremely important or very important (Gallup/CNN and *USA Today*, January 2000, 1,027).

Polls show a division of attitudes about solutions to the crime problem. In one survey about illegal drugs, about 40 percent of respondents supported anti-drug programs that emphasize either prevention or treatment. A somewhat higher proportion (46 percent) supported a tougher approach involving both law enforcement and stopping the production and movement of drugs to American shores and through its borders (TPC/Family Research Council, May 1998, 1,000).

Specific Circumstances

Various factors influence the perception of crime as a social phenomenon. For instance, as comparative studies show, in areas where violent conduct is rare, people are sensitive to any form of violence and aggression. But in communities where violence is common, such as a zone of ethnic conflict, people view crime and violence as an unfortunate norm (Frey & Hoppe-Graff, 1994). People tend to see the national crime situation as more worrisome than the local situation.

- When assessing the seriousness of the crime problem in 2000, 22 percent of respondents believed the problem is extremely serious, another 38 percent said the problem is serious, and 35 percent viewed it as moderately serious. Opinions changed when people were asked about the situation where they live. Only 12 percent thought the crime problem was either serious or very serious. Thirty-five percent called the situation moderately serious. The majority (53 percent) said it is either not too serious or not serious at all (Gallup Polls News Service, 2001).

- In 2002, 62 percent of Americans believed there was "more crime in the U.S. than there was a year ago" (Gallup, October, 1,002). At the same time, as discussed later in this chapter, significantly fewer people see crime increasing at the local level.

- Before September 11, America witness another tragedy caused by a terrorist act. On April 19, 1995, a bomb exploded near the Murrah Federal Building in Oklahoma City. The blast killed 168 people. Only 26 percent of Americans in 2000 thought this bombing was a random act unlikely to be repeated anywhere else. More terrorist incidents were anticipated by more than two-thirds (68 percent) of the surveyed (CBS, April 2000, 1,150). Nevertheless, 75 percent of respondents indicated they were not too worried or not worried at all about themselves or family members becoming victims of a terrorist attack similar to the bombing in Oklahoma City (Gallup/CNN and *USA Today*, April 2000, 1,006).

- When evaluating their personal treatment by the state police or state troopers, 86 percent said they were treated fairly and no more than 6 percent reported unfairness (Gallup, September/November 1999, 2,006). However, fewer people believed that in their communities police treat all groups fairly; 64 percent believed this is the case, while 26 percent said one or more groups are treated unfairly (Harris, March 2000, 1,013).

- Surveys indicate a general decline in serious violent incidents in public schools in the 1990s (Malico & Peterman, 1999). In 2003, 24 percent of Americans feared for their child's physical safety at school (Gallup, August 2003, 1,003). On the other hand, when a Harris poll asked educators how safe they felt in the schools, only 2 percent reported feeling "not very safe" or "not at all safe" (Hawley, 1997).

A 2001 national poll showed substantial public support (62 percent) for changing current laws so that fewer nonviolent offenses are punished by imprisonment. In particular, Americans supported alternatives for nonviolent offenders including mandatory education and job training (81 percent), compensation to victims (76 percent), and community service (80 percent). A majority of Americans drew sharp dis-

A CASE IN POINT 11.2 Survey Questions About Crime

Opinions about crime can be influenced by the structure of the questions asked. In a 1998 survey (WP/Kaiser and Harvard, August, 1,200), respondents were asked several questions, including the following.

"Would you say that being tough on criminals is much more important, somewhat more important, or only a little more important than protecting the rights of those accused of a crime?" Two-thirds of the respondents (66 percent) suggested that being tough on criminals is "much more important" than protecting the rights of those accused of a crime; one-quarter (25 percent) said it is "somewhat more important." In other words, 91 percent supported toughness against criminals compared to concerns for their rights. Then the respondents had to answer another question.

"Would you say that protecting the rights of those accused of a crime is much more important, somewhat more important, or only a little more important than being tough on criminals?" Forty percent of the surveyed in this case said that "protecting the rights" is "much more important" than being tough on criminals. Overall, in answering this question, 77 percent of the respondents supported concerns for the rights of the accused!

tinctions between punishment for trafficking in illicit narcotics and for lesser drug-related offenses. While a majority believed drug dealers should always be sent to prison, far fewer agreed that users (25 percent), minor possessors (19 percent), and buyers (27 percent) should always be locked up (ACLU/BRC, January 2001, 2,000).

Political Affiliations

The get-tough-on-crime policy was enthusiastically embraced by the majority of the Republican Party over the past 30 years. Along with issues such as cutting taxes and reforming welfare, this tough stance on crime is one of the most salient aspects of Republican electoral messages and campaigning (Kelly, 2001). On the other hand, Republicans try to avoid being portrayed as insensitive and remorseless, which is how Democratic supporters present Republicans with respect to crime, its causes, and anti-crime policies. Democrats also appeal to criminal justice issues that are popular with voters. For example, as mentioned earlier, most Americans prefer broader means of social intervention, including crime prevention programs.

In 2000, 42 percent of registered voters believed Republicans would do "much better" or "somewhat better" than Democrats in dealing with crime. On the other hand, 31 percent said Democrats would be better than Republicans on crime (Greenberg, October 2000, registered voters, 1,016). Certainly, these views are not determined only by people's rational assessment of the crime situation and partisan initiatives. Several factors, including partisan values, the local crime situation, media coverage, and personal experiences, contribute significantly to overall views on political parties and crime.

A CASE IN POINT **11.3** The Willie Horton Case

One of the most notable examples of public perception of crime and anti-crime policies is the Willie Horton case. This is remarkable because many Americans think it affected the outcome of the 1988 presidential election, when the major candidates were Republican Vice President George H. W. Bush and Democratic Massachusetts governor Michael Dukakis. This is what happened. Willie Horton, a convicted killer, had received a weekend release from prison in Massachusetts when Dukakis was governor. During this brief release, typical of those granted for good behavior, Horton raped a woman and stabbed a man. Although the furlough policy had been started under Dukakis's Republican predecessor, Frank Sargent, the Bush campaign set out aggressively to tie this case to Dukakis and his "soft-on-crime" policies (Gottlieb, 2000). First, Bush recounted the Horton case in June 1988 before the National Sheriffs Association meeting. Then the story received far-ranging national publicity after the Republican campaign aired a "revolving door" television ad in September blasting Dukakis as inefficient and overwhelmingly soft on crime. Figure 11.1 displays the swing of public attitudes toward Bush in terms of his ability to be tough on crime.

There is mixed evidence that the Horton ad was the reason so many people shifted their electoral intentions or that this shift decided the presidency of the United States. In fact, Dukakis was trailing Bush in other opinion polls before this ad was aired and received national publicity. Most likely, however, some people's belief that Dukakis was soft on crime became a contributing factor in decisions not to vote for him in November. In perception of many, the Horton ad attached the name of Dukakis to lenient policies against criminals (Rothenberg, 2000).

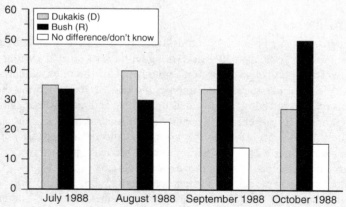

FIGURE 11.1

Question: "If elected president, which candidate—Michael Dukakis or George Bush—do you think would do a better job in being tough on crime?" (In percentages.)
Source: NBC/*WSJ*, July 8, 1988, telephone, 2,129; NBC/*WSJ*, August 5, 1988, telephone, 2,118; NBC/*WSJ*, September 19, 1988, telephone, 4,159; NBC/*WSJ*, October 17, 1988, telephone, 2,148.

DEATH PENALTY

Since 1930, more than 4,500 prisoners have been executed in the United States, where the death penalty has long been legal. In 1972, the Supreme Court outlawed the death penalty as unconstitutional, only to reverse itself four years later. Since the reinstatement of the death penalty, no state has repealed it, although in the wake of questionable convictions some legislatures and governors have established a death penalty moratorium or formed committees to study reforming the laws. By 2005, only 12 states did not have the death penalty: Alaska, Hawaii, Iowa, Maine, Massachusetts, Michigan, Minnesota, North Dakota, Rhode Island, Vermont, West Virginia, and Wisconsin. Washington, DC, also does not put prisoners to death. The vast majority of states allow judges or juries to sentence convicted criminals to life in prison without the possibility of parole (Lash, 1998). The United States and Japan are the only developed industrial nations that apply the death penalty. In contrast, the European Union has abolished this form of punishment.

General Arguments

What do Americans think about the death penalty? Overall, as noted in Chapters 4 and 7, the majority express support when asked "Do you favor or oppose the death penalty for persons convicted of premeditated murder?" A 2002 national Gallup poll showed that 72 percent of respondents supported and 25 percent opposed this measure (Gallup, May 2002, 1,012). A 2003 poll showed that 64 percent of Americans were in favor of "the death penalty for persons convicted of murder," 31 percent said they opposed it, and 5 percent did not give a definite answer (ABC, January 16, 1,006). More than one-third of a national sample (36 percent) wanted to see an increase in the number of executed convicted criminals. One-fifth (22 percent) supported decreasing the rate of execution; one-third (31 percent) supported no change (Harris, July 2000, 1,010).

The debate about the death penalty embraces a variety of arguments presented by both opponents and proponents. Overall, supporters of the death penalty argue that this punishment is lawful, effective as a deterrent to crime, and supported by public opinion. Opponents maintain that the death penalty is unfair, ineffective, and cruel and unusual punishment. A brief summary of arguments used by both sides of the death penalty debate is presented in Table 11.6.

In February 2001, Gallup Polls asked supporters of the death penalty, "Why do you favor the death penalty for persons convicted of murder?" (Gallup New Service, 2001). More than half of respondents (54 percent) used the retribution argument of "an eye for an eye," "they took a life," or "they deserved it" to justify their opinion. The high cost of imprisonment or the problems of prison overcrowding were mentioned by 22 percent. Deterrence and "setting an example" were mentioned by 10 percent. Incapacitation of criminals was mentioned in 6 percent of answers. Forty-four percent of respondents in a 2000 poll felt the death penalty deters serious crime; however, 50 percent did not think it did (Harris, July 2000, 1,010).

Deterrence of crime and the incapacitation of criminals are two points often challenged by opponents of the death penalty, who cite studies showing the ineffectiveness of the death penalty in deterring deter new crime. For example, the *New York Times* examined homicide rates in two groups of states: the 12 states without the death

TABLE 11.6

The Death Penalty: Arguments Pro and Con.

Pro	*Con*
The death penalty deters crime. Many potential criminals are frightened by this punishment and do not commit capital crimes.	The death penalty does not prevent crime. Some people are not frightened by this law and commit capital crime anyway.
The death penalty incapacitates criminals. Once sentenced to death, the criminal will never be able to commit crime again.	Life in prison without possibility for parole is a possible and reliable alternative to the death penalty and incapacitates offenders.
The cost of the death penalty is not as high as the price tag for keeping a convicted criminal in prison.	The death penalty conviction, appeals, and execution cost taxpayers more money than long-term prison sentences.
The death penalty is a form of retribution. This is what citizens want to happen to murderers.	The death penalty is brutal, cruel, and unusual punishment. It is premeditated murder performed by the state.
The death penalty is applied to the most vicious criminals, the waste of human society.	Innocent people are often put to death by mistake.
The death penalty is given to criminals convicted by the jury in accordance with the letter and spirit of the law.	The death penalty is discrimination. Minority group members and people in certain states are put to death more often than people from other groups or states.

penalty and the 36 states with it. The analysis found that homicide rates have not declined any more in the states that instituted the death penalty than in states that did not (Fessenden, 2000). Proponents of the death penalty argue, referring to these and similar studies, that capital punishment is not the only contributing factor to growing or declining crime rates, and therefore it is wrong to use the absence or presence of the death penalty in the state's criminal code as the only influence on criminal behavior.

Another powerful argument of death penalty opponents is that many innocent people have been executed because they were wrongfully accused of and prosecuted for a crime they did not commit. In a 2000 poll, only 1 percent of Americans believed there are no innocent people among death penalty convicts; 88 percent said there must be at least one (Gallup, February 2000, 1,050). Few people suggest that if the death penalty is truly a deterrent, it may be worth executing the occasional innocent person so that whole society is safer. Although most people support the death penalty in general, 53 percent express support for a nationwide moratorium on its implementation until each state better determines the accuracy and fairness of its administration. Forty percent oppose such a moratorium, demonstrating that opinions on this issue are split on the national level (Gallup, March 2001, 1,024).

Among the factors determining whether or not a death sentence is handed down, the quality of the suspect's legal representation stands out. Opponents of the death penalty argue that an overwhelming majority of death row inmates received inadequate legal representation at trial. Well-to-do or well-connected individuals have better access to high-quality lawyers. In contrast, court-appointed lawyers who usually represent defendants who cannot afford an attorney are often less experienced and busier than their high-paid colleagues at well-known criminal defense firms.

Overall, the population of death row is disproportionately poor and black compared to the general population. While African Americans constitute 12 percent of the U.S. population, they constitute approximately 35 percent of the death row population. In 1999, Gallup asked about perceptions of social justice with respect to the death penalty (Gallup News Service, 2001). A clear majority (65 percent) of respondents agreed that a poor person is more likely than a person of average or above-average income to receive the death penalty for the same crime; half as many (32 percent) disagreed. However, people's views on whether a black person is more likely than a white person to receive the death penalty for the same crime were split almost evenly. An even 50 percent agreed, and 46 percent disagreed.

Opponents of the death penalty often cite the role of location in the implementation of justice. Whether someone receives a death sentence, they argue, often depends on the state or county in which the trial and conviction takes place. In some states, death sentences are rare. Connecticut and Kansas, for example, have only a few people on death row. Other states, particularly Texas and California, have hundreds of convicts on death row (ACLU, 1999).

Supporters of the death penalty often refer to tradition, law, and public opinion. Opponents suggest that vengeance may have cultural roots but should no longer be a moral foundation for delivery of justice. Former Supreme Court Justice William Brennan said that the death penalty "more than any other area besmirches the constitutional vision of human dignity." He called it "barbaric and inhuman punishment that violates our Constitution" (WP, April 28, 1996). Opponents also argue that hanging, electrocution, gas chamber, firing squad, and lethal injection are not the ways by which a civilized state should punish convicted criminals, no matter how terrible the crime.

Specific Circumstances

Again, as detected in other polls, many opinions are influenced by the number of options presented in a question. For example, when a survey asks, "Do you favor or oppose the death penalty for persons convicted of murder?" support is typically expressed by 60–70 percent and opposition by 20–25 percent (Gallup, May 2002, 1,012; ABC, January 2000, 1,006; Gallup, February 2000, 1,050; and February 1999, 1,054). Seventy-one percent supported a mandatory death penalty for anyone found guilty of abducting and murdering a child (Fox, July 2002, registered voters, 900). Sixty-two percent of respondents favored the death penalty for a U.S. citizen found guilty of helping terrorists act against the United States (24 opposed) (Fox, June 2002, 900). However, when the question reads "Which punishment do you prefer for people convicted of murder, the death penalty or life in prison with no chance of parole?" the distribution of opinions tends to change substantially. A 2002 Gallup poll showed that 52 percent chose the death penalty, 43 percent selected life imprisonment, and 5 percent had no opinion (Gallup, May 2002, 1,012). A 2003 poll showed that 49 percent chose the death penalty and 44 percent selected life imprisonment (WP/ABC, January 2003, 1,133). In general, the gap between supporters of death penalty and supporters of life sentence without parole has decreased to 5–10 points, compared to the 40 percent gap between supporters and opponents of the death penalty in polls that ask the simpler questions (Gallup News Service, 2003).

Ethnic and racial groups express different opinions about capital punishment. For example, among blacks, 41 percent oppose the death penalty, and 36 percent support it. African Americans estimate that an average of 22 percent of all those convicted of murder are innocent, compared to whites and Hispanics, who estimate 11 percent and 12 percent, respectively (Taylor, 2000). Since 1973, estimates indicate that from 34 to more than 100 death row inmates have been exonerated (Campbell, 1999; ACLU, 2002), and that after 1900, from none to perhaps 11 to 23 or more innocents were executed (*National Review,* 2000; Bedau & Radelet, 1994). Men are significantly more supportive of capital punishment than are women. In 2003, nearly three-quarters of men supported the death penalty, in contrast to 55 percent of women. Fifty-six percent of men prefer death over life in prison, while 52 percent of women prefer life imprisonment. Men are 13 points more likely than women to oppose commuting the death sentences in their state (ABC/WP, January 2003, 1,133).

Voting Implications

Attitudes about the death penalty are correlated with party affiliation. However, being a Republican or Democrat in the United States does not determine exactly which side of the death penalty debate a person occupies. More than 8 out of 10 Republicans and more than 6 out of 10 Democrats tend to support capital punishment. However, more than one-third of Democrats do not endorse the death penalty, while only 14 percent of Republicans do not. More Republicans also prefer the death penalty (59 percent) to life in prison

---

A CASE IN POINT 11.4 Attitudes About the Death Penalty in Japan

Almost 80 percent of Japanese nationwide supported the death penalty, according to a 1999 survey of 3,600 respondents conducted by the prime minister's office in Japan. It was a record level of approval compared to six similar polls conducted since 1956. Only 9 percent of respondents said capital punishment should be abolished, marking a 5 percentage-point fall from the previous record low in a 1994 survey (when 41 percent preferred life imprisonment without parole). The higher approval probably reflects growing public concern about crime in recent years, including the poisonous gas attack on the Tokyo subway system in 1995 and the Wakayama mass poisoning in 1998. The results of the survey showed that 79 percent believed there can't be an alternative to the death penalty in some cases. Respondents were also asked why they favored the death penalty (they could select more than one answer). A significant proportion (49 percent) said the perpetrators of serious violent crimes should lose their lives for their wrongdoings. Another reason, cited by 49 percent of respondents, was that victims and their families would not be satisfied unless those convicted of crimes against them were executed. In addition, 48 percent said "more crimes would be committed" if the death penalty were abolished, while 45 percent said those who are convicted might repeat the same kind of crime (after their release from prison) unless the death penalty is kept in place (*Daily Yomiuri,* November 28, 1999, p. 1A).

without parole (35 percent), whereas Democrats divide their opinions almost evenly (45 percent for the death penalty versus 49 percent with 6 percent undecided) (Gallup, February 1999, telephone, 1,054). These survey results convince some Democrats not to run vigorous anti–death-penalty campaigns at either the state or the national level. Both presidential candidates in 2000 supported the death penalty (Wills, 2000), as did Bush but generally not Kerry in 2004. The situation could change if opponents of the death penalty gain in national surveys.

EDUCATION

In the United States, laws require that children must attend a public or private school or undertake home schooling at least through mid-high school. Historically, the American educational system is one of the most decentralized in the world. Local communities, through elected school boards, are in charge of education. State and federal agencies exercise only partial control over schools by distributing funds to disadvantaged schools, training teachers and specialists, and imposing guidelines or regulations. In the 1990s, from 50 to 60 percent of Americans, in assessing whether the schools are doing an excellent, good, fair, or poor job, expressed general satisfaction by replying "excellent" or "good" (Hochschild & Scott, 1998). The satisfaction level was somewhat lower according to a Gallup poll of January 2001; 37 percent of respondents said schools do either an "excellent" or a "good" job; 38 percent said "fair" and 28 percent said "poor" (Gallup News Service, 2001). About half of respondents would prefer, if cost were not a factor, to send their children to a private school (Gallup New Service, 2001). Generally, in response to open-ended survey questions, people rank education as a top issue. For instance, in 2000, Americans cited education as an issue that would influence their vote in the presidential elections (Fox, January 2000, registered voters, 900).

Basic Arguments

Discussions about education range across issues such as financing of public schools, educational standards, school violence, and school prayer. Many debates about education

TABLE 11.7

Schools and Government's Role in Educational System: Arguments Pro and Con.

Pro	Con
Federal and state governments should invest more money in education, especially in communities that cannot generate enough money for schools.	It is not the federal government's job to do what local communities are supposed to do, including paying for schools and the education of children.
Schools should not practice mandatory prayer, and the government should not promote religion in schools.	Prayer at school should be permitted, and nothing is wrong with government promoting moral values through religion.
Taxpayers' money should not be dispersed via a voucher system; moreover, most people do not understand how voucher systems work.	People, not the government, should be in charge of their money and decide where to send their kids to school; therefore, the voucher system should be supported.

address the role of local, state, and federal governments in schooling and which policies should and should not be implemented (Table 11.7).

Two views on the role of the government in schools have taken shape in recent decades. Supporters of policies based on active government involvement in school affairs argue that because there is uneven distribution of income across communities some schools are better funded than others (due to differences in revenues received from local property taxes). Therefore, state and federal governments ought to provide financial assistance to schools in poorer communities. Opponents reply that providing assistance to some schools but not to others is a preferential and irresponsible policy that can create a sense of entitlement and diminish the role of local communities in education.

Specific Circumstances

Most Americans believe the federal government should ensure at least a minimum level of spending per pupil in public schools. Nearly half say government should ensure an equivalent level of spending for all students. As a whole, support for increased spending on education is high. In 1997, for example, 62 percent believed the government spends too little money on education (Hochschild & Scott, 1998).

Most people (77 percent versus 20 percent) support the idea that public school students be required to pass a standardized test in order to be promoted to the next grade. They also express strong support (70 percent or more) for the implementation of national testing standards in basic school subjects. However, the majority of those surveyed (58 percent) oppose using such tests to determine whether or not to withhold federal funds from schools whose students perform poorly (Gallup News Service, 2001; CBS/*NYT*, March 2001, 1,105). While little less than 50 percent back the idea of **school vouchers,** this support evaporates by half if respondents understand that the money would be taken away from the existing public school budget (Table 11.8).

Most Americans believe schools should admit only local children and that the state or federal government should not interfere with this practice. In 1999, 82 percent of respondents supported the idea that students should go to the local school in their community, even if most students would be of the same race. Only 15 percent

TABLE 11.8
Attitudes Toward School Vouchers, 2001. (In percentages.)

	Agree	Disagree
Parents should get tax-funded vouchers they can use to help pay for tuition for their children to attend private or religious schools instead of public schools.	49	48
If public schools fail, they should be denied federal funds, and parents should get tax-funded vouchers to help pay their children's tuition at private or religious schools instead of public schools.	38	58
What if this meant the public schools in your community would receive less money, then would you agree or disagree that parents should get tax-funded vouchers they can use to help pay for tuition for their children to attend private or religious schools instead of public schools?	26	69

Source: CBS/*NY Times*, March 2001, telephone, 1,105.

supported transferring students to schools in neighboring areas or districts to create more integrated student populations, a practice often referred to as **busing.** Opposition to busing is strong across gender and party lines; for Republicans and Democrats, men and women, it is above 75 percent (Gallup/CNN and *USA Today*, July 1999, 1,031). However, the distribution of opinions about busing and integration is different among black and Hispanic respondents. For example, 43 percent of black respondents support busing while 49 percent support the idea that children should attend only local schools. Among Hispanic respondents, the support of busing is lower, but still twice as high (31 percent) as the national average.

Support for prayer in school is consistently high since the late 1990s; more than two-thirds of Americans support daily prayer (ABC News/*Washington Post*). For instance, 66 percent of people surveyed in 2001 expressed support for allowing spoken daily prayer in the classroom; 34 percent opposed prayer (Gallup/CNN and *USA Today*, February 2001, 1,016). Almost two-thirds of respondents (64 percent) supported an amendment to the U.S. Constitution that would allow organized prayer in public schools. Again, opposition to this measure (34 percent) was substantial but significantly lower (*Washington Post*/Kaiser and Harvard, May 2000, 1,225).

GUN CONTROL

According to surveys, at the beginning of the 2000s, between 34 and 40 percent of Americans had guns in their homes (Pew, July 2003, 2,002; Gallup, October 2002, 1,002; IPSOS-REID, May 2002, 1,000). Among those who own guns, 28 percent have only one gun, 41 percent own from two to five guns, and 21 percent have more than five guns in their possession (Gallup News Service, 2001). Although the Constitution includes the people's right to bear arms, the intensity of the debate on this topic has not subsided.

General Arguments

One of the most important themes in discussions about firearms is laws that would limit gun possession. Some people approve the idea of a total ban on private possession of firearms, but they have never been a majority. In 2000, 62 percent of respondents did not support a hypothetical law prohibiting firearms in private hands, and 36 percent supported the ban (Gallup, August–September 2000, 1,012).

Another topic is tougher laws limiting access to guns and increasing individual penalties for the misuse of firearms. Some people believe such laws are unnecessary. Overall, the majority favor stricter gun laws; 63 percent favor tougher gun laws, and 33 percent oppose such measures (ABC, April 2000, 1,083). Fifty-one percent of respondents to a 2002 poll felt the laws covering the sale of handguns should be made stricter, with 36 percent wanting to keep them as they are (Gallup, October 2002, 1,002). Nevertheless, most Americans do not want to prohibit sales completely. In 2000, 59 percent of those surveyed by ABC and the *Washington Post* were against a ban on handgun sales, with 38 percent in favor (ABC and WP, May 2000, 1,068).

Each side of the debate offers strong and emotional arguments to defend their beliefs and opinions. However, gun control has never been a top priority of respondents to surveys with open-ended questions; only 4 percent cited gun control as the most important issue in their vote for president in 2000 (Fox, January 2000, national registered voters, 900).

Opponents suggest that guns themselves are not the cause of crime. Rather, the problem is people who choose to use guns against other individuals. Supporters of gun control argue that if the government outlaws guns, society will become less violent. The opposing argument is that if such a ban is enforced, law-abiding citizens will be disarmed but criminals will not surrender their weapons and thus will have an advantage over those disarmed law-abiding citizens (Table 11.9).

Specific Circumstances

When answering questions on gun control, people with a high school education tend to not express strong preferences, while the majority of more-educated respondents (66 percent) strongly support stricter gun control (Edsall, 2001). Eighty percent of respondents support national child-access prevention laws that subject adults to criminal or civil penalties if they fail to store their firearms from children who then use the firearms, causing death or injury. Only 18 percent of respondents expressed their opposition to this measure (NORC and Johns Hopkins Center for Gun Policy and Research, November 1998, 1,204). Sixty-one percent of Americans support stricter laws covering the sale of firearms, twice the proportion of those who want no change in gun laws (Gallup/CNN and *USA Today*, April 2000, 1,006). Seventy-two percent of respondents support a federal handgun license. One-quarter of those surveyed opposed this idea (Yankelovich/*Time* and CNN, March 2000, 1,559).

As you might expect, opinions about gun laws change if the survey question allows for several options in the response. Overall, by 2000, the ratio of those who support stricter gun laws and those who do not was 2:1. However, when the question asks people to choose from two options, "pass new gun laws" and "stricter enforcement of current laws," responses are divided relatively evenly. A plurality (47 percent) support still tougher laws, whereas 41 percent prefer the enforcement of existing

TABLE 11.9

Arguments About Firearms and Gun Control.

Americans have the right to keep firearms; this right is guaranteed by the Constitution under the second amendment.	The Constitution is created by the people and for the people and therefore the people can reinterpret or amend it.
America does not need new gun laws; what it needs is the enforcement of the existing laws.	America needs stricter gun laws because the existing laws do not work.
People should stop blaming guns for gun violence. Guns do not kill; people kill.	People kill with guns; firearms are easy to obtain, sell, and resell. Access to guns should be substantially limited or eliminated.
Guns deter violence. If most citizens were armed, then potential offenders would be less likely to commit crime.	Guns in private possession are a leading cause of violence and crime.

regulations (Gallup/CNN and *USA Today*, April 2000, 1,027). Seven out of ten Americans support a ban on the manufacture, sale, and possession of semiautomatic assault guns (Gallup, February 1999, 1,054).

Support of gun owners' rights is generally stronger in rural areas than in cities. For example, in 1999, voters in Missouri cast ballots in support or opposition to a proposition that would allow people age 21 and older to apply for permits to carry concealed handguns. The proponents of this permit argued that concealed weapons should be a way to fight violent crime. While the measure won support in rural areas of the state, it lost heavily in big cities such as St. Louis, St. Charles, Kansas City, and St. Joseph (Ganey & Bell, 1999).

Extraordinary events, such as highly publicized crimes that involve the use of firearms, generate concerns among many people. These increased worries about guns are reflected in surveys. For instance, in the fall of 2002, millions of people in the Washington, DC, metropolitan area were terrified by a series of random sniper shootings that claimed the lives of several innocent victims. Major national cable television companies covered this story live over a two-week period. After the suspects were caught and the shootings stopped, a national survey showed that 36 percent of those interviewed said the shootings made them more likely to support stricter gun control laws. More people, however (49 percent), said their views were not affected (*Newsweek*/Princeton, October 2002, 1,001).

People perceive a small difference in the way major political parties deal with gun control. Thirty-seven percent of respondents believed the Republicans do a better job handling this issue, while 32 percent chose the Democrats. Other respondents either did not have a preference or believed neither party could handle this issue (*Newsweek*/Princeton, October 2002, 1,001). On the other hand, on the issue of gun safety, Democrats in the U.S. Congress were trusted by 43 percent of people, 9 points higher than the Republicans (PSB/DLC, January 2002, registered voters, 500). In general, men, people with postgraduate degrees, and Republican voters support less government intervention in gun ownership than do women, the less educated, and Democratic voters.

IMMIGRATION

At the beginning of the 2000s, more than 10 percent of the U.S. population was foreign-born. Before 2001, from 600,000 to 800,000 people were admitted to the United States each year as permanent residents (green-card holders). With the exception of Native Americans, however, *everyone* in the United States is either an immigrant or the descendent of voluntary or involuntary immigrants. However, from the earliest days of the nation, people had different opinions about how many people and what groups of immigrants should be welcome. Throughout U.S. history, various expulsion campaigns, restrictions, admission tests, national origin quota systems, repatriation crusades, and other legal and political barriers have been established to control and curb immigration. Many Americans supported those restrictive measures, and many did not. The debates continue about how many newcomers should be allowed; the matter may become one of the most important social and political issues American society faces today.

General Arguments

Many citizens of the "nation of immigrants" express strong and persistent anti-immigration sentiment (Reimers, 1998). They argue that the problem is not immigration itself but rather the high level of immigration. For example, only recently, the vast majority of Americans, 75 percent or more, believed immigration should either be decreased or remain at the same level. Only one in ten Americans wants the number of new immigrants increased (*Washington Post*/Kaiser and Harvard, June 1999, 4,614; Gallup News Service, 2001). Both supporters and opponents of immigration use a wide range of arguments to defend their views (Table 11.10).

The fact that most Americans do not want immigration increases does not necessarily mean that most have a negative opinion about immigrants. An anti-immigration stance may not derive from prejudice or xenophobia but rather from reason, supporters say. The rational basis is that immigrants take jobs from citizens and place a heavy burden on an already sagging social welfare system. Other Americans disagree, noting that immigration is economically beneficial. In fact, on many immigration issues opinions are split almost evenly. For example, no strong majority agrees or disagrees on whether or not immigrants improve the country economically and financially. Almost half of respondents in 1999 believed that, in the long run, immigrants become productive citizens and pay their fair share of taxes. On the other hand, 45 percent maintained that immigrants cost taxpayers too much by using government services such as public education and medical services. In 2002, 32 percent of respondents to a Gallup poll believed immigrants to the United States had a negative impact on the economy. In contrast, the same percentage thought immigrants had a positive impact, and 28 percent did not believe they made any impact at all (Gallup, June 2002, 1,360).

"Illegal immigration" in particular is the subject of vigorous debate. Some Americans believe that by allowing many undocumented immigrants to stay in the United States, the government is encouraging others foreign nationals to take their chances in getting here illegally. Others suggest that most undocumented aliens stay only temporarily, make money, and go back to their home country. Critics also say that

TABLE 11.10

Immigration: Arguments Pro and Con.

Pro	*Con*
Immigration should continue. This country was founded by immigrants and for those who sought safe haven within its borders.	Immigration should be regulated and placed under stricter control. This "nation of immigrants" lives in a different epoch now.
Most immigrants pay taxes. They take low-paying jobs most Americans do not want.	Immigrants take jobs from U.S.-born citizens and raise welfare costs. Immigration is a burden on the country and depletes its resources.
Most immigrants adjust and bring diversity to the American culture. They certainly enrich and strengthen it.	Most immigrants do not blend well into American society and threaten its cultural foundations.
Undocumented aliens, especially children, should receive reasonable benefits, such as schooling and medical care.	Undocumented aliens and their families should not receive any tax-sponsored benefits. These people should be deported.

undocumented immigrants steal jobs from working Americans. As a counterargument, people who support immigration note that immigrants take mostly low-paying jobs that American citizens do not want. In fact, more than 70 percent of Americans agreed with this argument (Gallup, February 1999, 1,013). Many people blame illegal immigration for draining national resources. However, researchers showed undocumented immigrants generate significantly more in taxes paid than they cost in services rendered (Espenshade, 1995; Durand & Massey, 2004).

Specific Circumstances

Immigration is seldom cited as the most important problem the nation faces. Nevertheless, answering a multiple-choice question about possible threats to the vital interests of the United States in the next ten years, the prospect of "large numbers of immigrants and refugees coming into the United States" was assessed as "critical" by 55 percent of respondents. Another 35 percent called this problem "important but not critical" (Gallup/CCFR, October–November 1998, personal, 1,507).

In 2001, little more than one-quarter of Americans expressed great worry about illegal immigration; another quarter said they worry a "fair amount," and another quarter reported they worry only a little. A smaller group (17 percent) said they do not worry at all (Gallup, March 2001, telephone, 1,024). Only 22 percent of Americans believed that **illegal immigrants** (technically, *undocumented aliens*) deserve the same benefits and privileges to which U.S. citizens are entitled, such as education, medical care, and welfare benefits (AV, October 1997, 1,000). When the question names a specific benefit, however, many people express softer views. As an example, one-half of respondents agreed that the children of illegal or undocumented immigrants should be eligible to attend public schools. The other half disagreed (WP/Kaiser and Harvard, July–August 1998, 2,025): Distributing benefits, such as food stamps to legal residents who are not U.S. citizens, was supported by 44 percent and opposed by 53 percent. The number of those who strongly opposed this measure (22 percent) was twice the percentage of the strong supporters (Princeton/Pew, February 1998, 1,007).

A 1998 survey offered two statements for evaluation.

Statement 1: "Some people believe that we should increase the number of immigrants who are let into the country, because they fill a number of jobs that many companies are having trouble filling."

Statement 2: "Others believe that we should not increase the number of immigrants who are let in, because they will take jobs that Americans should have and will ultimately result in higher unemployment."

Although the majority of Americans believe immigrants take mostly low-paying jobs that Americans do not want, in this particular poll, 72 percent of respondents agreed with the second statement. This attitude was perhaps influenced by the strong inclination of most Americans to keep immigration within limits (Hart & Teeter/NBC and *WSJ*, December 1998, 2,106). Almost one-quarter of respondents supported the idea of reducing the number of immigrants entering the United States (PSB/DLC, July–August 1998, telephone, 1,400).

On many immigration issues, most Americans express similar opinions. A 66-percent majority believe immigrants should be welcome to the United States but expected to live up to their responsibilities as American citizens; only 6 percent say immigrants should be able to maintain distinct ways of life. A general accord (86 percent) exists that immigrants should be required to learn English before they can become citizens (Rasmussen, March 1999, 1,000). Only a small fraction (7 percent) of respondents believe schools should teach children of immigrants in their native language (Rasmussen, October 1999, telephone, 1,000). The consensus (77 percent) is also that it is important for children of immigrants to learn to speak English as quickly as possible (Gallup, March 2001, telephone, 1,034). In fact, any person applying for citizenship must pass an English comprehension exam, so every citizen should have some knowledge of and skill in the English language.

The question's format may have a significant impact on responses, as may external circumstances. When the question about immigration was asked ten days after the events of the September 11, 2001, and attached to terrorism, almost all people (92 percent) expressed the same opinion, that stricter immigration and border crossing policies would be one way to deal with terrorism (Opinion Dynamics/Fox News, September 20, registered voters, 900). A year later, in September 2002, support for stricter immigration policies had not dropped significantly; 88 percent continued to support this idea (Opinion Dynamics/Fox News, September 9, registered voters, 900). Fifty percent of Americans believed in 2002 that immigrants to the United States were making the crime situation worse (Gallup, June 2002, 1,360).

ENVIRONMENT

Many Americans express concern about environmental problems and their solutions. For example, 52 percent believed in 2000 that during the past 30 years, overall progress on environmental problems was only minor. Although nearly one in five surveyed (18 percent) said major progress has occurred, nearly as many (16 percent) believed environmental conditions have worsened (*Newsweek*/Princeton, April 2000, 752).

When weighing two options, protecting the environment or producing energy, 61 percent chose environment and 29 percent energy (CBS, April 2001, 660). Most Americans believe global warming is occurring and is a problem; 38 percent of respondents in a 2002 national poll described global warming as a serious problem, and 37 percent believed it is a "somewhat serious" problem (Kaiser/WP/Harvard, July 2002, 1,603). In addition, 64 percent agreed in 2001 that emissions of gases such as carbon dioxide increase global temperature. A smaller proportion (23 percent) disagreed (CBS, April 2001, 660).

The majority of Americans support more active governmental involvement in the solution of environmental problems. However, in general, people are more cautious when asked about specific governmental regulations related to the environment or consumer safety; 42 percent support specific measures (DQRR/DC, July 2002, registered voters, 1,000). According to a survey conducted in March 2001, eight out of ten Americans agreed on setting stricter emissions and pollution standards for business and industry. Three-quarters of Americans approved higher emission standards for automobiles, and the same proportion approved of spending more government money on developing solar and wind power. Many people, but not a majority, supported ideas such as expanding the use of nuclear energy and opening up the Alaskan Arctic Wildlife Refuge for oil exploration; 44 percent favored nuclear energy, and 40 percent favored oil exploration in Alaska. On the other hand, a slight majority (53 percent) advocated tax breaks as an incentive for drilling for oil and gas in the United States (Gallup Polls News Service, 2001).

On several environmental issues, opinions are divided almost evenly. For example, no opinion about existing environmental laws and regulations predominates. Forty-three percent of respondents believe the laws are adequate or go too far. A slightly higher proportion (47 percent) believe these laws and regulations should go further than they do. A little more than half of the national sample believed it would be better to clean up the environment first and then spend on new energy-producing sources. The same distribution of answers occurred when people were asked whether they supported government actions to help reduce global warming if this would result in higher utility bills (Harris/*Time* and CNN, March 2001, 1,225). As a trend, individuals who hold predominantly left-liberal or egalitarian views tend to rate many contemporary technologies as dangerous. The liberal view is associated with the belief that conservatives pay almost no attention to environment. In contrast, economic conservatives tend to view these technologies as relatively safe. The conservative attitude on this issue is that liberals push for expensive environmental programs to fix something not yet been proven harmful.

HEALTHCARE

A majority of Americans believe the U.S. healthcare system needs major changes. According to surveys, the two issues Americans most want to see addressed are expanding health insurance coverage to more Americans and controlling healthcare costs. A strong 68 percent majority found convincing the argument that the government "has a responsibility to expand health insurance coverage" because some uninsured Americans "may face financial crisis if they or their children become ill." Additionally, 68 percent rejected as unconvincing the opposite argument, that "expanding health insurance coverage is another example of the government getting involved in something that is better left to individual initiative" (CPA, June–July 2000, 652). Some polls have found strong majority support for the idea that the government should guarantee medical coverage for all Americans. In October 1999, an NBC News/*Wall Street Journal* poll found that two-thirds (67 percent) thought the federal government should guarantee health insurance coverage for every American. Similarly, a July 1998 *Time*/CNN poll reported 69 percent in favor of the idea that government should guarantee universal health coverage (Kull, 2000).

In the 1990s, public opinion on government-sponsored health programs was changing. The majority of Americans generally supported an expanded role of the government in 1992 and 1993. During this time, President Bill Clinton proposed a plan to reform healthcare in the United States. The opinion of the majority changed by 1994 to support more conservative ideas that were in favor of less government intervention in healthcare. Why did this change occur? One answer is that most people began to recognize the very high cost attached to universal health insurance plans. Another explanation is based on an assumption that the structure of people's preferences changed in accordance with the prominence of arguments advanced by political elites. In other words, the tone in Washington influences what people express in polls (Koch, 1998).

It is also possible that public officials noted the changing opinion of the majority of Americans and changed their rhetoric accordingly. Americans had several voting opportunities in which to express their views on government-sponsored coverage of medical care. In the fall of 2002, residents of Oregon, for instance, rejected a ballot initiative that would have introduced universal health coverage for all Oregonians. The high cost of the plan and the threat of an influx of migrants into the state were among the reasons cited in rejecting this initiative (Knickerbocker, 2002).

Americans tend to express generally positive views about new medical procedures and methods. In the 1990s, approximately one-half of Americans supported genetic screening and testing for possible genetic defects. Less than a quarter of respondents expressed negative opinions about testing, and 20 percent did not have an opinion on the issue. Americans were increasingly supportive of genetic therapy as a possible cure for certain diseases. Three-quarters supported gene therapy. Yet, in the 1990s, from 75 to 93 percent, according to several national surveys, believed cloning of humans is inappropriate or should be banned (Singer et al., 1998). Genetic issues are closely connected with concerns for medical confidentiality (87 percent support, *Time*, February 23, 1996) and antidiscrimination laws (Sobel & Bursztajn, 2000).

SELECTED ETHICAL ISSUES: EUTHANASIA AND SEXUAL ORIENTATION

Among ethical issues, the rights of a person to end his or her life and to pursue a particular sexual orientation stand out. Views on **euthanasia** and homosexuality are likely to reflect beliefs with deep roots in an individual's socialization experiences and major life values. These views define a society's cultural climate and reflect people's fundamental beliefs about human rights, responsibilities, and social norms. (See the website for information on ethical issues.)

GOVERNMENT

Americans traditionally maintain ambivalent attitudes about government, tending to be ideologically against big and powerful government but still concretely supporting many specific governmental programs. On the one hand, most people agree that capable government means freedom, stability, and prosperity. On the other hand, people do not want their government to become so powerful that it intrudes on their daily lives. For instance, almost twice as many Americans believe the government has gone too far in regulating business and interfering with the free enterprise system (62 percent) than do not (34 percent) (Harris, March 2000, telephone, 1,013). In brief, as many surveys reveal, the public wants public officials to spend less but still assigns a long list of responsibilities to the government (Mitchell, 1998; Roth & Cantril, 1972).

Legal Systems and Institutions

Although the majority of Americans display confidence in the legal system, the proportion reporting very little or no confidence remains relatively high; during the 1990s, one-third of respondents were not confident (Biskupic, 1999). Several branches of the federal government, including the Federal Bureau of Investigation (FBI) and the Internal Revenue Service (IRS), draw persistent criticism from the media and ordinary citizens (Alvarez & Brehm, 1998). However, surveys show that only a modest percentage express general disappointment. For example, although many individuals did not have a particular opinion, 43 percent of respondents expressed a favorable opinion about the FBI, four times as many as those who expressed negative views (10 percent) (CBS, April 2000, 1,150). Perhaps surprising some observers, 58 percent said the IRS was doing a good job collecting the nation's taxes, and 8 percent said a "very good job." This is significantly higher than the percentage of respondents who assessed the IRS work as "poor" or "very poor" (28 percent) (Gallup/CNN and *USA Today*, April 2000, 1,012).

Most Americans over the past several decades generally approve of the way the Supreme Court is handling its job (Marshall, 1997). In 2003, 52 percent approved and 38 disapproved (Gallup, September, 1,025). Majorities of respondents to polls conducted between 1981 and 1995 also showed confidence in the police; however, from 38 to 44 percent had only "some" or "very little" confidence (Gallup Polls News Service, 2001). More people showed confidence in their local police departments; 81 percent said they had either a favorable or mostly favorable opinion (PSRA, May 1997, 1,228). Overall, 72 percent of respondents agreed that police in their community were friendly and helpful (74 percent), 69 percent said police were "excellent" or "very good" at preventing crime; 67 percent believed police treat people fairly; and 63 percent gave police "excellent" and "very good" marks for solving crimes (Harris, March 2000, 1,013). Confidence in the military has been consistently high since the end of the Vietnam War, and polls show that the military is the most trusted American institution (King & Karabell, 2003).

Presidential Approval Ratings

One of the most prevalent ways of describing attitudes toward current government activities is the presidential approval rating, or presidential popularity. Presidents are typically evaluated on issues such as job approval, issues approval, attractiveness, and personal characteristics. The most general question is "Do you approve or disapprove of the way [the president] is handling his job as president?" Based on answers to this question, we can establish overall averages of approval ratings of the most recent presidents (Table 11.11). Presidents are also evaluated retrospectively based on people's perceptions of past performance (Figure 11.2). Who were considered best and worse?

The highest average approval ratings were given to John Kennedy and the lowest to Jimmy Carter. However, Carter's ratings were not significantly lower than those of his predecessors, Richard Nixon and Gerald Ford. In the first six months of George W. Bush's presidency, his average approval rating was 58 percent, slightly above the

TABLE 11.11
Average Approval Ratings of Past Nine U.S. Presidents. (In percentages.)

Eisenhower *(1953–1960)*	*Kennedy* *(1961–1963)*	*Johnson* *(1963–1968)*	*Nixon* *(1969–1974)*	*Ford* *(1974–1976)*
65	70	55	49	47

Carter *(1977–1980)*	*Reagan* *(1981–1988)*	*Bush* *(1989–1992)*	*Clinton* *(1993–2000)*	*Bush* *(2001–2003)*
45	53	61	55	69

Source: Gallup Polls News Service, 2003.

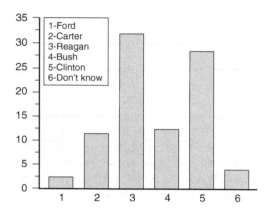

FIGURE 11.2

Who Was the Best President? *Question:* "Now thinking about the last five presidents before George W. Bush, which one do you think was the best president—Bill Clinton, George Bush, who is the current president's father, Ronald Reagan, Jimmy Carter, or Gerald Ford?" (In percentages.)
Source: Gallup/Kaiser/Princeton, September 1, 2002, 2,886.

average approval ratings of presidents during a similar period (55 percent). Bush's ratings, however, rose to 90 percent after September 11, and remained above 60 percent until summer 2003. This high support was expected because, historically, approval ratings "rally" during extraordinary events such as national crises or the start of military engagements abroad (see Chapter 12 on foreign policy). By early 2004, Bush's rating was around 50 percent (Gallup/CNN/USA, 2004).

Evaluating Congress

Congress typically earns lower approval ratings than presidents do. From April 1974 to April 2003, approval ratings based on the question "Do you approve or disapprove of the way Congress is handling its job?" were below 51 percent, ranging primarily between 20 and 40 percent. Only a few times did the approval ratings go higher than 50 percent. The highest disapproval rates were registered in the 1990s, first in March 1992, when 78 percent expressed their disapproval, and again in October 1994, when a 73-percent disapproval rating was followed by an electoral defeat of the Democratic Party, which controlled the House of Representatives in the early 1990s (Gallup Poll News Service, 2001).

People tend to think more highly of their own member of Congress than they do of Congress as a whole (Hibbing & Theiss-Morse, 1998). In the last decade, when answering the question "Do you approve or disapprove of the way your own representative in Congress is handling his or her job?" approximately 60 percent of Americans approved and less than 30 percent disapproved (ABC/WP). Individual representatives receive higher evaluations than Congress in general for several reasons. Typically, the performance of individual representatives gets less negative media coverage than the functioning of a big governmental organization, which is historically viewed critically. In addition, local representatives are often engaged in many activities in their district, so their work is more visible to constituents than is the work of the entire Congress.

PRIVACY AND SECURITY

What opinions do Americans have about domestic liberty and security in the wake of the terrorist attacks and other developments in the 2000s? Right after the events of September 11, 2001, part of the public expressed willingness to trade some liberty for security (Sobel, 2001). Since then, sensitivity to civil liberties shows a mixed pattern. At the end of 2001, two-thirds of respondents approved of military tribunals for trying suspected terrorists, and three-quarters (79 percent) supported the government's interviewing of 5,000 young Arabs in the terrorism investigation, ABC found. Half (53 percent) felt the government should be able to censor news stories threatening national security, according to a Pew poll. Yet three-quarters of Americans (73 percent) believed the media should show all points of view, rather than be pro-America. Though most (59 percent) people in 2001 thought the administration has had restricted civil liberties about the right amount in response to terrorism, more people felt in 2002 that the administration had not gone far enough in restricting civil liberties in the United States (23 percent) than too far (12 percent), according to *Newsweek*.

As grief over the events on September 11 has subsided, Americans remain resolutely determined to fight terrorism. The nation continues to be ready to use force against terrorism. But how long this already somewhat reduced unity will last and provide leeway for leaders to act depends on the effectiveness of the U.S. response both militarily abroad and in preventing terrorism at home.

ID cards and monitoring of mail and email provide good demonstrations of how public sentiment on privacy and civil liberties issues has changed over time. Historically, opinion about a national ID card has ranged from a majority (57 percent) opposed and a third (39 percent) in favor in 1985 (Yankelovich) to over 70 percent support during World War II. In 1979, 72 percent of the public felt police should not have the right to stop people on the street and demand identification if the person in question was not doing anything illegal. Eighty-four percent of congressional representatives and 45 percent of law enforcement officials agreed. In a 1985 poll, only 39 percent of Americans favored requiring "all U.S. citizens to carry a national identification card" (Harris, 1985).

In the post–September 11 climate, the call for a national ID was revived with more intensity and greater public approval than in the past. According to a Pew poll taken immediately after the attacks, 70 percent of Americans favored the idea that all citizens carry a national ID card as an antiterrorism measure. While surveys showed that a majority of Americans supported proposals for the ID cards, by early 2002 that majority was significantly lower than right after the attack.

By January 16, 2002, a Gallup poll showed that support had dropped significantly as the terrorist attacks receded somewhat in memory; only 54 percent supported required carrying of a government-issued national identification card. Forty-three percent opposed this requirement. By February 2002, according to a CBS poll, only a bare majority (50 percent) supported the idea. Forty-four percent were not willing to support such a policy. Yet a significant minority of 35 percent supported including religion on a national ID. Other countries, including Russia, list ethnicity (called *nationality*) on national ID documents.

Public sentiment, as shown in the polls, is that most Americans do not want their own rights denied even in the pursuit of terrorists. Opposition to "allowing government agencies to monitor the telephone calls and e-mails" of ordinary Americans rose from half (53 percent) in September 2001 to two-thirds (65 percent) in December in CBS News/*New York Times* polls. Voices from across the political spectrum, including conservative and liberal commentators, questioned the extent of the restrictions on civil liberties (Sobel, 2002).

In review.   Democracy and diversity of ideas are inseparable. A paradox and a major feature of contemporary Western society is that as people are free to express their ideas, and yet they must allow others to do the same, even with unpopular views. People must have freedom to argue about the death penalty or abortion, criticize and support presidents and local politicians, and hold opposite ideas about how to reduce crime and whether the rich have to help the poor. Contemporary American culture has developed in an atmosphere of persistent competition of ideas, values, and principles. To navigate comfortably within this whirlpool of opinions, one must adopt a critical thinking strategy in order to examine, evaluate, and understand the events and contextual factors that contribute to the opinions, individual beliefs, and values. These often determine what people say in polls, and they reveal individual biases that influence the way people think.

ASSIGNMENT 11.1 RECENT POLLS ON DOMESTIC ISSUES

Using search engines or other online sources such as the Roper Center's iPoll, find the most recent studies that measure the attitudes of Americans about the following political, social, and personal issues or problems:

Cigarette advertisement

Aggressive driving

Universal healthcare

Homeless people

Cheating on taxes

Cheating on a spouse

Granting statehood to Washington, DC

Legalization of marijuana

CHAPTER SUMMARY

- Americans express a range of opinions about domestic topics, such as abortion and education. Arguments of both pro-life and pro-choice advocates focus on the question of when life begins. People on the pro-life side argue that because human life begins at conception, all abortion is murder. People on the pro-choice side maintain that determining when life begins is a matter of debate. Supporters of pro-life arguments feel that women do not have the right to decide whether their unborn children should live or die. Backers of the pro-choice position argue that an embryo is a part of the woman's body and that she should be free to decide what to do with it.

- Approximately one-third of Americans today believe that abortion should be legal under any circumstances. Around 50 percent of respondents believe abortion should be legal under limited circumstances such as danger to the life of the mother. The remaining 20 percent want abortion illegal under all circumstances. The pro-choice position is mostly endorsed by residents of large metropolitan areas, the better educated, the moderately religious, and political liberals. Pro-life supporters are likely to be religious, politically conservative, rural residents, and older.

- Supporters of affirmative action believe this policy provides qualified people with a better opportunity to succeed in education, employment, and business. In contrast, one of the main arguments against affirmative action is that this policy is a form of reverse discrimination; in the attempt to remedy past injustice, white men were singled out as targets of new forms of bias. Attitudes about affirmative action are, in general, evenly split between opponents and proponents. Overall, in surveys conducted since 1980, notable majorities of Americans endorse equality of opportunity and the elimination of discrimination in all spheres of social life.

- Two clusters of opinions about crime exist. Proponents of the first view believe crime is inevitable and the only effective remedies are tough laws and their unremitting enforcement. Proponents of the second view consider crime, in most forms, the result of social problems. As long as society does not solve these problems, people will have to deal with crime and other forms of deviant behavior. Most Americans believe the criminal justice system in this country is not tough enough in its handling of crime. At the same time, most Americans believe in crime prevention and rehabilitation programs.

- Overall, supporters of the death penalty argue this punishment is constitutional, effective as a deterrent to crime, and supported by public opinion. Opponents reply that the death penalty is unfair, ineffective, unconstitutional, and cruel and unusual punishment. When answering the general question "Do you favor or oppose the death penalty for persons convicted of premeditated murder?" more than 60 percent of Americans favor capital punishment.

- Generally, in response to open-ended survey questions, people rank education as one of the top issues. Despite criticism, people express predominantly positive opinions about the educational system in the United States. In surveys, most people express the belief that the federal government should ensure at least a minimum level of spending per pupil in public schools. Nearly half say government should ensure an equivalent level of spending for all students. As a whole, support for increased spending is high. The vast majority of Americans endorse racial integration in schools, but most people oppose deliberate integration policies such as busing.

- Most Americans do not support laws that would prohibit private ownership of firearms, yet the majority favor stricter gun laws and support the federal government requiring people to get a license in order to own a handgun legally. Support of gun owners' rights is stronger in rural areas than in cities. In general, men, people with postgraduate degrees, and Republican voters support less government intervention in gun ownership than do women, the less educated, and Democratic voters. The strongest support for prohibitive actions against firearms, 60 percent, was registered in 1959. The highest level of opposition, 65 percent, was registered in 1980; 31 percent supported gun control.

- Immigration is one of the most important social and political issues American society faces. Although most Americans remain pro-immigration, many citizens express strong and persistent anti-immigration sentiment. Many argue the problem is not immigration itself but rather the high level of immigration. Most Americans hold negative opinions about undocumented aliens. Only one in five people believe undocumented immigrants are entitled to the same benefits and privileges as U.S. citizens are. A majority believe that immigrants should be expected to live up to their responsibilities as American citizens.

- The majority of Americans support more active governmental involvement in the solution of environmental problems. Opinions are split on many environmental issues. A majority of Americans believe the U.S. healthcare system needs major or fundamental changes. Some polls reveal strong support for the idea that the government should guarantee medical coverage for all Americans. According to surveys, the two issues Americans most want to see addressed are expanding health insurance coverage to more Americans and reining in healthcare costs. Americans tend to express positive views about new medical procedures and methods, and are concerned about medical privacy.

- Americans traditionally maintain ambivalent attitudes about the institution of government. On one hand, most people agree capable government means freedom, stability, and prosperity. On the other hand, people do not want government to become too powerful or to intrude on their daily lives. The public wants public officials to spend less but still assigns them a long list of responsibilities. Most Americans over the past several decades approve of the way the Supreme Court handles its job. Congress typically receives lower approval ratings than do presidents. Most people trust the military.

- Americans have periodically supported and opposed the idea of a national identity card. At the same time, public sentiment in the polls shows that most Americans are concerned about privacy and do not want their rights restricted or limited even in the pursuit of terrorists.

Looking Ahead.   After exploring issues about domestic policy here, the last chapter explores foreign policy knowledge, interest, and opinions. It examines the U.S. role in the world and types of foreign policy attitudes. It discusses the role of public opinion in policymaking and Americans' reactions to the war on terrorism.

DEFINITIONS OF KEY TERMS

Affirmative action—The creation and implementation of policies to end discrimination based on sex, race, color, religion, or national origin and to enchance the success of minorities.

Busing—The policy of transferring students to schools in neighboring areas or districts to create more racial integration.

Euthanasia—The practice of ending the life of the incurably ill. It is understood as action or inaction to encourage death of an individual suffering from a terminal condition.

Illegal or undocumented immigrants—Individuals who live in the United States but do not have legal status because they either came to this country illegally or outstayed the terms of their visas.

Pro-choice—A term that emerged in 1978 to designate those who favor the right of women to decide whether or not to have an abortion.

Pro-life—The term that has become a label to identify those people who oppose abortion.

School vouchers—The policy according to which the government allots a certain amount of money for the education of each child. The child's parent or custodian can then use that money to send him to any available public, parochial, or private school.

CHAPTER 12

Opinions About Foreign Policy

I have said this before, but I shall say it again, and again, and again: Your boys are not going to be sent into any foreign wars.

Franklin D. Roosevelt (1940)

During a discussion about public support for U.S. military actions in Iraq in 2005, a student in one of our classes suggested this operation was only the third military campaign (besides the 1991 Gulf War and the 2001 war in Afghanistan) the majority of Americans supported since the 1960s. The student, who called himself a pragmatist, said he regretted the "belligerence" of the American people, who over the last 12 years were ready to solve international conflicts with force, an approach the public had previously opposed for many years. The student was right in only one part of his argument. Indeed, the majority of Americans supported military actions against Iraq in 1991 and in Afghanistan 10 years later. But they also approved of the use of force on many other occasions. He forgot to mention that in 1995 and 1999, the public approved the United States and the NATO air strikes against Yugoslavia in response to that government's brutal actions against Muslims in Bosnia and Kosovo. Most Americans supported the invasion of Grenada in 1983. Public opinion sided with the government when American troops arrested Manuel Noriega, the president of Panama, in his own country in 1989. Most Americans supported the U.S. bombing of the palace of the Libyan leader in 1986 and retaliation against Syrian troops in Lebanon in 1982. Most Americans, at least initially, supported the war in Vietnam in the mid-1960s.

But wait. Do polls suggest that most Americans support the use of force on any occasion convenient to the government? If they do not, when have Americans expressed opposition to war? To what extent do their opinions matter in foreign policy?

Looking Forward. This final chapter explores the international counterpart of domestic opinions—in foreign policy knowledge, interest, and attitudes, and their overlap. It examines the nature of foreign policy attitudes, opinions about other coun-tries, preferences about America's role in the world, and sentiments about foreign aid and military interventions. It illuminates the parts that public opinion and politics play in foreign policy development, Americans' reactions to the war on terrorism, and crit-ical factors behind foreign policy preferences.

KNOWLEDGE AND INTEREST

Americans are not generally as interested in foreign affairs as they are in domestic issues, except when there are international crises like wars in Afghanistan and Iraq or terrorist attacks of September 11. Yet, Americans have opinions about many foreign policy and international issues with which they have limited familiarity.

There are at least three types of attitudes about international affairs. The first is the overall **climate of opinion,** or a general sense of the public mood, about certain international situations or about America's role in the world (Rosenau, 1961). The second type of opinion is **presidential approval** on handling foreign policy. Pollsters typically ask whether people approve or disapprove of the president's handling of for-eign affairs in general or of a particular international crisis. U.S. presidents normally care about their popularity related to foreign affairs because it affects their ability to obtain congressional support for their domestic policy initiatives (Neustadt, 1976; Wittkopf, 1990). Moreover, there is evidence that presidents' decisions about inter-vening in international conflicts are often affected by their approval rating (Ostrom & Job, 1988). However, the public's evaluation of presidential performance is affected not only by dramatic foreign events but also, importantly, by domestic developments, including national economic conditions.

The third type of opinion involves **attitudes about specific foreign policy options**. These can range from whether the United States should provide more for-eign aid to a specific country to whether or not Washington should intervene in a for-eign crisis or send troops to a particular territory. For instance, after World War II and throughout the second half of the 20th century, from 50 to 60 percent of Americans believed the number of U.S. troops in Europe was adequate and did not need to be either increased or decreased (Richman, 1993; 1996). Pollsters also ask questions about respondents' awareness of particular international problems (conflicts, wars, negotiations, diplomacy), their familiarity with the details, and their evaluation of the government's handling of them. Some surveys examine how Americans feel about problems, such as famine, military brutality, and health crises in other countries, and what the U.S. government should do about them.

According to a report compiled by the Program on International Policy Attitudes (PIPA), about 8 in 10 American adults typically pay at least some attention to what is going on in the world (Kull & Ramsey, 1997). Americans generally feel strongly about foreign troubles, as they do about domestic ones (PIPA, 2000), though national devel-opments tend to draw more attention than international news. Only during major inter-national tragedies and events, such as government overthrows, earthquakes, massacres, hostage situations, and deadly catastrophes, does the public move its focus and attention from domestic to foreign issues. Examples of these cases include the deadly explosions at a tourist resort in Bali (Indonesia) in October 2002, the sinking of the Russian nuclear submarine in August 2000, the allied bombing of Serbs in Bosnia in 1995, and the war in Iraq in 2003 through 2005. Many Americans express anxiety about possible wars and confrontations with other nations. In 2002, five months before the beginning of military actions against Iraq, 78 percent of Americans expressed either "a great deal" or "moderate" anxiety about the possibility of war (Gallup, October 2002, 1,018). But the focus of attention keeps switching back to domestic developments. For example, even during international crises, no more than 25 to 30 percent of the public considers foreign policy issues the most important problem the United States faces (LeoGrande, 1993). Table 12.1 provides a comparative analysis of the issues that drew the attention and concern of Americans from 1974 to 1992, a period within the Cold War era and right after the collapse of the communist bloc in Eastern Europe. From a list of 13 items, people selected the two or three issues about which they were "concerned most" at the time of the survey.

Only once in a 14-year period, in 1986, did foreign relations draw more attention and cause more concerns than domestic problems. A possible explanation is that during that year, both the United States and the Soviet Union were taking important steps to improve their relations. In other years, less than 20 percent of Americans considered foreign relations their top concern. The issue of potential war was relatively important in the 1980s, in part because of the ongoing nuclear arms race between the Soviet Union and the United States and also because of intense local conflicts around the world.

Polls show that the public is consistent in its tendency to identify domestic issues as more important than international developments. In 1976, one poll asked, "If you had to choose, which of these problems do you think is more important to the country: relations with Russia or crime and drug abuse?" (CBS News/*NYT*, April 15). Just 18 percent of respondents chose Russia, whereas 70 percent chose crime and drug abuse. A 1982 Roper poll (December 11) asked respondents to choose the two or three most important problems of the year from a list of 13 items. The Tylenol poisonings, a domestic event (see Chapter 6 on media), was chosen more often than other events (47 percent). Both the war between Great Britain and Argentina over the Falkland Islands (31 percent) and the Israeli invasion of Lebanon that attempted to crush the Palestinian military forces (29 percent) drew less attention. In 2002, in answering

TABLE 12.1

Foreign Relations Among Issues of Concern.

Respondents were asked to identify the two or three issues from a list of 13 items about which they were most concerned. (In percentages.)

Year	Recession and rising unemployment	Inflation and high prices	Foreign relations	Getting into another war
1974 (1,997)	15	56	18	7
1980 (2,005)	27	56	19	19
1986 (2,000)	17	27	37	24
1990 (1,994)	10	27	18	7
1992 (1,978)	41	33	15	5

Source: Roper Organization.

"What one issue would you most like to hear the candidates in your state or district talk about this fall?" respondents most frequently mentioned education (20 percent) (Pew, June 19, 1,212). Meanwhile, only 6 percent mentioned foreign policy. Of course, many domestic issues like trade, immigration, employment, environmental protection, and anti-terrorism increasingly overlap with international affairs.

How well informed are Americans about foreign policy and foreign countries? Estimates are imprecise because people show selective attention at various times to different events. In 1972, during the Cold War, for example, 52 percent said they knew most about Russia. Second on the list was China (25 percent), followed by India (24 percent), and South Korea (20 percent) (ODC/Hart, October 22, 1972). Factors such as religious and ethnic identity, general educational level, occupation, and business interests determine the part of the world and the foreign policy issues to which people pay most attention. Ironically, Americans may know slightly more about foreign affairs than domestic policy (Delli Carpini & Keeter, 1996, Tables 2.4 vs. 2.5). Table 12.2 displays data about how many Americans correctly identified issues related to foreign politics and international developments since the 1940s.

TABLE 12.2

Correct Identification of International Issues.

Percent of Americans correctly identifying issues related to foreign politics and international developments.

Year	Issue examined	%	Year	Issue examined	%
1942	Relation of England to India	51	1988	England has nuclear weapons	35
1948	Argentina ruled by a dictator	29	1988	USSR is a member of the Warsaw Pact	67
1950	What Marshall Plan is	63	1991	Who Boris Yeltsin is	34
1964	USA is a member of NATO	61	1995	More federal money spent on Medicare than on foreign aid	42
1967	Number of U.S. soldiers in Vietnam	29	2000	ABM rocket test failure	64
1977	U.S. has military base on Cuba	37	2000	Indira Ghandi associated with India	73
1978	Volkswagen is a foreign company	87	2000	Winston Churchill associated with Great Britain	70
1979	Countries signing Camp David accord	62	2000	Hitler associated with Germany	87
1985	Name of the current Soviet leader	24	2003	Names of at least three countries holding permanent seats on U.N. Security Council	48
1986	Whether or not USSR was an ally of the USA during WWII	37	2003	Names of all five countries holding permanent seats on the U.N. Security Council	18

Sources: Delli Carpini & Keeter, 1996; Shlapentokh & Shiraev, 2001; PIPA, 2000; Gallup/CNN/*USA Today*, May 2000; Harris, July 2000; TNS & GMF, June 2003.

It is obvious that some questions in these polls require more knowledge than others. In addition, many people are unaware of specific statistics, such as the number of casualties sustained in a military conflict. People often are better at retaining names of individuals and places, especially if they are frequently mentioned in the media. On the other hand, only 2 percent of Americans correctly identified the name of the prime minister of Canada in 2001 (CBS News, April 2001, 660).

The "attentive public" of perhaps one in six Americans who pays special attention to foreign affairs tend to be more knowledgeable than the general public about international issues but less so than the foreign policy elite who actually influence or make foreign policy decisions (Rosenau, 1961; Kull & Destler, 1999). An overwhelming majority of Americans correctly perceive that the world's population is increasing and believe global population growth is a significant problem. At the same time, 58 percent either did not know how many people are in the world or overestimated the number. About 22 percent of Americans underestimated the world's population, assessing it between 1 and 4 billion (Belden & Russonello, 1998, 1,500). The issue of overpopulation evokes less of a sense of urgency than it did early in the 1990s. This is perhaps because part of the public has heard that population growth has slowed in the developed world and that this seems to accompany economic development and rising education. In a 1992 Gallup poll, 29 percent said population growth is a major problem now; in 1999 the figure dropped to 18 percent. Those who chose the less urgent view that it "was not a problem now, but likely to be a problem in the future" rose from 45 to 59 percent. When respondents answer open-ended questions asking them to evaluate the most serious world problems, hunger does not appear as a high priority. In a 2002 poll, only 1 percent of respondents mentioned overpopulation, in contrast with the 42 percent that chose terrorism (WP/Kaiser/Harvard, June 13, 1,603). Since 2001, then, the problem of overpopulation has been significantly overshadowed by the threat of international terrorism.

In review.   People in the United States tend to pay more attention and assign greater importance to domestic events and issues than to international concerns. People tend to be less interested in international affairs and events in other countries, except during times of crisis.

OPINIONS ABOUT ENEMIES AND ALLIES

Not so long ago, public opinion about U.S. foreign affairs was considered "moody," "unknowledgeable," and "unstable" (Almond, 1950; Miller & Stokes, 1963; Cohen, 1973). This assessment has changed; the attitudes of the public about international issues are now considered rational and stable over time (Page & Shapiro, 1992). From the beginning of scientific polling in the 1930s, Americans have held relatively steady attitudes about several foreign countries and have evaluated their governments consistently. How were these opinions formed?

At least two related factors influence people's views on foreign nations: security and ideology. First, people tend to pay attention to whether a foreign nation displays hostility against one's own country. Then, they evaluate if that other country's ideology, or the basic principles on which its government is built, is acceptable. Americans

Toward which one of these foreign governments
do you feel least friendly? (selected answers)

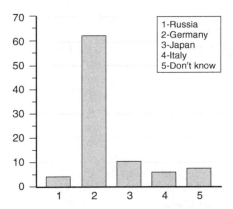

Toward which one of these foreign governments
do you feel most friendly? (selected answers)

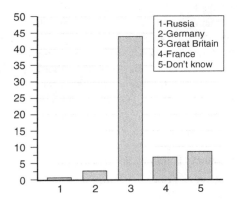

FIGURE 12.1

Distribution of Opinions About Least and Most Friendly Governments in 1938.
*Source: Fortune/*Roper, November 1938.

typically do not approve of totalitarian regimes. Americans held predominantly negative attitudes toward both Nazi Germany and Communist Soviet Union even before
these countries were direct military threats to the United States: Germany became an
enemy before World War II, and the Soviets became a U.S. adversary during the Cold
War. Figure 12.1 displays results of a 1938 national poll in which respondents were
asked to evaluate certain countries. The largest group held the least friendly views
toward Germany, whereas Germany's close allies and future enemies of the United
States during World War II, Italy and Japan, received few negative responses. Respondents felt most friendly toward Great Britain.

During the Cold War, from the late 1940s to the late 1980s, most Americans held
negative opinions about communist governments, such as those of Cuba, China,

Czechoslovakia, North Vietnam, East Germany, and the USSR. It is difficult to gauge whether ideological or national security reasons determined these negative evaluations, as anti-communism as an unofficial ideology and anti-Americanism as a foreign policy priority were largely inseparable (Thornton, 1988; Shiraev & Zubok, 2000). The majority of Americans in the 1980s and 1990s also evaluated negatively any country whose government was hostile to the United States. Among these countries were Iraq, Iran, and North Korea, which together President George W. Bush called the "axis of evil" in his 2002 State of the Union address. In particular, 80 percent of Americans in 2002 perceived the government of Iraq as evil; 70 percent felt the same way about Iran, and 54 percent felt so about North Korea.

Although the distinction between ally and enemy often reflects individuals' perception of other countries, it is too simplistic. Polls also measure a wider range of attitudes and determine whether respondents view a particular country as an "ally," "friend but not ally," "neither friend nor ally," or "unfriendly and enemy." For example, in 1990, 20 percent of Americans considered China either an ally or a friendly country; 21 percent called China an enemy, and 50 percent identified it as a neutral country (Hart/Teeter, registered voters, March 10, 1,003). Israel was called a "close ally" by 20 percent, "friendly but not a close ally" by 36 percent, and "enemy" by 10 percent (Harris, March 1990, 1,254). Did these opinions change over the last decade or so? Table 12.3 presents opinions in 1995, 2000, and 2003 about eight countries.

Public perceptions of a foreign country and its government generally correspond with the direction of official U.S. policy toward that country. This is true for practically any nation if most Americans have a predominantly positive or negative view about its government (Shiraev, 2000). For instance, according to a Gallup poll (May 2000, 1,011), Iraq, which the United States confronted on numerous occasions in the

TABLE 12.3

Distribution of Opinions About Foreign Countries. (In percentages.)

	Close ally			Friend, not close ally			Not friend, not enemy			Unfriendly and enemy			Don't know		
	'95	'00	'03	'95	'00	'03	'95	'00	'03	'95	'00	'03	'95	'00	'03
Russia	4	5	13	42	31	39	37	36	28	14	14	9	3	13	10
China	3	19	7	25	34	24	45	21	36	23	4	18	3	23	15
Israel	27	31	44	39	29	25	22	16	16	7	8	3	5	16	12
Japan	14	23	32	48	37	35	25	22	16	8	7	6	4	12	10
Mexico	24	28	33	54	40	39	15	16	17	4	4	3	3	11	8
Canada	62	63	57	35	23	27	3	5	9	0	2	1	1	7	5
Great Britain	59	63	74	30	19	12	6	6	4	1	2	2	4	11	7
Germany	22	29	19	55	38	42	14	16	20	5	4	8	5	13	10

Source: Harris, August 1995, telephone, 1,005; Harris, August 2000, telephone, 1,010; Harris, August 2003, 1,011.

1990s and later, was perceived as an enemy by 47 percent of Americans, long before it was declared by the White House as part of the "axis of evil." More than 39 percent of Americans saw it as an unfriendly country. Only 10 percent of respondents had a favorable opinion about Iraq. In 2002, more than 60 percent of Americans supported the idea of allied military action to remove Iraqi leader Saddam Hussein from power (Fox, October, 900). In contrast, South Africa, which was generally supported by the U.S. government for its post-apartheid reformation, was viewed positively; 44 percent of Americans believed South Africa was either a friend or close ally, and only 4 percent named it an enemy (Harris, August 2000, 1,010).

However, these patterns do not suggest that public opinion simply mirrors foreign policy. The official U.S. policy toward a country contributes to opinions about it. Table 12.4 reveals that, for instance, Arab countries such as Jordan and Egypt were viewed mostly favorably, whereas other Arab countries, including Gulf nations like Iraq, received less favorable evaluations.

Although official diplomatic or military policies play a major role in determining people's opinions, in general, a wide variety of socioeconomic, political, and cultural factors influence attitudes about foreign nations (Shiraev & Zubok, 2001). For example, during the Gulf War of 1991, Saudi Arabia received impressive military and diplomatic support from the United States and its allies. Although a slight majority of Americans in 2000 maintained positive attitudes toward Saudi Arabia, considering this country an ally (19 percent) or a friendly country but not an ally (37 percent), more than one-third of Americans (35 percent) considered Saudi Arabia an enemy or unfriendly to the United States. In 2002, 49 percent had an unfavorable opinion about this important U.S. ally. Consider another example. Overall, sympathies with Arab nations were consistently lower than sympathies with Israel. Gallup polls (Hinckley,

TABLE 12.4

Favorable and Unfavorable Opinions About Countries. (In percentages.)

Statement: "I am going to read you the names of some countries. After I read each, please tell me whether you have a favorable or unfavorable opinion of it." Totals less than 100 percent because "Don't know/No opinion" responses omitted.

Country	Total favorable	Total unfavorable
Great Britain	86	4
Israel	59	24
Egypt	52	22
Jordan	45	23
Kuwait	34	42
Saudi Arabia	32	49
Pakistan	24	56
Afghanistan	18	65
Iraq	5	81

Source: FMA, May 2002, 1,200.

1992) showed that support for Israel was around 50 percent from 1967 to 1981, compared to single-digit support for Arab nations or Palestinians. However, when international circumstances change, people's attitudes often change too; during the 1982 Israeli invasion of Lebanon, support for Israel dropped significantly and support for Arab nations grew to 32 percent. During the 1991 Persian Gulf crisis, support for Israel, the target of Iraqi missile attacks, climbed back to 60 percent (Sobel, 1998).

Most Americans agree with U.S. military assistance to friendly countries. A 1999 poll asked Americans whether they supported or opposed the use of U.S. troops to assist various countries. Expressing attitudes about a hypothetical scenario, 51 percent of respondents said they would support sending American troops to defend Japan from Russian attacks, and 38 percent said they would not. Almost the same distribution of opinions (52 percent versus 38 percent) occurred in the case of China attacking Japan. Fewer Americans (46 percent) were willing to support sending troops to protect Japan if North Korea attacked it, and 43 percent preferred to stay out of this hypothetical conflict. Likewise, 43 percent of respondents did not agree to send troops to aid South Korea in fighting North Korea, with a slightly larger proportion (48 percent) willing to send American soldiers. The least enthusiastic support was given to the idea of fighting Chinese troops if they were to attack Taiwan. A majority (52 percent) opposed this, and only 35 percent supported American military intervention in such a conflict (Sobel et al., 1999).

Now look at the distribution of attitudes about the U.S. responses to hypothetical invasions against certain allies and the willingness to commit American troops in those disputes (Table 12.5). This table displays public opinion between the late 1970s and mid-1990s in support or opposition to using U.S. troops.

While support for a hypothetical military confrontation with the Soviet Union or Russia, if it attacked Western Europe, remained relatively stable, support of military commitment almost doubled with respect to Israel and South Korea. From 80 to 90 percent of Americans considered "defending our allies' security" as a top foreign policy goal (Richman, 1993, 1996).

TABLE 12.5

Support and Opposition to Using U.S. Troops.

Respondents were asked to support or oppose use of U.S. troops if the following countries are attacked by the Soviet Union (Russia), any Arab country, or North Korea, respectively. In the 1978 and 1986 polls, "don't know" and "oppose" answers were combined. (In percentages.)

Year	Western Europe	Israel	South Korea
1978 (1,546)	54/46	22/78	21/79
1986 (1,585)	68/24	32/54	24/64
1990 (1,662)	58/31	43/43	44/47
1994 (1,492)	54/34	42/42	39/48

Source: Potomac & Lewis.

In review.   Most people evaluate foreign countries using at least two criteria: whether or not the country presents a direct threat and whether or not its government maintains an unacceptable or dangerous ideology. U.S. policy also matters.

THE U.S. ROLE IN THE WORLD

Which international role would you choose for your government: to be actively involved in the world's events or mostly to ignore them? Whether or not the United States should take an active role in the world, intervene in foreign conflicts, develop diplomatic agreements with adversary nations, or send humanitarian aid are key issues in people's opinions about foreign policy. Since polling began, the preferences of Americans have shifted between supporting a more active and interventionist role and a less active, noninterventionist role (Foster, 1983; Sobel, 1996, 2001). Before World War II, **isolationism** prevailed in Americans' views of the appropriate U.S. role in international relations. After the United States was attacked at Pearl Harbor in December 1941, Americans began to reevaluate the country's role in the world affairs, and the predominant opinion changed toward **internationalism** or interventionism. For instance, in February 1942, 60 percent of Americans believed the U.S. "will have the most to say about what kind of peace there will be" after World War II (Roper/*Fortune*, personal, 5,196). Following the war, internationalism remained the foundation of American foreign policy. As isolationism declined, a new consensus emerged about the nation's world role: that the United States should cooperate with other nations but might choose intervention alone, including military force, when necessary (Holmes, 1985; Kegler & Wittkopf, 1991).

Most Americans prefer a multilateral approach to foreign policy developed in cooperation with allies and international institutions like the United Nations or NATO to a unilateral one in which the United States acts alone or with few other nations, often in military action. Many Americans advocate more use of **soft power,** or the influence of the attraction of the American way of life, over traditional military, economic, or coercive, **hard power** (Nye, 2002, 2004).

The interventionist foreign policy post–World War II "consensus" lasted only until the mid-1960s (Figure 12.2). The Vietnam War then became a watershed for Americans' attitudes about their country's role in the world. Afterwards, Americans became more reluctant to get involved elsewhere until the end of the Cold War and the beginning of the age of terrorism.

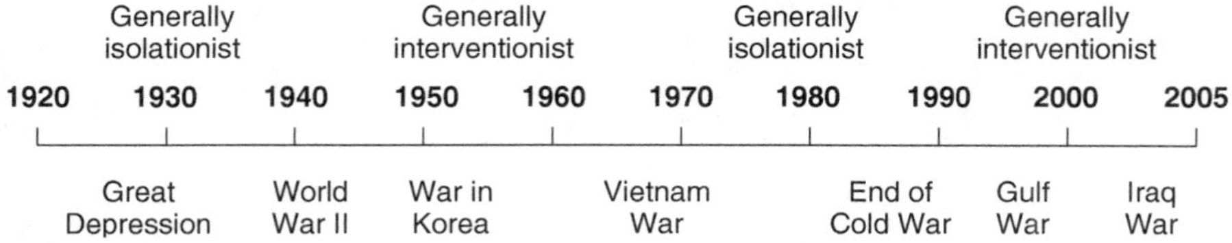

Generally isolationist		Generally interventionist		Generally isolationist		Generally interventionist	
1920	1930	1940	1950	1960	1970	1980	1990	2000	2005
	Great Depression	World War II	War in Korea		Vietnam War		End of Cold War	Gulf War	Iraq War

FIGURE 12.2

Isolationist and Interventionist Trends in Foreign Policy.
Source: Holmes, 1985; Sobel, 2001, p.28.

Division of Opinions

During and after the Vietnam War, foreign policy became the subject of bitter partisan and ideological disputes. Figure 12.3 displays the results of polls taken in 1967, 1969, and 1972 about whether the United States should continue or withdraw from fighting in Vietnam. The majority came to support withdrawal (Mueller, 1973). The development of the **Post-Vietnam** (or Vietnam) **Syndrome,** the belief that the United States should not intervene in other countries' problems, represented an extension of withdrawal sentiment.

Generally determined and supportive at the beginning of the conflict in Southeast Asia, public opinion changed dramatically by the 1970s. The debates caused by the Vietnam War challenged the assumptions on which the consensus had been built in the 1940s and 1950s. These assumptions included the belief that military power alone could achieve American foreign policy objectives; that containment underlay American foreign policy; that American political institutions worked well; and that a presidency preeminent in foreign policy was necessary to cope with the hostile world (Hodgson, 1976). The apparent foreign policy consensus of post–World War II America dissipated. People became divided not only over the question of *whether*

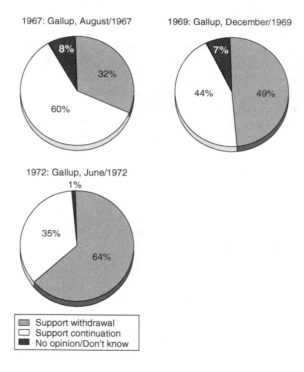

FIGURE 12.3

Changes in Attitudes About the War in Vietnam, 1967–1972.
Source: Gallup, August 1967, 1,525; December 1969, 1,521; June 1972, 1,535.

the United States should be involved in world affairs but also *how* it should (Witt-kopf & McCormick, 1993). Overall, the Post-Vietnam Syndrome was an important restraining factor in American foreign policy for the next two decades, discouraging many forms of interventionist behavior, including the prolonged use of military forces abroad (Sobel, 2001b).

The Post-Vietnam Syndrome is also an expression used to identify the American public's reluctance to accept the use of military force abroad. Comparative studies show that the same types of concerns influence opinion in other countries; after taking casualties or suffering a serious military defeat on foreign soil, a country's public opinion is typically far less committed to support future military engagements abroad (Shiraev, 2000).

The Post-Vietnam Syndrome alone did not initiate a new isolationist era in public opinion since new international realities continued to shape Americans' attitudes toward foreign policy. In the 1970s, concerns grew about the Soviet Union's increasing military might and geopolitical ambitions, particularly in Afghanistan, Southeast Asia, and Africa. Despite the existence of post-Vietnam restraining attitudes, these new concerns contributed to the support of many Americans for their country's active international involvement as an attempt to counterbalance Soviet expansionism.

New Concerns

With the collapse of the Soviet bloc and end of the Cold War, a new set of concerns developed in the 1990s. The source was the actions of so-called **rogue states,** relatively small countries with belligerent and anti-American governments, including Iraq (before 2003), Iran, and North Korea. In addition, international terrorism emerged as a dangerous and growing problem, especially in **failed states** like Somalia and Afghanistan. Three years before the tragic events of September 11, almost 80 percent of Americans agreed that combating international terrorism should be a very important foreign policy goal (Gallup/CCFR, 1998). In the 1980s, 50 to 60 percent of survey respondents agreed to support hypothetical military actions against "known terrorist facilities" in Libya, Iran, Syria, Cuba, and Nicaragua (Rielly, 1999). The terrorist attacks on the World Trade Center in New York City and the Pentagon in Washington, DC, in September 2001 further contributed to the public's attitudes about terrorism and the fight against it. In December 2001, public support for continuing the war against terrorist groups in Afghanistan was 89 percent. More than 65 percent of Americans approved giving U.S. military and intelligence agencies the power to assassinate terrorist leaders in the Middle East. Fifty-seven percent approved of expanding targeted killings to Africa and Asia, and 54 percent thought assassination of terrorist leaders should be carried out in Europe as well. Although the public was split on support for covert operations to assassinate individuals overseas who give major financial support to terrorists (45 percent support it and 48 percent do not), overall, support for forceful actions against terrorists and their sponsors remained high (*Newsweek*/Princeton, December 2001, 1,002).

U.S. Military Actions

Despite reservations about the use of military force abroad, in many years most Americans supported short-term military actions. In 1986, for example, 54 percent of Americans supported sending troops "somewhere abroad," if military fighting broke out there

TABLE 12.6

Public Support of U.S. Military Actions.
"Don't know" answers are not included. (In percentages.)

Country, Date	Poll	General approval	General disapproval
Military intervention in Grenada, 1983	ABC/WP; 11/83; 1,505	71	22
Air strikes against Libya, 1986	ABC/WP, 5/86; 1,506	75	23
Invasion and arrest of president of Panama, 1990	Hart-Teeter Research Companies; 1/90; 1,510	72	18
U.S. troops disarm the warring factions in Somalia, 1993	Harris, 1/22/93; 1,255	71	24
Air strikes against Serb targets in Bosnia, 1995	CBS, 9/95; 1,069	59	25
Air strikes against Iraq, 1998	ABC/WP, 12/98; 1,285	78	17
Air strikes against Sudan and Afghanistan, 1998	LA Times, 8/98; 895	75	16
Air strikes against Yugoslavia, 1999 (USA and NATO)	CBS, 4/13/99; 878	59	29
Military actions against terrorist groups in Afghanistan, 2001	Gallup, 10/01; 2,042	89	5
War against Iraq, 2003	ABC/WP, 3/20/03; 506	72	26

(Hinckley, 1992). In 2001–2002, after the end of the Cold War, four major U.S. military engagements—in Kuwait, Kosovo, Afghanistan, and Iraq—found substantial public support. An analysis of public opinion about international conflicts and crises from 1983 to 2003 shows the public largely approving of U.S. military actions (Table 12.6).

Tables 12.7, 12.8, and 12.9 display attitudes about the role the United States should play in international affairs. As you see, on the whole, people maintain supportive opinions about America's foreign policy commitments. However, in following the rules of critical thinking, pay attention to the context in which each poll was administered and each question asked. In general, polls ask about issues when there is a crisis, not during calm periods (Sobel, 1996a). In particular, when people are asked to choose between international engagement and solving domestic problems, most prefer to take care of "our own national problems." Notice that the large opinion gaps in favor of domestic problems in 1974 may have marked a symptom of the Post-Vietnam Syndrome. The gap narrowed in 1985, partly because the perceived threats from the Soviet Union and its satellites increased; many people felt countermeasures were necessary. In the 1990s, after the Cold War ended, the gap widened again toward domestic issues.

TABLE 12.7

Opinions About America's Internationalism.

Statement: "We shouldn't think so much in international terms, but concentrate more on our own national problems and building up our prosperity here at home." Agree/Disagree. (In percentages.)

1964 (3,215)	1974 (1,592)	1985 (1,018)	1995 (1,007)	1999 (1,008)
55/32	77/14	60/34	78/18	68/27

Sources: Potomac Associates/Gallup, 1964, 1974, 1985; *Times Mirror*, 1995.

Table 12.8 demonstrates relative attitudinal consistency across several generations about America's part in the world affairs. Time after time, more than 60 percent agreed the United States should take an active international role. The high points of activist attitudes were recorded in 1965 (79 percent) at the start of the Vietnam War escalation and again in March 1991 (79 percent), right after the end of the first Gulf War. Isolationist attitudes increased slightly in the 1970s and in 1999. On the whole, since the 1970s, the ratio of those expressing activist preferences and those expressing isolationist preferences was approximately 2:1. This pattern of activist attitudes continues into 2005.

Notice that these polls asked general questions about foreign policy engagements. When polls ask more specific questions, for instance, whether or not the U.S. should be involved in settling international disputes, the opinions tend to differ, depending on the crisis. Between 1964 and 2000, for instance, noninterventionist sentiment grew (Table 12.9). A substantial increase in noninterventionist opinions appeared in 1974, at the end of the Vietnam War, and again in the 1990s, but not to majorities. However, as you can see from the table, isolationist attitudes declined between these years.

Priorities about the overall goals of American foreign policy have not changed significantly since 1978 (Table 12.10). The majority of Americans consider combating world hunger an important foreign-policy goal. Human rights are a priority for more than one-third of Americans. The idea of protecting weaker nations also receives modest support, with the exception of the early 1990s. Promoting democratic governments elsewhere receives only lukewarm support compared to other goals; slightly more than a quarter of

TABLE 12.8

Opinions About America's Role in World Affairs.

Question: "Do you think it will be best for the future of this country if we take an active part in world affairs or if we stay out of world affairs?" (In percentages.)

N	1947 (532)	1953 (1,291)	1965 (1,469)	1973 (1,504)	1982 (1,506)	1990 (1,372)	1996 (1,608)	1999 (1,022)	2001 (602)	2002 (1,204)
Active part	68	73	79	66	61	69	66	61	81	71
Stay out	25	21	16	31	34	27	28	34	14	25

Sources: NORC, 1947, 1953, 1965, personal interviews; NORC/GSS, 1973–1993, personal interviews; Gallup/CNN/*USA Today*, 1999, telephone; PIPA, 1996, 2001; CCFR, 2002.

TABLE 12.9

Agreements on U.S. Isolationism.
Statement: "The United States should mind its own business internationally and let other countries get along as best as they can do on their own." (In percentages.)

1964 (3,215)	1974 (1,592)	1985 (1,018)	1991 (1,100)	1995 (1,007)	2000 (1,027)
18	41	34	33	41	46

Sources: Potomac Associates/Gallup, 1964–1991; *Times Mirror*, 1995; Gallup/CNN/*USA Today*, 2000.

respondents believed it was important. Support of the idea of improving living standards in other nations also declined (Rielly et al., 1999).

When asking about the top priorities of foreign policy, the distribution of responses reflects similar trends: World hunger receives the strongest endorsement. In 2001, as an illustration, 34 percent of adults considered the problem of the world hunger a top issue on a list of possible long-range U.S. foreign policy goals. Fewer people (27 percent) considered promoting and defending human rights in other countries a top priority. Helping improve living standards in developing nations was considered top priority by only 20 percent (Princeton, October, 1,281).

Among the most prominent events of the second to last decades of the 20th century was a series of military conflicts in Central America. Did Americans pay attention to these dangerous developments? What did they think about the conflicts and the U.S. role in fighting them? Nearly 60 percent of Americans had read about the events in Nicaragua in 1983–1984. When the conflict escalated, the number climbed to 80 percent (Hinckley, 1992; Sobel, 2001). Most Americans perceived civil wars in El Salvador and Nicaragua as threats to the security of the United States as well as other countries in Central America (Sobel, 1989, 1993). However, fear of U.S. involvement was also great. Many people believed the United States was at risk of becoming "entangled" in these crises (Gallup, March 1981; September 1983). Polls conducted by ABC/*Washington Post* (March 1982; May 1983) showed that from 30 to 46 percent of respondents believed Central America could become "another Vietnam." Backing for military aid to the contras (the anti-Sandinista government oppo-

TABLE 12.10

Thinking About America's Role.
Assessments of whether each of these problems should be a very important/not important goal for U.S. foreign policy. (In percentages.)

	1978 (1,564)	1986 (1,585)	1994 (1,492)	1998 (1,507)	2002 (1,106)
Combat world hunger	59/5	63/4	56/6	62/4	61/4
Promote human rights	39/14	42/9	34/13	39/10	47/10
Promote democratic form of government	26/21	30/17	25/22	29/16	34/15
Protect weaker nations	34/10	32/8	24/11	32/5	41/7
Improve living standards	35/12	37/10	22/17	29/14	30/12

Sources: Gallup/CCFR.

A CASE IN POINT **12.1** Self-defense

How can America defend itself? Soon after World War II, almost 68 percent of Americans approved the creation of a hydrogen bomb "a thousand times more powerful than the atom bomb" (Gallup, 1950, personal, 1,500). The Strategic Defense Initiative (SDI, also known as Star Wars) received support from 50 to 75 percent of Americans between 1983 and 1985 (Hinkley, 1992). As a partisan issue largely favored by Republicans and opposed by Democrats, SDI drew both support and opposition. The rise of opposition attitudes in the late 1980s was attributed to changes in the political climate as a result of Reagan administration policies and the transformations in the Soviet Union. In the early 1990s, survey respondents were asked to assess these two choices:

1. "Strong defense against nuclear missiles to keep them from reaching their targets in the United States."

2. "Have enough nuclear weapons to be able to inflict unacceptable damage in retaliation to an enemy attack."

Twice as many people favored SDI over accumulating missiles and nuclear weapons (Hinckley, 1992). When a 2000 poll asked Americans about their views of a comprehensive missile defense system, 44 percent favored the idea and 55 percent opposed (ABC, 1,004). Nevertheless, when asked whether the president and Congress should continue research on SDI, to be successfully tested before deciding whether or not to proceed, 66 percent of Americans favored testing before deployment. Less than one-fifth (19 percent) said they wanted the system to be built immediately (Harris, 2000, 1,000).

sition in Nicaragua) was modest: from 25 to 40 percent throughout the 1980s. Most Americans opposed sending military aid to the contra opposition. Democrats in Congress used this public disapproval as an argument to oppose appropriating funds to the contras requested by then Republican president Ronald Reagan.

In review.　Between World War I and World War II, American public opinion was mostly isolationist. During the second War and subsequent decades of the Cold War, it became more interventionist. Opinions about foreign involvement were generally mixed at the end of and after the Vietnam War.

FOREIGN AID AND FOREIGN TRADE

Many Americans overestimate how much the United States gives in aid to foreign nations, as shown in surveys by the Program in International Policy Attitudes (PIPA) and *Washington Post*/Kaiser. The median estimate was 15 percent of the federal budget; this is 15 times higher of the actual amount, 1 percent. Only 1 out of 100 respondents more or less correctly identified the amount (PIPA, 2000). Overall, Americans are split on the issue of whether or not the United States should provide foreign aid and, if it should, how much. From the 1970s through the 1990s, neither supporters nor opponents of foreign aid had a clear majority in opinion polls.

A CASE IN POINT **12.2** Stability and Rational Foundations of People's Opinions

As you remember from Chapter 4 on attitudes, some scholars suggest that few people make informed responses and use comprehensive knowledge when they reply to survey questions. These studies conclude that people's opinions are inconsistent and tend to be generated on the spot without prior consideration (Converse, 1964). Yet, an analysis of more than 3,000 surveys (1940–1991) related to the Soviet Union shows both logic and consistency in people's opinions about that country and communism.

Over more than 60 years of polling, the Soviet Union, its government, and its inhabitants evoked predominantly negative opinions from a clear majority of Americans. Between 1940 and 1991, most Americans did not like the Soviet social and political systems. The Soviet system was seen as oppressive, its military might was considered excessive, and the country's intentions were interpreted as aggressive. The Cold War years were associated with stable negativism and resentment toward the Kremlin's policies, the Soviet people, and the Soviet Union as a country.

The Soviets were not considered friends in the eyes of the majority of Americans as early as the 1940s and as late as 1990, when the Soviet Union was on the verge of collapse. When 32 percent of Americans said in a 1990 survey that they trust Russians "a little," this was a record-setting expression of positive feelings (Gallup, June 30, 1990). In 1972, the Soviet Union was named first on a list of three countries to which people least favor giving aid. An overwhelming 57 percent placed Russia high on this list and left China a distant second (39 percent) and Egypt third (12 percent) (ODC/Hart, October 22, 1972). The unenthusiastic sentiment about the Soviet Union and its system was so keen that in 1985, 53 percent of Americans surveyed by CBS and the *New York Times* said they would rather risk the "destruction of the United States" than be "dominated by the Russians" (September 19, 1985). In the same survey, 56 percent of respondents thought that average Americans and average Russians are "quite different," and only one in six Americans felt these two peoples were "pretty much the same."

Of course, elements of prejudice (irrational prejudice against Russia or Russians constitutes *Russophobia*) were present in these attitudes and the parallel views of Russians about Americans. The difference was that the average Russian perceived his enemies at the American extremes: the hawks, Pentagon militarists, Wall Street fat cats, Hollywood producers, and oil magnates from Texas. For many Americans, the enemies were average Russians, seen as civilization's outcasts, strong and vicious, yet obedient to their diabolical regime (Ebenstein, 1963). Nevertheless, negative views were not merely reflections of xenophobia. As the analysis of the selected surveys shows, (a) Soviet interventionist foreign policy and (b) oppressive domestic actions were two crucial factors that determined Americans' attitudes. Military competition against the United States, the lack of freedom and the violation of human rights, and the absence of free market and democracy were among the most compelling reasons that deter-

A CASE IN POINT **12.2** *(Continued)*

mined both the tone and content of the majority of American attitudes about the Soviet Union. The root of these negative opinions was not a lack of knowledge about the USSR but rather a response to specific Soviet policies. Because the Soviet Union was an adversary of the United States for a long time and

because of its repressive communist system, most Americans had enough information to form and maintain negative attitudes about the mightiest communist country in the world and to express these opinions with remarkable consistency.

Certain questions draw predictable responses. As a rule, when asked about Americans' taxes being spent on aid to foreign countries, respondents show lukewarm support. For instance, in a 1996 poll, 63 percent of respondents did not want their taxes spent on foreign aid (Richman, 1996). However, when additional arguments, such as explanations about where the aid will be delivered, are presented in the question, the distribution of opinion changes and responses become more balanced as the majority becomes more supportive of foreign aid.

The American public is likely to support foreign trade, economic aid, and the resulting economic recovery and stability in other countries. A strong majority of Americans believe it is in the national interest to see developing countries grow and that this will eventually benefit American businesses and the economy in general (PIPA, 2000). However, such support is conditional, depending on at least three factors: (1) the political situation in the other country, (2) the country's policy toward the United States, and (3) whether or not economic ties with the other country hurt American business or people in general.

For example, since the late 1970s, most Americans supported tariffs and other economic or financial restrictions aimed to protect American businesses from foreign competitors (Richman, 1996). Majorities or pluralities supported trade sanctions as a means of applying political pressure on North Korea (Potomac/Luce, October 1999, 1,200) and economic sanctions on Iraq (48 percent) (Gallup, February 1999, 1,014), Cuba (58 percent) (Gallup/CCFR, December 1998, 1,507), China (52 percent) (Gallup/CCFR, November 1998, 1,507), and countries harboring terrorists (86 percent) (WW, September 2001, 1,007).

In contrast, when a question poses a moral dilemma, Americans tend to select answers based on ethics rather than pragmatic considerations. For example, people are aware that many items they buy in shops and department stores are made overseas in so-called sweatshops. People who work in sweatshops, usually children, are paid a few dollars a day and often work in awful conditions. The vast majority of Americans agreed they would pay up to $1 more for a $20 garment if guaranteed it was not made in such a sweatshop (PIPA, 2000; Princeton/*Times Mirror*, 1993).

As you can see, particular points presented to respondents in survey questions and certain design features of those questions affect people's responses with respect to foreign aid and trade. Overall, public opinion about specific countries parallels U.S. government policy.

THE ROLE OF PUBLIC OPINION IN POLICYMAKING

When asked about the influence of public opinion on foreign policymakers, many politicians tell researchers that political decisions are made according to the "will of the people." But others insist their choices are based on their own expertise about what is best for the nation (Serafino & Storrs, 1993). In 1974, 54 percent of Americans (more than 60 percent in 1988) believed public opinion played either a very important or somewhat important role in determining the foreign policy of the United States (Harris/CCFR, December 1974, personal 1,513; Gallup/CCFR, November 1988, 1,547). In 1982, 77 percent of opinion leaders from the government, media, education, labor, and other fields said public opinion is an important factor in foreign policy. The public feels its opinions merit a more important role in policy formation (Kull, 1999).

Does public opinion influence foreign policy, and if so, how? The question debated today is not *whether* there is influence, which is now largely acknowledged, but rather under what conditions such influence takes place. Although public opinion does not set policy directly, it *can* set limitations or constraints on foreign policy, forming what V. O. Key (1966) called a "system of dikes." The climate of opinion and presidential approval are especially significant in setting the limits within which foreign policy must operate. Public opinion provides guidelines within which elites set policy. It affects policy because it is a proxy for the potential outcome of elections. Public opinion, in short, does not set policy but instead is capable of setting the range or limits of policy (Sobel, 2001).

The democratic formula requires that all policy, including foreign policy, depend on public approval, and that in order to succeed, the government must experience or engender a favorable climate of opinion (Rosenau, 1961). Every democratic government must maintain or win public support for its program.

In some cases, a president or prime minister senses that he has adequate support and that his election gives him a mandate to carry out certain policies (Kelley, 1983). For example, approval ratings of President George H. W. Bush for his handling of the first Gulf war were never lower than 59 percent (in November 1990) and peaked around 90 percent in January 1991 (Hinckley, 1992). In 2001, approval ratings of President George W. Bush's performance during the military action in Afghanistan were close to 90 percent. When the president lacks public support for his policies, however, he seeks to exercise presidential leadership and persuasion to swing opinion to his side, or he needs to modify the policy. As President Clinton's influential adviser Dick Morris (1997) noted, the president was reluctant to send American troops to Bosnia in the mid-1990s, because, among other reasons, he felt public opinion was largely against long-term engagement of American troops overseas (but see Sobel, 1998).

Most Americans are generally supportive of the government's spending on national defense and significantly outnumber the supporters of cutbacks (Table 12.11). The idea that the federal government should spend more on national defense even if that means spending less on social programs found more supporters (53 percent) than critics (34 percent) in 2002 (Fox, September, 900). Such sizable support gives national officials more flexibility in setting defense priorities, including overseas military operations (Bartels, 1991).

In Europe, between the mid-1990s and the beginning of the 2000s, the proportion of European voters who consider the European Union (EU) "a good thing" dropped from over 70 percent to under 50 percent. Because, typically, political decisions in European countries need to take account of public approval and voting, the decline in support for the EU contributed to many politicians' thinking about economic measures that could boost support (Black, 2001).

On the other hand, public officials may pay little attention to polls or ignore them altogether. In 2001, the Japanese government decided to send three military vessels to the Indian Ocean to help its Western allies in the Afghan conflict. This decision was made despite protests against the ships' departure and amid a low level of public support; only 8 percent of the Japanese public wanted Japan to play such an active role in the conflict. Since World War II, the Japanese constitution and public opinion there, responding against their government and military's aggressive role in starting that war, have generally opposed military activities at home and abroad. The deployment of small contingents of Japanese troops to Afghanistan and Iraq was the first foreign military intervention since 1945. The Japanese government's actions were determined, among other reasons, for strategic reasons to play a more active role in world affairs and the hope that this policy would eventually win the approval of the Japanese people (Maddox, 2001).

The relationship between opinion and foreign policy is mediated by a variety of conditions (Risse-Kappen, 1991; Page & Shapiro, 1992). Among these conditions are the nature of the international problem; the nature of the proposed policy; the effectiveness of the communication between elite groups; the government's awareness of public opinion; and the structure of domestic political institutions. Moreover, public opinion's influence on foreign policy is related to a relatively stable system of values developed over a long period of socialization; many children learn early about their country's foreign friends and foes (Page & Shapiro, 1994). For cross-national comparisons, mediating factors such as the structure of the parliamentary system, the views of elected officials, presidential leadership, the effectiveness of elite communication, and the elite's perception of public opinion are also critical to our understanding the links between opinion and policy (Powlick, 1991; Jentleson, 1992; Graham, 1986; Risse-Kappen, 1991).

TABLE 12.11

Opinions on Defense Spending.
Question: Do you think that we should expand our spending on national defense, keep it about the same, or cut back? (In percentages.)

Year (sample size)	Expand	About the same	Cut back	Don't know
1978 (1,546)	32	45	16	7
1986 (1,585)	20	54	23	3
1990 (1,662)	12	53	32	3
1994 (1,492)	18	53	26	3
1997 (2,000)	17	57	24	2
2001 (1,281)	50	41	7	2

Source: PSRA/Pew.

How do we make sense of the multiple factors affecting the impact of public opinion on policy? These variables can be examined on several dimensions or levels, as discussed here in Chapter 1 (Shiraev & Sobel, 2003).

1. The structure of political institutions and political communications in a country.
Special areas of influence include type of republic (e.g., parliamentary or presidential), formal distribution of roles among foreign policy institutions, frequency of national and local elections, the design and ownership of the media, and the use of opinion polls by the government. In the United States, studies of the links between opinion and policy must take into consideration the presidential political system and the relative weakness of parties and party factions in Congress. In contrast, the role of parties is much stronger in the European context. In parliamentary systems where executive power is based on the strength of the parliamentary majority, foreign policy is often influenced and directed by internal political considerations. Typically, the head of the government tries to avoid taking policy steps that could undermine the ruling parliamentary majority. In the French system, for instance, a president who lacks a parliamentary majority is often forced to appoint a prime minister from an opposing party and then try to find a formula to work together in what the French call "cohabitation"; this leads to relative responsiveness of the president to the views of the prime minister and foreign minister. In the Italian political system, political parties and the mass media (themselves heavily controlled by political parties and influenced by public opinion) shape the channels of communication between foreign policy administrators and the public.

2. The political context.
On the whole, foreign policy actions link to larger political battles. Areas of special attention include government coalitions among different parties; debates and struggle within the government; political struggle between the ruling party and other political forces; domestic and international political issues relevant to election campaigns; and decision makers' anticipation of public reaction to foreign policy decisions. At this level, specific political interests mediate the influence of public opinion on foreign policy under definable circumstances. Internal political considerations affect the degree of influence of public opinion, namely, the role of parties and interest groups in shaping and mediating linkages between mass opinion and foreign policy. On the one hand, the opposition seeking to criticize and denounce government officials in charge of foreign affairs focuses on foreign policy issues and, especially, mistakes in foreign policy. On the other hand, the government can use success in foreign policy to strengthen its own political standing and electoral prospects. The desire to be elected creates further incentives for politicians to respond to the majority of public opinion. Parliamentary approval of government policies in the international field may hinge on yielding to the opposition in other policy areas.

Not only domestic but also international public opinion matters when domestic policy is created or evaluated by the opposition. Consider the following illustration. A majority of Europeans in August 2001, well before the war in Iraq, already disapproved of President George W. Bush's foreign policy, believing he understood Europe less than other presidents, according to polling in four European countries. In a survey by the Pew Research Center, only a sixth of the French and British, a quarter of Germans, and slightly less than a third of Italians approve of the Bush's foreign policy (Wolfe, 2001). George Bush's Democratic opponents in Congress immediately sought to exploit the policy differences between the United States and Europe. Tom Daschle, at the time the Democratic Senate majority leader, repeatedly criticized the president for isolating the country from its allies.

3. General sociocultural factors.   Special areas of attention include predominant isolationist or interventionist values, religious beliefs, historic experiences, stereotypes, and prejudice toward particular decision makers and groups. Someone viewed as a war criminal by many Americans may be perceived in other countries as a legitimate representative of a struggling people. People's concerns about human rights, global environment, domestic issues (such as jobs, stock market, and immigration), and military security can mediate opinions about foreign policy (Richman, 1996). Historic periods are marked by public attitudes about foreign policy. For instance, as mentioned earlier, the U.S. public had maintained an activist orientation toward foreign policy since World War II, but the Vietnam War experience split public opinion between isolationism and interventionism. The military conflict in Kosovo in 1999 changed the isolationist attitudes of many Europeans.

4. Contextual and situational factors.   These areas of attention include the salience of a foreign policy issue, the presence or absence of media coverage that evokes specific opinions, and the individual characteristics of decision makers as political leaders. One should not overlook situational factors that can affect the perception of both the elite and the public of the linkages between opinion and policy. Among these factors are media, "rally-around-the-flag," "free rider," "body bag," and "innocent victim" effects (see Chapter 6 on media, and the website). The Sarajevo market massacre during the 1994 Bosnia war and its extensive coverage by the U.S. media shows how quickly a consensus between governments and public can be reached about the necessity for military action. The examination of opinion and policy should also take into consideration the level of unity or disagreement among the elites, including the media, regarding foreign policy issues. The Italian government, by way of illustration, at a crucial stage of the war in Bosnia in the 1990s was divided; the minister of foreign affairs was in favor of military intervention, while the minister of defense was opposed to it. Finally, the personal commitment of a leader to a particular decision affects policy. For example, the opposition of the late French president François Mitterrand to military involvement led him to argue against military involvement in the Balkans. Similarly, American leaders' commitment to help starving people in Somalia in the early 1990s resulted in Operation Restore Hope (La Balme, 2001).

The impact of public opinion on foreign policy is likely to be stronger if:

1. A national election is scheduled in the near future. Incumbent officials need public support for reelection, especially if the opposition is strong.
2. Support of or opposition to a certain foreign policy issue is overwhelming and consistent. Officials may argue they have the nation's mandate for a policy or decision.
3. The majority in public opinion corresponds with the position of decision makers. Officials are likely to use the results of polls as one justification for their action or inaction.

Americans' Reactions to the War on Terrorism

Though the anger over the terrorist acts of September 11 began to subside in the months after the attacks, support for U.S. intervention in Afghanistan remained strong. In the beginning of 2002, support of military action was near 90 percent, and approval of Bush's handling of the campaign against terrorism was almost as high, according to ABC polls. George W. Bush's approval rating of 86 percent before his 2001 speech to Congress in mid-September rose to 92 percent after the fighting in Afghanistan began three weeks later. At the end of the year, only the "American people" had higher approval (90 percent) than the president (87 percent) for handling the war on terrorism, according to Gallup polls (Sobel, 2001b).

Support for military actions against terrorism varied by risks, costs, and results. For instance, approval for military action (86 percent) in 2001 dropped in the polls to 77 percent if innocent civilians were killed. It fell to two-thirds (69 percent) if "a large number" of U.S. troops died, and to half (55 percent) for a ground invasion involving the loss of U.S. lives. In general, the American public felt the Afghan campaign was a success, a key factor in sustaining support. While the proportion that believed the United States and its allies were winning the war against terrorism rose from half (53 percent) in December 2001 to two-thirds (66 percent) in January 2002, according to Gallup, the proportion that felt the war was going very well in fact dropped from 51 percent in December to 38 percent in January 2003. Most felt the intervention would reduce (53 percent) rather than increase (17 percent) terrorism (Gallup). Three in four (77 percent) of Americans did not feel the intervention would turn out like the Vietnam War (ABC).

A majority of Americans felt in 2001–2003 that another terrorist attack with the United States was possible. Moreover, in December 2001, fully 88 percent felt the worst was yet to come in the fight against terrorism (ABC). Yet, two-thirds (62 percent) of registered voters did not worry about terrorist attacks taking place where they live or work (Fox), partly because they don't live near targets.

While the long-term Gallup trend of higher sympathy for Israel persists, most Americans want the U.S. government to be neutral in pressing toward an Israeli-Palestinian settlement. In particular, over two-thirds (71 percent) support neither side, 22 percent support Israel, and 2 percent support the Palestinians (Gallup). Half consider Israeli military actions to be part of a war (53 percent) and mostly justified (49 percent). On the other hand, 70 percent consider Palestinian tactics as "terrorism" and mostly unjustified (66 percent) (Gallup). A large majority of Americans feel both sides should stop the violence. In 2004, 83 percent of Americans said that the war on terror was equally or even more important than it was just months after September 11 (HT, NBC, and *WSJ*, March, 1,018).

THINKING CRITICALLY ABOUT FOREIGN POLICY ATTITUDES

Context

When analyzing surveys about foreign policy and international developments, try to identify particular events that could have influenced people's answers. It is understandable, for example, that some Americans, after the events of September 11, 2001, changed their opinions about the priority of international problems. Those saying that "dealing with the problems of hunger" should be a top priority dropped from 47 percent before September to 34 percent in October. Likewise, "dealing with global warming" fell from 44 percent to 31 percent (Pew, October 2001, 1,281). Overall, more Americans assigned a greater importance to national security issues than other world problems. As mentioned in Chapter 3 on critical thinking, among Israelis, support for a peaceful resolution of the Palestinian problem varies considerably and is linked to the most recent act of violence against Israel. Support for a Palestinian state strengthens when few terrorist acts are committed against Israel. Anti-American attitudes were expressed by a majority of people in Russia during NATO air strikes in Kosovo in 1999. In the following period, between 2000 and 2002, the proportion of Russians holding negative attitudes about the United States has dropped significantly. Anti-American sentiment increased again in 2003 during the war in Iraq but decreased in 2004.

Whenever possible, pay attention to the way survey questions are asked. As we learned earlier in this chapter, the majority of the U.S. public is often willing to let the military intervene overseas. The extent of this support, however, is based on several contextual conditions. Numerous polls show that in most people's minds, the benefits of U.S. military operations abroad should clearly outweigh the risks (Sobel, 2001b). In particular, support is greater if the military action is multilateral, that is, involves contributions from other nations (Bardes, 1998). However, most Americans tend to believe that the United States should stay out of other countries' internal conflicts, unless these conflicts result in genocide and substantial loss of human life. Overall, the public is more willing to intervene in humanitarian causes than in other scenarios. Historically, the public tends to support interventions as long as the involvement is expected to be brief and successful (Mueller, 1973; Brody, 1991; Jentleson, 1992; Jentleson & Britton, 1998).

One of the most important conditions of support of military response is the number of casualties; support drops if casualties are expected to increase or actually do grow. For example, the initial public support for U.S. military actions in Afghanistan was 89 percent (Gallup, September 14–22, 2001, 2,042). This proportion fell 13 points when people were asked to reconsider their opinions should military action continue for several years or should 1,000 American troops be killed. Yet, as noted earlier in the chapter, the American public is willing to sacrifice for good causes that are successful (Gelpi & Feaver, 2002).

The following example shows how different answers can become when respondents are asked to consider additional arguments or conditions. Also, notice the gender gap in responses (Table 12.12). Although the overall majority continues to support U.S. military actions, the decline in support under some circumstances is significant, especially among women.

Consider what you learned from examples introduced in other chapters about how question wording may significantly affect people's answers. Compare two polls. Among Americans asked to assess their perception of the U.S. role in the world in 1999, more than 70 percent felt the United States should play a leading role in developing new and better ways to prevent and react to international problems, such as those in Bosnia, Kosovo, Rwanda, and East Timor, while 25 percent disagreed (Harris, October–November 1999, 1,011). However, just six months later, when asked whether or not the country should take the leading role in trying to solve international

TABLE 12.12

Support for U.S. Military Actions in Afghanistan by Gender and Question's Context. (In percentages.)

	Men	Women	Gap
Overall support	90	88	2
If shortages of oil and gas would occur	84	75	9
If taxes would be increased	89	79	10
If there would be less money to spend on domestic programs	83	72	11
If further terrorist attacks would occur in the USA	85	72	13
If a prolonged economic recession would occur	84	71	13

Source: Gallup, September 14–22, 2001, 2,042.

problems, the majority preferred a more restrained approach. Answers were divided between a minority who said "should" (41 percent) and the majority, who objected to international leadership (55 percent) (Gallup, May 2000, 1,011).

Why is there an opinion gap? Of course, the timing of the surveys might have affected the responses. However, another plausible interpretation is that the survey questions were different. In one survey, the respondents were asked about whether the United States should play *a leading role* (presumably along with other countries); the other survey posed the question about *the leading role* (presumably played by the United States alone).

Bias

We learned in this chapter that large proportions of the population have only vague knowledge of international events and that many people make inaccurate assumptions about foreign politics. Some people are simply uninterested in world events, whereas others invest their personal interest and values in their perception of other countries and international events. People often interpret survey questions, therefore, in a biased way, whether they intend to or not. For example, in 1998, 45 percent of Americans believed that "strengthening the United Nations" should be a very important goal of the United States and 39 percent believed this goal was somewhat important. These results can be misleading if one attempts to estimate American's overall attitudes about the United Nations (Gallup/CCFR, 1998). The word "strengthening," however, can have different meanings to different people. Some individuals may think the question is about a growing independent role of the U.N. as a global government. Others may equate "strengthening" with an increasing involvement of the United States in U.N. activities. How would you interpret the results of this poll?

Knowledge about respondents' bias helps us evaluate surveys critically. However, we should not expect to find objective and unbiased attitudes; by definition, opinions are subjective evaluations. What we should look for are patterns of opinion or bias that distinguish certain polls or groups of respondents. An event or policy can be seen and evaluated in a certain way by the majority of American people. People in other countries may see the same event or policy differently.

A remarkable study conducted in 2001 interviewed a sample of the political, media, and business elite in 24 countries on five continents about a variety of international issues related to the struggle against terrorism and the role of the United States in this campaign. The findings were based on 275 interviews with persons identified as influential in government, politics, culture, the media, or business. About 40 interviews were conducted in the United States and approximately 10 each in Europe, Latin America, Asia, Africa, and the Middle East (Pew/Princeton/IHT, December 2001, 275 selected). Approximately 70 percent of American opinion leaders in the survey said the United States was acting jointly with its friends and cared about the interests of its partners. Large majorities of non-American experts, however, said they believed the United States was acting unilaterally. Furthermore, more American than non-American opinion leaders approved of military actions against countries found to be supporting terrorism. Slightly more than half of American opinion leaders believed the United States is admired because it does good things around the world. In contrast, a majority of those questioned outside the United States (from 63 percent in Western Europe to 86 percent in the Middle East) said that American scientific and technological advances are the main reason people in their countries like the United States (Richburg, 2001).

What do these figures suggest? Of course, the sample chosen for this survey was not random, and therefore it is difficult to say whether or not the opinions of participants accurately reflected their country's public opinion. Moreover, it is difficult to determine whether or not this poll accurately represented American and international opinion leaders since the selection criteria were vague. Nevertheless, we can learn one important lesson: Some U.S. opinion leaders do not see the world and their country's role in world affairs in the same way as some opinion leaders of other countries do. What is considered just on "our" side of the ocean may be seen as unjust elsewhere. Misperceptions of others' thoughts about our country can lead to misjudgments about its actions. These misjudgments can cause unpredictable and unpleasant consequences in politics and international relations.

Knowledge of other people's views serves an important educational role: It allows you to think critically about your opinions and those of others, and, if necessary, to make informed evaluations of them. Knowing the trends of public opinion in nondemocratic countries is most difficult, however.

Wording and Labeling

There are many examples, as we have noted, of how verbal biases, labels, and categories can distort people's opinions. Among the most common patterns in survey labeling is dichotomization. Attitudes about international events and military engagements do not, in most cases, fall into distinct categories. People are not necessarily hawks or doves, interventionists or isolationists. People have varying attitudes about different conflicts, and the circumstances of an international dispute can significantly affect attitudes about it. Let's illustrate by putting in one sentence the results of the five surveys displayed in Figure 12.4. In particular, if you were a journalist, how would you describe the results of these polls in a newspaper headline?

You can make the judgment, for example, that over the years, the gap between (a) those who believed the United States should cooperate with the United Nations

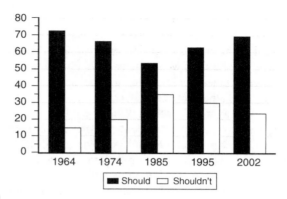

FIGURE 12.4

Opinions About Whether or Not the United States Should Cooperate with the United Nations. (In percentages.)
Source: Potomac Associates, 1964, 1974, 1985; Times Mirror, 1995; PIPA, 2002.

and (b) those who did not shrank 10 points, from 56 points to 46 points, and that opposition to such cooperation increased by 8 points. Thus, you could propose this headline: "Support for U.N. Declines Since 1964." However, this would be misleading. Why? When we compare the results of the 1964 and 2002 polls, a slight decline in support is evident. However, the opposite tendency is evident too. Since 1985, the proportion of people who support cooperation with the U.N. increased by 14 points, while that of those opposed declined.

It would be also incorrect to categorize people as hawks or doves simply according to their attitudes about U.S.–U.N. cooperation. The results of these polls do not show clearly whether some people did not want U.S. cooperation at all or whether they were disappointed with the U.N.'s limited success in settling world problems. Other people may want to see cooperation develop but do not want to endorse it at this moment.

You should be cautious of the standard phrase "the polls show" when it appears in media reports. Instead, look carefully at what the polls actually show and whether or not headlines are misleading or oversimplified. Of course, many headlines are accurate because they are based on verifiable facts. For instance, the 2001 newspaper headline that read "Polls Show the President's Popularity at Near-record Highs" was accurate. In fact, when this article was published in December 2001, the president's approval ratings were the highest among U.S. presidents in recent history (Cameron, 2001). This headline was correct if we ignore a small imprecision: The surveys did not measure the popularity of the president but rather people's approval of his performance in office.

Many headlines, though, are quite inaccurate. A Canadian front page featured this headline in 2001: "Canadians Sympathize with Protesters, But Want More Trade." The article reviewed popular attitudes about international trades, globalization, and the 2001 riots in Genoa, Italy, in which several thousand protesters took to the streets during a meeting of the leaders of the leading industrial nations known as G8. What would you think about the proportions of Canadians who sympathize with the pro-testers if you knew nothing about the actual percentages in the survey? In fact, not all Canadians, but a little more than 50 percent of those surveyed, said the protests "are about valid points that a great many Canadians care about." Moreover, only a major-ity of Canadians wanted more trade, according to the survey (*Gazette*, July 24, 2001, p. A12). How would you rewrite the headline for greater accuracy?

Explanations: Causes and Reasons

A wide variety of factors can affect attitudes about international events and foreign policy. Among them are fundamental religious or moral values, according to which a person weighs his views of world events. Ethnic and national affiliations, along with religious beliefs, can significantly affect people's attitudes about foreign pol-icy. In Great Britain, for instance, the Muslim population, according to polls, was more reluctant to endorse military strikes against targets in Afghanistan in 2001 than were people of other religions, including Christians, Hindus, and Sikhs. Religious and ideological values can be connected to general fundamental beliefs, such as acceptance of only peaceful solutions to international conflicts or concerns about human rights.

Political and other social affiliations can also influence people's views on inter-national politics. An individual's acceptance of a political party's domestic platform can seriously affect her views on international developments. For instance, left-wing voters in Europe typically express lukewarm attitudes about the United States and its policies, a stance that generally corresponds with their parties' political platforms. Political considerations affect a large number of individuals' views on world events. A certain foreign policy course conducted by a government is typically questioned, criticized, and challenged by political opponents. Congressional Democrats expressed serious opposition to the Gulf War of the early 1990s, which was led by the Republi-can presidential administration. During the Bosnian conflict in the mid-1990s, when Democrats were in the White House, the Republicans seriously questioned President Clinton's foreign policy. In late 2003 and through the election year in 2004, Democ-rats, especially candidates for president, began to criticize the incumbent President Bush's economic and military policies. Foreign policy experience and anti-terrorism policy became major issues in the 2004 presidential campaign pitting a Vietnam vet-eran and internationally oriented senator, John Kerry, against an incumbent president, George W. Bush, leading the war on terrorism after September 11.

Additional factors, such as individual experience, party affiliations, and idiosyn-cratic likes and dislikes, can also affect a person's opinions about international events. For instance, knowledge about war and military operations can be a substantial factor in the formation of attitudes about military actions abroad. Unlike in World War II, when nearly every able-bodied man under the age of 30 was in uniform, most Ameri-can families in the 2000s do not have a member in the service. In the 1940s and 1950s, the vocabulary of the military became part of the American language, transmitted by letters to home from training camps, airfields, and front lines. People knew more about basic military terms than they do today because their own family members might have instructed them in the differences between platoons, battalions, and divisions. Today the vast majority of Americans know about wars from the media only.

Remember that a single factor is not likely to explain why some people support foreign trade and others do not, or why some individuals favor the military solution to international conflicts whereas others categorically oppose it. As in other matters of opinion, multiple factors influence people's attitudes about foreign policy, and many views are the result of uneasy choices. For example, although the vast majority of Americans in 2002 supported the use of military force against international terrorism and even backed the assassination of foreign leaders to achieve victory (and a third supported government-sanctioned torture of suspects), these attitudes were not rooted simply in belligerent values and narrow-mindedness. For the most part, people struggled between at least two important options. One was general respect for individual freedom and other fundamental rights; the other was a strong desire to protect themselves and other people from harm (McLaughlin, 2001). Issues of unilateral versus multilateral foreign policy, and who could better handle America's relations with their allies and adversaries, including international terrorism, became important in the 2004 presidential campaign. The debates pointed to the enduring nature of foreign policy issues even for a nation more typically oriented to domestic affairs.

ASSIGNMENT 12.1   RECENT POLLS ON FOREIGN POLICY ISSUES

Using search engines or other sources such as the Roper Center's iPoll, find the most recent studies that measure the attitude of Americans about the following foreign policy issues:

Opinions about Foreign Countries
Support and Opposition to Using U.S. Troops
Opinions on America's Role in the World
Goals for U.S. Foreign Policy
Opinions on Foreign Aid
Opinions on Defense Spending
Opinion on Cooperation with the UN

CHAPTER SUMMARY

- Americans are generally less interested in foreign affairs, except during international crises or when domestic and international issues significantly overlap. Although critics have called public opinion about foreign affairs unknowledgeable, unstable, moody, and of little influence, today, opinion about foreign policy is recognized as possessing relatively high stability. Knowledge about foreign affairs was slightly higher than knowledge about domestic topics, such as politicians, institutions, and public affairs.

- There are three types of opinion about international affairs. The first is the public mood or climate of opinion. The second is conveyed by approval or disapproval of the president's handling of foreign affairs. The third type is a set of attitudes about specific foreign policy options.

- From the beginning of modern polling, Americans have held relatively stable attitudes about foreign countries and established their consistent evaluations, positive or negative, of their governments. Two major factors determine the general public's views on foreign nations: security and ideology. These are often but not always inseparable. Government policy also affects attitudes.

- Key issues in foreign policy attitudes include whether or not the United States should take an active role in the world, intervene in foreign conflicts, develop diplomatic agreements with other nations, and send humanitarian aid abroad. Since polling began, the preferences of Americans have shifted between more and less active roles, between support for foreign intervention and nonintervention. Before World War II, public opinion was mostly isolationist. During the Cold War, it became more interventionist. Opinions were more split at the end and after the Vietnam War. More recently, attitudes have become more activist again.

- Americans tend to overestimate how much the United States gives in aid to foreign countries. Opinions are typically split on whether and how much foreign aid the United States should provide, though favoring foreign trade.

- The climate of opinion and presidential approval affects the limits within foreign policy operates. Public opinion provides guidelines for elites within which to set policy. As a proxy for the potential outcome of elections, it influences public policy. In the final analysis, public opinion does not set policy, but rather sets the range or limits of policy.

- Americans today are generally willing to intervene in trouble spots around the world, depending on the perceived costs such as expenses and casualties and the likelihood of success. Terrorism has increased the willingness of U.S. public to support military actions abroad. Foreign policy attitudes differ by events, question wordings, background, and political orientations.

DEFINITIONS OF KEY TERMS

Climate of opinion—The general opinion environment about, for instance, America's role in the world.

Failed states—Nations whose governments have become unstable or nonfunctional.

Hard power—The use of military force or economic pressure to achieve foreign policy aims.

Internationalism or interventionism—The belief that the nation should take an active role in world affairs.

Isolationism—The belief that the nation should focus on domestic affairs and avoid international involvement and assistance.

Presidential approval—The approval or popularity of the president's handling of political matters such as foreign affairs.

Rogue states—Relatively small countries with belligerent and hostile governments, such as Iraq, Iran, and North Korea in the 1990s.

Soft power—The influence of the attractive aspects of American life to gain international stature and influence in foreign affairs.

Post-Vietnam Syndrome—The belief among the public and elites that the United States should not intervene in other countries' problems.

Thinking Critically About People and Their Opinions

To capture the interest of students and their instructors, *People and Their Opinions* has incorporated three distinct approaches to learning about public opinion in politics. First, it develops the **critical thinking approach** to creating the skills needed to understand and interpret public opinion, especially as represented in polls. While anyone can read the results of opinion polls in newspapers, on television, and on websites, the question is how to interpret the numbers. The tools of critical thinking this textbook presents help in conceptualizing polling data, finding trends in attitudes, and explaining similarities and differences in opinions. The discussion points, exercises, and pedagogical devices throughout the textbook help in applying tools of critical thinking to public opinion research.

Second, the textbook captures American public opinion in a **comparative perspective.** Beyond discussing U.S. polls based on national samples, the chapters provide information about political and social issues in other parts of the world and differences among ethnic, racial, national, and religious groups. These analyses pay special attention to culture, gender, social class, and other factors in political socialization. The book considers major social and political developments in the United States and over 40 other nations in the rest of the changing world.

The critical thinking and comparative approaches are essential, first, because knowledge of national elites' views and public opinion trends is increasingly significant for policy and national security analyses. Comparing trends in American and international public opinion also helps students understand the ideological, political, and psychological foundations of opinion formation and expression. In addition, the growing debates about multinational cooperation, understanding other countries' basic interests, and developments in international economic policies, international diplomacy, peacekeeping missions, and overall democratic transitions all require better understanding of domestic public opinions and their effects on policy.

Third, the book introduces **numerous practical examples** for understanding how the public thinks and feels about current political and social issues. Moreover, the **website** complements the text and provides current updates to the issues and applications discussed in the printed pages. Assignments help students apply the comparative and critical thinking approaches this book emphasizes.

REVIEW OF THE ISSUES OF *PEOPLE AND THEIR OPINIONS*

The twelve chapters of *People and Their Opinions* explored a wide range of public opinion issues. Chapter 1, "The Nature of Public Opinion," introduced public opinion and discussed three types: consensus, majority opinion, and plurality opinion. Considering how polls affect policy, the chapter addressed the social and practical value of opinion polls and explored in comparative perspective political and ideological values expressed in surveys. The impact of polls on government policy depends partly on whether people's representatives take a trustee or delegate view of the role opinion should play in government decisions. The influence of opinion also depends on the structure of government institutions and communications, the political landscape and elections, and political participation. Importantly, the chapter explored the relationship of the political system and elections, among types of political participation, to the impact of opinions on government. It introduced national polling organizations.

Chapter 2, "Measurement of Opinion," explored the difficult task of measuring human psychology and attitudes. The steps in survey research assist in creating meaningful measurements. Polling involves gathering information and selecting samples. In using convenience, systematic, or random samples, sampling and other errors affect the accuracy of polls. In searching for links, correlations help in identifying the size and direction of relationships between variables. Survey questions take several forms, primarily the multiple-choice and open-ended formats. The structure and order of questions affects the quality of responses since poorly worded questions may yield inaccurate information. Methods other than surveys help explore attitudes: experiments, content analysis, meta-analysis, focus groups, and qualitative approaches.

Chapter 3, "Thinking Critically About People's Opinions," explained how to apply the tools of critical analysis in survey research. It examined the survey process and evaluated survey questions. It examined cognitive errors of human perception. It directed attention to the question of wording and looked critically at descriptions, labels, and apparently obvious statements. In providing information about dichotomous and continuous variables, correlations, and multicausal explanations, it emphasized the importance of critical analysis of secondary sources of information in previous polls.

Chapter 4, "Attitudes and Opinions," dealt with the nature of attitudes, beliefs, and values. It examined approaches to understanding attitudes, including the cognitive, regulatory-adaptation, and rational actor approaches. The chapter discussed accessibility and cognitive balance theories. In explaining dogmatism as well as theories that attitudes may just be convenient and temporary constructions, the chapter examined critical thinking issues related to attitudes.

Chapter 5, "Political Socialization," described the stages of political socialization, or learning about politics, during childhood, adolescence, and adulthood. It examined family socialization and the impact of birth order on attitudes and explored political learning through issues such as quality of life and materialist and postmaterialist values. The chapter introduced approaches to political socialization, the stages of moral development, and education's role in learning about the political and social world. It closed with a critical evaluation of opinion studies in political socialization.

Chapter 6, "The Media and Opinions," emphasized the importance of critical thinking in studies about the media. The chapter discussed the problem of access to information and types of political, ideological, and moral censorship. It dedicated sections to the content of information and the impact of the media on people's attitudes and behavior. It emphasized name recognition and sensationalism and the process of information spread in contemporary society. In examining important factors such as agenda setting, media frames, and political bias, the chapter explored both positive and negative views of the media's impact on opinions.

Chapter 7, "Gender and Opinion," began the exploration of how other important factors in political socialization, such as the differences and similarities between men and women, influence their political attitudes. As a formative element of individuals and their social environment, gender affects people's social opportunities, attitudes about politics like party identification, and the likelihood of their political involvement. The gender gap represents differences between women and men in their attitudes on important social and political issues, and their partisanship in voting. In the "Thinking Critically" section, the chapter examined the gender gap on important issues such as the economy, social welfare, war and peace, and political participation from sociological, cultural, identification, sociobiological, and socioeconomic perspectives.

Chapter 8, "Social Class and Opinions," examined the impact of social class on opinions. It analyzed class as a concept, social class opinion gaps, and ideological identity and party identification. Then it examined class-related views on taxation, foreign aid, undocumented immigrants, affirmative action, the death penalty, abortion, free speech, privacy, and individual rights. Besides socioeconomic factors like inequality, it addressed variables such as class interests, perceptions of economic change, and views on merit and fairness. It highlighted class antagonism, self-identity, and access to information. The chapter discussed the influence of occupation, work involvement, and education on opinions and critically evaluated the social class gap in attitudes.

Chapter 9, "Race, Ethnicity, Religion, and Opinions," dealt with cultural issues and opinion expression and voting. It examined U.S. polls on opinions expressed by people who are black, Hispanic, and Asian. In addressing religion and its impact on attitudes and behaviors, it examined the voting patterns of Catholics, Protestants, Jews, and Muslims in the United States. The chapter explored theories of differences in culture-related views and the social power, prejudice, and cultural identity theories. Finally, the chapter critically explored culture's links to opinions.

Chapter 10, "Opinions and Voting," discussed the expression of opinion in electoral choices and voting as a political process. It explored the reasons people vote (or not), including socioeconomic factors, knowledge, legal and institutional factors, electoral format, and cognitive, moral, and personality factors. It paid special attention to the low voter turnout in most democratic countries and addressed online voting and its impact on the way people pick their preferences. The chapter explored ideological and partisan voting by means of critical thinking, paying special attention to the complexity of voting decisions, particularly in the 2004 presidential election.

Chapter 11, "Opinions About Domestic Issues," dealt with the diversity of opinion about key social and political issues in the United States. Among the topics were abortion, affirmative action, crime and law enforcement, the death penalty, education, gun control, immigration, the environment, and healthcare. The chapter examined other ethical issues such as euthanasia, sexual orientation, security, and privacy, and it explained people's views about the role of government. Contemporary updates on domestic issues appear on the website.

Chapter 12, "Opinions About Foreign Policy," explained the nature and dynamics of attitudes about foreign policy. While public interest in foreign affairs is typically lower than interest in domestic issues, Americans have relatively stable opinions about enemies, allies, the international role of the United States, national security, foreign trade, and foreign aid. Foreign policy attitudes are influenced by factors including security issues and terrorism concerns, ideology and partisan beliefs. Public opinion does not set foreign policy, but it constrains it. The chapter provided tools for critical thinking about foreign policy attitudes. The website presents a special section on international public opinion and the war in Bosnia and updates on the presidential elections in 2004, and beyond.

THE INFLUENCE OF PUBLIC OPINION ON GOVERNMENT POLICIES

While comedians joke about politics and politicians, most people notice and care about what the government does. Most vote in national or local elections, and many support political candidates, sign petitions, participate in rallies, and call or write the president and their representatives in both houses of Congress. Most people want their opinions to be reflected in government decisions. The doubling of emails to the House of Representatives between 1998 and 2000 and the proliferation of polls suggest that people want to be heard: yet, their messages may be like or unlike opinions expressed in polls. As Walter Lippmann reminded us, people want democratic government not for its own sake but for its results.

How should and does government respond to the people's voice, and to what extent does public opinion influence the policies governments enact? The two basic views on how public opinion should affect policy represented complementary models. The first holds that people's representatives should be independent decision makers, or trustees, who act on behalf of their constituencies but do not rush to deal with every citizen's grievance. The government needs to reflect only the true and enduring concerns of the public. In the second view, representatives in the government, or delegates, should make policy by responding to their constituents' wishes. Pioneering pollsters and advocates of democracy George Gallup and Louis Harris contended that the opinions of ordinary people should be taken into account by government.

Americans hold mixed views about public opinion polls and what their influence on the government should be. Many feel politicians should pay more attention to public opinion. On the other hand, many acknowledge that officials should develop reasonable and independent policy on behalf of the electorate but not under the influence of emotional responses from the public and the media.

So what is the impact of opinion on policy? Polls are becoming an increasingly significant factor in government decision making, even if some politicians "spin" the results to appear to support their policies. In general, public opinion constrains and stimulates policy but does not set it directly. Since the 1960s, comparing public opinion with policy outcomes shows relative consistency between the two, and that congruence appears to be strengthening. In short, the correspondence between public opinion and policy is generally stable; what most people want and what the government does are usually correlated.

Yet the public's strong and stable opinion about a specific issue does not automatically translate into a government policy. Around the world, different governments have varied ways of considering (or ignoring) public opinion as a factor in policy-making. Political institutions and communications, political competition, elections, and other forms of political participation affect this translation. National political systems and their organization affect the degree to which public opinion is a catalyst for domestic or foreign policy actions. Parties, bureaucracies, political competitors, the media, and interest groups all attempt to transmit opinions to the policy process. How does this happen?

A country's political structures and institutional communications influence how public opinion affects policies. Democratic governments care more about public opinion than nondemocratic ones. A dictator or military ruler may be able to ignore public opinion when the majority does not support his policies. Most authoritarian governments do not allow opinion polls to be conducted in their countries. Public opinion influences policy more directly in two-party parliamentary settings like the United States than in coalition-based multiparty systems like Germany or Italy. Stronger political parties are better conduits of public opinion than weaker ones. Political systems that have concentrated and sophisticated channels of communication between political parties, interest groups, bureaucracies, and the media provide better public opinion expression than those with underdeveloped, fragmented, or restricted communications.

Democracy is inseparable from elections, and people's opinions about how they are going to vote affect policy in remarkable ways, as the 2004 examples show again. Public opinion limits and encourages the actions of elected representatives because public officials want to be reelected. Mistakes cost politicians politically; they may be voted out of office. As a result, policymakers rarely act against overwhelming public support or opposition on issues. In the United States, major elected officials, cabinet secretaries, and other high-level administrators tend to be more responsive to public opinion than appointed, nonpolitical career officials. In sum, people running for election or reelection tend to be responsive to public opinion.

The anticipation of positive public reaction to a specific policy contributes to a permissive policy climate, while anticipated criticism contributes to a less permissive climate. While political opponents rarely challenge policy decisions of government officials if public support for these decisions is strong, opponents will challenge the government if the public reaction is, or is expected to be, negative or divided.

Political leaders and activists typically have more influence than people who are uninterested in public issues or do not want to express their views. People who pay attention to politics tend to know more about how government works and how to influence it. The ill-informed public is more subject to manipulation by leaders that have the power and resources to boost support for their policies. On the other hand, many public officials cite polls as supporting their decisions, and most politicians actively read polls, although some deny this, especially those results that support their views on issues.

In short, individuals who express their opinions actively, are engaged in the political process, join forces in effective groups, and command greater resources are typically more influential than the unorganized public. While people's opinions expressed in polls matter in democracies, there are more active ways to make your opinions known to fellow citizens, media, and government leaders. These may be final lessons for students who want not only to learn about public opinion and politics but also to influence them, perhaps in 2006 and 2008.

People and Their Opinions offers the essential tools for critical thinking in the field of public opinion and policy analysis. It presents public opinion as a captivating and powerful force with significant influence on contemporary politics and government in the United States and around the world. *People and Their Opinions* provides an illuminating entry into a fascinating adventure. We invite you to continue this invigorating journey further as an explorer in understanding, and perhaps influencing, how public opinion and democracy works in America and beyond.

Abbreviations of Polls

The following items are included in the survey references:

- The abbreviated name of the organization that conducted the survey and, in many cases, the survey's sponsor
- The month and year the survey was conducted
- If the survey was not conducted via telephone, the method (usually "personal")
- If the sample is not "national adult," the type of sample (for example, "registered voters")
- The size of the sample (number of respondents)

EXAMPLE:
(CBS and NYT, February 2000, 1,225)
This survey was conducted by CBS News and the *New York Times* in February 2000, via telephone, with a national sample of 1,225.

THE FOLLOWING ABBREVIATIONS OF POLLING ORGANIZATIONS AND POLL SPONSORS ARE USED IN THIS TEXT AND TABLES:

ABC—ABC News

ABC and WP—ABC News and *Washington Post*

ACLU and BRS—American Civil Liberties Union and Belden, Russonello, and Stewart

ANES—American National Election Study

AP—Associated Press

AP and ICR—Associated Press and ICR Survey Research Group

ATS—Americans Talk Security

AV—American Viewpoint

Barna—Barna Research Group

Black—Gordon Black Corporation

BRS and CV&K—Belden, Russonello, and Stewart; and Community Voices and W.K. Kellogg Foundation

CBS and NYT—CBS News and *New York Times*

CCD—Center for Communication Dynamics

CCFR—Chicago Council on Foreign Relations

CNN and *USA Today*—Cable News Network and *USA Today*

CPA—Center on Policy Attitudes

CSPA—Center for the Study of Policy Attitudes, University of Maryland (see also CPA, PIPA)

CSRA and FFMS—Center for Survey Research and Analysis and the Freedom Forum Media Studies

CSRA and AARP—Center for Survey Research and Analysis and American Association of Retired Persons

Discovery, *Newsweek,* and PSB—Discovery Health Media, *Newsweek,* and Penn, Schoen, and Berland

GQRR and DC—Greenberg Quinlan Rosener Research and Democracy Corps Poll (see also Greenberg)

FFMS—Freedom Forum Media Studies

FMA—Fabrizio, McLaughlin and Associates

***Fortune—*Fortune* Magazine Poll

Fox—Fox News

Gallup and CCFR—Gallup Polls and Chicago Council on Foreign Relations

***Glamour* and MCR—*Glamour* Magazine and Mark Clements Research

Greenberg—Greenberg Quinlan Rosener Research

Greenberg/POS and NPR—Greenberg Quinlan Rosener Research/Public Opinion Strategies and National Public Radio

GSS—General Social Survey

Harris—Harris Poll

Hart and Teeter—Hart and Teeter Research Companies

Harvard—Harvard University, Kennedy School of Government

HT, NBC, and WSJ—Hart and Teeter Research Companies, NBC News, and *Wall Street Journal*

HT, CNN, and *Time*—Hart and Teeter Research Companies, Cable News Network, and *Time*

ICR and AAOHN—International Communications Research and American Association of Occupational Health Nurses

ICR, Harvard, and Johnson—International Communications Research and Harvard School of Public Health and Robert Wood Johnson Foundation

ICR and Hearst—International Communications Research and Hearst Newspapers

Kaiser—Henry J. Kaiser Foundation

KRC and Kaiser—KRC Communications Research and Kaiser Foundation

**LAT—*Los Angeles Times*

MOR and ATS—Market Opinion Research and Americans Talk Security

NBC and WSJ—NBC News and *Wall Street Journal*

NBC and WSJ and Hart—NBC News, *Wall Street Journal,* and Hart and Teeter Research Companies

Newsweek—*Newsweek* Magazine

NFOR—National Family Opinion Research

NORC—National Opinion Research Center

NORC and GSS—National Opinion Research Center and General Social Surveys

NSIC—National Strategy Information Center

NYT—*New York Times*

OD and Fox—Opinion Dynamics and Fox News

OD and Hart and Teeter—Opinion Dynamics and Hart and Teeter Research Companies

Ogilvy—Ogilvy Public Relations Worldwide

PAF—Public Agenda Foundation

Pew—Pew Research Center for People and the Press

Pew/Princeton/IHT—Pew Research Center, Princeton Survey Research, *International Herald Tribune*

PIPA—Program on International Policy Attitudes, University of Maryland

Potomac and Gallup—Potomac Associates and Gallup Polls

Potomac and Lewis—Potomac Associates and Henry Lewis Foundation

Princeton—Princeton Survey Research Associates (see also PSRA)

Princeton and KR—Princeton Survey Research Associates and Knight Ridder

PSB—Penn, Schoen, and Bernard Associates

PSB and DLC—Penn, Schoen, and Bernard Associates and Democratic Leadership Council

PSRA—Princeton Survey Research Associates (see also Princeton)

PSRA, CRP, and Pew—Princeton Survey Research Associates, Center for Responsive Politics, and Pew Charitable Trust

PSRA and NCCJ—Princeton Survey Research Associates and National Conference for Community and Justice

PSRA and *Newsweek*—Princeton Survey Research Associates and *Newsweek*

PSRA and Pew—Princeton Survey Research Associates and Pew Research Center

PSRA and *Times Mirror*—Princeton Survey Research Associates and *Times Mirror*

POF—Public Opinion Foundation (Russia)

QUPI—Quinnipiac University Polling Institute

Rasmussen—Rasmussen Research Poll

Roper—Roper Center for Public Opinion Research

Roper and FAIR—Roper Organization and Federation for American Immigration Reform

Roper and TIO—Roper Organization and Television Information Office

RSM—Research Strategy Management

SRC—Survey Research Center (University of Michigan)

Tarrance and BAPAC—The Tarrance Group and Black America's Political Action Committees

Tarrance and MLL—The Tarrance Group and Mellman, Lazarus, and Lake

Time—*Time* Magazine

TNS and GMF—Taylor Nelson Sofres and German Marshall Fund of the United States

TPC—The Polling Company

USA Today—*USA Today*

US News—*US News and World Report*

VNS—Voters News Service

VS—Virginia Slims

WP, Kaiser, and Harvard—*Washington Post,* the Henry J. Kaiser Family Foundation, and Harvard University

WW—Wirthlin Worldwide

Yankelovich—Yankelovich Partners Poll

Yankelovich, *Time,* and CNN—Yankelovich Partners Poll, *Time,* and Cable News Network

References

Abramovitz, Alan. (1997). The cultural divide in American politics: Moral issues and presidential voting. In: Barbara Norrander and Clyde Wilcox (Eds.), *Understanding public opinion*. Washington, DC: CQ Press.

Abrams, Herbert L., and Brody, Richard. (1998). Bob Dole's age and health in the 1996 election: Did the media let us down? *Political Science Quarterly,* 113 (Fall), 471–491.

Abu Sada, Mkhaimar. (1997). *Party identification and political attitudes in an emerging democracy.* Paper presented at the annual meeting of the Midwest Political Science Association, April 10–12, Chicago, 1997.

Achen, Christopher. (1992). Social psychology, demographic variables, and linear regression: Breaking the iron triangle in voting research. *Political Behavior,* 14, 195–211.

Adler, Alfred. (1931). *What life should mean to you.* Boston: Little Brown.

Adorno, Theodore W., Frenkel-Brunswik, Else, Levinson, Daniel J., and Sanford, R. N. (1950). *The authoritarian personality.* New York: Harper and Row.

The Advertising Council. (1963*) Challenge to Americans: The struggle we face and how to help win it.* Second printing, 1963. Foreword by President John F. Kennedy.

Aikens, G. S. (1996). The democratization of systems of public opinion formation. 1996 International Symposium on Technology and Society. Technical Expertise and Public Decisions. Proceedings. Princeton University. Princeton, NJ, June 21–22.

Aldrich, John. (1993). Rational choice and turnout. *American Journal of Political Science,* 37, 246–278.

Allport, Gordon. (1954). *The nature of prejudice.* Cambridge, MA: Addison-Wesley.

Almond, Gabriel. (1950). *The American people and foreign policy.* New York: Praeger.

Almond, Gabriel, and Verba, Sidney. (1965). *The civic culture.* Boston: Little Brown.

Alvarez, R. Michael, and Brehm, John. (1998). Speaking in two voices: American equivocation about the Internal Revenue Service. *American Journal of Political Science,* 42, 2, 418–452.

Alwin, Duane, Cohen, Ronald, Newcomb, Theodore. (1988). *Persistence and Change in Socio-political Orientations over the Life Span: The Bennington Women.* 50 Years Later, Madison, WI: University of Wisconsin Press.

Alwin, Duane F., and Krosnick, Jon. (1991). Aging, cohorts, and the stability of sociopolitical orientations over the life span. *American Journal of Sociology,* 97, 169–195.

Amanpour, Christiane. (2001). Why do I do it? *Brill's Content,* January, 50–54.

American Association for Public Opinion Research. (1996). *Statement condemning push polls.* By Eleanor Singer. www.aapor.org.

American Association for Public Opinion Research. (1997). *Best practices for survey and public opinion research and survey practices that AAPOR condemns.* May.

American Association for Public Opinion Research. (1998). *Standard definitions: Final dispositions of case codes and outcome rates for RDD telephone surveys and in-person household surveys.* Ann Arbor, Michigan: AAPOR http://www.aapor.org/ethics/stddef.html.

American Civil Liberties Union. (1999). *The death penalty.* ACLU Briefing Paper. http://www.aclu.org/library.

American Civil Liberties Union. (2001). Materials posted on http://www.aclu.org on July 19, 2001.

American Civil Liberties Union. 2002. "Release of 100th Innocent from Death Row Underscores Urgent Need for Moratorium, ACLU say." April 9.

Ancheta, Angelo N. (1997). *Race and the Asian American Experience.* New Brunswick, NJ: Rutgers University Press.

Andersen, Kristi. (1997). Gender and public opinion. In: Barbara Norander and Clyde Wilcox (Eds.), *Understanding public opinion.* Washington, DC: CQ Press.

Anderson, C. A. (1987). Temperature and aggression: Effects on quarterly, yearly, and city rates of violent and nonviolent crime. *Journal of Personality and Social Psychology,* 52, 1161–1173.

Anderson, David C. (1995). *Crime and the politics of hysteria: How the Willie Horton story changed American justice.* New York: Random House.

Ansolabehere, Stephen, and Iyengar, Shanto. (1995). *Going negative.* New York: Free Press.

Ansolabehere, Stephen, Behr, Roy, and Iyengar, Shanto. (1993). *The media game.* Boston: Allyn and Bacon.

Archer, John. (1996). Sex differences in social behavior: Are the social role and evolutionary explanations compatible? *American Psychologist,* 51 (September), 909–917.

Aronson, Elliot. (1995). *The social animal.* New York: W. H. Freeman.

Aronson, Elliot, and O'Leary, Michael. (1982–1983). The relative effectiveness of models and prompts on energy conservation: A field experiment in a shower room. *Journal of Environmental Systems,* 12, 219–224.

Asch, Solomon. (1946). Forming impressions of personality. *Journal of Abnormal and Social Psychology,* 41, 258–290.

Asch, Solomon. (1956). Studies of independence and conformity: A minority of one against a unanimous majority. *Psychological Monographs,* 9, 416.

Astin, Alexander W. et al. (1997). *The American freshman: Thirty-year trends.* Los Angeles: Higher Education Research Institute, University of California, Los Angeles.

Baker, Gerard. (2001). Leap of faith that divides Europe and the US: Religious observance rather than cultural and economic differences may explain the lack of transatlantic understanding. *Financial Times* (London), August 23, 21.

Ball, George. (1962). Lawyers and diplomats. Address before the New York Lawyers Association, December 13. Department of State Bulletin, December 31, 987–991.

Ball-Rokeach, Sandra J., Grube, Joel W., and Rokeach, Milton. (1981). Roots: The Next Generation: Who watched and with what effect? *Public Opinion Quarterly* 45, 1, 58–68.

Ball-Rokeach, Sandra, and Loges, William. (1994). Choosing equality: The correspondence between attitudes about race and the value of equality. *Journal of Social Issues,* 50, 4, 9–18.

Balz, Dan, and Morin, Richard. (1999). Clinton-weary public has doubts about Gore. *Washington Post,* September 8, A01.

Banaszak, Lee Ann. (1998). East-West differences in German abortion opinion. *Public Opinion Quarterly,* 62 (Winter), 545–582.

Bandura, Albert. (1969). *Principles of behavioral modification.* New York: Holt, Rinehart, Winston.

Barber, Benjamin. (1998). Democracy at risk: American culture in a global culture. *World Policy Journal,* 15, 2 (Summer), 29–42.

Bardes, Barbara, and Oldendick, Robert. (2000). *Public Opinion: Measuring the American Mind.* Belmont, CA.: Wadsworth.

Bardi, Anat, and Schwartz, Shalom H. (1996). Relations among sociopolitical values in Eastern Europe: Effects on the communist experience? *Political Psychology,* 17, 3, 525–550.

Barner-Barry, Carol, and Rosenwein, Robert. (1991). *Psychological perspectives on politics.* Prospect Heights, IL: Waveland Press.

Baron, R. A. (1970). Magnitude of model's apparent pain and ability to aid the model as determinants of observer reaction time. *Psychonomic Science,* 21, 196–197.

Barone, Michael, Cohen, Richard, and Ujifusa, Grant. (2002). *The almanac of American politics 2002.* Washington, DC: National Journal Group.

Bartels, Larry. 1991. Constituency opinion and congressional policy making: The Reagan defense buildup. *American Political Science Review,* 85, 457–72.

Bass, Loretta E., and Casper, Lynne. (1999). *Population Division working paper no. 28.* Washington, DC: U.S. Bureau of the Census.

Bassili, John. (1995). On the psychological reality of party identification: Evidence from the accessibility of voting intentions and of partisan feelings. *Political Behavior,* 17, 4, 339–359.

Bassili, John, and Krosnik, Jon. (2000). Do strength-related attitude properties determine susceptibility to response effects? New evidence from response latency, attitude extremity, and aggregate indices. *Political Psychology,* 21, 1, 107–133.

Bassili, John N., and Roy, Jean-Paul. (1998). On the representation of strong and weak attitudes about policy in memory. *Political Psychology,* 19, 4, 669–682.

Beck, Paul. (1977). "The Role of Agents in Political Socialization," in Stanley Renshon, ed. *The Handbook of Political Science.* New York: Free Press.

Bedau, Hugo, and Radelet, Michael. (1987). Miscarriages of justice in potentially capital cases. *Stanford Law Review,* 40,1, November.

Bedau, Hugo, Radelet, Michael, and Putnam, Constance. *In Spite of Innocence,* Northeastern University Press, 1992.

Bedau, Hugo, Radelet, Michael, and Putnam, Constance. Convicting the innocent in capital cases: criteria, evidence, and inference. *Drake Law Review,* 52 (August), 2004.

Bekhterev, Vladimir. (1924/2001). *Collective reflexology.* New Brunswick, NJ: Transaction.

Belknap, George, and Campbell, Angus. (1951). Political party identification and attitudes toward foreign policy. *Public Opinion Quarterly,* 15, 601–623.

Bell, Daniel. (1960). *The end of ideology: On the exhaustion of political ideas in the fifties.* New York: Free Press.

Bellamy, Edward. (1888/2000). *Looking backward.* New York: Penguin.

Belli, Robert F., Traugott, Michael W., Young, Margaret, and McGonagle, Katherine A. (1999). Reducing vote overreporting in surveys. *Public Opinion Quarterly,* 63, 90–108.

Bellucci, Paolo, and Isernia, Pierangelo. (2003). Massacring in front of a blind audience? Italian public opinion and Bosnia. In: R. Sobel and E. Shiraev (Eds.), *International public opinion and the Bosnia crisis.* Lanham, MD: Lexington Books.

Bem, D. J. (1972). Self-perception theory. In: L. Berkovitz (Ed.), *Advances in experimental social psychology,* Vol. 6, 1–62. New York: Academic Press.

Benedict, Ruth. (1946). *The chrysanthemum and the sword: Patterns of Japanese culture.* Boston: Houghton Mifflin.

Benett, Rosemary. (2000). Sex bias costs women staff pounds. *Financial Times* (London), February 2, 7.

Bengston, Vern L., and Black, K. D. (1973). Intergenerational relations and continuities in socialization. In: K. Schaie and P. Baltes (Eds.), *Personality and socialization.* New York: Academic Press, 207–234.

Bennett, W. Lance. (1998). The uncivic culture: Communication, identity, and the rise of lifestyle politics. *PS Political Science and Politics,* 31 (December), 741–761.

Bennett, Stephen E. (1996). Why young Americans hate politics, and what we should do about it. *PS: Political Science and Politics,* 29 (March), 47–53.

Bennett, Stephen E. (1998). Young Americans' indifference to media coverage of public affairs. *PS: Political Science and Politics,* 31 (September), 535–541.

Bennett, Stephen E. (1999). The past need not be prologue: Why pessimism about civic education is premature. *PS: Political Science and Politics,* (December), 755–757.

Benson, John. (1999). The polls-trends. End-of-life issues. *Public Opinion Quarterly,* 63 (Summer), 263–277.

Berger, Kathleen S. (1995). *The developing person through the lifespan.* New York: Worth.

Berkowitz, Leonard. (1962). *Aggression: A social psychological analysis.* New York: McGraw-Hill.

Bernstein, Morty, and Crosby, Faye. (1980). An empirical examination of relative deprivation theory. *Journal of Experimental Social Psychology,* 16, 442–456.

Berry, John. (1967). Independence and conformity in subsistence-level societies. *Journal of Personality and Social Psychology,* 7, 415–418.

Berry, John W., Poortinga, Ype, Segall, Marshall, and Dasen, Pierre. (1992). *Cross-cultural psychology: Research and applications.* New York: Cambridge University Press.

Berry, John W., Pootinga, Ype H., Segall, Marshall H., and Dasen, Pierre R. (1992). *Cross-cultural psychology.* Cambridge: Cambridge University Press.

Berthoud, Joy. (1996). *Pecking order: How your place in the family affects your personality.* London: Victor Gollancz.

Bickman, Leonard. (1972). Social influence and division of responsibility in an emergency. *Journal of Experimental Social Psychology,* 8, 438–445.

Binson, Diane, and Caiana, Joseph A. (1998). Respondents' understanding of the words used in sexual behavior questions. *Public Opinion Quarterly,* 62 (Summer), 190–208.

Birch, Herbert G., and Gussow, Joan D. (1970). *Disadvantaged children: Health, nutrition, and school failure.* New York: Harcourt, Brace and World.

Bishop, George. (1999). America's belief in God. *Public Opinion Quarterly,* 63 (Fall), 412–434.

Biskupic, Joan. (1999). In jury rooms, a form of civil protest grows. *Washington Post,* February 8, A01.

Black, Ian. (2001). Only connect: It's now a question of when rather than whether the E.U. will enlarge. Yet it still has to deal with the disillusionment of those who are already in. *Guardian* (London), December 13, 21.

Blais, Andre, and Carty R. K. (1990). "Does proportional representation foster voter-turnout?" *European Journal of Political Research* 18:2, 167–81.

Blais, André, Fleury, Christopher, Lapp, Miriam, and Young, Robert. (1995). Do people vote on the basis of minimax regret? *Political Research Quarterly,* 48, 4, 827–836.

Blais, André, and Dobrzynska, Agnieszka. (1998). Turnout in electoral democracies. *European Journal of Political Science,* 33, 239–261.

Blauner, Robert. (1972). *Racial oppression in America.* New York: Harper and Row.

Bobo, Lawrence. (1988). Group conflict, prejudice, and the paradox of contemporary racial attitudes. In: P. Katz and D. Taylor (Eds.), *Eliminating racism: profiles in controversy.* New York: Plenum.

Bobo, Lawrence. (1997). The color line, the dilemma, and the dream: Racial attitudes and relations at the close of the twentieth century. In: J. Higham (Ed.), *Civil rights and social wrongs: Black-White relations since World War II.* University Park, PA: Pennsylvania State University Press.

Bobo, Lawrence. (2000). Reclaiming a Du Boisian perspective on racial attitudes. *Annals of the American Academy of Political and Social Science,* 568, 186–202.

Bobo, Lawrence, and Zubrinsky, C. (1996). Attitudes on residential integration: Perceived status differences, mere in-group preference, or racial prejudice? *Social Forces,* 74, 883–909.

Bolce, Louis, and De Maio, Gerald. (1999). Religious outlook, culture war politics, and antipathy toward Christian fundamentalists. *Public Opinion Quarterly,* 63, 29–61.

Bond, Michael. (1985). How are responses to verbal insult related to cultural collectivism and power distance? *Journal of Cross-Cultural Psychology,* 16, 1, 111–127.

Bond, Michael, and Tak-Sing, Cheung. (1983). College students' spontaneous self-concept: The effects of culture among respondents in Hong Kong, Japan, and the United States. *Journal of Cross-Cultural Psychology,* 14, 153–171.

Boninger, Faith, Boninger, D.S., Strathman, A., Armor, D., Hetts, J., and Ahn, M. (1995). With an eye toward the future: The impact of counterfactual thinking on affect, attitudes, and behavior. In: N. J. Roese and J. M. Olson (Eds.), *What might have been: The social psychology of counterfactual thinking,* 283–304. Hillsdale, NJ: Erlbaum.

Booth, William. (2000). A key constituency defies easy labeling. *Washington Post,* February 14, A01.

Bouton, Marshall, and Page, Benjamin. (2002). *Worldviews, 2002, American public opinion and U.S. foreign policy.* Chicago: Chicago Council on Foreign Relations.

Borisova, Yevgenia. (1999). The truth about polls. *Moscow Times,* November 13, 3.

Bovasso, Gregory. (1993). Self, group, and public interest motivating racial politics. *Political Psychology,* 14, 1, 3–20.

Bowen, William, Bok, Derek, and Loury, Glenn. (1998). *The shape of the river: Long-term consequences of considering race in college and university admissions.* New York: Princeton University Press.

Bowler, Shaun, and Donovan, Todd. (1995). Popular responsiveness to taxation. *Political Research Quarterly,* 48, 1, 79–91.

Bowles, Samuel, and Gintis, Herbert. (1976). *Schooling in capitalist America.* New York: Basic Books.

Boykin, A. Wade. (1994). Harvesting talent and culture: African-American children and educational reform. In R. Rossi (Ed.), *Schools and students at risk,* 116–138. New York: Teachers College Press.

Brace, C. L. (1995). Race and political correctness. *American Psychologist,* 50, 8 (August), 725–726.

Brandstatter, Herman, Davis, James, and Stocker-Kreichgauer, Gisela. (1984). *Group decision making.* New York: Academic Press.

Brigham, J. C., and Pfeifer, J. E. (1996). Euthanasia: Introduction. *Journal of Social Issues, 52,* 2, 1–11.

Brislin, Richard W. (1970). Back-translation for cross-cultural research. *Journal of Cross-Cultural Psychology,* 1, 3, 185–216.

Broder, David. (2000). It's an even split. *Plain Dealer,* December 12, B9.

Brody, Richard. (1991). *Assessing the president: The media, elite opinion, and public support.* Stanford, CA: Stanford University Press.

Brody, Richard, and Page, Benjamin. (1972). The assessment of policy voting. *American Political Science Review,* 66, 450–458.

Brody, Richard, and Rothenberg, Lawrence. (1988). The instability of partisanship: An analysis of the 1980 presidential election. *British Journal of Political Science,* 18, 445–465.

Bronfenbrenner, Urie. (1979*). The ecology of human development: Experiments by nature and design.* Cambridge, MA: Harvard University Press.

Brooks, N. R. (2000). Twenty-something men say family comes first. *Los Angeles Times,* May 3, C1.

Brown, Archie. (1996). *The Gorbachev factor.* Oxford: Oxford University Press.

Bryder, Thomas. (2003). *The psychology of anti-communism in visual propaganda: Nazi-German and McCarthyite American.* Paper presented at the Annual Scientific Meeting of the ISPP, Boston, MA.

Bukhari, Zahid, Zogby, John, Nyang, Sulayman, and Bruce, John. (2004). Muslims in the American public square: Shifting political winds and fallout from 9/11, Afghanistan, and Iraq. Washington, DC: Center for Muslim-Christian Understanding, Georgetown University.

Bull, R., and David, I. (1986). The stigmatizing effect of facial disfigurement. *Journal of Cross-Cultural Psychology,* 17, 1, 99–108.

Bullard, Monte. (1997). *The soldier and the citizen: The role of the military in Taiwan's development.* New York: Sharpe.

Burden, Barry, and Mughan, Anthony. (1999). Public opinion and Hillary Rodham Clinton. *Public Opinion Quarterly,* 63, 237–250.

Burke Information Communications and Entertainment Research for MTV Networks and Turner Entertainment Networks. (1999). October 8. http://www.internet.com.

Burnstein, Eugene, and Vinokur, Amiram. (1975). What a person thinks upon learning he has chosen differently from others. *Journal of Experimental Social Psychology,* 11, 412–426.

Burrell, Barbara. (1994). *A woman's place is in the House: Campaigning for Congress in the feminist era.* Ann Arbor: University of Michigan Press.

Cain, Bruce, Citrin, Jack, and Wong, Cara. (2000). *Ethnic context, race relations, and California politics.* San Francisco: Public Policy Institute of California.

Calvert, R., and MacKuen, Michael. (1985). *Bayesian learning and the dynamics of public opinion.* Paper presented at the annual meeting of the Midwest Political Science Association, Chicago.

Cameron, M. (2001). Empathy for dissent in the winter of '01. *Seattle Times,* December 2, B2.

Camilleri, Carmel, and Malewska-Peyre, Hanna. (1997). Socialization and identity strategies. In: J. W:. Berry, P. R. Dasen, and T. S. Saraswathi (Eds.), *Handbook of cross-cultural psychology: Basic processes and human development* (Vol. 2, 41–67). Needham Heights, MA: Allyn & Bacon.

Campbell, Angus. (1960). Surge and decline, a study of electoral change. *Public Opinion Quarterly,* 24.

Campbell, Angus, Converse, Philip, Miller, Warren, and Stokes, Donald. (1960). *The American voter.* New York: Wiley.

Campbell, David. (1967). Stereotypes and the perception of group differences. *American Psychologist,* 22, 817–829.

Campbell, Ward A. (2000). Critique of DPIC List ("Innocence: Freed from Death Row"), DPIC Innocence Critique. www.prodeathpenalty.com/DPIC.htm.

Caprara, Giano Vittorio, Barbaranelli, Claudio, and Zimbardo, Phillip C. (1999). Personality profiles and political parties. *Political Psychology,* 20, 1, 175–197.

Carmines, Edward, and Berkman, Michael. (1994). Ethos, ideology, and partisanship: Exploring the paradox of conservative Democrats. *Political Behavior,* 16, 2, 203–220.

Carriere, Erin, O'Reilly, Marc, and Vengroff, Richard. (2003). Service of peace: Reflexive multilateralism and the Canadian experience in Bosnia. In: Richard Sobel and Eric Shiraev (Eds.), *International public opinion and the Bosnia crisis.* Lanham, MD: Lexington Books.

Carroll, Susan. (1989). The socializing impact of the women's movement. In: Roberta Sigel (Ed.), *Political learning in adulthood: A sourcebook of theory and research,* 306–339. Chicago: University of Chicago Press.

Cashmore, Judith A., and Goodnow, Jacqueline J. (1986). Influences on Australian parents' values: Ethnicity vs. sociometric status. *Journal of Cross-Cultural Psychology,* 17, 441–454.

Center for the American Woman in Politics. (1987). *Gender gap facts sheet.* New Brunswick, NJ: Center for the American Woman in Politics.

Center on Alcohol Marketing and Youth, Alcohol Advertising on Television, 2001 to 2003: *More of the Same.* Washington DC: Center on Alcohol Marketing. http://camy.org/research/tv1004.

Chapman, G. (2000). The cutting age: Focus on technology. *Los Angeles Times,* March 20, C3.

Charters, W. W., Jr., and Newcomb, Theodore M. (1952). Some attitudinal effects of experimentally increased salience of a membership group. In: Newcomb, Theodore M. et al. *Readings in Social Psychology.* New York: Holt.

Chavez, Linda. (2000). Democratic attacks unmasked. *Denver Post,* August 2, B09.

Chen, Jie. (1999). Comparing mass and elite subjective orientations in urban China. *Public Opinion Quarterly,* 63, 193–219.

Chernyaev, Anatoly. (1993). *Six years with Gorbachev.* Moscow: April.

Cialdini, Robert B., Reno, Raymond R., and Kallgren, Carl A. (1990). A focus theory of normative conduct: Recycling the concept of norms to reduce littering in public places. *Journal of Personality and Social Psychology,* 58, 1015–1029.

Cialdini, Robert B., Schaller, M., Houlihan, D., Arps, K., Fultz, J., and Beaman, A. (1975). Reciprocal confessions procedure for inducing compliance: The door-to-face technique. *Journal of Personality and Social Psychology,* 31, 206–215.

Citizens for Tax Justice. (2000). Quoted in *Washington Post,* July 19, A8.

Citizens Juries/Policy Juries. (2001). The Jefferson Center for New Democratic Processes. http://www.jefferson-center.org.

Citrin, Jack, Green, Donald, and Sears, David. (1990). White reactions to black candidates: When does race matter? *Public Opinion Quarterly,* 54, 74–96.

Citrin, Jack, Sears, David O., Muste, C., and Wong, C. (1995). *Liberalism and multiculturalism: The new ethnic agenda in mass opinion.* Paper presented at the annual meeting of the American Political Science Association, Chicago.

Claritas, Inc. (2000). Referred by Bredemeier, K. County of riches. *Washington Post,* June 10, A01.

Clark, Mary E. (1995). Changes in Euro-American values needed for sustainability. *Journal of Social Issues,* 51, 63–82.

Clausen, Christopher. (2000). *Faded mosaic.* I. R. Dee.

Clifford, James. (1988). *The predicament of culture: Twentieth-century ethnography, literature, and art.* Cambridge, MA: Harvard University Press.

Cohen, Bernard C. (1973). *The public's impact on foreign policy.* Boston: Little Brown.

Cohen, Richard. (2000). Undeterred. *Washington Post,* June 1, A 25.

Cohen, Steven, and Liebman, Charles. (1997). American Jewish liberalism: Unraveling the standards. *Public Opinion Quarterly,* 61, 405–430.

Cohn, D'vela. (2000). A racial tug of war over census. *Washington Post,* March 3, B1.

Colleau, S., Glynn, K., Lybrand, S., Merelman, R., Mohan, P., and Wall, J. (1990). Symbolic racism in candidate evaluation: An experiment. *Political Behavior,* 12, 4, 385–402.

Connell, Robert. (1971). *The child's construction of politics.* Carlton, Victoria: Melbourne University Press.

Connell, R. W. (1972). Political socialization and the American family: The evidence reexamined. *Public Opinion Quarterly,* 36, 323–333.

Connelly, Marjorie. (2004). Election 2004: How Americans Voted: A Political Portrait. *New York Times,* November 7, w4.

Converse, Philip E. (1964). The nature of belief systems in mass publics. In: David E. Apter (Ed.), *Ideology and discontent.* New York: Free Press.

Converse, Philip E. (1966). Information flow and the stability of partisan attitudes. In: A. Campbell et al. (Eds.), *Elections and the political order.* New York: John Wiley and Sons.

Converse, Philip E. (1970). Attitudes and non-attitudes: Continuation of a dialogue. In: E. R. Tufte (Ed.), *The quantitative analysis of social problems,* 168–189. Reading, MA: Addison-Wesley.

Converse, Philip E., and Pierce, R. (1985). Measuring partisanship. *Political Methodology* 11, 143–146.

Cook, Elizabeth A. (1994). Voter responses to women senate candidates. In: E. Cook, S. Thomas, and C. Wilcox (Eds.), *The year of the woman: Myths and realities.* Boulder. CO: Westview Press.

Cook, Elizabeth A. (1997). Public opinion and abortion in the post-Webster era. In: B. Norrander and C. Wilcox (Eds.), *Understanding public opinion,* 131–149. Washington, DC: CQ Press.

Cooperman, Alan. (2002). Number of Jews in U.S. falls 5 percent. *Washington Post,* October 9, A03.

Costa, Paul T., and McCrae, Robert R. (1997). Personality trait structure as a human universal. *American Psychologist,* 52, 5 (May), 509–516.

Couch, Arthur, and Keniston, Kenneth. (1960). Yeasayers and naysayers: Agreeing response set as a personality variable. *Journal of Abnormal and Social Psychology,* 60, 2, 151–174.

Cox, Gary W. 1997. *Making votes count.* New York: Cambridge University Press.

Croteau, David. (1998). Examining the "liberal media" claim: Journalists' views on politics, economic policy, and media coverage. *Fair* (Fairness and Accuracy in Reporting). http://www.fair.org.

Culver, Virginia. (1999). Politics drawing U.S. Muslims issues, not parties focus, polls show. *Denver Post,* December 18, A26.

Cunningham, John. (1992). Too much faith in opinion polls. *Times* (London), April 4, Features 1.

Curry, George, and West, Cornell. (1996). *The affirmative action debate.* New York: Perseus Press.

Cutler, Neal E. (1977). Demographic, social-psychological, and political factors in the politics of aging: A foundation for research in political gerontology. *American Political Science Review,* 71 (September), 1011–1125.

Cutler, W. B. (1999). Human sex-attractant pheromones: Discovery, research, development, and application in sex therapy. *Psychiatric Annals,* 29, 54–59.

D'Souza, Dinesh. (1995). *The end of racism.* New York: Free Press.

D'Souza, Dinesh. (1999). The billionaire next door. *Forbes,* October 11, 50–62.

Dabbs, James M., and Morris, Robin. (1990). Testosterone, social class, and antisocial behavior in a sample of 4,462 men. *Psychological Science,* 1, 209–211.

Daily Yomiuri. (1999). [No title.] November 28, 1.

Darley, John, and Batson, Daniel. (1973). From Jerusalem to Jericho: A study of situational and dispositional variables in helping behavior. *Journal of Personality and Social Psychology,* 27, 100–108.

David, Leonard. (2001). *Poll shows space flights would be hot ticket.* November 30, 2001. http://www.space.com.

Davies, James. (1963). *Human nature in politics.* New York: Wiley.

Davis, Darren W. (1995). Exploring black political intolerance. *Political Behavior,* 17, 1, 1–15.

Davis, Darren W. (1997). Nonrandom measurement error and race of interviewer effects among African Americans. *Public Opinion Quarterly,* 61 (Spring), 183–207.

Davidson, Andrew R. and Thompson, Elizabeth (1980). Cross-cultural studies of attitudes and beliefs. In Harry C. Triandis and Richard W. Brislin (Eds.), *Handbook of Cross-Cultural Psychology: Vol. 5. Basic Processes* (pp. 25–35). Boston, MA: Allyn and Bacon.

Davis, James, and Smith, Tom W. (1990). *General social surveys, 1972–1990.* Chicago: National Opinion Research Center.

Davis, Rebecca. (1997). *Women and power in parliamentary democracies: Cabinet appointments in Western Europe.* Lincoln: University of Nebraska Press.

Dawson, Richard, Prewitt, Kenneth, and Dawson, Karen. (1977). *Political socialization.* Boston: Little Brown.

Delli Carpini, Michael. (1989). Age and history: Generations and sociopolitical change. In: Roberta S. Sigel (Ed.), *Political learning in adulthood: A sourcebook of theory and research,* 11–55. Chicago: University of Chicago Press.

Delli Carpini, Michael, and Keeter, Scott. (1996). *What Americans know about politics and why it matters.* New Haven: Yale University Press.

Dennis, Jack, and Owen, Diana. (1997). The partisanship puzzle: Identification and attitudes of Generation X. In: S. Craig and S. E. Bennett (Eds.), *After the boom: The politics of Generation X.* Lanham, MD: Rowman and Littlefield.

Deutsch, Karl. (1954). *Political community at the international level: Problems of definition and Measurement.* Garden City, NY: Doubleday. Reprinted in 1970 by Archon Books.

Deutsch, Morton, and Gerard, Harold. (1955). A study of normative and informational social influence upon individual judgment. *Journal of Abnormal and Social Psychology,* 51, 629–636.

DeVries, Walter, and Tarrance, Lance, Jr. (1972). *The ticket-splitter: A new force in American politics.* Grand Rapids, MI: Eerdmans.

deWitte, H. (1992). Unemployment, political attitudes, and voting behavior. *Politics and the Individual,* 2, 1, 29–41.

Diagnostic and statistical manual of mental disorders. Volume 4 (1994). Washington, DC: American Psychiatric Association.

DiClemente, Diane, and Hantula, Donald. (2000). John Broadus Watson, I-O Psychologist. Division 14 of the American Psychological Association Organizational Affiliate of the American Psychological Society. http://www.siop.org.

Dillner, Luisa. (1999). I do…but only with you. *Guardian* (London), November 9, Features 6.

DiVall, L. (2000). Women voters like Bush. *Los Angeles Times,* May 7, Opinion 2.

Detroit News Wire Services. (2000). NCAA officials gambling. *Detroit News,* March 30, Sports, 2.

Dolan, Kathleen. (1995). Attitudes, behavior, and the influence of the family: A reexamination of the role of family structure. *Political Behavior,* 17, 3, 251–265.

Dolan, Kathleen. (1998). Voting for women in the "Year of the Woman." *American Journal of Political Science.* 42, 1, 272–293.

Dole, A. A. (1995). Why not drop race as a term? *American Psychologist,* 50, 1 (January), 40.

Doll, Jorg, and Ajzen, Icek. (1992). Accessibility and stability of predictors in the theory of planned behaviour". *Journal of Personality and Social Psychology,* Vol. 63, 754–765.

Dollard, John, Doob, Leonard W., Miller, Neal E., Mowrer, O. H., and Sears, Robert R. (1939). *Frustration and aggression.* New Haven: Yale University Press.

Douglas, James W., and Blomfield, J. M. (1968). *Children under five.* London: Allen and Unwin.

Downs, Anthony. (1957). *An economic theory of democracy.* New York: Harper.

Du Bois, W. E. B. (1899/1996). *The Philadelphia Negro: A social study.* Philadelphia: University of Pennsylvania Press.

Du Bois, W. E. B. (1940/1995). *Dusk of dawn: An essay toward an autobiography of a race concept.* New Brunswick, NJ: Transaction.

Durand, Jorge and Douglas Massey, eds. (2004). *Crossing the Border: Research from the Mexican migration project.* New York: The Russell Sage Foundation.

Durkheim, Emile. (1924/1974). *Sociology and philosophy.* New York: Free Press.

Durkheim, Emile. (1925). *L'education morale.* Paris: Felix Alcan.

Dyal, J. A. (1984). Cross-cultural research with the locus of control construct. In: H. Lefcourt (Ed.), *Research with the locus of control construct,* Vol. 3, 209–306. New York: Academic Press.

Ebenstein, William. (1963). *Two ways of life.* New York: Holt, Rinehart, and Winston.

Eagly, Alice. (1995). The science and politics of comparing women and men. *American Psychologist,* 50, 3 (March), 145–158.

Easton, David, and Dennis, Jack. (1967). The child acquisition of regime norms: Political efficacy. *American Political Science Review,* 6, 25–30.

Easton, David, and Dennis, Jack. (1969). *Children in the political system: Origins of political legitimacy.* New York: McGraw-Hill.

Eckhardt, W. (1971). Eastern and Western religiosity. *Journal of Cross-Cultural Psychology,* 2, 3, 283–291.

Edley, Christopher. (1998). *Not all black and white: Affirmative action and American values.* New York: Noonday Press.

Edsall, Thomas. (2001). Voter values determine political affiliation. *Washington Post,* March 26, A1.

Edwards, Ward. (1954). The theory of decision making. *Psychological Bulletin, 51,* 380–417

Efron, E. (2001). Between the lines. *Brill's Content,* January, 29–30.

Ehrlich, Thomas. (1999). Civic education: Lessons learned. *PS: Political Science and Politics,* June, 245–250.

Eichenberg, Richard C. (2002). *Gender differences and the use of force in the United States, 1990–2002.* Paper prepared for delivery at the 2002 Annual Meeting of the American Political Science Association, Boston, August 29–September 1.

Eilperin, Juliet. (2002). Battle emerges over Latino votes. *Washington Post,* July 10, A06.

Elliott, Anthony. (1998). Celebrity and political psychology: Remembering Lennon. *Political Psychology,* 19, 4, 833–852.

Ellsworth, Phoebe C., and Gross, S. (1994). Hardening of attitudes: Americans' views on the death penalty. *Journal of Social Issues,* 50, 2, 19–52.

Elshtain, Joan Bethke. (1991). *Power trips and other journeys: Essays in feminism as civic discourse.* Madison: University of Wisconsin Press.

Erikson, Erik. (1950). *Childhood and Society.* New York: Norton.

Erikson, Erik. (1968). *Identity: Youth and crisis.* New York: Norton.

Erikson, Erik. (1977). *Toys and reasons: Stages in the ritualization of experience.* New York: Norton.

Erikson, Robert S. and Tedin, Kent L. (2005). *American Public Opinion: It's Origins, Content and Impact.* New York: Pearson/Longman.

Erikson, Robert, and Wlezien, Christopher. (1999). Presidential polls as a time series. *Public Opinion Quarterly,* 63 (Summer), 163–177.

Erskine, Hazel. (1971). The polls: Women's role. *Public Opinion Quarterly,* 35, 275–290.

Everts, Philip. (1998). *Public opinion and decisions on the use of military force in democratic societies.* Paper prepared for presentation at the workshop "Democracy, Public Opinion, and the Use of Force in a Changing International Environment," Joint Sessions of the European Consortium for Political Research, University of Warwick, Coventry, UK, March 23–28.

Ewell, Miranda. (1999). Gender bias limits careers, say high-tech women. *Ottawa Citizen,* September 25, J2.

Eysenck, Hans. (1954/1999). *The psychology of politics.* New Brunswick, NJ: Transaction.

Farley, Reynolds, Steeh, Charlotte, Krysan, Maria, Jackson, Tara, and Reeves, Keith. (1994). Stereotypes and segregation: Neighborhoods in the Detroit area. *American Journal of Sociology,* 100, 750–780.

Faux, Jeff. (1997). You are not alone. In: Stanley Greenberg and Theda Skocpol (Eds.), *The New Majority.* New Haven: Yale University Press.

Fazio, Russell H. (1989). *On the Power and Functionality of Attitudes: The Role of Attitude Accessibility,* in Anthony R. Pratkanis et al. (Eds.), *Attitude Structure and Function.* Hillsdale, NJ: L. Erlbaum Associates.

Fazio, Russell H., and Zanna, Mark P. (1981). Direct experience and attitude-behavior consistency. In L. Berkowitz (Ed.), *Advances in experimental social psychology* (Vol. 14, pp. 161–202). New York: Academic Press.

Fazio, Russell H., Williams, Carol J., and Powell, Martha C. (2000). Measuring associative strength: Category-item associations and their activation from memory. *Political Psychology,* 21, 1, 7–27.

Feaver, Peter, and Kohn, Richard. (2000). Project on the gap between the military and cvilian society. Triangle Institute for Security Studies. http://www.poli.duke.edu/civmil/.

Feldman, Kenneth, and Newcomb, Theodore M. (1971). *The impact of college on students: An analysis of four decades of research.* San Francisco: Jossey-Bass.

Feldman, Ofer. (1996). The political personality in Japan: An inquiry into the belief system of Diet members. *Political Psychology,* 17, 657–682.

Feldman, Ofer and Valenty, Linda. (2001). (Eds.), *Profiling Political Leaders: Cross-Cultural Studies of Personality and Behavior.* New York: Greenwood Press.

Ferguson, Neil, and Ed Cairns. (1996). Political violence and moral maturity in Northern Ireland. *Journal of Political Psychology,* 17, 4, 713–727.

Fessenden, Ford. (2000). Deadly statistics: A survey of crime and punishment. *New York Times,* September 22, A23.

Festinger, Leon. (1957). *A theory of cognitive dissonance.* Stanford: Stanford University Press.

Fine, Michelle, and Weis, Lois. (1998). *The unknown city: Lives of poor and working-class young adults.* Boston: Beacon Press.

Fiorina, Morris. (1981). *Retrospective voting in American national elections.* New Haven: Yale University Press.

Fiorina, Morris, and Peterson, Paul. (1998). *The new American democracy.* Boston: Allyn and Bacon.

Fischer, J. (1999). Fifty-seven percent of Russians believe December polls will be rigged. *Washington Times,* September 3, A1.

Fischer, J. (1999). Ukrainian poll stirs U.S. policy worries. *Washington Times,* September 3, A1.

Fletcher, Joseph F. (2000). Two-timing: Politics and response latencies in a bilingual survey. *Political Psychology,* 21, 1, 27–57.

Foster, H. Schuyler. (1983). *Activism replaces isolationism.* Washington, DC: Foxhall.

Fowers, Blaine J., and Richardson, Frank C. (1996). Why is multiculturalism good? *American Psychologist,* 51, 609–621.

Fowler, Floyd Jackson Jr., Roman, Anthony M., and Zhu Xiao Di. (1998). Mode effects in a survey of medicare prostate surgery patients. *Public Opinion Quarterly,* 62 (Spring), 29–46.

Fox, Richard, and Smith, Eran. (1998). The role of the candidate sex in voter decision-making. *Political Psychology,* 19, 2, 405–420.

Fraczek, A. (1985). Moral approval of aggressive acts. *Journal of Cross-Cultural Psychology,* 16, 1, 41–54.

Frager, R. (1970). Conformity and anti-conformity in Japan. *Journal of Personality and Social Psychology,* 15, 203–210.

Frankel, Lester R. (1983). The report of the CASRO Task Force on Response Rates. In: F. Wiseman (Ed.), *Improving data quality in a sample survey.* Cambridge, MA: Marketing Science Institute.

Frankenhauser, Marianne, Lundberg, Ulf, and Chesney, Maragaret. (1991). *Women, work, and health: Stress and opportunities.* New York: Plenum.

Fredrickson, George M. (1981). *White supremacy: A comparative study of American and South African history.* Oxford: Oxford University Press.

Freeman, Richard B. (1999). *The new inequality: Creating solutions for poor America.* Boston: Beacon Press.

Freud, Anna. (1946). *The ego and the mechanisms of defense.* New York: International Universities Press.

Freud, Sigmund. (1920). *A general introduction to psychoanalysis.* New York: Boni and Liveright.

Freud, Sigmund. (1938). *The basic writings.* New York: Random House.

Frey, Claudia, and Hoppe-Graff, Seigfried. (1994). Serious and playful aggression in Brazilian boys and girls. *Sex Roles,* 30, 249–268.

Friedman, Lawrence, and Levantrosser, William. (Eds.) (1987). *Richard Nixon: Politician, president, administrator.* New York: Greenwood Press.

Frost, Sheri, and Makarov, Denis. (1998). Changing post-totalitarian values in Russia through public deliberation methodology. *PS: Political Science and Politics,* 31 (December), 775–781.

Fukuyama, Francis. (2000). *The great disruption: Human nature and the reconstitution of social order.* New York: Free Press.

Fukuyama, Francis. (1998). Women and the evolution of world politics. *Foreign Affairs,* (September-October), 24–40.

Fund, J. (2000). Serious damage: Awkward candidate. http://www.msnbc.com. June 26.

Funk, Carol. (1998). Practicing what we preach? The influence of a societal interest value on civic engagement. *Political Psychology,* 19, 3, 601–614.

Galbraith, John Kenneth. (1998). *Created unequal: The crisis in American pay.* New York: Free Press.

Gallup, George. (1985). *The Gallup poll: Public opinion 1984.* Princeton: Gallup.

Gallup Polls News Service. (2001–2004). http://www.gallup.com/poll/indicators.

Ganey, Terry, and Bell, Kim. (1999). Gun measure splits votes along rural, urban lines. *St. Louis Post-Dispatch,* April 7, A1.

Garcia, Chris. (Ed.) (1997). *Pursing power: Latinos and the political system.* Notre Dame, IN: University of Notre Dame Press.

Gardiner, Harry, Mutter, Jay, and Kosmitzki, Corrine. (1998). *Lives across cultures: Cross-cultural human development.* Boston: Allyn and Bacon, Inc.

Gay, Claudine, and Tate, Katherine. (1998). Doubly bound: The impact of gender and race on the politics of black women. *Political Psychology,* 19, 1, 169–184.

Gay and Lesbian Victory Foundation. (2000). A survey by the Gay and Lesbian Victory Foundation. http://www.victoryfund.org.

Geer, John. (1996). *From tea leaves to opinion polls.* New York: Columbia University Press.

Gelman, Andrew, and Little, Thomas C. (1998). Improving on probability weighting for household size. *Public Opinion Quarterly,* 62, 398–404.

Gelpi, Christopher, Feaver, Peter, and Reifler, Jason. (2004). Paying the human costs of war in Iraq. Paper presented at the Weatherhead Center, Harvard University, March 5.

Gerber, Alan S., and Green, Donald P. (1998). Rational learning and partisan attitudes. *American Journal of Political Science,* 42 (July), 794–818.

Gerbner, George, Gross, Larry, Morgan, Michael, and Signorelli, Nancy. (1986). Living with television: The dynamics of the cultivation process. In: J. Bryant and D. Zillman (Eds.), *Perspectives on media effects.* Hillsdale, NJ: Laurence Erlbaum.

Gergen, K., and Black, K. (1965). Aging, time perspective, and preferred solutions to international conflicts. *Journal of Conflict Resolution,* 9, 177–186.

Gielen, Une P., Adler, Leonore Loeb, and Milgram, N. (1992). *Psychology in an international perspective.* Amsterdam: Swets and Zeitlinger.

Gilbert, Richard, and Shiraev, Eric. (1992). Clinical psychology and psychotherapy in Russia. *Journal of Humanistic Psychology,* 32, 3, 28–40.

Gilens, Martin. (1995). Racial attitudes and opposition to welfare. *Journal of Politics,* 57, 4, 994–1014.

Gilens, Martin. (1996). Race and poverty in America: Public misperceptions and the American news media. *Public Opinion Quarterly,* 60, 515–541.

Gilligan, Carol. (1982). *In a different voice: Psychological theory of women's development.* Cambridge: Harvard University Press.

Ginsberg, Steve. (2000). Officials fear bias in bus survey. *Washington Post,* June 28, V04.

Gish, Nancy. (2000). Town board oks extension of term limit. *Buffalo News,* June 8, 5B.

Glad, Betty. (1980). *Jimmy Carter: In search of the big White House.* New York: Norton.

Glad, Betty, and Shiraev, Eric. (1999). (Eds.), *The Russian transformation.* New York: St. Martin's Press.

Glanville, Jennifer L. (1999). Political socialization or selection? Adolescent extracurricular participation and political activity in early adulthood. *Social Science Quarterly,* 80, 2 (June), 279–290.

Glaser, James M., and Gilens, Martin. (1997). Interregional migration and political resocialization. *Public Opinion Quarterly,* 61 (Spring), 72–81.

Glass, David, Squire, Peverill, and Wolfinger, Raymond. (1984). Voter turnout: An international comparison. *Public Opinion,* 6 (December/January), 49–55.

Glenn, Norval D., and Hefner, Ted. (1971). Further evidence of aging and party identification. *Public Opinion Quarterly,* 36, 31–47.

Glock, Charles. (1962). On the study of religious commitment. *Religious Education,* 62, 4, 98–110.

Glaser, James M. and Gilens, Martin. (1997). Interregional migration and political resocialization. *Public Opinion Quarterly* 61 (Spring), 72–86.

Glynn, Carroll J., Hayes, Andrew F., and Shanahan, James. (1997). Perceived support for one's opinions and willingness to speak out. A meta-analysis of survey studies on the spiral of silence. *Public Opinion Quarterly,* 61, 452–463.

Goertzel, Ted. (1994). Belief in conspiracy theories. *Political Psychology,* 15, 4, 731–742.

Goldstein, Amay, and Morin, Richard. (2002). Young voters' disengagement skews politics: Graying electorate's issues predominant, fueling trend. *Washington Post,* October 20, A08.

Golovaha, Y. and Panina, N. (1999). Protestniy Potencial Ukrainskogo Ibshestva [Protest Potential of Ukrainian Society. Sotis, 1999, no. 10: 31–40.

Gonzalez, C. (1998). Puerto Rico voters reject statehood. *Daily News* (New York), December 14, 5.

Goodnow, Jacqueline J. (1990). The socialization of cognition: What's involved? In James W. Stigler, Richard A. Shweder, and Gilbert S. Herdt (Eds.). *Cultural psychology: Essays on comparative human behavior,* 259–286. Cambridge: Cambridge University Press.

Gordon, Milton. (1964). *Assimilation in American life: The role of race, religion, and national origins.* New York: Oxford University Press.

Gore, P. M., and Rotter, J. B. (1963). A personality correlate of social action. *Journal of Personality,* 31, 58–64.

Gottlieb, Martin. (2000). *Campaigns don't count: How the media get American politics all wrong.* http://www.coxnews.com/2000/reports/ebook.

Gould, Stephen Jay. (1994). The geometer of race. *Discover,* 15, 65–81.

Gould, Stephen Jay. (1997). This view of life: Unusual unity. *Natural History,* 106, 69–71.

Gozman, Leonid and Etkind, Alexander. (1992). *The psychology of post-totalitarianism in Russia.* London: Centre for Research Into Communist Economies.

Graber, Doris. (1989). *Mass media and American politics.* 3rd edition. Washington, DC: CQ Press.

Graber, Doris. (2002). *Mass media and American politics.* 6th edition. Washington, DC: CQ Press.

Graber, Mark A. (2002). Surf's up! Protecting the privacy of health information on the Internet; we need new privacy laws and better encryption of information. *The Western Journal of Medicine.*

Graham, Bradley. (1999). Civilians, military seen growing apart: Study finds partisan armed forces "elite." *Washington Post,* October 18, A17.

Graham, Thomas W. (1986). *The politics of failure: Strategic nuclear arms control, public opinion, and domestic politics in the United States, 1945–1980.* PhD dissertation, Massachusetts Institute of Technology, Cambridge, MA.

Graham, Thomas W. (1988). The pattern and importance of public knowledge in the nuclear age. *Journal of Conflict Resolution* 32, 319–34.

Green, Donald, and Palmquist, B. (1994). How stable is party identification? *Political Behavior,* 16, 4, 437–452.

Green, Donald, Gerber, Alan, and De Boef, L. (1999). Tracking opinion over time: A method for reducing sampling error. *Public Opinion Quarterly,* (Summer) 63, 178–192.

Green, Joshua (2002). The Other War Room. *The Washington Monthly,* April. http://www.washingtonmonthly.com/search#2002.

Greenberg, Edward. (1981). Industrial democracy and the democratic citizen. *Journal of Politics,* 43, 964–981.

Greenberg, Stanley B. (1995). *Middle-class dreams: The politics and power of the new American majority.* New York: Times Books.

Greenstein, Fred. (1965). *Children and politics.* New Haven: Yale University Press.

Greenstein, Fred. (1965). Personality and political socialization: Theories of authoritarian and democratic character. *Annals,* 361, 81–95.

Greenwald, Anthony G. (1968). Cognitive learning, cognitive response to persuasion, and attitude change. In: A. Greenwald, T. Brock, and T. Ostrom (Eds.), *Psychological foundations of attitudes,* 147–170. New York: Academic Press.

Griffin, Kwanza L. (1999). Minorities blame cost more than bias in health care access survey. *Milwaukee Journal Sentinel,* October 14, 7.

Grillo, Thomas. (2000). Harris ranks below peers in survey on workers' comp judges. *Boston Globe,* April 15, C1.

Gross, Michael. (1995). Moral judgment, organizational incentives, and collective action in abortion politics. *Political Research Quarterly,* 48, 4, 827–836.

Gross, Michael. (1996). Moral reasoning and ideological affiliation: A cross-national study. *Political Psychology,* 17, 2, 317–338.

Groves, Robert M., and Lyberg, Lars E. (2001). An overview of nonresponse issues in telephone surveys. In: R. Groves, P. Biemer, L. Lyberg, W. Nicholis, and J. Waksberg, *Telephone survey methodology.* New York: John Wiley and Sons.

Gruca, Thomas S. (1996). Reporting poll results: Focusing on point spreads instead of percentages can be misleading. *Marketing Research,* 8 (Winter), 29–31.

Grush, Joseph E. (1980). Impact of candidate expenditures, regionality, and prior outcomes on the 1976 presidential primaries. *Journal of Personality and Social Psychology,* 38, 337–347.

Gryzunov, S. (1995). So far, nothing threatens fascism in Russia. *Izvestia,* June 6, 5.

Guinier, Lani. 2000. Make Every Vote Count. New York: The Nation.

Guth, James L., Green, J., Smidt, Corwin E., Kellstedt, Lyman A., and Poloma, Margaret M. (1997). *The bully pulpit: The politics of Protestant clergy.* Lawrence: University Press of Kansas.

Habermas, Jurgen. (1984). *Theory of communicative action.* Boston: Beacon Press.

Hall, G. Stanley. (1904). *Adolescence.* New York: Appleton.

Hall, Peter A. (1997). The role of interests, institutions, and ideas in the comparative political economy of the industrialized nations. In: M. I. Lichbach and A. S. Zuckerman (Eds.), *Comparative politics,* 174–207. London: Cambridge University Press.

Harden, Mike. (2000). Let's not talk, if you must use uncivil cell phone. *Columbus Dispatch,* April 21, 1H.

Harkness, Sara (1992). Human development in psychological anthropology. In Theodore Schwartz, White, Geoffrey M., and Lutz, Catherine A. (Eds.). New directions in psychological anthropology, 102–121. New York: Cambridge University Press.

Harris, Louis. (1973). The Anguish of Change. New York: Norton.

Hawley, Chandra. (1997). *Violence in the schools: Media hype or stark reality?* Center for Adolescent Studies, Indiana University. http://education.indiana.edu/cas/tt. June 6.

Headlee, Sue, and Elfin, Margery. (1996). *The cost of being female.* Westport, CT: Praeger.

Heider, Fritz. (1959). *The psychology of interpersonal relations.* New York: Wiley.

Heilbroner, Robert. (1993). Don't let stereotypes warp your judgments. In: V. Cyrus (Ed.), *Experiencing race, class, and gender in the United States,* 144–146. New York: McGraw-Hill.

Heiman, Gary W. (1996). *Basic statistics for the behavioral sciences.* Boston: Houghton Mifflin.

Heith, Diana. (1998). Staffing the White House public opinion apparatus. *Public Opinion Quarterly,* 62 (Summer), 165–189.

Hellas, Paul, and Lock, Andrew. (1981). *Indigenous psychologies the anthropolgy of self.* London: Academic Press.

Hennessy, Bernard. (1981). *Public opinion.* Elmont, CA: Wadsworth.

Henshaw, Stanley K., Singh, Susheela, and Haas, Taylor. (1999). Recent trends in abortion rates worldwide. *International Family Planning Perspectives,* 25, 1, 44–48.

Herald (Glasgow). (1999). Secretaries meet age bias. November 22, 4.

Hermans, J. M., and Kempen, J. G. (1998). Moving cultures: The perilous problems of cultural dichotomies in a globalizing society. *American Psychologist,* 53, 10, 1111–1120.

Hershey, Marjorie R. (1977). The politics of androgyny: Sex roles and attitudes toward women in politics. *American Politics Quarterly,* 5, 261–387.

Hess, Robert D., and Torney, Judith V. (1967). *The development of political attitudes in children.* Chicago: Aldine.

Hibbing, John R., and Theiss-Morse, Elizabeth. (1996). Civics is not enough: Teaching barbarics in K–12. *PS: Political Science and Politics,* 29 (March), 57–62.

Hibbing, John R., and Theiss-Morse, Elizabeth. (1998). The media's role in public negativity toward Congress: Distinguishing emotional reactions and cognitive evaluations. *American Journal of Political Science,* 4 (April), 475–498.

Hill, Kim Quaile. (1998). The policy agendas of the president and the mass public: A research validation and extension. *American Journal of Political Science,* 42, 4, 1328–1334.

Hinckley, Ronald. (1992). *People, polls, and policymakers: American public opinion and national security.* New York: Lexington Books.

Hochschild, Adam. (1997). *The time bind: When work becomes home and home becomes work.* New York: Henry Holt.

Hochschild, Jennifer. (1981). *What's fair? American beliefs about distributive justice.* Cambridge: Harvard University Press.

Hochschild, Jennifer, and Scott, Bridget. (1998). Governance and reform of public education in the United States. *Public Opinion Quarterly,* 62 (Spring), 79–120.

Hodgson, J. (2001). Poll shows UK Asians support military action. November 23. http://www.guardian.co.uk.

Hofstede, Geert. (1980). *Culture's consequences: International differences in work-related values.* London: Sage.

Hofstede, Geert. (1996). Gender stereotypes and partner preferences of Asian women in masculine and feminine cultures. *Journal of Cross-Cultural Psychology,* 27, 5 (September), 533–546.

Holhut, Randolph T. (1996). The myth of "liberal bias" in the media. *The Written Word* (online journal of economic, political, and social commentary). http://www.mdle.com/WrittenWord.

Holmes, Jack. (1985). *The mood/interest theory of American foreign policy.* Lexington: University of Kentucky.

Holsti, Ole. (1992). Public opinion and foreign policy: Challenges to the Almond-Lippmann consensus. *International Studies Quarterly,* 36, 439–466.

Holsti, Ole. (1996). *Public opinion and American foreign policy.* Ann Arbor: University of Michigan.

Holtz, Rolf, and Miller, Norman. (1985). Assumed similarity and opinion certainty. *Journal of Personality and Social Psychology,* 48, 890–898.

Hooghe, Marc. (1999). Participatie en de vorming van sociaal kapitaal: Een exploratie van het causaal verband tussen participatie en maatschappelijke houdingen. *Sociologische Gids,* 46, 6 (November-December), 494–520.

Hoskin, Marilyn. (1989). Socialization and anti-socialization: The case of immigrants. In: Roberta S. Sigel (Ed.), *Political learning in adulthood: A sourcebook of theory and research.* Chicago: University of Chicago Press.

Houston Chronicle. Staff. (1999). Wide gaps: White and minority military personnel see race differently. Star Edition, December 4, A44.

Hout, Michael. (1998). More universalism, less structural mobility: The American occupational structure in the 1980s. *American Journal of Sociology,* 95, 6 (May), 1358–1400.

Hovland, Carl I., and Weiss, Walter. (1951). The influence of source credibility on communication effectiveness. *Public Opinion Quarterly,* 15, 635–650.

Hovland, Carl I., Janis, Irving L., and Kelly, Harold H. (1953). *Communication and persuasion.* New Haven: Yale University Press.

Huckfeldt, Robert, and Sprague, John. (2000). Political consistency and inconsistency: The accessibility and stability of abortion attitudes. *Political Psychology,* 21, 1, 57–81.

Hughes, John, and Conway, Margaret. (1997). Public opinion and political participation. In: B. Norrander and C. Wilcox (Eds.), *Understanding public opinion,* 191–210. Washington, DC: CQ Press.

Hunsberger, Bruce. (1995). Religion and prejudice: The role of religious fundamentalism, quest, and right-wing authoritarianism. *Journal of Social Issues,* 51, 2, 113–129.

Hunt, Linda M., Arar, Nedal Hamdi, and Akana, Laurie L. (2000). Herbs, prayer, and insulin: Use of medical and alternative treatments by a group of Mexican American diabetes patients. *Journal of Family Practice,* 49 (March), 3, 216–223.

Huntington, Samuel. (1993). Clash of civilizations. *Foreign Affairs,* 72, 22–49.

Hyman, Herbert. (1959). *Political socialization.* Glencoe, IL: Free Press.

Inglehart, Ronald. (1990). *Culture shift in advanced industrial society.* Princeton: Princeton University Press.

Iwao, Sumiko, and Triandis, Harry C. (1993). Validity of auto- and heterostereotypes among Japanese and American students. *Journal of Cross-Cultural Psychology,* 24, 4, 428–444.

Iyengar, Shanto. (1991). *Is anyone responsible?* Chicago: University of Chicago Press.

Iyengar, Shanto, and Kinder, David. (1987). *News that matters.* Chicago: University of Chicago.

Jackman, Robert. (1987). Political institutions and voter turnout in the industrial democracies. *American Political Science Review,* 81 (June), 405–423.

Jackman, Robert, and Miller, Ross. (1995). Voter Turnout in the Industrial Democracies During the 1980s. *Comparative Political Studies,* 27: 467–92.

Jacobs, Lawrence, and Shapiro, Robert. (1994). Issues, candidate image, and priming: The use of private polls in Kennedy's 1960 presidential campaign. *American Political Science Review,* 88, 527–540.

Jacobs, Lawrence R., and Shapiro, Robert Y. (2000). *Politicians don't pander: Political manipulation and the loss of democratic responsiveness.* Chicago: University of Chicago Press.

Jacoby, William G. (1999). Levels of measurement and political research: An optimistic view. *American Journal of Political Science,* 43, 271–301.

Javeline, Debra. (1999). Response effects in polite culture: A test of acquiescence in Kazakhstan. *Public Opinion Quarterly,* 63 (Spring), 1–29.

Jaynes, Gerald D. (2000). Identity and economic performance. *Annals of the American Academy of Political and Social Science,* (March), 128–139.

Jenkins, Adelbert. (1995). *Psychology and African Americans, Second Edition.* Needham Heights: Allyn and Bacon.

Jennings, M. Kent. (1992). Ideological thinking among mass publics and political elites. *Public Opinion Quarterly,* 56, 419–441.

Jennings, M. Kent. (1996). Political knowledge over time and across generations. *Public Opinion Quarterly,* 60, 228–252.

Jennings, M. Kent, and Niemi, Richard. (1974). *The political character of adolescence: The influence of families and schools.* Princeton: Princeton University Press.

Jennings, M. Kent, and Niemi, Richard. (1981). *Generations and politics.* Princeton: Princeton University Press.

Jennings, M. Kent, and Stoker, Laura. (1999). *The persistence of the past: The class of 1965 turns 50.* Paper presented at the annual meeting of the Midwest Political Science Association, Chicago.

Jennings, M. Kent, and Markus, Gregory. (1986). Yuppie politics. *ISR Newsletter,* August 1986. Ann Arbor: University of Michigan.

Jentleson, Bruce W. (1992). The pretty prudent public: Post post-Vietnam American opinion on the use of military force. *International Studies Quarterly,* 36, 49–74.

Jentleson, Bruce W., and Rebecca L. Britton. (1998). Still pretty prudent: Post-cold war American public opinion on the use of military force. *Journal of Conflict Resolution,* 42, 395–417.

Jones, Lloyd P., and Meinhold, Stephen S. (1999). The secondary consequences of conducting polls in political science classes: A quasi-experimental test. *PS: Political Science and Politics,* September, 32, 603–604.

Jones-Correa, Michael. (1998). *Between two nations: The political predicament of Latinos in New York.* Ithaca, NY: Cornell University Press.

Joshi, Mary Sissons, and MacLean, Morag. (1997). Maternal expectations of child development in India, Japan, and England. *Journal of Cross-Cultural Psychology,* 28, 2, 219–234.

Juviler, Peter, and Stroschein, Sherrill. (1999). Missing boundaries of comparison: The political community. *Political Science Quarterly,* (Fall) 114, 435–453.

Kagay, Michael. (1999). Public opinion and polling during presidential scandal and impeachment. *Public Opinion Quarterly,* 63, 449–463.

Kagitcibasi, Cigdem. (1996). *Family and human development across cultures: A view from the other side.* Mahwah, NJ: Lawrence Erlbaum.

Kahneman, Daniel, and Tversky, Amos. (1973). On the psychology of prediction. *Psychological Review,* 80, 237–251.

Kaiser, Robert G. (2000a). Predictions for 2000: Is this any way to pick a winner? *Washington Post,* May 26, A1.

Kaiser, Robert G. (2000b). Foreign disservice. *Washington Post,* April 16, B1.

Kallgren, C.A. and Wood, W. (1986). Access to attitude-relevant information in memory as determinant of attitude-behavior consistency. *Journal of Experimental Social Psychology,* 22, 328–338.

Kalyvas, Stathis N. (1994). Hegemony breakdown: The collapse of nationalization in Britain and France. *Politics and Society,* 22, 3, 316–348.

Kampwirth, Karen. (1998). Feminism, antifeminism, and electoral politics in postwar Nicaragua and El Salvador. *Political Science Quarterly,* 113 (Summer), 259–279.

Keeley, Lawrence. (1997). *War before civilization.* New York: Oxford University Press.

Keen, Sara. (1986). *Faces of the enemy. Reflections of the hostile imagination.* New York: Harper and Row.

Kegley, Charles W., Jr., and Eugene R. Wittkopf. (1991). *American foreign policy: Pattern and process.* 4th ed. New York: St. Martin's.

Kegley, Charles W., Jr., and Eugene R. Wittkopf. (Eds.) (1987). *The domestic sources of American foreign policy.* New York: St. Martin's.

Keim, Curtis A. (1999). *Mistaking Africa: Curiosities and inventions of the American mind.* Boulder, CO: Westview Press.

Keith, Bruce, Magleby, David, Nelson, Candice, Orr, Elizabeth, Westlye, Mark, and Wolfinger, Raymond. (1992). *The myth of the independent voter.* Berkeley and Los Angeles: University of California Press.

Kelley, Harold H. (1986). The process of causal attribution. *American Psychologist,* 28, 107–128.

Kelley, Stanley, Jr. (1983). *Interpreting elections.* Princeton, NJ: Princeton University Press.

Kelly, Michael. (2001). The monster and the minority. *Washington Post,* January 24, A15.

Kelly, Ursula. (1997). Schooling desire: literacy, cultural politics, and pedagogy. London: Routledge.

Keltikangas-Jarvinen, Liisa and Terav, Tuuli. (1996). Social Decision-Making Strategies in Individualist and Collectivist Cultures: A Comparison of Finnish and Estonian Adolescents. *Journal of Cross-Cultural Psychology,* 6, 714–732.

Kennedy, John F. (1963). Foreword. In: *Challenge to Americans: The struggle we face and how to help win it.* Approved by the Department of State, Washington, DC. New York: Advertising Council.

Kerbel, Matthew. (2000). *If it bleeds, it leads: An anatomy of television news.* Boulder, CO: Westview.

Kern, Marian, and Just, Montague. (1995). The focus group method, political advertising, campaign news, and the construction of candidate images. *Political Communication,* 12, 127–145.

Key, V. O. (1966). *The responsible electorate.* New York: Vintage Books.

Kharchev, D. (1994). *Mnenia o Mire i Mir Mneni.* [Opinions about the world and a world of opinions]. Issues 1–4. Moscow, Russia.

Kimball, D. C. (1995). *Public approval of Congress: To what extent do people respond to cues provided by current events and elite discourse?* Paper presented at the annual meeting of the Midwest Political Science Association, Chicago.

Kinder, Donald, and Sanders, Lynn. (1996). *Divided by color: Racial politics and democratic ideals.* Chicago: University of Chicago Press.

Kinder, Donald, and Kiewiet, D. Roderick. (1979). Economic discontent and political behavior: The role of personal grievances and collective judgments in congressional voting. *American Journal of Political Science,* 23, 3, 495–527.

Kinder, Donald and Kiewiet, D. Roderick. (1981). Sociotropic Politics: The American Case. *British Journal of Political Science,* 11 (April), 129–61.

Kinder, Donald, and Mendelberg, Tali. (1995). Cracks in American apartheid: The political impact of prejudice among desegregated whites. *Journal of Politics,* 57, 2, 402–424.

King, David C. and Karabell, Zachary. (2003). *The generation of trust: public confidence in the U.S. military since Vietnam.* Washington, DC: AEI Press.

Kirkpatrick, Samuel A., and Jones, Melvin E. (1974). Issue public and the electoral system: The role of issues in electoral change. In: A. Wilcox (Ed.), *Public opinion and political attitudes.* New York: John Wiley.

Kirschenman, Joleen, and Neckerman, Kathryn M. (1991). We'd love to hire them, but: The meaning of race for employers. In: C. Jencks and P. Peterson (Eds.), *The urban underclass,* 203–234. Washington, DC: Brookings Institution.

Klapper, Joseph T. (1960). *The effects of mass communication.* New York: Free Press.

Klicperova, Martina. (2002). The Czech Republic: Transitional worries. In: V. Shlapentokh and E. Shiraev (Eds.), *Fears in post-communist societies,* 29–50. New York: Palgrave.

Knäuper, Bärbel. (1998). Filter questions and question interpretation. *Public Opinion Quarterly,* 62 (Spring), 70–78.

Knäuper, Bärbel. (1999). The impact of age and education on response order effects in attitude measurement. *Public Opinion Quarterly,* 63 (Fall), 347–370.

Knickerbocker, Brad. (2002). In Oregon, a bold healthcare proposal. *Christian Science Monitor,* September 24, 1.

Koch, Jeffrey W. (1998). Political rhetoric and political persuasion: The changing structure of citizens' preferences on health insurance during policy debate. *Public Opinion Quarterly,* 62 (Summer), 209–229.

Kohn, Melvin. (1969). *Class and conformity.* Homewood, IL: Dorsey.

Kohn, Melvin. (1980). Job complexity and adult personality. In: N. Smelser and E. Erikson (Eds.), *Themes of work and love in adulthood,* 430–439. Cambridge, MA: Harvard University Press.

Kolata, Gina. (1996). One in five nurses tell survey they helped patients die. *New York Times,* May 23, A14.

Kolbert, Elizabeth. (1993). New Jersey experts try to figure out where they went wrong. *New York Times,* November 4, A9.

Kohlberg, Laurence. (1981). Essays on Moral Development. New York: Harper and Row.

Kon, I. S. (1979). Psychologya yunosheskogo vozrasta [Psychology of adolescence]. Moscow: Prosveshenie.

Korotich, Vitaly. (2000). *Ot pervogo litsa* [From the personal account]. Moscow: ACT.

Koulish, Robert. (1998). Citizenship service learning: Becoming citizens by assisting immigrants. *PS: Political Science and Politics,* 31 (September), 562–567.

Kravitz, David A., Turner, Marlene E., Levine, Edward L., Chaves, Wanda, Brannick, Michael T., Denning, Donna L., Russell, Craig J., and Conrad, Maureen A. (1997). *Affirmative action: A review of psychological and behavioral research.* Bowling Green, OH: Society for Industrial and Organizational Psychology.

Krieger, Samuel. (2001). Russian Immigrants in America: Fears and Hopes. In Shlapentokh, V. and Shiraev, E. (Eds.), *Fears in Post-Communist Societies.* New York: Palgrave.

Krugman, Paul. (1997). Superiority complex. *New Republic,* November 3, 20–21.

Krysian, Maria. (1998). Privacy and the expression of white racial attitudes: A comparison across three contexts. *Public Opinion Quarterly,* 62 (Winter), 506–544.

Kuhn, Thomas E. (1962/1970). *The structure of scientific revolutions.* Chicago: University of Chicago Press.

Kull, Steven. (1999). *Expecting more to say: The American public on its role in government decision making.* Washington, DC: Center on Policy Attitudes.

Kull, Steven. (2000). *Americans on health care policy: A study of US public attitudes.* Washington, DC: CPA.

Kull, Steven, and Destler, I. M. (1999). *Misreading the public: The myth of a new isolationism.* Washington, DC: Brookings.

Kull, Steven, and Ramsay, Clay. (1997). *The foreign policy gap: How policy makers misread the public.* Washington, DC: Program on International Policy Attitudes.

Kurtz, Howard. (2000). Are the media tilting to Gore? *Washington Post,* September 25, A01.

LaBalme, Natalie. (2000). Constraint, catalyst, or political tool? The French public and foreign policy. In: R. Shapiro et al. *Decisionmaking in a glass house.* Lanham, MD: Rowman and Littlefield.

Lafferty, William. (1989). Work as a source of political learning. In: Roberta S. Sigel (Ed.), *Political learning in adulthood: A sourcebook of theory and research.* Chicago: University of Chicago Press.

Lagosi, Nick. (2000). Village considers whether to disband police department. *Milwaukee Journal Sentinel,* November 17, 2B.

Laino, Charlene. (2000). *Many don't wash hands after using public restrooms.* http://www.msnbc.com. September 19.

Langaney, André. (1988). *Les hommes, passe, present, conditionnel* [The men, past, present, conditional]. Paris: Armand Colin.

Langton, Kenneth. (1969). *Political socialization.* New York: Oxford University Press.

Lapinski, John, Peltola, Pia, Shaw, Greg, and Yang, Alan. (1997). Immigrants and immigration. *Public Opinion Quarterly,* 61, 356–683.

Larson, Eric. (1996). *Casualties and consensus: The historical role of casualties in domestic support for U.S. military operations.* Santa Monica, CA: Rand.

Lasalandra, Michael. (2000). Women docs cite pervasive bias at medical schools. *Boston Herald,* June 6, A29.

Lash, Steve. (1999). Executions are highest since 1951; Texas tally of 33 tops the national toll of 96. *Houston Chronicle,* December 13, A1.

Latané, Bibb, and Nida, Steve. (1981). Ten years of research on group size and helping. *Psychological Bulletin,* 89, 2, 308–324.

Latané, Bibb. (1981). The psychology of social impact. *American Psychologist,* 36, 343-356.

Lau, Richard R., Lee Sigelman, Carolyn Heldman, and Paul Babbitt. (1999). The effects of negative political advertisements: A meta-analytic assessment. American Political Science Review 93: 851–875.

Lavine, Howard, Bordiga, Eugene, and Sullivan, John L. (2000). On the relationship between attitude involvement and attitude accessibility: Toward a cognitive-motivational model of political information-processing. *Political Psychology,* 21, 1, 81–107.

Lavine, Howard, Bordiga, Eugene, Sullivan, John L., and Thomsen, Cynthia J. (1996). The relationship of national and personal issue salience to attitude accessibility on foreign and domestic policy issues. *Political Psychology,* 17, 2, 293–316.

Lawson, Edwin D. (1975). Flag preference as an indicator of patriotism in Israeli children. *Journal of Cross-Cultural Psychology,* 6, 490–499.

Layman, Geoffrey C. (1997). Religion and political behavior in the United States: The impact of beliefs, affiliations, and commitment from 1980 to 1994. *Public Opinion Quarterly,* 61, 288–316.

Lazarsfeld, Paul, Berelson, Bernard, and Gaudet, Hazel. (1948). *The people's choice: How the voter makes up his mind in a presidential campaign.* New York: Columbia University Press.

LeBon, Gustave. (1896). *The crowd: A study of the popular mind.* London: Ernest Benn.

Lem, Sharon. (2000). Guys are living it up: Life expectancy, gender gap narrowing. *Toronto Sun,* June 7, News 8.

Lenart, Silvio. (1994). *Sharing political attitudes: The impact of interpersonal communication and mass media.* Thousand Oaks, CA: Sage.

LeoGrande, William M. (1993). The controversy over contra aid, 1981–1990: An historical narrative. In: R. Sobel, *Public opinion in U.S. foreign policy: The controversy over contra aid.* Lanham, MD: Rowman and Littlefield.

Leung, Kwok, and Drasgow, Fritz. (1986). Relation between self-esteem and delinquent behavior. *Journal of Cross-Cultural Psychology,* 17, 2, 151–167.

Levin, Shana, Sidanius, Jim, Rabinowitz, Joshua L., and Federico, Christopher. (1998). Ethnic identity, legitimizing ideologies, and social status: A matter of ideological asymmetry. *Political Psychology,* 19, 2, 373–404.

Levine, J., Carmines, Edward, and Sniderman, Paul. (1999). The empirical dimensionality of racial stereotypes. *Public Opinion Quarterly* 63, (Fall), 371–384.

Levine, Myron A. (1992). *Presidential campaigns and elections: Issues, images, and partisanship.* Itasca, IL: Peacock.

Levine, Robert V. (1992). Social time: The heartbeat of culture. In: T. Hurscheberg (Ed.), *One world, many cultures.* New York: Macmillan.

Levine, Robert V., and Bartlett, K. (1984). Pace of life, punctuality, and coronary heart disease in six countries. *Journal of Cross-Cultural Psychology,* 15, 2, 233–255.

Levinson, Daniel. (1978). *The seasons of a man's life.* New York: Knopf.

Levinson, Daniel. (Ed.) (1989). *Family violence in cross-cultural perspective.* Newbury Park, CA: Sage.

Levy, David. (1997). *Tools of critical thinking.* Needham Heights, MA: Allyn and Bacon.

Lichter, Robert. (1986). *Media Elite: America's New Powerbrokers.* New York: Woodbine House.

Lien, Pei-te. (1994). Ethnicity and political participation: A comparison between Asian and Mexican Americans. *Political Behavior,* 16, 2, 237–264.

Lien, Pei-te. (1997). *The political participation of Asian Americans.* New York: Garland.

Link, Michael W., and Oldendick, Robert W. (1999). Call screening: Is it really a problem for survey research? *Public Opinion Quarterly,* 63 (Winter), 577–589.

Lippmann, Walter. (1922). *Public opinion.* New York: Harcourt Brace.

Lipset, Seymour Martin. (1960). *Political man.* Garden City, NY: Doubleday.

Littlewood, Thomas. (2000). *Calling elections: The history of horse-race journalism.* Notre Dame, IN: University of Notre Dame Press.

Lloyd-McGarvey, E., Sheldon-Keller, A., and Canterbury, R. (1996). Date rape on the college campus: Does alcohol use make it excusable? Unpublished manuscript.

Lord, C., Ross, L., and Lepper, M. (1979). Biased assimilation and attitude polarization: The effects of prior theories on subsequently considered evidence. *Journal of Personality and Social Psychology,* 37, 2098–2109.

Loth, Renee. (2000). Safe choice, high price: Women trade rights for security, creating a "freedom gap." *Boston Globe,* June 25, Focus E2.

Lovell, J., and Stiehm, J. (1989). Military service and political socialization. In: Roberta S. Sigel (Ed.), *Political learning in adulthood: A sourcebook of theory and research.* Chicago: University of Chicago Press.

Lublin, David. (2002). The real story in Georgia. *Washington Post,* August 27, A15.

Lucas, Greg. (2000). *San Francisco Chronicle,* January 14, News 20.

Luker, Kristin. (1996). *Dubious conception: The politics of teenage pregnancy.* Cambridge, MA: Harvard University Press.

Luttwak, Edward. (1990). *Strategy: The logic of war and peace.* Cambridge, MA: Belknap Press of Harvard University Press.

Ma, Hing Keung, and Cheung, Chau-Kiu. (1996). A cross-cultural study of moral stage structure in Hong Kong Chinese, English, and Americans. *Journal of Cross-Cultural Psychology,* 27, 6, November, 700–713.

Maccoby, Eleanor E., Mathews, Richard E., and Morton, Anton S. (1954). Youth and political change. *Public Opinion Quarterly,* 18, 23–39.

Macionis, John. (2003). *Sociology.* Upper Saddle River, NJ: Prentice Hall.

Maddox, Bronwen. (2001). Japan dips toe in military waters. *Times* (London), November 29, Overseas News 1.

Madse, M. (1986). Developmental and cross-cultural differences in the cooperative and competitive behavior of young children. *Journal of Cross-Cultural Psychology,* 2, 365–371.

Mair, Peter. (2000). Apathy on the march: As voter turnout continues to fall across most of Europe, we have little to feel smug about in relation to the US election results. *Guardian* (London), November 20, 21.

Malico, Melinda, and Peterman, Kara. (1999). School violence continues to decline: Multiple homicide in schools rise. October 19. www.ed.gov/PressReleases/10-1999/violence.html.

Mann, Sheilah. (1999). What the survey of American college freshmen tells us about their interest in politics and political science. *PS: Political Science and Politics,* 32 (June), 263–268.

Marsella, Anthony J. (1998). Toward a "global-community psychology": Meeting the needs of a changing world. *American Psychologist,* 53, 12, 1282–1291.

Marcuse, Herbert. (1964). *One-dimensional man.* Boston: Beacon Press.

Margolis, Michael, and Mauser, Gary. (1989). *Manipulating Public Opinion: Essays on Public Opinion as a Dependent Variable.* Pacific Grove, CA: Brooks/Cole.

Markman, Stephen, and Cassell, Paul. (1988). Protecting the innocent: A response to the Bedau-Radelet Study. *Stanford Law Review,* 41, 1 (November).

Marshall, Thomas. (1997). Public opinion and the Supreme Court: The insulated court? In: Barbara Norrander and Clyde Wilcox (Eds.), *Understanding public opinion,* 269–280. Washington, DC: CQ Press.

Martin, Elizabeth. (1999). Who knows who lives here? Within-household disagreement as a source of survey coverage error. *Public Opinion Quarterly,* 63, 220–236.

Maslow, Abraham. (1954). *Motivation and Personality.* New York: Harper & Row.

Mathi, Braema. (2000). Only 8 countries have closed gender gaps. *Straits Times* (Singapore), June 10, World 18.

Matsuda, N. (1985). Strong, quasi-, and weak conformity among Japanese in the modified Asch procedure. *Journal of Cross-Cultural Psychology,* 16, 83–97.

Matsumoto, David. (1994). *People: Psychology from a cultural perspective.* Pacific Grove, CA: Brooks/Cole.

Mayton, Daniel, Ball-Rokeach, Sandra, and Loges, William. (1994). Human values and social issues: An introduction. *Journal of Social Issues,* 50, 4, 1–9.

McBride, A. (1998). Television, individualism, and social capital. *PS: Political Science and Politics,* 31 (Fall), 542–553.

McBurney, Donald. (2001). *Research Methods.* Belmont, CA: Wadsworth.

McCann, James A. (1995). Nomination politics and ideological polarization: Assessing the attitudinal effects of campaign involvement. *Journal of Politics,* 57, 1, 101–120.

McClain, Dylan L. (2000). A growing gender gap (and it's not what you think). *New York Times,* June 14, G1.

McClosky, Herbert. (1964). Consensus and ideology in American politics. *American Political Science Review,* 58, 2, 361–382.

McCourt, Kathleen. (1977). *Working-class women and grass-roots politics.* Bloomington: Indiana University Press.

McCullough, David. (1992). *Truman.* New York: Simon and Schuster.

McDonagh, Eileen. (1999). Assimilated leaders: Democratization, political inclusion, and female leadership. *Harvard International Review.* October. http://www.hir.harvard.edu.

McGuire, William J. (1968). Personality and susceptibility to social influence. In: E. F. Borgatta and W. W. Lambert (Eds.), *Handbook of personality theory and research,* 1130–1187. Chicago: Rand-McNally.

McLaughlin, Abraham. (2001). How far Americans would go to fight terror. *Christian Science Monitor,* November 14, 1.

Merida, Kevin. (1996). New parents voting for three. *Washington Post,* October 2, A1.

Merom, Gil. (1999). Israel's national security and the myth of exceptionalism. *Political Science Quarterly,* 114, 3, 409–434.

Merriam, Charles E., and Gosnell, Herbert F. (1924). *Nonvoting: Causes and method of control.* Chicago: University of Chicago Press.

Milgram, Stanley. (1963). Behavioral study of obedience. *Journal of Abnormal and Social Psychology,* 67, 371–378.

Miller, J. (1984). Culture and the development of everyday social explanation. *Journal of Personality and Social Psychology,* 46, 961–978.

Miller, Joanne M., and Krosnick, Jon A. (1998). The impact of candidate name order on election outcomes. *Public Opinion Quarterly,* 62 (Fall), 291–330.

Miller, Warren E., and Shanks, J. Merrill. (1996). *The new American voter.* Cambridge, MA: Harvard University Press.

Miller, Warren E., and Stokes, Donald. (1963). Constituency influence in Congress. *American Political Science Review,* 57, 45–56.

Mills, C. Wright. (1959). *The Sociological Imagination.* New York: Oxford.

Mitchell, Susan. (1998). *American attitudes: Who thinks what about the issues that shape our lives.* New York: New Strategies.

Mohai, Paul, and Bryant, Bunyan. (1998). Is there a "race" effect on concern for environmental quality? *Public Opinion Quarterly,* 62 (Winter), 475–505.

Monroe, Alan. (1998.) Public opinion and policy. *Public Opinion Quarterly,* 62, (Spring), 6–28.

Monroe, Kristen. (1995). Psychology and rational actor theory. *Political Psychology,* 16, 1, 1–21.

Monroe, Kristen, and Kreidie, L. (1997). The perspective of Islamic fundamentalists and the limits of rational choice theory. *Political Psychology,* 18, 19–44.

Moodie, E., Markova, I., and Plichtova, J. (1995). Lay representations of democracy: A study in two cultures. *Culture and Psychology,* 1: 423–453.

More, David W., and Jones, Jeffrey M. (2002). Higher turnout among Republicans key to victory: Major divisions among Americans across the country. Gallup News Service. November 7. http://www.gallup.com.

Moreno, E. (1999). *Explaining voter turnout in presidential democracies: A comparative analysis.* Paper presented at the 1999 Western Political Science Association Annual Meeting, Seattle, WA, March 25–27.

Morin, Richard. (2000). The exit polls face extinction. *Washington Post,* March 16, A19.

Morin, Richard. (2004). Surveying the damage: Exit polls can't always predict winners, so don't expect them to. *Washington Post* National Weekly, November 21, B01.

Morris, Aldon D., Hatchett, Shirley J., and Brown, Ronald E. (1989). Black political socialization. In: Roberta S. Sigel (Ed.), *Political learning in adulthood: A sourcebook of theory and research.* Chicago: University of Chicago Press.

Moscovici, Serge. (1981). Foreword. In: P. Hellas and A. Lock, *Indigenous psychologies.* London: Academic Press.

Moskowitz, David, and Stroh, Patrick. (1994). Psychological sources of electoral racism. *Political Psychology,* 15, 2, 307–329.

Mueller, John. (1973). *War, presidents, and public opinion.* New York: Wiley.

Mueller, John. (1994). *Policy and opinion in the Gulf War.* Chicago: University of Chicago.

Murphy, Caryle. (2000). Muslims see new clouds of suspicion. *Washington Post,* November 27, B01.

Naito, Takashi, and Gielen, Uwe P. (1992). Tatemae and Honne: A study of moral relativism in Japanese culture. In: U. Gielen, L. Adler, and N. Milgram (Eds.), *Psychology in international perspective.* Amsterdam: Swetsand Zeitlinger.

National Review Online. (2000). The Guilty are Executed. June 23. http://www.nationalreview.com

National Voter Registration Act of 1993. Public Law 103-31, May 20, 1993. 103rd Congress.

Naumetz, Tim, and O'Neil, Peter. (2000). Don't impose mandatory voting in elections. *Gazette* (Montreal), December 20.

Neal, Terry, and Morin, Richard. (1998). For voters, it's back toward the middle. *Washington Post,* November 5, A33.

Neuman, W. Russell. (1986). *The paradox of mass politics: Knowledge and opinion in the American electorate.* Cambridge, MA: Harvard University Press.

Neustadt, Richard E. (1990). *Presidential power and the modern presidents: The politics of leadership from Roosevelt to Reagan.* New York: Free Press.

Newcomb, Theodore. (1943). *Personality and social change: Attitude formation in a student community.* New York: Dryden Press.

Newport, Frank. (1999). Some change over time in American attitudes towards homosexuality, but negativity remains. *Poll Releases,* March 1. Gallup News Service. http://www.gallup.com/poll.

New York Times Editorial Desk. (2000). Harassment of gays in the military. *New York Times,* March 28, A22.

Nie, Norman, Verba, Sidney, and Petrocik, Jon. (1976). *The changing American voter.* Cambridge, MA: Harvard University Press.

Niemi, Richard, and Junn, Jane. (1998). *Civic education: What makes students learn.* New Haven: Yale University Press.

Nimmo, Dan. (1970). *The Political Persuaders: The Techniques of Modern Election Campaigns.* Englewood Cliffs, NJ: Prentice-Hall.

Nisbet, Robert. (2000). *Twilight of authority.* Indianapolis, IN: Liberty Fund.

Nisbett, Richard E., and Ross, Lee. (1980). *Human inference: Strategies and shortcomings of social judgment.* Englewood Cliffs, NJ: Prentice Hall.

Noelle-Neumann, Elizabeth. (1986). *The spiral of silence: Public opinion—our social skin.* Chicago: University of Chicago Press.

Norrander, Barbara. (1997). The independence gap and the gender gap. *Public Opinion Quarterly,* 61 (Fall), 464–476.

Norrander, Barbara. (1999). The evolution of the gender gap. *Public Opinion Quarterly,* 63 (Winter), 566–567.

Norris, Pippa. (2000). *A virtuous circle: Political communications in post-industrial societies: Communication, society, and politics.* New York: Cambridge University Press.

Norris, Pippa. (Ed.) (1997). *Passages to power: Legislative recruitment in advanced democracies.* Cambridge: Cambridge University Press.

Norris, Pippa, and Lovenduski, Joni. (1995). *Political recruitment: Gender, race, and class in the British Parliament.* Cambridge: Cambridge University Press.

Nye, Joseph S., Jr. (2002). *The paradox of American power: Why the world's only superpower can't go it alone.* New York: Oxford University Press.

Nye, Joseph S., Jr. (2004). *The power game: A Washington novel.* New York: Public Affairs.

Nye, Joseph S., Jr. (2004a). *Soft power: The means to success in world politics.* New York: Public Affairs.

O'Connor, Karen, and Sabato, Larry. (1997/2002). *American government: Continuity and change.* Needham Heights, MA: Allyn and Bacon.

Offe, Claus. (1996). *Varieties of transition: The east European and east German experience: Studies in contemporary German social thought.* Boston: MIT Press.

Ong, Paul, and Nakanishi, Don. (1996). Becoming citizens, becoming voters: The naturalization and political participation of Asian immigrants. In: B. Hing and R. Lee (Eds.), *Reframing the immigration debate,* 275–305. Los Angeles: LEAP and UCLA Asian American Studies Center.

Opotow, Susan, and Clayton, Susan. (1994). Green justice: Conceptions of fairness and the natural world. *Journal of Social Issues,* 50, 3, 1–11.

Oppenheimer, Martin. (1972). What is the new working class? *New Politics,* 15, 29–43.

Osborn, Alex. (1957). *Applied imagination.* New York: Scribners.

Owen, Diana. (1997). Mixed signals: Generation X's attitudes toward the political system. In: S. Craig and S. Bennett (Eds.), *After the boom: The politics of Generation X.* Lanham, MD: Rowman and Littlefield.

Owen, Virginia. (2000). An interview by Katie Sampson. *Independent* (London), July 5, 7.

Page, Benjamin I., and Shapiro, Robert Y. (1988). Foreign policy and the rational public. *Journal of Conflict Resolution,* 32, 211–247.

Page, Benjamin I., and Shapiro, Robert Y. (1992). *The rational public: Fifty years of trends in Americans' preferences.* Chicago: University of Chicago Press.

Page, Benjamin I., and Shapiro, Robert Y. (1994). Democratic responsiveness? Untangling the links between public opinion and policy. *Political Science and Politics,* 27, 25–28.

Page, Susan (2000). The male vote stands as Gore's Achilles' heel. *USA Today,* April 26, A1.

Paine, H. J. (1977). Attitudes and patterns of alcohol use among Mexican Americans: Implications for service delivery. *Journal of Studies on Alcohol,* 38, 544–553.

Panagakis, Nick. (1989). Incumbent races: Closer than they appear. *Polling Report,* February 27, 1–3.

Panagakis, Nick. (1999). Response to "Was 1966 a worse year for polls than 1948?" *Public Opinion Quarterly,* 63 (Summer), 278–281.

Paniotto, V., and Kharchenko, N. (2000). *Poverty and social policy in Ukraine in 1995–1999.* A study conducted by Kiev International Institute of Sociology (KIIS) and presented at a conference sponsored by Michigan State University on post–Cold War fears, Washington, DC, April 15.

Paolino, Phillip (1995). Group-salient issues and group representation: Support for women candidates in the 1992 Senate elections. *American Journal of Political Science,* 39, 294–313.

Parillo, Vincent. (1997). *Strangers to these shores.* Needham Heights, MA: Allyn and Bacon.

Parsons, Talcott. (1964/1951). *The social system.* New York: Free Press.

Patterson, Thomas. (1993). *Out of order.* New York: Knopf.

Perkins, Anne. (1999). What is it with women and the Euro? *Guardian,* January 7, 6.

Petersen, Anne C. (1988). Adolescent development. *Annual Review of Psychology,* 39, 583–607.

Petrovsky, A. (1978). *The psychological theory of the collective.* Moscow: Academy of Sciences.

Petty, R. E., and Cacioppo, J. T. (1979). Issue involvement can increase or decrease persuasion by enhancing message-relevant cognitive responses. *Journal of Personality and Social Psychology,* 37, 1915–1926.

Piaget, Jean, and Weil, A. (1951). The development in children of the idea of the homeland and of relations with other countries. *International Social Science Bulletin,* 3, 561–578.

Pitkin, John R., Myers, Dowell, Simmons, Patrick A., and Megbolugbe, Isaac F. (1997). *Immigration and housing in the United States: Trends and prospects*. Report of early findings from the Fannie Mae Foundation Immigration Research Project.

Plous, S. (1996). Ten myths about affirmative action. *Journal of Social Issues,* 52 (Winter), 4, 25–32.

Plutzer, Eric, and Zipp, John F. (1996). Identity politics, partisanship, and voting for women candidates. *Public Opinion Quarterly,* 60 (May), 30–57.

Plutzer, Eric, Maney, Ardith, and O'Connor, Robert E. (1998). Ideology and elites' perceptions of the safety of new technologies. *American Journal of Political Science,* 42 (January), 190–209.

Pollock, J. (1975). Early socialization and elite behavior. In: D. Schwartz and S. Schwartz (Eds.), *New directions in political socialization.* New York: Free Press.

Pomper, Gerald. (1975). *Voters' choice.* New York: Dodd, Mead.

Popkin, Samuel. (1991). *The reasoning voter: Communication and persuasion in presidential campaigns.* Chicago: University of Chicago Press.

Portes, Alessandro, and Bach, Robert. (1985). *Latin journey: Cuban and Mexican immigrants to the US.* Berkley: University of California Press.

Powell, G. B. (1986). American voter turnout in comparative perspective. *American Political Science Review,* 80 (March), 17–43.

Powlick, Philip J. (1991). The attitudinal bases for responsiveness to public opinion among American foreign policy officials. *Journal of Conflict Resolution,* 35, 4, 611–642.

Pratkanis, A. (1988). The attitude heuristic and selective fact identification. *British Journal of Social Psychology,* 27, 257–263.

Pratto, Felicia, Tatar, Deborah G., and Conway-Lanz, Sahar. (1999). Who gets what and why: Determinants of social allocations. *Political Psychology,* 20, 1, 127–150.

Prendergast, William B. (1999). *The Catholic voter in American politics: The passing of the Democratic monolith.* Washington, DC: Georgetown University Press.

Presidential Debates (2000). *The first 2000 Gore-Bush presidential debate: October 3, 2000.* Transcript. Clark Athletic Center at the University of Massachusetts in Boston. Moderator: Jim Lehrer.

Price, D. (1999). Opposing anti-gay bias becomes the consensus. *Detroit News,* August 2, Opinion A9.

Program on International Policy Attitudes. (2000). *Americans on globalization: A study of U.S. public attitudes.* March 28. A special report. http://www.policyattitudes.org.

Program on International Policy Attitudes. (2001). *Americans on population.* July 17. http://www.policyattitudes.org.

Pruitt, Dean, Rubin, Jeffrey F., and Sung, Hee Kim. (1986). *Social conflict: Escalation, stalemate, and settlement.* New York: Random House.

Punetha, D., Giles, H., and Young, L. (1987). Ethnicity and immigrant values: Religion and language choice. *Journal of Language and Social Psychology,* 6, 229–241.

Putnam, Robert. (2000). *Bowling Alone: The Collapse and Revival of American Community.* New York: Simon and Schuster.

Putnam, Robert D. (1995). Tuning in, tuning out: The strange disappearance of social capital in America. *PS: Political Science and Politics,* 28 (December), 664–683.

Raden, D. (1994). Are symbolic racism and traditional prejudice part of a contemporary authoritarian attitude syndrome? *Political Behavior,* 16, 3, 365–381.

Raghubr, Priya, and Johar, Gita V. (1999). Hong Kong 1997 in context. *Public Opinion Quarterly,* 63 (Winter), 543–565.

Rahn, Wendy. (1998). *Decline of American national identity among young Americans: Diffuse emotion, commitment, and social trust: A data essay.* Future of Democracy Workshop, Annenberg Center, Washington, DC, April 20.

Rao, P. V. L. N. (2002). Should opinion polls be banned? *Hindu,* February 12. Online edition.

Raviv, Amiram, Raviv, Alona, Sadeh, Ari, and Silberstein, Ora. (1998). The reaction of the youth in Israel to the assassination of Prime Minister Rabin. *Political Psychology,* 19, 2, 255–278.

Reimers, David. (1998). *Unwelcome strangers: American identity and the turn against immigration.* New York: Columbia University Press.

Reinish, Jane. (1979). Prenatal influences on cognitive abilities. In: M. Wittig (Ed.), *Sex-related differences in cognitive functioning.* New York: Academic Press.

Renshon, Stanley. (1975a). The role of personality development in political socialization. In: D. Schwartz and S. Schwartz (Eds.), *New directions in political socialization.* New York: Free Press.

Renshon, Stanley. (1975b). Birth order and political socialization. In: D. Schwartz and S. Schwartz (Eds.), *New directions in political socialization.* New York: Free Press.

Renshon, Stanley. (1989). Psychological perspectives on theories of adult development and the political socialization of leaders. In: Roberta S. Sigel (Ed.), *Political learning in adulthood: A sourcebook of theory and research.* Chicago: University of Chicago Press.

Renshon, Stanley. (1994). The psychology of the Clinton presidency: First appraisals. *Political Psychology,* 15, 375–394.

RePass, David. (1971). Issue salience and party choice. *American Political Science Review,* 65 (June), 389–400.

Rice, F. Phillip, and Dolgin, Kim Gale. (2002). *The adolescent.* 10th edition. Boston: Allyn and Bacon.

Richburg, Keith B. (1997). Asians, West clash over human rights. *Washington Post,* July 29, A1.

Richburg, Keith B. (2001). Divergent views of U.S. role in world. *Washington Post,* December 20, A34.

Richler, Howard (1999). New terms cropped up as needed. *Gazette* (Montreal), December 24, Books and the Visual Arts G2.

Richman, Alvin. (1993). The polls-trends. American support for international involvement. *Public Opinion Quarterly,* 57 (Summer), 2, 264–276.

Richman, Alvin. (1996). The polls-trends. American support for international involvement: General and specific components of post–Cold War changes. *Public Opinion Quarterly,* 60 (Summer), 2, 305–321.

Richter, Anthony. (1998). "Blood and soil": What it means to be German. *World Policy Journal,* 1998/1999 (Winter), 91–98.

Riker, William, and Ordeshook, Peter. (1968). A theory of the calculus of voting. *American Political Science Review,* 62 (March), 25–42.

Risse-Kappen, Thomas. (1991). Public opinion, domestic structures, and foreign policy in liberal democracies. *World Politics,* 43, 4, 479–512.

Rivera, Ray. (2000). Bias hurts U.W. climate, survey of students says. *Seattle Times,* May 25, B2.

Robinson, Claude E. (1932). *Straw votes: a study of political prediction.* New York: Columbia University Press.

Robinson, John P., and Godbera, Geoffrey. (1997). *Time for life: The surprising ways Americans use their time.* University Park: Pennsylvania State University Press.

Rogoff, Barbara. (1990). *Apprenticeship in Thinking: Cognitive Development in Social Context.* New York: Oxford University Press.

Rohier, I. (1975). A social-learning approach to political socialization. In: D. Schwartz and S. Schwartz (Eds.), *New directions in political socialization.* New York: Free Press.

Rokeach, Milton. (1973). *The nature of human values.* New York: Free Press.

Rokeach, Milton. (1954). The Nature and Meaning of Dogmatism. *Psychological Review,* 61:194–204.

Rokeach, Milton. (1968). Beliefs, attitudes and values. San Francisco: Jossey-Bass Inc.

Roll, Charles W., and Cantril, Albert H. (c1972/1980). *Polls, their use and misuse in politics.* Cabin John, MD: Seven Locks Press.

Rosenau, James. (1961). *Public opinion and foreign policy: an operational formulation.* New York: Random House.

Rosenau, N. (1975). The sources of children's political concepts: An application of Piaget's theory. In: D. Schwartz and S. Schwartz (Eds.), *New directions in political socialization.* New York: Free Press.

Rosenberg, Shawn. (1988). *Reason, ideology, and politics.* Princeton: Princeton University Press.

Ross, Lee. (1977). The intuitive psychologist and his shortcomings: Distortions in the attribution process. In: L. Berkowitz (Ed.), *Advances in experimental social psychology.* Volume 10. New York: Academic Press.

Rothenberg, Stuart. (2000). Tuned out: TV ads unlikely to play major role in Bush-Gore race. *Roll Call,* September 7. http://www.rollcall.com.

Rothman, Stanley, and Lichter, Robert. (1987). Elite ideology and risk perception in nuclear energy policy. *American Political Science Review*, 81, 383–404.

Rotter, J. B. (1966). Generalized expectations for internal vs. external control of reinforcement. *Psychological Monographs*, 80, 1–28.

Rusk, J. G. (1970). The effect of the Australian ballot reform on split ticket voting, 1876–1908. *American Political Science Review*, 64 (December), 1220–1238.

Safire, William. (1978). Safire's Political Dictionary. New York: Random House.

Sanders, Stephanie A., and Reinisch, June Machover. (1999). Would you say you "had sex" if...? *Journal of the American Medical Association*, 281 (January), 275–277.

Sangster, Roberta, and Reynolds, Robert. (1996). A test of Ingelhart's socialization hypothesis for the acquisition of materialist/postmaterialist values: The influence of childhood poverty on adult values. *Political Psychology*, 17, 2, 253–270.

Savage, J. (1985). Post-materialism of the left and right. *Comparative Political Studies*, 17, 4, 431–451.

Sax, L. J., Astin, A. W., Korn, W. S., and Mahoney, K. M. (1998). *The American college freshman: National norms for fall 1998*. Los Angeles: Higher Education Research Institute, University of California.

Scarrow, Susan. (1996). *Parties and their members: Organizing for victory in Britain and Germany*. Oxford and New York: Oxford University Press.

Schaeffer, David, and Dilman, Don. (1998). Development of a standard e-mail methodology: Results of an experiment. *Public Opinion Quarterly*, 62 (Fall), 378–397.

Schaffer, Frederick. (1998). *Democracy in translation: Understanding politics in an unfamiliar culture*. Ithaca: Cornell University Press.

Scheepers, P., Felling, A., and Peters, J. (1992). Anomie, authoritarianism, and ethnocentrism. *Politics and the Individual*, 2, 1, 43–59.

Schickler, Eric. (1996). *The grim reaper, the stork, and partisan change in the North and South, 1952–1994*. Paper presented at the annual meeting of the Midwest Political Science Association, Chicago.

Schickler, Eric, and Green, Donald P. (1997). The stability of party identification in western democracies: Results from eight panel surveys. *Comparative Political Studies*, 30, 450–483.

Schlesinger, Arthur Jr., Israel, Fred L., and Frent, David J. (1994). *Running for president: The candidates and their images: 1789–1896 and 1900–1992*. Volume 2. New York: Macmillan Library Reference.

Schlichting, Kurt C., and Tuckel, Peter S. (1994). *A spatial analysis of contextual effects on voter participation in the 1992 presidential election*. Paper presented at the annual meeting of the American Association for Public Opinion Research, Danvers, MA.

Schneider, F. W. (1970). Conforming behavior of black and white children. *Journal of Personality and Social Psychology*, 16, 466–471.

Schneider, Howard. (2000). Independent TV gives Arabs a new perspective on the news. *Washington Post*, November 7, A22.

Schönpflu, Ute. (1990). Perceived Decision-Making Influence in Turkish Migrant Workers' and German Workers' Families. *Journal of Cross-Cultural Psychology*, 213, 261–282.

Schooler, C., Basil, M. D., and Altman, D. G. (1996). Alcohol and cigarette advertising on billboards: Targeting with social cues. *Health Communication*, 8, 109–129.

Schorow, Stephanie (2000). Will a new generation of girls narrow computing's gender gap? *Boston Herald*, June 26, P31.

Schubert, Glendon. (1991). *Sexual politics and political feminism*. Greenwich, CT: Jai Press.

Schudson, Michael. (1999). *The good citizen: A history of American civil life*. Cambridge, MA: Harvard University Press.

Schuman, Howard, and Presser, Stanley. (1981). *Questions and answers in attitude surveys: Experiments in question form, wording, and context*. New York: Springer.

Schwartz, David, and Manella, C. (1975). Popular music as an agency of political socialization: A study in popular culture and politics. In: D. Schwartz and S. Schwartz (Eds.), *New directions in political socialization*. New York: Free Press.

Schwartz, David, and Schwartz, Sandra. (1975). *New directions in political socialization.* New York: Free Press.

Schwartz, D., Garrison, J., and Alouf, J. (1975). Health, body images, and political socialization. In: D. Schwartz and S. Schwartz (Eds.), *New directions in political socialization.* New York: Free Press.

Schwartz, Norbert, and Sudman, Seymour. (Eds.) (1992). *Context effects in social and psychological research.* New York: Springer.

Schwartz, Sandra. (1975). Patterns of cynicism: Differential political socialization among adolescents. In: D. Schwartz and S. Schwartz (Eds.), *New directions in political socialization.* New York: Free Press.

Schwartz, Shalom. (1994). Are there universal aspects in the structure and content of human values? *Journal of Social Issues,* 50, 19–45.

Sears, David. (1988). Symbolic racism. In: P. Katz and D. Taylor (Eds.), *Eliminating racism: Profiles in controversy,* 53–84. New York: Plenum Press.

Sears, David. (1996). Presidential address: Reflections on the politics of multiculturalism in American society. *Political Psychology* 17, 3, 409–420.

Sears, David, and Funk, C. (1990). Self-interest in Americans' political opinions. In: J. Mansbridge (Ed.), *Beyond self-interest,* 147–170. Chicago: University of Chicago Press.

Sears, David, Citrin, J., Vidanage, S., and Valentiono, N. (1994). *What ordinary Americans think about multiculturalism.* Paper presented at the annual meeting of the American Political Science Association, New York.

Sears, David, Taylor, Shelly O., Peplau, Letitia Anne, and Freedman, J. (1995). *Social psychology.* Upper Saddle River, NJ: Prentice-Hall.

Sears, David O., Van Laar, Colette, Carrillo, Mary, and Kosterman, Rick. (1997). Is it really racism? The origins of white American's opposition to race-targeted policies. *Public Opinion Quarterly,* 61 (Spring), 16–53.

Sechrest, Lee, Fay, Todd L., and Hafeez Zaidi, S. M. (1972). Problems of translation in cross-cultural studies. *Journal of Cross-Cultural Psychology,* 3, 1, 41–56.

Semetko, Holli A., Blumer, Jay G., Gurevitch, Michael, and Weaver, David H. (1991). *The formation of campaign agendas: A comparative analysis of party and media roles in recent British and American elections.* Hillsdale, NJ: Erlbaum.

Sentinel staff and wire reports. (1999). *Milwaukee Journal Sentinel,* December 26, Real Estate 1.

Servin-Gonzalez, Mariana, and Torres-Reyna, Oscar. (1999). Religion and politics. *Public Opinion Quarterly,* 63 (Winter), 592–621.

Shapiro, Robert Y., and Mahajan, Harpreet. (1986). Gender differences in policy preferences: A summary of trends from the 1960s to the 1980s. *Public Opinion Quarterly,* 50, 42–61.

Shapiro, Robert Y., and Jacobs, Lawrence. (1999). Public opinion and policymaking. In: C. Glynn, S. Herbst, G. O'Keefe, and R. Shapiro (Eds.), *Public opinion.* Boulder, CT: Westview.

Sharp, Dudley. (1997). Death penalty and sentencing information in the United States. Justice for All. October 1. http://www.prodeathpenalty.com/DP.htm.

Shaw, Greg M., Shapiro, Robert Y., Lock, Samuel, and Jacobs, Lawrence R. (1998). Crime, the police, and civil liberties. *Public Opinion Quarterly,* 62 (Fall), 405–426.

Shen, Fern. (2000). More than half of America's voters don't. *Washington Post,* October 9, C15.

Shi, Tianjian. (1997). *Political participation in Beijing.* Cambridge, MA: Harvard University Press.

Shiraev, Eric. (2000). People say, advisers advise, and officials decide: Toward a comparative analysis of opinion-policy linkages. In: R. Shapiro, B. Nacos, and P. Isernia (Eds.), *Decisionmaking in the glass house,* 297–304. Lahnam, MD: Rowman and Littlefield.

Shiraev, Eric, and Bastrykin, A. (1988). *Fashion, idols, and the self.* St. Petersburg: Lenizdat.

Shiraev, Eric, and Fillipov, A. (1990). Cross-cultural social perception. *St. Petersburg University Quarterly,* 13, 53–60.

Shiraev, Eric, and Levy, D. (2004). *Cross-cultural psychology: Critical thinking and contemporary applications.* 2nd edition. Needham Heights, MA: Allyn and Bacon.

Shiraev, Eric, and Livingston, Steven. (1996). *A preliminary exploration of the post–Cold War schemata.* Paper presented at the annual meeting of the International Society of Political Psychology, July, Washington, DC.

Shiraev, Eric, and Sobel, Richard. (2003). Public opinion and foreign policy: A comparative analysis of linkages. In: Richard Sobel and Eric Shiraev (Eds.), *International public opinion and the Bosnia crisis.* Lanham, MD: Lexington Books.

Shiraev, Eric, and Tsytsarev, S. (1995). *Addictive behavior in addictive societies.* Paper delivered at the annual meeting of the International Society of Political Psychology, Washington, DC.

Shiraev, Eric, and Zubok, Vladislav. (2001). *Anti-Americanism in Russia: From Stalin to Putin.* New York: St. Martin's Press/Palgrave.

Shlapentokh, Vladimir, and Shiraev, Eric. (2002) (Eds.) *Fears in post-communist societies.* New York: Palgrave.

Shweder, Richard A. (1990). Cultural psychology—what is it? In James W. Stigler, Richard A. Shweder, and Gilbert S. Herdt (Eds.), *Cultural psychology: Essays on comparative human development,* 1–43. New York: Cambridge University Press.

Sidanius, James, and Pratto, Felica. (1993). Racism and support of free-market capitalism: A cross-cultural analysis. *Political Psychology,* 14, 3, 381–401.

Sidanius, James, and Pratto, Felicia. (1999). *Social dominance: An intergroup theory of social hierarchy and oppression.* Cambridge: Cambridge University Press.

Sigel, Roberta. (1970). *Learning about politics.* New York: Random House.

Sigel, Roberta. (1989). Introduction: Persistence and change. In: R. Sigel (Ed.), *Political learning in adulthood: A sourcebook of theory and research.* Chicago: University of Chicago Press.

Sigel, Roberta. (1996). *Ambition and accommodation: How women view gender relations.* Chicago: University of Chicago Press.

Sigel, Roberta, and Reynolds John V. (1979–1980). Generational differences and the women's movement. *Political Science Quarterly,* 94, 635–648.

Sigelman, Lee, and Tuch, Steven A. (1997). Metastereotypes: Black perceptions of whites' stereotypes of blacks. *Public Opinion Quarterly,* 61 (Spring), 87–101.

Simon, Herbert. (1957). *Models of man.* New York: Wiley.

Simon, Herbert. (1983). *Reason in human affairs.* Stanford, CA: Stanford University Press.

Simon, Rita J., and Landis, Jean M. (1989). The polls—A report: Women's and men's attitudes about a woman's place and role. *Public Opinion Quarterly,* 53, 265–267.

Singer, Eleanor, Groves, Robert, and Corning, Amy. (1999). Differential incentives: Beliefs about practices, perceptions of equity, and effects on survey participation. *Public Opinion Quarterly,* 63, 2, 251–260.

Singer, Eleanor, Corning, Amy, and Lamias, Mark. (1998). The polls-trends: Genetic testing, engineering, and therapy: Awareness and attitudes. *Public Opinion Quarterly,* 62, 4, 633–664.

Singer, Eleanor, Van Hoewyk, John, and Maher, Mary P. (1998). Does the payment of incentives create expectation effects? *Public Opinion Quarterly,* 62 (Summer), 152–164.

Skjeie, Hege. (1991). The rhetoric of difference: On women's inclusion into political elites. *Politics and Society,* 19, 2, 233–263.

Slote, Walter. (1996). Conflict in action: A psychological study of a Venezuelan revolutionary. *Political Psychology,* 17, 2, 229–251.

Smith, Adam. (1937/1776). *An inquiry into the nature and causes of the wealth of nations.* New York: Modern Library.

Smith, Dita. (2000a). Home, violent home. *Washington Post,* March 18, A13.

Smith, Dita. (2000b). What on earth? *Washington Post,* September 2, A16.

Smith, M. B. (1997). The authoritarian personality: A re-review 46 years later. *Political Psychology,* 19, 4, 669–682.

Smith, Rogers. (1997). *Civic ideals: Conflicting visions of citizenship in U.S.* New Haven: Yale University Press.

Smith, Tom W. (1999). The JAMA controversy and the meaning of sex. *Public Opinion Quarterly,* 63 (Fall), 385–400.

Smith, Tom W. (2001). *Public opinion on abortion. General Social Surveys (GSS), 1972–1996: Cumulative Codebook.* Chicago: NORC. University of Chicago. www.norc.uchicago.edu/library/abortion.htm.

Smith, Peter, and Schwartz, Shalom. (1997). Values. In John Berry, Marshall Segall, and Cigdem Kagitcibasi (Eds.), *Handbook of Cross-Cultural Psychology.* (Vol. 3., pp 77–118). Needham Heights, MA: Allyn and Bacon.

Snarey, John R. (1985). Cross-cultural universality of social-moral development: A critical review of Kohlbergian research. *Psychological Bulletin,* 97, 202–232.

Sniderman, Paul. (1975). *Personality and democratic politics.* Berkeley: University of California Press.

Sniderman, Paul, Brody, Robert, and Kulinski, James. (1984). Policy reasoning and political values: The problem of racial equality. *American Journal of Political Science,* 28, 75–94.

Snyder, Mark, and Swann, William B., Jr. (1978). Behavioral confirmation in social interaction: From social perception to social reality. *Journal of Experimental Social Psychology,* 14, 148–162.

Sobel, Richard. (1989). *The white-collar working class: From structure to politics.* New York: Praeger.

Sobel, Richard. (1989a). Public opinion about United States intervention in El Salvador and Nicaragua. *Public Opinion Quarterly,* 53, 1, 114–128.

Sobel, Richard. (1990). Staying power in Mideast. *Dallas Morning News,* October 10, A19.

Sobel, Richard. (1993). *Public opinion in U.S. foreign policy: The controversy over contra aid.* Lanham, MD: Rowman and Littlefield.

Sobel, Richard. (1993a). From occupational involvement to political participation: An exploratory analysis. *Political Behavior,* 15, 4, 339–353.

Sobel, Richard. (1994). The politics of the white-collar working class: From structure to action. *Research in Micropolitics,* 4, 225–242.

Sobel, Richard. (1995). What people really say about Bosnia, *New York Times,* November 22, A23.

Sobel, Richard. (1996). U.S. and European attitudes about intervention in the former Yugoslavia: *Mourir Pour la Bosnie?* In: R. Ullman, (Ed.), *The world and Yugoslavia's wars,* (145–181) New York: Council on Foreign Relations.

Sobel, Richard. (1996a). Polling on foreign policy crises: Creating a standard set of questions, *Public Perspective,* 7, 2, 13–16.

Sobel, Richard. (1997). America's place in a changing world, *Public Perspective,* 338–40.

Sobel, Richard. (1998). The polls: United States intervention in Bosnia, *Public Opinion Quarterly,* 62, 2, 250–278.

Sobel, Richard. (1998a). Portraying American public opinion toward the Bosnia crisis. *Harvard International Journal of Press/Politics,* 3, 2, 16–33.

Sobel, Richard. (1998b). U.S. Public Opinion Still Favors Israel. *JUF News,* July, 39–40.

Sobel, Richard. (1999). "The Authoritarian Reflex and Public Support for the U.S. Military." Paper for the Meetings of the Midwest Political Science Association, Chicago.

Sobel, Richard. (2000). To intervene or not to intervene in Bosnia. In: Brigitte Nacos, Robert Shapiro, and Pierangelo Isernia (Eds.), *Decisionmaking in a glass house* (111–132). Lanham, MD: Rowman and Littlefield.

Sobel, Richard. (2001). *The impact of public opinion on U.S. foreign policy since Vietnam: Constraining the Colossus.* New York: Oxford University Press.

Sobel, Richard. (2001a). Immigration and identification: Interview with Alan Simpson. *Migration World,* 29, 3, 2.

Sobel, Richard. (2001b). Constraining the colossus. *Kennedy School Bulletin,* 3, 8.

Sobel, Richard. (2001c). Anti-terror campaign has wide support, even at the expense of cherished rights. *Chicago Tribune,* November 4, 2: 1, 6.

Sobel, Richard. (2002). A new wound to medical privacy. *Los Angeles Times,* August 23, B15.

Sobel, Richard. (2002a). The degradation of political identity under a national identification system. *Boston University Journal of Science and Technology Law,* 8, 1, 37–74.

Sobel, Richard. (2002b). The demeaning of identity and personhood in national identification systems. *Harvard Journal of Law and Technology,* 15, 2, 319–387.

Sobel, Richard. (2003). Maintaining informed consent for doctor-patient confidentiality: More serious failings in the HHS medical records regulations. *Journal of Biolaw and Business,* 6, 2, 61–65.

Sobel, Richard. (2005). License to Spy—A National Driver's License. *The Boston Phoenix.* April 22, 22.

Sobel, Richard, and Bursztajn, Harold. (2000). Ban genetic discrimination. *Boston Globe,* August 7, A15.

Sobel, Richard, and Loughlin, Kevin. (2005). "The Health of the Supreme Court." *Chicago Tribune.* July 3, 2, 1.

Sobel, Richard, and Shiraev, Eric. (Eds.) (2003). *International public opinion and the Bosnia crisis.* New York: Lexington.

Sobel, Richard, et al. (1999). National and international security. In: John Rielly (Ed.), *American public opinion and U.S. foreign policy 1999.* Chicago: Chicago Council on Foreign Relations.

Sommerville, John C. (1999). *How the news makes us dumb: The death of wisdom in an information society.* Downers Grove, IL: Intervarsity Press.

Sowell, Thomas. (1981). *Ethnic America.* New York: Basic Books.

Spencer, Herbert. (1954). *Social statics.* New York: R. Schalkenbach.

Sperry, Paul. (2002). U.S.–Saudi oil imports fund American mosques. April 22. www.worldnetdaily.com.

Steckenrider, J., and Cutler, N. (1989). Aging and adult political socialization: The importance of roles in transitions. In: Roberta S. Sigel (Ed.), *Political learning in adulthood: A sourcebook of theory and research.* Chicago: University of Chicago Press.

Steeh, Charlotte, and Krysan, Maria. (1996). Affirmative action and the public: 1970–1995. *Public Opinion Quarterly,* 60, 128–158.

Stein, Robert M. (1998). Early voting. *Public Opinion Quarterly,* 62 (Spring), 57–69.

Steinhorn, Leonard. (2000). Does the reliance of the news media on polls distort reporting? *Insight on the News,* 25 (December), 40.

Stoker, Laura, and Jennings, M. Kent. (1995). Life-cycle transitions and political participation: The case of marriage. *American Political Science Review,* 89 (June), 421–33.

Stroble, Warren. (1997). *Late-breaking foreign policy, The news media's influence on peace operations.* Washington DC: U.S. Institute of Peace.

Strong, Bryan, Christine DeVault, and Barbara Sayad. (1998). *The marriage and family experience.* Belmont, CA: Thomson/Wadsworth.

Suellentrop, Chris. (2000). Why online polls are bunk. *Slate,* January 11.

Sullivan, Harry. (1954). The psychiatric interview. New York: Norton.

Sulloway, Frank. (1996). *Born to rebel.* Boston: Little Brown.

Summer, William. (1970). *What social classes owe to each other.* Caldwell, ID: Caxton.

Sumner, William. (1906). *Folkways.* Boston: Ginn.

Sunar, D. G. (1982). Female stereotypes in the United States and Turkey. *Journal of Cross-Cultural Psychology,* 13, 4, 445–460.

Swanson, David L., and Mancini, Paolo. (Eds.) (1996). *Politics, media, and modern democracy.* Westport, CT: Praeger.

Sycheva, V. (1994). Impoverishment of the "people's masses" of Russia. *Sotsiologitheski Zhurnal,* 1, 66–69.

Tajfel, Henri. (Ed.) (1982). *Social identity and intergroup relations.* Cambridge: Cambridge University Press.

Tajfel, Henri. (Ed.) (1984). *The social dimension: European developments in social psychology.* Volume 2. Cambridge: Cambridge University Press.

Tarde, Gabriel. (1903). *The laws of imitation.* New York: Holt, Rinehart and Winston.

Taylor, Donald N., and Simard, Lise M. (1972). The role of bilingualism in cross-cultural communication. *Journal of Cross-Cultural Psychology,* 3, 1, 101–108.

Taylor, Humphrey. (2000). Support for death penalty down sharply since last year, but still 64% to 25% in favor. *Harris Poll # 41.* August 2, 2000. http://www.harrisinteractive.com.

Taylor, Ronald. (2002). *Minority families in the United States.* Upper Saddle River, NJ: Prentice Hall.

Taylor, S. E., Peplau, L. A., and Sears, D. O. (1997). *Social Psychology.* Englewood Cliffs, NJ: Prentice Hall.

Tedin, Kent. (1974). The influence of parents on the political attitudes of adolescents. *American Political Science Review,* 68, 1579–1592.

Teixeira, Ruy Antonio. (1987). *Why Americans don't vote: Turnout decline in the United States, 1960–1984.* New York, Westport, CT, and London: Greenwood Press.

Thornton, Thomas P. (Ed.) (1988). *Anti-Americanism: The annals of the American Academy of Political and Social Science.* Volume 497. Newbury Park, CA: Sage Publications.

Thornton, Arland, and Freedman, Deborah. (1979). Changes in the sex role attitudes of women, 1962–1977: Evidence from a panel study. *American Sociological Review,* 44, 831–842.

Tiger, Lionel. (1969). *Men in groups.* New York: Random House.

Tiger, Lionel, and Fox, Robin. (1971). *The imperial animal.* New York: Holt, Rinehart and Winston.

Tilove, Jonathan. (2000). A new force in American politics is being born: Asian Americans who plan to make their voices heard. *Seattle Times,* May 28, B5.

Timpone, Richard. (1998). Structure, behavior, and voter turnout in the United States. *American Political Science Review,* March, 145–158.

Titarenko, Larissa (2002). Fears, hopes, and paradoxes of the transformation. In Shlapentokh, V. and Shiraev, Eric. (2002). (Eds.), Fears in Post-Communist Societies. NY: Palgrave.

Tobacyk, J., and Tobacyk, Z. (1992). Comparisons of belief-based personality constructions in Polish and American university students. *Journal of Cross-Cultural Psychology,* 23, 3, 311–325.

Tourangeau, Peter, and Rasinski, Kenneth. (1988). Cognitive processes underlying context effects in attitude measurement. *Psychological Bulletin,* 103: 299–314.

Tourangeau, Robert, and Smith, Tom W. (1996). Asking sensitive questions: The impact of data collection mode, question format, and question context. *Public Opinion Quarterly,* 60, 275–304.

Toynbee, Polly. (2000). What Blair needs to do to woo back the women. *Guardian* (London), June 21, Guardian Leader 22.

Trevor, Margaret C. (1999). Political socialization, party identification, and the gender gap. *Public Opinion Quarterly,* 63, 62–89.

Triandis, Harry. (1989). The self and social behavior in differing cultural contexts. *Psychological Review,* 96, 506–520.

Triandis, Harry. (1994). *Culture and social behavior.* New York: McGraw-Hill.

Triandis, Harry. (1995). *Individualism and collectivism.* Boulder, CO: Westview.

Trump, T. M. (1991). Value formation and postmaterialism: Inglehart's theory of value change reconsidered. *Comparative Political Studies,* 11, 63–74.

Tuch, Steven, and Sigelman, Lee. (1997). Race, class, and black-white differences in social policy views. In: Barbara Norrander and Clyde Wilcox (Eds.), *Understanding public opinion,* 37–54. Washington, DC: CQ Press.

Tuckel, P., and O'Neil, H. (1996). Screening out. *Marketing Research,* 8, 1, 34–43.

Tullock, Gordon. (1967). *Toward a mathematics of politics.* Ann Arbor: University of Michigan Press.

Turner, Frederick C. (Ed.) (1992). *Social mobility and political attitudes: Comparative perspectives.* New Brunswick, NJ: Transaction.

Ullman, Richard. (1996). *The World and Yugoslavia's Wars.* New York: Council on Foreign Relations.

U.S. Bureau of the Census (1999). *Region of birth of U.S. foreign-born population.* March 9.

USA Today. (1999). Rising doubts on death penalty. December 22, News A17.

Valentino, Nicholas. (1999). Crime news and the priming of racial attitudes during evaluations of the president. *Public Opinion Quarterly,* 63 (Fall), 293–320.

Van den Berghe, Pierre. (1978). *Race and racism.* New York: Wiley.

Vassiliou, Vasso, and Vassiliou, George. (1973). The Implicative Meaning of the Greek Concept of Philomoto. *Journal of Cross-Cultural Psychology,* 4, 3, 326–341.

Verba, Sidney, and Nie, Norman. (1972). *Participation in America.* New York: Harper and Row.

Verba, Sidney, Schlozman, Kay L., and Brady, Henry. (1995). *Voice and equality: Civic voluntarism in American politics.* Cambridge, MA: Harvard University Press.

Volkan, Vamik. (1988). *The need to have enemies and allies.* Northvale, NJ: Jason Aronson.

Vrij, A., and Winkel, F. (1994). Perceptual distortions in cross-cultural interrogations. *Journal of Cross-Cultural Psychology*, 25, 2, 284–295.

Wallace, David. (1959). A tribute to the Second Sigma. *Public Opinion Quarterly*, 23, 311–315.

Waltzer, Michael. (1995). Liberalism and the Jews: Historical affinities, contemporary necessities. In: P. Medding (Ed.), *Values, interests, and identity: Jews and politics in a changing world: Studies in contemporary Jewry*, Volume 11, 3–10. New York and Oxford: Oxford University Press.

Ward, Martin. (1999). Who are the many? *Ottawa Citizen*, August 2, B6.

Ware, Alan. (1998). Parties and their members: Organizing for victory in Britain and Germany. *American Political Science Review*, (June), 491.

Washington Post. (1993). Exactly how many unemployed? Opinion editorial. November 28, C6.

Washington Post. (2002). Most Hispanics say they're Democrats. Those polled also show ambivalence. October 4, A08.

Washington Post. (1995). July 23, 1995.

Washington Times, 1999. "AMA releases old survey on oral sex just in time for President's trial." January 15.

Watanabe, Teresz (2000). Farrakhan questions Lieberman's loyalty. *Washington Post*, August 12, A10.

Watson, John B. (1922). What cigarette are you smoking and why? *J. Walter Thompson News Bulletin*, 88, 1–17.

Wattenberg, Merton. (1990). *The decline of American political parties, 1952–1980*. Cambridge, MA: Harvard University Press.

Wayne, L. (2000). One consulting firm finds voter data is a hot property. *New York Times*, September 9. http://www.nytimes.com.

Weaver, Mark. (1998). Weber's critique of advocacy in the classroom: Critical thinking and civic education. *PS: Political Science and Politics*, (December), 799–801.

Weber, Max. (1946). Science as a vocation. In: H.H. Gerth and C.W. Mills (Eds.), *From Max Weber: Essays in sociology*, 524–555. New York: Oxford University Press.

Weber, Max. (1968/1922). *Economy and society: An outline of interpretive sociology*. New York: Bedminster Press.

Weber, Paul. (2000). *Catholics and the 2000 election*. Posted October 28. Copyright ©2000 by America Press. http://www.amaericapress.org.

Weigel, R., Loomis, J., and Soja, M. (1980). Race relations on prime-time television. *Journal of Personality and Social Psychology*, 30, 724–728.

Weissberg, Robert. (1976). *Public opinion and popular government*. Englewood Cliffs, NJ: Prentice Hall.

Welch, S., and Sigelman, Lee. (1982). Changes in public attitudes toward women in politics. *Social Science Quarterly*, 31, 312–321.

West, Maureen. (2000). Boomer women return to battle. *Arizona Republic*, May 14, J1.

West, Tom. (1997). *Vindicating the founders: Race, sex, class and justice in the origins of America*. Lanham, MD: Rowman and Littlefield.

Wilbanks, William. (1994). The myth of a racist criminal justice system. In: R. Monk (Ed.), *Taking sides: Clashing views on controversial issues in race and ethnicity*. Guilford, CT: Dushkin Publishing Group.

Wilder, David A. (1981). Perceiving persons as a group: Categorization and intergroup relations. In: D. Hamilton (Ed.), *Cognitive processes in stereotyping and intergroup behavior*, 1361–1374. Hillsdale, NJ: Erlbaum.

Will, George. (2000). Forget values, let's talk virtues. *Washington Post*, May 25, A37.

Willie, Charles V. (1979). *Caste and class controversy*. New York: General Hall.

Wills, Gary. (2000). Prosperity mellows us on death penalty. *Chicago Sun-Times*, January 1, A28.

Wilson, Thomas C. (1996). Cohort and prejudice: Whites' attitudes toward blacks, Hispanics, Jews, and Asians. *Public Opinion Quarterly*, 60, 253–274.

Wilson, William Junius. (1978). *The declining significance of race*. Chicago: University of Chicago Press.

Wilson, William Junius. (2000). Rising inequality and the case for coalition politics. *Annals of the American Academy of Political and Social Science,* (March), 78–99.

Wirt, Frederick. (1997). *We ain't what we was: Civil rights in the new south.* Durham, NC: Duke University Press.

Wirzbicki, Alan. (2004). Late polls are seen as largely accurate. *Boston Globe,* November 5.

Witt, April. (2000). Elian impasse widens Miami's ethnic divides. *Washington Post,* April 16, A01.

Wittkopf, Eugene R. (1988). American foreign policy beliefs, preferences, and performance evaluations. Paper presented at the International Society of Political Psychology, New York.

Wittkopf, Eugene R. (1990). *Faces of internationalism: Public opinion and American foreign policy.* Durham, NC: Duke University Press.

Wittkopf, Eugene R., and McCormick, James M. (1993). The domestic politics of contra aid: Public opinion, congress, and the president. In: R. Sobel, *Public opinion in U.S. foreign policy: The controversy over contra aid.* Lanham, MD: Rowman and Littlefield.

Wolf, Frederic M. (1986). Meta-analysis: Quantitative methods for research synthesis (Sage University Paper Series on Quantitative Applications in the Social Sciences, No. 07–059). Beverly Hills, CA: Sage.

Wolfe, Richard. (2001). European thumbs-down for Bush policies. *Financial Times* (London), August 16, 8.

Wolfinger, Raymond E., and Rosenstone, Steven J. (1980). *Who Votes.* New Haven: Yale.

Wong, Martin. (2000). Poor people lazy and a burden: Public's attitude "barrier to easing plight." *South China Morning Post,* October 7, 5.

Woodward, Kathryn. (1997). *Identity and Difference.* Thousand Oaks, CA: Sage.

World Health Organization. (1999). Press release. WHO/28. May 17.

Wrangham, Richard, and Peterson, Dale. (1997). *Demonic males: Apes and the origins of human violence.* New York: Houghton Mifflin.

Wright, Debra L., Aquilino, William S., and Supple, Andrew J. (1998). A comparison of computer-assisted and paper-and-pencil self-administered questionnaires in a survey on smoking, alcohol, and drug use. *Public Opinion Quarterly,* 62 (Fall), 331–353.

Wyman, Matthew. (1997). *Public opinion in postcommunist Russia.* London: Macmillan.

Yadov, Vladimir. (1978). *About the dispositional regulation of the social behavior of the personality* (in Russian). Leningrad: Academy of Sciences.

Yang, Alan S. (1997). Attitudes toward homosexuality. *Public Opinion Quarterly,* 61 (Spring), 477–507.

Yin, Chi Kin, and Kannan, P. K. (1999). Consumer behavioral loyalty: A segmentation model and analysis. *Journal of Business Research,* 44, 75–92.

Young, John, Hemenway, David, Blendon, Robert, and Benson, John. (1996). Trends: Guns. *Public Opinion Quarterly,* 60 (Winter), 634–649.

Zajonc, Robert. (1968). The attitudinal effect of mere exposure. *Journal of Personality and Social Psychology,* Monograph supplement, 9, 1–27.

Zaller, John. (1992). *The nature and origins of mass opinion.* New York: Cambridge University Press.

Zaller, John. (1996). The myth of massive media impact revisited: New support for a discredited idea. In: Diane Mutz, Richard Brody, and Paul Sniderman (Eds.), *Political Persuasion and Attitude Change.* Ann Arbor: University of Michigan.

Zechman, M. (1979). Dynamic models of the voter's decision calculus. *Public Choice,* 34, 297–315.

Zogby, John. (1998). U.S. Jewish voters in the 1998 elections. *Mideast Mirror,* July 27, 12.

Index

Note: Page numbers followed by the letters *f* and *t* indicate figures and tables, respectively.

A

AAPOR. *See* American Association for Public Opinion Research
AAUW. *See* American Association of University Women
Abbreviations, list of, 321–24
ABC
  Disney as parent company of, 117
  election coverage by, 132
  political bias in, 128–29, 128*t*
  polls by, 73, 130, 217–18, 255, 269, 279, 298, 306
  quantitative framing by, 125
Abortion, 250–55
  accessibility of attitudes toward, 75
  arguments for and against, 251–52, 251*t*
  rates of, 250, 252
  social class attitudes by and, 170*t*, 172*t*, 175
  specific circumstances of, 253–55, 253*t*, 254*t*
  and voting behavior, 57, 255
Accessibility
  of attitudes, 73–75, 124
  of information
    media and, 118–20
    social class and, 181
  of resources
    in quality of life, 102
    and social class, 167
    and social power, 204–7
Adolescents
  computer-assisted surveys of, 29
  definition of, 98
  political knowledge of, 98, 99*t*
  political socialization in, 98–99
  rebelliousness of, 98–99
Adults, political socialization in, 99–100
Advertisements
  for beer, 139–40
  political candidates' use of, 123
Advisory referenda, 225
Advocacy polls. *See* Push polls
Affective component, of attitudes, 68–69, 75
Affirmative action, 255–58
  arguments for and against, 256, 257*t*
  attitudes about, 256–58
  black views of, 197, 258
  context for polls on, 84–85
  decline in support for, 87
  definition of, 255–56
  economy and, 177–78
  media coverage of, 197, 244–245, 245*t*
  political party affiliation and, 258
  as reverse discrimination, 151, 256

social class and, 170*t*, 171*t*, 174, 177–78, 257–58
Afghanistan
  U.S. attitudes toward, 291*t*, 295
  U.S. intervention in, 295, 306, 307, 311
African Americans. *See* Black Americans
Age
  and party affiliation, 239, 241
  and political beliefs, 101
  and prejudice, 209
Agenda setting, by media, 124
Aggression, gender gap in, 152–53, 155
Agree-disagree questions, response bias in, 34
Agreement bias, 33–34
Aid. *See* Foreign aid
Alienation, of voters, 232
Aliens, undocumented/illegal, 102, 272–73
  benefits and privileges for, 273
  content analysis with, 38
  political tolerance of, racial differences in, 195
  social class attitudes by and, 170*t*, 172*t*, 173–74
Allende, Salvador, 105
Allies, *vs.* enemies, 288–92
Amanpour, Christiane, 5, 137
Ambiguity, of survey questions, 35–36
Ambivalence, in attitudes, 68, 75
American Association for Public Opinion Research (AAPOR)
  Code of Ethics of, 10
American Association of University Women (AAUW), 154
American Institute of Public Opinion, 16
American Muslim Council, 203
American National Election Studies, 149
The American Voter (Campbell et al.), 240
American Women's Opinion Poll, 144
Anderson, John, 242
"Angry white men," 151
The Anguish of Change (Harris), 13
Antagonism, class-related, 179
Anticipatory socialization, 154
Approval ratings. *See also* President(s)
  for Congress, 278
  for federal institutions, 276–77
Arab countries, U.S. attitudes toward, 290–92, 291*t*, 306
Arab immigrants, 203
Armstrong, Neil, 121
Aronson, Elliot, 130
Asian Americans
  discrimination against, 199
  diversity of opinions among, 193–96, 194*t*–195*t*, 199
  political attitudes, 194*t*, 199
  population of, 199
  post hoc errors regarding, 61

Assumptions, among survey respondents, 53–55
Attentive public
  definition of, 4
  foreign policy knowledge of, 288
  political participation by, 6
Attitude(s), 67–88
  accessibility of, 73–75, 124
  affective component of, 68–69, 75
  ambivalence in, 68, 75
  cognitive approach to, 73–78
  cognitive component of, 68–69
  cognitive dissonance among, 76–77
  critical thinking about, 84–88
  definition of, 68
  depiction of, 68
  dogmatism and, 77–78
  impact on behavior, 69
  as learned reactions, 78–79
  public *vs.* private, 84
  regulatory-adaptation approach to, 73, 78–84
  strength of, 69, 74
  as temporary constructions, 80–82
  types of, 72–73 (*See also* Beliefs; Value(s))
Attitude accessibility theories, 73–75
Attribution, social, 51
Australia, compulsory voting in, 226
Authoritarian regimes
  censorship in, 118–19
  as context for opinion, 6–7
  impact of opinion on policy in, 318
  political socialization in, 94, 97–98, 109, 119
Authority, in workplace, 184
Autonomy, *vs.* social order, values of, 72
Availability heuristic, 54
Available news, 120
Average person
  common usage of term, 1
  generalizations about, 1–2, 62, 266
"Axis of evil," 290–91

B

Balance theories, cognitive, 75–77, 84
Ballot initiatives, 224
Banner districts, 227
Barna Research Group, 212
Beck, Paul, 97
Beer commercials, 139–40
Behavior. *See also specific types*
  consistency between attitudes and, in cognitive balance theories, 75–77, 84
  impact of attitudes on, 69
  impact of prejudice on, 209
  impact of values on, 71
Belarus, context of surveys in, 48–49

CPSIA information can be obtained
at www.ICGtesting.com
Printed in the USA
BVHW04s0441200718
522123BV00011B/98/P